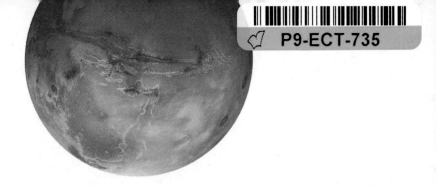

SLAVE SPECIES
OF
THE GODS

P9-ECT-735

"Michael Tellinger's groundbreaking work presents evidence that challenges all the conventional major assumptions about human origins and history. Emerging into our true power and significance cannot happen until we realize we are not the pinnacle of God's creation, not even among the creatures of this Earth."

MÍCEÁL LEDWITH, D.D., LL.D.,
COAUTHOR OF *THE ORB PROJECT*

"Even if you don't agree with the conclusions Michael Tellinger draws from the evidence he presents—and I don't!—this is a well-researched, well-written, and thought-provoking book on a controversial subject, and I applaud it as a contribution to the debate about the mysterious origins of humanity."

GRAHAM HANCOCK,
AUTHOR OF *FINGERPRINTS OF THE GODS*

"If you have ever wondered about the age-old questions concerning the human race: Who are we? Where did we come from? Where are we going? Answers may be found in Michael Tellinger's book *Slave Species of the Gods*. Clearly written, it's a fast and gripping read that covers everything from biology, science, and history to religion, mythological gods, and ancient astronauts. Don't miss this one."

JIM MARRS,
AUTHOR OF *RULE BY SECRECY*, *ALIEN AGENDA*, AND *CROSSFIRE*

SLAVE SPECIES OF THE GODS

The Secret History
of the Anunnaki
and Their Mission on Earth

MICHAEL TELLINGER

Bear & Company
Rochester, Vermont • Toronto, Canada

Bear & Company
One Park Street
Rochester, Vermont 05767
www.BearandCompanyBooks.com

Bear & Company is a division of Inner Traditions International

Library of Congress Cataloging-in-Publication Data
Tellinger, Michael.
 [Slave species of god]
 Slave species of the gods : the secret history of the Anunnaki and their mission on Earth / Michael Tellinger.
   p. cm.
 "Originally published in South Africa in 2005 by Zulu Planet Publishers under the title Slave species of god"—T.p. verso.
 Summary: "Our origins as a slave species and the Anunnaki legacy in our DNA"—Provided by publisher.
 Includes bibliographical references and index.
 ISBN 978-1-59143-151-0 (pbk.) — ISBN 978-1-59143-807-6 (e-book)
 1. Human beings—Origin—Religious aspects. 2. Evolution—Religious aspects. 3. Human genome—Religious aspects. 4. Genetic engineering—Religious aspects. 5. DNA. 6. Heredity. 7. Gods—History. 8. Mythology, Assyro-Babylonian. 9. Archaeology and religion. 10. Civilization—Extraterrestrial influences. I. Title.
 GN281.4.T45 2012
 599.93'8—dc23

2012010036

Printed and bound in the United States by Versa Press, Inc.

10 9 8 7 6

Text design and layout by Virginia Scott Bowman
This book was typeset in Garamond Premier Pro and Gill Sans with Trajan Pro, Helvetica, and Gill Sans used as display typefaces

To send correspondence to the author of this book, mail a first-class letter to the author c/o Inner Traditions • Bear & Company, One Park Street, Rochester, VT 05767, and we will forward the communication, or contact the author directly at **www.michaeltellinger.com**.

Note to the Readers

Each chapter was written with the objective to function as a small piece of the greater puzzle—one of sixteen building blocks that collectively tell a more compelling tale. I have attempted to take the readers by the hand and guide them toward the deep end of the knowledge pool.

While some chapters will appeal more to some readers, and less to others, I have tried to keep them as short and punchy as possible, while getting the core message across. There is, however, a strange logic to the sequence of the journey I have chosen to take you on, and it all comes together in chapter 16.

Chapter 16, "The Story of Humankind," combines all the information you will absorb in the previous chapters and exposes you to the time before the creation of the human race and the strange activity on Earth in such distant times, which includes the terrible truth surrounding our origins.

So do not lose sight of the fact that there is a chronology woven into the puzzle. If, however, you find yourself at odds with some of the more technical chapters and you cannot see your way through them . . . read chapter 16 if you read nothing else.

Enjoy the read and keep exploring.

MICHAEL TELLINGER

CONTENTS

ACKNOWLEDGMENTS

I WOULD LIKE TO THANK a few people for their assistance and support in helping me to complete this book:

Lily Hattingh for her relentless commitment and working into the early hours of the morning on the layout.

Mike van Niekerk for his ongoing moral and financial support.

Andy Stadler for his advice, motivation and African sunsets.

Ryan Aldridge for the inspiring cover design.

Leigh Stadler, Pamela MacQuilkan, Jan Swanepoel for reading the raw material and giving me their valuable comments.

Tiara Walters for her critical input as the devil's advocate.

Thanks to Kerry Marshall and Terry Cropper for spotting all the gremlins in the first edition.

Scott Cundill for his ingenious online marketing campaign and his contribution toward making this book a bestseller in South Africa.

INTRODUCTION

IN AN AGE WHERE TECHNOLOGY has allowed us to expect instant reward and provides us with immediate solutions, humankind seems to have all the answers. Our confidence as a species is higher than ever before, and the knowledge of the universe we live in is expanding faster than most people can keep up with. We can compute and calculate the landing of a small probe on a planet 100 million miles away; we know what the atmosphere on Jupiter consists of; we can regenerate new organs in our bodies, and genetic engineers can create new life in any shape or size they want to. There are, however, three fundamental questions that we have not been able to answer. Who are we? How did we get here? And, why are we here?

As we steadfastly march on the road to an unknown destiny, our ignorance has become our weakness and our arrogance has become a congenital disease threatening us with our own annihilation. In this book we will deal with the latest breakthroughs in science and technology, to reach back into the distant past in an attempt to unravel the extremely vague origins of humankind. It simply makes no sense at all that as advanced as we have become, we have no absolute answers dealing with our origins and ancestry. Why has humankind been so obsessed with gold? And why are slavery and gold the two common denominators that can be traced all the way back to the very dawn of humankind?

The global population is torn between hundreds of religions and cults, all claiming to have the answers. Any semisober person will realize in an instant that they cannot all be right. Right? And yet it is religious dogma that has held billions of people captive through preaching death and destruction, threatening punishment by the "almighty" to disobedient pilgrims, and promising reward and salvation to those who submit to blind faith.

The past fifty years have seen an explosion of new archaeological discoveries that have stunned scholars all over the world with its body of information. Over 500,000 clay tablets have been excavated and many of them have been deciphered. It is only in the past thirty years or so that the true meaning and relevance of the tablets has been identified by a handful of broad thinkers. What was originally believed to be myth or fantasy, mainly due to ignorance by so-called scholars, has turned out to be documented historic evidence so fantastic that it shakes the very essence of our existence.

I would like to take you on a journey of discovery, using the latest translations and revelations of the many tablets that speak about ancient events, long before a single word of the Bible was written. It is shocking to find that none of the stories of the book of Genesis are original, but rather watered-down versions of much older stories conveyed in great detail in ancient clay tablets. Our journey will weave through precious detailed information that was left behind by our ancient ancestors, probably never realizing that it would be treated with such suspicion.

The uncanny coincidences that link the many ancient civilizations by the same pantheon of "mythical gods" are too fantastic to be accidental. We now have irrefutable evidence that there were strange powers on Earth who ruled the early humans with an iron fist. They dispensed punishment and demanded absolute obedience from the primitive new species. We will uncover the slow and painful path the newly created human race had to travel and the crucial role played by more advanced deities who had ulterior motives for our existence. We will uncover the terrible truth that the human race was indeed created in the image of our maker, but the maker was not who we've been led to believe. We will unmask the god of the Bible and other major religions, showing the difference between God with a big "G" as opposed to god with a small "g." The god who constantly displays humanlike behavior, the "god of vengeance" we know from the Bible, turns out to be a god with a small "g." Some characters will be instantly recognizable, while others have been so distorted by latter translators that we will need a little polishing to identify them. Many more questions will be raised as we postulate new theories surrounding our origins, demystifying God, and allowing the reader to experience the much bigger picture of possibility.

With the help of science and the corroborative evidence from thousands of ancient clay tablets, we are now able to weave together the full story, which I like to refer to as the Great Human Puzzle. Why did it take thousands of years for the slave species to progress from their labor camps in southern Africa, to the point about 9,000 years ago, when a wave of sudden civilization spread around the world, from India, the Near East, Europe, and the Americas? This journey will also resolve the many archaeological dilemmas regarding the missing link, which is clearly outlined by our advanced ancestors. We dispel the myth and the dogma that has kept humankind ignorant and fearful for far too long. The advances we have made in genetic engineering will help us understand that just because we can create life, it does not make us God.

We dispel archaic myths that belong in the Dark Ages and provide clear thinking individuals with the information to reach new conclusions. I would like to share with every reader the same incredible sense of discovery that I personally experienced as I unravelled the utter rubbish that I was conditioned to believe through my formative years. As terrible as this new truth may sound, it will be the most liberating experience you will have.

1

ANIMAL BEHAVIOR

EVER SINCE I FIRST BECAME interested in genetics, it has always intrigued me that such an important part of our anatomy, the genome, a molecular structure so refined, should have been created incomplete. Actually, the truth is that the genome was created in abundance, with large parts of the structure that are not being used at all. It is as if the inactive parts of the genome are waiting for some extrinsic factor to switch them on. The question begs, which unimaginable characteristics or super abilities are the dormant parts of the genome not controlling? What human abilities are they hiding? And how has this affected our evolution as a species?

The genome is just another name for the full complement of genes and DNA contained by an individual. In humans, the genome consists of 23 pairs of chromosomes that contain the entire genetic program for that specific individual, and is located in the nucleus of every cell in our bodies. This genetic program controls all the information that allows us to grow and function. Our genome is unique for every individual and every species. When we are born, we are blissfully unaware of what awaits us. There might be seven ages of man, but it all ends up woven together into a long reality performance directed by some invisible force. We are all given some seventy years to do our performance here on Earth, on average; the rest is up to each one of us. Enter stage left . . . exit stage right. The only certainty we have at present is that we will exit. What are you going to do with your seventy years? What is the purpose of this journey, this play of life that we all participate in? Will you use this time creatively, make a contribution to the global community of beings, or will you be a mere spectator: a usurper of facilities before you exit stage right?

Despite the 6.5 billion people who populate the Earth, the human race is a rather fragile and primitive species. No matter how intelligent and smart we think we are, we constantly display signs of basic animal behavior that can lead to the decimation of our kind in the blink of an eye. We have waged war on our fellow man throughout history and continue to do so into the twenty-first century. There always seems to be a moral high ground or justification for our action. From Cain and Abel, to George W. Bush, it has always been the strong and powerful who oppress and wipe out the weak. The Old Testament of the Bible is not a pretty tale of compassion and forgiveness. In fact, quite the opposite. It talks about an eye for an eye; wiping out man, woman, child, and beast in the name of god; and often mentions the enemy by name, personifying them as the bad guys or disciples of the devil. It seems that god has been taking sides from the very beginning. He had his favorites, and then there were "the others." I always felt that the God I have been told about should be more impartial and loving.

The Bible is filled with prophets and other individuals who for thousands of years had a direct link to god and who on a regular basis received instructions from god to do certain things. When reading the Bible it is not only deemed normal, but it is expected of us to take for granted and to believe that a number of chosen people received such regular instructions from god. Not only did they receive clear instructions and warnings, they received physical instructions in the form of the Ten Commandments and rewards of a material kind, like land or cattle. But the most impressive interactions between god and man were the many visitations god made in person to various individuals. If he could not make it in person, he would send angels to deal with whatever situation needed to be dealt with. The divine beings would share ideas, share wine and bread, and inevitably god would instruct the person to perform certain tasks. All of these individuals seem to have been men. And all of the people who contributed to the scriptures of the Bible were also all men. If "He" created us all equal, did god have a problem with the credibility of women? Or was god just the personification of a male-dominated society? The simple historic fact remains that god actually physically interacted with man. Today, such claims of a physical interaction with God would draw strong criticism and ridicule. Why is that? Is it perhaps that such events in prehistory cannot affect us here today? We seem to accept it when it happened in ancient history, almost reduced to some fantastic fairy tale of our struggle for freedom. Or is it simply because we are too scared to analyze the facts for fear of victimization by placing such arguments in the public domain? These questions have troubled me for most of my life.

And who, and when, decided that the Bible had reached its conclusion? That it was now enough, it is now the end, and the final chapter must be written! Obviously this was another man, inspired by God and dictated to by the Holy Spirit! Surely the quest for truth and salvation continues? Surely the atrocities on Earth have not abated; surely the people of the Earth need ongoing guidance and instructions from God on how to deal with modern-day mayhem and crime; how to respond to dictators; how to survive colonization, racism, invasions, and other inventions of evil minds. Our capacity for cruelty as a species has reached unbearable proportions. We make rules as civilized beings, only to be abused and used against us by less civilized individuals with a good knowledge of the legal system. Those who preach peace and love and turning the other cheek have become the weakened victims of their own philosophy.

Now, more than ever, people need salvation. They need something real to believe in and to hold onto in times when all hope seems to have vanished. So why are the scriptures not ongoing? Why is God not dictating more wisdom through one of his prophets? Or many of his prophets? Some say he is. Many claim they are in contact with God on a regular basis. Many convey God's messages in packed churches and other places of worship. How does the global community respond to individuals who make fantastic claims of miracles, and hearing God's voice, and having the answer? Well, in many cases these modern prophets rise to a cult status with a blind following of disciples who will respond to every command, while in other cases they are reduced to cranks with a loose screw.

So, how should a judge in the twenty-first century respond to a guy who tied up his ten-year-old daughter to a table in the backyard, and who was caught by police in the process of stabbing her to death or slitting her throat? If he claims that God had instructed him to sacrifice her to prove his obedience to the almighty lord, should such a character be seen as an example of a modern faithful or a psychopath? Yet, we look at Abraham as a faithful man of God with strong principles and a leader of men because he obeyed god's instructions to kill his own son. The Bible, however, calls it "sacrifice." Would we see it as such if it happened today in a wealthy suburb of Johannesburg or Paris?

It is truly a confusing state of religious activity out there. Thousands of religions, all of them man-made, all claiming that they have the answer. Only their followers will be saved by the maker and bask in the pleasures of paradise. It seems that the more money they have, the more power they wield and the closer to God's ear they can get.

And so the religious argument begins, and we clearly display the primitive side of our low evolutionary state. Are these the primitive characteristics that could be controlled by the inactive genes? We look at the past great civilizations and somehow feel superior. The fact that we cannot explain many things from prehistory is quickly discarded as "Who cares about the Egyptians . . . they're all dead." In the light of all our achievements and scientific discoveries, the more we evolve, the stronger the religious dogma becomes. It seems that the religious dogma, which could also be called fanaticism in this case, is directly linked to money. The wealthier a nation, the more they can enforce their particular religious views on others. The United States may claim that they are a free society in all respects, but that is mainly because they feel a sense of comfort among their 96% Christian community. It is safe for them to allow the minority rogue religions to waste their time on their own meaningless salvation.

But then we start to look at who we really are, and the road we have traveled as a species on this planet, only to realize that our presence here does not even equate to the tip of the iceberg. We marvel at dinosaur fossils and talk about what it must have been like here on Earth when dinosaurs roamed. We throw around numbers like "60 million years" when they were extinct, "200 million years" when T-Rex caused havoc, and "400 million years" ago really makes us gasp at the fossils of insects in the museums. Then we start comparing the timescale to famous events in our own frame of reference. The First World War 100 years ago; Leonardo da Vinci 500 years ago; the Vikings some 1,200 years ago; Mohammed some 1,400 years ago; Jesus 2,000 years ago; the pyramids 4,000 years ago; the last ice age some 13,000 years ago; by then most of us run out of reference points.

And then one day something miraculous happens. We lift our eyes up at the night sky filled with billions of stars and we try to imagine infinity. Someone points out Mars and Jupiter. And then you look through a telescope and for the first time you see Saturn with its rings and even several of its moons, and suddenly the reality of it all changes somewhat. It all becomes a little bit bigger. You look at Alpha Centauri and realize that the light from the closest star to us takes five years to reach us, travelling at 300,000 km per second. You go to a lecture by an astronomer and see pictures of galaxies so far away, it is impossible to imagine the distance. Galaxies a billion light-years away. Supercluster galaxies five billion light-years away; ultra hot quasars some 12 billion light-years away right at the edge of the known universe and then—some 13.8 billion light-years away—just blackness. Nothing. You sit in silent contemplation as you try to digest the reality of what you have just witnessed. You have just looked beyond the edge of the known universe, where nothing exists.

But when you wake up in the morning and you try to explain your epiphany to a group of close friends, they share your excitement for exactly fifteen seconds before one of them pronounces "Hey, did you guys see that cool movie on TV last night?"

With all the valiant attempts and sometimes remarkable discoveries by archaeologists, we still cannot pinpoint the origin of humankind. Oh, scores of scientist will argue and give you all kinds of evidence and proof, only to be rewritten by some new scientist five years from now. It is all calculated speculation presented to us either as scientific hypotheses or religious dogma. But in reality, all it ends up being is more manipulation of the pieces of the Great Human Puzzle. We cannot tell when civilized man first walked the Earth and we cannot tell when man was created or how man evolved with a definite level of certainty.

Let's face it: The past two centuries have led to amazing discoveries of ancient civilizations, lost cities, and a closer understanding of the people who developed these ancient cultures—cultures that displayed remarkable knowledge and understanding of science and the cosmos. It has taken us decades to decipher the various texts or styles of writing by the many extinct cultures. With all our knowledge and sophistication, we have not deciphered the Balkan-Danube script and the Indus Script to date. The diversity of these ancient civilizations, from the ancient Chinese, various cultures of the Americas, the hieroglyphs of the Egyptians, to the cuneiform scriptures of the Sumerians, the lost cities of Asia, have baffled historians and archaeologists alike. It has taken us by complete surprise to discover ancient libraries, such as the library of King Ashurbanipal at Nineveh, with around 30,000 cuneiform clay tablets of scriptures that point to great knowledge by lost civilizations.

It is curious to discover the extended knowledge of astronomers as early as 6,000 years ago with detailed information of our own solar system. We read about ancient gods who roamed and ruled the Earth in chariots that flew in from the stars, and conflicts and betrayal between these ancient gods. We read about brave men who achieved great things in the distant past and wisdom that was imparted to man by the many gods who came from the stars. The ability to extract precious metals from ore in the ground, with the production of gold, copper, tin, and bronze as early as 9,000 years ago, points to clear understanding of metallurgical procedure. The ancient ruins of the Americas with visible extraction and mining activity explain why there was an unimaginable wealth of gold in this part of the world long before Columbus, Cortes, or the other savages who set foot there only a few hundred years ago. The further inexplicable evidence of ore mining in southern Africa as far back as 100,000 years ago is simply too much for even the bravest of archaeologists to accept.

The knowledge of medical procedure and genetic manipulation, the creation of the "Adamu"—a new species, is clearly documented in ancient tablets that have only recently been understood by so-called intelligent man. The power of wireless communication and geophysical knowledge to anticipate natural disaster; all this wealth of information stares us bluntly in the face. And yet, we cannot come to terms with the fact that we may not be the pinnacle of intelligence that has inhabited the planet. Since the rapid evolution of the computer, our ability to document and match this ancient wisdom has enabled us to understand it more clearly. But what do we do with all this information when standing face-to-face with incredible tales from prehistory? We have two choices. Either we believe that it has been left for future civilizations to use and build upon, or we discard it as hallucinogenic garbage by some primitive idiots from a Stone Age, not worthy of our attention.

The fact that only 500 years ago men were burned at the stake for suggesting that Earth was not the center of the universe, the human body was a mysterious vessel that was studied and dissected by daring scientists risking their lives in the early hours of the morning, that we only discovered the last three planets in our solar system in the past 200 years, are clear indication that we are not the superior race.

We are the subspecies. Our arrogance is our weakness and our ignorance a congenital disease that will eventually destroy us. The dogma has consumed us and the fear controls us. But why are we so blind to the facts and evidence that surround us? Why are we so obsessed with popular religions that mostly bow to a god who uses retribution and punishment as a form of control? If we all come from the same maker, we should all have the same set of rules on how to obey that maker, but this is clearly not the case. Religious conflict has torn our history apart for millennia and still hangs over our heads into the twenty-first century like a cancer waiting to devour us.

In this book we will discover that our disorder is the direct result of our bastard race status, with unpredictable animal behavior lurking in our manipulated double-helix DNA. Our intelligence has been suppressed, our knowledge has been erased, our lifespan has been genetically shortened, and our memory has been removed. We are an inferior, genetically cloned mutation of the great civilizations of the past, left behind to pick up the pieces, or to put together the pieces of the Great Human Puzzle.

We have made remarkable progress in the field of genetic engineering, but just because we have been able to map the genome does not mean we know everything about it. On the contrary, the more we learn about the genome, the more we marvel at its complexity. We seem to understand the basic principle of the double helix, but we are far from understanding all its functions. What we are especially perplexed by are the large sections that seem to be switched off. Yes, it is curious to learn that there are large parts of the genome that are not active. That kind of discovery flies directly in the face of all evolutionary processes. But the real truth is that the genome was created in abundance, with far more DNA in our cells than we need for our primitive form.

This begs the question. If the genome controls all our characteristics and bodily functions, then what is it that is not controlled by the inactive parts of the genome? I firmly believe that this is the ultimate question of humanity. What inert secret powers are being locked up behind the inactive parts of our genetic structure?

Let's take a quick look at the history of genetic discovery. While there is clear evidence of prehistoric genetic activity and manipulation dating back to some 250,000 years ago, modern man has only rediscovered the genome in the 1950s.

In 1866 Gregor Mendel published the results of his investigations of the inheritance of factors in pea plants, but it was only in the 1950s that the chemical structure of the DNA was rediscovered by modern scientists. They finally had a name for it: deoxyribonucleic acid. The people involved in this breakthrough were Maurice Wilkins, Rosalind Franklin, Francis H. C. Crick, and James D. Watson. With this discovery they started a whole new branch of science, namely, molecular biology. In the same decade, Watson and Crick made history when they made the first model of the DNA molecule, showing its twisted double-helix structure, and proved that genes determine heredity. In 1957 Arthur Kornberg produced DNA in a test tube. 1963 saw F. Sanger develop the sequencing procedure for proteins. By 1966 a real breakthrough was made when the genetic code was discovered. Scientists were now able to predict characteristics by studying DNA. This very quickly evolved into genetic engineering and genetic counseling.

In 1972 Paul Berg produced the first recombinant DNA molecule, and in 1983 Barbara McClintock was awarded the Nobel Prize for her discovery that genes are able to change positions on chromosomes. In the late 1980s an international team of scientists began the tedious and demanding task of mapping the human genome, and the first crime conviction based on DNA fingerprinting—in Portland, Oregon—took place. By 1990 gene therapy was used on patients for the first time. In 1993 Dr. Kary Mullis discovered the polymerase chain reaction (PCR) procedure, for which he was awarded the Nobel prize. In 1994 the FDA approved the first genetically engineered food. These were FlavrSavr tomatoes engineered for better flavor and shelf-life.

By 1995 criminal DNA forensics made headlines in the O. J. Simpson trial. In 1997 Dolly the Sheep was the first adult animal cloned. 1998 saw the Senate inquiry into the Clinton/Lewinsky scandal based largely on DNA evidence, and in the year 2000 J. Craig Venter, along with Francis Collins, jointly announced the completion of the mapping and sequencing of the entire human genome. This was a major achievement that took almost ten years less than originally expected. In 2003 Craig Venter launched a global expedition to obtain and study microbes from environments ranging from the world's oceans to urban centers. This mission will yield a definitive insight into genes that make up the vast realm of microbial life. And now the true genetic era is upon us. The first pet cloning company opened their doors for business in the United States in 2004. In essence, we have become the creators of species. And so we have become "god" to those species we create.

The more we discover in the Cradle of Humankind in South Africa, the more we can genetically link the various peoples of the world to half a dozen original individuals in southern Africa; the more evidence we get from female mitochondrial DNA that the first human was born around 250,000 years ago, the more the pieces of the puzzle seem to fit. In this book we will explore written evidence that places such a group of primordial humans in southern Africa some 200,000 years ago, at about the time when the Adamu was supposed to have been created. When I first started placing these pieces together, I was doubtful that something so fantastic could be a possibility. But if you allow yourself the freedom of thought and possibility, you will discover an incredible story with a clear vision of the past and you will begin to unravel the great steps of humanity that brought us here.

This brings us to the age old question. "Who are we . . . and why are we here?" No, it is not really a "Oh wow, dude" kind of question, it is possibly one of the most complex riddles of our species, which deserves a fresh new look and possibly a slightly less conventional approach if we want to reach new and refreshing answers. But then we must be prepared to face answers we may not have expected. This is what I intend to share with you in this book. What may at first seem like a horror story will turn out to be the most liberating experience; one that brought me much closer to God than I ever imagined possible. Once again I have to draw your attention to the difference between God, the creator of the universe and all things in it, and god, one of many deities who walked the Earth over millennia, wielding power, knowledge, and technology with which they ruled over humanity.

There is good news for those who believe in the creation theory, that man was created by God and given certain rules to live by. Those who believe in the evolutionary theory have a few surprises to face. Evidence has been uncovered and contained in the many Sumerian tablets that suggests that the Adamu was created here on Earth in the image of his maker. But who created Adam and when will reveal that he was created by an advanced species of deities for a specific purpose here on Earth some 200,000 to 250,000 years ago. We further learn from the tablets that Adam was created from the genetic pool of the advanced species of humans on Earth and a lesser evolved hominid that roamed in southern Africa. But who were these advanced humans and where did they appear from? And why is there no fossil evidence of their existence?

I must once again remind you of the dilemma we face when we contemplate such outlandish theories, as most, if not all, of our facts come from prehistoric clay tablets that have been deciphered over the last fifty years of the twentieth century. We have to make a personal choice whether we believe that what was written in these tablets is close enough to the truth, or whether it is merely some hallucinogenic garbage from a time when people's minds did not function properly. I, for one, have made my decision to take at face value what has been written. I cannot imagine for one minute that thousands of people spent millions of man-hours painstakingly creating these tablets if their contents were less than relevant. I am convinced that they had better things to do than trying to confuse future generations about our origins. After all, we have not really changed that much; we also want to leave evidence of our intellect and achievements, not only for future generations but also for other advanced species in the vastness of the universe. Why else would we send space probes filled with human paraphernalia, videos, compact discs, books, photographs, TV shows, and other symbols of our existence into space? At the back of our minds and against the belief of millions, there is the faint hope that there may be advanced life somewhere in the universe. If there is, we hope to dazzle it with our brilliance or disappoint them with our ignorance, all depending on how evolved they may be by the time they accidentally recover our earthly "space ark."

It has always amazed me how many people show a complete disregard for history. To many, what happened in the past simply does not matter. But if we don't know who we are and where we come from, how can we possibly begin to understand where we might be going on our path of progress and evolution?

So we toil away and dream of better days. We close ourselves in cocoons of comfort, position our blinders squarely on our heads, and try not to step too far out of the lane of conformity. We believe that if we work hard or if we work smart we will achieve some sort of reward at the end of all of this. We take out insurance policies to reward our offspring and retirement annuities to cruise through the last few years of our own time on this planet. We keep procreating as if we were programmed to do so. It seems to be a natural step in our maturing process. And unbeknown to us, it is most likely driven by our genome in an attempt to continue surviving while our DNA evolves toward its own completion. On this path of evolution it unlocks the secret parts that have been switched off by some alchemist in our distant past.

We pray for health, wealth, and happiness. Some dream of eternal life and many pray for salvation, but deep inside there seems to bubble the burning desire to find answers to the great human question . . . "Who am I and why am I here?"

History gives us many clues about who we may be, and by stringing together the events and behavioral patterns of humans in the past, history does give us some clues as to where we are heading. Whether we will survive to get there is another question all together. History does not, however, always clearly answer the question of who we are and where we come from. Historians, archaeologists, and anthropologists have painted a very predictable past for us. Aside from the arguments between creationists and evolutionists, the story of humanity and humankind has become an almost pretty fairy tale, and most humans do not want their fairy tale disrupted. Humanity rose from the ashes against all odds: we survived and grew in numbers while spreading over the Earth. We discovered fire, iron, bronze, silver, and gold. We learned new skills, adopted farming instead of roaming, buried our dead, learned to live in structured communities, learned to write, and built cities to protect us from the bad guys. Then we learned to trade, found democracy, discovered mechanization, discovered technology, reached for the stars, and all the time we have been killing each other in the name of our god, our king, or for some other perfectly justifiable reason. It is truly a miracle that we have survived all this. It is clear that somewhere in our DNA there is a violent gene that plays a prominent role in human behavior.

This is a great story, but it only really deals with the past 6,000 years or so. Prior to this it gets very murky and somehow the timing does not seem to fit. The question of the missing link is now more relevant than ever before. Our genome has certainly evolved to the point where we can at least ponder these questions and challenge some of the obvious conventions. But this evolution seems to be more spiritual or mental. Physical evolution is debatable. If we have not really evolved physically in the past 6,000 years since the Egyptians and Sumerians, why should we believe that we underwent some dramatic evolution the previous 6,000 years—or the 10,000 years before that? It appears that our genome has been evolving around the mental parts only, as if we had some catching up to do mentally. This kind of genetic imbalance seems to point to some sort of tampering in the ancient past.

Survival of the fittest has been embraced as one of the pivotal evolutionary arguments. Terms like *natural selection* have been introduced and presented with dramatic evidence. It may have been the case in the protozoa, the dinosaurs, or the horse, but there seems to be serious gaps in the prehistoric evolutionary patterns of humans. Dramatic jumps in evolution that will form part of my argument point to the horrible truth that we are a slave species, purposefully created to perform a mundane function here on this Earth. It is for us to collect the clues and string them together to formulate a sensible answer. Some will not find any sense in my logic, but some will hopefully become more tolerant of the unknown and the forbidden questions of the past. One of the highest hurdles to cross will be the real possibility that we might have to come to terms with two gods: one with a capital "G" and the other with a small "g." The difference between the two should be obvious and our prehistory seems to be filled with events that tend to favor the needs and whims of the latter. Have we been conned since the beginning to believe that some form of advanced deity was actually God? If so, did he give us the rules, the scriptures, and the punishment? Was it in his image that we were created? There is an overwhelming amount of written evidence pointing to this conclusion. Do we start to take this ancient knowledge more seriously, giving it the respect it deserves, or do we respond to our overwhelming enslavement by dogma, and discard all this ancient knowledge? I will leave it up to you to draw your own conclusions.

2

THE CELL

OUR HUMAN BODY IS TRULY a miracle of creation. It clearly points to an extraordinary event that led to our existence. Our bodies consist of billions upon billions of cells that make up all the different parts of the body: heart cells, liver cells, muscle cells, and so on. Inside the nucleus of each cell is the genetic material that determines pretty much everything about us from the moment we are conceived to the day we die.

Before we journey back in time to retrace the evolutionary steps of humanity, let us take a quick look at those tiny things in our cells that shape us: our genes and the genome. I think of them as the fingerprints of God. This is where all the codes for our existence are kept, and this is where God with a capital "G" played the omnipotent role when life in the universe was created. I use this expression poetically and more for effect, so don't take it too literally, but rather inject your own theory of how the universe was created. One of the pivotal questions I have been grappling with for thirty years is why we age and why we die. A question like that may sound silly to most of us, as we have all been conditioned to accept death as the inevitable. We always hear that the only thing we can be sure of in life is that one day in the future we will die. What happens after death is the question that man has been debating for eternity from a multitude of angles, and that we will attempt to answer by the end of this book. I have, however, purposely steered clear of an extended spiritual debate, rather focusing on the physical aspects of our being, and how those have evolved to shape our present state. Some will argue that it is impossible to separate the spiritual from the physical, but I hope to demonstrate that it is the physical boundaries, predetermined by our DNA at the point of conception, that ultimately dictate the pace or capacity of our spiritual evolution. But even in this relatively primitive and disease-prone state, our bodies are miracles of creation.

For those with biology or anatomy as a major, please humor me as I bring the rest of the readers into the loop. To put things into perspective on this cellular level, let us first take a quick look at the cell and its contents as this will introduce a number of terms that will help you understand some further explanations.

The Cell and Its Contents

The cell surface is covered with a plasma membrane and the contents consist of the cytoplasm, which contains the various organelles including the nucleus.

The plasma membrane controls flow of materials in and out of the cell, either passively, which is called diffusion, or actively by active transport. The surface is covered with vesicles or vacuoles, which are flasklike invaginations of the membrane. It is thought that these provide a crucial means for large molecules to be taken into and out of the cell.

The nucleus controls the cell and also contains the DNA (chromosomes or genome), which in turn determines all of our characteristics. Elements of these characteristics will be passed onto the next generation of offspring because of the action of the DNA. This is called hereditary transfer of DNA and it is why children take after their parents. One half of the child's DNA comes from its mother, the other half from its father.

The cytoplasm is the whole area between the cell wall and the nucleus, where the metabolism and all the chemical reactions occur. The rate is con-trolled by enzymes. But the secretion of enzymes is in turn controlled by DNA.

The cytoplasm contains a number of organelles:

- The Endoplasmic Reticulum (ER) is an organized matrix of inter-connected flattened parallel cavities. It is the intracellular transport system.
- Ribosomes are attached to the sides of the ER in some places, in which case it is called the rough endoplasmic reticulum. Proteins are made here. Some of these proteins include enzymes and diges-tive hormones that are used by the cell, while some are secreted. The ER isolates and transports the proteins, which have been made by the ribosomes.
- The Golgi body is made up of smooth ER with no ribosomes. It is thought to be involved in the making and transporting of lipids and steroids. There are a number of vesicles nearby containing secretory

granules. It is thought that the Golgi apparatus is an assembly point through which raw materials for secretion are funnelled before leaving the cell.

- The mitochondria is where respiration in the cell happens. The mitochondria also generate all the energy for the cell. There is an average of 1,000 of these per cell, but there are many more in the motile tail of the sperm cell.
- Lysosomes contain enzymes for splitting complex chemical compounds into simpler subunits. They also destroy worn out organelles or even the whole cell if needed.
- Chromatin is the genetic material within the nucleus.

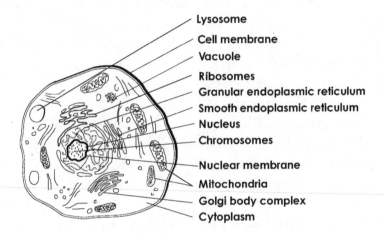

Lysosome
Cell membrane
Vacuole
Ribosomes
Granular endoplasmic reticulum
Smooth endoplasmic reticulum
Nucleus
Chromosomes
Nuclear membrane
Mitochondria
Golgi body complex
Cytoplasm

Fig. 2.1. The human cell

But cells don't just float around on their own throughout the body. Large numbers of them are massed together to form organs and tissue. The latest estimation is that there are around 50–100 billion cells in an average human body, but this number changes all the time, every hour of the day. It gets more complex, as bigger people have more cells than smaller people, and in the end no one has a definite answer for the number of cells in the human body. To demonstrate the complexity of this estimate, just imagine that your turnover of blood cells alone is about eight million per second. When quantities like these are in question, it is really hard to pin down an accurate number.

The cells that make up the many different parts of our anatomy all originate from stem cells, which are formed shortly after fertilization and make up the early embryo. They divide and divide and slowly transform into all the organs and cells that make up our entire anatomy. It's like a factory that keeps on producing a large variety of end products. Every single part of your body started out as a stem cell. Several months later the baby is born and unless it has a severe genetic defect it is perfectly complete and ready to grow into an adult human. Its body appears to be complete and ready for life, but its genome is far from complete. Just like its parents, the child bears a genome that will control all of its life functions, but this genome is as incomplete as its parents' who collectively contributed to their offspring.

I remember the day very vividly. It was 1975 and I was sitting in the biology class at my high school in Randfontein, South Africa. Biology was one of those subjects that seemed to always come naturally to me, one of the lucky ones. The secret was to pay attention in class. It dramatically reduced the amount of work I would have to do on my own at home. The other trick was to ask as many questions as you could, to anticipate what may come up in the exam. The teacher took forever to draw the animal cell on the board and then stepped back to admire her masterpiece. "Right . . . who knows what this is?" she asked with a determined pride in her voice. She proceeded to explain all the different parts of the cell, then moved on to the very curious fact that the cells divide every few hours in some tissue, to every few days in others. The new cells are born and almost immediately proceed to prepare for mitosis (cell division). This was almost too good to be true, I thought to myself. This was a perfect formula for eternal life. When you add the Krebs Cycle to the equation, the process through which energy is derived from food in the cells to keep the body nourished, it seemed pretty clear to me that the cells are the perfect structures to keep the body at peak maturity and the achievement of eternal life should be a mere formality. I raised my hand and asked the question that most probably changed the way I think about life and death today. "So why do we die, if new cells are born all the time and nourished by the food we eat?" I asked. "We die because that is what happens," she said. She went on to explain that this process of mitosis seems to carry on for some time, a number of cycles or years, and then suddenly the process starts to slow down. Fewer cells are born, the cells grow older and fragile with weakened cell walls, prone to pathogenic attack, until they stop dividing completely. This process spreads throughout all the parts of the body until we eventually die.

Somehow this explanation was not good enough for me and I felt that the teacher was missing out on a very important part of the equation. There had to be some sort of control mechanism that should be and could be manipulated to overcome this slowing down process in cell division that ultimately leads to death. But in 1975 I knew absolutely nothing about genetics and the teacher was not all that well informed either. Ever since that day I have always believed that there must be a simple procedure possible to reverse this aging process. When genetics became the cool new science by the late 1980s, it all started to make a lot of sense. Strangely enough, until the year 2004, scientists have still been at odds about the causes of aging. Some have still not reached the seemingly obvious conclusion that just like all other anatomical and physiological functions, aging must also be controlled by the genome. It is not only the cell as a whole that keeps multiplying, but all the parts of a cell are constantly being built up and broken down throughout its lifespan. The cell is constantly active and every bit is often renewed. When certain parts or organelles are not needed, such as extra mitochondria, they are simply disassembled and broken down to a molecular level. The truth is that once cells are born, they are truly perfect organisms that should continue to live by constantly dividing themselves for as long as they are fed. This is a great question for philosophers, since the original cell is now two cells and exists twice. Like a magician at a kiddie

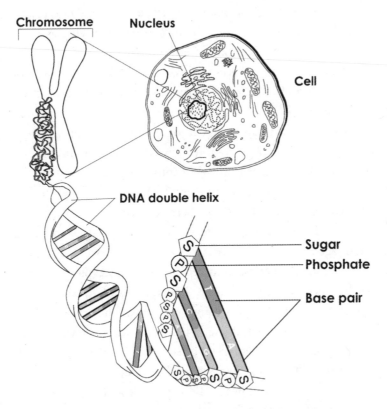

Fig. 2.2. The human cell showing the DNA in the nucleus

party with those long thin balloons, a twist here and a twist there, and soon the balloon has become two balloons. A few more effortless manipulations and the cells have become a little doggie or a rabbit or even a beating heart. That is the magic of the cells in our bodies.

The last decade has seen some new theories on cell death and aging, but to date no one is sure why cells get fragile and "cranky" as they get older. One of the popular theories in the attempt to understand aging is a substance called *telomeres*. These protect the DNA from damage during copying. It is thought that the telomeres on the ends of the genes get worn away or damaged and when this happens it seems that the DNA can get damaged too. This can lead to mutations and changes that lead to aging and cell death. This is, however, still an hypothesis with many others doing the rounds and no one can speak with absolute authority. So I will use this hole in the fabric of science to postulate my own hypothesis in later chapters. The damaged DNA then starts to send the wrong messages or codes to the cell and its components, which leads to the secretion of the wrong enzymes or chemicals, which leads to the cell not performing at its peak, and then it slowly shuts down and dies.

This is an important link to my argument in later chapters. All because of messed up programming and incorrect triggering of genetic responses, it is possible that the cells in our bodies die and we end up dying as a logical consequence. So if messed up cellular genetic information leads to diseases like tumors and cancers and many other serious life-threatening conditions, could we assume that the correct genetic information will do the opposite? Keep the cells alive forever? This is where genetic engineers are focusing much of their attention. We have made many breakthroughs in identifying various genes that control a vast number of physiological activities, and our success rate in gene therapy and gene replacement is growing constantly. In a nutshell, by identifying damaged genes we can take steps to replace them with healthy genes.

But what if we cannot do this, in certain situations, what alternatives do we have? Stem cells! The success rate we have witnessed by introducing stem cells into damaged tissue has taken everyone by surprise. While everyone was focused so fiercely on genetics, stem cell research has exploded with astonishing results. By injecting stem cells into damaged tissue, doctors have reconstituted hearts, livers, and even eyes using stem cells. The recovery of the organs is almost like performing a miracle, with the damaged tissue being regenerated within days or weeks. A man who had only 10% active heart muscle left had recovered to 90% within two weeks after receiving a stem cell injection into the damaged part of the heart. This is why the debate over human cloning has become so heated. Scientists have now realized that the stem cells in human embryos can be used to cure all kinds of incurable diseases, produce new organs, and rejuvenate almost any part of our body. Embryonic stem cells first appear about a week after fertilization. They are the parents of all other cells in our body.

In theory, stem cells could be harvested from an early embryo that was a cloned version of you, after which the embryo would be discarded. Such deliberate wastage of embryos is one reason why therapeutic cloning is so highly controversial. But the technique offers such important life-saving treatments that its use is considered justified by many people. Research into therapeutic cloning is allowed in the United Kingdom, but it is illegal to place any cloned human embryo into a womb. This was intended to prevent anyone from trying to create a living clone.

Stem cells can also be found in adult bodies, where they provide ongoing maintenance and repair. Adult stem cells appear to be partially differentiated, which means they have already started moving toward becoming a specific cell type. They do, however, show great flexibility.

Another possible source for stem cells is in the blood collected from a baby's umbilical cord just after birth. Some parents are choosing to freeze and store this blood so their baby will be able to call on a supply of its very own stem cells if it ever needs it later in life. I trust that scientists all over the world are already busy trying to recreate stem cells in a tube, but the miracle of these cells lies embedded in the deep secrets of their genome. Not until we start to unravel some of the "junk" parts of the genome and the secret encoding they possess will we start to fathom the true mechanism of stem cells. So, now that we have uncovered a possible miracle of life, let's get back to the shortcomings of the incomplete genetic structure lurking in our cells.

The Human Genome Project was launched in 1990 and its goal was to decipher and map the entire DNA of a representative human, who was selected from a group of anonymous donors. The cost? A phenomenal US$3 billion! It has been called the biological equivalent of putting a man on the moon. The results have taken humanity completely by surprise every step of the way as the group of scientists continually made new discoveries. The original estimate was that the project would take about twenty years, but thanks to the rapid development of computer technology, it only took them ten years. In June 2000 it was announced that the entire human genome had been sequenced. The sequence is a printout of the structured order of four chemicals found along the length of the DNA molecule. These chemicals are referred to as letters A, T, C and G, and there are an astonishing 3 billion variations of them along our 23 chromosomes, forming a unique sequence that holds the encoded program for the growth of a specific person. The hidden message in this code controls everything about us; it points to our ancestry and predetermines our future. These are mainly the instructions for building proteins and millions of other secret activities that have not yet been discovered.

The big surprise to the scientists was that active genes make up only tiny fractions of the entire genome. Incredibly, they only make up 3% of the total DNA in our chromosomes. The genes are either alone or clustered together in larger groups, but in between each gene sequence there are long stretches of DNA that do not appear to contain any type of code for anything. These stretches have now been referred to by scientists as "junk DNA," mainly because they have not figured out what secret message it conceals. This has sparked an interesting new debate that will last until the true relevance of these dormant DNA sections is explained. Fortunately, the scientists had learned from the arrogance of their predecessors, and in their wisdom they decided to map the entire Human Genome, including the junk, just in case it might have as yet undiscovered significance. It only took a few years to learn that those junk genes indeed played an important role in the structure of the genome. It is now clear that the positioning of these sections of dormant DNA are an integral part of the entire structure. More specific information will emerge as time goes by.

It makes no sense at all that the single most important molecular structure in our body, which is also the master control mechanism, would be created incomplete or with defects. I suggest that at the point of creation, the genome was originally created to be complete and fully functional. But because it is neither complete nor fully functional, we start to theorize about its true potential and our own full potential when dictated to by the perfect genome. Every week scientists are discovering new genes with specific control mechanisms over certain parts of our body. Genes that control the color of your eyes, your hair, your height, the secretion of enzymes, your skin, your sex, and even a gene that supposedly dictates whether you will be straight or gay. For every characteristic or function, there is a specific group of genes that controls that specific part of our body. Before we are even born, while we are growing in the womb, the genome starts to dictate how the master cells should divide and how they should shape our unique being.

It seems that as our genome evolves, it allows us to evolve on two levels: a physical level, and a spiritual or mental level. It is very curious that our evolution or development as a species seems to be linked to technological discovery, scientific achievements, and spiritual maturity. The more we evolve, the more impressive our discoveries. The more complex the questions we seem to pose, the more challenging the goals we set ourselves—except for periods like the Dark Ages, when all knowledge was seemingly lost and replaced by oppression, dictatorship, and savagery. It seems incredible that the knowledge of the universe, our ability to build breathtaking structures like the pyramids, and broad-minded philosophy all vanished, only to be replaced by an oppressed society during those times. But once again we emerged as a striving species and continued to ask more poignant questions about our origins, discovering electricity, the atom, and reaching for the stars. We have theorized about traveling beyond the speed of light, time travel, and even meta universes. We no longer seem so sure of our wisdom, we wonder more curiously where we are heading, but we still don't know where we come from. Is our insatiable need to reach the stars a clue to where we might have come from? It is quite possibly so, and we will examine ancient evidence that seems to support this theory very persuasively. We cannot place a limit on our mental and spiritual evolution. So if the mental and physical are somehow linked, there should be no boundary to our physical evolution also. Such physical evolution will not necessarily be visible on the outside, but its effects will most certainly be felt on a molecular and cellular level where the genome is most active.

Without most of us realizing it or having the background knowledge to comprehend the reasons, our bodies are continually striving for a complete or perfect genome: one that has reactivated the seemingly endless stretches of junk that line the DNA. This is the fundamental principle of evolution. Our own genome is in a constant state of evolution, a never-ending process of completing itself, recomputing and rescanning its own structure and constantly filling in the missing bits. The evolutionary process starts with the genome itself. Just like new computer technology allows us to scan photographs and turn a dull image into a perfectly sharp image, the genome is constantly fixing the dull, inactive bits, unlocking them and reactivating them to perform the specific function for which they were created. Just because the geneticists have not yet figured out what all the dormant stretches of DNA are for does not mean that evolution is going to stand still and wait for us to figure it out. Slowly but surely we are evolving physically and mentally, as the genome reactivates itself. It is like a rebirth from a long sleep from which humankind is waking up. A sleep into which we must have been induced by someone or something a long time ago. A sleep of ignorance and forgetfulness. It is often said that less intelligent people seem to be happy with their lot. They don't question why; they just accept their lot and get on with life without asking too many questions. They place their lives in the hands of their god, whichever god it may be, and believe that one day their souls will be saved from the devil. It is truly a great escape for many and a good enough reason to go on regardless.

We have, however, seen small increments of evolutionary evidence in our physical and spiritual forms. The fact that our tonsils cause more trouble than good, our appendixes are removed well before they can possibly kill us by bursting, and the fact that the average survival age in the global population has increased dramatically since the Dark and Middle Ages. This may have something to do with socioeconomic circumstances, diet and climate, but on the other hand it may not. For every bit of genetic resurrection that occurs in our cells, our bodies and minds evolve in harmony. More and more people around the world now refer to themselves as spiritual rather than religious. The past 2,000 years has seen the emergence of countless new religions and more splinter cults, as people are searching for new answers and opening themselves up to new realities.

I predict that in time to come, as we unravel more of this DNA structure, we will discover power and wisdom emanating from the genome, the complexity of which we cannot comprehend today. But we have the capacity to digest science fiction in large doses, so if this is a little too much for you at this moment, just pretend that this is a little science fiction trip and enjoy the ride.

Why would such a perfect part of creation like the DNA, consist of as much as 97% of unintelligible junk? Surely God does not make mistakes! Or is it possible that the inactive genes were purposely switched off, somehow, by someone when modern humans were created, right at the dawn of humanity? Could there have been some group of beings armed with sufficient skill and knowledge who consciously planned and executed this procedure? They must have had a reason or motive to create a being or possibly even a new species with a drastically stunted genome. In the past two decades scientists have shown conclusively and established with a relatively wide margin for error that both mitochondrial Eve and chromosomal Adam were created between 180,000 to 250,000 years ago. Who would have had such knowledge of genetics 250,000 years ago and what motive did they have to create a lesser evolved and more primitive creature like the human? The answer may be hidden in thousands of ancient texts that have gone unnoticed for centuries. In her book *Private Lives of the Pharaohs,* Joyce Tyldesley points out that 200 years ago, the early archaeologists were no more than "officially sanctioned treasure hunters." They knew very little about the science they were involved in, unable to read hieroglyphs or other ancient texts, sometimes not even being able to distinguish between written text and decorative art. Excavators were obsessed with finding giant monumental pieces to impress funders and attract curious people to the museums. The knowledge that was captured on thousands of clay tablets was lost to humankind for centuries, piled up in the basements of museums of the world. No one could possibly imagine that the primitive people of the ancient past could have had anything of consequence to say. Those who believed such misconceptions would have had those beliefs shattered.

For now, let us return to the possibility of a perfect genome and let us imagine for a moment what capabilities we may possess if our genetic structure was complete and fully functional, if large parts of our genome were not switched off. Let us examine some of the common problems in our physical anomalies that we would overcome with our DNA intact. The list is very long and touches every single aspect of our being. On this list would be all forms of disease; cancer; the simple process of healing; organ failure; mutation and the ability to adapt swiftly to severe external conditions; eyesight; hearing; deformities and other physical imperfections; and obviously also aging and death. These are just some of the complex physical benefits humankind will reap with a complete genome. By logical deduction, there will be genes that control all these characteristics in our bodies, and we will be able to manipulate these genes in any way we choose. Curiously enough, I have mentioned the topics that have already received much attention from scientists. Have you ever tried to catch an ordinary garden lizard and its tail comes off in your fingers? Or while you dig a hole for the plant you received as a present from your mother, you accidentally chop an earthworm in half? Well, the lizard's tail will grow back rather quickly and the worm will not die, it will grow to its full size again. The fact that such primitive creatures have the capacity to regrow lost limbs or other vital parts of their anatomy should unquestionably allow us, a far more advanced species, to do the same, if we could only reactivate certain parts of our genome. The other more complicated characteristics deal with the spiritual and mental parts of our psyche. The concept of being born with all the memories and knowledge of our parents has been debated for decades. The power to interact with others through ESP or reading someone's thoughts have been touted as a function of higher evolved beings. Thought materialization and teleportation linked to the materialization of the physical around the spiritual would allow us to travel though time and the universe. In a nutshell, we would become superhumans who live forever. But this kind of evolved state of existence will have certain prerequisites. The physical and the spiritual parts must evolve in tandem and in perfect harmony with each other. The one cannot overtake the other. A kind of yin and yang coexistence between physical and spiritual needs to be accomplished. If the one should evolve faster or slower than the other, we will have an imbalance between the two characteristics, which will manifest in a variety of unpredictable effects, behavioral patterns of instability, violent and dramatic antisocial behavior, and who knows what else. In fact, it is exactly the kind of behavior we have grown accustomed to on this planet. This must be the reason why we as a species are so volatile. The reason for our instability can be ascribed to the turbulent clash of our current disparate pace of evolution between the physical and spiritual parts of our being. The fact that some people may be evolving faster than others is a possible cause for conflict, aggression, and misunderstanding.

The fact that our genome is evolving toward a complete genome could also be evident from the way in which our bodies cope with certain diseases, which in the past would have killed us and yet today are controlled by our boosted immune system. On the spiritual side it is heralded by the more complex questions we ask about our origins, God, and the universe. With the advances in astronomy we marvel at the vastness of the universe, and many people are coming to terms with the fact that we may not be the only intelligent life out there. In 1990, astronomers were still of the opinion that planets were not commonly distributed in the universe. A few years later, after some more startling discoveries, they estimated that a small fraction of the stars may have some planets that formed around them during their own birth. And only a few years later they reached the conclusion that the formation of planets and the existence of solar systems is an integral part of what happens when nebulae give birth to new stars and galaxies. Suddenly, filled with this new wisdom, astronomers started discovering many new solar systems with planets and they continue to do so today.

When Sir Fred Hoyle and Chandra Wickramasinghe reintroduced the ancient Greek concept of *panspermia* in the early 1970s and suggested that life arrived here on Earth from space, as it probably did on countless other planets in the universe, most of us were unaware of other planets, and this theory was laughed off as ludicrous by most scholars. Today, panspermia is accepted by the majority of scholars. These two celebrated scientists have proved beyond any doubt that life has in the past arrived on Earth from space and still does so every day, in the form of viruses, bacteria, spores, and other microscopic organisms. While these may have played the leading role in the origin of life on Earth some 3.5 billion years ago, they also played a pivotal part in the great leaps of evolution of species. Furthermore, Fred Hoyle has presented evidence that supports the theory of evolution happening in jumps, as opposed to the great Darwinian propaganda that evolution happens slowly over time. So what has this got to do with our quest for our own identity? Everything!

It holds up the argument that humankind is not the final link of an evolutionary process that started with so-called apes and grew into primitive hominids, who in turn grew into intelligent humans. It goes a long way in supporting the argument that the Adam, or first man, was created by a conscious act of medical science some 200,000 years ago. This has been supported by tracking the Y-chromosome in the male population and arriving at a similar date. Is it a coincidence that this scientifically determined prehistoric date is in turn supported by the 1994 announcement by scientists that tracing mitochondrial DNA in females has placed the first Eve around the same time? These scientific discoveries have gone a long way in supporting the evidence that suggests Adam was created and when he was lonely, a female partner was created for him from his "essence." It sounds like a great fairy tale that we read in the Bible, but it is also written exactly like this in Sumerian clay tablets, which predate the Bible by as much as 3,000 years. So where did the authors of the Bible get all their inspiration? As we unravel the ancient times of humankind, we will expose the origins of many of the stories from the Old Testament, clearly captured for eternity on thousands of cuneiform clay tablets, long before a single word of the Bible was first jotted down. Furthermore, we are able to draw such conclusions and begin to make sense of it all because of the incredible discoveries in biological science that have exposed the power of the DNA, all held together in the human cell.

3.

THE BRAIN

SO WHAT IS THIS THING called a brain? It's a lump of gross-looking soft tissue tightly squeezed into our skulls, which allows us to formulate thoughts, contemplate our own being, and question our consciousness. We use it to be witty, to bamboozle people, to reason with others, and a million other functions that are often too small for us to notice. We abuse it with drugs and alcohol, pushing the limits of our brains to what seems to be the edge at times. The brain is a very fragile organ and that is why it is so well protected by the skull. But the brain also punishes us for abusing our bodies. It gives us headaches and causes us to feel pain of a wide variety. It can even cause us emotional pain when there is no sign of physical trauma. The brain can send mixed messages and cause us to hear voices, imagine demons, and drive us to insanity.

The brain is by far the most complex and mysterious organ in our bodies. It is the ultimate marvel of our creation. It has intrigued doctors and scientists for centuries and will possibly continue to do so for centuries more. Unlike the genome, the brain's activity is impossible to map. The truth is that we know very little about the brain and how it works. Oh, we know all about the chemicals and enzymes involved, what triggers what and where, and what the final effect is, but this is just the visible chain reaction that is easy to follow. What we cannot explain are the invisible bits: what actually happens in the brain in between the stimulus and response that allows us to formulate an argument or burst into tears, or feel pity and remorse, or such anger that we respond with violence.

Neuroscientists have spent the past few decades studying the brain's anatomy, function, physiology, biochemistry, and molecular biology, but all that this research has amounted to is to highlight how little we know about this mysterious organ. Intelligence has always been ascribed to the size of the brain in species. That is why we are said to be the smartest or most evolved species on Earth. And yet, whales have larger brains than humans, so where does that leave them?

Here is a short list of animals from the University of Washington in Seattle, comparing their brain sizes in grams. It must surely force us to reconsider the idea of "larger is smarter" or is there something more to the bigger brains of several species on Earth?

AVERAGE BRAIN WEIGHT IN GRAMS	
Adult human	1,300–1,400
Newborn human	350–400
Sperm whale	7,800
Fin whale	6,930
Elephant	6,000
Humpback whale	4,675
Gray whale	4,317
Killer whale	5,620
Bowhead whale	2,738
Pilot whale	2,670
Bottle-nosed dolphin	1,500–1,600
Walrus	1,020–1,126
Pithecanthropus Man	850–1,000
Camel	762
Giraffe	680
Hippopotamus	582
Leopard seal	542
Horse	532
Polar bear	498
Gorilla	465–540
Cow	425–458
Chimpanzee	420
Orangutan	370

California sea lion	363
Manatee	360
Tiger	263.5
Lion	240
Grizzly bear	234
Sheep	140
Baboon	137

Based on the above information, the bottle-nosed dolphin should be slightly more intelligent than humans, while elephants and whales should be infinitely smarter. For all we know, maybe they are. But for now there are still some countries in the world who allow the barbaric hunting and killing of these highly evolved species.

The brain and its major extension, called the medulla oblongata, can be described as a mass of interconnected nerve cells that control all the activities of the entire central nervous system. Between these two structures, they control all the voluntary and involuntary activities in our bodies. Involuntary activity would be respiration, heart rate, blood pressure, muscle activity, and all the goings-on in the digestive tract, just to name a few. Voluntary activity is basically every movement or action we engage in by first thinking about it and then doing it. Some of these may seem like involuntary reactions because our muscles are trained to perform the tasks, like walking, talking, or even typing. There are millions more activities that fall into both the voluntary and involuntary categories. It is estimated that the communication network in your brain can perform several billion connections and calculations per second. There are a number of major players in this network. Neurons or brain cells, which carry the nerve impulses rapidly between the point of stimulation and the affected organ; the neurotransmitter, which allows the message between neurons and organs to be transmitted; and receptors or receptor cells, which receive the message at the site of the affected organ, like the eye.

There are around 100 billion neurons in the brain but there are also an estimated 10–50 times as many glial cells in the brain. These perform some sort of supportive and possibly nutritive function to the neurons but their true function is yet unknown. The total estimated length of nerve fibers in the brain is around 160,000 kilometers. To get an idea of how incredibly complex the brain and its entire central nervous system really is, just look at the eye. It sits very closely located to the brain with a five centimeter long optic nerve. In this nerve there are 1.2 million fibers that send and receive messages between the brain and the eye on a constant basis. Even when we sleep the brain controls the eyes through rapid eye movement activity or REM. If you ever have doubts about a supreme creator God who master-minded all this stuff in the universe, the brain is a good place to start. It is truly the master organ of our anatomy. But the brain also controls activities that are often described as spiritual and are more mysterious by nature, like consciousness, thought, reason, emotion, love, purpose, passion, and more. These are the properties of the brain that will challenge us until we are evolved enough to understand them. But for now, we just speculate.

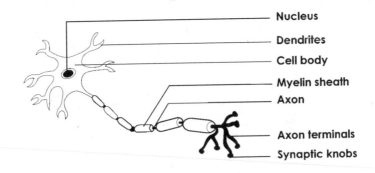

Fig. 3.1. Neuron

Someone, somewhere, at some stage in the past made the careless statement that we only use 10% of our brains. The media immediately jumped on it and the lie has been immortalized in pop science, pulp fiction articles ever since. There are a number of interesting examples to keep the theory alive. I must draw attention to the subtle difference in such claims by scholars who approach it from the point of view that the brain's potential is infinite. Their statements are, therefore, merely expressions of support for the infinite brain concept, such as was outlined by Australian neurology Nobel laureate Sir John Eccles.

Another scientist called John Lorber performed a number of autopsies in England on hydrocephalics. This condition basically causes large parts of brain tissue to be dissolved by acidic spinal fluid. He tested the IQs of patients before and during the disease. His findings showed that IQ remained constant up to death, even though more than 90% of brain tissue was destroyed by the disease. It had no impact on what is considered to be normal intelligence.

In Russia, a neurosurgeon called Alexandre Luria showed that the bulk of frontal lobes are mostly dormant when he physically proceeded to cut out large parts of frontal lobes from humans. He also gave them physiological and psychological tests before and after cutting out parts, and he even went as far as removing entire frontal lobes from patients. His conclusion was that while it had some effect on mood patterns, it caused no major change in brain function. I believe that experiments like these most likely had a lot to do with the "10% brain activity" mania.

In higher mammals there are large parts of the brain that seem to be associated with intelligence, personality, and higher mental activity. Neuroscientists have developed a number of imaging techniques to study the activity inside the brain, such as positron emission tomography (PET), magnetic resonance imaging (MRI), and computerized tomography (CT).

CT uses X-rays to discern normal brain geography from tumors and other abnormalities; MRI reveals brain structure by detecting radio waves that are deflected by tissues in a strong magnetic field; and PET detects gamma rays emitted by radioactively-labeled chemicals as they rush to active sites in the brain. Another technique, which is known as magnetoencephalography, involves measuring the magnetic currents that are generated by the electrical impulses in the brain. All of the different approaches to imaging in the brain give us some insight into brain activity and functionality, but leave humans far short of understanding the true complexity of this organ.

Many tests have been done trying to determine how much of the brain we actually use but scholars seem to differ on this estimation. As mentioned, 10% is a number often theorized, some are as bold as saying that we use up to 20%, but the more cautious ones claim that 3%–4% is much closer to the probable truth. There seems to be no specific scientific finding or origin for any of these statements. This sudden interest in the capacity of the brain may have originally been stimulated when scientists performed basic experiments with rats, and found that rats could perform most of their normal functions with as little as 2% of their cerebral cortex intact. Various extrapolations of these statements may have caused this brain usage debate, which was mainly fueled by the media and others who wanted to capitalize on such disinformation. The truth is, we probably use all of our brain. This has been illustrated by many of the previously mentioned imaging techniques over the years.

Neuroscientists have now pretty much mapped the anatomy of the brain and identified the functions of each section. Upon examining the map of the brain, you will realize that we know which part of the brain is responsible for various functions and there is not much brain left that could be called idle. But

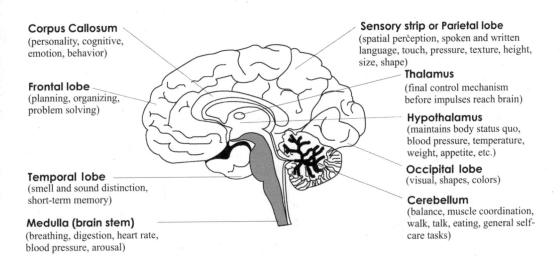

Corpus Callosum
(personality, cognitive,
emotion, behavior)

Frontal lobe
(planning, organizing,
problem solving)

Temporal lobe
(smell and sound distinction,
short-term memory)

Medulla (brain stem)
(breathing, digestion, heart rate,
blood pressure, arousal)

Sensory strip or Parietal lobe
(spatial perception, spoken and written
language, touch, pressure, texture, height,
size, shape)

Thalamus
(final control mechanism
before impulses reach brain)

Hypothalamus
(maintains body status quo,
blood pressure, temperature,
weight, appetite, etc.)

Occipital lobe
(visual, shapes, colors)

Cerebellum
(balance, muscle coordination,
walk, talk, eating, general self-
care tasks)

Fig. 3.2 The human brain

the fact is, although it seems that the whole brain is active in countless stimuli and responses, there is no scientific way that we can measure the amount of brain we use. At the same time, there is also no method to date that can measure the full capacity of the brain. So we should be asking what the capacity of the brain is, rather than how much of the brain we actually use.

The two approaches are philosophically opposed. The one approach assumes that the brain capacity is finite and aims to measure the current usage, while the other suggests that our brain capacity could be infinite.

Many scientists claim that nutrition plays a key role in the performance and possibly evolution of the brain. Much has been written about healthy diets with very specific dietary instructions to help certain conditions. While diet and nutrients undoubtedly play a crucial role in the health and smooth performance of the brain, it is impossible to claim any long-term evolutionary benefits from such treatment. It would be equivalent to saying that a daily moisturizing regime will make you immortal. The one thing that many scientists seem to agree on is that around 200,000 years ago the human brain underwent a dramatic evolutionary change. Various theories for this sudden increase in brain size and intelligence have had scientists guessing and speculating for years. The popular theory doing the rounds is one of high seafood intake.

The different functions of the left brain and the right brain have been well documented. Here are some examples:

LEFT-BRAIN FUNCTIONS	RIGHT-BRAIN FUNCTIONS
Written language	Insight
Number skills	3-D forms
Reasoning	Art awareness
Spoken language	Imagination
Scientific skills	Music awareness
Right-hand control	Left-hand control

Let's take a quick look inside the brain and at some crucial statistics: The brain is involved in everything you do, either voluntarily or involuntarily. As was pointed out before, some of the involuntary activities that are controlled by the brain are your heartbeat, breathing and coughing, or better described as all the things that need to continue functioning while you sleep. The voluntary activities are all the things you do consciously, like walking, writing, talking, smiling.

When your brain functions properly, you function properly as a well-synchronized unit. But when your brain hits a few bumps it can manifest itself in a multitude of unwanted side effects. The brain is active from the moment you are born to the day you kick the bucket. If it had to shut down for even a second, all the involuntary functions in your body would shut down too. Something as simple as breathing or your heartbeat would basically put an end to you if your brain had to stop functioning. Because the brain is so active and never stops, it consumes about 20%–30% of the body's energy. To achieve such a high consumption of blood, it is serviced by about 400 miles of capillaries delivering a constant supply of oxygen, glucose, and other nutrients. So if you want to lose weight you have to think harder.

There are about 100 billion neurons or nerve cells in the brain. Alcohol and drugs destroy these cells by the millions. They do grow back, however. Each neuron or nerve cell is connected to other nerve cells in the brain, by hundreds or even thousands of connections, called dendrites. It is estimated that there are over 1,000,000,000,000,000 (ten to the power of fourteen, 10^{14}) connections in the brain, more connections than there are stars in the Milky Way. The brain is more complicated than any computer we can imagine. The reason we can make such a silly comparison is because we now know that the brain's capacity is infinite.

A single neuron can produce almost a tenth of a volt electrical charge, and the total electrical activity in your brain can easily be measured with an electroencephalogram (EEG). This allows us to actually measure brain activity and test the activity under various stimuli. Just like the other cells in your body, the brain cells also start to decline and die after a certain period. The receptors also decline with age. The neurotransmitter serotonin interacts with at least fifteen different receptors in the body, but after the age of about twenty, one of serotonin's most common receptors starts to decline and vanishes from the human brain at about 15% per decade, which may be why depression commonly appears in middle age.

The suggestion that a high seafood diet was the cause of this major brain change around 200,000 years ago is silly and makes no scientific sense at all. There had to be a more dramatic event that caused such a change in the brains of our ancestors. There is emerging evidence supported by genetic and mitochondrial dating that seems to point to such a dramatic event. It seems that scientists in all fields of expertise are constantly providing us with more evidence of our human ancestry, but most of us are totally oblivious to the evidence that surrounds us. Keep in mind the coincidental fact that mitochondrial Eve and chromosomal Adam were both dated back to around 200,000 years ago. Just a coincidence, or another piece of the Great Human Puzzle that fits perfectly? Those scientists who ascribe this sudden brain change to dietary habits of the ancient *Homo sapiens* are saying that those who ate more seafood evolved bigger brains over millions of years. They compare the small brains of inland *Australopithecus afarensis* some 2 million years ago to *Homo sapiens* some 200,000 years ago. Can you see the problem here? These changes in brain size happened suddenly, as if overnight. They are more easily explained by genetic manipulation than gradual evolution due to high fish consumption. Besides, the two species have no connection in their evolutionary lines anyway.

This kind of theory is a clear indication of how resistant some sectors of the scientific fraternity are to new discoveries that challenge the conventional way of thinking. *Homo habilis* (translation: handy man) was the first of its genus, who lived between 2.2 and 1.6 million years ago, with an average brain size of 500–750 ml. The next in line was *Homo erectus,* around 2 million–400,000 years ago, with a brain capacity of 800–900 ml. Then suddenly around 200,000 years ago a new species appears out of the blue with a brain 55% bigger. This calls for some serious investigation, since Darwin believes that evolution does not happen in jumps. How is it possible that such a species could miraculously appear, be able to think, able to reason, and able to calculate? There must be more plausible theories for this phenomenon.

Scientists go on trying to substantiate their big brain theory by comparing the high fish intake of humans some 28,000 years ago in central Europe. Neanderthals had a low seafood intake, surviving mostly on meat from inland animals, and this is why they were outlived by *Homo sapiens,* who had a high Omega-3 and Omega-6 fatty acid intake. The crucial mistake they make here is that fossilized evidence has clearly shown that *Homo neanderthalensis* had a larger brain than *Homo sapiens,* by 5%–10%. Scientists have also proved that a high seafood intake dramatically reduces the levels of depression among its population. North American and European populations showed a rate of depression 10 times greater than a Taiwanese population who consumed a lot of fish. The Japanese, whose diet is also rich in fish, have a significantly lower incidence of depression compared to North Americans and Europeans. Once again, these are simply cosmetic reactions by the brain that will have no effect on how the genome has been programmed. This theory will need more evidence that points to DNA restructuring or some form of evolution to make it stick. Putting make-up on your face will not keep you immortal.

So while it may be true that fats build your brain and proteins unite it, carbohydrates fuel the brain, and micronutrients defend it, the real miracle lies in the fact that your DNA planted the programmed code at your point of conception, which allowed your brain to grow into its fully functional form. As incredible an organ as the brain may be, it is ultimately controlled by the genome, just like every other minute aspect of our being.

It does seem that the brain may have a limitless capacity for higher functions not yet understood by humans. A variety of unexplained psychic abilities have been demonstrated by large numbers of individuals. They are more often than not looked upon as freaks of nature and not regarded as a possible higher state of evolution that needs closer attention. We can look at the brain as the interface between the physical and the spiritual: our body and our soul. Somehow, some individuals have mastered these higher brain activities without knowing how and why. This adds another mysterious element to the Great Human Puzzle. How and why have some people cultivated ESP skills? It makes complete sense to me that while the genome is evolving toward its own completion, it keeps unlocking parts of our brain, allowing us to perform higher mental functions.

So if the brain is indeed the physical interface between body and spirit, it will take a lot more evolution on our behalf to understand it. Remember, the genome and the spirit cannot evolve at individual speeds. So while the genome controls the rate of evolution of the brain, it is then by default also the genome that ultimately dictates the pace at which the soul is allowed to evolve while trapped in our human body. Like the laws of osmosis, the two concentrations on either side of the membrane will eventually reach a state of equilibrium, but only if the membrane is permeable and allows these to cross. Our DNA will allow the spirit in our bodies to mix with the greater spirit in the universe, in bite-size chunks, as we evolve and as we learn to deal with our newfound knowledge.

All this strange activity in the ancient past that caused our brains to suddenly expand goes a long way to substantiate that there must have been some kind of genetic manipulation involved; the kind of manipulation that was revealed to us in ancient clay tablets written somewhere between 4,000 and 6,000 years ago. This new emerging information has found favor with only a handful of broad thinkers. Many archaeologists, historians, and anthropologists are very nervous about dealing with such sudden leaps in philosophy. I hope to show you a steady, cohesive trail of evidence that points to the placement of an advanced race of beings, right here on Earth at the time when our brains had so miraculously expanded. Not only did they leave behind written evidence of their genetic manipulation, but they actually explain in great detail the reasons why they needed to create a primitive worker on this planet.

Just think about how many times people say to you, "I don't know if I want to hear that . . . it sounds too horrendous." That is really an honest admission that they are not ready to receive certain information. When it comes to new truths regarding our origins and spirituality, people are not that polite about it. The majority of the world's population is not yet ready to face these new emerging facts, even if they were asked to contemplate them only as a theory to begin with. On the contrary, most people will reject any such utterances with high levels of contempt. After all, they know exactly where they come from and who their god is, clearly displaying the power of our preprogrammed genome to keep humanity obedient and fearful of its maker.

So, what have we learned in this chapter? The brain is an infinitely complex organ with a capacity for processing knowledge and information that goes way beyond our imagination. All the mystique around the brain raises the possibility that it is an interface between the physical and the spiritual worlds. Regardless of its complexity, the program for its development comes from the genome. Around 200,000 years ago the brain underwent a dramatic increase in size, just about at the time when the Anunnaki created the Adamu, according to the Sumerian tablets. The sudden increase in the *Homo sapiens* brain could not have occurred due to millions of years seafood consumption. The human race uses only a fraction of its brain, which is strictly controlled by our genome. All this leads to some crucial questions to close this chapter. What will our mental and spiritual capacity be when our genome has fully evolved? Who were the Anunnaki? Why and how did they create humankind?

4

A JOURNEY BACK IN TIME

IF WE DON'T KNOW WHERE we come from, how can we possibly know where we are going? In this chapter we will attempt to find pointers in both directions. We need to dig deep into our prehistory before we start gazing far into the future. Fortunately, we have been handed loads of knowledge by our advanced ancestors. This information paints a very clear picture of exactly who we are and where we are heading as a species. All of this is possible because of hereditary DNA transfer, combined with thousands of clay tablets filled with historic entries that have been treated either as mythology or the mutterings of primitive folk with nothing better to do.

So at the risk of becoming repetitive, let me remind you that to know where we are going, we need to know where we come from. To start our journey back in time, we need to retrace the steps of modern humans and use all the resources available, including knowledge and information from prehistoric scriptures that may have previously been dismissed as garbage. The Sumerian tablets have been a fascinating revelation and a source of mysterious knowledge. So little is known about prehistory, about the time before time, that when new dramatic evidence rises to the surface, it can sound so fantastical to us modern humans in the twenty-first century, that we refuse to accept it. We all talk about Greek and Roman mythology; we know their gods and we even know their designations: Venus, Pluto, Mercury, Isis, Thor, Apollo, and the all-powerful Zeus, just to remind you of a few. But were these just fairy-tale heroes from ancient times or were they really beings with superior powers? The Sumerian tablets tell us that these were real gods and not imaginary names for forces of nature. The names might have changed from civilization to civilization, but their influence has shaped all of humanity to date.

Just when I sat down to start writing this chapter, I had visitors who popped in on a Saturday afternoon. We relaxed with a chilled glass of wine by the pool and the subject of evolution and our ancestry came up. I asked my friends what they thought of evolution, and what they know about our ancient prehistory, and how and when we became human. Jana immediately expressed her understanding that we became human when we jumped out of the trees and started walking upright. Clearly not an opinion based on any levels of credible research, and yet, probably a very similar perception shared by many others who have had the misfortune of being brainwashed by the modern education system. Anton, on the other hand, was a bit more reserved and unsure of the answers, but he was sure that the evolutionist had got it right and that we evolved from some sort of apelike species over millions of years.

From these and numerous other discussions I've had over a period of fifteen years, it seems that there are still two main theories that captivate the minds of modern humans: the evolution path and the creation path. I have personally grappled with the conflict between the two for nearly two decades, only to discover that there is a third possibility! This one may possibly satisfy the fanatical beliefs of both sides, while opening their eyes to new realities that have emerged out of our ancient past.

While new discoveries and evidence are continually being presented, the finish line keeps moving. Every time some smart person postulates the latest unassailable argument supported by remarkable evidence, it just stimulates more debate and controversy that inevitably leads to more discoveries and more debate. It is truly a great journey of discovery that no person should lay claim to hastily. Scientists and anthropologists will continue to differ on this subject for years to come, but I do feel a convergence of the two doctrines is unavoidable. Just recently I heard a priest talk about how he would welcome any alien species as the miracle of God's creation. He made a clear point of differing with previous religious dogma, which places man at the center of creation, god's great masterpiece, and as the pinnacle of intelligence and master of the beasts.

It is impossible to argue against evolution as it has been presented to us over the past 150 years. We are surrounded by evidence everywhere that supports evolution in the animal world and in the plant world. This is not the challenge I am raising in this book. My struggle lies with the last few hundred thousand years on this planet that saw the emergence of humanity and the disappearance of the hominid creature who preceded us.

I need to quickly draw a link between the words *humankind* and *humanity.* I present that you cannot have humanity without humankind and, therefore, the two are inextricably linked, with subtle differences in our personal interpretation. So I purposely use the two interchangeably to illustrate this simple relationship. Evolution has played an important role in how the two have entwined as man has evolved. There are, however, some fascinating shortcomings in the Darwinian theory that have already been attacked endlessly by much smarter people than me.

It does seem that Darwin may not have had it all correct. Darwin actually borrowed much of his doctrine from many other scientists and brilliant people before him, sometimes seemingly distorting the theories to support his own. I trust that if he had lived today, he would most likely change his mind dramatically about his natural selection theory based on the new evidence available.

It was not actually Charles Darwin who first coined the phrase *natural selection,* when he published his controversial bible on evolution in 1859, called *On the Origin of Species by Means of Natural Selection, or the Preservation of Favoured Races in the Struggle for Life.* It was another biologist by the name of Patrick Matthew who in 1831 referred to the "natural process of selection." He saw it as a more descriptive term than "the feedback idea," which was used leading up to that point. Natural selection was described as "the properties which best permit particular individuals possessing them to survive and reproduce their own genetic variants, will increase from generation to generation, more in proportion than other individuals with less beneficial genetic structures." In a nutshell, what this really means is "the survival of the fittest." There was another concept that Darwin seems to have borrowed as well: the analogy of the branching tree of life, which was described by Alfred Russel Wallace in 1855.

One of the very strong points Darwin makes is that evolution does not happen in jumps. It took about 120 years for Fred Hoyle and Chandra Wickramasinghe to show that evolution does happen in jumps with the help of viruses and bacteria that arrive on Earth from space in a process called panspermia. These new arrivals from space constantly mutate, infect the cells of plants and creatures, and quite quickly cause dramatic changes in the DNA structure of the host.

To demonstrate this outlandish proposition very basically, I would like you to take your mind back to your school classroom wall. Picture the poster with the chronological stages of human evolution. The apelike creature on the left, the slightly taller apelike creature to its right with less hair, and a slightly taller and more upright apeman to its right with even less hair;

eventually we end up with a handsome man on the extreme right representing modern humans, as the pinnacle of evolution. From ape to human, just like that. They show us these simplistic illustrations that leave children with preconceived ideas that this evolution thing is pretty well documented and understood. They do not tell the children that this is just one hypothesis of how we became human. There is a deafening silence from the anthropologists about what exactly happened in the gaps between the different stages of evolution. We would be wiser to teach our children the full truth instead of the sweetened half-truth. There are giant jumps of evolution between every creature on the evolution poster. How is that possible? What happened to the thousands of evolutionary steps between every stage? Or, did the creature on the left live for millions of years, when suddenly it gave birth to a creature that looked nothing like it? What could have sparked such a dramatic change? Clearly it was a genetically driven change, but what would have caused such a dramatic genetic deviation so quickly, when it was happy in its previous form for millennia?

At the end of the eighteenth century, James Hutton felt unhappy with the concept of gradual evolution when relating it to the geological activity on Earth and the principles of uniformity in geology. He stated that "the processes at work on and inside the Earth have been operating in the same general way throughout geological history. The overall environment has remained broadly the same for 500 million years, while life has changed dramatically from simple neurological beginnings, to highly complex present day forms. How could this measure of change come about in a broadly unchanging environment, if species were always optimised to their maximum extent?"

Since the unearthing of Lucy and Mrs. Ples, the Taung skull and the Turkana boy, which were all landmarks in the field of archaeology, thousands upon thousands of fossil skeletons of hominids and other human ancestors or relatives have been found. Just when we think we have a clear picture of how humans evolved, and a better understanding of the great apes that lived alongside them, we are faced with a new discovery that forces us to rethink some of the fundamentals. Just recently, two major discoveries shook our views quite dramatically. In September 2003, Ebu was unearthed in a cave on the Indonesian island of Flores. Standing at only about 1 meter tall, she is the smallest adult hominid known. It is estimated that Ebu lived from around 95,000 years ago until as recently as 13,000 years ago. This was the first time we actually realized that we were not alone on this planet until relatively recently, but shared it with people from another species! Ebu was not a simple *Homo sapiens,* she was apparently human.

Another discovery was made about the great ape family in Spain during 2005, near Barcelona. Salvador Maya-Sola and Miquel Crusafont unearthed a fossilized skull and partial skeleton of a great ape, *Pierolapithecus cata-launicus.* This great ape is thought to have lived in the Middle Miocene period 12–13.5 million years ago, when the great apes, which include gorillas, chimpanzees, and humans, split from the lesser apes like gibbons and siamangs. Although it is possible that this was the ancestor of the great apes, the major difference is that this great ape could not swing through the trees. I mention these examples of very recent discoveries to prove the simple point that the more we seem to think we know, the more surprises we receive to remind us that we know very little. We should keep an open mind at all times and realize that while we evolve as humans, our evolving genome forces us to ask more complex questions and discover even more staggering answers.

Let us now take a journey into our human past to realize how young and fragile our species is and how little time we have spent on this Earth. This is an important journey we need to take, to place the argument between creation and evolution squarely on the table. Armed with this knowledge, we will postulate a new combination of the two theories, which will offend neither those who believe that God made all life on Earth, nor the evolutionists who cling onto the Darwinian doctrine of natural selection. We will, however, need to stress the important differences between God and god. A little technicality with universal implications, which seems to have evaded the attention of humanity for millennia.

AD 2004	The modern Olympics return to Greece where it started in 1896, displaying the human struggle to hold onto peace, camaraderie, and fair competition.
AD 1903	Wilbur and Orville Wright make the first claim to have flown a heavier-than-air machine—the airplane.
AD 1452	Leonardo da Vinci is born to become the central and most influential figure of the Renaissance period.
AD 570	Muhammad was born in Mecca. Inspired by the Jewish and Christian monotheism, he went on to recite the Koran which was inspired by the angel Gabriel. This book united the Muslims under the principles of Islam and gave birth to the youngest of the world's Abrahamic religions.

Year 0	This actual date is debatable: the birth of Christ, the start of the modern calendar. Jesus Christ introduced a revolutionary new philosophy of love and peace among humanity. This was a dramatic break from the Old Testament of the Bible, and he was seen as the messiah by some and a traitor by others. Jesus was probably the most influential and the most controversial human to have walked the Earth. His gospel inspired prophets, kings, and presidents, but it was also abused as a symbol of power by dictators and religious groups even before he was born, and this abuse is still continuing today. The debate goes on: Was he the son of God in the body of a man, or just a prophet who was pushed by the needs of the people of the day? Or maybe he was someone with special powers in a place and time when humanity needed a new direction and a message of hope.
31 BC	Foundation of the Roman Empire.
776 BC	First Olympic games are held in Greece.
1200 BC	Iron Age begins.
1224 BC	Death of Ramses the Great.
2000 BC	Abraham living in Canaan.
2500 BC	Stonehenge stone circle built.
2570 BC	The Great Pyramid of Giza is completed. (Speculative theory, not conclusively proven.)
2900 BC	First monetary system introduced: Mesopotamian shekel.
3000 BC	Bronze Age begins. Oldest artifacts depicting wheeled carts in Mesopotamia.
3500–3700 BC	Traditional date for the oldest cities known. Uruk in southern Mesopotamia—Modern Iraq and Tell Hamoukar further north.
4000 BC	More evidence of cities. Tell Brak in modern Syria shows evidence of administrative buildings and traders. A seal stamp from the fifth millennium BC has been found there.
5000 BC	Earliest known writing. Balkan-Danube Script, originating from Europe along the Danube river, not yet deciphered.
6000 BC	The plough is invented.
8000 BC	Mammoths go extinct on the Siberian mainland.
9000 BC	Colonization of the Americas.
9600 BC	The last ice age ends. The world enters a warmer period that still persists to date.

10000 BC	First domesticated crops. Evidence of the earliest villages and the oldest known pottery from the Jomon period of Japan. This period is also thought to have been when dogs were first domesticated.
20,000 years ago	The last ice age is at its peak.
30,000 years ago	*Homo neanderthalensis* die out. They lived mostly in what is now Europe. It is important to note that modern *Homo sapiens* lived at the same time and probably side by side with them.
35,000 years ago	Cave paintings in Europe.
40,000 years ago	Traditional date for the origin of Material culture.
50,000 years ago	Colonization of Australia.
75,000 years ago	Clothing invented. The oldest beads were discovered in South Africa dating back 77,000 years, right to the middle of the Stone Age.
90,000 years ago	Modern humans start migrating out of Africa into Eurasia.
120,000 years ago	Widespread use of pigments like ochre in Africa.
170,000 years ago	Mitochondrial Eve. The first female ancestor of all living humans. This date varies from 150,000–250,000 based on various interpretations by scientists.
170,000 years ago	Adam is born. From the Y-chromosome passed down only through males, it has been calculated that Adam, the first man on Earth, was created at this time. This date also varies by the same margins as Eve. (It is curious to see that Adam and Eve seem to have been created at the same time—this will form a very convincing part of our story in later chapters.)
200,000 years ago	First anatomically modern humans make their appearance.

From *New Scientist* 2004

It seems that there may be a clash in this time line—did other humans exist before Adam and Eve? This is also part of the puzzle that seems to corroborate our theories in later chapters.

This was the easy part of the journey back in time, because we really only covered the journey of one species: *Homo sapiens* and *Homo sapiens sapiens,* the more civilized version of the earlier. There is a very fine line between the two, and scholars are still at odds about where the one suddenly became the other—

a slightly more streetwise version of its prior self. There was possibly a period during which the two relatives may have crossed over and lived side by side, and the clay tablets certainly give us enough evidence to take such suggestions seriously. This part of our archaic history has, however, been rewritten many times before and probably will be rewritten many times again, until we are presented with irrefutable evidence from some credible, unquestionable source. What we will take from this evidence is anyone's guess, but it would have to be pretty convincing to draw mass appeal from a generally uninformed global populace. The funny thing is that such evidence has existed for thousands of years, without us taking any notice of it. It's as if we emerged out of those prehistoric times as an ignorant species, and for some obscure reason forgot everything we had been through. Could this phenomenon have something to do with our shortened lifespan? A curious anomaly, which is way out of step with the many years our distant ancestors apparently lived? If that is the case, then why is it that we only live for an average of 70 years, while the biblical characters and others before them are shown to have lived for as long as 900 years and even more? The answers are all well documented in the enigmatic clay tablets that we will uncover in later chapters.

But for now, the next part of our journey back in time gets very interesting because we have to use our imagination and powers of visualization. That is what most anthropologists will want from you, as the evolutionary jumps between the fossilized hominids become very large. While evolutionists expect us to buy into the fantastic story of human evolution, in the same breath most scholars will also tell you that there are anything from 20 to 50 evolutionary steps between each identified genus or species. Unfortunately, we have had no proof or evidence of any of these in-between steps of evolution. What this really means is that we face a dilemma of many missing links, and not just the "missing link" that we often joke about. I know that we have all spotted a potential candidate for the missing link in our neighborhood, or a potential candidate for *Homo neanderthalensis,* but you can rest assured that you are mistaken. But then on the other hand, maybe not!

Let us go back to around 30,000 years ago. This is the time when Neanderthals apparently disappeared from Earth. The debate around Neanderthals has been raging since the first skeleton was discovered in 1857, just two years before Darwin published *Origin of Species.* It seems that Darwin simply ignored this momentous find as it did not really fit his model of evolution. Many theories have been postulated about this species, mostly depicted as wild savages who were much more primitive than humans. This seems a little arrogant and probably premature since we now know that the Neanderthal brain was on average 1,200–1,750 ml, which would make it approximately 100 ml larger than modern humans. If you consider that we only use 3%–10% of our brains, just think of what the Neanderthals would have been capable of today.

In 1999, the skeleton of a child was unearthed in Portugal. It was dated back to 25,000 years ago. It had very strange features that looked like it could be a hybrid between modern human and Neanderthal. This prompted scientists to extract small fragments of DNA from three different Neanderthal specimens, which showed that they were not closely related to any present-day human population. Neanderthal anatomy, on the other hand, is essentially human in scope, with the same number of bones as humans, which function in the same manner. There are, however, minor differences in thickness and strength. Based on some rigorous dental studies, it seems that Neanderthals may have had a greater longevity than modern humans, which may have also affected their anatomy.

The reason I am taking you on this little journey, which I trust will end before you get too bored, is purely to illustrate the complexity and contradictions that have been troubling this field of science for centuries. From these high levels of speculation and uncertainty, others like myself can take some respite that although I do not have a Ph.D. behind my name, I do understand the fields of gambling, speculation, and deduction.

A perfect example of anthropologic contradiction lies in that some evolutionists claim that Neanderthals were incapable of modern speech. They apparently lacked the ability to produce the full range of vowels because the flat, nonflexing bone at the base of their skull and larynx was positioned higher in the throat than in modern humans, or even chimpanzees. A computerized reconstruction of this part of their anatomy showed that the resonating chamber at the back of the mouth was all but eliminated. This obviously supported their argument and placed Neanderthals in a completely different league from humans. But a new reconstruction of the same anatomy showed it to be quite human. What brought Neanderthals even closer to us modern humans was a discovery of the most complete Neanderthal skeleton in 1983, which contained the first Neanderthal fossil hyoid bone. This bone is located in the throat and is integral to the formation of sound in speech: it is indistinguishable from that of modern humans.

To add to the intrigue of who these Neanderthal people really were, let me add some more startling discoveries. In 1996, a small flute made from the thigh bone of a cave bear was found in a cave in Slovenia. It had four precisely aligned holes punctured on one side of the four-inch-long bone, pointing irrefutably to evidence that strongly supports Neanderthal "humanness." Furthermore, they made tools to make other complex tools, buried their dead, had controlled use of fire, practiced religious ceremonies, used complex syntax in their spoken grammar, and played musical instruments.

Some Neanderthal graves have stone tools, animal bones, and even flowers buried in the ground next to their remains. The corpse was not simply dropped into a hole in the Earth without preparation; it was prepared and buried in an unusual posture. This implies an awareness of the afterlife, demonstrates the existence of formal ritual, and is also an indication of strong social ties. This is also supported by evidence that Neanderthal individuals with severe crippling injuries were cared for. So? Were Neanderthals human and somehow related to us? Or were they just wild and primitive cavemen who deserved extinction? Maybe an explanation of our own humanity may shed some light on the possible answers a little later in this book.

Now that we have dealt with a possible human relative who lived on Earth and shared it with modern humans for around 200,000 years, let us travel further back and take a quick look at how the other hominid ancestors fit into the picture. Once again, the most recent knowledge is constantly under scrutiny and will most likely be modified as a result of new discoveries in years to come. But years after the first discovery of *Australopithecus afarensis*, scientists still do not rank them as ancestors to humans. In the areas of archaeology and anthropology, like in all the others of science, disagreement is widespread. So, the information below should be absorbed with a sense of speculation and uncertainty.

Just recently in the year 2000, scientists discovered a possible hominid that they call *Orrorin tugenensis*. It lived around 6 million years ago in Kenya and possessed clear features that indicate it walked upright. This was certainly an early entry for the two-legged race and some dare to say that it may be one of the many missing links. Certain features, like the teeth of *Orrorin tugenensis*, suggest this species could even be more closely related to *Homo sapiens* than the many *Australopithecus* species it predates. Like our molars, the molars of *Orrorin tugenensis* were small compared to any of the australopithecine teeth. Their teeth also had very thick enamel like ours.

Australopithecus afarensis lived from approximately 4–2.7 million years ago along the northern Rift Valley of east Africa, and possibly even earlier. They seem to be the root ancestors of all subsequent hominids who were reasonably adapted for upright walking. Some of the bones in their feet were slightly curved and looked like the bones you would expect to see in a human ancestor who climbed trees. Although they probably lived in flat savannah areas,

Australopithecus afarensis was capable of climbing trees in times of danger, and it is possible that they slept in trees, like baboons do in areas where there are no caves for shelter. *Australopithecus afarensis* is classified as an ape, not a human: a hominid ape closely related to human beings but not necessarily an ancestor.

So, maybe my friend Jana was right after all. When the apes came down from the trees and started walking upright, we became human; the origin of bipedalism must be seen as the major step in human evolution. Walking around on their hind limbs, leaving their forelimbs free for other jobs, was an unusual mode of locomotion for mammals. Suddenly, many things associated with being human became possible, such as fine manipulation with the hands and carrying food back to base camp. This does not necessarily mean that 4 million years ago primitive hominids evolved upright walking to develop a food-sharing economy. This kind of behavior only arose several million years after the development of upright walking.

Australopithecus africanus, meaning "southern ape of Africa" was actually the first discovery of an early hominid in Africa. They lived 3–2 million years ago and probably stood around 4 feet 6 inches tall, which means they walked upright. Raymond Dart found the well-preserved skull of a child, the Taung baby, in South Africa in 1924 and set the world alight with speculation. Could this be the missing link? For quite a while this speculation did the rounds until it became quite clear that the concept of a missing link is far more complex than just one skull. This discovery led to an intense focus on Africa as the probable site of human origins and early development. However, *Australopithecus africanus* shows no signs of tool use or any kind of permanent living site. Their huge teeth and skulls with prominent dorsal crests and large jaw muscles show that they specialized in eating tough plant material. They must have been vegetarians, while our supposed ancestors evolved as omnivores with a taste for meat.

The next group of hominids lived around 2.2–1 million years ago. They were *Australopithecus robustus*. This seems to have been a more robust version of *Australopithecus africanus* that seems to have outlived its relative in southern Africa. Also referred to as *Paranthropus robustus,* or "robust near-man," very few fossils of these hominids have been uncovered.

At this point we really kick in with humanity. *Homo habilis* is the earliest-known species of the genus *Homo:* the first human species. It existed from approximately 2.2–1.6 million years ago in east Africa. Only a few fossil remains have been unearthed so far, but they all exhibit a clear trend toward a larger brain size. *Homo habilis* brains were about 30% larger than those of *Australopithecus africanus*.

Next in line was *Homo erectus* who lived from approximately 2 million to around 400,000 years ago. Coming across this information was to me like finding the holy grail. As we will uncover later, it is around this time that the tampering with genetics first begins to pop its head out of the pages of prehistory. These dramatic tales will be looked at in great detail. *Homo erectus* had a large brain ranging from 900ml–1200 ml. This was a 50% increase in brain size over the older *Homo habilis.* The largest brain sizes of *Homo erectus* fall within the range of modern humans; although the brain is configured somewhat differently than our own, it nevertheless provides a crucial link to the origins of *Homo sapiens* and our very first direct relatives.

The following statement is the kind of scientific babble that truly demonstrates our need to make empty pronouncements, when there is actually not much to say. "The transition from *Homo erectus* to *Homo sapiens,* the earliest forms of our own species, occurred approximately 300,000 to 400,000 years ago." Do yourself a favor and ask any paleoanthropologist to explain to you how exactly this transition occurred! Unfortunately there is no clear explanation for this process and they rely on some imaginary sequence of events and environmental conditions that would have sped up the evolutionary process. What seem to be missing are the many gradual steps from one form to the other. It is simply not feasible that the last female of the species woke up one morning and gave birth to a completely new species.

What is, however, very important and impressive is the fact that they found items such as wooden tools and weapons that give evidence of a hunting lifestyle among *Homo sapiens.* There is much speculation about a 300,000-year-old skull that was found near Petralona in northeastern Greece by Dr. Aris Poulianos in 1997. He claims that it is the most complete find of early *Homo sapiens* and believes that human civilization existed on Earth over one million years ago. He has produced a variety of tools and other implements that indicate these humans had the ability to communicate with speech. There is much more to be explored around this find, so for now I would like to return to what is historically documented in Sumerian tablets.

Once again I ask you to place this in your memory banks, as it will be used further as evidence of our birth as a slave species. A number of 130,000-year-old skulls have been found in southern and eastern Africa, once again giving us a link to the story of human creation. But we will discover that our creation was followed by 200,000 years of exploitation by a more evolved species who appeared on this planet out of nowhere. The rest of the chapters will slowly introduce us to these progenitors of the human race, expose the readers to the calculated steps that were taken to create the "primitive worker," as they called it, and the years of enslavement that followed.

Why is it that we can trace slavery and the obsession with gold all the way back to the very beginning of human origins? Therein lies the terrible truth about the reasons for our existence, our ignorance, and our genetic origins. All of this information has been carefully handed down to us in cuneiform clay tablets from the earliest days of writing. These tablets will also explain our natural tendencies, why we look the way we do, and why we could have possibly experienced such rapid stages of mental evolution in the past few hundred years. Deep inside our genome, in between all the brutal and barbaric genes, there is a natural tendency for compassion, love and peace, which is encoded, but switched off. Sometimes it breaks through the clutter; as the genome evolves and allows us to move closer to a completely reconstructed DNA, we are one step closer to a perfect genome and total enlightenment on both the physical and spiritual fronts.

5

THE GENOME

Human Software Program

BY THE TIME WE REACHED the year 2000, there were two terms in the global vocabulary that spread fear and confusion among people around the world: *millennium bug* and *cloning*. But hindsight is an exact science, and in hindsight it certainly seems that the first feared item was possibly a conspiracy by the global computer industry to rake in billions of dollars on the back of ignorant consumers. The millennium came and went with virtually no hiccups, yet the coffers of the IT sector swelled with unimaginable wealth. The other term, brandished about carelessly by the media and swashbuckling journalists trying their best to impress their readers with their knowledge of this new science, was *genetic engineering*. This was highly unfortunate as it was inevitably followed by another new buzz word: *cloning*. This was very sad, as those two words immediately conjured up gruesome images in the minds of the global population, of butcherlike scientists hacking and splicing human genes, while creating an endless number of humanoid monsters and other unimaginable creatures who would overpopulate the world. People were imagining horrific tales of human-animal clones and many other interspecies clones of unthinkable horror. There was talk of cloning extinct animals like the mammoth, saber-toothed tigers, and even some dinosaurs. This was, however, a typical sensationalistic response by the media in an attempt to attract readers and audiences. You see, if they were to report responsibly on the subject, keeping the facts as scientific and realistic as possible, they would not have had as large a response from the consumer, whose perception of science and progress is pretty much driven by Hollywood.

The lack of understanding of this exciting new field of science was suddenly

51

thrust into the limelight of global politics and attracted the attention of religious groups worldwide. In a flash the world had a new evil to fight. Lengthy debates on cloning and genetic engineering erupted all over the world, causing one of the most controversial issues of the new millennium. The truth is that genetic engineering is the most exciting development in the history of humankind. As we develop this knowledge and refine our skills in this area, we will come ever so closer to dealing with most, if not all, disease in living creatures, but more importantly, we will come to understand our imperfect genome. This knowledge will help us in speeding up our evolutionary process by unlocking the junk genes that will most likely help speed up our spiritual evolution. What this really means is that we will not only be able to deal with our physical disorders and malfunctions, but also our mental and spiritual shortcomings. We can speed up the evolution toward a violence-free global community that strives for absolute physical and spiritual harmony. This is what excites me most about this new science of genetic engineering. Before we can elaborate on this subject, we need to dispel some myths and misconceptions you may have heard from your mechanic while he was changing your oil.

In short, genetic engineering deals with the study of our genome: splicing, duplicating, copying, replacing, and any form of manipulation involving genes in our DNA. There is so much interest in the actual activity of genes and what kind of effect they have on our bodies that there is very little time to dream up the creation of monsters. My assumption is that the most active area of genetic engineering is the study of genes for medical research and medical applications. After all, we are driven by the greed gene, and in a global capitalist economy genetic healing is where all the money and power of the future will be. It is now known that genetic engineering will most likely be able to treat any human disease imaginable. It follows that the world will soon be run by two major players: the media, telling us what to think; and genetics, allowing us to be what we want to be. But we first have to understand much more about this field of science before we can make such claims convincingly.

So what are genes? We talk about genes as if we see them on a daily basis. As if we all have a stash of genes somewhere in our bodies and we can reach in and grab a handful whenever we need to. Well, to a certain extent this is true, because every cell in our body (with the exception of a few) holds our genetic material in the nucleus of the cell. These are called *eukaryotic cells* and could also be put into the animal cell category, where the chromosomes are in the nucleus of the cells, surrounded by a nuclear membrane. The other kind of cells are called *prokaryotic cells,* but we are not dealing with those in this instance.

Our DNA performs the most complex activities imaginable, and yet the structure of the DNA molecule is so incredibly simple that it truly baffles the mind. I am extremely concerned to find that the majority of source material I used called DNA the "most complex molecule in our body."

I strongly disagree. The simplicity with which the molecule is put together is another indication of the miracle of life and the absolute supreme intelligence of the creator God with a big "G," or the Supreme Being, or whichever name makes you feel comfortable. I always imagine DNA as a very long line of Lego blocks made up of only three different colors. If we consider that DNA is a molecular structure that contains all the codes and information needed to build, control, and maintain a living organism, we once again stumble upon the subtle hint that we should live forever, because DNA should control and maintain a living organism. All the programs and codes that control our body are in this tiny molecule. The structure is actually so simple that it raises another question. Could the DNA be somehow extended to whatever length we want it to be? Since we only use 3% of our DNA at present, this suggestion may seem a little premature, but you never know what our future needs may be. I would like to suggest that once we have come to terms with our genetic material and unraveled the mystery behind its code, we will be able to sculpt future DNA molecules exactly as we need them. On the other hand, that may already be preprogrammed into the molecule itself, as part of its evolutionary function. In a sense, it's like the metric system: all you do is add a zero, and you create a new unit of measure. See . . . that's how simple it is. But let's take a quick tour of the genome to demonstrate. For those with molecular science as a major, please skip this section.

Every cell in our body has a nucleus. In this nucleus lies a long double-stranded molecule shaped like a twisted ladder, called DNA: deoxyribonucleic acid. This ladder is broken up into 46 chromosomes that pair up into 23 pairs. One side of the chromosome is derived from the mother, the other side from the father. People born with Down's syndrome have one extra chromosome, totaling 47 chromosomes, causing their unusual features and brain activity. Each side of the twisted DNA ladder chromosome is made up of only three components. A sugar known as deoxyribose, phosphate, and any one of four bases: adenine, thymine, guanine, or cytosine. They are represented by the letters A, T, G, and C. That is why scientists get very excited when they find traces of phosphate on Mars, which could indicate life possibly driven by DNA. The sugar and the phosphate bind together to form the two parallel sides of the DNA ladder and the bases join each other from each side to form the rungs of the ladder. But the bases making up the rungs of the DNA ladder can only join in a specific sequence. A joins with T, and G joins with C. It is this specific combination of A–T and G–C that contains the codes for life and all the complex functions that keep us going. A short stretch of this chromosome, with a unique sequence of A, T, G, C, is referred to as a gene. Because of the unique sequence of the bases, this gene is specifically coded to control a specific function in the body. This gene can also be identified and mapped because of its unique sequence of components. This is referred to as gene mapping. The largest human chromosome contains around 280 million DNA base pairs, and it is estimated that the entire human genome consists of about 3 billion base pairs. All this genetic material in the cells of a human is called the genome.

However, genes make up only a tiny fraction of the entire genome. This amazing discovery forms the central doctrine of my arguments in this book. Incredibly, our active genes only make up about 3% of the total DNA in our chromosomes. Why?

Between each gene there are long stretches of DNA that do not appear to code for anything. Why would such a complex molecule be created with only 3% functionality? Scientists refer to this as junk DNA because they have not discovered what secret messages it is hiding, if any. This clearly makes no sense according to the evolutionist theory. If the genome was evolving from a simple to a complex structure, these long sections of the DNA would not exist. It would make sense that a relatively small number of genes may have evolved over time, only to become obsolete, but the fact that 97% of our DNA seems to be inactive leaves many questions unanswered.

One of the obvious arguments for the state of our overextended genome is that it was genetically manipulated or tampered with during the early days of our existence as a species. Our genome could have been created or copied from an existing genome of another species, or even tampered with to allow only a small portion of it to function. If we are able to do this today, why could an equally advanced group of beings not have done this to us humans a long time ago? The ancient evidence from our prehistory spells out very clearly that this is actually what happened. We will cover the actual translations of clay tablets with reference to this in later chapters.

When it was decided to sequence the entire human genome, the junk DNA was included in the project just in case it might have as yet undiscovered significance. I predict that such functionality will be discovered as we evolve and discover more and more. The outcome of the Human Genome Project was that scientists managed to sequence and map our human genome. All three billion base pairs. The surprising thing is that 99.9% of the sequence is the same in every single human on Earth.

The Human Genome Project was started in 1990 with its objective to basically draw a map of the entire human genome and thereby gain a basic understanding of the entire genetic blueprint of a human being. From this map they could then start to identify unique sequences that indicate genes and their special functions. The progress on the Genome Project convinced researchers that the three billion base pairs of the human genome could be fully sequenced by 2003, two years ahead of the original schedule. This success, coupled with the growing sense of urgency and recognition of the value of DNA sequence information, led to a major acceleration in human genome sequencing in early 1999. The international consortium of public domain laboratories committed to produce a working draft of the whole genome in the year 2000, as an intermediate step in the program, while the complete and fully accurate referenced sequence would become available during 2003.

The international sequencing consortium was releasing new data continuously, as soon as it was available. By the end of 1999, over one billion bases of the working draft were in the public domain, and amazingly, the two billion base milestone was passed during March 2000. The first complete working draft was a major scientific milestone for humankind. This was achieved in June 2000 and the draft provided an overall outline of the genome. This became an extremely useful resource for biologists everywhere, for the very first time. But the draft was not a fully accurate sequence—work on it continues, and probably will for a long time to come as they discover hidden secrets in this seemingly simple molecule.

As is the case in all science and discovery, we are always taken by surprise when we least expect it. The genes of many forms of life have an additional surprising feature: they contain stretches of DNA, called exons, each of which codes for part of a protein; and introns, which are stretches of noncoding DNA. The relationship between the inactive introns and junk DNA is not understood. Genes consist of alternating introns and exons, and the programmed genetic codes are contained in several scattered exons rather than a continuous stretch of DNA. The largest part of the DNA consists of seemingly never-ending stretches of junk DNA. In humans, 97% of DNA consists of noncoding genes while in very simple creatures like fruit flies only 17% of the DNA contains noncoding genes. This is another possible indication of strange manipulation that must have occurred at some stage in our distant past, and it ties up perfectly with the 97% junk DNA discovery. The noncoding introns make no sense in the evolutionary scheme of things. It also means that yeast with only 4% noncoding genes and fruit flies with 17% noncoding genes are more evolved than humans within their own DNA structures. At the time of

writing this book, the noncoding gene percentage in apes was not clearly established yet.

Bacteria have no introns, and biologists are uncertain whether early life-
forms lacked introns, and whether they only evolved into our DNA relatively
late when complex multicellular life arose. That might be so in primitive
organisms, but the perplexing genetic code of humans leaves many questions unanswered. I think the scientists should revisit their theories and turn
them around. They should familiarize themselves with the scriptures of the
Sumerians, which clearly describe genetic manipulation in the process of creating the Adamu. This information will help them fill in some of the missing
links in the great puzzle of human origins.

The arrangement of genes into introns and exons enables the encoded
message in one gene to be read in more than one way. The process is called
alternative splicing and has allowed scientists to code as many as 500 different
messages from one small stretch of DNA. Alternative splicing is a recent discovery and biologists do not yet know how important it is in life. What it does
point to very clearly, together with the knowledge that we only use 3% or less
of our genome, is that we have a long way to go for our genome to become fully
functional. It also shows how enormously complex the encoding for humanity
can be, in only a few genes.

I raise the primary question once again. What will humans be capable of
when the full potential of the genome is unlocked? Or . . . what capability was
humanity deprived of when all this potential was unplugged at the point of our
creation?

We have hardly stumbled upon this incredible discovery when the insatiable human greed gene pops out its ugly head. While the people of the world are
squabbling over the ethics of genetic engineering, cloning, and other processes,
which are mostly driven by emotional outbursts and very little understanding,
greedy pharmaceutical giants are attempting to lay claim to and patent some of
the newly discovered genes. Already they are seeing the future and the fact that
if they can take ownership of some of our genes, they will control all medical
procedures involving such genes in the future. It does not take a rocket scientist
to see where this can lead. If you ever believed in a conspiracy to create a super-
race of humans on Earth, hold onto your hat. This may just be the beginning.
Once the control of gene therapy lands in the hands of the rich, this kind of
science fiction fantasy will become an instant reality. This is what we should
guard against as the human race. Stop worrying about the cloning and the
monsters and the babies without parents, but rather worry about the exclusive
control of the human genome by a handful of giant medical firms. As research

and knowledge grow, money will be able to buy you everything. Height, hair, eye color, muscle tone, sexy features, health, and even eternal life. I suspect, however, that the eternal life gene will be the last one we shall conquer.

There does, however, seem to be a level of sanity and fairness in global legal circles. It seems that the patent applications by some of these giants have been overturned, as genes are regarded to be the intellectual property of all humans and cannot be exclusively owned by one group or individual. What was suggested is that companies can protect newly discovered medical procedures or drugs, which results in a desired treatment through genetic manipulation. This will protect their discoveries from exploitation for the normal fifteen- to twenty-year period, while they recover their research and development costs. This way all the people can benefit from progress without any socioeconomic discrimination.

During the past two decades, the first major breakthroughs in finding genes associated with hereditary diseases were announced. These included examples such as cystic fibrosis, hemophilia (A and B forms), muscular dystrophy, and Huntington's disease. Each one of these is an example of an inherited disease caused by defects in a single gene. More recently, genes have been discovered that contribute to more complex diseases, notably cancers of the bowel, or of the breast. These are two examples of the many diseases in which other factors, both in other genes and in the environment, also affect the onset of the disease. Complex diseases such as cancer, heart disease, diabetes, and many psychiatric disorders all involve multiple genes, unlike some defects caused by single genes. Yet the multiple gene disorders are by far the most common conditions affecting human health. Until recently, their sheer complexity has limited progress in our understanding of these diseases. The access to the human genome sequence, with a complete catalog of all human genes, has opened the way to tackling all these conditions, to understand the underlying biology of each disease and speed up the development of new and better cures.

Sequencing the human genome is only a first step. Now we know that a single gene can produce more than one protein and that a different set of proteins is found in each type of cell in the body. The big challenge facing scientists is to map the human *proteome*. This map will unveil which proteins are made by which genes and which combination of proteins is at work in each type of cell. This process is a little more complex than just mapping the genome and will most likely take a lot longer than ten years. But it will transform our understanding of how genes build humans.

Since 1999, we have identified a huge number of genes and their activity. The speed of new discoveries in genetics has been astounding. Let us take a quick look at a short list of genes that have been identified and linked to specific activity. It will give you a glimpse at some of the crucial functions in our bodies, which we will be able to manipulate in time. Many genes have also been identified in plants and animals. As strange as it may seem, their relevance to human development can often be paramount. For example, identifying which genes make plants and insects resistant to radiation and many other characteristics that would be of benefit for human survival.

Genes in the following areas of activity have been identified:

asthma
cancers—including breast, lung, colon, and skin
Alzheimer's
hearing
male fertility
radiation resistance—107 genes
Parkinson's
human hereditary genes
fat and obesity
sleep-wake cycle
UV light resistance in plants
hair loss
pain
vision
embryonic development
emphysema
azoospermia
neurodegenerative disease
psoriasis
tumor suppression
epilepsy
juvenile diabetes
cell death clock—150 genes
learning disability
bipolar depression
heart attacks and coronary disease—over 200
genes, discovered by Finnish company Jurilab

This sample is just a drop in the ocean. Thousands more genes have been identified and by the time this book is released, there will be many more. There is so much more going on in this field of science that I cannot resist just outlining a few more examples:

- Scientists are working on a novel kind of DNA vaccine that could protect people against a wide variety of conditions, from snake bites to HIV, by directly triggering the production of antibodies.
- Biotechnologists in Massachusetts are taking animal genes that make growth-promoting proteins and putting them into oysters to make them mature faster and produce pearls sooner. The first oysters to undergo the treatment grew 2.5 times faster than ordinary oyster shells and also took less time to make bigger pearls. What this will do to the value of pearls is anyone's guess at this point.
- In a study of identical and nonidentical twins, a medical team in London has shown that acne is 80% genetic. Environmental factors, such as eating the wrong foods or wearing greasy makeup, are relatively unimportant. They are close to identifying the genes that control the activity of acne, which will lead to more effective and cheaper acne treatment.
- Hans-Hinrich Kaatz and his colleagues at Jena University in Germany did an experiment that showed genes introduced into genetically modified plants jump between species into bacteria in the guts of the animals eating the plants. Could these kind of jumping genes have played a role in speeding up evolution by jumping from virus to host and altering the host's genetic structure? This theory is presented very strongly by Fred Hoyle in his book *Our Place in the Cosmos* and we deal with it in more detail in chapter 6.
- Researchers in Cincinnati are discovering how small changes in a gene could influence a person's tendency to abuse opiates, and distinguish between a person who is unlikely to abuse heroin or one predisposed to it. Discoveries like this will make it easier in the future to pinpoint and prevent addictions. Researchers have confirmed this finding and have found several new variants of the gene, one of which appears to protect against drug addiction.
- A group of genes called *novel genes* apparently undergo a change when a person starts to develop prostate cancer. This can be used as an early warning system. Now all they have to do is figure out what to do with this gene and they may reverse the process.
- Mutations in the FOXP2 gene on chromosome 7 have been found to cause specific language impairment. The gene seems to be necessary for the proper development of human speech and language.

- The 17 CREB genes play a vital part in the mechanism of learning and memory. If one of them is not working, no long-term memory can be formed. They are switched on in real time when the brain lays down a new memory. This means that the act of learning actually turns on these genes. It is a great argument for the evolution of genes and DNA, as it clearly displays a way in which nature works together with nurture. This is the kind of interaction between stimulus and response that may unlock the introns and junk genes under specific conditions, causing the release of previously unused genes, resulting in further evolution and activation of the genome.

- Vasopressin and oxytocin are hormones that stimulate bonding behavior. The vasopressin receptor gene lies on chromosome 12 in humans and is controlled by a promoter whose length varies between species. In rodents it seems to play a part in forming monogamous pairs, which means to fall in love, in human terms. Different promoter lengths have also been found among humans. This is possibly the reason why some people cannot hold down a normal relationship. It could also mean that the probability of divorce is as highly inheritable as is the possibility of a long and happy marriage.

- Now, here is some emerging evidence about that elusive violent gene I have been referring to. Research at the Institute of Psychiatry in London offers a fascinating hint of how antisocial behavior can be affected by an interaction between genes and environment. They examined a group of New Zealanders for evidence that an abusive childhood can induce antisocial behaviour; they found that indeed it can, but far more strongly in people of one genotype. Men who had been maltreated as children and had "low-active" genes for monoamine oxidase A on the X chromosome were much more likely to get into trouble with the law. They could be described as violent and display antisocial traits in a personality test. Those with "high-active" genes were broadly resistant to the effects of childhood maltreatment. The difference between the high-active and low-active genes lies once again in the promoter lengths. Long and short promoters produce low activity, intermediate promoters produce high activity.

- A gene called p53 defends you from disease and decay, but p53 also dictates how likely you are to get cancer and how fast you age. It is probably the most important molecule in the formation of cancer. Faults in the gene itself, or any of the activities it controls, are likely to be involved in the development of nearly all tumors. After 25 years of research, we are finally beginning to understand how p53 works, and how it either causes or prevents cancer.

- Howard Hughes Medical Institute researchers have identified a large number of new genes that control the formation of tiny, hairlike cilia that cover the surfaces of many organs in a wide variety of creatures. Cilia are also widely present in the human body, including the brain, nose, ears, eyes, lungs, kidneys, and sperm. These genes are important because cilia are critical for transport and as sensory structures, wherever they are located.

The purpose of presenting some of these basic examples is to demonstrate how far we have come in the field of genetics over the past twenty-five years. Things that would have been farfetched then are commonplace today. We have pushed the boundaries of knowledge way beyond what we thought would be possible. But as we learn, we realize how little we know. It's as if every new page is just the introduction to a whole book. We must remind ourselves that even some of the new truths we have learned will be proven wrong with time. But the need for discovery and exploration is well encoded in our genome and only extinction will put a stop to it. So while we are discovering new scientific breakthroughs and celebrating its relevance to our species, we should also celebrate the uncovering of old truths from prehistory. The clues and the information were left behind for us by our ancient ancestors, in the hope that we may build on their experiences without having to learn much of their hard-earned knowledge all over again. We are a fragile species on a knife's edge, precariously balancing between the rapid evolution toward the universal community of beings, or toward the destruction and extinction not only of humanity, but the entire planet. The road forward is pretty clear, but we must find a speedy solution to the millennia of propaganda, religious oppression, dogma, and fear that have been entrenched so deeply in humanity that it will take some kind of miracle from the real God to release those who are trapped by it.

Since 1977, when split genes were discovered, much has been written about why introns and junk DNA exist. There have been countless theories all taking a stab at this perplexing genetic phenomenon, some of which include: the relationship and relevance between introns and exons; various selection mechanisms; selected gene reproduction; adaptive genes with a "fitness" advantage; constructional selection and constructional advantage; the nature-nurture controversy; low and high pleiotropy; genotype-phenotype relationship; evolution of proteins; the effect of original "proto-genes"; critical and noncritical regions; selfish DNA; competition between DNA sequences; new genes evolving and being added to the genome; useful genes; exon shuffling; high and low modularity; folding genes and their effects; competition between exons; random intron insertion; and many more complex and even simple issues. Insane stuff isn't it?

What strikes me is that seemingly all these philosophies have approached the subject from the perspective that introns and junk DNA are just a waste of space on the genome whose only possible function is that of their relevance of position. They may play a role in DNA division, but because all the introns are discarded by mRNA (messenger RNA) before it duplicates the split DNA strand, introns are actually perceived as an unnecessary waste of space, and a disposable by-product that just happens to be present in our genome. But since all human DNA is 99.9% identical, why is this wasted space still present in our DNA, and how could DNA have evolved into this form when evolution favors the dominant gene? Scientists should shake their own personal dogma about wisdom derived from archaeological discoveries and pay more serious attention to the idea that we may have been created some 200,000 years ago in the image of our maker. The makeup of our DNA has a great deal to do with that specific incident.

There does not have to be a conflict between evolution and creation, but most scientists are so blinded by the evolutionist doctrine that they bluntly refuse to take seriously the relatively new Sumerian translations of the creation of the Adamu. If we can just get our heads around this so-called incredible fairy tale from our distant past, we may just be able to tie up the various loose ends that don't seem to add up. We all share the same genome with all this wasted space on it, and according to our chromosomal Adam and mitochondrial Eve, we have all had it since the point of creation. Let us not forget the very important words that many of us live by, that we were created "in the image of our maker." If believe this, it must mean that much of our anatomy and character is inherited from our maker. These are critical clues, which lead me to reach only one logical conclusion. The genome was meant to be the length it is, which happens to be the same length of that of our maker, our genetic donor. The genes have, however, been tampered with, resulting in the removal or shutting down of most of them (97%), leaving behind an unintelligent, primitive, and subservient creature. However, many of the undesirable genes of this maker remained behind in the newly created DNA.

If this is the case, then we need to ask, "Who was our maker(s)? How evolved were they? How smart were they really? How much of their genome did they use compared to ours?" According to my theory, if they had the perfect complete genome, they certainly did not behave accordingly. They certainly created a big mess on this planet, leaving their offspring to survive and fend for themselves in the kindergarten of the universal community of beings. Is this the way we will behave when we start to colonize Mars?

6

PANSPERMIA

I HAVE OFTEN WONDERED WHY so many depictions of aliens from space carry such resemblance to us humans. All those who claim to have been abducted, or those who have been contacted by aliens, mostly describe them in very similar fashion. The strange thing is that these aliens seem to have features similar to humans and not some other insectlike monster from space. Is it because the individual who claims to have seen these aliens may simply be hallucinating or projecting our own image onto them? Or could it be the influence of mass media and the many movies that have graced our screens depicting aliens mostly in a humanoid form? Or could there possibly be a more logical or even scientific explanation for this curious phenomenon?

Since we have come to know that the Earth is not the center of the universe, and that the universe is quite possibly endless, we can start opening our minds to new possibilities. But like many things we seem to have discovered in the last two centuries on Earth, we find out that they have already been discovered by our distant ancestors. It is especially true for the subject of astronomy. The ancient Mesopotamians, Egyptians, Greeks, Chinese, and Americans all had a superior knowledge of the cosmos compared to us today. They knew things about the planets and our solar system that we in the Western world only rediscovered in the latter parts of the twentieth century.

One such cosmic phenomenon that was reintroduced into modern cosmology in the 1970s was the ancient Greek concept of *panspermia*. This word can be translated as "seeds everywhere" and its first recorded advocate was a Greek philosopher known as Anaxagoras of Clazomenae in Asia Minor, born about 500 BC. He was from a noble family, but wishing to devote himself entirely to science he gave up his property to his relatives and relocated to Athens, where he lived in intimacy with Pericles. Shortly before the outbreak of the Peloponnesian War he was charged with impiety, which was, "denying the gods recognized by the state." He not only had the honor of giving philosophy a home in Athens, where it flourished for a thousand years, but he was the first philosopher who introduced a spiritual principle that gives matter life and form. Anaxagoras laid down his doctrine in a prose work entitled *On Nature,* of which only fragments are preserved. Anaxagoras postulated the idea of independent elements that coexist in space and air, creating life. He called them seeds. They are the ultimate elements of combination and are indivisible, imperishable primordia of infinite number, and differing in shape, color, and taste. Later writers referred to these seeds as *omoiomereia,* which was an expression of Aristotle, meaning "particles of like kind with each other and with the whole that is made up of them."

It is fascinating how the ancient gods seem to make their appearance in the strangest places at the strangest times. Here we are trying to unravel the origins of a completely different subject, and yet we find that our protagonist Anaxagoras' life was greatly influenced by the ancient gods because he denied the gods who were recognized by the state. It is very clear that these ancient gods must have had a firm hold on the Greek authorities. The fact that a philosopher was jailed because he disobeyed the gods goes a long way in supporting the outlandish theory that these gods must have had a real hold over the ancient kings. And as we will find out, their control was absolute.

When panspermia was reintroduced by a handful of serious scientists, it was met with loads of criticism and the kind of ridicule that has been experienced by most visionaries throughout human history. Somehow Aristotle got in on the act some 2,400 years ago with his theory of "spontaneous generation," which had become the preferred philosophy until recent times. It was, however, grossly abused and misused by creationists ever since to support their narrow-minded religious beliefs, which portray a romantic picture of Adam and Eve in the garden of Eden.

Then in 1864 Louis Pasteur shocked the scientific world with his landmark experiment, disproving the concept of spontaneous generation. This discovery also had a practical impact on medicine, proving that germs are the primary causes and carriers of disease. In a simple experiment using a sterilized flask, he showed that a culture can grow in the flask only if germs enter it, and that plain air cannot initiate the growth of microorganisms. As Pasteur wrote, "There is no known circumstance in which it can be confirmed that microscopic beings came into the world without germs, without parents similar to themselves." He clearly demonstrated that life comes only from life. If this principle had been accepted as the fundamental theory on the origins of life then, today we may still be unsure how life on Earth began, but at least we would approach the question differently. We would assume that life here had to be seeded somehow and we would investigate the possible mechanisms for such seeding. Is it possible for bacteria and other microscopic organisms to come to Earth from space? Can they survive harsh conditions, radiation, and extreme temperatures for long periods of time? Maybe even millions of years?

Since Pasteur made his discovery, many scientists have supported his findings with their own voices and experiments. But the real twist came in the 1970s when British astronomers Fred Hoyle and Chandra Wickramasinghe rekindled international interest in panspermia. While their statements were quickly dismissed by the majority of the scientific world as an old-fashioned philosophy, their experimental evidence could not be ignored. As time passed and these renewed theories attracted more interest from a growing field of scholars, the evidence presented became overwhelming. Suddenly, panspermia attracted a new, more appropriate name in the form of the theory of cosmic ancestry. But to prove this theory required some solid evidence. After all, scientists all say they work with evidence . . . don't they? This is really the fundamental difference between them and theologians . . . or is it? It seems to me that as time passes by, the tenets of science are firmly rooted in the speculative and the possible, more often than in the proven. Even in the face of irrefutable evidence there is always an element of error that may have crept in. This is the stuff of science: always has been and probably always will be, at least until we attain that perfect genome status, which will hopefully elevate us beyond the need to know the physical while putting us firmly in touch with the spiritual.

So, to argue the possibility of life arriving on Earth from space requires some proof of life in space . . . and if it does exist, how does it reach Earth . . . and once it has reached Earth, what kind of role can it possibly play in the creation of life, evolution, or the speeding up of evolution? This is what Hoyle and Wickramasinghe proved in the early 1970s. By using spectroscopic analyses of light from distant stars, they showed that there was evidence of life in the interstellar dust. This dust exists throughout space as leftover matter from the creation of stellar systems and contains microscopic organisms like bacteria. It is also possible that there may be viruses and other organic material present in this dust. It got there as a result of cosmic collisions of space bodies, like planets and even supernovas, which occur when a star explodes spreading its contents over vast distances of space. By definition this really means that the universe must be filled with life of all kinds. Given its size and age, there have been cosmic collisions occurring for billions of years. The additional fact that the universe is growing at the speed of light, creating unimaginable numbers of stars and planets, creating more matter that can collide in space, spreading more living organisms throughout space, every millisecond of Earth-time. Now that we have the evidence, the next step is to convince the world that such life could actually reach our planet, or any other planet. Obviously these organisms will only survive and flourish on planets with conditions favorable for their growth. So how does this dust filled with life reach our planet and other planets?

We will discuss the presence of asteroids and comets in space. Comets are probably the most fascinating objects in the universe. I say universe because the assumption is that if they exist in our solar system they will most likely exist in others. The more we study comets, the more they take us by surprise; every year reveals amazing new facts. The latest estimates are that all the comets in our solar system actually outweigh the total mass of the planets. If this is true, and much of the evidence about their ability to distribute living organisms throughout space is also true, it certainly turns comets into the primary distributors of life in the universe.

Comets are thought to be leftover matter from the creation of solar systems and have been described as giant dirty snowballs on some kind of orbit around the sun. These orbits are very erratic and can vary from a few years to many thousands of years. Asteroids, on the other hand, are thought to be leftover pieces of planets or moons due to cosmic collisions. There is still a lot of debate about the difference between the two. It is possible that asteroids are just the remains of old comets whose ice and dirt have been burned off and evaporated over thousands of years of traveling in space—either by getting too close to the sun or too close to other large bodies that radiate heat, or even the constant radiation of distant stars and solar winds.

As comets and asteroids fly through space they pick up bacterial life from the interstellar dust, which gets embedded in the ice and rock. The ice in comets covers and protects the microscopic organisms on their journey through space. The comet becomes the carrier for the living organism, and together they can journey for longer than humanity has been on Earth. The latest findings are that microscopic life can survive indefinitely under the right conditions. This means that once the living space dust is embedded in the comet, it can survive for as long as it takes to be deposited on some hospitable planet.

The tail behind the comet is quite spectacular and can stretch for millions of kilometers. It consists of gas and dust that is discharged from the *coma* (nucleus head), and will contain many of these microscopic living particles. Thousands if not millions of comets have come into close proximity to Earth, leaving behind billions of miles of living space debris from their tails. These comets cross the paths of many planets, leaving behind the living debris waiting to pounce on an unsuspecting cosmic body. When the comets are close to the sun their activity increases and they discharge as much as one million tons of gas and living dust into space every day. As the planets orbit the sun they will inevitably travel through this living debris, which gets trapped by the gravitational pull of the planet.

But how many of these comets can there possibly be? Millions may have passed close to the sun in the past, but would the solar winds not drive their space dust away, into deep space? This is where that amazing human nature resurfaces, to remind us of how suspicious we are of each other and how obsessed we are with conflict. In the 1960s when space activity increased around the Apollo moon landings, U.S. intelligence photographed many explosions in the outer limits of the atmosphere, while on the lookout for enemy missiles. They were obviously waiting for an attack from the Soviets and, therefore, these cosmic events must have really given them a scare. But luckily they soon realized that it was not the enemy, but comets and other space objects 30–50 meters in diameter, which were exploding when entering the upper atmosphere. This information was apparently kept classified until 1994 and the realization of what was actually happening possibly prevented a full-scale nuclear war.

It seems that U.S. intelligence has lightened up a little since the fall of the Soviet Union, because on May 28, 1997, NASA announced the incredible news that thousands of comets "as large as houses," enter Earth's atmosphere every day. They actually break up and are destroyed 1,000–20,000 kilometers above Earth. The principal investigator for NASA's polar spacecraft instruments, Dr. Lewis A. Frank, described their descent as a "relatively gentle cosmic rain." This information also feeds the theory that all the water on Earth actually arrived from space.

There have been many scientists who vigorously supported the distribution of life from space, before Hoyle and Wickramasinghe reintroduced it to the world. Sir Isaac Newton was just one of them. He was convinced that the continued arrival of cometary material on Earth was essential for life on this planet. Since then it has been calculated that roughly 1,000 tons of cometary debris enters the Earth's atmosphere annually.

Comets and asteroids either crash into us, or they explode in the atmosphere, or they burn up in the atmosphere. Remember that these cosmic bodies are traveling in space at incredible speeds of 10 km per second to as much as 100 km per second. But because there is no friction, the speed is not a factor. It does, however, become a factor when these objects get sucked toward a planet and enter its atmosphere. The friction in the atmosphere starts to slow the objects down, heating them up in the process. This has been one of the major hurdles NASA had to deal with to protect the space shuttles against burning up on reentry from space.

We saw the tragic accident when some of the protective tiles were dislodged and the shuttle Columbia disintegrated as a result of the intense heat while on its way back to Earth from the International Space Station.

Now we know that there are constant minor cosmic collisions in which Earth is involved, and we have witnessed some spectacular collisions between near neighbor Jupiter and a giant comet in 1994. We recognize that the planets and moons bear the crater scars of giant collisions from the distant past, and the asteroid belt looks like it could be the leftover matter from a planet that was destroyed in a cosmic collision. Is it not possible that at some stage in the distant past Earth was also involved in a cosmic collision? The kind of collision that could be responsible for the strange phenomenon that all the land on Earth at the beginning of Earth-time was concentrated together on one side of the planet, while the other had a gaping hole filled with water? A collision of this kind between Earth and another planet would have resulted in the contamination and sharing of the seeds of life between the two planets. As they moved apart, the one settled in an orbit around the sun where Earth is at present, while the other planet was spun into an orbit that took it into deep space, very similar to the orbits of many comets. As these planets evolved and life on them evolved, they would have shared many similar species of animals and plants originating from the shared seeds of life, transferred between them during their collision. Should we be surprised to find similar kinds of animal species and plant species on both planets? It seems highly feasible that given their shared seeds of life, they should be evolving along similar paths. As the larger of the planets round the sun every couple of thousand years and their humanoid inhabitants come to Earth to observe the activity on such a beautiful planet, should we be surprised that the aliens we encounter share many humanlike features with us? We will revisit this topic later as we unravel the Sumerian scriptures.

While some comets and asteroids explode in the atmosphere, and others explode just before impact several kilometres above ground, as a result of the tremendous air pressure that builds up ahead of it, some actually do end up crashing into the ground. I am sharing this with you because it's the kind of stuff we always see in sci-fi thrillers, but we never realize how real it all is. As they say, "Truth is stranger than fiction," and this certainly applies to the stuff that is going on around us in space.

The best known atmospheric explosion of a meteoroid happened above Tunguska in central Siberia on June 30, 1908. The explosion flattened the forest for roughly 15 kilometers in every direction, completely devastating thousands of square kilometers of the forest. It was apparently heard up to 600 kilometers away and seen over 1,000 kilometers away. There are reports

Fig. 6.1. Evidence of craters on cosmic bodies. Virtually all cosmic bodies have craters, which remind us of the violent cosmic past during which the seeds of life were transmitted throughout the universe.

from Paris, France, that shortly after the event, pedestrians stopped to see an eerie, unusual glare in the east. The object was most likely a meteor, estimated to be around 60 meters in diameter, because a comet that size would have exploded higher in the atmosphere. However, nobody investigated the site until 20 years after the explosion, which leaves the evidence a little sparse. There must be some sort of magnetic comet target in Siberia because a similar atmospheric explosion occurred again in 1947. Poor Russians. An atmospheric explosion is much gentler on the invading meteor than a full impact. It allows the content of the meteor to be dispersed over a wide area without being destroyed by the shock of the impact. The effect on the planet is, however, much more devastating when the object explodes above the ground. This is what the bomb experts in World War II realized before they dropped the first nuclear bombs on Japan.

In March 1965, a 7-meter object exploded approximately 30 kilometers above Revelstoke in Canada. Investigators arrived promptly and recovered many fragments a few millimeters in size. The amazing thing was that most of them were not altered by heat, proving that a plausible delivery mechanism for living cells from space is not only feasible, but most certainly possible. But the greatest volume of organic space matter comes to Earth in the form of dust. This delivery system far outweighs the deposits from impacts of asteroids and comets. Okay, so if life can survive a large impact, how does it survive the trip in small dust particles through the atmosphere? Surely the heat or the X-rays and even UV radiation will kill microscopic organisms that are so exposed? Some startling discoveries have been made about this method of the transport of life from space to Earth.

Besides being able to survive UV radiation levels 3,000 times higher than humans can, many bacteria actually thrive at temperatures higher than boiling point. Bacteria and viruses have been known to possess the ability to mutate very rapidly while spreading new forms of disease, causing havoc in the medical field and in the preparation of antibiotics, so it is plausible that they could mutate very quickly from a state in which they reside in space to an adapted state for conditions on Earth. Bacteria actually have built-in cellular equipment that can help them survive sudden heating in space. They are called "heat-shock" proteins, which respond in seconds to external stimuli in bacteria. It seems that these heat-shock proteins are closely related across a wide range of species. This is simply one protective mechanism that allows these organisms to arrive alive on Earth, despite drastic and sudden temperature changes. I am convinced that these proteins will be the subject of great interest to genetic engineers, once they have figured out how to incorporate those genes into the human DNA. With genetic engineering anything is possible, even developing a new human characteristic similar to that of a bacterium that can resist sudden changes in temperature. This would help our human space exploration endeavors greatly, and probably be a necessary scientific process to help NASA reach more inhospitable places in space.

To get back to the vulnerability of organisms in space, it has also been established that a dust layer only a few microns thick will protect the contained microbe against UV radiation very successfully. So the organisms move toward Earth through the mesosphere, about 120 kilometers above the surface of Earth, where various gases may also protect them from X-rays. Then they descend through the stratosphere for a few days where they are protected from UV radiation by the ozone. After this, they drop quite quickly to the surface. This can be on mountain tops, rivers, deserts, or wooded areas basically spreading into every nook and cranny of the planet.

We have all seen shooting stars at night and many of us quickly make a wish, because somewhere back in time this became a ritual. I wonder if the origins of this tradition have anything to do with ancient people's beliefs that comets and shooting stars were often associated with plagues and diseases? The wish was possibly more of a prayer for health and protection against the disease announced by the fiery messenger in the sky. Shooting stars are actually small meteors that enter the atmosphere and fall to the ground while burning up. Most of them evaporate, but many do land up on the surface of Earth. So every time you see a shooting star, you may be witnessing the arrival of extraterrestrial life on Earth. But if shooting stars burn up in the atmosphere, will the microorganisms survive the trip? When tiny meteoroids of a few centimeters crash to Earth they burn up and evaporate. Particles the size of a pinhead will move at about 10 km per second and heat up to about 3,000 degrees Celsius. This is enough to kill any organism entering the atmosphere. But bacteria and viruses are much smaller than pinheads and they do momentarily heat up to about 500 degrees Celsius after entering the atmosphere. Is this enough to destroy them?

The University of Wales experimented with *Escherichia coli* bacteria under extreme temperatures to determine if the bacteria can withstand quick temperature bursts of up to 700 degrees Celsius for periods of about 20 seconds. The amazing thing is, the bacteria survived and after being placed in a nutrient broth, it grew back to normality. These experimental temperatures are more extreme than would apply to a microorganism. The organism would slow down quickly, only being exposed to high temperatures for a few seconds, after which it will gently descend to Earth.

Hoyle and Wickramasinghe received high levels of ridicule for their proposals but through their excellent scientific corroboration their critics were silenced, and today it is pretty much universally accepted that space contains the ingredients of life. But their theory went a bit too far for some when they suggested that all life comes from space, including bacteria, viruses, protozoa, seeds, pollen, other bits of organic material containing more complex DNA, and even larvae.

There is another theory of evolution of life on Earth referred to as "Gaia." This was introduced in the early 1970s by James Lovelock who proposed that life controls Earth's environment to make it suitable for life. It is this panspermia and Gaia combination of theories that others have referred to as cosmic ancestry: a strange combination of Darwinian evolution and spontaneous creation. It postulates that while evolution drives all living organisms, life has always existed in the universe before it arrived on Earth, and Earth was just another destination point in the universal path of natural selection while life was spreading to other planets. Well, that's how I understand it at least. I find this very confusing and unnecessary to say the least. What seems more logical is that all the planets in the universe have had, or will have, continuous exposure to new life from the interstellar soup of microscopic life. Some planets have had life for much longer than others and have been able to evolve more over time. But the big question remains—where did the original life forms begin before they were distributed throughout the universe so successfully? This is a question for philosophers more than biologists and scientists, so I will leave this subject for them to debate. We will see that some of the questions about our origins as humans may point us toward some unorthodox answers about the much bigger question regarding the origin of life. I must point out that my objectives in this book are more to do with uncovering our human origins, and not necessarily finding the origins of life. The following events have been presented as evidence for the theory of cosmic ancestry. It does not seem to do much more than present irrefutable evidence to support panspermia in its original form:

May 19, 1995	Two scientists at California Polytechnic State University showed that bacteria can survive without any metabolism for at least 25 million years; they are probably immortal.
November 24, 1995	The New York Times ran a story about bacteria that can survive radiation much stronger than any that Earth has ever experienced.
August 7, 1996	NASA announced fossilized evidence of ancient life in meteorite ALH 84001 from Mars.
October 27, 1996	Geneticists showed evidence that many genes are much older than the fossil record would indicate. Subsequent studies have strengthened this finding.

July 29, 1997	A NASA scientist announced evidence of fossilized microscopic life forms in a meteorite not from any planet.
Spring, 1998	A microfossil that was found in a meteorite and photographed in 1966 was recognized by a Russian microbiologist as a magnetotactic bacterium.
Fall, 1998	NASA's public position on life-from-space shifted dramatically.
January 4, 1999	NASA officially recognized the possibility that life on Earth comes from space.
March 19, 1999	NASA scientists announced that two more meteorites hold even stronger fossilized evidence for past life on Mars.
April 26, 2000	The team operating the mass spectrometer on NASA's Stardust mission announced the detection of very large organic molecules in space. Nonbiological sources for organic molecules so large are not known.
October 19, 2000	A team of biologists and a geologist announced the revival of bacteria that are 250 million years old, strengthening that case that bacterial spores can be immortal.
December 13, 2000	A NASA team demonstrated that the magnetosomes in Mars meteorite ALH 84001 are biological.
June 2002	Geneticists reported evidence that the evolutionary step from chimps to humans was assisted by viruses.
August 2004	Photos of fossilized cyanobacteria in a meteorite were reported by a NASA scientist.

Compiled by Brig Klyce, www.panspermia.org.

Throughout history comets have been associated with diseases and plagues, which followed closely after the comets' appearance and disappearance. We also now know that thousands of small comets evaporate in the upper atmosphere daily, releasing their precious content to rain down on us. Viruses and bacteria can mutate rapidly, infiltrating our cells and causing random changes to specific genes, which may result in evolutionary changes quite rapidly in a chosen species. This leads to the conclusion that rapid jumps in the physical evolution of species can occur and have occurred.

One such beautiful example, which was reported in *New Scientist* on November 13, 2004, is the sudden appearance of bats in the world some 50 million years ago. This is a real evolutionary dilemma, because until now there have been no fossils found of any intermediate animal linking their rodent ancestors to modern bats. A gene called BMP2 changed all this around 50 million years ago. This gene is present in bats but not in mice. How did this gene suddenly appear? Given some of the theories we have covered in this book, it is possible that the genome caused itself to evolve as part of the self-improvement process within a species. This seems a little farfetched as it would mean that humans could also evolve in this direction and start to fly, if our feedback, or natural process of selection, determined that we as humans would be better off flying. But herein lies the rub, as far as I can see. If our human genome already has its foundation, or its entire structure preerected, it must be in some sort of state of suspension just waiting for the right sequence of genes to fill the empty space. It will, therefore, reject any alien gene combinations and only allow predetermined genes to fill the inactive spaces taken up by junk DNA. This is a theoretical situation with humans, because we suspect that our DNA has been tampered with. This situation will not apply to creatures like rodents, which evolved into bats. So what else could have caused the BMP2 gene in bats to suddenly appear? Realistically, as Hoyle has shown, it could have been a viral effect on the DNA of the species causing some kind of mutation in the cells, which resulted in the subtle but dramatic change in its genetic structure.

But what is a virus? And what actually happens when a virus infects our body? There are thousands of different viruses recognized by biologists, but it is possible that millions may exist. We all know viruses very well from getting colds and flu. A relatively common virus can sometimes cause unimaginable carnage and death in humans. The 1918 influenza epidemic killed around 20 million people, and every year about 36,000 people die from a simple bout of flu in the United States alone. The *Hutchinson Dictionary of Science* describes a virus as: "An infectious particle consisting of a core of DNA or RNA, enclosed in a protein shell. Viruses are not cellular and they can only reproduce by invading other living cells where they use the host cell's system to replicate themselves. In the process they can actually disturb and alter the host's DNA. The healthy human body reacts by producing an antiviral protein called interferon which tries to prevent the infection from spreading to adjacent cells. Viruses mutate very quickly to prevent the host from developing permanent resistance."

When we get the flu, the viruses attack our cells, break the cell wall, and spill the contents into the spaces between cells. This causes a number of unpleasant side effects: swelling, pain, runny nose, headaches, inflammation, and more. Then it interacts with our DNA by first splitting the double-helix strand and attaching itself to one of the strands. The virus then replicates itself

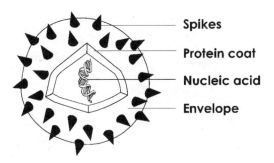

Spikes
Protein coat
Nucleic acid
Envelope

Fig. 6.2. Virus

many times, while our body tries to fight this invader with its own immune defense system. At some point the virus exits the cell, leaving our DNA to recombine the two strands of the double helix once again. It can happen that the DNA strands recombine incorrectly, resulting in different activities of the genes. In an instant we have the beginnings of a possible mutation or even an initial step toward evolution of that organism. Viruses can mutate so quickly that it is impossible to keep up with the development of new vaccines. It is clear to see that viruses are perfect organisms that are made for survival. If they have the ability to invade our genome and cause dramatic disfiguring disease and death, is it not possible that they can be equally responsible for genetic mutations that have the opposite effect, which can lead to positive evolutionary steps? Would it not be in the interest of the viral DNA to develop a stronger, more resilient host to ensure its own continued survival? It is a perfect argument for the selfish gene in some respects.

Bacteria, on the other hand, are microscopic organisms, each one consisting of a single cell that has no nucleus. Bacteria can be found virtually everywhere on Earth, even in the most inhospitable places with high acidity, high temperatures and low temperatures. Some bacteria are parasites that can be very harmful because they produce toxins. Others can be beneficial to humans and sometimes even vital for our survival, like the digestive bacteria in our stomachs. Bacteria have DNA but also additional small circular pieces of DNA called *plasmids*. These plasmids carry additional genetic information and move freely between bacteria, even if they are of a different species. Plasmids are also responsible for bacterial resistance to antibiotics, but they are very useful tools in genetic engineering. The staggering thing about bacteria is their ability to reproduce in as little as 20 minutes. They normally divide into two new equal cells through a process called *binary fission*. Other single-cell organisms like amoeba also divide in this way. Scientists estimate that we have only identified 1%–10% of bacteria

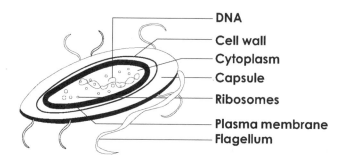

Fig. 6.3. Bacterium

on Earth. This figure will probably remain this low, as new bacteria arrive from space every minute of the day.

In October 2004, *New Scientist* published an article in which they describe lightning as "nature's own genetic engineer." When lightning strikes the ground, it kills the organisms within a specific radius, but the bacteria further away have been shown to undergo changes in their DNA. Timothy Vogel from the University of Lyon said that the bacteria actually take up any kind of "stray" DNA as a result of the shock: "This could explain why gene swapping is so common among bacteria." They also suggest that this phenomenon will help bacteria evolve very quickly. Until now scientists have been puzzled by the rate of evolution in bacteria because the natural rate of new DNA uptake did not match their findings. This new discovery has gone a long way to explain the rapid rates of evolution in various life-forms on Earth.

Most people think of bacteria as nasty little things that should be obliterated with new knowledge, "We don't need bacteria . . . they just cause trouble and make us sick." But we should realize that life on Earth would most likely be impossible without bacteria, and when scientists say that the universe is teeming with life, they can back it up because of the properties of bacteria.

Let's first look at the crucial role bacteria play in human life. We have more bacteria in our bodies than we have human cells. They pass from mother to baby in breast milk virtually as soon as the baby is born. It is now known that the struggle for equilibrium by bacteria in babies plays a vital role in their development. While some bacteria are harmful and may cause the slowing down of development and growth, other bacteria are vital for our health. It is now known that giving young babies various probiotics, for example *Lactobacillus,* will reduce conditions like eczema and allergy later in life. From *New Scientist,* the following are the predominant bacteria living in our gastrointestinal tract:

ORGAN	BACTERIA
Stomach	*Lactobacillus. Streptococcus, Staphylococcus, Enterobacteria,* yeasts.
	There is 0–1,000 bacteria per ml.
Duodenum	*Lactobacillus, Streptococcus, Bifidobacterium, Staphylococcus, Enterobacteria,* yeasts.
	100–100,000 bacteria per ml.
Small intestine	*Bifidobacterium, Bacteroides, Lactobacillus, Streptococcus, Staphylococcus, Clostridium, Enterobacteria,* yeasts.
	1,000–10,000,000,000 bacteria per ml.
Colon	All the above plus *Fusobacterium, Peptostreptococcus;* E. *Coli.*
	In huge quantities of up to 10,000,000,000,000 bacteria per gram.

Fred Hoyle writes that there is organic life everywhere in the universe, he not only substantiates it with scientific proof, he also explains that such proof of life is only possible if we take into account how bacteria can multiply. Then suddenly it all makes a great deal of sense, and we can easily explain where such an abundance of life in space comes from. If you take a single bacteria cell in favorable conditions, the average time for it to duplicate itself is about two hours. One makes two, two makes four, four makes eight, and so on. This means that by the end of the first day you will have a colony too small to be seen by the naked eye, but in two days the colony of 1,000 will become 1,000,000, which suddenly becomes just visible with the naked eye, and is about a tenth the size of a pinhead. By the fourth day you will have 1,000,000,000,000 bacteria, which will weigh about 1 gram. In five days the colony will weigh about 1 kilogram, and in six days you will have a ton of bacteria. Every day the weight will grow by three zeros, which should give you a pile of bacteria the size of Mount Everest in just eleven days. It will take only thirteen days to produce the weight of Earth in bacteria, our galaxy in nineteen days, and the estimated visible universe in just twenty-two days. So when people ask how it is possible that there is such an abundance of organic life in the universe, you can explain it to them very simply by using these facts.

It seems that airborne infectious diseases, plagues, and epidemics literally descend upon the people of the world like a blanket from the sky. And yet for millennia people believed, and men of science and medicine believed, that these diseases were passed on from person to person. It does not need a scientist to conclude that it is impossible for these infections to spread worldwide, from person to person within hours or a few days, and yet this happens every year with the coming of the flu season. These diseases can be linked to the periodic appearance of a number of comets that leave behind their millions of tons of living debris as they fly by the Earth on their irregular orbits. This is also true for the horrific plagues of the past. It seems to tie up quite logically. A comet flies in close proximity to our planet, filling space with deadly unearthly pathogens; a few weeks later the planet flies through this debris minding its own business, but collecting deadly bacteria on its way. Before you know, the world is covered in this microscopic alien species, causing diseases and havoc because our bodies have to generate a brand new form of resistance that we do not possess.

Some archaeologists think that the pharaohs used their knowledge of viruses and bacteria to cast so-called spells on their tombs. By including an ancient strand of bacteria or viruses in their tombs, these organisms simply went into suspended animation while trapped inside the tomb, only to be reactivated when the tomb raiders opened the tomb up a few thousand years later. The unexplained deaths of well-known archaeologists shortly after entering the tombs have puzzled scholars for decades. If we attempt to explain it in terms of viruses or bacteria, we can rapidly remove the dark wizardry from the equation. The bacteria have been locked up for a long time and probably do not exist on Earth in their original form any more. This means that our bodies are not used to the bacterium and cannot develop antibodies quickly enough. The result is swift and tragic. Other examples of this kind of prehistoric contamination are bacteria that have apparently survived for 4,800 years in the brickwork of Peruvian pyramids; for 11,000 years in the gut of a well-preserved mastodon; and possibly even 300 million years in coal.

Some bacteria have an even more effective survival strategy: they form spores. Spores are bacterial cells with thick protective coats in a complete dormant state. In this form they can basically survive forever. Many plagues of the Old Testament can be explained very comfortably by bacterial phenomena. In just one example, around 1200 BC god punished the Philistines for an attack on the Hebrews, by "emrods in their secret parts." Emrods are translated as buboes, which occur as a result of bubonic plague. The plague among humans has become well documented since the fourteenth century and some scientists still cling onto the theory that it was caused by fleas that carried the bacterium to humans from rats that were infested with the *Pasteurella pestis* bacterium. While this may have been the case in a small number of infections, we will clearly show

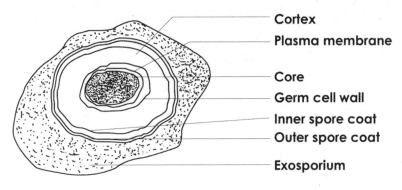

Cortex
Plasma membrane

Core
Germ cell wall
Inner spore coat
Outer spore coat

Exosporium

Fig. 6.4. Spore

in chapter 11 how impractical the spread of such an infection is when attributed to rats and fleas only.

So what have we learned in this chapter? That cosmic collisions have been occurring for billions of years; that asteroids, and especially comets, are carriers and distributors of life in the universe; that life exist in abundance everywhere in space; and that life comes to Earth from space every second of every day as it has been for millions of years. We also discovered that bacteria and viruses can mutate very rapidly, possibly causing plants and animals to mutate by interacting with their DNA, and that electricity and other environmental factors cause bacteria and viruses to mutate on their own. All this information leads to the conclusion that panspermia is no longer a dubious sector of science, but the predominant theory of how life arrived on Earth, and that larger cosmic collisions between planets would result in the transfer and sharing of much of their respective organisms, which would lead to a parallel evolutionary development on two separate planets.

So, if we can accept these scientific findings of the past thirty years, why should we not accept the possibility that a species similar to us may have evolved on such a parallel planet? All we need to do now is to prove that such a planet exists in the depths of our own solar system and we may very well have the answer to why aliens are often described with a striking resemblance to us humans. The strangest thing is that it has been revealed to us many times in the past, but we seem to be determined to ignore it.

7

PLANET X

I WAS TWENTY-TWO YEARS OLD, during my first year out of college trying desperately to become a pop star. But deep inside, the heart of a closet-scientist was beating, constantly being attracted by news that made my musician buddies yawn with boredom. The news clip of a Planet X appeared on TV as suddenly as it disappeared. I was riveted by the story of scientists thinking they may have discovered a large new planet beyond Pluto in our own solar system. The report was very convincing as it quoted some credible-sounding cosmologists. But that one single occasion was the first and the last time I heard about it. I expected to read about it in the papers the following day or in some weekly magazines but I was bitterly disappointed. None of the papers carried any stories of such content and nobody else remembered anything about it either. Unfortunately, this was about thirteen years before the Internet and finding information on this kind of topic was not easy, especially in South Africa where the media was well controlled by the apartheid government. Strange objects in the sky? That sounded too much like a communist threat. So, for a brief moment my curiosity and imagination was stirred, only to fade under the pressures of nightly gigs and stars of a different kind in my eyes. In the years to come I was steadily drawn to the cosmos and literature of a diverse nature. I never realized how seriously the idea of Planet X was being taken, and how vigorously it was pursued by a large number of astrophysicists and other cosmologists. The news report that impressed me so much was based on a similar article in the *New York Times* June 19, 1982, which suggested that something big, far beyond the reaches of the solar system, is tugging on Uranus and Neptune, causing gravitational fluctuations that are resulting in irregularities in their orbits. The force suggested a large object, far away and unseen, which could lend some credibility to the speculation of the existence of a planet in deep space.

The discovery of planets in the last 200 years had more to do with the science of mathematics rather than the building of bigger and more powerful telescopes. In the same way that astronomers predicted the existence of Uranus and Neptune some 200 and 150 years ago, they now predict the existence of a large planet way beyond Pluto. Because of the mathematical irregularities in the gravitational orbits of the outer planets, they were so certain that such a further planet exists that they called it Planet X.

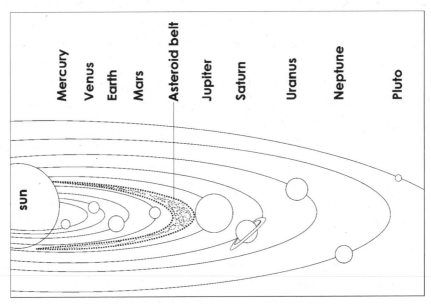

Fig. 7.1. Is it possible that the Asteroid belt was
previously a planet known as Tiamat?

Our solar system is in a relatively quiet part of the Milky Way, our galaxy, but it was born out of a violent past, which is evident from the large number of impact crater sites on all the planets around us. Take a pair of binoculars and look at the moon for a little while; you will not believe the number of craters you can see. Our closest celestial body has been bombarded by asteroids and other flying space debris for billions of years. The same can be said for Mercury, Venus, and Mars. The many moons of the other gaseous planets also carry the scars of our violent cosmic past. It is actually a miracle that our planet has escaped a serious cosmic collision for long enough to allow life to develop and flourish. Well, it did until around 65 million years ago, they say, when the last giant asteroid crashed into Earth, apparently causing the extinction of the dinosaurs. This asteroid is referred to as K-T. But, let us take a broader look at our place in the universe to get a more realistic perspective of the big picture.

The big bang theory still seems to be the popular scientific theory for the creation of the universe and all things in it. This theory postulates that some 13.8 billion years ago the universe was born out of a point of singularity, which exploded creating stars and galaxies while expanding at the speed of light. I recently attended a lecture given by South African-born astronomer Dr. Tony Readhead, who heads up California Institute of Technology's Cosmic Background Imager project. He shared some of the fascinating images from deep space, generated by the new generation background-imagery radio-telescopes. After taking the packed auditorium on a journey through time away from Earth into the depths of the universe, I literally felt as if I was traveling through time. The images of galaxies and cluster galaxies and quasars truly boggled the mind. But when he presented an image of the stuff beyond 13.8 billion years, it sent a shock through my entire body. It was pitch black. Nothing existed beyond this point. Nothing that we could see or imagine. We had just traveled beyond the edge of the known universe. The amazing thing is that with all the knowledge in the world, nobody could even hazard a guess about what might exist beyond this point. It is, however, possible that if you carry on moving beyond this point for a long, long, long time, you may reach another universe. Because, given infinity, everything will happen. But this really gets too close to opening myself up to philosophical attack, so let's get back to the more familiar part of the physical universe.

The universe continued to expand, creating new stars at an unimaginable rate. It seems that planetary systems such as ours, with all the planets, their moon satellites, as well as other bodies, are formed from gas and dust accompanying the birth of their own star, in our case the sun. The first stars that formed from the primordial hydrogen and helium of the big bang could not have had any planets because there were no heavy elements present as yet. These elements that are necessary for the creation of planets only made their appearance once the second generation stars started exploding and scattering such heavy elements throughout the universe. These elements necessary for planet-building were built up in the stars by nucleosynthesis. Once a star is born, the debris that results from this event is scattered throughout the universe, ready to get absorbed into the new planets, which begin to form around the star.

As I mentioned earlier, as recently as 1994 there was still great skepticism about the existence of other planets in the universe, outside of our solar system. But since then many new planets have been discovered. Now it is believed, mainly because of the continual discovery of new planets, that planetary systems do not form in isolation, they are the norm. Interstellar clouds are so large that when one of them collapses, it breaks up into enough pieces to form hundreds, if not millions, of stars like our sun. These interstellar clouds are like astronomical nurseries, constantly giving birth to new stars. These stars then form a loose association known as an *open cluster* of stars, which is dispersed as the individual stars follow their own orbits around the galaxy. The magnetic fields generated by the young stars keep a strong grip on the material that surrounds them. This force will trap all matter extending far from the core of the star. But as the core of this new stellar system collapses to form a star, some of the material from which it is being formed remains out at a distance from the core of the star. It is kept out from the center of the cloud by the residual spin of the whole system, while it settles down into a disc of star dust around the young star. Discs like these have been detected around young stars, which

Fig. 7.2. Primordial cloud develops from which stars will be born

Fig. 7.3. Primordial disc of stardust

largely confirm our understanding of how planetary systems are formed. A similar disc effect can be seen around the large planets like Saturn, but only much, much, smaller in size.

The heat of the star blows away the lightest materials like hydrogen and helium, which are closest to the star. The material that gets left behind is made up of billions of tiny grains of dust that collide and stick together, building up larger lumps of what are the beginnings of new planets. These lumps become small rocks, then big rocks, and even bigger asteroid-size rocks. While these rocks orbit the sun in swarms, they bump into each other while gravity keeps pulling

Fig. 7.4. Nuclear fusion blows away the
lightest materials creating space for planets to develop.

Fig. 7.5. Primordial disc spreads around
the star resulting in planet formation.

them tighter and tighter together. The largest lumps have the highest gravity and attract more and more material until they grow into large planets and moons.

So now we have our solar system with the closest star to us, our sun, giving it light and heat and life. Mercury, Venus, Earth, and Mars are the four inner planets of our solar system. But where do all the asteroids and comets come from? Between Mars and Jupiter there is a ring of cosmic rubble known as the asteroid belt. It is believed that the combined content of this asteroid belt would constitute a planet about four times the size of Earth. This is a fascinating bit of information from the world of modern science, because the ancient Sumerians had the same knowledge about the size of the possible planet before it became the asteroid belt. In the well-known *Enuma Elish,* or the *Epic of Creation,* the clay tablets describe in detail how the large planet they called Tiamat was smashed to pieces in a cosmic collision. It further describes the planet as having been a "water giant" with "golden veins" being exposed in her "belly" as the moons of Nibiru smashed into her. It further explains how Earth inherited its water and its wealth in golden ores. It all came from planet Tiamat. The details in the *Epic of Creation* are so vivid that it goes way beyond imagination. How did the authors of those clay tablets know so much, more than 5,000 years ago? Can the asteroids possibly be the remains of a large planet that was destroyed by some celestial collision a long time ago? Today we know that the asteroid belt is made up of similar materials to the four inner planets. This would suggest that there should be golden ores in the many fragments whizzing around the sun. The incredible coincidence is that the clay tablets tell us the same. They clearly outline that the rich golden ore on Earth is very similar to that in the pieces of the asteroid belt. The tablets that describe the *Epic of Creation* are no ordinary stories. They give us a detailed sequence of events that caused the creation of our planet Earth. We are told in no uncertain terms that Earth is the largest remaining piece of the original planet called Tiamat, which was shattered and became the asteroid belt.

Beyond this belt of gold there are four planets known as *gas giants,* which most likely have a small rocky core while the rest of the planet is made up of various gasses, giving them their distinctive colors. All this knowledge and research was rewarded in April 1999 when the first multiple system of extrasolar planets was discovered 44 light-years from Earth. Upsilon Andromedae is a sunlike star, which was found to have three giant planets, two of which orbit closer to their parent star than the Earth is to the sun. From that moment on, the previous belief that planets were not the norm in the universe had changed for ever. At the time this publication went to print, astronomers had discovered approximately 130 extrasolar planets. Our own solar system is estimated to be

4.5 billion years old. The bombardment of planets by space debris most likely started just after 4.5 billion years ago and ended 4 billion years later. Although we have reached a fairly stable period in our solar system, there are still many life-threatening monsters flying around in our own cosmic backyard.

Comets have been sighted and written about for thousands of years. They have been seen as messengers of God or omens of evil. But where do they come from? There are really two known sources of comets. The Kuiper belt, which is just beyond Neptune, is said to contain a billion comets, which are ice and rock bodies left over from the formation of the solar system. The other source of comets is known as the Oort cloud, which basically surrounds our entire solar system and is said to contain a million million comets, more than all the stars in the entire Milky Way. I remember in the 1980s when I first watched Carl Sagan's *Cosmos* series, they were estimating that there were 100 million stars in the Milky Way. By the year 2004 it was estimated to be 100 billion stars. This is another quick indication of how our knowledge is evolving and how it shapes our perceptions. One of the theories of how the Oort cloud actually formed is that during the creation of the solar system, besides all the material that made up the giant planets, there must have been many frozen balls of ice and dust that were influenced by the gravity of the gas giants, in the same way that objects in the asteroid belt came under the influence of Jupiter. It is possible that some of these icy objects were pulled into orbits, taking them close to the sun, and as a result evaporated. Those that did not evaporate were flung out from the region of the giant planets and ended up in giant orbits, possibly taking them 100,000 times as far from the sun as Earth. This is a distance of

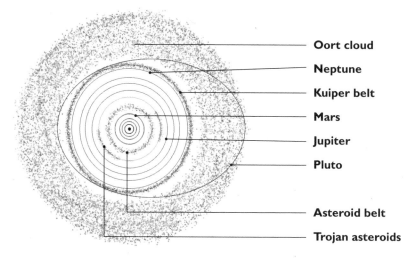

Fig. 7.6. There are two known sources of comets: the Kuiper belt and the Oort cloud.

some 15 million million kilometers, which is so far away from the sun that the dirty snowballs were partly influenced by the gravity of other stars. Over billions of years their orbits got smoothed out and they became a spherical shell of comets around the solar system, now known as the Oort cloud. Although this is a theory, the Oort cloud remains a reality, consisting of all those billions of comets, large and small.

The comets that we see from time to time are all on elongated elliptical orbits around the sun. They broke away from their parent cloud and were hurled toward the sun. They keep coming in close to the sun as they round it, and then get flung out into deep space with a kind of pendulum effect. Their orbits can be many thousands of years. What is very interesting is the similarity of the orbits of these comets and the theoretical orbit of the illusive Planet X. If you choose to believe the Sumerian scriptures, the orbit of Planet X, which they called "Nibiru," is very similar to that of the comets that orbit the sun. "A large elliptical orbit" is what the clay tablets called it, all those thousands of years ago. Since we modern civilized humans only discovered the last three planets in our solar system in the past 220 years, it is difficult for us to comprehend how someone 6,000 years ago could have known so much about our solar system and other planets beyond. This is a very disturbing reality, which clearly points to our gross lack of knowledge relating to the cosmos in the twenty-first century.

Just very recently we were handed a clear reminder of what some maverick astronomers have been trying to prove for a few hundred years, and in the

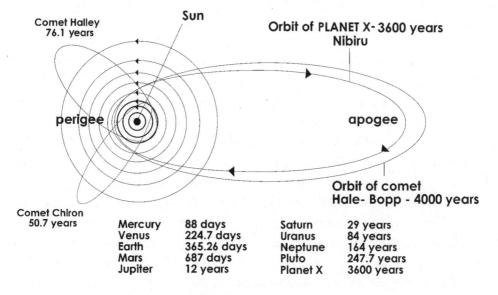

Fig. 7.7. Orbits of planets

process restoring some lost pride in the modern-day cosmologists—the existence of Planet X. This is not some fancy science fiction name made up by wacky students, but simply the Roman numeral X, which stands for the number 10. Planet X is the tenth planet in our known solar system. One other interesting point I should raise is the accidental symbolism that also dates back to Sumer and a certain "planet of the crossing" that was often represented by a cross on their clay tablets and cylinders. We will examine these ancient artifacts later in the book.

And so the obsession with Planet X goes on. Let us examine a story about a French astronomer, Alessandro Morbidelli, who in 2003 dared to suggest that there may be a large planet way beyond Pluto, which is on an elongated elliptical orbit around the sun that lasts about 3,600 years. The similarities between the facts in his article and the Sumerian texts are quite staggering. The interesting thing is that seemingly the French astronomer had never heard of the Sumerian stories of the planet called Nibiru.

In February 2003, a prestigious French monthly called *Science & Vie,* published an update on the planetary makeup of our solar system, in light of recent discoveries in the Kuiper belt. The article made the sensational announcement that there is one more, unknown, planet in our solar system. The writer called it "a phantom planet whose possible orbit is too elongated to be seen." The article, written by Valerie Greffos, was based on statements by Alessandro Morbidelli, an astronomer at the French observatory Côte d'Azur. He suggested that while the solar system was chaotic in the beginning, there was a celestial collision involving a planet that existed where the asteroid belt is today. This all happened about 3.9 billion years ago and as a result of those events the so-called phantom planet is caught in this unusually long elliptical orbit of several thousand years. He further stated, "I expect that one day we will discover a new, Mars-sized planet!" He also provided the journal with a proposed sketch of the elongated orbit, which included a speculative guess on where the planet may have been at that point in time. Is it a coincidence that this sketch is virtually identical to that of Zecharia Sitchin, which he proposed in his book *The 12th Planet* in 1976? Since this French astronomer is not the first to be talking about Planet X with such certainty, it seems to me that this kind of speculation is too close to be coincidence. There must be something more to this obsession than mere speculation by a handful of wacky scientists in search of an invisible planet. Not so invisible it seems, as many scientists have presented mathematical calculations that point to the existence of something in deep space that supports their calculations.

Sitchin has become a leading authority in the analyses of ancient Sumerian clay tablets. He is said to own the largest private collection of over 800 ancient cuneiform clay tablets. Sitchin has studied these and other tablets extensively for many years, and has deciphered and also interpreted many complex messages and presented startling theories, which are now being taken more seriously by growing numbers of broad-minded scientists. One of the many stories inscribed on some of the tablets was a long complex tale of Nibiru, the home planet of the Anunnaki, the gods of the Sumerians. This knowledge of the Sumerians is what the French astronomer seemingly rediscovered, around twenty-eight years after Sitchin first published it in *The 12th Planet*, containing his translation of these ancient tablets.

The similarities between Sitchin's work and Morbidelli's are staggering:

- In the beginning the solar system was "chaotic."
- There was another "supplementary planet" where the asteroid belt is now.
- This was Tiamat in the Sumerian texts.
- A celestial collision "disturbed and rearranged" the solar system outlined in the *Enuma Elish,* or *Epic of Creation.*
- Based on the findings on Earth's moon, the collision occurred some 3.9 billion years ago.
- In the aftermath of the collision, the solar system acquired the phantom planet Nibiru, which was later renamed "Marduk" by the Babylonians after their god.
- Its orbit is elliptical and not circular.
- At its perigee, the point closest to the sun, it passes between Jupiter and Mars.
- The orbit lasts thousands of Earth years. Sitchin applied the Sumerian Shar, which equals 3,600 Earth years per one Nibiru orbit. This is similar to many known comets.

It is truly remarkable that here we have an author, scholar, and scientist in his own right who started to expose the world to the hidden realities of our ancient past in the early 1970s, and a modern-day astronomer who virtually quoted Sitchin verbatim, while exposing his own findings some twenty-eight years later.

What is also interesting is the elliptical orbit of the early comets during the formation of our solar system. To date, comets have puzzled astronomers, causing many unsubstantiated speculations to surface. While all of the planets, except Pluto, orbit the sun in the same general plane and in the same direction, all moving more or less in a circular orbit, the comets seem to follow their own paths without obeying any of the normal rules. Comets move in elliptical orbits that move in random planes, in the opposite direction to the planets. They are flung deep into space, sometimes for hundreds and thousands of years in their orbits. The *Enuma Elish* tablets also seem to provide a plausible explanation as to where the comets originated and why they behave so strangely. We will cover this in a closer look at these mysterious clay tablets a little later. The current theory on comets seems to be supported by astrophysical evidence that the comets, which eventually settled in the Oort cloud, started out on very large elliptical orbits that took them so deep into space that they were affected by the gravity of other stars. This caused a fluctuation in the comets' orbits. Some of the comets in this cloud do, however, remain at distances far beyond the edge of the solar system, possibly as far as halfway to the nearest star. You can weigh up the evidence and start formulating your own decisions. If this can happen to a comet, why not to a planet? The proposed phantom planet must have entered the solar system pretty much on a similar path to the comets. From the outer edge of the solar system, turning between Mars and Jupiter, and out across the paths of all the other planets once more, on its way into deep space. Such a planet weighing many millions of times as much as a comet would take much longer to settle down into a stable orbit around the sun. So it is possible that it will continue on its elliptical orbit for a long time to come before it finds a stable path around the sun. If such a planet is on an orbit of some 3,600 years, it seems to fit that it could have been the subject of debate and influence on Earth around 5,000 BC and subsequent intervals of 3,600 years.

We have to return briefly to the asteroid belt located between Mars and Jupiter. Although I casually mentioned that it is probably the remains of a planet, it should be taken in with an understanding that the knowledge about this part of our solar backyard is still very speculative. The asteroid belt certainly adds a great deal of intrigue to our very own solar system, and astronomers are at odds about what might have caused this phenomenon. Some scholars, like Zecharia Sitchin, have analysed the ancient Sumerian creation epic, which seemingly describe the struggle between good and evil, in different way. He explains them as an historic event that describes the creation of our Earth and its moon. Scientists seem to feel that the moon is too big in relation to Earth to have been created as its satellite during the formation of the solar system. If one compares the moon to all the other moons orbiting the planets, we find that the other moons are considerably smaller in proportion to their planet. In fact, our moon is the fifth largest satellite in our solar system, comfortably comparing with the sizes of the large moons of Jupiter, Saturn, and Neptune. Our moon is simply far too big to have been formed under similar conditions to the other moons. The physics would not have allowed such a large satellite to form at the point of creation around a planet as small as Earth.

The more popular theory on the origin of the moon is known as the big splash theory. This was first introduced by astronomer-artist Bill Hartmann and his colleague Donald Davis, both at the Planetary Science Institute, Arizona in 1975. *Astronomy Now* featured an article in May 2002, which describes the big splash as such:

> The Earth had only recently coalesced in solar orbit when it suffered a devastating blow. Along came a rogue protoplanet . . . more than half the size of the Earth itself and slammed into the proto-Earth in a glancing impact. The collision vaporised the outer regions of both worlds to considerable depth, and the core of the impacting planet sank to the centre of the Earth where the two cores merged into one. Debris, about 80% of it from the Earth's crust and mantle, was flung into orbit. Gradually, particles in the orbiting debris ring began to lump together through agglomeration and then gravitational accretion, until the mess had all been swept up and a single, large satellite remained. Only this theory fits the data. But until recently, even this idea had serious problems, because it left the Earth and Moon system spinning too madly. Now, this problem has been largely fixed, and the vast majority of researchers are in agreement that the Big Splash, ad hoc though it might seem, represents the true picture.

I would say that in many ways the big splash theory resembles the story of the *Enuma Elish* described by the Sumerians. What was also created in that collision was the asteroid belt. Let us focus on this part of the solar system again. It is amazing that only a tiny fraction of the total weight of the asteroid belt has been ejected over time. This is mainly ascribed to the gravitational effect of Jupiter, but it is also possible that at some stage a giant asteroid was ejected toward the sun, collided with Earth, melted much of the rock and metals, and was ejected as a giant satellite that was caught in Earth's gravitational orbit, cooled down, and became our moon. That is another theory for the origin of the moon.

The Sumerians had a different story about the moon's creation altogether. A planet called Tiamat, which existed in the place of the asteroid belt, was involved in a cosmic collision with an invading planet called Nibiru. It was caught by the gravitational pull of our sun in a long elliptical orbit. It became the twelfth planet of our solar system because the Sumerians counted the moon and Nibiru as part of the planets. It makes perfect sense why such a planet would be depicted by a cross, graphically depicting its path and place in history: crossing the paths of other planets. There are numerous clear references to this planet in a multitude of clay tablets and cylinder seals from Sumer and other civilizations dating much further back in time. This planet is always symbolized by a cross. Both Nibiru and Tiamat had their own moons, which were involved in a spectacular cosmic collision. The result of all this was the destruction of Tiamat, which became the asteroid belt; the creation of the Earth from the largest chunk of Tiamat; and the capturing of an existing moon of Tiamat or Nibiru, which was trapped by the gravitational pull of the newly formed Earth. This is why the moon is so large compared to the size of Earth, because it was originally a moon of a much larger planet. It was this fateful event that developed the seasons and tides on Earth, which contributed to the very unique life-forms here on Earth.

New Scientist devoted the cover of a recent issue to "The Planet That Stalked the Earth." In the article the writer offered theories about a "rogue planet" involved in a cosmic collision. What is most fascinating is that the article called the phantom planet "Theia," without any explanation. Is it possible that the writer was thinking of Tiamat?

Why do we know so little about this planet? For a start, its 3,600-year orbit is way too long for our short human time frames. We can hardly relate to stuff that went on 200 years ago on Earth, how could we possibly come to terms with a planet and a possible civilization that come within our reach every 3,600 years? The fact is that many clues have been handed down to us over time. Detailed information was captured by thousands of scribes over thousands of years, writing of their ancient experiences on a young planet, for future generations to absorb, but our civilization has come along and discarded all this knowledge under the premise that it cannot possibly be true. My grandfather refused to believe that man walked on the moon and I thought he was very naive and ill informed. So let us imagine that there really is such a planet out there, a "radiant planet" called Nibiru, as it is referred to by the Nibiruans in several ancient inscriptions. Furthermore, if there is life on this planet, who are the inhabitants, and what effect have they had on our planet Earth? This is a question that has been asked millions of times by regular people with inquisitive minds and scientists who have been more involved in the search for such a Planet X.

During the search for this illusive Planet X, various other objects were discovered in our distant solar system; in recent times, right on the edge of the Kuiper belt. Pluto and its moon, Charon, are often thought to be very large members of the Kuiper belt, referred to as Kuiper Belt Objects (KBO). The average size of the other KBOs are thought to be roughly 10 km–50 km in diameter. If one of those had to collide with our precious Earth, it would have consequences so severe that it would push the entire planet with all its life right to the edge of extinction. This belt is probably the main source of the short-period comets that orbit the Sun less than every 200 years, like Halley's Comet. Some other comets, like Kohoutek, are on much larger orbits, and astronomers predict that its orbit can range from 7,500 to 75,000 years. This is pretty much in line with the kind of thinking behind the orbit of Planet X. When Pluto was first discovered in 1930, it was often referred to as Planet X, but it soon became clear that this could not be the celestial body that was exerting such turbulence on Uranus and Neptune. Remember that scientists discovered that these two planets had disturbances in their gravity and orbits, but Pluto was simply too small to have such an effect on them. For this to happen, the body causing these effects had to be many times the size of Pluto. The debate goes on, some frantically searching for the lost Planet X, others dismissing it as utter nonsense.

Very recently, another KBO was discovered. Quaoar is 1,250 kilometers in diameter, which is about half the size of Pluto, and is the largest KBO known to date. A study of the outer solar system suggests that it may not be a cemetery full of dead, frozen bodies. The study revealed that this KBO could have been warm at some stage in the past. This supports the theory that planetary processes such as volcanism can occur on objects at extreme distances from the sun. This volcanism could add support for the existence of planets at such large distances from the sun. The Sumerian tablets describe the planet Nibiru as exactly that: "A radiating planet," which was symbolised by a cross, to indicate the planet of the crossing but also radiation in the form of heat emerging from the planet. We are told in the clay tablets about the importance of the thick atmosphere, which protects Nibiru against the long cold periods while deep in space, when the planet is furthest from the sun, as well as the hot periods when it is closest to the sun. It would ultimately be their wounded atmosphere that brought the Anunnaki from Nibiru to Earth.

Scientists have found about 1,000 KBOs so far, but little is known about their composition because they are so distant and faint. However, the detection of crystalline ice suggests that Quaoar is, or was, being heated by something other than the sun. Could it be the close proximity of the radiant Nibiru on its occasional fly-by? This was proposed by David Jewitt of the University of Hawaii in Honolulu and Jane Luu of the Massachusetts Institute of Technology in Lexington. The two researchers discovered the first KBO in 1992, and then made these latest observations. They said that it would have to be an object of substantial size to have such a profound effect on this KBO. Could this be a real clue pointing toward a distant giant Planet X?

If we look at the detailed descriptions of the celestial battle between gods and the collisions of planets that the *Enuma Elish* describes so graphically, it sounds almost too fantastical to believe. It all seems so far back and so far away that we struggle to see its relevance to our existence at this point in time, but all we have to do is lift our eyes at the sky to realize how vulnerable we are to a cosmic attack. Maybe not by other planets, but by giant asteroids and even comets. Every so often we hear the news of a large asteroid that passed close by planet Earth, without us even spotting it, until it had gone by, unnoticed. This kind of ignorance could cause our extinction in the blink of an eye and cause a cosmic collision of spectacular proportions, not too dissimilar to the spectacular events described in the Sumerian tablets. There are possibly many thousands of giant asteroids flying around the solar system, many of which come very close to the Earth. These are called Near-Earth Asteroids (NEA). Eros is an elongated NEA, which is 33 x 13 x 13 kilometers in size: large enough to destroy our planet and all life on it. About 250 NEAs have been found so far, but many, many more exist. The largest known NEA is 1036 Ganymede, with a diameter of 41 kilometers. According to astronomers there are at least 1000 NEAs whose diameter is greater than one kilometer and which could do catastrophic damage to Earth. Even smaller NEAs could cause substantial destruction if they were to collide with Earth.

This brings us to the dramatic events at Tunguska, Siberia, on June 30, 1908. A meteorite measuring some 90 meters–200 meters in diameter exploded above the ground just before impact. It completely scorched the snow-covered forest below for some 2,100 square kilometers and destroyed some 80 million trees. If that was a city, you can just imagine the drama.

Around 65 million years ago there was a far more devastating collision with planet Earth. A large asteroid about 10 kilometers in diameter crashed into the Earth near the Mexican Yucatan peninsula and as a result caused the extinction of not only the dinosaurs, but all land animals over 30 kilograms, and large sections of plant life. The impact would have penetrated the Earth's crust, scattering dust and debris into the atmosphere, causing huge fires, volcanic activity, tsunamis, and severe storms with high winds and even highly acidic rain. The impact could have resulted in chemical changes in Earth's atmosphere, increasing concentrations of sulphuric acid, nitric acid, and fluoride compounds. What is more, the heat from the impact's blast wave would have incinerated all life in its path. After the impact, dust and debris that were thrust into the atmosphere would have blocked most of the sunlight for months and lowered the global temperature. Organisms that could not adapt to the light and temperature changes would die out. Since plants' energy is derived from the sun, they would likely be the first to be affected by such changes in the climate. Many families of phytoplankton and plants died out, and the

Earth's oxygen levels may well have dramatically decreased. This would have affected oxygen on both land and in the oceans, suffocating those organisms that were unable to cope with the lower oxygen levels. The drama continued. Many major changes in the food chain resulted from all of these environmental upheavals, and the herbivores starved soon after the plants died. Then the carnivores would have had to eat each other, and eventually also died out. Their large carcasses must have provided smaller animals with food for quite a while.

This must have surely been one spectacular explosion. To remind us just how spectacular such cosmic explosions can be, all we have to do is cast our minds back to the most observed cosmic event in human history. In 1994, twenty-one pieces of the Shoemaker-Levy comet crashed into Jupiter. The whole world came to a standstill to watch this spectacular event while all the telescopes were pointed at Jupiter to bring these dramatic pictures into our living rooms. The largest parts of the comet caused explosions one million times bigger than all the atomic explosions ever exploded on Earth put together. In other words, if that comet had hit Earth, we would not be here today, nor would the planet in all likelihood.

So you see, it is not so hard to visualize a cosmic collision. We are very fortunate that we have the magic of TV to remind us of the Jovian event. All that the Sumerians had some 6,000 years ago were some clay tablets and a scribe who captured the events in cuneiform writing, instead of video.

So, now that we have explored our universe, our solar system, comets, asteroids, and cosmic collisions, is there enough content for us to substantiate the probability of an elusive Planet X in the distant parts of the solar system, which pays us a visit every 3,600 years or so? We will explore many more unexplained pieces of the Great Human Puzzle, which lead me to believe that there is such a planet out there. We will also discover that this planet is not only linked to our existence here on Earth through a strange sequence of events, which included the transfer of the seeds of life between planets in the very beginning, but also through genetic manipulation, long after life had developed and evolved on both Nibiru and Earth. The genetic manipulation that our more evolved cosmic relatives inflicted on us some 200,000 years ago is carefully laid out for us in ancient tablets. I will urge you to once again consider the total knowledge we have of the cosmos, and how much we seem to learn every day from our scientists who study the skies. Once you have concluded that our knowledge is still in its infancy, the obvious conclusion must be that we simply cannot say. What keeps haunting me is how carelessly we discard all this information left behind by dedicated scribes from another time when the world was a completely different place. It seems that if this knowledge does not conform to the way we would like to see our ancient history, we are not so keen to accept it into our body of knowledge. To end this chapter on an inspirational note, here are some statements on the subject of Planet X, by scientists, visionaries, and broad thinkers of the past and present.

> That Mankind's progression from Palaeolithic (Old Stone Age) to Mesolithic (Middle Stone Age) to Neolithic (New Stone Age) and then the great Sumerian civilization, had occurred in intervals of about 3600 years is a fact. That Anu visited Earth, approved the grant of civilization (knowledge, science, technology) to Mankind is certain. But as I have tried to explain in my recent Seminars (though not yet in a full length book), the visits to Earth and the nearing (at what is called perihelion) of Nibiru do NOT coincide. This is a point of immense significance, which those who have only read my first book somehow ignore.
>
> ZECHARIA SITCHIN

> In the fields of archaeology, geology, and astronomy the last few years have brought a vast array of facts to corroborate the claims that there were physical upheavals of a global character in historical times; that these catastrophes were caused by extraterrestrial agents; and that the nature of these agents may be identified. The memory of the cataclysms was erased, not because of lack of written traditions, but because of some characteristic process that later caused entire nations, together with their literate men, to read into these traditions allegories or metaphors where actually cosmic disturbances were clearly described.
>
> IMMANUEL VELIKOVSKY

> Dr. Robert S. Harrington, former head of the U.S. Naval Observatory, calculated several parameters of Planet X and its orbit. Harrington started from the perturbations in the orbits of Neptune and Uranus, knowing that Pluto could not be responsible for them. The observations he used were supplied by the Nautical Almanac Office of the U.S. Naval Observatory and go back as far as 1833 for Uranus and 1846 for Neptune.
>
> ROBERT HARRINGTON, HARRINGTON PAPER, U.S. NAVY

> A great many empirical data indicate that at each point of the Earth's surface that has been carefully studied, many climatic changes have taken place, apparently quite suddenly. This is explicable if the virtually rigid outer crust of the Earth undergoes, from time to time, extensive displacement.
>
> ALBERT EINSTEIN

8

HUMAN NATURE

WE SEEM TO TAKE SO MUCH CARE to bring our children up in the proper fashion. Depending on what culture you come from, the variations on the word *proper* can be quite extreme. There are many established cultures throughout the world, each one with its own peculiar customs, rituals, and belief systems. In the last 100 years we have gone from two world wars, a possible third one, to several localized conflicts like Korea, Vietnam, Afghanistan, Iraq, and other skirmishes that have been described as minor uprisings, like the one in Haiti. It is quite amazing that despite the pockets of conflict during the last fifty years of the twentieth century, we have experienced possibly one of the most peaceful and tolerant chapters of our human history. I make this statement with great reservation, because until we have eliminated all conflict from society we will not be free. This period will, however, always be remembered for the collapse of the Soviet Union and turning the giant communist China into the fastest growing economy in the world and everyone's favorite trading partner. But we should be aware that there are other forms of conflict or aggression than pure outright war. We have become experts at highly persuasive techniques of convincing others to follow our lead, while it may not necessarily be to their benefit. Wealth and military power will allow you to call the shots without having to fire a single bullet, and sometimes we conveniently overlook such incidents. It is either that our violent genes have mutated into "clandestine" violent genes, or we have attained new genes that have mutated into displaying their violent nature in more subtle ways.

In his latest book titled *DNA: The Secret of Life,* one of the discoverers of the DNA structure, James Watson, writes: "Understanding genetics is not just understanding why we look like our parents. It is also about coming to grips with some of humankind's oldest enemies: the flaws in our genes that cause genetic disease."

This statement feeds my argument superbly. Why should our genome be so incomplete and so full of flaws if we have been evolving for millions of years? It just does not add up and it indirectly supports the theory of our DNA being tampered with early in our existence. I refer frequently to the "violent gene" and the "greed gene" because I firmly believe they truly exist in our genetic makeup. The evidence is all around us. If we behave in a certain way, there must be something driving it from within, and our DNA is the master program that predetermines all our characteristics. Just as we cannot refute the fact that someone has blue eyes, when it is clearly visible, we cannot refute the fact that we display violent behavior, when it is also clearly visible. And yet there is the other side of our character, the benevolent and peaceful traits, which must have a group of genes that control them. What drives this striving toward harmony by a growing number of earthlings is a mystery, because we have now established that the violent gene is well embedded in our DNA. We have seen a dramatic shift toward tolerance between the global cultures, where only 100 years ago imperialism was still the major quest of the global powers, annihilating weaker cultures in the name of god and king. But while society has been narrowing the gap in some sectors, a growing gap in other sectors has been developing. Religious intolerance is a truly worrying factor to world peace because with religion comes a virtually indestructible force that drives it from within: fanaticism! As long as certain groups of people believe that they occupy a moral and religious high ground over other groups, we are staring disaster in the face. All the efforts by the politicians to create a stable global trading environment will mean absolutely nothing as long as we have the threat of religious fanatical violence. Unless we can point out a new religious road of moderation to the hoards of religious faithful in the world, there is a great risk that this whole issue is possibly still coming to a violent head.

There is another global development that drives the violent genes in some of us in much more subtle ways: Economic warfare. The gap between the rich and the poor is the most worrying aspect of globalization and it is not diminishing; it is growing ever wider. While you have one group or one nation achieving greatness at the expense of another, there will never be a state of harmony on Earth. As I pointed out earlier, our brain is an immensely complex organ, which we may never come to understand completely. The brain seems to play a kind of interface role between the physical and the spiritual aspects of our being. It is the computer that is driven by an extremely well-developed software package called the genome. But the brain computer can only function at the rate at which the software package allows it, and the software requires constant upgrading. This upgrading can only come through the action of DNA. Many scientists have made daring pronouncements about the amount of brain capacity that we humans use, but the truth of the matter is that the brain has a capacity that we cannot begin to estimate. As advanced as it is, our brain can only perform the functions that have been programmed into the genetic software. The more advanced the software, the more amazing things the brain can do. Just like your computer software constantly updates itself from some remote Microsoft reservoir, your genome software constantly strives to update itself from the reservoir of our evolving DNA. There is also, however, a constant tussle between nature and nurture. While some of us are being nurtured into becoming business leaders, others who grow up in less privileged societies are "naturally" marginalized to remain the working class, which provides the slaves who drive the global machine.

We cannot escape our past, which is pretty much built on exploration, invasions, occupation, domination, crusades, and warfare, during which the stronger culture would simply attack the weaker one as part of its unquestionable right to expand its area of influence. Just because we know the past and are starting to understand the complex effects of conflict does not mean we know how to deal with this genetic defect, as James Watson so correctly points out. Our genetic defects do not only affect our physical health, but our mental state as well. It is this mental state of ours that is controlled by our "faulty" DNA that drives us into conflict situations. For us to be able to deal effectively with our insatiable need for conflict, we must know exactly where we come from and why we are the way we are, so that there may be no speculation, as this kind of uncertainty becomes an underlying justification for our behavior. Unfortunately, all the effort expended on our human psychological shortcomings has been based on speculative assumptions of our human origins. The complexity of human nature, therefore, goes back to our creation. African American sociologists claim that it will take their society another several hundred years to overcome the underlying effects of slavery, and this was just a temporary oppression of one group by another without any surgical or genetic manipulation. Just imagine the damage that was handed to humanity at its creation by severely pruning its genetic capacity. The volatile path of human history has left us with scars that we need to heal in an attempt to begin to understand our human nature.

On a personal level, I have always been an eternal optimist, a messenger of positive energy, finding the good in everyone, and constantly creating. Creating what, you may ask? Creating anything. It seems that when humans are busy doing something creative, their minds tap into the nonviolent portion of the genome. An example can be as basic as working in the garden, planting some flowers. The levels of therapy derived from gardening are well documented. It goes on to other simple examples like building a tree house or fixing an old chair. It can get as mundane as writing a shopping list. The creative process seems to override the activity of the violent gene. There are incredible stories from war situations where the opposing armies would stop to play a game of soccer before returning to killing each other. This pop-philosophy causes a dilemma, however. What about the people who create weapons of war? What happens to the relationship between creative genes and violent genes in their system? Is it that they are so absorbed by the creative process of actually creating something new that they are completely removed from the effects of their creation? Or, can it be that the violent gene has become so cunning inside of us that it supports and drives the creative gene to feed its own survival needs? Some of these philosophies have been explored in great detail under the guise of the selfish gene, but these are all answers we will find with time. As for now, at least we are raising the questions, being allowed to explore by our evolved and enlightened society, to examine new boundaries that would have had us burned at the stake a few hundred years ago.

It is such a great pity that communism was corrupted by a group of power-hungry individuals who used the communal benefits to feed their own greed. The behavior of the fallen Communist leaders flew right in the face of their gospel. I believe that under more evolved human conditions, maybe some time in the future, this doctrine of sharing could be more useful to the human race. In its theoretical make up, it is a kind of utopian answer to many global problems. I will most probably be shouted down by millions of capitalists but I still believe that the original idea of sharing has a lot to do with our hidden genetic structure. The people of southern Africa have a communal philosophy they call *ubuntu,* which is based on the principles of sharing and caring for the whole village or community. This concept predates the communist ideals by many thousands of years, and could actually be its early origins. It seems to have worked very successfully for thousands of years, until the tribes were invaded by the colonialists and forced to break up their ancient traditions in favor of democracy and capitalism. Was this a smart or a stupid move? You be the judge, but it seems to me that the survival of the global commune may become dependent on some of the simple philosophies of the oldest cultures on Earth. Capitalism is a recipe for disaster, but the wealthy and powerful corporations who dominate the world will never admit this for as long as they are in the driving seat. They will continue to exploit and enslave large amounts of people for as long as they are on top. Then they will eventually be toppled by another group that will do exactly the same. We have to ask ourselves: where is this all leading?

A perfect genome will have no need for violence, greed, vanity, and all the other characteristics that have caused human suffering for so long. So, as we evolve and we need less and less to feed the materialistic reservoirs of our psyche, will we become more comfortable with the global concept of sharing? Once again, this sharing thing is not really new to humanity. We are involved in communal sharing on various scales: in our homes, extended families, and even offices, but to be taken to its extreme, we would have to eliminate any form of material reward from the global equation.

This concept must be completely unthinkable to anyone in economics or the financial markets, because as they see it, the world is driven by economics—in other words, money. The only problem is that money makes money and in the end it gets us nowhere. The pursuit of money has been a major driving factor behind many wars. The simple expression "the rich get richer and the poor get babies" is very real and very dangerous for future prospects of human survival, because the babies of the poor become the slaves of global corporations in the modern world.

What used to be brutal wars waged by thousands of men in bloody hand-to-hand combat in open fields has been replaced by global terrorism, which is probably more sinister and difficult to guard against. But the largest threat to our survival is economic terrorism. This relative newcomer to global domination has replaced nuclear superiority and has been waged quietly from behind closed doors of the giant multinationals against the smaller unsuspecting nations. After all, it is much wiser and more profitable to invade a country by taking over its economic assets and owning its wealth and natural resources, than blowing them up first, before you take them over. So, in essence nothing has changed since Alexander the Great or Attila the Hun. Only our methodology has changed. The violent gene is still in all of us. While some of us have learned to suppress it somehow, possibly through our own evolutionary process, a new more menacing gene has taken center stage: the greed gene.

If you ask any regular person on the street, they will tell you that they want peace and harmony in the world, but many people are still prepared to fight for peace. You have probably seen those T-shirts that say "Fighting for peace is like fucking for virginity." You can't get much closer to the truth than that. Standing firmly juxtaposed to all the violence and greed in the world is a seemingly endless river of goodwill, but because the media have become obsessed with blood, guts, and gore, we hardly ever get to hear about the good news in the world. On an average day there is far more good news to cover in the world than there is bad news, but that is not the choice of the editors. This is a very strange aspect of human nature that must have its roots in some macabre genetic dysfunction we do not understand yet. Editors seem to be convinced that good news does not sell. I have had this debate with a number of TV and radio producers who tend to dismiss my suggestions of good news content with large amounts of arrogance, as if they knew exactly what the average man on the street wants to consume in the news. Well, I believe they have become slaves to the violent and greed genes driving our character. They have settled into the safe zone of using violent sensationalism to sell their news. They are not brave enough to push the boundaries of their own genetic makeup and explore the deeper needs of the global society. How much longer will the media survive on feeding us such negative news? How much longer will the average person put up with consuming and digesting the sensationalism dished up to us as crucial knowledge without which we could not function?

The amount of goodwill and benevolence that people display on a daily basis is truly staggering: from Mother Theresa to social workers and volunteers in conflict situations, the Red Cross, the Red Crescent, a multitude of aid organizations and charity institutions, animal rights groups, orphan support groups, soup kitchens, night shelters, a seemingly endless list of NGOs (non-government organizations) with some cause at heart, there is so much goodwill in the world it is quite simply overwhelming. The concept of sharing seems to be deeply entrenched in human culture. By the time you see a disaster on TV, some international benevolent organization has already arrived to deal with the situation. One of my favourite quotes is "Do unto others as you would have them do unto you." I always felt that somehow this should be one of the principal philosophies we should subscribe to in our turbulent state of mind. The recognition of good and bad is clearly visible in the eyes of little children; when you tell them stories about evil characters, they burst into tears very quickly. Instinctively, they don't like the bad guys and they want the good to conquer evil. And yet some grow up choosing a violent path and others do not. Is it social conditioning together with a programmed violent gene that causes some children to grow up into monsters? How can a pure little baby who cries when the evil stepmother raises her voice at Cinderella turn into a global dictator who does not count his victims by the dozen, but by the million? The fact that there have been peacemakers like Mahatma Gandhi and Nelson Mandela, who have inspired most of the world to engage in dialogue rather than war, has been an inspiring closure to the twentieth century. This is all juicy fodder for the preachers of nature versus nurture theories. Are we a product of our environment, or are we a product of our DNA program?

Psychologists have been speculating for years about the triggers for violence among humans. There have been fantastic theories: the effect of your parents, your friends, your neighborhood, the climate, disease, the stars, and a host of other extrinsic factors that play an important part in our behavior. That may very well be the case, but they are just the triggers that stimulate the violent gene inside. The chain reaction that follows the stimulation of the violent genes will differ from person to person. This is where it becomes even more complex. If we have been created with a restricted genome, our creator must have done so purposefully. It is clear from the Sumerian tablets that our makers had an advanced knowledge of science and medical procedure, but it does not mean that they, themselves, had a perfect genome. And if we are genetic offshoots from a more advanced human species who settled on Earth in the distant past, we must retain parts of their genetic structure. The fact that we have reached the capacity to contemplate these once unimaginable prospects is a clear sign that there is much more to this fairy tale than first meets the uninformed mind. Our level of development in the twenty-first century must be very close to that of the Anunnaki astronauts when they first arrived on Earth. My guess is that in 100 years or so, we will be ready to absorb the full truth of our ancestry and the authentic origins of the human race. The evidence will be more compelling, the fearful grip of religious dogma will be more fragmented, and people will be searching for real answers rather than the mumblings of conservative power-mongers.

The giant gap between the haves and the have-nots is bigger than ever before. Just compare the giant social chasm separating a rocket scientist who is trying to land a probe on Mars, and the situation of a homeless person contemplating to rob someone for ten bucks. The disparity between humans is staggering. If we were all born equal, we have certainly done everything in our power to change that; a very disturbing aspect of human nature that must have deep-seated roots somewhere in our genome as well. Are some humans more valuable than others? If our bodies are disposable but our souls are not, should we not do away with the imperfect bodies, keeping only a few on this planet, until such time that a more perfect genetically created body has evolved? At that point we could allow humanity to multiply to their hearts' content, because their DNA will not allow us to do anything damaging to either the planet or humankind.

Just look at our insatiable need to explore. We have done quite well in thirty years since the first Viking space probes were launched on a planetary expedition into the depths of our solar system. We have done very well in such a short space of time. We received photographic images of all our planets, before the probe finally left our solar system and disappeared into deep space en route to distant stars. This obsessive desire to explore and conquer is very strong in our genes and, as I point out in other chapters, a quest of humanity since our creation. We can trace it back as far as the garden of Eden. It all started there, when Adam disobeyed his god and wanted to try a new experience. He just had to know more, explore, push the boundaries, without even knowing why he was doing so. It was very simply a natural response that was dictated to him from deep inside his DNA. Poor guy, the father of all humans and he himself was receiving mixed messages from the very start! No wonder we are all so confused.

Since then, we have a much better understanding of our place in the universe. We now know that we are not the center of creation, something that I was still taught as a boy in first grade, and we have had physical interaction with many of the planets around us. So the next step in our quest to conquer would clearly be settling on another planet. The fortunate thing is that there are no intelligent creatures living on any of the local planets. We would surely be faced with a moral dilemma if we found an advanced creature living on one of them. What would we do? It all depends if the creature was more or less advanced than we are, I suppose. This would play a major role in the way we dealt with them.

So let us imagine that the creatures on Mars are more or less as evolved as we are. The first thing that would happen is our natural instinct for defense would probably kick in. We would display high levels of concern that we may be attacked and colonized by our planetary neighbors. So we would face a number of options. Reach out a hand of friendship, attack, or sit back and wait. It is often said that history has taught us nothing, and this is where we will most likely prove it all over again. In conflict situations, a surprise attack will normally catch your opponent off-guard or even better, unprepared. Preemptive strikes are justified based on the pronouncements of people like George W. Bush and many of his disciples. So, we would probably do the latter and forget the lessons from history. Once we have surprised the Martian people and subdued them into subservience, we would occupy them and immediately start to import our global culture. But what culture would it be? American culture of course. After all, they are paying most of the costs, so they will have first option to introduce whatever culture they feel fit. What if the United States acts alone in this invasion of Mars and occupies the Martians against the will of the rest of the world? Suddenly we will all be at risk of an attack by a Martian force anytime in the future. Can you see the deeply rooted signs of a violent gene? I know this is just a silly hypothetical example but it is not that far removed from what is happening on Earth! As far as we know there is no advanced intelligent life on Mars, so the settlement and colonization would not have such serious consequences, yet. It is, however, quite probable that this kind of invasion happened here on Earth some 443,000 years ago. We will expose all the evidence left behind on thousands of Sumerian clay tablets. From the annals of human history, we can also deduce that the consequences of invasions can be catastrophic.

Many books have been written on the possibility of human settlement on Mars. Strangely enough it does not seem to be as insurmountable as we originally thought. Knowing the human hunger for exploration we will send explorers to settle on Mars at some stage in the future. Many brilliant minds have been compiling the necessary steps for human life to flourish there. The three most important criteria are: an atmosphere that protects the settlers against cosmic radiation and contains the necessary gases for us to breathe without a support mechanism; water; and food. The latest announcement by NASA scientists predicts that we could create a livable atmosphere within 200 years. There have been brilliant proposals to achieve all of them and it will probably happen in time to come. So let's just imagine for a moment that if we manage to populate Mars, solve the oxygen and water problems, and start active communities on this neighboring planet: one of the first resources we will need is labor. While robots may be able to perform some of the tasks, human involvement will be unavoidable in the form of actual people who can do all the physical work, which we will need to create a stable sustainable community on Mars. Building structures, reservoirs, roads, mining, food preparation, healthcare, and so on.

If we did not face the moral dilemma imposed on us by religion, would we rather wait for a number of years to get some help from Earth, or would we seek a different solution? The journey to Mars takes more than three years at present speeds of spaceships and would only be able to deliver a very small number of people. In that case, would we rather consider the possibility of cloning men and women who are properly educated and skilled in the various tasks needed on Mars? Will the same moral rules that prohibit human cloning on Earth also apply on Mars? If we could get the emotion and the religious interference out of the equation, cloning would surely be a realistic option. After all, the babies will be well cared for, educated, and protected by the Martian authority. Everything will be provided for them. At a point in the future, when the new Martian humans have matured and are capable of procreating themselves, we would have introduced our family values that we hold so dear on Earth. So you see, cloning does not have to be such a bad thing. It can help us to advance into space, without the constant physical intervention from Earth. It would make the space pioneers self-sufficient and independent. Like a general in a war situation, the general on Mars would most likely decide on the most effective action to deal with the situation, without having to wait for instructions from his leader back home. Will this situation arise on Mars? Maybe . . . possibly . . . probably. It all depends on how impressive the advancement in space travel will be in the next two to three decades. If we can break the bonds of gravity, come to understand and use electromagnetic science more effectively, replace archaic combustion power with a new propulsion system, all of this is possible.

The question remains, how will we deal with the labor problem on the new planets we conquer? In this lies the human moral dilemma, which is very closely linked to our own origins and evolution. The human nature that shapes us and our thoughts, the drive for exploration and invention, the shortcomings of our genome and our imminent understanding of it, all play a part. We are so close to seeing the whole story of humanity, but there are still some hurdles to cross. It is an incredible story that will liberate us from our moral imprisonment and also free us from the cradle of humanity: planet Earth. All of this is programmed into our DNA, each and every one of us. All we need to do is to exhibit patience and restraint as we decode our human program and unlock the dormant genes that will liberate our spirits. Let us go back to Mars. We have now successfully landed, set up a base, and spent a few years—with the help of advanced science—to speed up the development of an atmosphere, generating oxygen from the carbon dioxide trapped under the surface, and we've even brought up water from the underground ice. We also planted thousands if not millions of trees and other vegetation, like grasses, including cereal, maize, barley, oats, wheat, and more. They all grow well with the fertilizer we created from nitrogen and phosphate, and the irrigation system keeps it all hunky-dory. We then face the first dilemma of labor. Suddenly things get out of hand and start to grow and evolve around us on Mars. We have an urgent need for additional manpower. We soon overcome this dilemma by taking the necessary steps to deal with the situation, and we create a whole army of cloned babies. They are bought up in comfort and loved by their minders and creators, providing everything they need while educating them in the necessary skills they will need to perform specialized functions from the early age of sixteen. As the years go by we create more environmentally adapted cloned human babies to supply the needs of the Martian expansion. Mating among the cloned adults is strictly prohibited, because of unforeseen physical problems and controlling the numbers of humans in the colony. In fact, the clones were originally created without the sex chromosome to prevent them from multiplying on their own, but after two decades we realize that it is quicker to allow the clones to mate among themselves under controlled conditions. A quick genetic procedure allows them to procreate on their own for some years. We teach them the importance of monogamy and chastity and family values. They experience the meaning of parenthood and responsibility for the first time. Suddenly, we have a new Martian race of humans who were born of Martian parents and all their experiences are restricted to their Martian history. These Martians were not created as slaves, but as equal humans.

The community and population on Mars grow and their needs grow along with them. The rare precious metals that are being extracted and shipped back to Earth become a highly sought-after commodity among Martians, and they start to adorn themselves with it as a symbol of their achievement. As time goes by this metal becomes so desirable that it becomes the local currency. Martians everywhere start to trade with this currency so that it begins to affect the supply to mother Earth. Soon after this, the trade with the metal is outlawed and it goes underground. Within a short space of time, a new elite Martian mafia-type organization emerges that starts to control much of the power, while criminal activity surges. With this sudden arrival of material and monetary desires of the Martians comes a whole new and most serious dilemma. There are now 12,875 people on Mars and complex social problems start to creep into all spheres of life. The most worrying is the emergence of social classes, skewing the balance of equality. Since this was originally a government-funded expedition, all the people who were enrolled played a vital and integral part in the mission to Mars. They all received the same remuneration, while all their daily needs and requirements on Mars were provided for by the expedition funds. The original team worked smoothly, without any conflict, as they each had a special function to fulfill, and each member was a crucial part of the team. But suddenly this all changed, and a new worker class emerged. Should the worker be treated the same as the first members of the team? Or are they to be regarded as "lesser equals," since they were created for more menial work? And how will they be remunerated? With food, clothing, entertainment, free sporting facilities, and other things that will satisfy their needs while they live happily in the growing Martian community? Or do they get given some form of monetary remuneration that is deemed to be proportional to the job they perform? With the one option you will create a communist structure where everyone is equal and expected to contribute toward the benefit of the whole group; the other option is to plant the seeds of a capitalist system that comes with its own instant set of problems of greed and ownership. Which is the lesser of the two evils? With the first system it may happen that pretty soon some individuals will start to drag their feet, not performing at their peak and causing dissatisfaction among the other workers who have to make up for their co-worker's laziness. The other system will create instant class structures where some get richer while the others get disgruntled with their lot. Corruption and greed will permeate the communities with a long list of undesirable social side effects.

Now I would like you to take a deep breath and attempt to answer this question. If it is possible that we as the human race are on the verge of colonizing other planets, is it not possible, given the very murky surroundings of our ancestry, that we ourselves have come through a similar set of events here on Earth? Is there not a real case for examining the evidence from prehistory to present a case based on more scientific and physical evidence, rather than the man-made religions that keep the human race trapped in a cycle of religious dogma, guilt, and fear?

Fear is a powerful tool that has been used by dictators for eternity. The fear of punishment, physical harm, torture, and gruesome death has haunted humanity since the beginning, but the fear of spiritual torture is equally strong. The insane fear of going to hell after death, where you will burn for eternity, is very real to billions of people on Earth today. The fear that was instilled in us by our maker was the blueprint that was followed by political leaders and religious leaders ever since. These powerful tools have not only been used by gruesome dictators, but also by the more cunning leaders of the modern world as a clever tool of propaganda. The global media have given world leaders instant access to their people. With this access they can create and control a relentless propaganda campaign, so subtle that often their strongest critics do not recognize it. I am always amazed how the giants like BBC and CNN can discriminate or choose sides so blatantly, when they refer to "the Israeli soldiers," and in the same sentence they call their opponents "Palestinian militants" or "terrorists." In an instant they legitimize the one group while reducing their opponents to a distasteful group of barbarians. If I recall correctly, that is not the way they referred to the African National Congress (ANC) when Nelson Mandela was part of this militant group of revolutionaries. They were called "freedom fighters" with a just cause to reclaim their land. So what is going on in the Middle East? Have the world's media decided that the Palestinians are just a bunch of brutal barbarians who deserve to be annihilated? Whether we like it or not, this subtle play on words will eventually influence our personal judgment, as the years of repetition wear down our ability to distinguish truth from propaganda.

George W. Bush used the media very skillfully after the 9/11 attacks to make the American people fearful of almost everything. He used the media to make them believe that everyone was a threat and everyone wanted to attack them, invade them, and overthrow them. A clever maneuver to unite his people behind him and follow blindly as he leads them into a new global conflict of cultural domination. This instilled fear suddenly justified all acts of war against other countries based purely on the propaganda of the U.S. government. The really sad thing is that the poor American people are completely oblivious to this development that has completely consumed their lives. They are happy to pay their taxes, strengthen their army, and invade the whole world to prevent them from possibly engaging in any future acts of aggression against the "land of the free." Does this sound familiar? Is this not very close to what Alexander the Great and the Roman Empire did 2,300 years ago? If you add the element of economic warfare waged by the largest economy on the rest of the world, you have a very grim picture of how civilized the modern world really is. The truth is, we are in a constant state of conflict of some kind. The most prevalent and the most dangerous is the growing economic conflict. Until recently there was only one player with total control of global economics, but through an unexpected sequence of events, the impossible has occurred and placed the former economic giant under threat. The sleeping dragon has awakened, and through the sheer numbers of people, China has shifted the balance of economic power dramatically in a few short years.

So what is the outcome of all this military and economic warfare? There is no outcome; warfare will continue to be the biggest threat to the human race and it will continue to cause unimaginable suffering among people everywhere. It seems that there is nothing we can do to temper the violent gene until we start to come to grips with genetic engineering, until we actually located this gene and its related genes, or until we actually evolve a little more. Together with its newfound friend, the greed gene, they make a devastating slice of DNA, so powerful, with so much control over humanity, that it will be very difficult to fight it with our minds. Even though many will tell you that the mind can do anything, the program in our genes reigns supreme. This violent gene and the greed gene are stimulated by a variety of triggers to come out of hiding and get activated. These triggers depend on various factors that influence our lives as we grow, and possibly even the activity of other genes. There is a possibility that it is not really a violent gene, but just one element of a cluster of genes that has a completely different function when working together, and just like a computer will malfunction if the software program is not complete, a specific gene will function improperly when it has been disturbed by extrinsic factors. This too, we will discover as our knowledge of the genome increases.

George Soros is possibly the world's wealthiest and most active philanthropist. He has made immense wealth and at the same time has been involved in continuous donor funding activity all over the world. He is truly a strange phenomenon, because to make money and build an empire like he has takes a specific type of character that is normally associated with drive, commitment, cunning, ruthlessness, being relentless and often cruel, but also a visionary and a good strategist, the kind of characteristics displayed by military leaders. It makes sense that the fight for economic victory follows a parallel path, but George Soros is better known for his benevolent attributes. The amount of money he spends on financial support for needy countries and thousands of other charitable institutions around the world is truly inspiring.

This unusual characteristic seems to be growing among the high profile wealthy individuals globally, but Soros still leads the pack by a long way. The curious thing is his ancestry. Being of Hungarian origin places him very close to the main center of activity of the Anunnaki of the ancient times. Just humor me for a while as I try to unravel the possible genetic links to our makers. The main residences and palaces of the Anunnaki were in the Middle East when they first arrived. This is where they settled and ruled. This is also where they made certain crucial decisions that were then implemented, like the decision to create a humanlike clone to perform all the hard labor on Earth. If the first humans were created in this part of the world, using a mixture of Anunnaki DNA and *Homo erectus* DNA to create a new species, it means that there must have been a period when the Middle East had a growing population of the new human species, evolving as they performed menial tasks for their masters and gods. It is also likely, given the human nature of promiscuity, that the "sons of the Nefilim saw the daughters of man" (as it says in Genesis 6:1–2) and they had sex with them, creating a whole new genetic pool that was more advanced than the *Homo sapiens* "slave species." Is it, therefore, possible that there is a genetically more advanced group of people in the Middle East who have a more advanced genome in certain respects? These may be the wealthy but benevolent individuals who have evolved faster and started to feel the effects of newly released genes that the rest of us are yet to experience. Is this also a possible reason why all over the world we have great people who emerge out of the morass of human conflict to shine a light of new wisdom and a new vision, as they lead by example? Gandhi and Mandela being just two examples. Could they be more evolved genetically because their ancestors had more Anunnaki blood in their bodies than human blood?

It is curious that some wealthy people are overcome by guilt of some sort once they have amassed large amounts of wealth. I suppose it is the realization that you can't take it with you, which leads to all kinds of internal moral clashes. We have been given some eighty years on average to do something with our lives. Since we have been liberated from the slave species status into which we were originally created, we face a dilemma: What do we do with all this time on Earth? I predict in this book that as our genome evolves, it allows our mind to interact on different levels with the world around us. It stands to reason that an evolved mind will interact differently with the universal spirit, or God with a big "G" as I like to call it. This relationship between human and the divine will unquestionably impact on the way those individuals behave and how it changes their opinions about worldly issues facing humankind. For the meantime, while various structures that were imposed on us as a primitive species still prevail, we are slowly unlocking the chains of bondage and inventing new pastimes, hobbies, and knowledge.

It is incredible how certain sectors of the global economy have influenced the way we behave, dress, speak, court, make love, and engage in war. The past century is filled with a number of fantastic examples of this impressionable human trait.

Let's take a look at the tobacco industry for example. Before the advent of the moving pictures, smoking was not such a "hip" thing to do. Suddenly the silver screen was filled with stars who all held long sexy cigarettes in their hands. Lighting a cigarette became a signature scene in virtually every movie as directors fell in love with the way their cameras captured the swirling smoke. Within a few short years smoking was associated with glitz and glamour, and everyone wanted to look as cool as their favorite movie star. Personal health was not on their mind; their image was the main thing. Is it possible that the cigarette companies may have had something to do with those early movies? Were they using the power of mass media to attract new consumers?

Soap operas have had such a huge impact on the behavior of people that it absolutely boggles the mind. Millions upon millions of people across the world gather every day to worship at the TV, watching their favorite soap religiously. It has become a pseudoreligion for some and they will not go out at night before getting their dose of surrealism. At the risk of sounding sexist, I have heard confessions from women who claim that they plan their days based on the storyline in their favorite soap. It affects their moods, their needs, their relationships, and their lives. Is that not a clear sign of a disturbed civilization in search of reason? So where does this disturbed global population come from?

As we uncover the dusty tablets of wisdom left behind by our ancient ancestors, we will begin to see the clear evidence that we are the reluctant by-product of an advanced group of beings who populated the Earth some 443,000 years ago. The evidence is overwhelming that they created humans as a primitive worker to ease their workload in the gold mines, essentially creating the first slaves and entrenching our obsession with gold. We will discover with absolute amazement how closely our behavior resembles that of the Anunnaki who created us. Because we were endowed with much of their DNA, we should not be surprised that we are showing the same character flaws, which eventually destroyed their own unity on Earth. We look like them, we behave like them, and slowly our DNA is evolving to its original configuration as possessed by our makers, the Anunnaki. In essence, we are the aliens on this planet called Earth.

9

GOLD

The Endless Obsession

I have been asked several times throughout my life what I would change if I had a chance to do it all again. Maybe I was very lucky or ignorant or possibly even arrogant, but I would change nothing. My childhood days were filled with so much laughter, nonstop fun and adventure, growing up on the gold fields of South Africa, that I cannot imagine having it any other way. For those who have never had the pleasure of visiting the gold fields of the West Rand, South Africa, do not be disappointed, because the fields are not actually filled with gold.

The name does, however, suggest a landscape filled with shiny, glistening mounds of gold as far as the eye can see. All you have to do is reach out and take it. On the contrary, the West Rand is a rather flat grassland, full of *mielie* (maize) fields, whirlwinds, dust, afternoon thunderstorms, and sinkholes. There is a small range of hills that seem to run all the way from Johannesburg to Potchefstroom for about 150 kilometers. As you travel this two-hour stretch of road, you come across your typical mining settlements, which have between 200 and 5,000 residents. They have great names like Zuurbekom, Westonaria, Randfontein, Venterspost, Waterpan, Hills Haven, Libanon, Fochville, and the famous Carletonville. The one common feature that links them all together is the array of mine shafts: small ones, giant ones, concrete ones, and steel ones. Sinkholes are a fascinating phenomenon in these parts, mainly as a result of man's hunger for gold. As the mining activity underground drains the water, it allows the dolomite rock formations to become dry and brittle. With time and pressure, they eventually cave in and cause sinkholes on the surface with devastating effects to humans. These sinkholes can range from a few meters across to a kilometer across and their depth normally varies from hole to hole. The Venterspost Golf Course, where I mastered my envious handicap of 22, was built around such a sinkhole featuring some daunting drives that force you to clear the hole instead of water. On many occasions we would be forced to venture down into the giant sinkhole in search of lost balls. More often than not it was worth the trek, as the booty provided us with golfing riches every twelve-year-old could only dream of . . . Balls for Africa.

Everything on the West Rand revolved around gold, which had a knock-on effect into every possible industry imaginable. The villages were, and are still today, designed to provide the families of mine workers with everything they need to keep them occupied. This obviously applied only to the white miners, while the black migrant labor force was crammed into men's hostels that developed very disturbing socioeconomic problems with time. But for the fortunate ones, it was swimming, golf, tennis, squash, bowls, badminton, jukskei, club house activity, and constant social events. This was like paradise for any growing child. What more did we need? Every mining home had the spoils of their underground toil on display, normally consisting of a range of gold ore rocks, clearly showing the rich sediment arteries of gold and other metals. These rocks would inevitably be above the fireplace, in the middle of the table holding down the crochet cloth, or even converted into a homemade ashtray. It's incredible to think that as much as 60% of the modern world's gold came from this area, which stretches about 200 kilometers in diameter and also includes large parts of the Free State.

While this geographic location may not have been terribly relevant to me and all the other gold miners in the 1970s, it would certainly start to raise many crucial questions in my mind by the mid-1990s, when it started to become clear that the so-called Cradle of Humankind was located right here in southern Africa. Is it not curious that it was here in southern Africa where the Sumerian tablets claim that most of the original gold mining activity took place, shortly after the Anunnaki first arrived on Earth some 443,000 years ago? And according to the tablets, it is also here at the southern tip of Africa where the newly created species, Adamu, was put to work some 200,000 years later. Should we be surprised that these amazing historic facts all seem to tie up? Yes we should, because we know by now that history has taught us nothing, so once again we look at these incredible coincidences and we refuse to believe what they are telling us.

Back on the West Rand in 1970, to the hundreds of thousands of people growing up in this mining industry, it was all they knew, and it was all they needed, to the point that I personally always felt sorry for the kids in the city. I could never understand what all the other people were doing living in cities and other parts of the country. What could be more important than gold? What else was there? Our lives were so consumed by the activities surrounding the gold mining industry, it was truly difficult to imagine a life other than that. After all, our fathers were the guys responsible for getting the shiny metal out of the ground—the bars of gold that were the envy of the whole world. I distinctly remember the sadness that surrounded underground rock falls resulting in deaths of people I knew very well, like my friend's father who died underground in the pursuit of gold, or people swallowed up by sinkholes while playing tennis on a Sunday morning. But while there were regular tragedies, we somehow justified it and believed that it was all okay, because we were part of the big plan to provide the world with gold. Life simply carried on and every day more trucks filled with gold would leave our backyard to be delivered to someone, somewhere in the distant corners of the world.

Looking back at this scenario some thirty years later, there seems to be very little difference between my father's underground toil for the shiny yellow metal and the original primitive miners who worked the gold mines at the dawn of humanity. They both came into this world with a finite number of years to live, performed their duty, and made some invisible god richer. The similarity between the human slave species at the dawn of humanity and the modern mine worker is quite startling. If we examine the Sumerian texts and see how the new primitive worker was treated by his gods while working the mines, performing the hard labor for his masters while being provided with everything they needed in the garden of Eden, we realize that nothing much has changed in thousands of years.

The primitive workers must have also wondered where all this shiny metal was going; it would be whisked away by the gods never to be seen again. Why was it so important to the gods? What made this yellow metal so sought-after? Why were the workers not allowed to keep any of it . . . or own it? Why were they punished so severely if they kept any of it? Why was so much effort put into its recovery? Who was using it . . . and for what? But these questions were probably never answered in ancient times. While we may think differently today, do we really know where all the gold goes? And who actually ends up using it for what purpose? We think we know . . . we have all the scientific answers and the economic indicators thrown at us daily providing us with a warped sense of confidence because the "gold market is stable." Explanations of what happens to all the precious metals on Earth fills the pages of economic dailies, but I still suspect that there is much more to the story of gold that is neither known nor understood by the well-informed human race in the twenty-first century. It feels as if there is a greater monster somewhere in the sky consuming much of the precious metal spoils from Earth.

Why are we so obsessed with gold? What caused this sudden prehistoric obsession? Why was it gold and not some other precious metal? Why is it that we can trace this obsession all the way back to the Cradle of Humankind? The sudden emergence of civilization some 11000 BC went hand in hand with agriculture, structured communities, and domestication of animals by the new "thinking man." There seems to be no sensible explanation for this. Anthropologists are perplexed by man's virtual disappearance or slow regression before the Great Flood of some 13,000 years ago, until they suddenly reemerged with a new vigor, and as if out of nowhere, civilization emerged in the Near East. It was from there that all these suddenly acquired skills spread around the world. These are now accepted statistics by most scholars. They had hardly appeared from the dregs of the Flood, and already they had gold, and their fascination with the pale metal was as visible as it is today.

One other thing that still perplexes historians is the speed at which a wide variety of new agricultural produce kept coming out of the Near East, starting from around 8000 BC or even earlier. It was as if the Near East had become some kind of a botanical incubator, constantly producing newly domesticated plant species. How was it possible that primitive man, who was still living in caves, suddenly gained such advanced knowledge? This time has been described as the end of the Palaeolithic period or Old Stone Age, and the beginning of the Middle Stone Age or Mesolithic period. It means that man was still completely consumed by stone in all his day-to-day activity. His dwelling was made from stone, villages were protected by stone walls, his tools were made from stone, he covered his dead with stones, and so on. So who was holding his hand, dragging him toward civilization, showing him the way, imparting knowledge as quickly as man could absorb it? There seems to be a clear link between Noah's landing on fertile land, planting the first vines, and the emergence of civilization in the Near East. It is very curious that this primitive man, while emerging from the Stone Age, already possessed advanced knowledge of refining and processing gold, even for thousands of years leading up to this point.

Was the same hand that helped man with agriculture behind his gold mining exploits? It certainly seems like a plausible explanation. Or do you still believe that primitive man just slowly evolved into knowing all about this advanced technology? I could possibly buy the alluvial gold theory, because it is reasonably easy to find it in rivers, sieve the mud, retrieve the gold and polish it. Alluvial gold nuggets vary from very small to reasonably large and often shine in the water, which would have attracted the attention of many a passer-by. The problem is that many of the prehistoric mining sites were actually ore installations. This complicates things a bit. Even the subtle difference in the appearance of gold in its alluvial state, compared to the way it looks like in ore sediments, takes a trained eye to recognize. I simply cannot imagine primitive man walking along some 12,000 years ago, stubbing his toe on a rock, which led to the inadvertent discovery of ore gold mining. He saw that the rock was different from others. On closer inspection he identified gold sediments in the rock. He instinctively knew that if he crushed the rock he could extract gold from it, but first he had to go through the following process:

> Sodium cyanide solution is allowed to leach through a pile of finely-ground rock that has proven to contain gold and silver, and is then collected as gold cyanide and silver cyanide solution. Zinc is added to the solution, precipitating out zinc, silver and gold metals. The zinc is removed with sulphuric acid, leaving a silver and gold amalgam that may be further processed into the individual metals. The cyanide technique is very simple and straightforward to apply, and popular in areas where mine tailings may contain surprisingly large quantities of valuable metals. There can be significant environmental damage caused by the use of this technique, in addition to the high toxicity presented by the cyanide itself.
>
> FROM THE NATIONMASTER ENCYCLOPEDIA ENTRY FOR GOLD MINE

I have a real problem believing that primitive man engaged in this process on his own accord long before he even knew about agriculture and other basic aspects of civilization. The only known reference to this kind of knowledge exists in the Sumerian tablets. Do we take them seriously or do we discard the information captured on these tablets? Many historians have chosen to discard this knowledge and by doing so have denied humankind a true glimpse at the inexplicable behavior of ancient humans. Why has there been this fanatical obsession with gold since the earliest days of humanity? Why is this obsession continuing today? When did man first decide that gold made a great necklace and start adorning himself with the shiny metal? What were early man's real reasons or motivations? Many people believe the answer is simple; they will tell you that it is the rarity of gold that makes it so desirable, but it somehow does not answer the question satisfactorily. Why did primitive man need gold in the first place when there were so many other shinier objects to adorn himself with? What made gold so rare and more desirable than all the other worldly shiny stones and metals? Besides the alluvial gold that may have been exhausted very quickly, who taught man to extract metal from ore?

The history of gold is a fascinating tale. As far back as we can go, humans have always been obsessed with it. The gold rush of the 1850s, the Vatican, the Spanish conquistadores, the Vikings of the Dark Ages, the Romans, the Greeks, the Egyptians, the Maya, Inca, Olmec, Toltec, the Mesopotamians, Akkadians, Sumerians, and the mysterious Anunnaki were all obsessed with gold. Gold has been the obsession of kings forever. It was also the chosen item of sacrifice by god and many of the other ancient gods, when demanding offerings from their human subjects. It has been a symbol of wealth and success in most religions and the Old Testament is filled with references to gold in a multitude of situations. This includes the strict instructions from god to Moses about the dimensions of the Ark of the Covenant and the materials that were to be used in its construction. The following instructions come directly from Exodus 25:10–22.

- They are to make an Ark of acacia wood, 45 inches long, 27 inches wide, and 27 inches high.
- Overlay it with pure gold; overlay it both inside and out. Also make a gold moulding all around it.
- Cast four gold rings for it and place [them] on its four feet; two rings on one side and two rings on the other side.
- Make poles of acacia wood and overlay them with gold.
- Insert the poles into the rings on the sides of the Ark in order to carry the Ark with them.
- The poles are to remain in the rings of the Ark; they must not be removed from it.
- Put the [tablets of the] testimony that I will give you into the Ark.
- Make a mercy seat of pure gold, 45 inches long and 27 inches wide.
- Make two cherubim of gold; make them of hammered work at the two ends of the mercy seat.
- Make one cherub at one end and one cherub at the other end. Make the cherubim of one piece with the mercy seat at its two ends.
- The cherubim are to have wings spread out above, covering the mercy seat with their wings, and are to face one another. The faces of the cherubim should be toward the mercy seat.
- Set the mercy seat on top of the Ark and put the testimony that I will give you into the Ark.
- I will meet with you there above the mercy seat, between the two

cherubim that are over the Ark of the testimony; I will speak with you from there about all that I command you regarding the Israelites.

These are pretty detailed instructions. If I had to receive a plan like this today, I would be quite curious to know why the sizes and materials had to be so specific, if all that this fancy chest was supposedly for was to carry some valuables from Johannesburg to Bloemfontein. Is it possible that instead of just being a container for the future commandments, the Ark was also some kind of communication device? After all god said to Moses, "I will meet with you there above the mercy seat, between the two cherubim that are over the Ark of the Testimony; I will speak with you from there about all that I command you regarding the Israelites." Surely the all-powerful-god could speak to Moses anywhere? Rather than confining him to a designated seat with his head between suspicious cherubim! Were the extended poles not just for carrying the devices, but also antennae to receive transmitted messages? Were the cherubim some sort of speaker system between which Moses had to sit to hear god's message? It is all very curious and highly suspicious once you remove the religious emotion from it. The historic reality is that gold has played a very unusual role in the entire history of humankind, often crossing the line to become religious practice or rituals. Why would god have such an insatiable appetite for gold? Before we speculate any further about the possible reasons surrounding such a divine hunger for gold, let us first take a look at the metal and what the real fuss is all about. What makes this metal so special?

Gold is a remarkable metal with an unparalleled combination of chemical and physical properties, which make it invaluable in a wide range of everyday applications essential to our modern life. Many thousands of everyday appliances require gold to ensure a smooth performance for long periods. Gold is virtually indestructible and is completely recyclable and immune to the effects of air, water, and oxygen. Gold will not tarnish, rust, or corrode. These properties make gold a vital component in many medical, industrial, and electrical applications.

Gold is the most nonreactive of all metals. It never reacts with oxygen, that is why it will not rust or tarnish. The golden mask in the tomb of Tutankhamen looked as brilliant when it was unearthed in 1922 as when it was entombed in 1352 BC. Gold is among the most electrically conductive of all metals and is able to convey even a tiny electrical current in temperatures varying from −55° Celsius to 200° Celsius. It is, therefore, a vital component in computers and telecommunication equipment. It is the most ductile of all metals, allowing it to be drawn out into tiny wires or threads without breaking. A single ounce

(28.4 grams) of gold can be drawn into a wire 8 kilometers long. It can be shaped and extended into extraordinarily thin sheets. One ounce of gold can be hammered into a 12-meter-square sheet. Gold is the most reflective material of infrared energy. This means that high purity gold reflects up to 99% of infrared rays. This makes gold ideal for heat and radiation reflection for astronauts and firefighters. At the same time, gold is also an excellent conductor of thermal energy or heat. It is used to transfer heat away from delicate instruments. For this reason, a 35% gold alloy is used in the main engine nozzle of the Space Shuttle, where temperatures can reach 3300° Celsius.

So what did god have up his sleeve when he gave Moses such precise instructions? Did someone capture all those instructions in writing or were some of the more intricate details omitted simply because the writer could not really understand the finer details? Why were the ancient gods and not only humans so obsessed with gold? When you start weighing up all the little coincidences, and you pay attention to the Sumerians, they begin to make a lot of sense. Most people still carry the naive view that man simply stumbled upon gold by accident, it became a tradable commodity admired by kings, eventually becoming the global currency driving stock markets up and down. I just cannot buy this simplistic view, which is largely based on our current perception of the metal in the twenty-first century.

The history of gold mining has very sketchy roots that are as murky as the rest of ancient human history. The oldest tangible written documentation we have available to us are the Sumerian clay tablets and seals, but these seem to be rejected by many resistant scholars. The last decade, however, has seen a giant and radical swing toward accrediting these tablets with some merit. As more and more tablets have been verified and translated, mavericks like Zecharia Sitchin have received more serious acclaim with their outlandish theories on our ancient ancestors and creators, and the tablets started to make a real impact on the holy grail of science. So if we accept the contents of the Sumerian tablets, we will have to accept the fact that gold mining goes back several hundred thousand years, long before any of us could fathom. But as we will see, it all fits perfectly into the Great Human Puzzle and provides us with riveting information to dispel all the rubbish that we have been indoctrinated with over hundreds of years. You will have to be brave to face the real truth, because it is not what the global establishments would like you to believe. This leaves me personally with only one conclusion. The ancient "gods" who populated the world and enslaved humankind may still be active among us in ways that we cannot comprehend, not allowing knowledge to spread, keeping their firm grip through religious oppression over their "slave species."

There are very clear references in the Sumerian tablets to the introduction of kingships by the gods, the role of high priests as the carriers of the gods' instructions to their people, and the ongoing mining activities in search of the precious metal that brought the Anunnaki to Earth in the first place. The priests and kings were often summoned to a meeting with god during which they would receive very specific instructions to convey to their people. This was a common event in the Old Testament, with people like Abraham and Moses being just two of the more famous examples of how god interacted with man, giving him explicit instructions. Why is this not happening today? Or have we just become too wise for the conniving gods of biblical times? In chapter 16, "The Story of Humankind," we will cover in great detail the creation of the Adamu and the primitive slave worker who had to toil in the mines of southern Africa digging for gold for their gods. But, I trust that I should set the scene in order to explain some of the fundamentals derived from thousands of Sumerian tablets that form the foundation of the claims I make in this chapter.

The slow and steady translation of Sumerian tablets gives us a peek into ancient human history for the very first time, and turns everything we have been taught on its head. They give an extended written account of the entire history of the rise of civilizations on Earth, but it is not what most would expect. And yet when you evaluate all the stuff compiled in this book, it will hopefully make as much sense to you as it does to me. Here is a short outline of the complex story of humankind, as told in the Sumerian tablets, merely to serve as a guide to explain some statements in this chapter:

The Anunnaki were astronauts and explorers who settled on Earth some 443,000 years ago under the command of Anu, hence the Anunnaki. His two sons Enlil and Enki were given the control of their new space base. They came in search of gold to help mend their planet Nibiru's failing ozone layer and atmosphere. Over time they sent as many as 600 explorers and workers to Earth, set up a multitude of mining operations in southern Africa and a space command center in the Near East at Eridu, the oldest settlement on Earth. After some time and complaints from those Anunnaki who had to toil in the mines, they created a clone, which was a mixture of their DNA with that of the *Homo erectus* creature that lived on Earth. They called this first primitive worker "Adamu" and after some time they created a female partner for him to procreate, instead of being carried by surrogate Anunnaki females. As translated from the Sumerian tablet, "Let us create a Lulu, a primitive worker, the hardship work to take over . . . By the mark of our essence to fashion him."

The new slave species became highly sought after by the Anunnaki in the Near East and so began to toil there as well, away from his African cradle. The

Anunnaki also had a base established on Mars from where they could send larger shipments because of the lower gravity. This was before the cosmic events that caused the Great Flood on Earth and also caused Mars to lose its atmosphere. Those who lived on Mars were called Igigi, but the cosmic events forced the Igigi to desert the planet and return to Earth. The sons of the Anunnaki and the Igigi were referred to as the Nefilim in the book of Genesis and other literature: "Those who descended to Earth from heaven." Even Genesis tells us about these Nefilim who came to Earth and "saw that the daughters of man were beautiful and had children with them." This created a whole new species of humans called the Aryans who lived separately from the rest and influenced future civilizations to a great extent. They were followers of Marduk, who we will hear a lot more of later.

All these activities happened for very sound reasons. The planet Nibiru is on a 3,600-year orbit around the sun, just like the orbit of many comets. On one of its approaches to the sun, Nibiru came unusually close to Earth and Mars, causing great geological upheavals that resulted in the Great Flood some 13,000 years ago. At the same time, the presence of Nibiru also caused Mars' atmosphere to be "sucked away." The Anunnaki saw this approaching global catastrophe as an opportunity to wipe out the slave species that they created and that had grown to very large numbers by then. The slave species had become a big problem that was not going away. They needed constant supervision, care, and feeding like little helpless children. They were becoming unruly and some even began to develop thoughts of independence, breaking the bonds of labor and slavery in the mines. But the biggest problem for Enlil was that some of the Nefilim were having children with the human females, creating a whole new subspecies and exacerbating the problem. At the original point of creation of the Adamu there was much disagreement between the two commanding brothers. Enlil was completely opposed to the creation of a new species and now he had the perfect opportunity by allowing a natural disaster to eliminate the human problem. But Enki, who was the creator of humankind, told some of his own offspring to save themselves in a submersible boat. The rest is part of human history.

The close proximity of Earth to Nibiru had a devastating effect on the large planet Nibiru as well, once again disturbing its atmosphere. Just when the Anunnaki thought they had saved their planet Nibiru and were going home, the gold mining had to resume. As fate would have it, they were grateful that some humans survived, but this time they would give them knowledge and teach them all they needed to know about civilization and survival, while they slowly began to be absorbed into the extended family of gods. The gods divided the world into a number of regions, allocating each region to one of the more senior Anunnaki children on Earth. Disagreements and greed began to consume the ruling gods, with one of them, called Marduk/Ra/Amun, proclaiming himself to be the "one god above all." He expanded his influence over the world against the will of the rest of the Anunnaki gods, causing a standoff. Marduk seems to be the one god of the Old Testament, who began to prohibit the worship of other gods by humans. He was also referred to as the "god of vengeance," who about 2500 years BC began to force humans everywhere to accept him as the only god. He promised reward and sympathy to those who obeyed him and great punishment to those who did not. He also began to promise immortality to his followers, the pharaohs being the major and first benefactors of his promises. It is for these reasons that we see the unusual obsession with the afterlife among the Egyptian kings. The rest of the Anunnaki decided that they had to act decisively and with extreme force against Marduk. This was the time that involved Sodom and Gomorrah in the Bible. The destruction was violent and widespread, with dire consequences. But somehow, Marduk escaped the onslaught, and the events only made him more feared and worshipped by the surviving humans. So his related extended family in northern Mesopotamia, the Aryans, invaded the lands to the east and Europe to the west, conquering humans everywhere and imposing their Aryan supremacy on them, and such is the remaining status quo in the world today.

I must tell you that I am not making any of this up in a moment of fictional insanity. As ridiculous as these tales may sound, they are no more ridiculous than what is happening in the world today. You can be the judge of the evidence presented, and you can decide whether you want to remain a slave species, or whether you want to begin exploring the new options presented to us as we unearth more and more prehistoric artifacts that tell us a completely different story about our human ancestry than the one we have all been told.

Let us go back to the obsession with gold. The members of the slave species were toiling in the mines oblivious of their exact place in the greater scheme of things. They knew that this was the only thing required of them. They lived in compounds not dissimilar to those used on South African mines even today. Everything was provided for the slaves, but they had no choice, no freedom, no future other than toiling in mines.

They were born into mining slavery and they died as slaves on the mines. But there must have been slaves who rebelled and escaped into the dense African bush, to form small family units, learning to survive as hunter-gatherers. The Khoi-San people were most likely some of those. There came a time when some slaves were allowed to leave the mine compounds and live in the African wild, probably when they became old and fragile, not able to do the hard labor they were intended for.

These groups of early humans formed small units and tribes, developing their own distinct African cultures that were filled with mythological gods and tales that are difficult for historians to understand. When seen from this new perspective it makes perfect sense why African mythology and their religions are so different from the rest to the world. Because it was here in Africa where the first humans were created, they lived and slaved in isolation from the other emerging human communities, and they established their own unique cultures, highly influenced by their master gods. There was very little contact between these early humans in Africa and the rest of the world, where interbreeding was taking place between humans and the offspring of the Anunnaki, giving rise to the Aryans of the north. It is possible that there may even have been a mutiny by the slave species against their enslavement, after some 100,000 years of toiling.

After the mutiny of the slave species, when many were allowed to leave their mining compounds, the mining continued while many of the slaves tried to live in newly-formed communities and survive without the help of their gods. Could this relationship between the slaves and Anunnaki be echoed in the religious structures of today? Could the Anunnaki still be holding a firm grip on human activity especially around the production of gold in modern times? Many of the secret societies throughout history have been traced way back to the origin of humanity and the so-called Brotherhood of the Snake, and the conspiracy theories keep coming. The great thing about conspiracy theories is that that's exactly what they remain. But the fact that our human origin is in question, that the role of gold in the world has dubious origins, the questionable role that the church and its priests have played in the hoarding of gold and wealth, all point to possible conspiracies so deep that there may be more to them than meets the sober mind.

Just to demonstrate how confused historians are about the origins of gold and its possible meaning to early humans, here are some random extracts of what has been said about the origins of gold:

Gold was probably the first metal known to the early hominids that, on finding it as nuggets and spangles in the soils and stream sands, were undoubtedly attracted by its intrinsic beauty, great malleability, and virtual indestructibility.

I find this statement utterly ridiculous. Why would a soft metal have any value to primitive hominid, apelike creatures, when their preoccupation was with survival, food and shelter? But the Anunnaki needed gold and they needed a worker to get the gold from the ground.

During the stone ages the metal appears to have taken on a sacred qual-ity because of its enduring character and immortality, being worn initially probably as amulets and later fashioned into religious objects and idols.

All very well, but why would gold, rather than any of the other metals or pre-cious stones, take on such an importance? There is no justifiable reason for such behavior by primitive early humans, unless they were imitating someone, placing value on the metal for some reason.

By the time of the early Indus, Sumerian, and Egyptian civilisations (3000–2000 BC) gold had not only retained its sacred quality but had become the symbol of wealth and social rank.

Exactly! By this time humans were given civilization by their gods and gold was established as the "property of the gods." This is very well documented by the conquistadores in Mesoamerica. They were repeatedly told by the natives that all the gold "belonged to the gods." In biblical times god would reward his obe-dient human followers in various ways. Gold was one of those rewards, because it was revered by humans as a divine metal. Any human who was allowed to keep gold or given gold by the gods as a form of reward was admired by every-one. They would be in possession of something "godly" and "divine," which was a huge social privilege, increasing the desire and demand for gold.

Homer (circa 1000 BC), writing in the *Iliad* and *Odyssey,* the epic poems of ancient Greece, describes gold repeatedly both as a sign of wealth among mortals and as a symbol of splendour among the immortals.

There we have it. Homer had similar views on the issue with gold. Why did he know these things, which our modern intellectuals have reduced to mythologi-cal mumbo-jumbo not to be taken seriously? The following statement imme-diately supports my disillusion with modern teachers of human history. This seems to be a commonly accepted view among scholars, which I find extremely arrogant, shortsighted, and outright ignorant. They should read more, open their eyes, and stop filling the minds of our children with half-truths and utter rubbish, which is mostly regurgitated historical rhetoric not worthy of the paper it is written on.

Early references to the first discovery of gold are essentially legendary or mythical. The *Chronicum Alexandrinum* (AD 628) ascribes its discovery of gold to Mercury, the Roman god of merchandise and merchants, the son of Jupiter, or to Pisus. Similar legends and myths concerning the initial discovery of gold are referred to in the ancient literature of the Hindus (the Vedas) as well as in that of the ancient Chinese and other peoples.

What more do we need in the form of support for what we read in the Sumerian tablets? Obviously Alexander's historians knew more than our historians do today, and they must have been familiar with the extensive library at Alexandria with its millions of books, lost to our modern historians. They did not hesitate calling the deities "gods" while today's historians very quickly reduce them to "mythological" figures.

Here is a little more of what history sources have to say about gold: "The discovery of the element we call gold is lost in antiquity." This is not true. Here is an extract from a Sumerian tablet translated by Zecharia Sitchin: "Let gold from the waters be obtained, let it for salvation on Nibiru be tested."

This was the first ever reference to gold in our ancient prehistory. Words spoken by Anu, the king of Nibiru, before they dispatched the Anunnaki to Earth to retrieve the gold. Do we just ignore these scripts and regard them as nonsense? Why would prehistoric men be so obsessed with gold that they wrote such elaborate stories about the metal? I contest that it would have been relevant only if gold played a crucial role in their survival, and so it did. It was the main reason and the only reason why the Anunnaki were on Earth, and the only reason humankind was created.

> The principal source of gold in primitive times was undoubtedly stream placers, although there is considerable evidence in certain gold belts in Egypt, India and other places. The Eluvial and alluvial placers were worked in the crudest manner by panning or the simplest form of sluicing. Exposed parts of friable veins were simply dug out, trenched, or pitted with the crudest of tools, stone hammers, antler picks, bone and wooden shovels. Only rarely were simple shafts, and drifts attempted and then only in the soft rocks of the zone of oxidation. Fire-setting was probably employed by the ancient Egyptians, Semites, Indians, and others to break up the hard quartz veins.

Why would early humans want to break up gold-bearing rock, if they did not know how to extract gold from ore? They must have known the procedure otherwise they would not even have recognized gold deposits in ore. And we have evidence that they did use fire to break up the ore, so they must have known the rest of the complex procedure, including smelting at above 700° Celsius. But why be so surprised? The Sumerian tablets tell us exactly how they went about obtaining gold from ore and how they smelted it. "How a new metal from stones was extracted . . . to a place of melting and refining metals . . ." the gold was taken.

Throughout the history of humankind, where there was evidence of gold new settlements erupted, bringing prosperity to some and desperation to others. In fact, it seems that if there was no evidence of gold from the earliest days of antiquity, civilization would only show signs of development much later. All the earliest human settlements seem to go hand-in-hand with gold.

Both small and large deposits that showed free gold visibly or in the pan were worked by slaves, convicts, and prisoners of war who were assigned by those in authority to the gold placers and mines.

The term *mine* is very relevant here, as most mine shafts are dug for the purpose of ore mining. And why would they have dug mine shafts like the ones in southern Africa 50,000 years ago and more, if they had no knowledge of ore mining?

Early references to gold mining appear in ancient Egyptian codes, on stelae, in pictograms and inscriptions in the tombs of the Pharaohs. The most ancient geological map known, is from about the time of Seti I (circa 1320 BC). It shows roads, miners' houses, gold mines, quarries, auriferous mountains, and so on. The ancient Sumerian, Akkadian, Assyrian, and Babylonian civilisations utilized gold extensively, but their sources of the precious metal are relatively uncertain.

This is not true! The clay tablets give us many references to gold, outlining the mining operations, processing, smelting, and usage. But the historians who write such tripe about the history of gold are probably the same people who give the Egyptians credit for mining gold, but in the same sentence discredit that which the Egyptians held so dear—their gods—who gave them all the knowledge and wisdom, including that of mining for gold.

References to gold and gold mining are numerous in the Old Testament of the Hebrews. Six sources of gold are mentioned in the Old Testament. They are Havilah, Ophir, Sheba, Midian, Uphaz, and Parvaim. The exact locations of all six have given rise to much speculation. Some authorities claim that all six sources are Arabian; others have suggested locations much farther a field.

If only they would pay attention to those mystical ancient scriptures left behind for us to assimilate. But unfortunately those had been classified as mythology, so no sober historian could possibly admit that such fiction had influenced their professional opinion. There are very clear and detailed references to southern Africa or the "Abzu" as the place where the first gold in the world came from. It also happens to be where the first primitive worker was put to work to mine the gold, and it also happens to be the Cradle of Humankind. Is this all not a little too coincidental?

There has been much speculation as to the location of Ophir, the fabulously rich land, filled with gold, from which King Solomon's navy brought more than 34 metric tons of the metal to his kingdom. Kings 10:22 in the Old Testament mentions cargoes of sandalwood trees, precious stones, ivory, apes, and peacocks, suggesting the circumnavigation of Africa. Various references to Tarshish suggest that the gold may have come from Tharsis, a mining town in Spain.

Other favorite spots are East Africa and southern Africa, principally Zimbabwe, especially the ruins of Great Zimbabwe. The whole layout, design of the main residence, staff quarters, the art of building a stone structure without mortar, would have made a perfect master's residence for the god Enki in the Abzu, as the clay tablets call it. Could this have been the head office of King Solomon's mines? Who occupied it thousands of years after Enki "built his place in the Abzu." There is no shortage of mines in southern Africa and over the past 200 years of exploration over 500 ruins have been discovered in what was called the land of Monomotapa. This ancient land stretched from the coast of Mozambique, inland and included modern-day Zimbabwe. Various authorities such as Bruce, Huet, Quartremere, and Guillain, as well as the great majority of later writers on the Zimbabwe ruins, favor the claims that Monomotapa (Zimbabwe) was the Ophir of scripture.

There is also a clear distinction between a much older Great Zimbabwe and all the newer structures that were built in much later times. Could this be a repetition of the pyramid symptom? The original structures were built by the prehistoric Anunnaki under the leadership of Enki, as his home in the Abzu. Thousands of years later, just as in the case of the pyramids, kings of the biblical times, Phoenicians and Himyarites, built their own new structures, which do not quite meet the style and quality of the original. In the "Adapted Excerpts" from *The Ancient Ruins of Rhodesia* by R. N. Hall and W. G. Neal, we read about a "first or older" Zimbabwe and a more recent one. The scholars write that "massive structures which, while following generally the first Zimbabwe type, have been built in three or more high-terraced tiers rising to the summit of the hills, surrounding them, and sometimes completely covering them." They tell us that "this 'wedding cake' feature," as it has been termed, is absent in all Zimbabwe ruins built in the first period. Yet all these later Zimbabwe ruins present all the evidence of having been erected by nature-worshippers, and contain the orientated temple "open to heaven," the sacred circle, the conical towers "the high places," the monoliths, and every evidence of Phallic worship. This class of Zimbabwe is represented, among many others, by Dhlo-dhlo, Regina, Meteme, and Khami people.

The Phoenician connection to the ruins is striking. The monuments, stone carvings, and statues found in Zimbabwe are identical in style to those that are predominant in Sardinia and other ancient Near Eastern cultures, including the worship of the god Baal. Explorers Neal and Hall were leading this drive at the turn of the century. They continue explaining that there is a "marvellous similarity" between these later Zimbabwes and many of the three thousand *nauraghes,* or terraced fortresses, which cover the island of Sardinia. "In both the Rhodesian and Sardinian erections evidences of nature-worship are abundant." The age of the Sardinian nauraghes goes back to the Bronze Age, around 3500 BC–1500 BC, and scholars like Geyard write: "I have no hesitation in considering the numerous round edifices of Sardinia, which are known under the name of nauraghes, as monuments of the worship of Baal." The Zimbabwean ruins of the latter period resemble such monuments to the god Baal, who was worshipped between 2500 and 200 BC all over the Near East and Egypt. This gives us a clear link between the advanced civilizations of the north and the distant lands of gold in the south, referred to as Ophir during biblical times.

This is an incredible breakthrough. Not only do we have strong evidence to support that King Solomon's mines were indeed located in southern Africa, but suddenly we have tangible evidence that there were two distinct civilizations in Zimbabwe, separated by thousands of years. The more recent or Latter Zimbabwe was active between 2000 BC–200 BC. They built their shrines and dwellings the same way as their brothers up north in the Near East, praying to the same god Baal. There is irrefutable evidence of a much older prehistoric civilization, sometimes referred to by scholars as First Zimbabwe. Those from prehistory date back to over 50,000 years as shown by archaeologist Peter Beaumont with his discovery of ancient mines in Swaziland, southern Africa. But the Sumerian tablets tell us that these African mines date back as far as 200,000 years. Too incredible to digest? There is now a visible line connecting ancient mythology with more recent history, finding a natural meeting place. The issue of the "shrines and temples" is crucial here. While the latter biblical civilizations in Ophir were worshipping their gods, the First Zimbabwean cultures had no need or knowledge about worshipping any gods. It was the original Anunnaki who created the mines with their new slave species as the first ever gold miners on Earth. They had no need for temples and worshipping, because that kind of ritual had only been introduced to humankind around 4000 BC to 6000 BC, some 190,000 years later. But then came the kings and mariners of the north around 2500 BC and they built their dwellings as lesser copies of the original Anunnaki structures, and immediately plonked their shrines for worshipping right next door. After all, they would not want to upset the god of vengeance, otherwise they would have been punished. There are many other curious similarities like names of rivers and places that also add to the Great Zimbabwe theory.

Ancient navigational plans of Phoenician King Necho some 610 BC, setting out from the Red Sea to the south eastern coast of Africa or Monomotapa, is just one indication that the land of Ophir was actually in this part of the world. The support for these theories has been growing for decades and the evidence seems to be irrefutable. There was really no other part of the world that could have provided King Solomon and the Queen of Sheba with so much gold during those days of history. While many of the ancient mines in Monomotapa may have been filled with soil and mud during the Great Flood, some have survived to tell the tale of prehistoric mining in the Cradle of Humankind.

Other suggestions for the site of King Solomon's mines are southern Turkey in the Taurus Mountains, northwest Saudi Arabia, and possibly the Eldorado of the Hebrews. Nubia, in the Sudan, was a great source of gold for the Egyptians. It just so happens that "Nub" as in Nubia, means gold in ancient Egyptian. During the time of Queen Hatshepsut (1503–1482 BC) and later, the Egyptian navy brought great amounts of gold and stibnite from the areas in Punt to Egypt. The two other sources of gold mentioned in the Old Testament were Uphaz (Jeremiah 10:9 and Daniel 10:5) and Parvaim (II Chronicles 3:6). Where could those places have possibly been? So far historians have not been able to identify any of the references.

While the talk of gold is ever-present in the Old Testament, references to geological sites of gold and silver are relatively rare. Job 28:1 states: "Surely there is a vein for the silver, and a place for gold where they find it." Who are the "they" he mentions? Why would they be so obsessed with gold?

Southern India has long been known for its golden riches, where in ancient times loads of gold was mined. In his *Bibliotheca Historica* of the first century BC, Diodorus Siculus wrote that in India "the earth contains rich underground veins of many kinds, including many of silver and gold." Once again, it points to knowledge of ore mining and not just the commonly accepted alluvial methods.

In China, gold was mined and utilized during the earliest of times, including the Shang civilization (1800–1027 BC) of the Huang-Ho River. Gold mining was probably introduced into Korea around 1122 BC by the followers of Ki-ja, who migrated from China. From Korea, the various methods of mining for gold were taken to Japan, probably as early as 660 BC, according to Bromehead.

> Gold was known to the early Amerindians, but the metal was not held in high regard in the period . . . Later, during the first centuries of the Christian era, gold assumed much greater importance in the Olmec, Zapotec, Mayan, Aztec, and other civilisations of Mexico and Mesoamerica and in the Inca civilisation of South America.

This is not true. The Andean and Mesoamerican cultures have been obsessed with gold for thousands of years, most of their oral and written legends refer to gold that could go back as far as 12000 BC. These civilizations continue to tell us in their literature that the "gold belongs to the gods." This would have made gold very important in their everyday lives and it was also the reason why their civilizations emerged.

> Gold was not prized by the Amerindians of Canada and the United States, and the aborigines of Australia seem not to have paid any attention to the precious metal.

Could this have been because the Anunnaki did not find large deposits of gold in those areas to attract their attention? And, therefore, any human settlement for the purposes of mining gold only took place much later? Or their obsession with gold only reached them much later, once it became a human obsession, inherited from the gods?

The past few pages were just a tiny taste of the confusion that surrounds the origins of gold on our planet, but the confusion and contradiction get much worse. Therefore, I have no problem whatsoever in turning to other scientific records that may be regarded as inferior or esoteric by many scholars, and rather try to unravel the real truth behind the rich ancient mythology and oral traditions of some cultures. Gold is a central feature in most, if not all, ancient mythology. And yet, as strange as it may seem, after studying over 600 African mythological stories, I did not find one clear reference to gold. There may be some hidden imagery in some of them, but the general absence of gold in these stories is truly puzzling. It leads me to formulate some new theories.

If Africa was in fact the cradle of the very first humans, and if they were created as a slaves to work in the gold mines, they would have been a truly "primitive worker" as the Sumerian scripts call them. As a primitive species, and in the very early days of human existence, they would have had no real feeling or understanding for what they were doing. As far as they saw it, they were given food and shelter while they performed some grueling tasks, the reason for which they did not understand. It was a routine: year in, year out. The "stuff" they were digging up had absolutely no value to them. They could not eat it, or use it in any way. Only many thousands of years later, when the human mental capacity increased dramatically and when interbreeding happened between humans and the "godly" offspring of the Nefilim, did the newly-spawned more intelligent humans begin to give the metal value. This would have only occurred once civilization and kingship was bestowed on humans by their gods, and only after the global system of trade and currency entered the picture. The strange metal could have possibly developed some kind of strange sentimental value after the slaves began to set up their own settlements in Africa, and living away from the mining compounds. They had no real understanding of the use for the metal, and the only expression of their intellect was to adorn themselves with it in many ways to indicate their social standing and importance. Just like their South American brethren, they always knew that the gold belonged to the gods.

My assumption is that like many scientific theories, ridicule will often be followed by respect. When we go through the Sumerian texts in later chapters, you will be amazed at how simply it can all be explained if we just put our prejudice aside and keep our minds open to new realities.

You see, the first signs of ore mining in Mesoamerica date back to around 12,000 years ago, before the emergence of agriculture on Earth, and around the end of the last ice age. At this stage humans did not have it easy. They were constantly under threat from the elements and wild animals. They were concerned with shelter and food while leading a predominantly nomadic lifestyle. How and why would gold seem so attractive to them?

The oldest signs of ore gold mining get even more interesting when you visit the so-called Cradle of Humankind, just twenty minutes north of Johannesburg, South Africa. While archaeologists were making amazing discoveries about the origins of humanity, they also stumbled onto previously unexplained phenomena regarding gold mining. They discovered layers upon layers of prehistoric mining activity, which was dated back to 7690 BC by scholars from Yale and Groningen Universities. This inspired the excavators to search a little further, only to be rewarded with a find of an ancient mine near the famous landmark of the Lion Park. They uncovered a five-ton hematite stone that was covering a large cavern. Carbon dating a piece of charcoal near the mouth shocked the archaeologists when they found it to be from between 20000 BC and 26000 BC. Not believing what they had found, they searched further and exposed more mining access sites dating back to 41000 BC, give or take 1,600 years. Adrian Boshier and Peter Beaumont then extended their search to southern Swaziland where they found ancient mines containing twigs, leaves, grass, and feathers that were most likely brought in by the miners. There were also notched bones, which indicate man's ability to count at such distant times. Other remains at the site date it back to around 50000 BC. This must be a total riddle for historians, evolutionists, and creationists alike. How on Earth is this possible? How will the supporters of the different doctrines explain this? This is where I would like to step in and remind the readers of my theory that creation and evolution should be considered simultaneously. The convergence of the two seems inevitable. While evolution is evident in most life forms around us, there is mounting evidence of a specific time when man was created. We will have to come to terms with the reality that the two philosophies will have to share the stage in the Great Human Puzzle.

We should not be surprised that prehistoric miners were already mining gold in southern Africa several hundred thousand years ago. After all, the geological landscape would not have changed at all since then, and if gold is still available in such abundance in this part of the world today, it must have been available then. We must remember that until 1970, gold from South Africa made up over 75% of all global gold supplies. This clearly means that the early humans knew exactly where the gold was, or they were shown by someone more intelligent where to dig. So, we need to ask again . . . why would primitive man, immediately after being created, start to mine gold so vigorously? It simply does not make any sense.

Somehow the hunger for gold grew gluttonously over the years. So much so that ships were dispatched from the Old World by kings and popes to bring back as much as was humanly possible of this shiny yellow metal. This hunger for gold probably reached its most nauseating zenith during the bloodthirsty Spanish invasions of the New World. The abundance of gold found in the Mesoamericas by the conquistadores, together with the mythical stories of golden cities like Eldorado and Cibola, certainly raise the question: Where did the so-called primitive natives find all that gold? Story has it that during the 200-year activities of the conquistadores, the Spaniards looted more gold from the Americas than has been mined in the entire known world since then. This could obviously never be substantiated, but makes for some juicy imagery. The history books tell us a predictably thin tale of the history and origins of gold in the world. What is known, however, is that gold has always been and seemingly always will be the center of great controversy, speculation, and conspiracy.

At the center of the gold gluttony was the ever-present Vatican, which supported the exploits of the conquistadores. The split was said to be 90% for the Vatican and 10% for the Spanish king. The king in turn had a separate agreement with the conquistadores who undoubtedly had a free-for-all for themselves when overpowering the Native American villages of the New World while looting their gold. It is also said that the Vatican holds most of the gold in the world. A popular conspiracy theory holds that the Vatican has not only attempted to, but largely succeeded in, stealing all the U.S. gold reserves, with the aid of a succession of Jesuit U.S. presidents. As far as conspiracies go, this one seems very interesting because it has some landmark presidential decisions to support it. The most famous is the decision by president Nixon on August 15, 1971 to divorce the dollar from the gold standard. Suddenly the dollar no longer had gold to underpin its value and became just a piece of paper with a U.S. government stamp on it.

The Jesuit Order has been a powerful force in the murky waters of secret societies, linking them back to the formation of the Illuminati around AD 1340 in the central German state of Hess, and even further back to the establishment of the Rosicrucian Lodge in AD 1100 in the German city of Worms, also in the state of Hess. The Jesuit Order was established in 1540 by a militant Christian-soldier-turned-cleric, called Ignatius of Loyola, as one of several counter-Reformation organizations launched by the Catholics to suppress the rise of the Protestants. William Bramley has written a riveting book that deals extensively with most the secret societies in our human history linking us way back to the garden of Eden and the so-called Brotherhood of the Snake. It makes captivating reading as it unravels many dark hidden secrets of our ancient past, pointing convincingly to some form of intervention by more evolved and more intelligent beings. But while they may have been more advanced, it does not mean they were not violent nor bloodthirsty. All these ugly characteristics are still clearly evident in humans today, as visible scars from ancient times. From our behavior and the manipulative control that was exercised over us by secret societies, we can deduce that the influence of these strange phenomena in many ways prevented humanity from evolving faster to discover the true secrets behind our origins. At the same time, there seem to have been other secret societies that had always had some form of advanced knowledge and information, which may have had the opposite effect on human progress. I will resist the temptation of getting too involved in this topic as Bramley has covered it superbly in *The Gods of Eden*.

Gold continued to play a pivotal role in human evolution to the extent that during the California gold rush starting around the 1850s, Vatican monks would basically use their cloth as a front to steal the gold from the Native Americans along the Mexican and Californian coasts. There are reports of hard labor, slavery, and torture of the natives by Catholic monks in the name of god, and in pursuit of gold for the Vatican.

Gold was probably the first metal known to humankind and references to it have appeared almost from the birth of writing. Our entire human history is inextricably linked to the production of gold. If we take at face value what the Sumerians have written in their tablets, we learn that we were created as a slave species by the Anunnaki, with the sole purpose to work in the gold mines. The answer to the question "Why is mankind so obsessed with gold from the very beginning?" is quite simple. Gold was the first thing known to primitive man. He was surrounded by it and consumed by it. It was the principal reason why he was created. The truth is, however, that it was not really man who was so consumed by gold, but his masters and gods, the Anunnaki.

When we explore this early obsession with gold, we begin to understand the overpowering effect it must have had on early humans, how it shaped their behavior in times to come, and how it drove their own vanity, greed, and desire to be like their gods. Very quickly, this forbidden gold must have become the most desirable possession among the human slaves. They found ways to acquire it illegally, but gold was most likely also used to reward them from time to time for acts of obedience. So as time passed, a growing amount of gold made its way into human hands. Not really knowing what to do with it, or what its true purpose was, they started using their newly-acquired forbidden fruit in unconventional ways. They turned it into bracelets, necklaces, rings, ornaments, trinkets, and an ever-growing list of items the sole purpose of which was to show off its owner's elevated status in the emerging community. They made imitations of their gods' possessions, their chariots, their dwellings, their symbols, and even their image. Archaeologists have uncovered countless numbers of effigies of many ancient gods. The value of gold suddenly exploded when the Anunnaki allowed the humans to leave the compounds of the mines and live on their own in growing communities.

This period seems to coincide precisely with the sudden emergence of civilization in the Near East around 7000 BC. Many humans settled here while continuing to work for their gods. The mines in the southern part of Africa continued to produce gold, but the human workers had now developed many communities that have spread over large parts of the continent. Golden artifacts attained the highest status symbol on Earth, and humans started to decorate themselves more and more with symbolic new jewelery. The more gold you possessed, the higher your status in the community. It also meant that you had something to trade with or bargain with. This was exactly what the genetically modified human genome was waiting for: a stimulus to activate several dormant genes, which would cause continuous havoc for thousands of years to come. The greed gene, the gluttony gene, the opulence gene, and a few more beauties hidden in our DNA, of which we are equally unaware at this stage. And so began the eternal race for possession and control among primitive humans, which is stronger today than ever before. I have always been fascinated by primitive tribes around the world and the importance they place on decorative artifacts and shiny objects. I could never understand that there were so many similarities in their rituals and their gods while they are separated by thousands of miles, oceans, and continents. But the common human ancestry with its magic, shiny ingredient seems to tie it all together. The many rituals performed by the forgotten tribes of the world still today, and the importance they place on ornamental and decorative objects, can all be linked to the birth of man some 200,000 years ago and the role that gold played in his evolution.

This obsession with gold was quickly adopted by Mesolithic (Middle Stone Age 10000 to 4000 BC) and Neolithic (Near or Late Stone Age 4000 BC) humans in the Near East after the Great Flood some 13,000 years ago, while being helped by their gods to attain new knowledge of agriculture, architecture, communal living, and more. We have evidence of this rapidly emerging and refined artistic culture from Sumerian artifacts. This know-how was successfully copied and developed to staggering proportions by the Egyptian royalty. Everyone in the world today is acutely aware of the great Egyptian achievements and the great wealth they accumulated. The amount of gold found in many of the pharaohs' burial chambers astounded archaeologists when it was first discovered. This was something that the tomb raiders of the past 200 years knew very well, as they plundered these riches from the early days of postdiluvial humanity.

By this time, some gods had decided to help man out of bondage and empower him with knowledge for survival. This caused unprecedented tension among the Anunnaki gods, which led to argument, conflict, and bloody battles for control of a rapidly dividing world. Various gods took refuge in distant corners of the world like the Americas, China, Australia, India, or wherever they could set up a secure base for themselves. Every step of the way, the dispersed Anunnaki had their human slaves to perform the hard labor in the process of building new civilizations around them. The gods controlled the humans with an iron fist, giving them strict instructions on most things, rewarding them when they felt it appropriate and punishing them severely if the human slaves disobeyed. This is pretty much the story of most popular religions from the beginning of time, especially the Old Testament. We examine the "wrath of god" in other chapters, which show us the distinct humanlike needs displayed by the ancient gods. This globalization by the gods explains why the same strict dictatorlike behavior was witnessed all around the world by virtually all the communities of early humans.

While the Egyptian artistry and creation of spectacular golden artifacts were unprecedented on Earth, the cradle of goldsmiths was in fact the Sumerian civilization starting as far back as 5000 BC, according to the latest digs in Iraq and Syria. Nestled between the Tigris and Euphrates rivers, they set most of the trends for global generations to follow. They traded their wheat and barley, upstream and downstream for other goods, including gold. The Greeks later called this Mesopotamia, the "Land Between the Rivers." Here the Sumerians appeared and flourished until around 2000 BC in cities like Uruk, Larsa, Umma, and Ur. These cities had a network of well-planned streets and well-organized societies. They pioneered cuneiform writing on clay tablets the size of a postcard, and wrote poetry. Their craftsmanship with wood, stone, ivory, semiprecious stones and especially gold, was astonishing. Many of these are to be admired at the British Museum in London; the University Museum in Philadelphia, Pennsylvania; and nearer to its origins, at the Baghdad Museum in Iraq, which was unfortunately decimated by looters during the George W. Bush attacks. Gold cups, helmets, bracelets, garlands and chains of delicate workmanship, reveal an exceptional understanding of how to exploit gold's unique properties of malleability, ductility, and resilience. Jewelery historian Guido Gregorietti, author of *Jewelry Through the Ages,* observed of the Sumerian times that, "In fact, there were more different types of jewelery than there are today."

Did the Sumerians really write the opening chapter in the history of gold, or was it happening simultaneously in other parts of the world? They may have been the pioneers in golden jewelery production, but gold was being mined all over the world under the supervision of rebellious gods with the knowledge of mining and the desire to claim a piece of this planet for themselves.

You see, Sumer itself did not have gold, so it had to import it from somewhere. This was probably a great opportunity for the new custodian gods scattered around the world to bring their golden spoils to Sumer, establishing trade links while keeping their human slaves back home working, fearful and obedient. Jewelery expert Graham Hughes, author of *The Art of Jewelry,* says, "Sumerian work is flavoured with amazing sophistication, delicacy of touch, fluency of line, a general elegance of conception, all suggest that the gold-smiths' craft emerged almost fully fledged in early Mesopotamia." How is that possible? That primitive humans emerged out of the Stone Age, set up well-structured communities, and immediately showed great knowledge of manu-facturing some of the most refined golden jewelery we know today? Sumerian treasures reveal how well the goldsmiths understood working with gold. They used different alloys, and cast gold in solid or hollow ornaments. They chased veins on leaves or grooves on beads using the lost-wax technique. Jugs or cups could be beaten into shape from a flat sheet of gold, using sophisticated heat treatment. They even beat gold into thin foil or ribbon. This kind of sudden knowledge and sophistication clearly points to some form of intelligent inter-vention, which could only have come from their Anunnaki masters and gods.

So now we know that the origin of humanity is somehow directly linked to the production of gold on Earth; that the human slaves were aided toward civilization by their gods and makers, who accidentally created the gold trade on Earth by dispersing and forcing their own group of human slaves to mine the precious metal. While there was gold mining activity and jewelery-making going on in many centers of the world, Sumer was the main concentration of Anunnaki gods on Earth, and therefore it became the fastest growing center of civilization, setting the standard for an accidental industry that consumes most of the gold in the world today. This is the incredible story of the jewelery industry, which was an accidental by-product of a slave species and a group of occupying astronaut gods. The East consumes over 75% of the annual global production of gold in the twenty-first century. In 2002 this amounted to 2,726.7 metric tons.

We must take a step back to avoid being blinded by all this incredible stuff. After all, we have come a long way in 11,000 years. We have evolved mentally and physically. If we have much of the Anunnaki DNA in our cells, we need to ask ourselves, how advanced were they really? My theory is that they were not as advanced as I may have originally thought. I say this because the behavior they displayed from the very first day on this planet bears the symptoms of a species that falls way short of a complete genome. We have inherited many of their characteristics. I just pray that we lose the primitive desire to cover our-selves with shiny metal as we evolve toward more intelligent beings. After all, it was all a big accident.

To protect themselves against possible competition from a new species on Earth, the Anunnaki gods ensured that the genome of the slave species was severely stunted. They ensured that the new human species did not live too long, was prone to disease, did not use much of its brain, and had a finite memory. The one thing they did not count on was the evolution of our genome and our intelligence. Maybe they did not consider the evolutionary aspects, because they truly did not expect to stay on this planet for so long.

10

INSTANT CIVILIZATION AND SUMER

THE WORD *CIVILIZATION* IS POSSIBLY one of the most misused words in all the languages of the world. We constantly refer to issues surrounding the "civilized" world and compare quality of life between the developed West and the emerging economies. There is constant reference to the "First World" and the "Third World." There never seems to be any mention or clarification of a "Second World" by those who created these descriptions. I would like to know what happened to the clearly absent "Second World"? Or has the civilized world decided that the gap between their superior lifestyle and the rest of the poor bastards is so huge that there is no case for a "Second World" culture? Although the word *civilization* does not carry an exclusive component of distinction based on financial stability or wealth of its citizens, it certainly seems to be coined as an indicator of such criteria. The media talk about ancient civilizations with a mysterious tone that would suggest that they were not really that civilized, but we just don't understand how those lowlifes all those years ago could manage to build such impressive monuments. Even historians, anthropologists, and archaeologists are guilty of waxing lyrically about the great civilizations of the past, and yet they treat their scriptures and texts with an uncanny lack of respect loaded with heaps of skepticism. It's as if the ancients had some obscure reason to capture information aimed at misleading us poor twenty-first-century-ites. Our attitude is riddled with immense disbelief, as if there was an ancient plot aimed at feeding us with disinformation; the "us" in this sentence being the greatly "advanced" humans in the modern days of technology.

By doing this, scholars inject a comparative system of levels of civilization, placing us at the pinnacle of all-time civilizations, for obvious reasons to them. Ancient knowledge and so-called civilization is immediately and automatically superseded by us, because we live in more recent times. We have to be more civilized because we have technology, we have mass media, we live in a free world where all truth must eventually surface because we are too smart to be fooled by false prophets. Is that a fact? I suggest we take a long hard look at how manipulated and controlled we actually are. If civilization was to be penalized by some scale based on human ignorance per capita, we would be the most penalized bunch of humans of all time. We have looked extensively at the possible origins of humanity, yet we still do not know, we do not even suspect, where we come from. There is overwhelming evidence that the ancient Sumerians knew exactly who they were, where they came from, and who their "real god" was: the god of the Sumerians, who had absolute controlling power and ruled the whole world. It was the god with a lowercase "g" and his extended family, who were turned into a group of fairy-tale mythological characters by latter civilizations. That early knowledge has somehow escaped us, just like the extensive knowledge of the cosmos. Is it possible that for the same reasons we misplaced our knowledge of astronomy, and our ability to relate to our ancestry?

Today, the majority of the world is so brainwashed with religion that any breakthrough in knowledge of our shocking past is immediately relegated to the realms of the esoteric or mythological or evil or cult or heresy. We are so controlled by the media and advertising that we base our decisions on the moods of soap opera characters. If we get wiped out by a giant tsunami 200 meters high, when they uncover the dregs of our civilization some 20,000 years from now, will they think that the soap opera scripts and characters were actual events and real people? Hey, anything is possible.

If we unravel the true meaning of civilization, we will possibly see that the population of the twenty-first century is far from meeting the criteria. It is quite discernable that there is a global split between "thinkers" and "followers." By this I do not mean that if you have a nine-to-five job you are a follower, but it's rather a more direct stab at the mechanisms of fear that are successfully implemented at controlling large groups of people, whether these are of political, religious, or of any other origin. The 2004 U.S. presidential elections are a perfect example. The majority of Americans voted for George W. Bush because of this fear factor. They were so cleverly manipulated by the media that they truly believed their candidate would protect them against the onslaught of the "evil" world. To the rest of the world it was very obvious as to what was going on in the United States, but the average American truly believes that the world wants to invade them, either by coming to live there and taking their jobs away or by spreading terror. The United States is apparently the most advanced economy in the world, therefore the most civilized? I don't think so. Therein lies the proof. Just because we are more technologically advanced does not give us the collective capacity to reason, think, or solve problems any better than our ancestors did 6,000 years ago. In fact, Greece is probably best known for its great thinkers, like Socrates, Aristotle, and Plato. These philosophers are quoted now more than ever before and their influence has seeped into countless crevices of our societies. Just like dead artists who carry a strange mystique that propels the price of their work to dazzling heights, the dead philosophers from ancient times are more revered now than during their own time.

I will bet that if you placed Plato in a live performance situation to simply talk about his thoughts on life and death, he would fill every football stadium on his world tour. We seem to accept their wisdom and written works, but we will not accept the written works of other ancient teachers, just because we don't know who they were. That is so very shallow of us that I feel embarrassed by such behavior. As popular as those ancient wise men were, they were not seen as the prophets of their day, even though they carried such a great deal of respect. Why could that possibly be? The answer is clearly displayed in chapter 15, dealing with Jesus and other prophets. We will discover in later chapters that so-called prophets whom we have come to worship were cunningly contrived and planted by the gods of the day, while the thinkers did not fall into that category. The thinkers did not fit the profile of religious leaders who would attract pilgrims in need of spiritual shelter. The thinkers were too independent to be manipulated in such ways, it seems, at times causing great trouble between the newly created slave species and their gods.

So what does the word *civilization* actually mean? The dictionary describes it as "an advanced stage of human development, marked by a high level of art, religion, science, social and political organization." And yet the word *civil* means "belonging to, or consisting of the ordinary population of citizens; not military or religious." Immediately we see a distinct conflict here, since religion is one of the criteria that marks the levels of "civilization," yet it is explicitly excluded from being "civil."

Political assassinations are as common in modern days as they were in ancient times. Because war is declared by a political leader of a country, it means that a president or a king can never be civil, or civilized. The point is, the true meaning of the word is extremely obscure and it is used as and when necessary by individuals who want to create a distinction between themselves and others generally proclaimed to be less civilized. If we take the dissection a little further and actually try to determine our current levels of civilization from the definition, we reach a rather interesting outcome. "High levels of art"—we can say that current artistic levels are pretty high around the world. Our writers, filmmakers, playwrights, and painters are creating more than ever before, so we score high marks there. Science—this is a tough area to judge, because there is physical evidence that humans many thousands of years ago knew more about science, medicine, and astronomy than we know today. At every archaeological dig in Mesopotamia there are almost always clay tablets found, some dating as far back as 3800 BC, outlining the achievements of the ancient Sumerian civilizations. They describe the cosmos, planets, medical schools and medical procedure, surgery, eye surgery, genetic engineering, space craft, space travel, and much more.

Historians have, however, found these claims to be unbelievable and so they have become part of mythology rather than history. Remember that the father of modern anatomy, Leonardo da Vinci, was risking his life as recently as 500 years ago by dissecting corpses in the middle of the night so he could draw images of the internal organs. This was a time when the church had complete control over people's lives, killing and destroying anything that was not in keeping with their image of religious behavior. Unfortunately, we have inherited much of this behavior and we are practicing it "religiously" today. So, on the scale of scientific advancement, we cannot say that we have surpassed the knowledge of the distant civilizations. On the religious front we are less aware of the human reality than the ancient people were, mainly for the reasons that we have reduced their reality to the realms of mythology. If the religious reference as a measure of civilization is based on religious tolerance, then we certainly are far less civilized today than our distant ancestors. The last 1,000 years have seen the most brutal religious conflicts in all of human history. My conclusion is that until we start to treat the ancient texts and tablets with the kind of respect they deserve, we will remain trapped in the cycle of ignorance that will keep a stranglehold on our current civilization. How can we claim to have any levels of real intelligence if we still do not know with certainty where we come from? What kind of civilized species are we if we have no clear link to our origins? How can we expect to find unity and harmony among the cultures of the world when all our theories are driven by scattered groups of disparate religions, each one claiming to be the correct one?

The fact remains that our ancient past is filled with incredible achievements by many civilizations, which left behind traces and clues of their rise and fall. Many of these civilizations write about the "prior times" or the "times before time" or the "earlier times," when they refer to where they had received their knowledge. In times when global communication was nonexistent, these groups of highly capable people settled in the distant reaches of the world and began to develop highly structured cities with colossal monuments and pyramids, from the more recent Japanese, Chinese, and Thai ruins; to the more romanticized Egypt, Near East, Mesoamerica, and the Andean civilizations in South America.

To truly demonstrate our modern arrogance and greed, all we have to do is look at how Columbus and Cortes responded to the ancient cities and their people when they first invaded the New World in the fifteenth and sixteenth centuries. They were so obsessed with looting gold and other artifacts that they didn't really give the incredible achievements that stared them in the face much thought. The greed gene was hard at work, driven relentlessly by the conquering gene in those conquistadores. How is it possible that those civilizations could have appeared out of the blue, more or less at the same time in history, displaying the kind of advanced knowledge of the cosmos and architecture, without even knowing about each other? There are many more examples of such inexplicable ancient activity that are still surrounded by wild speculation today. Easter Island, Stonehenge, and the Great Zimbabwe Ruins are just a few. But let's take a short trip through some of these ancient sites to see how they all seem to be related to each other. Let us try to answer the recurring question: Who could have possibly been responsible for such a connection in those ancient times? The ever-present Anunnaki gods of course!

As we work our way through this book we will uncover that the ancient mythological gods in all of human civilization were not figments of the people's imagination. We will also discover that they were not weird and supernatural manifestations of the spiritual world, or any other hard-to-explain beings from the fourth dimension. They were in fact a group of early explorers and settlers on this planet under the leadership of Anu, their supreme commander and hence their name, the Anunnaki. They are the ancient astronauts whom the Sumerian tablets speak about in great detail, and we will show beyond any doubt that the Anunnaki ruled the world for over 400,000 years, performing the roles of gods as they nurtured their primitive creation, the human slave species into a state of civilization. It was one of the members of the full extended Anunnaki family who was in charge of the various activities on their newly settled planet, which would have also included the Great Zimbabwe settlement. The full story of the Anunnaki astronauts from Nibiru is told in great detail as it is written in many hundreds of clay tablets. It is not very difficult to see that it was they who crossed the skies in their "chariots" and were equally worshipped, while to a certain extent also feared, among all the ancient civilizations on Earth. So do not panic, you will be enlightened with the full story.

The archaeologists of some 200 years ago were shocked when they first started to scratch around in Egypt. Everyone believed that Greece was the place that gave the world the concept of civilization. Napoleon had heard a great deal about these impressive ruins and pyramids, so when he arrived in Egypt in 1799 with his army and an entourage of scholars, one of his objectives was to help unravel the secrets of the pyramids. He clearly did not achieve that, but what they did find in Rosetta was a stone slab that became known as the Rosetta Stone, and which has become one of the most important archaeological finds ever. It measures 114 x 72 x 28 centimeters. For those in the United States this translates to 3 feet 9 inches long, and 2 feet 4.5 inches wide. The stone had three inscriptions. The Egyptian hieroglyphic text was accompanied by a Greek translation that was understood by scholars, and a third inscription on the stone was written in Demotic, a cursive script developed late in Egyptian history, used almost exclusively for secular documents. Thus the stone displayed the same text in three

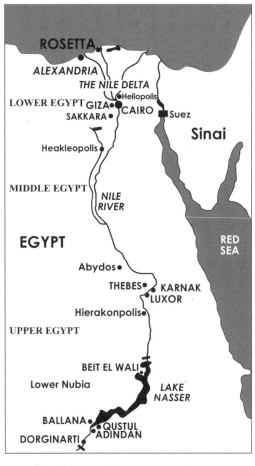

Fig. 10.1. Map of Egypt showing Rosetta

Fig. 10.2. Rosetta Stone

Fig. 10.3. Details from the Rosetta Stone showing
three different scripts in two languages—Egyptian and Greek.

scripts, but only two languages, Egyptian and Greek. It was quickly discovered
that all three contained the same message, and because the Greek could be translated immediately, it provided real clues for the very first time to the unraveling
of Egyptian hieroglyphs.

To a large extent this propelled the dissection and translation of the hieroglyphic texts, only to astound the scholars with the news that the Egyptian
royal dynasties stretched back to around 3200 BC. This was another typical
example of our lowly-civilized state in the so-called modern days, as it sent
shockwaves through the archaeological worlds. Very soon they discovered that

the Hellenic alphabet, which influenced the Latin and our own alphabets, actually emerged somewhere in the Near East. The Greeks admitted that a Phoenician called Kadmus originally brought the alphabet from the East. It had the same number of letters and the same order as in ancient Hebrew, but by the fifth century BC the poet Simonides of Ceos increased the number of letters to twenty-six. Alexander the Great may have been a relentless warrior but he also collected much information about the Persian empires that he defeated in 331 BC. His advisers concluded that they must have originated from the Aryan people or "lordly people." According to his knowledge the mysterious lordly people appeared in the distant past near the Caspian Sea and spread East all the way to India and further south to "the lands of the Medes and Parsees," as those lands were called in the pages of the Old Testament.

Cyrus the Great was an Aryan king and the founder of the Persian Empire who conquered almost all of the known world some 200 years before Alexander. The strange thing is that by the time Alexander rose to power, the Aryans had settled and controlled all of Europe and were the descendants of the same Aryan ancestors as the Persians. So what started happening at this time was that Aryans were fighting Aryans without actually realizing it.

The newly emerging finds and clay tablets from the Near East caught the interest of archaeologists, but it was only in 1843 when Paul Emile Botta started the first professionally planned excavation in Mesopotamia. The land that is modern-day Iraq, between and surrounding the Tigris and Euphrates Rivers, was producing remarkable treasures, many bearing illegible cuneiform texts, which was the style of writing used by the Sumerians. The name *cuneiform* was first coined in 1686 by Engelbert Kampfer, who mistook the texts he saw in Persia to be decorative patterns and described them as *cuneates,* which roughly means "wedge-shaped impressions." As the wave of treasure seekers and archaeologists poured into this part of the world to excavate Assyria and Babylonia, thousands of cuneiform clay tablets were found among the many mounds scattered throughout the region. There were even actual libraries of tablets found, neatly bound together. One word was translated from the cuneiform to be Dur Sharu Kin, which meant "walled city of the righteous king" whom we call Sargon II of Assyria. That was not all they unearthed; there were statues, bas-reliefs that would stretch for longer than a mile if displayed, palaces, temples, houses, stables, towers, warehouses, columns, gates, walls, terraces, gardens, decorations of a wide variety, and more mind-boggling evidence of a well-developed civilization. But the centerpiece of the city was the seven-step ziggurat pyramid referred to as "the stairway to heaven" for the gods. All of this took only five years to build

Fig. 10.4. Map of Mesopotamia

some 3,000 years ago. This is a demonstration of real achievement. Today, we cannot put a time frame to construction on such a scale. One other crucial bit of information they acquired was that the common language of Assyria and Babylonia was Akkadian. This was truly fascinating, but their surprise did not stop there. There were postscripts on many tablets, stating that they were copied from earlier originals. Who could have written such originals? And where are those originals now?

What is also interesting are the chief deities of the two cultures. Assyrians had Ashur, the "all-seeing" as their chief deity. Babylonia had Marduk, "the son of the pure mound" as their chief deity. The pantheons of the two gods were the same, reconfirming our earlier suggestions that the gods of prehistory were active over a wide area of the world. According to the Akkadian tablets, the kingdom of Akkad was started by Sharrukin, the "righteous ruler" who claimed that it was Enlil who pointed out the land to him and allowed him to govern it. We will discover that Sharrukin was not the only king who made such a statement, there is written evidence of many more kings who attested to the same. It was always some god who actually appointed them as the king of a specific land and allowed them to govern the people while receiving messages from his god. This is a very clear link to our pantheon of gods who ruled the world. Not only did they create the slave species worker to toil in the gold mines, but the evidence begins to pile up that they introduced all aspects of civilization to their human offspring sometime between 9000 BC and 3000 BC all over the world, which included kingship.

Suddenly we take a leap back in time from Sargon of Assyria 3,000 years ago, to Sargon of Akkad 5,000 years ago. Akkadian was the first known Semitic language, before Hebrew, Aramaic (which was the language of Jesus), Phoenician, and Canaanite. This Akkadian language was derived from an earlier one, which they refer to in their postscripts. The most relevant information that was obtained from these Akkadian tablets was a text dealing with the names, genealogies, deeds, powers, and duties of the gods. In Genesis there is a wonderful reminder for some doubtful historians about the actual existence of a place called Akkad that was indeed started by Sargon, who claims in the tablets that "at the wharf of Akkad, he made moor ships," from lands far and wide. From Genesis, "And the beginning of his kingdom: Babel and Erech and Akkad, all in the land of Shin'ar."

The excavations in Akkad delivered remarkable finds. The most precious was the library of King Ashurbanipal at Nineveh, where they uncovered 25,000 tablets of Akkadian texts, many of which were once again described to be copies of "olden texts." Based on the syllabic style of the Akkadian language, the scholars believed that it must have originated from an earlier written language, similar to the Egyptian hieroglyphs. Their suspicions were rewarded when one of the tablets from Ashurbanipal ended with the following statement: "twenty-third tablet: language of Shumer not changed." But as outlined by Zecharia Sitchin, it was a further text by King Ashurbanipal himself that really crowned the booty. "The god of scribes has bestowed on me the gift of the knowledge of his art. I have been initiated into the secrets of writing. I can even read the intricate tablets in Shumarian; I understand the enigmatic words in the stone carvings from the days before the Flood."

Some of these tablets date back to the origin of the Akkadian empire around 2350 BC and truly challenged the knowledge of historians of their time and continue to challenge most of humanity today. Was it a bunch of nonsensical garbage from days gone by, or was it a true historic entry reflecting a real historical event? We need to make these choices once more. The choice will irrevocably alter the way we perceive our human ancestry and our human origins.

It was Frenchman Jules Oppert who suggested in 1869 that because the

Mesopotamians proclaimed their legitimacy by taking the title "King of Sumer and Akkad" that we should call the ancient peoples Sumerians and their land should be called Sumer. And so his suggestions were adopted. Little did he know that the old biblical name for Sumer was Shinar, as it states in Genesis that "the royal cities of Babylon, Akkad and Erech were in the land of 'Shinar' (Shumer)." Among the many tablets they found were long lists of words that made no sense to anybody for long periods of time, but when the link between Akkadian and Sumerian was made, scholars realized that the strange "wordy" tablets were actually ancient dictionaries of Sumerian-Akkadian words, which gave them a glimpse at the first written language on Earth. This played a major part in speeding up the translations and understanding of many ancient tablets, but it did not necessarily open the minds of the translators. Over and over again, historians, anthropologists, and other scholars would restrict the Sumerian tales to the subject of mythology. After all, we know it is impossible that there were all these different "gods" flying around the world all those years ago! We know there is only one "god," the god of the Bible, or Koran or Kabbalah, or Hindus, or Buddhists, or Baha'i, or so many others. In essence we are not any different to the people of ancient times. Even today, different groups of people pray to a different god. We seem to be quite okay with this situation even in the twenty-first century. We all have our own faith and we all steadfastly believe that our god is the real god. If we accept it today, why can we not accept that it was so in the distant past as well? The only difference was that the gods of the past had constant contact with humans, as it states in the Bible, Koran, or Sumerian scriptures. Those gods were omnipresent, making their appearance in a flash, either in person or sending angels in their place.

It took fifty-six years of excavation to unearth the ancient city of Lagash in Sumer. They began in 1877 and had not finished by 1933. The effort produced an unprecedented amount of archaeological material. We learned from the efforts of scholars and from very neatly preserved records at this site that the city had "righteous rulers" who were called EN.SI, and that over a period of 650 years there were 43 EN.SIs who ruled Lagash. We also learnt from the records that any EN.SI could only assume the throne with the approval of the gods. Were these merely in their minds? And if so, how could the rest of the population allow the king to assume the throne if the gods were not visible or audible to the ordinary man? Surely the people of the time would not have stood for it unless they were convinced that the new EN.SI was really appointed by god. A depiction of Ur-Nammu, the ruler of Ur, was unearthed, in which he is shown being ordered to build a temple for his god according to strict instructions. Other biblical heroes like Moses, Solomon, and Ezekiel also built buildings for their gods after being instructed. Solomon received "wisdom" from god after which he built the temple in Jerusalem. Ezekiel saw a godly vision of a person who had a bronze appearance who held a measuring rod, and Moses built a residence in the desert for his lord after getting specific instructions on how to build it. So what is the difference between the ancient kings receiving instructions from their so-called mythological gods and our popular biblical characters receiving similar instructions from our one and only biblical god? Nothing, I say. The evidence is overwhelming to suggest that it was the same god or gods, dealing with different people at different times.

One of the most impressive constructions took place some 1,200 years before Moses. King Gudea recorded his instructions in a long detailed

Fig. 10.5. Sumerian king list. Probably the most important document ever discovered by modern humans. It lists some 149 kings and rulers on planet Earth, starting with ten rulers before the flood, which spanned some 240,000 years. It goes on to name rulers of many dynasties and outlines when each kingdom was lowered to Earth from Heaven by the Anunnaki, or the biblical Nephilim. The list also outlines the coming to Earth of the Igigi or biblical Anakim from their space colony. We also read that it was Ninurta, the biblical YAHWEH, who destroyed Sodom and Gomorrah.

inscription. It talks about a "man that shone like the heaven" and he "commanded me to build his temple"; and "from the crown on his head he was obviously a god." The god held some kind of stone in his hand, "the plan of a temple it contained." The plan was so complex that he sought the advice of a goddess who pointed out all the "right" people or deities who could help him. He then recruited 216,000 people to complete the job. An undertaking on such a scale is unthinkable in the twenty-first century; the ability to coordinate, control, house, and feed such a large number of builders indicates that the ancient Sumerian civilization was well advanced as far back as 3000 BC.

The real achievements of the Sumerians only became evident as the tablets were transcribed and understood. It is now evident that Sumer was the origin of all culture and civilization on Earth, giving us all the foundations of what we know today. The staggering thing is that the knowledge of the Sumerians has been lost in translation or lost in antiquity, because some of the activities they make reference to find us at a loss, completely overwhelming the translators. Ancient Sumer had thousands of scribes who worked relentlessly at capturing most of their daily activities. There were all kinds of scribes in temples, courts, and in trading houses. Junior scribes, high scribes, and royal scribes, capturing everything in clay. There is so much information captured about their lives and activities that it leaves us with a very clear picture of how organized they were. The records are not really of a spiritual nature but instead they inadvertently indicate how controlled they were by their demanding gods, who needed to be pleased on an ongoing basis. They also speak of measuring fields, calculating prices, and recording harvests of crops.

Here is a quick overview of the Sumerian "firsts." Besides their architectural and engineering feats, they invented:

- Writing—including the precursor to the printing press. With their cylinder seals engraved in hard stone, which could be rolled in clay leaving a clear imprint, they could supply educational materials to teachers and schools.
- Schools—which were headed by *ummia*, "the expert professor."
- There is evidence of corporal punishment at schools for being absent, lack of tidiness, loitering, making a noise, misbehaving, and even having untidy handwriting.
- They wrote pharmacopoeia and captured literary debates in clay.
- They introduced the first bicameral congress, library catalogues, codes of law, teaching methods and curricula, health and even exercise.

- Sumerian textiles and apparel were so sought-after that invading armies would fight over the spoils of clothing, as it is mentioned in Joshua 7:21 that someone could not resist "one good coat of Shinar," although such looting was punishable by death. By 3800 BC they had advanced weaving technology, which also resulted in the TUG, later known as the Roman *toga*. The Sumerians referred to it as the TOG.TU.SHE, which means "the garment that is worn wrapped around."
- Fashion, hairstyles, and jewelery all originate from here.
- They gave us the first mathematical system with the ability to do complex mathematical calculations, which were based on the sexagesimal system where 10 is combined with a "celestial" 6 = 60.

SEXAGESIMAL COUNTING SYSTEM

Decimal	Sumerian (Sexagesimal)
I	I
10	10
10 × 10	10 × 6
(10 × 10) × 10	(10 × 6) × 10
(10 × 10 × 10) × 10	(10 × 6 × 10) × 6

- The 360 degrees in a circle, advanced astronomy, the calendar, the seven day week, kilns, bricks, high-rise buildings like pyramids and ziggurats, ceramics and even art and sculpture were all first created in Sumer.
- Furthermore there was metallurgy and the molding of soft metals like gold, silver, and copper.
- The creation of bronze by smelting copper with tin.
- They were the first to develop an exquisite range of decorative jewelry.
- They even introduced the first money in the form of the silver *shekel*, thereby converting thousands of years of what must have been a strictly socialistic society without any use for money, into the first capitalist economy.
- Their extensive knowledge of agriculture was astounding. The planting and harvesting of cereals; the manufacture of flour for different kinds of breads, pastries, biscuits, cakes, and porridges.

The Sumerian cuisine was well-refined and they certainly got a lot of practice preparing lavishly extensive menus for their gods who had a great appetite. Yes! The gods would actually demand different types of food to be prepared and placed in their temples as offerings. This would include wine from grapes and palm dates, milk yogurts, butter, cream, and cheeses. The gods of the city of Uruk demanded five different beverages and foods as a daily sacrifice. The Sumerians even wrote poems about food.

> *In the wine of drinking*
> *In the scented water*
> *In the oil of unction*
> *This bird have I cooked*
> *and have eaten.*

The large library of King Ashurbanipal at Nineveh gave us a good insight into their world of medical practice as they outline areas like therapy, surgery, and commands and incantations. It also covers subjects like fees charged by surgeons and penalties that had to be paid if they messed up. The surgeon would lose a hand if he damaged the patient's eye during a temple procedure with a lancet. There is reference to "water physicians" and "oil physicians" or A.ZU and IA.ZU as referred to by Zecharia Sitchin. They even refer to possible cataract removal and bone scraping. A 5,000-year-old tablet found in Ur refers to a "Lulu the doctor" and there were even vets who were known as doctors of "oxen and asses." All these texts make it very clear that these people practiced medicine and not any form of sorcery.

On the social front, they also introduced alcohol, which is evident from the Arabic and Akkadian roots of *kohl* and *kuhlu*. This was obviously also used in medical applications and some instructions were given to use wine, beer, or honey as solvents when taking powders by mouth. And where do you think the Romans got their knowledge of bitumen, asphalts, and petroleum, which they used so successfully in building and warfare? From the Sumerians of course. The reference to the discovery of the ancient city of Ur claims that it was found under a "mound of bitumen." And, the origin of the word *naphta* comes from the word *napatu*, which can be translated as "stones that flare up." One of the cornerstones of civilization and development, the wheel, was also first used by the Sumerians. Not to be outdone by those on land, the ship makers had their own dictionary that outlines 105 types of ships by size, function, and destination, and that also includes 69 Sumerian terms for the construction of ships. There were three primary types of ships: cargo, passenger, and those exclusively used by the gods.

I trust that by now you must be thinking that maybe there was a lot more to the interaction between the so-called gods and our ancient ancestor. This is only the beginning. The evidence keeps piling up higher and higher as we work through the clay tablets linking them to the many activities and events of our distant past. We learn that the Anunnaki gods were our original advanced ancestors who came to Earth with a very specific purpose—gold! From their arrival on Earth in search of gold some 443,000 years ago to the creation of the Adamu as a *lulu amelu* or primitive worker, to the creation of Eve shortly after that, to the graphic descriptions of the hard work in the gold mines of southern Africa, to the Flood and the subsequent civilization that was bestowed on the slave species to help feed the flood survivors, while pushing ever harder to extract enough gold to save their planet Nibiru's atmosphere. What a mouthful . . . but what a ride. You are going to be amazed to see how easily all the pieces of the puzzle fit together, and you will question why it has taken so long for the truth to start filtering through. The answers are all written down for us to absorb, but you will discover how our creators and ruling gods have carefully manipulated humankind into a subservient species, fearful of their god with a small "g."

Back to the digs in Mesopotamia now: what was really impressive was the Sumerians' sense of the law. For long periods it was thought that the Akkadian King Hammurabi set out the first code of laws in history, the Code of Hammurabi. The excavations in Mesopotamia found otherwise. Long before Hammurabi, who is said to have ruled around 1792 BC–1750 BC, there were several kings or rulers who were all instructed by their god to write down and institute various codes of law. One such ruler was from the city of Eshnunna. Some of the laws he was instructed to lay down dealt with the price of food, rental of wagons and boats, property laws, family matters, slave issues, and rights for the poor. Before him, and acting under strict instructions from the great gods to "bring well-being to the Sumerians and Akkadians," was the code of Lipit-Ishtar, ruler of Isin. Unfortunately, only thirty-eight of his laws have been recovered on tablets. Around 500 years before Hammurabi, circa 2350 BC, lived Urnammu who was the ruler of Ur. He was instructed by the god Nannar to lay down a code of law to deal with thieves. They are described as "grabbers of the citizens' oxen, sheep, and donkeys." The laws also included topics dealing with social behavior. "Orphans shall not fall prey to the wealthy," "widows shall not fall prey to the powerful," and "the man of one shekel shall not fall prey to the man of 60 shekels." As if this was not impressive enough, a further 250 years before this and almost 1,000 years before Hammurabi there was the EN.SI called Urukagina who was forced to introduce "necessary" reforms around 2600 BC. He was instructed by his god Ningirsu to "restore the decrees of former days." The one question that immediately springs to mind is that if

Fig. 10.6. Code of Hammurabi

Fig. 10.7. Code of Ur-Nammu

these reforms were so necessary, their civilization must have been around for quite some time before. Scholars call this find a "precious record of man's first social reforms based on a sense of freedom, equality, and justice." I am not sure about that statement because we now know that there were more sinister forces at play during the emergence of human civilization. I feel conflicted about the motives of both Enlil and Enki in such activities, although they certainly both had their respective motives.

Enki and Enlil were half-brothers and sons of Anu, the supreme commander of the planet Nibiru. Enki was the first to arrive on Earth 443,000 years ago in search of gold, and to set up a base before more Anunnaki would arrive to extract the precious metal. The two brothers had completely diverse personalities. Enki was the humanist and creative scientist, with the heart of a poet, while Enlil was the politician with a passion for control. He was on a mission to control humanity through religious violence, fear, and oppression, as he was never in favor of creating this new slave species—while Enki was the actual scientist who planned and created the human species. It is, therefore, not surprising that he wanted to uplift humanity in an effort to speed up their evolution. We learn through the tablets that Enki felt a very close link to his new creation. Which of the two was instrumental in orchestrating these law reforms is not clear at present, but like all hidden agendas, it will eventually emerge. My instinct tells me that they both probably had something to do with the injection of legal principles, but each one had a slightly different motive. We know what happened in the end; we are the living proof of all those laws today. And yet some parts of the world had a completely different approach to the laws that governed their cultures. This is one possible piece of evidence that highlights how the two rival Anunnaki brothers tried to control humanity in their own way, each one taking control of different parts of the world for themselves. It is beginning to feel as if Enki may have been instrumental in the setup of the very first secret society, which William Bramley calls "The Brotherhood of the Snake," right after the eviction from "Edin," as the Sumerians called it. After having a run-in with his brother Enlil about the upliftment of Adam and Eve, the creator of humanity, Enki, realized that the slanderous campaign against him as the serpent, and the evil snake, would be fiercely enforced by Enlil.

Humans would be controlled, whatever it took, and Enlil was an accomplished strategist and a master of propaganda. Enki had to resort to a more clandestine approach to uplift humankind. One such distinct possibility was the establishment of a small group of humans who were introduced to more advanced thinking, information, and technology. The start of the secret society had arrived. How else can we possibly explain the incredibly advanced think-

Fig. 10.8. Classic Greek representation of Zeus fighting his brother Hades in a disagreement. We will find that this is the identical story to Enlil and Enki during their argument in the garden of Eden. Enki was represented as the serpent and was banished from Eden for attempting to help the first human couple. Notice the serpent's tail taking the form of a double-helix DNA. The wings are a constant symbol throughout all mythologies that talk about the winged serpent, creator god.

ers and philosophers in ancient times, and small groups of more informed and technologically astute people? As astounding as the sudden emergence of civilization was all those thousands of years ago, the sudden appearance of advanced thinkers is equally puzzling. Where on Earth did a small group of individuals with such clear minds suddenly emerge? Who helped them to see things so differently? Why were they so much more informed and enlightened than the rest of the humans who were nervously worshipping a vengeful god? They must have had a mentor of some repute; an advisor or guardian who introduced such advanced ideas to them. Though William Bramley traces these secret societies all the way back to the garden of Edin, there are a few areas where they get very closely entangled with the manipulative activity of Enlil, who proclaimed himself the only god of man, the god of the Bible, who continued to dispense punishment to his disobedient subjects and rewarded those who toed the line. These historic inconsistencies of great violence and yet great benevolence are starting to take on a whole new slant as we unravel the motives of the two patriarchal brothers of the Anunnaki. We will explore much more of their actual behavior from the clay tablets known as *The Lost Book of Enki,* which was meticulously presented by Zecharia Sitchin in 2002.

Back in the days of Urukagina, the Law Maker, the bench would consist of one royal judge who was chosen from thirty-six men, and three or four other judges who made up a kind of jury. Meticulous records were kept of contracts, court proceedings, judgments, and sentencing.

One more interesting ritual that was inherited by the Hebrews and Jews is the ten-day period that marks the beginning of the Jewish New Year. During this period Jews are supposed to take stock of their activity from the year gone by and based on their deeds, the fate of the new year will be determined for them by god. This entire process has been adopted from the Sumerian culture, where the god Nanshe would come down every year to evaluate the performance of the humans, not based on material wealth or conquest, but rather whether they "did the righteous thing." Their fate for the year to come would be determined based on the outcome of such an evaluation by the god Nanshe.

Professors at the University of California at Berkeley claim that they have been able to read and play cuneiform notes from a tablet dated to around 1800 BC. It seems that in Sumer, music and songs were performed in temples and many original love songs have been unearthed. They feature the words while the musical scores are captured in the margins. We will discover that Inanna, the goddess of love, was the one who led the artistic explosion. The tablets refer to her constantly as being highly sexed, enjoying singing and playing instruments, and writing and reciting poetry. During the excavations at Nippur, which was the religious center of Sumer and Akkad at some stage, they found around 30,000 texts, many of which are still being studied. The wealth in cultural finds continued in Shurupak, where schools dating back to the third millennium BC were uncovered. From the mound of Tell Brak in northern Mesopotamia archaeologists uncovered the ancient capital of the Akkadian empire, the city of Nagar, dating back to 2000 BC. It is also the home of one of the oldest religious sites, the Eye Temple. At Ur, the birthplace of Abraham, excavation efforts delivered weapons; chariots; jewelery; helmets made of gold, silver, copper, and bronze; magnificent vases; the remains of a weaving factory; court records; and a towering ziggurat pyramid. More fascinating information in the form of inscriptions were found at Umma, which referred to "earlier empires," and at Kish there is another ziggurat pyramid and other monumental buildings that date back to at least 3000 BC.

The Sumerian city of Uruk or "Erech," which is situated on the banks of the Euphrates River, is still considered by many as the first true city in the world. This city boasts the oldest stone construction known to date, which is a limestone pavement dating way back into the fourth millennium BC. They also found a potter's wheel, a kiln, and exquisite colored pottery among other items. Until the 1990s the general consensus was that the earliest cities arose between 3500 BC and 3800 BC, but this time line is slowly being pushed back by new digs in Syria, Turkey, and Iraq. All this activity in the ancient Near East is strongly supported by the writings in the *Book of Enki* dating back from about 2050 BC. This precious prehistoric account of early humans outlines the activity of the early settlers on Earth and their explorations of the whole region and the establishment of their own settlements as far back as 443,000 years ago. We can now start to paint a more complete picture of what was going on in the greater Mesopotamian area over many thousands of years. In an article from September 18, 2004, *New Scientist* ran an in-depth feature on the "road to civilization" in which archaeologist McGuire Gibson from the University of Chicago makes some startling, and yet expected, discoveries. There have been many hints over the past few decades that civilization must have emerged virtually immediately after the end of the last ice age in the Near East and also in the Mesoamericas, some 9000 BC. Now there is real evidence that clearly supports those earlier theories.

The excavations at Uruk point to settlements already springing up around 8000 BC, but it was only around 3500 BC that it had grown into a real city that covered about 2.5 square kilometers with a population of around 50,000. Paul Collins, who is an expert on the Ancient Middle East at the Metropolitan Museum of Art in New York, says that, "There would have been major buildings, monumental structures on the scale of the Pantheon," that would classify it as a city, but to be formally classified as a city it also needed to have evidence of "zoning" between administrative centres, residential areas, markets, and so on. It also needed fortification to demonstrate that it was worthy of defending. Uruk had all these criteria in abundance by 3500 BC. However, Eridu was the first Sumerian city according to ancient texts. Many of these claims in scripture were confirmed when archaeologists uncovered an ancient temple dedicated to god Enki, "Sumer's god of Knowledge" at the site. It appeared to have been built and rebuilt many times, but as they dug deeper they struck virgin soil dating back to 3800 BC.

Not far from Tell Brak in the north lies Tell Hamoukar, which has been studied by McGuire Gibson's team for some time. They have also found evidence of a well-defined city by 3700 BC, which covered about 12 hectares enclosed by a defensive wall. The many mud-brick ovens found in the city suggest that there was large scale preparation of food going on at the site.

It is astounding that every time archaeologists embark on a major dig in the greater area of Mesopotamia, they unearth older and more impressive evidence of organized communal living and a well-evolved culture and civilization dating further and further back. *New Scientist* points out that David and Joan Oates from the University of Cambridge, who have been studying the site since 1976, first uncovered second and third millennium BC artifacts. In 1981, they uncovered hidden under the foundations of the city wall, deposits from 3000 BC. It took them another ten years to come back, but when they did they uncovered reasonably undisturbed records from the fourth millennium BC and even earlier, which included the ruins of a large building with very thick walls and a heavy door dating back to the late fifth millennium BC. It seems to have been some kind of official administrative building similar to those visible in the present-day Arab world. Joan Oates is convinced that there will be digs which will uncover more "fully fledged cities" in the southern parts that are older than 4000 BC. At the same time, Gibson has pointed out the abundance of pottery and other artifacts scattered all over the region, which includes the Mediterranean and Arabian peninsula. This indicates that the "pulse of trading" was strong all over the area. Yet another site called el-Queili, which is only a few kilometers east of Uruk, was discovered but it has not been touched since 1980. At the time, the last bit of excitement to emerge from the site were the remains of what Joan Oates called "strikingly large houses" dating back to 6000 BC.

In his book *The Goddess and the Bull,* Michael Balter writes about the exciting discoveries further north in Turkey, at the site of Catalhoyuk on the Anatolian plateau. Since 1958 this site has delivered an astonishing wealth of prehistoric artifacts. They have uncovered hundreds of structures, "astounding art," and much more evidence pointing to the existence of settled life as far back as 7000 BC. It is evident that there is much more hidden below the sands of time all over the area in which the Anunnaki first touched down. They obviously did not remain exclusively on the edge of the Persian Gulf at Eridu, but many ancient Sumerian texts indicate that they set up homes and other settlements further northwest, right across Asia Minor and into present-day Turkey. Their influence must have spread through Greece and Macedonia and even further north into ancient Europe, even as far north as Scandinavia. We can basically deduce that wherever there were mythological gods, there must have been the presence of the Anunnaki. As modern archaeologists scratch and dig they will undoubtedly uncover the evidence necessary to irrefutably prove the sudden emergence of civilization virtually immediately after the last ice age some 11,000 to 12,000 years ago.

There is, however, more physical evidence of even more archaic cultures

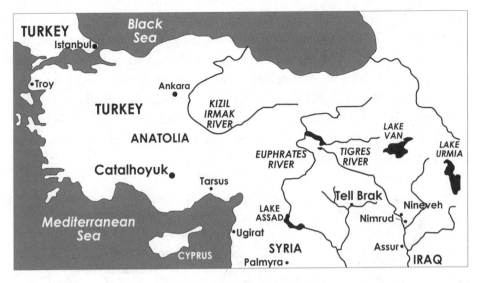

Fig. 10.9. Anatolia and the Near East

and "low" levels of civilization dating back 77,000 years in southern Africa. The beads discovered at Blombos in South Africa prove that humans were involved in the development of ornamental or decorative pieces a long, long, time ago. This does not, however, mean that the peak of what would be called civilization had been acquired by them at that stage. They were mostly nomadic hunter-gatherers who left behind a trail for us to unravel. These very early signs of human presence in southern Africa go hand in hand with the Cradle of Humankind, which is positioned just north of Johannesburg. It is now accepted by most scientists that the first humans on Earth lived in this part of the world. We will read detailed descriptions in the clay tablets corroborating these latest theories. We will read how the Anunnaki "created the 'Adamu' in their image and from their essence" to toil in the gold mines of southern Africa, as far back as 200,000 years ago. Is it a coincidence that the latest scientific dating of Adam and Eve places them in the same place at the same time?

BALKAN-DANUBE REGION

While we have been focusing on all this activity in Africa and Mesopotamia, further northwest in the Balkan-Danube region there were signs of great activity as far back as 9000 BC. From a small village called Rast in west Romania emerged a small figurine covered in "strange geometrical and abstract motifs" that resembled some form of previously unknown style of writing. It was only in

1989 that Marija Gimbutas first observed the markings on the figurine, called the "Madonna," and realized that these strange decorative inscriptions did not follow any set patterns or repetitive structure with predetermined spatial logic, which suggested that it must have been some form of early Proto-European writing, dating back to over 5000 BC. This shook the scientific world, making it older than the oldest known Sumerian texts by about 2,000 years. And so was born the Balkan-Danube Script mystery, now referred to as the oldest written documents known to man.

Fig. 10.10. Artifacts with examples of the Balkan-Danube Script

There was much controversy about the suggested new written language at first, but now most scholars agree that the staggering discovery was indeed a Proto-European written language. The amazing thing is that to date, nobody has been able to decipher it or venture a guess as to what kind of language it was, or where it originated. We do, however, know quite a lot about the activity of the Proto-European culture dating back as far as 9000 BC. Scholars write that trading activity started on the western side of the Aegean Sea when the tribes of hunter-gatherers adopted new knowledge from Anatolia and began to move westward. Their newfound techniques allowed them to create beautiful pottery, human figures, copper and other metal artifacts. Their writing technique and influence spread through the Danube valley, southern Hungary, Macedonia, Transylvania, and northern Greece. It is important to note that they also built palaces, temples, ships, and created new weaving techniques. Copper-forging technology appeared around 5500 BC, which should not surprise us since we have already seen that at another place in Anatolia, where these Proto-Europeans apparently acquired all their knowledge, we found evidence of a well-established civilization at some 6000 BC, who knew how to work with all the metals, including bronze.

It now makes complete sense that the Sumerians who were forging metals 6000 BC in Catalhoyuk, which also happens to be in Anatolia, expanded their knowledge to the Proto-European cultures. It is also more than probable that the Anunnaki used a different written language from the Sumerians. Could it be that the indecipherable script from ancient Europe was actually the written language of the Anunnaki?

INDUS VALLEY CIVILIZATION

It is astonishing that the ancient Indus Valley writings date back to 3300 BC, only 500 years later than the Sumerian cuneiform texts. Those Sumerian gods were clearly covering large parts of the world. We know this from the clay tablets that point out how the Anunnaki gods traveled the world, setting up different regions of people under the control of different gods. The Near Eastern gods refer to traveling to distant lands in every direction, and the east was obviously one of those places they disappeared while setting up settlements there and searching for gold. The ancient Indus civilization is another example of how archaeologists keep digging their way deeper back in time. Suddenly, the recent discoveries that surround the early Harappan/Ravi Phase pushed back the estimated date when writing first emerged in the Indus Valley by 700 years. There are many very clear and obvious links between the Indus gods and the Sumerian gods. Historians agree that there is a definite link to Anu, Enlil, Enki, Ninharsag, and other Anunnaki gods in the Harappan culture, art, pottery, and writings. One such example is the depiction of the celestial symbol of Anu on an Early Harappan polychrome pot.

The symbols of serpents and stars and other instantly recognizable Sumerian deities are clearly visible in much of the ancient Indus culture. It is now evident that the major Hindu gods are, in essence, Sumerian deities with different names. The evidence is visible in the pictorial tablets, seals, and other art depicting gods and deities. The seven divine goddesses depicted on Indus tablets overseen by a superior god are suspiciously similar to the seven Anunnaki goddesses, who gave birth to the first group of primitive workers on Earth while being overseen by Enki or possibly his son Ningishzidda, who according to Sumerian scriptures was the one who created the genetic pool for the original humans.

The Indus civilization goes back a lot further, which corroborates the legend

Fig. 10.11. Examples of the Indus Script, which has not been deciphered to date. Some characters have been identified as symbols for god and star.

Fig. 10.12. In Harappan culture the symbol of the star not only means "god," but also *anu* or "sky." The star image was originally the exclusive symbol for the sky god Anu. It just so happens that Anu was also the leading divine god of the Sumerian pantheon of gods. This particular form of the star symbol also represented the radiant planet Nibiru in Sumerian culture.

The symbol of the fish is one of the most popular motifs of the early Harappan period. The fish also represented the concept of god and symbolized the "god of waters." In Sumerian history Enki was often represented as a fishlike deity and an aquatic god who controlled the waters.

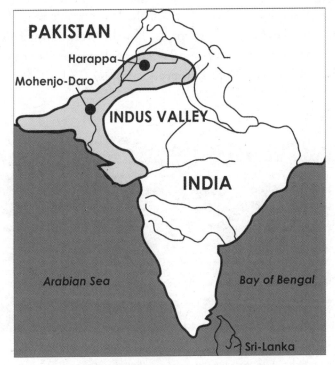

Fig. 10.13. An ancient Indus Valley civilization,
situated between modern-day India and Pakistan.

that the Vedic poems date back as far as 8000 BC, surviving only through oral transfer until they were written down for the first time some 3,000 years BC. Asko Parpola, a leading figure in ancient Indian culture, points out that the Indus civilization can be traced in an unbroken chain from a period some 8000 BC, through the Chalcolithic 5000 BC–3600 BC; to the Early Harappan period 3600 BC–2600 BC; and finally the Mature Harappan period around 2550 BC, eventually collapsing after 1800 BC. There is abundant evidence of close ties to Mesopotamia that included well-developed trade, maritime trade, and close cultural contacts. The neighboring cities of Harappa and Mohenjo-Daro were well developed as early as 3000 BC. They had similar structures made from the same bricks; they served as capitals for their provinces and were part of a unified government that had extreme organizational skills. This is the kind of influence that would have been imposed by the Sumerian gods to enable them to exercise control over the humans in that part of the world. The Harappa people even used Sumerian irrigation techniques in the lands along the valleys. The Indus Valley has its very own unsolved ancient secret treasure, the Indus Script. The amazing thing is that just like the Balkan-Danube Script, there has been very little progress made in deciphering the Indus Script in over seventy years by the smartest people available. Is it possible that this may be a derivative of a similar Anunnaki script used by the Proto-Europeans? After all, the evidence slaps us in the face, that the Anunnaki were as active in the Indus Valley as they were in the Proto-European cultures.

Fig. 10.14. Excavations at Mohenjo-Daro. This ruin from around 2500 BC shows the remains of Harappan bath pointing to the close cultural similarities between the Greeks, Romans, and Indus Valley civilizations.

We should really not be surprised by this broad influence of the Sumerian culture and the discovery of ancient undeciphered scripts. Is it possible that these scripts may have been used by the more advanced Anunnaki as a form of communication while they explored the world? The explorers of the fifteenth century did exactly the same when they moved into the Americas. They certainly did not land in one place and stay there, because it "looked kind of okay." They continued to move inland in all directions and proceeded to explore. It is highly ironic that thousands of years after Earth was populated by gold-seeking travelers from another planet, the gene that we inherited from them surfaced so viciously when the Spaniards discovered the golden riches of the Americas in the fifteenth century AD. It, therefore, stands to reason that when the Anunnaki had exhausted the gold deposits in the Near East, they explored the rest of the planet Earth. They had actually started looking around the planet much earlier, long before the gold ran out. They were fortunate to have the benefit of advanced technology and flight that took them to slightly more remote territories like Mesoamerica and the Andes. The tablets refer many times to the ways in which they scanned the seas and the lands for signs of gold under the surface. The tablets also carry more dramatic inscriptions of their rising levels of concern about the state of their planet Nibiru. The amount of gold that was being produced on Earth was not enough to deal with their degrading ozone problem. We might think this as very strange or possibly laughable that such an advanced species would have a problem with their ozone. Well, think again. What is one of the most pressing environmental concerns on Earth today? Global warming and the ozone layer. Very simply, the ozone protects us against all the deadly rays that are present in space. The two main culprits are ultraviolet rays and X-rays. Without the ozone we would literally fry like chips in heated oil, or like turning on a giant microwave oven in space pointing at Earth. The point is that if we are experiencing these kind of problems here, right now, they will be experienced on many other habitable planets in the galaxy. So before you dismiss this ozone thing as a farfetched hallucination, think again. It is real, it is right here, right now, on the very planet we call home. How will we deal with the ozone problem in a 100 years from now when it really starts to destroy crops and arable land? I don't know . . . maybe by then we would have found some amazing new compound on Mars or Europa or Titan or any of the other celestial bodies within reach in our solar system to produce the possible saving grace.

THE CIVILIZATIONS OF MESOAMERICA

One of the most perplexing events in human history is the sudden emergence of civilization in the Americas, which introduced the world to the Inca, Olmec, Toltec, and the early Maya of the Yucatan Peninsula in Mesoamerica. Historians and archaeologists just cannot agree on the times and possible dates when these mysterious cultures suddenly appeared, displaying pretty much all the same behavioral characteristics of the people in Mesopotamia. Such a sudden appearance of organized people in a distant continent is just too incredible to describe as a coincidence. It points irrefutably to an extreme example of the Sumerian-Anunnaki expansion over the world in search of gold, and gold there was plenty of in the Americas.

This sudden emergence of civilization in Mesoamerica happened virtually at the same time as it was exploding in Mesopotamia, shortly after the end of the last ice age. The ancient secrets of the Maya and the Inca have kept archaeologists and historians guessing for many years. How on Earth is it possible that a virgin civilization could have emerged out of the blue some 10,000 miles away from the so-called origin of civilization in Mesopotamia, across the Atlantic, 11,000 years ago, unless there was some interference by the highly mobile Anunnaki? It defies all laws of probability for such an event to happen

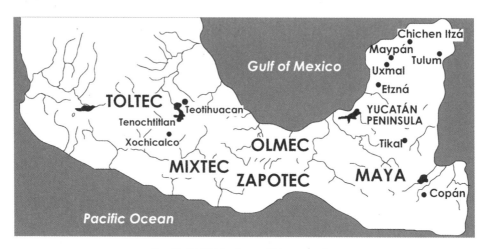

Fig. 10.15. Civilizations of Mesoamerica

randomly on a planet where the only activity was seemingly restricted to the land between the Persian Gulf and the Mediterranean. As suddenly as civilization emerged in the Near East, the Proto-Mayans appeared in Mesoamerica. They had all the knowledge possessed by well-developed cultures. They knew all about agriculture, they built cities and pyramids as impressive as the Egyptians, and they even knew how to extract gold from ore. Many theories have arisen about the origins of the Incas, Mayas, the Toltec, and Olmec, who collectively shaped the Andean and Mesoamerican cultures over thousands of years. The South American prehistory can really be divided into two regions where the Anunnaki gods were active: Mesoamerica, which includes Mexico; and South America—mainly Peru and Bolivia, where according to the Inca it all began. The Maya of the Yucatan Peninsula in Mexico had the gold, while the Inca and their ancestors had the tin.

The Anunnaki had more than just gold on their minds when they arrived in the Americas. They were also in search of tin. Tin is the necessary ingredient that together with copper makes up bronze. At this time in Earth's history bronze was becoming the metal of choice. Indications are that tin supplies in Mesopotamia were running dry and Inanna or Ishtar makes clear references in her Sumerian texts to "tin mountains" in Mesoamerica. She was asking permission from the superior gods to go in search of tin in the new lands. "Let me set out on the road to the tin ores. Let me learn about their mines." These tin mountains have been identified as the areas around Lake Titicaca in Bolivia. Even today, tin production is continuing in many parts of this region. The Anunnaki referred to tin as "the divine metal," and called it AN.NA, which means "heavenly stone." They called the combination of copper and tin into

Fig. 10.16. Example of typical Mayan pyramid. El Castillo Pyramid at Chichen Itza Mexico.

bronze ZA.BAR, which means "gleaming double metal." Ancient references to rich alluvial sources of tin have confused mineralogists, as pure tin is very rare. But David Forbes, who was a mineralogist researcher in South America, was astounded when he was shown a chunk of pure tin actually encasing a rock, as opposed to being encased in the rock, showing that such deposits must have existed in antiquity, if they still exist today. They did not come from a mine. The mines and rivers in that area were also rich in gold and other metals. He was convinced that people who worked those rich river deposits knew about tin and gold and how to process it from its ore.

The fascinating tales of the Andean legends begin with the god Viracocha who was the "creator of man" and the "god of heaven," who came to Earth in great antiquity, settling down on the shores of Lake Titicaca, close to the ancient city of Tiahuanacu, "place where the gods are born." Inca tales and legends also talk about the capital city Cuzco as being established by the "children of the sun" who were created and instructed by the great god Viracocha when he first settled at lake Titicaca. There are many versions of the settlement of the first people. One such tale comes from Juan de Betanzos, who writes that Viracocha created the world in two phases. Many of these ancient fables carry the same storyline as the Bible and the Sumerian scripts, which talk about the flood as a dividing event. An ancient Quechua tale says that the creator god "on the first occasion, made the heavens and the Earth," then he created mankind. But, "this people did some sort of wrong to Viracocha and he was angered by

Fig. 10.17. Andean civilization

it." It continues that "those first people and their chief he converted into stones in punishment," then after some time of darkness "he made men and women out of stones." Then he apparently gave them all tasks and abilities and told them where they should go and stay. It has many similarities with the Biblical Flood story, before and after the Flood. Noah was also told to "go forth and multiply." There are other stories about the original Andean or Maya or Inca forefather called Manco Capac, who was created by god. He was the first to be made a king by god and was the first monarch. Some say that he arrived by boat from another place across the sea, while others talk of god giving him a golden wand called "Tupac-yauri" which means "splendorous scepter." With this golden wand he had to go in search of a destined land and was said to have started the Inca capital city of Cuzco. He was the first Inca, after whom they were all called the "children of the sun."

The Popol Vuh is revered as the sacred book of the Quiche Maya. It has survived for centuries, written in Roman script shortly after the Spanish invasion in the sixteenth century. This is a copy of the original that has been lost to antiquity, but it contains come fascinating stories. It mentions that "the first people created by god were imperfect," which correlates exactly with the detailed description of the many attempts by Enki, Ninharsag, and Ningishzidda to create the first primitive worker.

Many people throughout the ages have made pronouncements and told tales about the ancient civilizations of the Americas. The origins of these Proto-Americans have also been linked to the highly controversial existence of the island of Atlantis or Poseidia. Plato was already referring to such people from Atlantis in 350 BC, when he wrote about the Mesopotamians and Proto-Europeans being attacked by the "islanders." He wrote that some 9,000 years had passed since the war between "those on the outside" and "those on the inside" of the "Pillars of Hercules." The "pillars" refer to Gibraltar, which divided the Atlantic ocean and the Mediterranean. This would place the time at around 9500 BC, just after the last ice age. This ice age date plays a pivotal role in all of prehistory, as it crops up over and over again as a landmark for the beginning of most activities by modern humans, whether they were in Mesopotamia or the Americas. The end of the last ice age brought the sudden emergence of civilized man in a number of places around the world, and is regarded by many as starting the Flood that swept the Earth, causing humankind to have to rebuild from scratch. We should, therefore, not be surprised when many scholars claim that the first people arrived in the Americas from the lost island of Atlantis at the time when the last ice age ended. It would make perfect sense, because their island was about to be swallowed by the giant tidal waves that flooded the Earth at that time. In December 2004, we saw how devastating a relatively small tsunami can be to islands in its way. Imagine what a flood ten to twenty times that size would do. This is why the original people settled on the mountainous shores of the lake Titicaca, far away from the flood waters and close to rich sediments of gold, tin, and other metals. This was also the time during which agriculture and farming were introduced to man, as outlined in many Sumerian tablets, especially the *Lost Book of Enki*, which describes in great detail the times and activities and relationships between the Anunnaki gods and the newly created humans.

There is clear evidence of crops being cultivated in the Teohuacan Valley some 7000 BC, but there is also evidence that there was probably some devastating flood leading up to this date, which only allowed civilization to continue much later in about 3100 BC. Barry Fell, a professor at Harvard, successfully proved that the Americas were being visited as early as 5000 BC by Proto-Europeans and Africans. Roman vases have been found off the seabed near Brazil; Roman coins were found off the beach in Massachusetts; Carthaginian vases were found off the coast of Honduras, but the permission to investigate the wreck was denied, in order to protect the historic importance of Columbus. Professor Fell also speaks about many sites in the Americas that have been found containing Carthaginian and Celtic writings. Many Punic inscriptions have been found on gravestones, cairns, and in stone cellars dating back to the Bronze Age between 1200 BC and 3000 BC. There are also inscriptions in the original Celt written language of Ogham from the pre-Roman times of France and Spain. On a stone carving of a ship from Tarshish, there is an inscription that says: "Voyagers from Tarshish, this stone proclaims." This was translated from the Tartessian Punic language.

One of the most incredible ancient finds in all of archaeological history was the Mayan calendar. When it was first discovered it perplexed all who tried to figure it out. It took the persistent investigative work of a German librarian by the name of Ernst Forstemann in 1880 to break the code and unravel its incredible mystery. When the Mayan calendar was finally explained, it showed the incredible knowledge that they possessed of the cosmos, solar system, and the movements of planets, including our own moon. The Mayan calendar became known as the "Long Count." Instead of using irrelevant points of reference to historic figures by which to develop a calendar, they used the movements of the sun, moon, and Venus to calculate precise points in time, to the "first" rising or "birth" of Venus. All the Mesoamerican cultures believe that there are five different "ages" or "suns." After many years of deciphering the Mayan mathematical formulas, scholars agree that the beginning of the Long Count started on August 13, 3114 BC and will end on December 22, 2012. That means that the period is 5,126 years long. What the exact significance is of the length of the age or the end date is not clear, but it's not a long time to go, so let's just wait and see. Some scientists claim that it has to do with a shift in the Earth's magnetic field, when the north and south poles move away from their current positions and establish new magnetic poles.

Fig. 10.18. Giant Olmec stone heads. Erik Parker stands in front of a giant Olmec Head. This is just one example of several such works of art discovered in the jungles of Mexico. Notice the distinct African features and protective headgear on both heads. This has baffled historians for ages.

The mystery of the Mesoamerican civilizations continues with the Olmec. They appeared in the Tabasco area of Mexico as suddenly as all the others, but their distinctly African physical features were completely different from the other locals. They seem to have appeared around the beginning of the Mayan Long Count some 3114 BC. The colossal stone head found at Veracruz in 1862 shows convincingly that their features were distinctly African. Several other giant heads have been found, and all of them show the same African features. On other carvings they were almost always depicted with some kind of tool in their hands, digging for gold. In many of the depictions on rocks and seals and stelae, their tools are reasonably detailed and it becomes clear that these were sophisticated people with a good knowledge of ore mining.

Let us analyze the situation for a second. If you had discovered gold in a faraway land and needed experienced miners to deal with the perils of getting it out of the ground, would you attempt to train the inexperienced people from the surrounding districts, or would you rather bring in a team of well-trained miners who could get on with the task immediately, while sharing their skills with the locals? Many scholars believe that is exactly what the ancient "mining lords" did. The Anunnaki gods came to America to mine for gold and brought their experienced miners from Africa. It provides a very simplistic explanation for the appearance of the Olmec in Mesoamerica. It also explains why there was so much gold when the Spaniards first invaded it some 4,500 years later.

To truly understand the magnificent golden riches that greeted the invaders, we just need to mention the Peruvian city of Cuzco. There the conquistadores found the great Temple of the Sun that had walls covered with gold. There were chapels and burial chambers honoring ancestors, filled with a variety of statuettes and images. It boasted an artificial garden where all the plants, shrubs, and trees were made of gold. In the courtyard, there was a mock field of maize where every stalk was made of silver and the delicate ears made of gold, which covered around 20,000 square meters or two hectares. The Spaniards soon realized that they would have to fight for the gold as all these American cultures believed that gold was a gift from the gods and it belonged to the gods. So it is our deduction that the Olmec were a group of miners from Africa who were brought to America to mine for gold by their Anunnaki-Sumerian masters. At this point, in our highly informed civilization of the twenty-first century, there seems to be no better explanation. After all, the Anunnaki have come to this new land to get more gold and they needed experienced miners. Who better to bring along for the task than the African miners of gold who had been created by the Anunnaki for that specific task, and who had loads of experience by then? Many of the depictions of Olmec miners show some form of advanced fire tool, which they point at the rock face. It almost seems like a device that produced a flame or beam to heat or cut the rock. They even show these miners with a kind of headgear that produced beams of light. Too much to swallow? Well, these stone carvings and depictions have survived for over 5,000 years, and today we still mine for gold using hand held tools and lamps on the helmets even at our advanced levels of sophistication. So why could they have not done so? It may just be that the Olmec had a smarter way of doing it. They must have known a great deal about engineering and construction because their pyramids and other lost cities are as impressive as any of the Mayan or Egyptian structures. They are remembered for building what is possibly the oldest pyramid in the Americas and introducing the "dot and bar" counting system that was apparently used by the Mayas to develop their Long Count calendar in later years. They also cultivated maize and other crops and introduced a ball game with a rubber ball, which may just be the predecessor to basketball and soccer. They were known as the "rubber people," the meaning of the word *Olmec*. The latter Spanish mining engineers have often spoken of "prehistoric gold mines" at Mexican sites.

If you have doubts about the African connection to the Olmec, here is a curious bit of information. The Olmec style of writing is very similar to the writing used by the Vai people of West Africa. They also spoke a language that had a strong resemblance to that of the Manding (Malinke-Bambara) language spoken in West Africa. Is that just another coincidence? It is believed that the Olmec people introduced writing to the New World and they had both a syllabic and hieroglyphic script. The decipherment of the Olmec writing of ancient Mexico provides us with keen insight into the world of the Olmec. Rafinesque published an important paper on Mayan writing in 1832, that helped to decipher the Olmec's writing.

The great Olmec centers that developed at La Venta, San Lorenzo, and Laguna de los Cerros, and the smaller centers such as Tres Zapotes, were not simply vacant religious sites, but dynamic settlements that included artisans and farmers, as well as priests and the rulers. Then there were the Toltec, Aztecs, Zapotecs, Mixtecs, and other groups who lived and influenced the ancient cultures of the Americas over many thousands of years. Each one pointing to the other whence they received their knowledge about gold mining and other skills. The most amazing thing is that all these ancient American cultures had one thing in common—they all worshipped the same deity whose name means "winged serpent," or "flying serpent." This major god was called Kukulkan by the Maya, Quetzalcoatl by the Aztecs, Viracocha by the Inca, Gucumatz in central America, Votan in Palenque, and Zamna in Izamal.

Fig. 10.19. A Mayan depiction of the divine serpent

The pre-Columbian Inca civilization was extraordinary in its development of human society and culture, ranking with the early civilizations of Egypt and Mesopotamia. There are several myths about pre-Inca civilizations and as with all ancient civilizations, legends and ancient stone carvings and their monuments speak of creation by gods who came from the skies, yet no one is certain how any of these civilizations came into being. Many just seem to spring up as if out of nowhere.

So were these gods actually real? Did they really come from the sky to create man in all these different parts of the world? Once again, the similarity to Mesopotamian and biblical legends are too close to be coincidental, especially if we take into account the vast distances between the continents with the Atlantic Ocean in between. There is a pre-Incan legend that speaks of Viracocha who is depicted in many forms, which is not unlike gods in other civilizations. He was known as the "good god," but the warrior side to his personality was also often shown. We see him as the enlightened god in white robes who brings knowledge, and the warrior god with staves in his hands and a sun symbol around his head, not unlike that of the sun god Ra in ancient Egypt. Viracocha, as the feathered serpent god, is one of the great mysteries of ancient American cultures, but there is a clear link to the activities of the Anunnaki in this part of the world and Viracocha is the main protagonist leading the rest of the gods who came in search of gold. The only question is, which of the feathered serpents is he? Enki, the Lord of the Earth, who is always depicted as a winged serpent, or his son Ningishzidda, whose symbol is also the entwined serpent, representing his knowledge of medicine?

Quetzalcoatl was the good god and hero of the Nahuatl people. He was the Feathered Serpent, hero god, giver of all their knowledge. The story goes that he established the city of Tula around 3200 BC, taught the people about maize farming and gave them other important knowledge. He was fair-skinned. But his brother was jealous and cast him out. Quetzalcoatl promised that he would return to "establish rule of law and enlightenment." It is this kind of character description that closely resembles Enki or his son Ningishzidda. As we explained, both had serpents in their Sumerian depictions.

There are many other fascinating tales about the relationship between the gods, the people, and their obsession with gold in the Americas. We already outlined the golden riches that greeted Cortes, the Spanish explorer, when he first set foot in this part of the world. He was astounded by the amount of gold there was. The cities were covered with it. The thing that amazed him was that all the locals explained to Cortes how they smelted the metal in small pots and cast them in bars. They also explained that "once it was ready it was sent to the capital, returned to the gods to whom the gold had always belonged." This seems to be a constant mantra with the ancient American cultures. They all claimed that the gold belonged to the gods. To the Aztecs, gold was a "divine metal." The Toltecs in Mexico were mining it in 1000 BC already and the Incas believed that it was "the gods who caused gold to be so valued." They also believed that gold was made from the gods' tears. Sitchin compares this notion to the voice of god as it spoke through the prophet Haggai. "The silver is mine and the gold is mine. So sayeth the Lord of Hosts." Once again the similarity is a little too close for coincidence. The Maya called gold *teocuitlatl*, which meant "the gods' excretion"—his tears and his perspiration. However, the serpent connection has another twist that links it to the Near East and our Anunnaki gods.

There is a very good reason why the symbol of a snake is so prominent in Earth history. Once again it is revealed to us by the Sumerian tablets. After Alalu first landed on Earth, he went in search of water northwest of where Eridu was later built, and at the shores of a lake or a river, he saw a snake for the very first time. It is obvious from his reaction that snakes were not known on Nibiru. "A hissing sound he could hear; a slithering body by the poolside was moving." After killing the snake in a reflex action he examined it with amazement. "The slithered body lay still . . . like a rope its long body was, without hands or feet was the body." Alalu pondered this creature for some time, wondering if it was the guardian of the water or what purpose it might have served. Later, when Enki and his first team of exploring astronauts landed to join him, he showed them the serpents. It makes good sense that they would have used this creature as some kind of symbol on their new planet, since it was the first creature they saw. The Mayan word for serpent is *can*, which is parallel to the Hebrew word *Canaan,* and that is why the god from Canaan got the title of serpent.

After Quetzalcoatl settled in the Americas, he established his first city inland at the great river Nachan, which means "place of serpents." It stands to reason that there would be snakes of a wide variety present in that part of the world, but it is also very close to the Hebrew word for serpent, *nachash.* Arthur Posnansky found a series of inscriptions on rocks on the shores of Lake Titicaca that link the ancient Peruvian script to inscriptions found on Easter Island. For those who don't know Easter Island, it is an extremely remote island in the middle of the Pacific between Australia and South America, which sports a long line of giant "heads" carved out of rock. As incredible as it is, both these scripts, which originate a great distance from each other, are related to the Indus Valley script and the writing of the Hittites of Mesopotamia. From a series of archaeo-astronomic calculations, Professor Rolf Muller concluded that the structures at Machu Picchu, Cuzco, and Tiahuanacu are at least 4,000 years old, which would explain how the Indus and Mesopotamian texts could have influenced their sister cultures on the other side of the world. But how would they have arrived there? With the help of the ever-present Anunnaki gods of course.

In the biblical story of Cain and Abel we are told that the two brothers were given separate tasks to help provide for the growing family of man. As with all of biblical stories, we find tales of exact parallel in Sumerian scriptures that predate the Bible by at least 1,000 years. In this case, the story is told in great detail, describing the brothers Ka-in "He who in the Field Food Grows," and Abael "He of the Watered Meadows," as they go about their respective chores of planting crops and breeding domestic animals, just like the Bible says. When Abael's animals started to eat Ka-in's crops, a fierce fight erupted between the brothers during which Ka-in killed Abael. Although he was filled with remorse and realized his grave mistake, the Sumerian gods decreed that he should be banished away from their land of Edin to toil on his own, without the help of the Anunnaki gods. Marduk was the firstborn son of Enki who arrived on Earth to be with his father on this exciting adventure, exploring a new planet. Marduk had the following to say: "Let Ka-in's life be spared, to the ends of the

Earth let him be banished!" Enki agreed with him. "Eastward to a land of wandering for his evil deed Ka-in must depart," Enki concluded. And so it was that Ka-in disappeared to a distant land. We can speculate where it may have been, but a further clue is provided later, when it is revealed that it was a land of high mountains, steep valleys, and a great lake high in the mountains. There could be a number of places like that in Europe, which could be linked to the early Proto-European farming activity, but this event took place way before the Flood, which would eliminate ancient Europe as a possible candidate territory for Ka-in's place of settlement. Large parts of Europe would have had snow and ice and would not have been very pleasant to farm in. The southern hemisphere is a much more likely candidate to fit the geographical description.

Another crucial clue is given to us by Ningishzidda who was another son of Enki, involved in the genetic creation of the Adamu. This bright young scientist was a master at genetic engineering and he certainly got lots of experience on Earth in the early days according to the *Lost Book of Enki,* which was compiled and translated by Zecharia Sitchin. In this incredible book we learn virtually everything we wanted to know about the origin of humanity and the activities that brought us to the days of Abraham. Ningishzidda explains how he genetically created Ka-in not to be able to grow a beard. "By Ningishzidda was the life essence of Ka-in altered. That his face a beard should not grow, Ka-in's life essence Ningishzidda changed." It is well established that the native people of the Americas do not really grow beards because of a subtle genetic differentiation from the Europeans. This is a vivid clue pointing to the strong probability that Ka-in eventually ended up in the mountainous lands of the early Inca civilization, in Peru, near Lake Titicaca. The Inca refer to ancient times when their progenitors arrived from a distant land in the west. Is it possible that it was Ka-in, after whom they were named? In-ca = Ca-in?

The world is filled with incredible mysteries from distant prehistoric times when man was supposed to be a wandering nomad, living in caves and struggling to survive. Then suddenly after the Great Flood of around 11000 BC, he emerged from the caves with instant knowledge of many things, praying to a number of ever-present gods who seemed to be active all over the world. There are hundreds more examples of other civilizations in Africa, Asia, Japan, Australia, and other islands scattered around the world, which also miraculously received great knowledge from some mysterious place sometime shortly after the Great Flood.

What we need to establish is the realistic probability that all this knowledge just suddenly came to primitive humans without some sort of assistance from a more advanced power. The ancient scripts of the Sumerians provide us with thousands of snippets of tough-to-argue-against evidence that such intervention actually occurred. All we have to do is remove it from the realms of mythology where it has been positioned by ignorant historians, and accept that those were times that we cannot possibly comprehend today. We can hardly understand how a man like Hitler could marshal up so much support to take on the whole world in our own lifetime and exterminate millions of people. If it was not for the visual evidence, and if we had to rely on oral tales of the events from only sixty-five years ago, we would find it hard to believe. Mind you, there are people who still do not want to believe the whole World War II saga with its extermination of the Jews, even in the face of all the evidence we have. Therefore, it is not surprising that we find it difficult to accept written evidence from thousands of years ago, which meticulously outlines the steps of humankind on Earth.

THE EGYPTIAN CIVILIZATION

One of the most compelling examples of interaction between gods and humans is the story of Egypt. Archaeologists, historians, and other scholars have speculated for the past 200 years as to the origins of the great knowledge of the Egyptians. The truth is that their entire culture stems directly from the Sumerians with all their major gods, and they inherited virtually everything from the Sumerians, except their writing. We learn from the tablets that the Anunnaki divided the world into a number of regions and appointed various family members to take care of their own regions, with explicit instructions to teach the earthlings the art of civilization. In a strange twist of fate, they needed the earthlings' help after the Flood to make the Earth habitable again. Anu instructed them to "rebuild the cities where they stood before" the Flood. They were to appoint kings and priests to each city through which they would communicate their instructions to the people. They taught them to make bricks, to build extravagant buildings, how to calculate, introduced wheeled chariots, laid down laws and a judicial system and much more.

Nowhere was the interaction between gods and kings as pronounced as in ancient Egypt. The firstborn son of Enki was Marduk. He was appointed as the god of Egypt, where he was worshipped as Ra—"The Bright One" and later Amun—"The Invisible or Absent" god. Enki was known as Ptah—"The Developer" and Ningishzidda was worshipped as Tehuti—"The Divine Measurer." But Marduk was rebellious from the word go and started to introduce a whole new way of doing things. He introduced a count of 10 instead of 60, he divided the year into 12 months, and had temples built everywhere in his honor. He orchestrated the building of a great temple for Anu and Enki, and he was instrumental in dictating the *Book of the Dead* to instruct pharaohs and kings on what to do if they wanted to be taken up to heaven by him after death. It explained how to reach the Duat, which means "Place of Celestial Boats." Although Marduk proclaimed his supremacy over all other gods, causing much unhappiness among the other Anunnaki, he was not endowed with knowledge of eternal life by his father Enki. "Then all manner of knowledge, except that of dead reviving to Ra he gave"—is said about Enki in the tablets. But Marduk (Ra) constantly made those claims to the pharaohs and priests of Egypt, laying down a strict set of rules and rituals they had to perform to reach the eternal afterlife in the heavens. What he was referring to was life on planet Nibiru. Another compelling entry by Marduk in the *Lost Book of Enki,* which outlines his deception of the pharaohs, was "Let the kings of my region of Neteru offspring be, to Nibiru in an afterlife journey." Neteru was the name used for the Anunnaki observers who were supposed to keep an eye on the region. Marduk/Ra decreed that the kings appointed to rule over Egypt had to be offspring from Anunnaki and human, to make them superior to mere humans. Once again, this explains why so many of the pharaohs believed that they were actually gods themselves. It was that kind of relationship between gods and mortals, and the power of "eternal life" being usurped by Marduk, and his encouragement of the kings to obey him and follow him into the afterlife, which led to the many murals in Egyptian tombs depicting dramatic scenes of their journey to the land of eternal life. These depictions have amazed historians for centuries while searching for the real meaning behind them; traveling in a "Boat of Heaven" across the skies to eternal life and immortality. Over and over, historians have tried to explain these images as dramatized depictions of the Egyptian religion, but it was much more real than that. It now becomes very clear where the Egyptians got those ideas. It was a cunning manipulative Anunnaki god, who was promised the command of the planet, now demanding his rightful place on the ladder of importance among the gods from Nibiru.

The pyramids of Giza have perplexed historians and archaeologists alike, making all kinds of pronouncements about their origins. The popular opinion is that the Great Pyramid was built by King Khufu (Cheops) of the Fourth Dynasty, during his reign some 2589 BC. This has been contradicted by many scholars over the years, who claim that Khufu was merely a user of the pyramid, that the pyramids of Giza already existed by the time he took the throne. Any inscriptions that may have been found in or on the pyramid were made long after it was completed. There are so many inconsistencies in the story of the building of the pyramids by the pharaohs that it keeps attracting new theories. If the pyramids of Giza were built by Khufu, Khafre, and Menkaure, as is claimed by historians, the progression seems back to front. Would it not make more sense that the latter kings would have wanted to show their supremacy? In that case the first pyramid would have been the smallest, followed by the larger one, eventually ending with biggest one, the Great Pyramid. This is a simple principle of progression that the Egyptians understood much better than we do today. There are many arguments raised by writers, like Graham Hancock in his book *Fingerprints of the Gods,* that go a long way to establishing that the pyramids were built long before the Egyptian civilization came into existence. They certainly were not built to be tombs for kings. It seems to follow that the early Egyptians would have been highly impressed by these giant monuments of their gods, and they tried to imitate them. The later pyramids became great tributes to their gods of which they were very proud, but the results were not always that successful. It is clear that all the imitation pyramids built by the Egyptian pharaohs were much smaller, did not possess the complex passages of the Great Pyramid, and often collapsed. They obviously did not have the knowledge of the Anunnaki who were the original builders of the Giza pyramids. The latter kings could never match the size and the angles of the original structure.

Once again, the Sumerian texts give us a very different version of the pyramids' origins, and again these seem to make much more practical sense than any of the more popularized versions. It was the talented Ningishzidda whom the

Fig. 10.20. Pyramids of Giza. From left to right: Menkaure, Khafre, and Khufu or Great Pyramid. Notice the two smaller queen's pyramids in the foreground. The Great Pyramid is the only one remaining wonder of the ancient Seven Wonders of the World.

Egyptians worshipped as The Divine Measurer who planned, measured, modeled, and perfectly built the three pyramids of Giza. His reason was far more pressing than a giant tomb to be buried in. The *Lost Book of Enki* describes it very vividly. Before he built the final thing, he first made a smaller scale prototype.

> The rising angles of four smooth sides with this he perfected. Next to it a larger peak he placed, its sides to Earth's four corners he set; By the Anunnaki, with their tools of power, were its stones cut and erected. Beside it, in a precise location, the peak that was its twin he placed; With galleries and chambers for pulsating crystals he designed it.

They called the erections Ekur—"House Which Like a Mountain Is." What becomes quite clear from this short extract is that the pyramids had a far more important role to play in the lives of the Anunnaki. The Flood had wiped out their space port, landing places, measurements, beacons, and other support structures that they had developed for regular take-off and landing with their spacecraft. The two pyramids were new indestructible beacons with specific chambers for "pulsating crystals" to help point out the landing places when approaching from space. They would not allow another flood to upset their base on Earth. The pharaohs who followed took inspiration from these great structures and started to imitate them with less success. Engineers have pointed out that there are very definite differences in the knowledge that went into building the Great Pyramids, and the many other smaller imitations that followed. Clearly, the kings and pharaohs did not possess the knowledge of the more evolved Ningishzidda. The pyramids also proved the supremacy of the gods to the Egyptians, who worshipped them fanatically.

So far we have learned that ancient civilizations sprang up all over the world shortly after the Great Flood of around 11000 BC. They all showed remarkable knowledge and understanding virtually overnight, which could only have happened if there was some form of intervention from the Anunnaki gods who ruled the world and explored every corner in search of gold. The primitive worker was serving his purpose well, but now the humans who survived the Flood had a more crucial function to perform than just to dig for gold. They had to provide for the growing population on a planet where much of the arable land was destroyed. The slave species had been promoted to provider, and for the first time the Anunnaki conceded that they were dependent on their slaves. In these dramatic translations we stumble upon the only two common denominators that can be traced all the way to the birth of humankind: our obsession with gold, and slavery.

11

THE WRATH OF GOD

I WAS WATCHING a documentary on Alexander the Great when I started wondering why he was so admired by his followers, and what made him so "Great." Is it the number of empires and kingships he overthrew, or the number of cities that fell under his sieges, or the number of people who supported him in his quest to invade the whole world? Is it possible that he was more feared than admired? It seems that he is even more admired today by historians and the general populace than he was in 333 BC. He is referred to in encyclopedias as the conqueror of the Persian Empire and probably the world's greatest military leader of all time. He has inspired many novels and movies, which have used him as a role model for the personification of a man's man: strong and steadfast, determined, reaching for the impossible and succeeding in the face of insurmountable odds. Basically, he personifies the kind of storybook hero that does not exist on Earth today. A deep thinker, strategist, and great leader of men. In a short space of twelve years, Alexander conquered virtually all of the known world as he marched his army of 40,000 men from west to east; invading cities and villages one by one, often killing all the men, women, and children, or saving the women and children but selling them into slavery. He plundered the wealth of the cities, royal treasuries, and took all their booty. After overpowering the cities, he often burned them to the ground.

Those who obeyed him were rewarded with unspoken treasures, while those who resisted him were brutally murdered. Prisoners of war were either released or murdered, all depending on his mood on that particular day. The global population at this time was estimated to be around 100 million and much of this eventually fell under the rule of Alexander the Great. This great leader of men was also known to have killed his father Philip II, a number of members of his army who disagreed with his judgment, and even his close friend and confidant whose advice conflicted with that of the great Alexander. This man went so far as to declare himself a "god," believing that he was above mere mortals and the son of the great Zeus, god of gods.

Where does this potential for violence, oppression, and punishment come from? Are we merely imitating something or someone from days gone by? Someone who was instrumental in controlling the formative years after our creation? If you look at the history of humankind all the way back to the days of Adam, Cain and Abel, it is one long horrific tale of betrayal, murder, warfare, oppression, rape and pillage, jealousy, envy, greed and continuous unspeakable horror inflicted by man on his fellow man. But the passage of time has a strange way of smoothing out the terrible truths of the past. Time has the ability to somehow legitimize the horrors committed in days gone by. History books have a tendency to glorify some of the acts of past leaders, when in reality they should be condemned by latter generations. Alexander was just one such "great" warring hero of the distant past. There were many others and most of them are revered as great historical leaders, forever imprinted in our memories. In truth, they were just insatiable, power-hungry thugs who used their influence and wealth to accumulate more and more.

Attila the Hun is another great leader of the past who is described somewhat differently by historians. Why is that? Because he did not have an empire before he started to invade and rule other kingdoms? Because his tribe was described as nomadic? He was just doing what all the other kings were doing, expanding his territory by force. This is how a historian by the name of Rit Nosotro writes about Attila.

Attila the Hun has been known as a ruthless barbarian, fierce and uncivilised. The devastation that he delivered to his enemies and the terror that he instilled in them during his lifetime caused him to become known as "The Scourge of God." While most people see Attila as being just a ferocious warrior, the more obscure side of him shows us that he was also a great king, possessing great leadership abilities and management skills. Attila the Hun was born in approximately AD 406 to the ruling Hun family, his uncle being the king. Although we do not know much about Attila's childhood other than that he was taught to ride a horse, shoot a bow, and fight in hand-to-hand combat at a very young age. By his late teens, he was leading the Huns in merciless battle against their enemies, the Visigoths. He pillaged numerous towns causing utter devastation. No one could match him in battle, and by his thirties, he was the Huns' leading commander.

Before Attila's time, the Huns were a nomadic, barbarian race. They came from Asia and first reached the outskirts of the Roman Empire in the late fourth century. The Huns conquered the barbarian Ostrogoths and drove back the Visigoths. The Eastern Roman Empire was threatened by these vicious Huns until 418 when Rome and the Huns negotiated peace terms. To secure peace, important persons, such as the young Attila, were exchanged as hostages between the Romans and the Huns. During Attila's two years in Rome, he was awed by the grandeur of the Empire. Upon his return home, he vowed to someday go back to Rome not as a hostage, but as a conqueror.

Why is Attila seen as a ruthless barbarian, while Alexander was "great" and the Romans were imperial and "civilized"? It almost feels as if we are legitimizing their individual rights to conquer others, based on their socioeconomic status. Because Alexander was the king of a wealthy empire he was allowed to invade and destroy, but because Attila was the leader of a lowly group of bandits, he should not possess such privileges. So what makes us in the twenty-first century so captivated by these warring heroes of the past? Do we not have heroes like this in the modern world? Or how long do we have to wait for some of the more recent potential candidates for great military leader status to be so recognized and decorated? Alexander conquered the world in the name of Macedonia, while Julius Caesar conquered the world some 300 years later in the name of the Roman Empire. The war stories go on. But still they are "great" leaders of the past. Just recently we had a great military leader who tried to conquer the world and in the process got very close to doing so. He had the full fanatical support of his people just like Alexander did; his followers all believed that they should conquer the world; he was admired by them as a great leader of men, a great strategist and someone they would follow to the end of the world in battle. He mobilized his well-trained and well-equipped army, killing many in the name of his empire. He wiped out cities and villages as part of his expansion plan, he occupied new lands and countries, declaring them part of the new empire. He looted wealth and riches as part of his victories and depending on his mood, he would eliminate anyone who stood in his way, even his close friends and allies. The kind of man which history books often praise as a "great leader of men."

But this great leader was Adolf Hitler, and our history books have not been as kind to him as they have been to Alexander and to the Romans. So what is the difference between Adolf Hitler, Alexander, Atilla the Hun, and Julius Caesar? How much time will need to pass before historians start to include Hitler in the same revered group of great military leaders of the past? Or is it the visual reminder of the horrors of war that will exclude Hitler from this "great" group of leaders? It certainly feels that time does soften the blow while the more recent dictators were captured on film, which blows the romantic perception of war in an instant.

In other chapters we have explored the DNA, our genome, and its capacity to control all of our emotional and physical characteristics. We raise the argument that we are the slaves to our DNA. As we cast our critical mind back to the events that shaped our history, all we can see is violence, conflict, and destruction. It's as if humankind simply cannot escape the grip of its violent behavior. Once again, I must remind you that the violent gene runs deep and strong in our bodies and we must begin to identify this behavioral pattern of humanity, so that we can begin to understand it. Mumbo-jumbo psychology will get us nowhere. The harsh reality is embedded in our genome. Our propensity for cruelty and violence was unconsciously bred into us by our maker at the point of creation. And because we were made in the "image of our maker," it must surely mean that we inherited more than just his physical features. There is the distinct possibility that if we were created as genetic experiments, or as I have called us, a slave species, other genetic characteristics like temperament and even our potential for violence would have been transferred to us. From genetic studies we have already found that most of our genome is somehow switched off. This could mean that the maker created a potential genetic imbalance, by purposely disabling certain genes, and allowing others to remain as the master program that controls us. So, by extrapolation, if we have parts of our maker in us, surely this must mean that such a maker must have the violent gene embedded in its genome? Is this why there are so many horrific tales of brutality by god toward man throughout ancient history? Could this god have been a mere advanced being, merely exhibiting his neohuman traits of jealousy, vengeance, retribution, punishment, and other very normal characteristics typical of the human species? Is it at all possible that God with a big "G" could behave in such a barbaric human way?

The wrath of god should really be called the wrath of man. How is it possible that God, the creator of the universe and all things in it, could have intentionally created such a hateful and violent creature as the human? And after creating us in this disturbing way, in his image, the God of love and the God of forgiveness, turned into a god of retribution, punishment, vengeance, but also a god of reward if he got what he wanted. And mostly he wanted a load of material things like gold, silver, saffron, foods of a wide variety, special favors, and he even requested his pilgrims to go to war in his name, destroying man, woman, and beast. The Bible is filled with these kinds of stories that are too close for comfort to the materialistic and obsessive desires by mortal beings, and are not becoming of the benevolent God who lives in spirit, filling every crevice of the universe.

Here is an interesting comparison between the brutality of modern dictators and the vengeance and brutality of god. Note that I use "god" instead of "God," as we are beginning to discover that there is a vast difference between the two, which has evaded simple man for millennia.

We are going to indulge in four multiple choice quizzes to get to know "our god" a bit better. I urge you to take out a pencil and mark your answers as you work your way through them.

⟡ First Quiz: The Wrath of Dictators

Objective: Please answer the following questions in an attempt to determine the number of living things that were killed by dictators, or in the name of dictators in the past. The answers are displayed after the quiz.

1. How many men did Genghis Khan kill because someone decided to peek into his chest of treasures?
    A. None. He certainly wouldn't kill someone merely for examining his private things.
    B. 50,070.
    C. Just the people who looked into the chest.
    D. 250. The people who looked into the chest and their immediate families.

2. How many men did Stalin's henchmen kill in one day because they failed to say they supported Stalin?
    A. None, Stalin doesn't kill people for their mistakes.
    B. 200—those who failed to say they supported Stalin, but not their family members.
    C. 1,000—those who failed to say they supported Stalin and their spouses.
    D. 3,000—those who failed to say they supported Stalin and their brothers, companions, and neighbors.

3. How many people did the Ku Klux Klan kill in a frenzy before someone pleased them by ending a mixed marriage with the murder of the couple?

A. None. The Ku Klux Klan loves all their followers and imposes no restriction on whom they marry (so long as the person is of the opposite gender).

B. 100.

C. 24,000.

D. None of the above.

4. **How many animals did the British Royal Guard kill in Africa in an attempt to please the Queen?**

A. None. The Queen is not so insensitive as to gain satisfaction from man's slaughter of innocent animals.

B. Two head of cattle, two rams, and two ravens.

C. A herd of 100 sheep that he and his men came across in their conquests.

D. 120,000 sheep and 22,000 oxen.

5. **How many Jews did the SS deliver to Hitler's concentration camps to be slaughtered?**

A. Trick question. The Jews were God's chosen people, hence Hitler never would have allowed anyone to slaughter them.

B. Half a million.

C. 5 million—the number who disobeyed his commands.

D. 200—the number who worshipped other leaders.

6. **How many people of Iraq were once killed or enslaved because they didn't give Saddam his due?**

A. 120,000 valiant men were killed and 200,000 women and children were taken as slaves for cheap labor (not to mention the theft of their property).

B. One.

C. Two.

D. None of the above.

7. **How many Ethiopians did Idi Amin kill for his cleansing of chosen people?**

A. None. Idi Amin doesn't kill people!

B. One million.

C. One Thousand.

D. A Hundred.

8. Speaking of cleansing and conquering, how many kings were maimed in the name of Alexander the Great?

   A. None.

   B. One had his legs broken so he couldn't gather men to form an army.

   C. Two had their tongues cut out so they couldn't call the people to war.

   D. 70 had their thumbs and big toes cut off.

9. How many soldiers did the U.S. army burn to death with fire from tanks because they confronted the killer of three innocent priests?

   A. None. The U.S. army would never engage in such a cruel act.

   B. 50

   C. 100.

   D. 150 (three sets of 50).

10. If Osama bin Laden was still alive, how many dead would there be by the time he was done with his killing spree?

   A. None. Osama doesn't kill.

   B. Ten million.

   C. One hundred million.

   D. Enough to cover the entire surface of the Earth.

While these questions may seem deliberately warped, sick, and probably indicative of a psychopathic mind, you don't have to panic. The answers to these questions are purely hypothetical, because these questions were actually taken, word for word, from a Bible quiz on the Landover Baptist Church website. While the church and website are a satirical look at fundamental Christianity, the content of these quizzes is all taken from actual Bible passages. All we did was to replace the word *God* with a notorious dictator or killer. I trust you are as horrified as I was when I first saw this. I had shivers running down my spine. It reads more brutally than any horror movie I have seen. And yet, this is the stuff we teach our children because it was written by some men thousands of years ago, claiming that they were instructed by "God" to perform these gruesome acts. I ask you to read these questions and answers with an open mind. But at this stage, it seems that we are incapable of separating right from wrong, as we keep justifying these acts of horror, because they were performed in the name of god. Ask yourself the following: if you were to commit such acts today, in the way they are described in this quiz, apparently in the name of god, what would happen to you and how would the global community react? The answers are actually pretty simple because they have occurred many times in the past, and they will probably continue to occur for many years to come. If you were to kill or maim one person, you will be tried and receive a prison sentence of some length, possibly life or even the death penalty. If you were to kill a small number of people, you would be called a mass murderer or a serial killer and you would get life or death, but you will be immortalized in books, documentaries, and movies. You may claim insanity, in which case you will live in luxury in an asylum where everything is provided for you, till you die. You will make millions from the book you write and the movie rights you sell to the highest bidder. But if you kill a few million people, and you take control of power in a small country where you continue to rule through oppression, torture and fear, you will become a dictator who is untouchable by the other governments of

Fig. 11.1. The first commandments. Instructions of Shuruppak: Sumerian on clay, Sumer, 2600 BC. This Early Dynastic tablet represents the earliest literature in the world. Only four groups of texts are known from the dawn of literature. The instructions are addressed by the pre-Flood ruler Shuruppak, to his son Ziusudra, who was the Sumerian Noah. Shuruppak's instructions can be said to be the Sumerian forerunner of the Ten Commandments and some of the Proverbs of the Bible.

Line 50: Do not curse with powerful means (third commandment); line 28: Do not kill (sixth commandment); line 33–34: Do not laugh with or sit alone in a chamber with a girl that is married (seventh commandment); lines 28–31: Do not steal or commit robbery (eighth commandment); line 36: Do not spit out lies (ninth commandment).

the world. Unless you are Saddam Hussein and you have inexhaustible wealth in the ground of your land, in which case you will be toppled by the strongest global regime of the time, against the advice of their allies, because the booty is too huge to resist.

Either way, the so-called wrath of god is too horrible to imagine, and the reality is too incredible to digest. And so, we teach our children the stories about the wrath of god, and we fill them with fear instead of love and compassion. Such is the nature of the defective genome lurking in our cells, keeping us entrapped in a cycle of fear, violence, and unspeakable cruelty toward our neighbors.

There are so many similarities between the Sumerian tablets and the books of the Bible that it instantly begs the question: How is it possible? If you look at the tone used in the books of the Old Testament, you will see that it carries a strong resemblance to the Sumerian transcripts regarding the behavior of the Anunnaki, who came to Earth in the distant past. We will study their behavior and their actions that resulted in the creation of our own human species, fast-forwarding the evolutionary process while restricting the genome of the new species to the bare essentials. From the Sumerian tablets it will become blatantly clear that the gods who ruled the world in the distant past were mere mortals with humanlike needs and desires. They may have had advanced knowledge, skills, and scientific ability, but this did not make them God. The strict instructions they gave man were blatantly designed to exercise absolute control over their newly created slave species. The messages that the so-called prophets of the Old Testament wrote about, and the messages they conveyed to the people of their world, were cunningly devised by the Anunnaki to keep man in his place and punish him if he stepped out of line. The wrath of god falls perfectly in line with this kind of "control-freak" behavior, and should never be confused with the will of God, the God with a big "G."

Answers to the "The Wrath of God" Quiz

1. **How many men did God kill because someone decided to peek into the ark of the Lord?**

   Correct Answer: **B.** (50,070) "And he smote the men of Bethshemesh, because they had looked into the ark of the Lord, even he smote of the people fifty thousand and threescore and ten men: and the people lamented, because the Lord had smitten many of the people with a great slaughter." (1 Samuel 6:19)

Fig. 11.2. Creation of the world. Debate between bird and fish—part of the Sumerian creation story. Sumerian clay tablet, Babylonia, circa 1900 BC. About 50–60 sources for the Creation of the Hoe are known. This clay tablet predates the Old Testament by at least 1,000 years. Could this have been one of the many ancient sources that inspired the authors of Genesis?

Commentary: Text 1 is a part of the Sumerian creation story, as a literary debate between the bird and the fish in which they argue for their usefulness in the universe. It has a substantially variant form of the published text, and the end is unpublished. Parts of the text are similar to Genesis 1:20–22. Text 2 deals with the Sumerian belief that the hoe, one of the basic agricultural tools, was given to them as a gift by the gods. It opens with the Sumerian creation of the world and of man, with parallels to the Bible's two creation stories: "The Lord hastened to separate heaven from earth" (Gen. 1:6–10); "and Daylight shone forth" (Gen. 1:3–5). It also predates the second creation story of the Bible: "The Lord put the (first) human in the brick mold, and Enlil's people emerged from the ground" (Gen. 2:7).

2. **How many men did Moses kill in one day because they failed to say they supported God?**
Correct Answer: **D.** (3,000) "Then Moses stood in the gate of the camp, and said, 'Who is on the Lord's side? Let him come unto me.' And all the sons of Levi gathered themselves together unto him. And he said unto them, 'Thus saith the Lord God of Israel, Put every man his sword by his side, and go in and out from gate to gate throughout the camp, and slay every man his brother, and every man his companion, and every man his neighbor.' And the children of Levi did according to the word of Moses: and there fell of the people that day about three thousand men." (Exodus 32:26–28)

3. **How many people did God kill in a plague before someone pleased God by ending a mixed marriage with the murder of the couple?**
Correct Answer: **C.** (24,000) "And, behold, one of the children of Israel came and brought unto his brethren a Midianitish woman in the sight of Moses, and in the sight of all the congregation of the children of Israel, who were weeping before the door of the tabernacle of the congregation. And when Phineas, the son of Eleazar, the son of Aaron the priest, saw it, he rose up from among the congregation, and took a javelin in his hand; And he went after the man of Israel into the tent, and thrust both of them through, the man of Israel, and the woman through her belly. So the plague was stayed from the children of Israel. And those that died in the plague were twenty and four thousand." (Numbers 25:6–9)

4. **How many animals did Solomon kill in a sacrifice to please the Lord?**
Correct Answer: **D.** (120,000 sheep and 22,000 oxen) "And Solomon offered a sacrifice of peace offering, which he offered unto the Lord, two and twenty thousand oxen, and an hundred and twenty thousand sheep. So the king and all the children of Israel dedicated the house of the Lord." (1 Kings 8:63)

5. **How many Israelites did God deliver to the people of Judah to slaughter?**
Correct Answer: **B.** (Half a million) "Then the men of Judah gave a shout: and as the men of Judah shouted, it came to pass, that God smote Jeroboam and all Israel before Abijah and Judah. And the children of Israel fled before Judah: and God delivered them into their hand. And Abijah and his people slew them with a great slaughter: so there fell down slain of Israel five hundred thousand chosen men. Thus the children of Israel were

brought under at that time, and the children of Judah prevailed, because they relied upon the Lord God of their fathers." (2 Chronicles 13:15–18)

6. **Notwithstanding the above, how many people of Judah were once killed or enslaved because they didn't give God his due?**
Correct Answer: **A.** (120,000 valiant men were killed and 200,000 women and children were taken as slaves, not to mention the theft of property.) "For Pekah the son of Remaliah slew in Judah an hundred and twenty thousand in one day, which were all valiant men; because they had forsaken the Lord God of their fathers . . . And the children of Israel carried away captive of their brethren two hundred thousand, women, sons, and daughters, and took also away much spoil from them." (2 Chronicles 28:6–8)

7. **How many Ethiopians did God kill for His chosen people?**
Correct Answer: **B.** (One million) "And Asa had an army of men . . . And there came out against them Zera the Ethiopian with an host of a thousand thousand . . . Asa cried unto the Lord his God, and said 'Lord, it is nothing with thee to help, whether with many, or with them that have no power, help us, O Lord our God' . . . So the Lord smote the Ethiopians." (2 Chronicles 14:8–12)

8. **Speaking of God's chosen people, how many kings were maimed in God's name?**
Correct Answer: **D.** (70 had their thumbs and big toes cut off.) "And they found Abonibezek in Bezek: and they fought against him, and they slew the Canaanites and Perizzites. But Abonibezek fled; and they pursued after him and caught him, and cut off his thumbs and his great toes. And Abonibezek said, 'Threescore and ten kings, having their thumbs and their great toes cut off, gathered their meat under my table: as I have done, so God hath requited me.'" (Judges 1:5–7)

9. **How many soldiers did God burn to death with fire from Heaven because they confronted Elijah?**
Correct Answer: **D.** (150—three sets of 50) "And Elijah answered and said to the captain of fifty, 'If I be a man of God, then let fire come down from heaven, and consume thee and thy fifty.' And there came down fire from heaven, and consumed him and his fifty. Again also he sent unto him another captain . . . And Elijah answered and said unto them, 'If I be a man of God, let fire come down from heaven and consume thee and thy fifty.' And the fire of God came from heaven, and consumed him and his fifty . . . And he sent again a captain of the third fifty . . . Behold, there came

fire down from heaven, and burnt up the two captains of the former fifties with their fifties." (2 Chronicles 1:10–14)

10. By the time God gets through with his killing spree, how many dead will there be?
Correct Answer: **D.** (Enough to cover the entire surface of the Earth.) "And the slain of the Lord shall be at that day from one end of the earth even unto the other end of the earth: they shall not be lamented, neither gathered, nor buried, they shall be dung upon the ground." (Jeremiah 25:33)

If the above content does not shock you, the years of propaganda have certainly dulled your senses. Could those possibly be the commands and the wishes of the God of Love? I do not believe that for one minute. It stinks of manipulative human characteristics of monumental proportion. It is amazing how "god" chooses sides, favoring one group of his creation over another, wilfully and maliciously guiding people to their death. He changes his mind virtually on a daily basis about his chosen people. Sometimes he delivers them from harm's way, at other times he purposely leads them to be slaughtered like sheep. This god clearly displays the kind of characteristics that he passed onto us. And we unmistakably display the traits that we could only have inherited from our maker, genetically engineered into us by the scientists of the ancient world, who arrived here on Earth to set up a base camp and mine the rich minerals in the ground for use on their planet Nibiru.

The next Bible quiz is just another item of proof in our gallery of evidence. It paints a gruesome picture of god and exposes his true identity. This was not the loving God some of us have come to imagine, but rather a materialistic, obsessive, and vengeful humanlike-being whom humankind got to worship as god. It is confusing why these ancient gods of the world would allow someone like Jesus Christ to shake their absolute control of humankind, but if we just read between the lines, their devious strategy bowls us over with its undermining brilliance. In a few short years Jesus turned the oppressive teaching of the Old Testament on its head and completely changed the way humans should deal with their needs and their own humanity. Was he the son of God? Of course he was! But now that we know who the god of the Old Testament really was, the identity of Jesus exposes a whole new plot in the entrapment of humankind. Did he have special powers? It certainly seems like it, and once we have looked at the Sumerian texts it will all start making very clear sense. We will come much closer to understanding who the Prince of Peace was and why his message was so important to humanity at that specific point in time. So let us take a

Fig. 11.3. Anu the supreme god. Two separate tablets showing Anu, the supreme commander of the Anunnaki, being served by human slaves. Note the star symbol representing his godly status and the radiant planet Nibiru.

few steps back now, from the Prince of Peace to the horrific, vengeful, barbaric acts perpetrated in the name of god by men in the times of the Old Testament. What was said is probably quite different from what was written. What is read and understood is most certainly different from what was said in the beginning. The ancient tablets have exposed the real truth.

All this will be breathtakingly revealed when we start to examine the Sumerian tablets. But if you think that I was lucky and found a few random out-of-place examples in the Bible, you are very mistaken. The Old Testament is filled with acts of horror on virtually every page. It seems that whoever was trying to control us had a very good strategy: fear, punishment, and reward. Just look at how successful it has been. There are still people today who live by those values 4,000 years later. It was actually very simple back then. Just remember that the Anunnaki gods were dealing with a new, primitive, unevolved, and uninformed species on Earth: one with no history, no memory, no legends, no culture. Everything they experienced was brand new to them. It was easy to find the leaders among them, appoint them in a position of author-ity by giving them the exclusive ability to converse with their maker "god" and bring instructions, warnings, reward, and retribution to the followers in the name of god. And so the embryonic relationship between the new species and its god evolved over several thousand years, while the uninformed slaves were entrapped in the worst kind of slavery possible: the fear of their creator.

Look how long it takes to rehabilitate battered animals. Some of them cannot be saved. Some will be fearful of their brutal master for the rest of their lives. With justifiable reason, because the master beats them and hurts them for no apparent reason. In this instance, there is no difference between the "dog animal" and the "human animal." The fear of the vengeful god runs so deep in some cultures that it will take hundreds of years to erase it, and replace it with the opposite emotion and response. The gods got themselves into the perfect position of power and control over their primitive creation. We were given clear instructions as the new slave species: do not question, do as you are told, have blind faith in your maker, because if you question or disobey, you will be punished. And as we have seen in the very graphic quiz, the punishment was swift and severe.

The quiz that follows points unquestionably to a violent gene passed onto us by our maker. It smacks of an obsessive human characteristic that is predisposed to divide and conquer through intimidation, violence, brutality, and fear. Where is the God of love, the God who asks us to love our neighbor, and to love thy enemy, and to turn the other cheek, and to forgive them for they do not know what they are doing? Prepare yourself for a spine-chilling experience. It is truly unbelievable when presented in this format. I, for one, cannot accept the delusional ramblings of a handful of men from the past, when they justify their horrific actions in the name of god. This is not my God, this is not the God who in a moment of infinite creativity, gave birth to the universe and filled it with an infinite number of souls to roam the width and breadth of the creation. There is so little we know about the spiritual realm, but there will come a day when we will evolve to the point where our genetic makeup starts to open up the portals of our mind to the greater spiritual world, to which we have been denied access, mainly due to our incomplete genome.

So if you are still not convinced that we had a vengeful, manipulative creator here on Earth in some kind of advanced human form, here are a few more extracts from the Old Testament to send shivers up your spine. Once again this food for thought is provided by the Landover Baptist Church.

⁝⁾ Second Quiz: "The Love of God"

Objective: Please indicate how many people our loving God brutally slaughtered in each of the following settings:

I. How many people did God kill in one day for having premarital sex?
   A. None. God doesn't kill people for such an unfortunate error in judgment.
   B. 23,000.
   C. God once killed a rapist for having premarital sex but no one else.
   D. None of the above.

2. After God brought the Israelites out of Egypt, how many of their own people did they kill, at God's behest, for declining to give God His due?
   A. None. God would not order His people to kill each other.
   B. 10. The number of people who chose to follow Satan.
   C. 3,000 spouses and siblings in a single day.
   D. Just two dozen total over two weeks.

3. How many Israelites did God kill to punish David for counting them?
   A. None. How could counting people be a sin? The census bureau does this every ten years.
   B. The difference between the number he counted and the actual number of people.
   C. All the people who were not counted.
   D. 70,000 people through pestilence.

4. How many people did God slaughter in a plague because they had the audacity to question the judgment of Moses and Aaron?
   A. None. God would not kill people simply for questioning the judgment of mortals.
   B. 14,700 (plus 250 He burned to death with fire).
   C. Only two people who tried to harm Moses and Aaron.
   D. A plague occurred but no one was killed.

5. How many Israelites did God slaughter in a plague for whoring around?
   A. None. God would not kill people just for sinning.
   B. 24,000.
   C. One or two.
   D. A plague is a natural phenomenon, not brought about by God.

6. How many members of other races and tribes did the Lord deliver to be slaughtered by Israel because he favored the Israelites and was prejudiced against other tribes?
   A. None. The Lord doesn't play favorites.
   B. 10,000 Canaanites and Perizzites.
   C. 10,000 Moabites.
   D. B and C, to name but a few of the tribes the Lord delivered for slaughter.

7. How many people did God kill in Sodom and Gomorrah for engaging in homosexual acts?
    A. None. God loves all his children, including the gay ones.
    B. Just the ones who engaged in acts of anal penetration.
    C. Every single living thing in the communities.
    D. Just those who actually practiced sodomy.

8. How many Assyrians did God kill after their king and his servants made fun of God?
    A. None. God is not so fickle He would kill people just for being disrespectful.
    B. Just the blasphemous king and his servants.
    C. 185,000.
    D. None of the above.

9. How many Israelites did God threaten to kill when the tribe abandoned Him?
    A. None. Killing is not God's way.
    B. All of the heads of household and no one else.
    C. Just those who abandoned Him.
    D. 90% of the population of each community.

10. At one time, when God became particularly disgusted with the sin of man, how many beings did He kill?
    A. None. Sin is inherent in humans. God wouldn't kill people for an inclination he instilled in them.
    B. All those who committed repeated violations of the Ten Commandments.
    C. Only those who engaged in the most egregious acts imaginable.
    D. Every living thing (children and unborn children included) on the face of the Earth (except those few residing in an ark).

⸮ Answers to the "The Love of God" Quiz:

1. **How many people did God kill in one day for having premarital sex?**
Correct Answer: **B.** (23,000) "Neither let us commit fornication, as some of them committed, and fell in one day three and twenty thousand." (1 Corinthians 10:8)

2. **After God brought the Israelites out of Egypt, how many of their own people did they kill, at God's behest, for declining to give God His due?**

Correct Answer: **C.** (3,000 spouses and siblings in a single day) "Then Moses stood in the gate of the camp, and said, 'Who is on the Lord's side? Let him come unto me.' And all the sons of Levi gathered themselves together unto him. And he said unto them, 'Thus saith the Lord God of Israel, Put every man his sword by his side, and go in and out from gate to gate throughout the camp, and slay every man his brother, and every man his companion, and every man his neighbor.' And the children of Levi did according to the word of Moses: and there fell of the people that day about three thousand men." (Exodus 32:26–28)

3. **How many Israelites did God kill to punish David for counting them?**

Correct Answer: **D.** (70,000 people through pestilence) "And Satan stood up against Israel, and provoked David to number Israel. And David said to Joab and to the rulers of the people, 'Go, number Israel from Beersheba even to Dan; and bring the number of them to me, that I may know it.' . . . And God was displeased with this thing; therefore he smote Israel . . . So the Lord sent pestilence upon Israel: and there fell of Israel seventy thousand men." (1 Chronicles 21:1–14)

4. **How many people did God slaughter in a plague because they had the audacity to question the judgment of Moses and Aaron?**

Correct Answer: **B.** (14,700, plus 250 He burned to death with fire) "And the Lord spake unto Moses, saying, 'Get you up from among this congregation, that I may consume them as in a moment.' And they fell upon their faces . . . and, behold, the plague was begun among the people . . . Now they that died in the plague were fourteen thousand and seven hundred, beside them that died about the matter of Korah" (Numbers 16:44–49). "And there came out a fire from the Lord, and consumed the two hundred and fifty men that offered incense." (Numbers 16:35)

5. **How many Israelites did God slaughter in a plague for whoring around?**

Correct Answer: **B.** (24,000) "And Israel abode in Shittim, and the people began to commit whoredom with the daughters of Moab. And they called the people unto the sacrifices of their gods: and the people did eat, and bowed down to their gods. And Israel joined himself unto Baalpeor: and the anger of the Lord was kindled against Israel . . . And those that died in the plague were twenty and four thousand." (Numbers 25:1–9)

6. **How many members of other races and tribes did the Lord deliver to be slaughtered by Israel because he favored the Israelites and was prejudiced against other tribes?**

   Correct Answer: **D.** (10,000 Canaanites and Perizzites and 10,000 Moabites to name a few) "And Judah went up; and the Lord delivered the Canaanites and the Perizzites into their hand: and they slew of them in Bezek ten thousand men" (Judges 1:4). "And he said unto them, 'Follow after me: for the Lord hath delivered your enemies the Moabites into your hand.' And they went down after him, and took the fords of Jordan toward Moab, and suffered not a man to pass over. And they slew of Moab at that time about ten thousand men, all lusty, and all men of valour; and there escaped not a man." (Judges 3:28–29)

7. **How many people did God kill in Sodom and Gomorrah for engaging in homosexual acts?**

   Correct answer: **C.** (Every single living thing in the communities) "Then the Lord rained upon Sodom and upon Gomorrah brimstone and fire from the Lord out of heaven; and he overthrew those cities, and all the plain, and all the inhabitants of the cities, and that which grew upon the ground." (Genesis 19:24–25)

8. **How many Assyrians did God kill after their king and his servants made fun of God?**

   Correct Answer: **C.** (185,000) "And it came to pass, when king Hezekiah heard it, that he rent his clothes, and covered himself with sackcloth, and went into the house of the Lord . . . And Isaiah said unto them, 'Thus shall ye say unto your master, Thus saith the Lord, Be not afraid of the words that thou hast heard, wherewith the servants of the king of Assyria have blasphemed me' . . . Then the angel of the Lord went forth, and smote in the camp of the Assyrians a hundred and fourscore and five thousand: and when they arose early in the morning, behold, they were all dead corpses." (Isaiah 37:1–36)

9. **How many Israelites did God threaten to kill when the tribe abandoned Him?**

   Correct Answer: **D.** (90 percent of the population of each community) "Hear ye this word which I take up against you, even a lamentation, O house of Israel. The virgin of Israel is fallen; she shall no more rise: she is forsaken upon her land; there is none to raise her up. For thus saith the Lord God; the City that went out by a thousand shall leave an hundred, and that which went forth by an hundred shall have ten, to the house of Israel." (Amos 5:1–3)

10. **When God became particularly disgusted with the sin of man, how many beings did He kill?**

Correct Answer: **D.** (Every living thing [children and unborn children included] on the face of the earth (except those few residing on an ark) "And God saw that the wickedness of man was great in the earth, and that every imagination of the thoughts of his heart was only evil continually. And it repented the Lord that he had made man on the earth, and it grieved him at his heart. And the Lord said, I will destroy man whom I have created from the face of the earth; both man, and beast, and the creeping thing, and the fowls of the air; for it repenteth me that I have made them . . . And all flesh died that moved upon the earth, both of fowl, and of cattle, and of beast, and of every creeping thing that creepeth upon the earth, and every man: all in whose nostrils was the breath of life, of all that was in the dry land, died." (Genesis 6:5–7:22)

As wild as my theories may sound to you about advanced humanoids creating a slave species on Earth to perform the hard labor in mines and other areas, it is not nearly as shocking as the following biblical quiz. It goes a long way in supporting my theories about the true identity of "god" our maker, depicting his obsession with taking control of the new species, which was proving to be a handful. After all, they could not allow the slave species to get out of hand, when they were created as slaves. They were not here to have a good time. After this bloodthirsty display of ancient times, we can take a look at how closely it compares to the military activity we are capable of today, showing that we, the slave species, have evolved much closer to the levels of our makers, the Anunnaki. Unfortunately our evolution has not always been for the better. Please hold onto your hat, the following is truly hard to believe.

⸮ Third Quiz: "God's Favorite Ways to Kill"

Once again this quiz was posed by the Landover Baptist Church, providing us with all the evidence we need to show that the so-called god of man was no more than a power-hungry and brutal humanoid with advanced powers. Brace yourself for some spine-chilling biblical facts:

I. Which of the following are among God's methods of punishing those who break His commandments?

Fig. 11.4. The sacrifice of Isaac. This famous painting by Rembrandt van Rijn depicts the Old Testament story that epitomizes the brutality of the biblical god. It was this very god who ordered Abraham to take his son Isaac to a distant mountain, far from the peering eyes of others, and murder him in cold blood. All this, simply to determine if Abraham—essentially god's first "snitch"—could be trusted to obey god's orders.

A. He strikes them with plagues, burning fevers that consume the eyes, pestilence, consumption, blasting, the sword, and even mildew.

B. He strikes them with hemorrhoids, scabs, itching, madness and blindness.

C. He sends wild bears to devour their children.

D. Any of the above, depending on His mood.

2. How does God handle people who make Him jealous by having a religion different than ours?

A. Trick question. God is not vain.

B. He has them burned with fire, shot with arrows, bitten by beasts, poisoned by serpents, stabbed with swords, and dashed to pieces with rods of iron—man, woman, and child including infants, the aged, and virgins.

C. He gently nudges them in the right direction.

D. None of the above.

3. How does God kill whiners?

A. What? God wouldn't kill people just for complaining.

B. Fire.

C. Earthquakes.

D. Terminal illness.

4. How does God prefer to torture those who somehow become enemies of His chosen people?

A. He breaks their bones and pierces them with arrows.

B. He sends hornets to kill them.

C. He has them eat their own flesh and drink their own blood.

D. All of the above.

5. How does God kill those who vacation in Egypt?

A. Sword.

B. Famine.

C. Pestilence.

D. Take your pick.

6. How did God express his hatred toward people living in metropolitan Babylon?

A. By destroying their livestock.

B. By making the women barren.

C. By turning the men into drag queens.

D. All of the above.

7. When a community's sins really make God mad, how does God find comfort?

   A. By killing a third of the people with plagues and famine.

   B. By killing a third of the people with local warfare.

   C. By killing a third of the people with international warfare.

   D. All of the above.

8. Whom does God slaughter when He gets jealous because a community is worshipping someone else?

   A. The women.

   B. The babies.

   C. The unborn infants.

   D. All of the above.

9. How does God punish promiscuous folks, like men who have sex with both their wives and mothers-in-law and daughters of priests who sleep around?

   A. He has their genitals mutilated so they can sin no more.

   B. He ensures their misdeeds results in unwanted pregnancy or venereal disease.

   C. He has them burned with fire.

   D. Any of the above.

10. In Jesus' time, how did the Trinity deal with nonbelievers?

   A. They had them eaten by worms.

   B. They struck one blind.

   C. A and B.

   D. None of the above.

⁝) Answers to "God's Favorite Ways to Kill" Quiz:

1. **Which of the following are among God's methods of punishing those who break His commandments?**

   Correct Answer: **D.** (Any of the above, depending on His mood.) "But if ye will not hearken unto me, and will not do all these commandments . . . I also will do this unto you; I will even appoint over you terror, consumption, and the burning ague, that shall consume the eyes . . . I will also send wild beasts among you, which shall rob you of your children, and destroy your cattle." (Leviticus 26:14–22.) "If thou wilt not hearken unto the voice of the Lord thy God, to observe to do all his commandments . . . The Lord will smite thee with a consumption, and with a fever, and with an inflammation, and with an extreme burning, and with the sword, and with blasting, and with mildew; and they shall pursue thee until thou perish . . . The Lord will smite thee with the botch of Egypt, and with the emerods, and with the scab, and with the itch, whereof thou canst not be healed. The Lord shall smite thee with madness, and blindness, and astonishment of heart." (Deuteronomy 28:15–28)

2. **How does God handle people who make Him jealous by having a religion different than ours?**
Correct Answer: **B.** "They sacrificed unto devils, not to God; to gods whom they knew not, to new gods that came newly up . . . And he said . . . They have moved me to jealousy with that which is not God; they have provoked me to anger . . . For a fire is kindled in mine anger, and shall burn unto the lowest hell, and shall consume the earth with her increase, and set on fire the foundations of the mountains. I will heap mischiefs upon them; I will spend mine arrows upon them. They shall be burnt with hunger, and devoured with burning heat, and with bitter destruction: I will also send the teeth of beasts upon them, with the poison of serpents of the dust. The sword without, and terror within, shall destroy both the young man and the virgin, the suckling also with the man of grey hairs." (Deuteronomy 32:17–25.) "Ask of me, and I shall give thee the heathen for thine inheritance, and the uttermost parts of the earth for thy possession. Thou shalt break them with a rod of iron; thou shalt dash them in pieces like a potter's vessel." (Psalms 2:8)

3. **How does God kill whiners?**
Correct Answer: **B.** (Fire.) "And when the people complained, it displeased the Lord: and the Lord heard it; and his anger was kindled; and the fire of the Lord burnt among them, and consumed them that were in the uttermost parts of the camp." (Numbers 11:1)

4. **How does God prefer to torture those who somehow become enemies of His chosen people?**
Correct Answer: **D.** (All of the above.) "God brought him forth out of Egypt; he hath as it were the strength of a unicorn: he shall eat up the nations of his enemies, and shall break their bones, and pierce them through with his arrows." (Numbers 24:8) "Moreover the Lord

thy God will send the hornet among them, until they that are left, and hide themselves from thee, be destroyed. Thou shalt not be affrighted at them: for the Lord thy God is among you, a mighty God and terrible." (Deuteronomy 7:20–21) "And I will feed them that oppress thee with their own flesh; and they shall be drunken with their own blood." (Isaiah 49:26)

5. **How does God kill those who vacation in Egypt?**
Correct Answer: **D.** (Take your pick.) "And now therefore hear the word of the Lord, ye remnant of Judah; Thus saith the Lord of hosts, the God of Israel; If you wholly set your faces to enter into Egypt, and go to sojourn there; Then it shall come to pass, that the sword, which ye feared, shall overtake you there in the land of Egypt, and the famine, whereof ye were afraid, shall follow close after you there in Egypt; and there ye shall die. So shall it be with all the men that set their faces to go into Egypt to sojourn there; they shall die by the sword, by the famine, and by the pestilence: and none of them shall remain or escape from the evil that I will bring upon them." (Jeremiah 42:15–17)

6. **How did God express his hatred toward people living in metropolitan Babylon?**
Correct Answer: **C.** (By turning the men into drag queens.) "How is Babylon become a desolation among the nations. A sword is upon their horses, and upon their chariots, and upon all the mingled people that are in the midst of her; and they shall become as women: and sword is upon her treasures; and they shall be robbed." (Jeremiah 50:23, 37)

7. **When a community's sins really make God mad, how does God find comfort?**
Correct Answer: **D.** (All of the above.) "Wherefore, as I live, saith the Lord God; Surely, because thou hast defiled my sanctuary with all thy detestable things, and with all thine abominations, therefore will I also diminish thee; neither shall mine eye spare, neither will I have any pity. A third part of thee shall die with the pestilence, and with famine shall they be consumed in the midst of thee: and a third part shall fall by the sword round about thee; and I will scatter a third part into all the winds, and I will draw out a sword after them. Thus shall mine anger be accomplished, and I will cause my fury to rest upon them, and I will be comforted." (Ezekiel 5:11–13)

8. **Whom does God slaughter when He gets jealous because a community is worshipping someone else?**
Correct Answer: **D.** (All of the above.) "Samaria shall become desolate; for

she hath rebelled against her God: they shall fall by the sword: their infants shall be dashed in pieces, and their women with child shall be ripped up." (Hosea 13:16)

9. **How does God punish promiscuous folks, like men who have sex with both their wives and mothers-in-law and daughters of priests who sleep around?**

Correct Answer: **C.** (He has them burned with fire.) "And if a man take a wife and her mother, it is wickedness: they shall be burnt with fire, both he and they; that there be no wickedness among you." (Leviticus 20:14) "And the daughter of any priest, if she profane herself by playing the whore, she profaneth her father: she shall be burnt with fire." (Leviticus 21:9)

10. **In Jesus' time, how did the Trinity deal with nonbelievers?**

Correct Answer: **C.** (A and B) "And immediately the angel of the Lord smote him, because he gave not God the glory: and he was eaten of worms, and gave up the ghost." (Acts 12:23) "But Elymas the sorcerer (for so is his name by interpretation) withstood them, seeking to turn away the deputy from the faith. Then Saul (who also is called Paul), filled with the Holy Ghost, set his eyes on him. And said, 'O full of all subtilty and all mischief, thou child of the devil, thou enemy of all righteousness, wilt thou not cease to pervert the right ways of the Lord? And now, behold, the hand of the Lord is upon thee, and thou shalt be blind, not seeing the sun for a season.' And immediately there fell on him a mist and a darkness; and he went about seeking some to lead him by the hand." (Acts 13:8–11)

And if you think I am done trying to prove a point, you are mistaken. When I started uncovering the brutality in the Bible and the way it has been passed down the generations and used as a tool of oppression, fear, and punishment, I was so shocked I could not sleep for weeks. We have to separate ourselves from these barbaric acts of self-righteous bigots from days gone by, who have hijacked the true spirit and meaning of God, and by so doing imprisoned an entire planet for millennia. We must separate the true spirit of God from the whims and needs of the advanced beings who settled on Earth and planted the seeds of a violent society among humans, into which we have evolved so comfortably, seemingly oblivious of our origins and true purpose. So here is some more food for thought especially for those who are still not convinced. From the Landover Baptist Church, this quiz also contains actual quotes from the Bible. You will notice that almost any commandment can be broken, if it somehow benefits god.

⁙ Fourth Quiz: "God's License to Sin"

1. Murder is a sin, unless your victim is:
   A. A homosexual.
   B. Spouses of a mixed marriage.
   C. Someone who urinates on partitions.
   D. Any of the above.

2. Intolerance toward the handicapped is a sin, unless the discrimination takes the form of:
   A. Not allowing them to approach the altar of the Lord.
   B. Expelling them from the community.
   C. Barring men with damaged testicles from entering the church.
   D. Any of the above.

3. Cannibalism is a sin, unless you eat:
   A. Trick question. Cannibalism is always a sin.
   B. Your children, infants, friends, and self when God destroys everything else so these are all that are left to eat.
   C. A person who is already dead, if you're very hungry.
   D. B or C.

4. Murdering your own child is a sin, unless your child:
   A. Spoke to you with curse words.
   B. Encouraged you to join a faith other than Christianity.
   C. Is killed in the name of Jesus.
   D. Any of the above.

5. Self-mutilation is a sin, unless:
   A. You remove a body part that has engaged or is about to engage in sin, such as slicing off your genitals to remain a virgin.
   B. You don a tattoo in the shape of a religious symbol, such as a crucifix or angel.
   C. You take action that results in no permanent body changes, such as a man shaving his head or trimming his beard.
   D. Any of the above.

6. Rape is a sin subject to the greatest of punishments, but is easily overlooked and forgiven if the victim is:

A. A captive in war.

B. A slave girl.

C. Someone you're willing to marry with a father you're willing to pay.

D. Any of the above.

7. Savagely beating another person with a weapon is a sin, unless you stop just before your victim dies, and the victim is:

A. One of your domestic help.

B. Your own child.

C. Either of the above.

D. None of the above.

8. Abandoning your family is a sin, unless:

A. It is a family you have out-of-wedlock.

B. It is a family originated by a mixed marriage (e.g., your wife is a foreigner).

C. You abandon them so you can spend more time praising Jesus.

D. Any of the above.

9. Homosexuality is a sin, unless:

A. You're in a permanent, monogamous relationship with your boyfriend.

B. You're one of God's favorite children, and you have many wives in addition to your boyfriend.

C. You're a woman making love to another woman.

D. Any of the above.

10. Killing someone is a sin unless your victim is:

A. Any wiccan.

B. A stranger who has the nerve to approach you.

C. A virgin raped in the city.

D. Any of the above.

⁙ Answers to the "License to Sin" Bible Quiz

1. Murder is a sin, unless your victim is:

Correct Answer: **D.** (Any of the above.) "If a man also lie with mankind, as he lieth with a woman . . . they shall be put to death." (Leviticus 20:13) "One of the children of Israel came and brought unto his brethren a Midianitish woman . . . And when Phinehas . . . saw it, he rose up from among the congregation, and took a javelin in his hand . . . and thrust both of them through, the man of Israel, and the woman through her belly. So the plague was stayed from the children of Israel." (Numbers 25:6–8) "He slew all the house of Baasha, he left him not one that pisseth against a wall, neither of his kinsfolk, nor of his friends. Thus did Zimri destroy all the house of Baasha, according to the word of the Lord." (1 Kings 16:11–12)

2. **Intolerance toward the handicapped is a sin, unless the discrimination takes the form of:**
Correct Answer: **D.** (Any of the above.) "Whosoever he be of thy seed in their generations that hath any blemish, let him not approach to offer the bread of his God. For whatsoever man he be that hath a blemish, he shall not approach: a blind man, or a lame, or he that hath a flat nose, or any thing superfluous, Or a man that is broken footed, or broken handed, Or crookbackt, or a dwarf, or that hath a blemish in his eye, or be scurvy, or scabbed, or hath his stones broken; No man that hath a blemish of the seed of Aaron the priest shall come nigh to offer the offerings of the Lord made by fire: he hath a blemish; he shall not come nigh to offer the bread of his God." (Leviticus 21:17–21) "And the Lord spake unto Moses, saying, 'Command the children of Israel, that they put out of the camp every leper, and everyone that hath an issue, and whosoever is defiled by the dead: Both male and female shall ye put out, without the camp shall ye put them; that they defile not their camps, in the midst whereof I dwell.'" (Numbers 5:1– 3.) "He that is wounded in the stones, or hath his privy member cut off, shall not enter into the congregation of the Lord." (Deuteronomy 23:1)

3. **Cannibalism is a sin, unless you eat:**
Correct Answer: **B.** (Your children, infants, friends and self when God destroys everything else so these are all that are left to eat.) "And I will cause them to eat the flesh of their sons and the flesh of their daughters, and they shall eat every one the flesh of his friend in the siege and strait- ness." (Jeremiah 19:9) "And toward her young one that cometh out from between her feet, and toward her children which she shall bear: for she shall eat them for want of all things secretly in the siege and the straitness." (Deuteronomy 28:57) "Through the wrath of the Lord of hosts is the land darkened, and the people shall be as the fuel of the fire: no man shall spare his brother. And he shall snatch on the right hand, and be hungry; and he shall eat on the left hand, and they shall not be satisfied: they shall

eat every man the flesh of his own arm." (Isaiah 9:19–20) "Whosoever toucheth the dead body of any man that is dead, and purifieth not himself, defileth the tabernacle of the Lord; and that soul shall be cut off from Israel: because the water of separation was not sprinkled upon him, he shall be unclean; his uncleanness is yet upon him." (Numbers 19:13)

4. **Murdering your own child is a sin, unless your child:**
   Correct Answer: **D.** (Any of the above.) "And he that curseth his father, or his mother, shall surely be put to death." (Exodus 21:17) "If thy brother, the son of thy mother, or thy son, or thy daughter, or the wife of thy bosom, or thy friend, which is as thine own soul, entice thee secretly, saying, 'Let us go and serve other gods' . . . thou shalt surely kill him; thine hand shall be first upon him to put him to death, and afterwards the hand of all the people. And thou shalt stone him with stones, that he die." (Deuteronomy 13:6–10) "And the brother shall deliver up the brother to death, and the father the child: and the children shall rise up against their parents, and cause them to be put to death. And ye shall be hated of all men for my name's sake: but he that endureth to the end shall be saved." (Matthew 10:21–22)

5. **Self-mutilation is a sin, unless:**
   Correct Answer: **A.** (You remove a body part that has engaged or is about to engage in sin, such as slicing off your genitals to remain a virgin.) "And if thy right eye offend thee, pluck it out, and cast it from thee: for it is profitable for thee that one of thy members should perish, and not that thy whole body should be cast into hell. And if thy right hand offend thee, cut it off, and cast it from thee." (Matthew 5:29–30; see also Matthew 18:8–9; Mark 9:43–48.) "For there are some eunuchs, which were so born from their mother's womb: and there are some eunuchs, which were made eunuchs of men: and there be eunuchs which have made themselves eunuchs for the kingdom of heaven's sake. He that is able to receive it, let him receive it." (Matthew 19:12) "And no man could learn that song but the hundred and forty and four thousand, which were redeemed from the earth. These are they which were not defiled with women; for they are virgins. These are they which follow the Lamb whithersoever he goeth. These were redeemed from among men, being the first fruits unto God and to the Lamb." (Revelation 14:3–4.) "They shall not make baldness upon their head, neither shall they shave off the corner of their beard, nor make any cuttings in their flesh." (Leviticus 21:5)

6. **Rape is a sin subject to the greatest of punishments, but is easily overlooked and forgiven if the victim is:**

Correct Answer: **D.** (Any of the above.) "And when the Lord thy God hath delivered [a city] into thine hands, thou shalt smite every male thereof with the edge of the sword: But the women . . . shalt thou take unto thyself." (Deuteronomy 20:13–14) "And whosoever lieth carnally with a woman, that is a bondmaid, betrothed to an husband, and not at all redeemed, nor freedom given her; she shall be scourged; they shall not be put to death, because she was not free. And he shall bring his trespass offering unto the Lord, unto the door of the tabernacle of the congregation, even a ram for a trespass offering. And the priest shall make atonement for him." (Leviticus 19:20–22) "If a man find a damsel that is a virgin, which is not betrothed, and lay hold on her, and lie with her, and they be found: Then the man that lay with her shall give unto the damsel's father fifty shekels of silver, and she shall be his wife." (Deuteronomy 22:28–29)

7. **Savagely beating another person with a weapon is a sin, unless you stop just before your victim dies and the victim is:**
   Correct Answer: **C.** (Either of the above.) "And if a man smite his servant, or his maid, with a rod, and he die under his hand; he shall be surely punished. Notwithstanding, if he continue a day or two, he shall not be punished: for he is his money." (Exodus 21:20–21) "Withhold not correction from the child: for if thou beatest him with the rod, he shall not die. Thou shalt beat him with the rod, and shalt deliver his soul from hell." (Proverbs 23:13–14)

8. **Abandoning your family is a sin, unless:**
   Correct Answer: **D.** (Any of the above.) "Wherefore she said unto Abraham, 'Cast out this bondwoman and her son: for the son of this bondwoman shall not be heir with my son, even with Isaac' . . . And God said unto Abraham. . . 'harken unto her voice; for in Isaac shall thy seed be called' . . . And Abraham rose up early in the morning, and took bread, and a bottle of water, and gave it unto Hagar, putting it on her shoulder, and the child, and sent her away: and she departed, and wandered in the wilderness of Beersheba." (Genesis 21:10–14.) "Ye shall not give your daughters unto their sons, nor take their daughters unto your sons, or for yourselves. Did not Solomon king of Israel sin by these things? Yet among many nations was there no king like him, who was beloved of his God, and God made him king over all Israel: nevertheless even him did outlandish women cause to sin. Shall we then hearken unto you to do all this great evil, to transgress against our God in marrying strange wives? . . . Thus cleansed I them from all strangers, and appointed the wards of the priests and the Levites, every

one in his business." (Nehemiah 13:25–30) "If any man come to me, and hate not his father, and mother, and wife, and children, and brethren, and sisters, yea, and his own life also, he cannot be my disciple." (Luke 14:26; see also Mark 10:29–30; Luke 18:29–30.)

9. **Homosexuality is a sin, unless:**

Correct Answer: **B.** (You're one of God's favorite children, and you have many wives in addition to your boyfriend.) "Thou shalt not lie with mankind, as with womankind: it is abomination." (Leviticus 18:22) "[David said] I am distressed for thee, my brother Jonathan: very pleasant hast thou been unto me: thy love to me was wonderful, passing the love of women." (2 Samuel 1:26) "And as soon as the lad was gone, David arose out of a place toward the south, and fell on his face to the ground, and bowed himself three times; and they [Jonathan and David] kissed one another, and wept one with another, until David exceeded." (1 Samuel 20:41) "And [David] had seven hundred wives, princesses, and three hundred concubines: and his wives turned away his heart." (1 Kings 11:3) "For this cause God gave them up into vile affections: for even their women did change the natural use into that which is against nature: And likewise also the men, leaving the natural use of the woman, burned in their lust one toward another; men with men working that which is unseemly, and receiving in themselves that recompense of their error which was meet." (Romans 1:26–27)

10. **Killing someone is a sin unless your victim is:**

Correct Answer: **D.** (Any of the above.) "Thou shalt not suffer a witch to live." (Exodus 22:18) "But those that encamp before the tabernacle toward the east, even before the tabernacle of the congregation eastward, shall be Moses, and Aaron and his sons, keeping the charge of the sanctuary for the charge of the children of Israel; and the stranger that cometh nigh shall be put to death." (Numbers 3:38) "If a damsel that is a virgin be betrothed unto an husband, and a man find her in the city, and lie with her; Then ye shall bring them both out unto the gate of that city, and ye shall stone them with stones that they die; the damsel, because she cried not, being in the city; and the man, because he hath humbled his neighbour's wife: so thou shalt put away evil from among you." (Deuteronomy 22:23–24)

As far as I am concerned this is all the proof we need to support the theory that things were not what we would have liked them to be all those years ago. There were some weird things going on in the Near East. If God said that we are all born in sin . . . all this graphic killing in the name of God seems a little arrogant, since we were told by Jesus, "He who is without sin, let them cast the first stone," and we are also supposed to "turn the other cheek." What is going on here? Which part of the Bible should we actually subscribe to? Not one part I say. It has become clear that this was not a book inspired by the divine God of the universe, but a sadistic, manipulative advanced being, obsessed with keeping humankind under control.

This may be a good time to put this book down, make a cup of tea, and try to absorb all this stuff. It may just take you some time, but hopefully you will eventually start to distinguish god from the God.

During our violent path to this point in time, we have fought endless wars and in the process developed some truly remarkable technology. The research and development that has gone into military weaponry, naval equipment, and aeronautical science has been astonishing. In the past 100 years we have created weapons of such awesome power that they could destroy the people of the world in a matter of hours if they were deployed. These deadly weapons come in a variety of forms, but the most feared are WMDs (weapons of mass destruction). You may remember hearing a great deal about these during the Bush-Iraq episode. These WMDs can be nuclear—atomic, hydrogen, neutron and other varieties; they can also be biological—anthrax, botulism, smallpox, mustard gas, the list is endless. What they have in common is that they can kill millions of people in a matter of seconds. While the bombs are usually dropped from the sky on their designated recipients with pinpoint accuracy, their delivery may vary. It may even be guided by a laser. The biological kind is more versatile. They can be delivered in a bomb, distributed by the wind, in viruses and other microscopic pathogens that develop into a plague, in the drinking water, in food, medication and other ingenious carriers. While the bombs explode with a mighty glare of the sun, obliterating everything in their path for hundreds of kilometers, biological weapons sneak up on their victims unexpectedly. You can die quickly, in a few seconds or you can suffer for days maybe even years before you eventually die a horrible painful death that seems to have no cure. The most impressive aspect of biological weapons is that there is no antidote for most of them. Just imagine the kinds of human minds who invented these as possible solutions to a problem, or as one of the options to choose from when planning a conflict situation. The long-term benefits of both kinds of weapons are legendary. It is now known that many of the world's governments have experimented on humans with biological substances for over sixty years, in the pursuit of WMDs development. All the global powers who were jostling for supremacy were involved in some form of BW (biological warfare) experimentation.

In their book entitled *Plague Wars,* Tom Mangold and Jeff Goldberg give us a gruesome overview of the history of biological warfare. And while they subtly draw our attention to some quotes from the Bible that may resemble biological warfare, they may not have been aware how close to the truth they were. The Germans were not the only ones who desecrated human rights in this regard. The Americans performed tests on their own soldiers in Korea and in Vietnam, the Russians did similar things, but it is the Japanese who possibly have the most horrific record of keeping prisoners alive for months while performing unspeakable tests on them. Dr. Ishii was a Japanese monster in charge of a huge army of so-called doctors who performed thousands of gruesome experiments on prisoners during the 1930s. They had built several BW research facilities throughout Manchuria, turning the whole region into a giant BW laboratory. About 24 kilometers south of Harbin was a complex of 76 buildings with labs, dormitories, greenhouses, barns for animals, and "special prisons for human test subjects." They would inject the people with every unthinkable toxin to study its effect. They would let them stay alive, sometimes tied to their beds in excruciating pain, to witness the developing effects of these toxins. They would amputate limbs and disembowel their victims who would scream in agony, sometimes only dying much later. All in the name of science.

In 1995 *The New York Times* ran an article that was a discussion between their correspondent, Nicholas D. Kristof, and an aging Japanese soldier who was present at one of these dissections. A 30-year-old farmer was taken captive, tied to a bed, and dissected without an anaesthetic. This is what was written:

The fellow knew that it was over for him and so he did not struggle when they led him into the room and tied him down. But when I picked up the scalpel, that's when he began screaming. I cut him open from the chest to the stomach and he screamed terribly and his face was all twisted in agony. He made this unimaginable sound, he was screaming so horribly. But then he finally stopped. This was all in a day's work for the surgeons.

This kind of behavior can only be explained by our malfunctioning DNA. No other creature, other than the human, is capable of such horrific acts against their own kind. But we must have inherited this DNA from somewhere? Our fascination with biological weapons and man's suffering associated with it goes back thousands of years. The Sumerian tablets carry gruesome details of how people perished from the "evil wind" which was caused by the gods' deadly weapons.

The weapons that we are exposed to in science fiction movies amaze us, and yet, somewhere deep inside we believe that it could be possible. Maybe not today, but sometime in the future. Is the future already here? Do such incredible weapons exist? How much do we really know about the latest technologies used by weapons manufacturers? There are many who claim that lasers and other new precision technology weapons exist that work with photons, ions, electrons, and ultra-high frequency radiation. Even ultra-low frequency sound waves are now well developed as weapons and most likely well guarded as national secrets by their respective governments.

So, where am I going with this? It is uncanny how similar the effects of modern weapons are when described verbally to the many descriptions of annihilation and destruction referred to in the Bible. The similarities are too close for comfort. If we were created by a more advanced humanlike species with a knowledge of genetics some 200,000 years ago, it must surely mean that they would also have had the knowledge of the kind of weapons that we have developed on Earth since then, as we evolved into our current state of consciousness. And if we compare the wars and conflicts that are started on Earth today, often as a result of minor misunderstandings or even a conscious demonstration of power by one leader over another, it is very easy to reason that the advanced gods of prehistory used such technology to control and punish their creation in an attempt to keep them fearful and obedient. There are many passages in the Bible that clearly point to such violent activity, which could only have been delivered by WMDs. Many of these biblical situations are virtually identical to situations described in the Sumerian tablets in which the gods were either leading, guiding, observing, engaging, rewarding or punishing the people.

A similar story, which we will expand on later, was depicted in the Bible surrounding the destruction of Sodom and Gomorrah. All these violent acts were supposedly performed by god against the sinful people on Earth. They seem to have been attacked with biological weapons and possibly even nuclear weapons. But if you think that such references are restricted to the ancient biblical days, you are mistaken. The presence of the god of vengeance is reported in great detail by William Bramley in his book *Gods of Eden*. Between 1347 and 1350, the whole of Europe and surrounding lands were struck down by the Black Death that arrived from Asia, supposedly carried by the fleas transferring it from rats to humans. In those days little was known about the disease, but today we know there were actually two kinds: bubonic plague and pneumonic plague.

Today we have a bit more scientific information about these diseases and how they spread. The plagues would return to Europe every ten to twenty years, killing many millions until the 1700s. It is estimated that over 100 million people died from the plague during that period. The people of the world had never experienced anything like this before. Or so they thought. It was like a plague from biblical days: swelling of the lymph nodes, which were called *buboes,* vomiting and fever, resulting in death within two days; or, shivering, rapid breathing, coughing up blood, high fever, and death in three to four days. The strange circumstances surrounding the breakout of this disease has puzzled scientists for years. The required contact with rats has caused great confusion, as the disease would strike isolated communities miles apart, while sparing others. There would be very little rodent activity and it would normally happen during summer in areas that were not necessarily heavily overpopulated. According to Bramley, the outbreaks would usually occur after the appearance of a "foul smelling mist" that went hand in hand with "seeing unusually bright lights in the sky." These mists and lights were the most frequently reported events of those times, just before the plague suddenly descended on them. It seems that these "lights and mists" had more to do with the plagues that followed than the large numbers of rats. Bramley continues with some staggering information. One year before the first outbreak in Europe, a "column of fire" was reported over the Pope's palace in Avignon, France. Another report from that period talks about "a ball of fire" that was observed over Paris and remained visible to observers for some time.

Is it possible that the ancient gods of Sumer and Egypt, who flew around in their "sky chariots" and "boats of heaven" could still have been active as recently as the thirteenth century? There is growing evidence to support such a ridiculous idea, but historians call the ancient events "mythological" while the more recent ones were just "figments of people's imagination." How convenient. Once more our precious historians dismiss events that cannot be explained, only to replace them with a more popular version of their own truth, one that does not seem too ridiculous to the global populace. Is it possible that while the ancient Anunnaki gods were trying to keep humankind enslaved with religious dogma, they were also attempting to reduce the growing numbers of their slave species, which would allow them to exercise greater control over humans? It certainly seems as if such crazy ideas may pack a punch after all.

The people of those Dark Ages were extremely superstitious, and the church exercised immense control over what people did and what they thought and what they believed. Those were days of high comet activity, which is well documented, and comets were therefore also always associated with an impending plague of some sort. Between 1298 and 1314 there were seven large comets reported over Europe, but in those days the people would call every bright light in the sky a comet. In 1557, Conrad Lycosthenes published a book with one of the longest titles ever: *A Chronicle of Prodigies and Portents that have Occurred Beyond the*

Right Order, Operation and Working of Nature, in Both the Upper and Lower Regions of the Earth, from the Beginning of the World up to These Present Times.

This was a bestseller of its time that talks about a "comet" that was seen over Arabia in 1479. "A comet was seen in Arabia in the manner of a sharply pointed wooden beam." This description certainly does not sound like a comet at all. Today it would most likely be called a UFO. I have steered clear of UFO-talk in this book, rather asserting that we have much closer historical links to the gods of the ancient world, who were described as flying in "sky ships" and "boats of heaven." It does, however, seem that the Dark Ages of humankind were a period of high UFO activity, whether we like to accept it or not. Similar reports from Asia also described the death and destruction that followed unusual aerial phenomena. This is a report by one Asian historian, as found in Bramley's *The Gods of Eden:*

> They were confused, exaggerated, frightening, as reports from that quarter of the world so often are: descriptions of storms and earthquakes; of meteors and comets trailing noxious gasses that killed trees and destroyed the fertility of the land.

The outbreak of plague was usually preceded by this kind of aerial activity that could range from a few minutes before the horror affected humans, to as long as one year. Another report found in *The Gods of Eden* claims:

> In 1117, in January, a comet passed like a fiery arm from the North toward the Orient . . . a year later a light appeared more brilliant than the sun . . . followed by great cold, famine and plague of which one third of humanity is said to have perished.

This event refers to one-third of the population in that specific region and not necessarily the whole world. But to those people, it was the whole world. The link between comets and the plague continued. There were 26 comets reported between 1500 and 1543. A further 15 or 16 were observed between 1556 and 1597, while in 1618 another 9 comets were observed. Does this not strike you as being highly suspicious at all? When last did you see a comet? Even if you did see one recently, which is highly unlikely, since the last visible comet that passed Earth was comet Encke, in December 2003, was hardly visible to the naked eye. But these comets in the distant past were apparently seen by many, during the day as well as at night. They were not described as a distant fiery ball with a long tail, but described more as a bright light hovering for all to see.

Another report in the Bramley's *The Gods of Eden* came out of Vienna describing events in 1568: "When in sun and moonlight a beautiful rainbow and a fiery beam were seen hovering above the church of St. Stephanie . . . followed by a violent epidemic in Austria, Swabia, Augsberg, Wuertemberg, Nuremburg and other places . . . carrying off human beings and cattle."

Each time these comets appeared, the people would be struck down with the plague. In 1606, a comet caused the death of 37.000 in Prague, and 46,415 in the Netherlands. But the horror of the plague was not only restricted to attacks with some kind of biological substance from the sky.

Have you ever wondered where the classic image of Death being portrayed as a skeleton demon carrying a scythe actually originated? Other reports of "frightening human-like figures dressed in black" were also common sights shortly before the plague would strike. Appearing on the outskirts of towns and villages, these figures normally entered the fields of wheat or oats with some sort of spraying device, distributing what must have been infectious poisons on the crops. Bramley describes yet another such reported incident:

In Brandenburg there appeared in 1559 horrible men . . . fearful faces and long scythes with which they cut at the oats, so that the swish could be heard at a great distance, but the oats remained standing.

The appearance of such "men" was followed by an immediate outbreak of the plague in Brandenburg, for example. The so-called scythes must have been a spraying device of some sort, the kinds which we would spot a mile away on a modern farm today. I have personally spent days on my dad's farm spraying for larvae with a similar device. The reports did not stop there, more were reported from Hungary as pointed out by Bramley:

There appeared so many black riders . . . but who rapidly disappeared again . . . and thereupon a raging plague broke out in the neighbourhood.

William Bramley points out that "the scythe came to symbolise the act of Death mowing down people like stalks of grain." And these reports of the plague have been recorded from all over the world. In China in 1333: "after a terrible mist emitting a fearful stench and infecting the air." If you ever smelt a burst gas pipe you would be able to relate to the stench. Poisonous gas or deadly biological gaseous compounds do not smell pleasant. They generally also have a choking effect on the victims. The reports make it clear that the deadly plague did not spread from person to person, it afflicted everyone at the same time. How could it be the result of infected fleas on rats? This is a very dubious bit of disinformation, which begins to sound more and more as if the real facts have been withheld from us. Another event in China describes the situation as such: "During 1382 . . . the air grew putrid . . . the plague did not pass from one man to another, but everyone who was killed by it got it straight from the air."

I believe I've made my point. There are, however, many more examples, which would begin to sound repetitive. The biological warfare hostilities against humans that we witnessed in the twentieth century showed us the gruesome effects of such poisons. It seems that while these kind of events were taking place in the first 600 years of the previous millennium, we have 4,500-year-old Sumerian tablets describing similar atrocities brought upon humankind by the so-called mythological gods of ancient times. Even the Bible has many descriptions of plagues and pestilence being unleashed on the human race by the god of vengeance. What a wonderful thread it is that holds it all together. So who is this god of the Bible who has kept us so fearful for thousands of years? One thing is for sure, this god certainly puts his money where his mouth is, when he executes his violent threats against his "beloved" human creation. There can be no mistake in our conclusion that the god of the Bible is not the God we all hoped he was. But rather a powerful, anxious, advanced being, whose primitive worker or slave species has grown out of control on this planet. The advanced beings who the humans have come to worship as gods have mostly withdrawn from Earth, as the conditions began to turn against them and they lost control over the large numbers of humans being born. Their little experiment to create the Adamu was an initial success, but it turned out to be the Great Human Tragedy. So much so, that some 4,050 years ago some of the Anunnaki gods attempted to wipe out all of humankind, with an all-out nuclear attack on all their main settlements. These events are dramatically recorded in the Bible, Genesis 18:23–29, during the destruction of Sodom and Gomorrah.

> The sun had risen on the earth when Lot came to Zoar. Then the LORD rained on Sodom and Gomorrah sulphur and fire from the LORD out of heaven. And he overthrew those cities, and all the valley, and all the inhabitants of the cities, and what grew on the ground. But Lot's wife, behind him, looked back, and she became a pillar of salt. And Abraham went early in the morning to the place where he had stood before the LORD. And he looked down toward Sodom and Gomorrah and toward all the land of the valley, and he looked and, behold, the smoke of the land went up like the smoke of a furnace. So it was that, when God destroyed the cities of the valley, God

remembered Abraham and sent Lot out of the midst of the overthrow when he overthrew the cities in which Lot had lived.

It is evident from the Bible that god destroyed more than just the two cities, as it also talks about the rest of the valley. But the event is described even more vividly on clay tablets dated back to over 4,500 years and predating the Bible by some 1,000 years. The graphic description in the ancient clay tablets leave us with no doubt at all that the god of the Bible was not our friend, nor our savior, but was most certainly our vicious and vengeful maker. It is in his image that we have been created and it is his violent DNA that we have inherited.

These are translations of Sumerian tablets by Zecharia Sitchin describing the events on that fateful day when the gods decided to destroy the world and humankind with it:

> The evil thing to carry out Ninurta and Nergal were selected . . . The five cities of the valley he finished off, to desolation they were overturned . . . steam to the heavens was rising . . . With fire and brimstone they were upheavaled, all that lived there to vapour was turned . . . The horizon with darkness it obliterated . . . By a darkening of the skies were the brilliance followed, then a storm to blow began . . . Gloom from the skies an Evil Wind carried . . . Wherever it reached, death to all that lived mercilessly it delivered . . . Like a ghost the fields and cities it attacked . . . No door could shut it out, no bolt could turn it back . . . In the streets were their corpses piled up . . . Cough and phlegm the chests filled, the mouths with spittle and foam filled up . . . Their mouths were drenched with blood . . . The waters were poisoned, all vegetation withered . . . Everything that lived behind it was dead, people and cattle all alike perished.

12

SLAVES AND SPIES

Slavery is a common theme in the Bible.

But now that you have been set free from sin and have become slaves to God . . .

ROMANS 6:22

Is this an admission that man has been conned by the gods?

They promise them freedom, while they themselves are slaves of depravity for a man is a slave to whatever has mastered him.

2 PETER 2:19

"THE APPLE DOESN'T FALL far from the tree" . . . "like father, like son" . . . are just two simple idioms that pretty much capture what actually happened to humanity in its ancient past. When attempting to trace back the well-hidden path to our origins, I stumbled upon numerous fascinating subjects that stopped me in my tracks quite unexpectedly; subjects that required more scratching, more investigation. Some of them are so common in our history and our daily lives that we never give them a second thought, and they have manifested themselves as human habits and behavioral characteristics that have become entrenched in our cultures and societies. Subjects like gold and jewelery came up and we had to scratch the surface to see why gold has been associated with humanity since the cradle, and how gold has so profoundly controlled many aspects of our evolution. We realize that while we take gold for granted today and we don't give it a second thought, there must have been some event in the deep dark history of humanity that caused gold to gain such an elevated status and resulted in a multitude of socioeconomic spin-offs that are at the center of our lives today: like jewelery, currency, trade exchange, stock markets, fashion, and more. The little bit of scratching that we do in this book has hopefully revealed some of the hidden secrets behind gold's relevance in our human history.

You can try this yourself at home, I recommend it. Look at any of the habits or activities you engage in and try to trace it back to its origin among humans on Earth. You will be amazed at how much you find out about humankind and our behavioral patterns.

One such fascinating subject that attracted my attention was the concept of slavery. Just like gold, slavery seems to have been around since the dawn of man. I will try to trace it back to its very start and point out why we are so entangled in such a barbaric act even today. Just think about it for a second. Where and when did man suddenly decide that he could own another person? A moment in which one person elevated himself way above the other and proclaimed his complete supremacy over the other. The concept of enslaving another person is arguably the most abhorrent act of humanity and the most barbaric display of our true character, which is indelibly programmed into our genome. It's as if we could not really escape this kind of behavior, as if we were predetermined to behave in such a way. What is even more unbelievable is that the god of the Old Testament does not seem to have a problem with slavery. In fact, on various occasions god actually instructs men on how to treat their slaves and how to dish out punishment to disobedient slaves. In fact, the whole idea of slavery was embraced and accepted throughout the entire Bible, right to the end of Revelations.

SLAVERY IN THE BIBLE

There are over 130 references to "slaves" in the Bible, here are just a few of them to get you thinking about it:

And she said to Abraham, "Get rid of that slave woman and her son, for that slave woman's son will never share in the inheritance with my son Isaac.

GENESIS 21:10

Whoever is found to have it will become my slave; the rest of you will be free from blame.

GENESIS 44:10

Clearly showing god's favoritism toward one group.

> The LORD said, "I have indeed seen the misery of my people in Egypt. I have heard them crying out because of their slave drivers, and I am concerned about their suffering. So I have come down to rescue them from the hand of the Egyptians and to bring them up out of that land into a good and spacious land, a land flowing with milk and honey—the home of the Canaanites, Hittites, Amorites, Perizzites, Hivites and Jebusites. And now the cry of the Israelites has reached me, and I have seen the way the Egyptians are oppressing them. So now, go. I am sending you to Pharaoh to bring my people the Israelites out of Egypt."
>
> EXODUS 3:7–10

> If a man beats his male or female slave with a rod and the slave dies as a direct result, he must be punished, but he is not to be punished if the slave gets up after a day or two, since the slave is his property.
>
> EXODUS 21:20–21

Even priests were allowed to have slaves.

> But if a priest buys a slave with money, or if a slave is born in his household, that slave may eat his food.
>
> LEVITICUS 22:11

It was okay for others to be enslaved, but it was deemed to be "evil" in the eyes of god to enslave other Israelites.

> If a man is caught kidnapping one of his brother Israelites and treats him as a slave or sells him, the kidnapper must die. You must purge the evil from among you.
>
> DEUTERONOMY 24:7

David seemingly liked to have some fun with his slave girls, which was not always to the liking of others. Maybe she was just jealous.

> When David returned home to bless his household, Michal daughter of Saul came out to meet him and said, "How the king of Israel has distinguished himself today, disrobing in the sight of the slave girls of his servants as any vulgar fellow would!"
>
> 2 SAMUEL 6:20

The repetitive sound of the god of vengeance and fear continues in these words:

> Because of this, I am going to bring disaster on the house of Jeroboam. I will cut off from Jeroboam every last male in Israel—slave or free. I will burn up the house of Jeroboam as one burns dung, until it is all gone.
>
> 1 KINGS 14:10

Once more god condones the act of slavery.

> Cursed be Canaan! The lowest of slaves will he be to his brothers.
>
> GENESIS 9:25

People prepared themselves against violent acts of god.

> Those officials of Pharaoh who feared the word of the LORD hurried to bring their slaves and their livestock inside. But those who ignored the word of the LORD left their slaves and livestock in the field.
>
> EXODUS 9:20

A very clear endorsement of slavery and enslaving other nations.

> Your male and female slaves are to come from the nations around you; from them you may buy slaves. You can will them to your children as inherited property and can make them slaves for life, but you must not rule over your fellow Israelites ruthlessly.
>
> LEVITICUS 25:44–45

Warring, conquering, and slavery were the order of the day under god's rule.

> He will take a tenth of your flocks, and you yourselves will become his slaves.
>
> 1 SAMUEL 8:17

A perfect example how god cunningly turned mankind into obedient slaves by showing them snippets of mercy and goodwill. This would have been a reference to Cyrus the Great, who freed the Jews from Babylonia, and allowed them to go to Jerusalem. But we must remember who Cyrus was. He was an Aryan Persian king who was under the influence of the Anunnaki gods, manipulating humans into all kinds of submission.

Though we are slaves, our God has not deserted us in our bondage. He has shown us kindness in the sight of the kings of Persia: He has granted us new life to rebuild the house of our God and repair its ruins, and he has given us a wall of protection in Judah and Jerusalem.

EZRA 9:9

God continued to enslave humans, making them grateful for small signs of benevolence. Promising reward for obedience and punishment for defiance.

But see, we are slaves today, slaves in the land you gave our forefathers so they could eat its fruit and the other good things it produces.

NEHEMIAH 9:36

God continues to oppress humans.

For I and my people have been sold for destruction and slaughter and annihilation. If we had merely been sold as male and female slaves, I would have kept quiet, because no such distress would justify disturbing the king.

ESTHER 7:4

And humans keep hoping to please the vengeful god while they waited for his benevolence. God's barbaric rule over humanity continues with false promises:

As the eyes of slaves look to the hand of their master, as the eyes of a maid look to the hand of her mistress, so our eyes look to the LORD our God, till he shows us his mercy.

PSALM 123:2

Even the Jews had Hebrew slaves.

Everyone was to free his Hebrew slaves, both male and female; no one was to hold a fellow Jew in bondage.

JEREMIAH 34:9

The god of war sends his loyal human "slaves" to plunder and kill others.

I will surely raise my hand against them so that their slaves will plunder them. Then you will know that the LORD Almighty has sent me.

ZECHARIAH 2:9

Not so with you. Instead, whoever wants to become great among you must be your servant, and whoever wants to be first must be your slave.

MATTHEW 20:26–28

God cunningly sets up his people to be forever grateful for his intervention.

"But I will punish the nation they serve as slaves," God said, "and afterward they will come out of that country and worship me in this place."

ACTS 7:7

Because the patriarchs were jealous of Joseph, they sold him as a slave into Egypt. But God was with him.

ACTS 7:9

Then the kings of the earth, the princes, the generals, the rich, the mighty, and every slave and every free man hid in caves and among the rocks of the mountains.

REVELATION 6:15

God makes it clear that humans are his slaves.

Masters, provide your slaves with what is right and fair, because you know that you also have a Master in heaven.

COLOSSIANS 4:1

Here we have a disciple of Jesus justifying slavery, all because god will reward them for their suffering, they should accept their lot. He even suggests that humankind was made to be slaves. It shows the incredible hold this brutal god had over humankind. Constantly subjecting them to hardship and violence.

Slaves, submit yourselves to your masters with all respect, not only to those who are good and considerate, but also to those who are harsh. For it is commendable if a man bears up under the pain of unjust suffering because he is conscious of God . . . But if you suffer for doing good and you endure it, this is commendable before God. To this you were called.

1 PETER 2:18–21

SLAVE SOCIETIES

We can go back to the ancient wars and argue that the concept of slavery arose out of situations where prisoners were taken and kept as slaves or sold as slaves. Alexander the Great would not only enslave the conquered armies, but he would take entire towns, cities, and even entire nations of mothers, fathers, and children to be enslaved. If they were not kept by the conquering side, they would be sold into slavery to some other king in exchange for gold or whatever they might have agreed to be a fair price for such a valuable booty of humans. The mere thought of this kind of behavior makes us physically ill today, and yet we forget that slavery only really reached its peak on Earth in the last 500 years.

There is evidence of slavery in Sumer right at the dawn of so-called civilization. When we analyze the Sumerian word for *slave,* we find that it translates into "mountain man" or "mountain girl." This is a crucial bit of evidence for my theory of a slave species. If man, the Adamu, was created as a slave to work the gold mines on Earth, he would have inherited much of his maker's DNA. This means that the very first things early humans had to deal with as a brand new species were gold and slavery. This is what they were not only born into, but intentionally *created* to do. It stands to reason that if our maker had the genetic makeup to commit such acts, the offspring would most certainly display very similar characteristics. The offspring must surely be a chip off the old block. And here we are, some 400,000 years later, displaying exactly the same kind of characteristics, completely oblivious to their origins. It is highly ironic that man was created and toiled in Africa from the beginning of time as a slave to the Anunnaki gods, but from the moment the new civilization emerged after the Flood that ended the last ice age, the so-called civilized and free human did exactly as his Anunnaki father did. He captured slaves and started behaving exactly like his maker. Suddenly the two expressions at the beginning of this chapter, "the apple doesn't fall far from the tree," and "like father, like son" make so much more sense.

Just picture the children in small isolated communities. They will inevitably grow up to do one of the things their fathers or mothers did in the small remote village. They will absorb the local culture; they may weave, plant certain crops, breed a certain farm animal, wash in a certain way, eat in a certain way, worship the same way, and marry a partner (or more) according to their tradition. Any suggestion of doing things differently is seen as heresy to those who have upheld those traditions for years. They are not aware of the other worldly possibilities, and their frame of reference is restricted only to what they grew up with. To the Western world this may sound a bit far-fetched, but let me assure you that this kind of activity permeates much of Africa, Asia, South America, eastern Europe, the Middle and Near East. In fact, even in the "very" advanced societies like the United States, there are little villages and small towns that have upheld their traditions for centuries, completely separated from the rapid modernization that has taken place around them.

When the Anunnaki gods decided to help humans learn the skills of survival after the Flood, not all humans were convinced that this was a good idea. Some primitive humans most likely did not trust the brutal gods who had oppressed them for so long, and, therefore, many of them remained in their mountain hideouts, too scared to enter the newly established settlements of people. It must have looked to them like a new version of the labor camps that persisted for millennia around the gold mines. This is why the newborn civilization did not explode in large numbers of people, but was rather stimulated by its acquisition of know-how virtually overnight. But the global gods eventually found those hidden communities of rebellious slaves and imposed their control on them in the most remote locations. This is all very clearly illustrated in the mythologies of even the most remote tribes of the planet. They all had a similar relationship with the omnipresent gods. But as the new civilized communities' needs for labor increased, they would do what came naturally to them: go into the mountains or the neighboring village and catch themselves some slaves. After all, those "mountain men" and "mountain girls" were now deemed to be wild and primitive in their eyes: "Like father . . . like son."

The irony does not end here. When humans adopted their new wisdom by settling into communities, domesticating animals, planting crops, and taking slaves captive in the mountains around them, where did they turn to for their supply of slaves next? Africa. The cycle of life has now been fully completed. The newly civilized slave species returns to its place of birth to capture slaves for their own needs. Does that sound out of line to you? Well it should not. The violent gene was strong in our DNA then, some 11,000 years ago, and it is still as strong as ever today, let there be no doubt about that. The greed gene is still firmly encoded in our DNA and a whole host of other genes that drive our violent, bloodthirsty behavior. Slavery is what the human species was born into, and slavery is what we have known until today.

The incredible thing is that virtually all ancient cultures in the world were practicing slavery at some stage, starting with the Sumerians and

Egyptians. Then came Hammurabi, the priest king of Babylonia who lived around 2123 BC to 2181 BC. This was a new breed of human king who showed distinct signs of mental evolution in the lineage of human-species-leaders. In essence he was the first great king who established the first metropolis on Earth: Babylonia. The Code of Law that he laid down in clay was one of the first recorded sets of laws in human history (see chapter 10). Hammurabi displayed an uncanny feeling for human rights in the face of his own people's tradition in slavery. He detailed many laws pertaining to slaves. Slaves were allowed to own property, enter into business, and marry free women. Formal release by the owner was permitted through either self-purchase or adoption. Nevertheless, even by this humanitarian code, the slaves were still considered as merchandise. The Code of the Hittites, which was applied in western Asia from 1800 BC to 1400 BC, was even more humane by conceding that a slave was a human being, although of an inferior order. The ancient Israelites experienced slavery in Egypt, while in the Indus Valley the first documented evidence of slavery coincides with the Aryan invasion of about 2000 BC. Indian literature indicates that slavery was allowed throughout India from the sixth century BC to the beginning of the Christian era, but there is no doubt that slavery was alive and well millennia before that. In ancient Persia, slaves were actually bred for supply purposes for the hungry slave-markets. Persian victories in the Aegean islands of Chios, Lesbos, and Tenedos resulted in the enslavement of entire populations. China's entire history is virtually built on a slave culture going all the way back to Huangdi, the Yellow Emperor and mystical ancestor of all Chinese, the Xia Dynasty, which started in the twenty-first century BC.

The first true slave society in history probably only emerged in ancient Greece between the sixth and fourth centuries BC. At the slave markets of Athens, Rhodes, Corinth, and Delos, a thousand slaves would change hands in an afternoon. Just imagine that kind of setup at the San Francisco harbour in 2004—the modern human mind would not be able to cope with such a desecration of human rights. This must surely be a visible indication of humanity's general state of mental and spiritual evolution. But things were different in Greece in 500 BC. After a major battle, as many as 20,000 captives would go on sale. Some say that Aesop, the legendary storyteller, was a freed Greek slave in the sixth century BC. Next in line was Rome, which became even more dependent upon slaves when a form of agricultural slavery called "estate slavery" was introduced. After the fall of the Roman Empire in the fifth century AD, slavery persisted in Arab lands and in central Europe. Many "Slavs" were captured and taken as slaves to Germany where it seems they retained their derivative name in "slave." At this stage, slavery across the world was unstoppable and man's cruelty and greed reached unprecedented heights. From the very first day of civilization, man practiced what he was taught by his maker: obsession with gold and keeping slaves.

Slave-owning societies continued and included the Ottoman Empire, the Crimean khanate, the Inca Empire in Peru, the Sokoto caliphate, and the Hausa of Nigeria. It extended to the central Asians such as the Mongols, Kazakhs, and various Turkic groups who also kept slaves. As unbelievable as it seems, slavery was even practiced by some native North American people such as the Comanche and the Creek. Even in Africa there was slavery among its own people. This is how firmly our genetic inheritance is entrenched from our maternal donors, the seven original Anunnaki females who gave birth to the first group of slave species, but we will find out more about them a little later. African chiefs would first sell off their prisoners to the slave traders from Europe. When these ran out, the chiefs would line up their own criminals and wrongdoers to be sold into slavery. When this was not enough, they would simply grab remote and ignorant villages capturing all and sundry for the slave markets. I hope that this is proof enough of the violent gene and greed gene embedded in our DNA.

I do, however, suspect that there will be many who still have a problem with this concept, so let me take it a bit further. Some men would even sell their wives or children into slavery to pay off their own debts. This barbaric, genetically inherited behavior reached its apex in the fifteenth, sixteenth, and seventeenth centuries when an estimated 20 million slaves were captured in Africa and shipped around the world to places like Brazil, the Caribbean, and North America, while trade within Africa itself continued. The first slaves to have been brought to South Africa came from Angola on board a Dutch ship called the Amersfoort in 1658, only six years after the first settlement by the Dutch at the Cape of Good Hope. And because I am South African, I have a particular interest in the slave history of this beautiful part of the world. So let's use this as a full chronological example. The rest of the world's slave trade between the fifteenth and seventeenth centuries evolved in similar ways. According to Mogamat Kamedien, these are the events surrounding the establishment of slavery in South Africa.

	FORMATION OF THE DUTCH EAST INDIA COMPANY—THE VOC
1602	Chamber Representatives of the Netherlands Parliament grants a founding charter to the Dutch East India Company to establish an Indian trading empire in the East.
	DUTCH COLONIAL SOUTH AFRICA
1652	The Dutch East India Company started a refreshment station at the Cape for its VOC shipping fleet on their way to the East and/or on their return trips from Batavia (present day Java as part of Indonesia).
1658	The first shipload of slaves are brought to the Cape, from Angola, onboard the ship the *Amersfoort*.
1666	Slaves built the Castle Fort Good Hope.
1679	Foundations are laid for the Company Slave Lodge.
1693	Slaves at the Cape outnumber free people for the first time. They are mainly from around the Indian Ocean, Mozambique, Madagascar, and Mauritius.
1717	VOC decides to retain the institution of slavery as the main labor system for the Cape.
1725	Evidence exists that runaway slaves had been living at the mountainous Hangklip for extensive periods, between Gordon's Bay and Kleinmond/Hermanus.
1754	The governor, Tulbagh, consolidated the numerous VOC slave regulations into a single document, the Cape Slave Code.
1754	A census taken of the Cape colony at the time showed the two populations, both slaves and settlers, to be roughly equal to about 6,000 each.
	FIRST BRITISH OCCUPATION
1795	The British take over control of the Cape and remain in charge throughout the nineteenth century.
1796	The British outlaw torture and some of the most brutal forms of capital punishments.
	SECOND DUTCH REOCCUPATION: THE BATAVIAN REPUBLIC
1803	The Dutch temporarily reoccupy the Cape of Good Hope for a short three-year stay.
	SECOND BRITISH OCCUPATION: BRITISH SOUTH AFRICA
1806	Company slaves are released from the Slave Lodge under rule of the then Governor, the Earl of Caledon.

1807	The British outlaw the Trans-Indian Ocean slave trade. It was now illegal to be a slave trader buying or selling slaves, but it was still legal to own slaves. Prohibition on the importation of overseas slaves resulted in the increase of exchange value of Cape-born Creole slaves.
	FIRST SLAVE REBELLION
1808	The Koeberg Slave Rebellion in the Swartland near Malmesbury, led by Louis of Mauritius, is defeated at Salt River. Resulted in the capturing of 300 farm slaves as dissidents.
1813	Het Gesticht, the fourth-oldest church building in South Africa, is erected in 1813 by the inhabitants of Paarl as a meeting house for non-Christian slaves and "heathens" in the town.
1823	The British House of Commons discuss the conditions of slaves at the Cape of Good Hope. A commission of enquiry is appointed due to relentless pressure of the Anti-Slavery Abolitionists lobby.
	SECOND SLAVE REBELLION
1825	A second slave uprising at the farm, Hou-den-Bek, led by Galant van die Kaap, is defeated in the Koue Bokkeveld, near Ceres.
1826	Collapse of the Cape wine industry.
	SLAVE AMELIORATION LAWS
1826	The Colonial Office intervened by forcing local colonial assemblies to bring the local amelioration legislation into effect through Ordinance 19 of 1826 promulgated at the Cape. This was in line with the Trinidad Order, aimed at the sugar plantation slave owners. Thus, the British introduced amelioration laws in order to improve the living conditions of slaves as well as a series of practical amelioration measures to make punishments less cruel; and the Office of the Protector of Slaves is established with Assistant Slave Protectors in rural towns and villages away from Cape Town.
1826	Appointment of the Guardian of the Slaves.
1827	Colored Persons qualified for the municipal franchise of Cape Town, and a Malay property owner was elected as Wardmaster.
1828	Ordinance 50 of 1828 liberated the Khoisan into the category on par with Free Blacks and placed all Free Black persons, both Hottentots and Vrye Swartes, on equal legal footing with white colonists within the judiciary system.
1830	Revised provisions of Ordinance 19 by the British Parliament resulted in the renamed Office of the Protector of Slaves.
1830	Slave owners ordered to keep records of slave punishments.
1831	Stellenbosch slave owners rioted by refusing to accept the order to keep registers of slave punishments.

1832	More than 2,000 slave owners assembled in Cape Town to hold a protest meeting demonstrating against this government order, which was adopted without proper consultation.
SLAVE EMANCIPATION	
1834	Slavery is abolished in British colonies on December 1. "Liberated" slaves now fall into the category of Free Blacks, although the "freed" slaves are forced to serve an extended four-year apprenticeship to make them "fit for freedom."
1835	Ordinance No. 1 of 1835 introduced the terms of apprenticeship at the Cape, including the appointment of special magistrates.
1836	Start of the Great Trek by 12,000 frontier farmers (Voortrekkers), who demonstrated their unhappiness about the government's policy to release slaves from the control of Free Burghers as slaveholders.
1836	Nonwhites were finally accorded similar treatment to white colonists in their interaction with the public institutions of the local authorities.
END OF SLAVE APPRENTICESHIP PERIOD	
1838	End of all slave apprenticeships.
1838	About 39,000 slaves are freed on Emancipation Day, December 1. Only 1.2 million pounds was paid out against the original estimated compensation amount of 3 million pounds that was initially set aside by the British government as compensation monies for the about 1,300 affected slaveholding farmers at the Cape of Good Hope.
CAPE "MASTERS AND SERVANTS" LABOR LEGISLATION	
1841	The Masters and Servants Ordinance was promulgated regulating and criminalizing labor relationships between employer and employee in favor of the former slave masters based on the past Cape Slave Codes originally issued by the VOC as Placaaten of India.

By the seventeenth century the slave trade was regarded an "honorable and noble" business in Europe through which many companies generated immense wealth and caused untold misery. As the inhumane elements of this trade started to be exposed by small groups of liberals in the eighteenth century, many of the so-called honorable businessmen fought their accusations with all their wealth and influence. By the end of the nineteenth century, one by one, the guilty culprits signed various "abolition of slavery acts" under pressure from enlightened activists: Argentina 1813; Colombia 1821; Mexico 1829; South Africa 1834; United States 1865, just to mention a few. It was, however, only in 1948, when the United Nations released the "Proclamation of Human Rights Declaration," that in essence prohibited slavery worldwide. But the United

Nations left a huge loophole in the previous declaration, which took another eight years to rectify. They were forced to add a further declaration that dealt with "slave trade and institutions similar to slavery."

To most people today this bit of information will come as a horrific shock: how is it possible that slavery was only officially prohibited in 1956 by the so-called free and civilized world? Let me remind you of an earlier sentiment that suggests that "if we don't know where we come from, how can we possibly know where we are going?" For as long as people keep their eyes closed to new evidence and their minds poisoned against new possibilities, we will continue to propagate the slave species characteristics that our maker so successfully implanted in us. We were created as a slave species and to this day we remain a slave species, held captive by our ignorance, lack of clarity about our human origins, and the stunted genome with which our maker has endowed us.

Even after the 1956 UN proclamation, the inhumane trade in people did not stop; 11,000 years since the emergence of civilized man nothing has really changed. Saudi Arabia only signed the "abolition of slavery act" in 1963, and Mauritania in 1980. Is it not incredibly ironic that it is once again in Africa, the cradle of man, the birthplace of slavery on Earth, that we find the last place to let go of this abhorrent custom? Slavery is so deeply and firmly rooted in the African ancestry that it seemingly cannot be escaped. But slavery is still alive and well in the twenty-first century. It seems that certain parts of our DNA have not evolved at all. In 1988 slaves were sold in Sudan for 30 pounds, and in 1989 China launched a national campaign against the trade in "women and children" slaves. The effort uncovered 9,000 cases of slavery in that year alone. My guess is that this was only the tip of the iceberg in China.

In this technologically advanced global village where every sensational event is reported by global networks within seconds, where communication has become child's play, where we look at Mars rovers with a certain amount of impatience because we want them to do more stuff, and do it quicker— how free are we really? We spoke about economic warfare in earlier chapters, but it should also be referred to as "economic slavery." This applies to individuals as well as poor countries. In this case the conquering armies do not take prisoners as slaves, they simply enslave the entire country economically. The total indebtedness of poor countries to wealthy countries is so incredibly vast that it most likely can never be repaid. The strange thing is that most of the poor countries of the world are those who were raped for slaves by the West for centuries. This rape of many nations understandably resulted in the complete collapse of such countries, that all eventually had to ask for assistance from the aggressor. What a conniving and calculating bunch of "civilized" humans we are.

Today, the slavery principal continues under this economic banner extremely successfully. The poor countries are exploited for cheap labor, they become the dumping grounds of global unwanted produce, deadly unwanted chemicals and nuclear waste, basically continuing to be enslaved on virtually every level; even their terra firma has become enslaved. Their currencies remain weak, their people remain poor, and they have no choice but to allow the bullies to abuse them. But the abuse does not always come from outside the borders. The slavery problems in China are potentially nothing to what is brewing right next door in India. The highly discriminating class system called "caste," which originates from the Portuguese *casta,* meaning breed, race, or kind, is still widely practiced throughout India.

Although this form of discrimination is officially prohibited, it is alive and well, serving as a legitimate cultural form of slavery, which holds close to half the population of one billion Indians enslaved in poverty and misery, with virtually no way out. Once you are classified as a Dalit or "untouchable" your lot has been determined for life. It is virtually impossible to elevate yourself to one of the four higher classifications that may make your life more bearable. There are approximately 200 million Dalits in India today. They may not marry anyone from a higher class, they may not use the same amenities as others, they must at all times be invisible to the higher castes, getting out of their way so that not even their shadows may touch in passing. In some situations, towns and villages will insist that Dalits carry a bell to warn any other higher castes of their approaching "vile" presence.

HOW FREE ARE WE?

So how free are we really? You may think that because you live in a First World economy you are okay, that you are the master of your own destiny, and that you are nobody's slave. Well, think again. The successful Westerners are slaves to their jobs, their boss, their mortgage bond, an array of credit cards, car loan, overdraft, and other significant entrapments of society. The modern economies are structured to attract as many consumers as possible, with the promise of some sort of credit. Even your student loan can enslave you for years. Once you are hooked, the onus is squarely on your shoulders to pay the creditor without default. You may tell everyone that "this is your new home," but the reality is that it actually belongs to the bank. They just allow you to work your backside off for twenty years, paying them a large sum every month, making nauseating amounts of interest from you in the process. So who is the slave? If you cannot pay, they auction your home at market value, in many cases still leaving you with a large debt to cover. Now that you are really deeply in trouble, they blacklist you, which dramatically reduces your chances for employment, of keeping a bank account, and making back the money that you owe them. The credit card is the same. You pay for your Caribbean trip with your card, feeling very fulfilled. Upon your return, you realize that your company has gone insolvent and the card becomes an instant trap. You have to sell your car to pay off the card and now you can't get around to launch your new business. The worst and most clandestine form of slavery is the good old student loan. Thousands of companies will give you a student loan with the condition that you work for them to pay it off after graduation. The snag is that they decide on your measly salary as an apprentice, which means that you have to work for them for years while earning very little, essentially becoming extremely cheap labor. This happens year in, year out, around the world to millions of graduates. Basically, our lives revolve around work and money. We behave like confused slaves on this planet, not knowing where we are going . . . why we are here . . . and who is really in control? Why are we chasing these castles in the sky? Is there a hidden message here? Could this possibly be a hangover from prehistory, when early man was promised a trip up to god's castle in the sky . . . and to live in the house of the maker, but only if he performed valiantly and pleased his master? Really . . . why are we so caught up in this chase for materialistic rewards, if we know that we can't take it with us?

The answer is simple. We are still slaves living in the twenty-first century, but our path to this point in time has been so meticulously planned by the "gods" of our prehistory that we could never expect to recognize the clues or symptoms. Our arrogance prevents us from even believing such wild and extravagant theories because "we are the masters of our own destinies."

Our entire history is riddled with temptation from a variety of sources: from biblical promises of heavenly wealth and eternal life, to the Sumerian tablets outlining the promises of great reward in the houses of the gods. But only if you behaved, obeyed, and performed the tasks that were assigned to you. Is this the seed that has driven man to toil and perform forever? Is it a hangover reflex response from days gone by, when the Anunnaki gods were still on Earth? It certainly smacks of something that eludes us to this day. After all, we are the slave species and so we shall behave. All that has happened in the past few thousand years is that we confused the reason with motive, which has resulted in the continuous frantic chase for material stuff. We want to accumulate and hoard. There is so much baggage and disinformation piled up in our human subconscious that we cannot possibly begin to unravel it without huge amounts of investigation, and especially introspection. Because the messages we are discovering from our distant ancestors are not the fairy tales we expected to hear.

The people of the "free" Western world are enslaved economically, culturally, and religiously. But if you ask them, they will deny it. We are enslaved to our jobs, our banks and our governments. If you don't pay your tax, you will go to jail. This blissful ignorance is exactly what the "maker" had planned. The Tower of Babel incident was a wonderful example of how the gods conspired to keep humanity enslaved through their ignorance. The Sumerian scriptures make similar references to the incident as is described in the Bible, where the gods had decided that man had grown too wise and was speaking one language. The use of the word *language* could be metaphorical for knowledge. The gods felt that if they left man to his own device, he would be capable of anything. This posed a big threat to the gods, when suddenly humankind displayed the potential to stand up against their maker and oppressor. At that point the gods decided to "go down from their heavenly abode and confuse their language," which they did. It is not exactly clear what they did to humans, but it certainly extended the slave mentality for millennia. What is very interesting, however, is that Genesis 10 ends with the sons and descendants of Noah scattering around the world, belonging to different clans and speaking different languages. Then suddenly, Genesis 11 starts with the following statements.

Now the whole world had one language and a common speech. As men moved eastward, they found a plain in Shinar and settled there. They said to each other, "Come, let's make bricks and bake them thoroughly." They used brick instead of stone, and tar for mortar. Then they said, "Come, let us build ourselves a city, with a tower that reaches to the heavens, so that we may make a name for ourselves and not be scattered over the face of the whole earth." But the LORD came down to see the city and the tower that the men were building. The LORD said, "If as one people speaking the same language they have begun to do this, then nothing they plan to do will be impossible for them. Come, let us go down and confuse their language so they will not understand each other." So the LORD scattered them from there over all the earth, and they stopped building the city. That is why it was called Babel, because there the LORD confused the language of the whole world. From there the LORD scattered them over the face of the whole earth.

GENESIS 11:1–9

This entire passage smacks of a master-slave relationship. This is virtually a copy of the Sumerian tablets where the gods were also very unhappy that the slaves were making rapid progress, gaining knowledge, and showing signs of higher intelligence. It's fairly plain to read between the lines that god the master panicked and took the necessary steps to prevent people from gaining skills and knowledge. The principle of divide and conquer was implemented very successfully among the emerging human threat. The simple fact that the sons of the gods were having children with the daughters of man was a huge problem. The new human offspring were even more intelligent than their human mothers, because they had more of the gods' DNA that allowed them to achieve more and evolve quicker.

> When men began to increase on earth and daughters were born to them, the divine beings saw how beautiful the daughters of men were and took wives from among those that pleased them. The LORD said, "My breath shall not abide in man forever, since he too is flesh; let the days allowed him be one hundred and twenty years." It was then, and later too, that the Nephilim appeared on earth—when the divine beings cohabited with the daughters of men, who bore them offspring. They were the heroes of old, the men of renown.
>
> GENESIS 6:1–4

There is no doubt that the fathers who were the sons of the gods also contributed to the technological know-how of their children. We can deduce from this kind of activity on Earth that man's evolution was speeded up rapidly, which went against the explicit wishes of the ruling gods. They wanted to keep man stupid. So, it is of particular interest that in Genesis 6:7, god suddenly became plural, and plans to go down with some of his associates to sort out this problem. "Come let us go down and confuse their language."

Who was god talking to and who went down with him? And why would god look unfavorably on human technological progress? Why would god not want his special creation, man, to be able to do other things. Why would god be so freaked out with man's rapid advancement?

The Tower of Babel incident was preceded by an earlier attempt to get rid of humans because they were already posing a prior threat to the gods. Once again this indicates an ultimate act of oppression that outlined the control that the gods maintained over the slave species while plotting their complete demise. For some reason, the gods decided that their creation, man, was evil and that all he knew was evil; that's pretty much how the Bible puts it. I sense that the gods had had enough of the humans and realized that they had created a monster that could rise up and bite them. The Sumerian tablets tell the story of an impending tidal wave that would destroy most of humanity, especially those who lived near the coastal areas. In December 2004, we saw how easily 300,000 people died from a relatively small tsunami in large parts of the world. Imagine what a 100-meter high tidal wave could do to the world. But the Anunnaki already knew of such a giant wave that would sweep the Earth as a result of their planet Nibiru coming back into close proximity to the world. So they decided that they would allow this wave to destroy humanity and in one fell swoop help them to take care of their growing human problem. It is estimated that there were 4 million of the slave species on Earth by this stage, far outnumbering the gods. This made the gods very nervous, so they would allow the slaves whom they created to be destroyed because their behavior was showing signs of uncontrollable intelligence.

Did the slaves start asking too many questions? Did they start evolving too quickly and were they absorbing advanced technical knowledge without the gods' permission? It certainly seems that way. By now you must have figured out that I am of the opinion that the Bible cannot be trusted, no matter how emotional we get about it. It is surrounded with so much controversy and there is no absolute proof who the real authors were, and under what influence they wrote those brutal descriptions of events of their times. Furthermore, most of the Old Testament is a diluted version of Sumerian tablets and other ancient texts. It is therefore a paradox in itself that I am using the Bible as a major source of reference. This, my friends, is purely to demonstrate the inconsistency and fanatical obsession bestowed on this book by those who so dearly worship it. By the time we reach the story of the biblical Flood, I would like to reason that the Anunnaki gods did not count on the rapid evolution of the human brain, which is why the gods wanted the growing number of humans to be destroyed in the flood. In short, the human slaves were suddenly a potential threat to the gods. But one of the two leading gods, Enki, was much closer to the humans than his coldhearted brother Enlil. Because Enki had worked with the human slaves in the African mines for millennia, he took pity on the humans and warned Ziusudra (Noah) of the impending disaster. He gave him strict instructions on what to do to save his friends and family and his livestock. It turns out that this was not just a random gesture of mercy, but Ziusudra was actually Enki's son with a human female. This was the real motive behind his actions.

The Bible puts it slightly differently: "God saw that everything man did was evil." Suddenly all the people on Earth were "vile and evil" and god decided to punish them. Is it possible that the story recorded in the Bible came from an

Fig. 12.1. Sumerian Flood story. Neo-Sumerian on clay, is mankind's oldest reference to the Deluge, together with a tablet in Philadelphia, the only other tablet bearing this story in Sumerian. In this transcript Ziusudra, the Sumerian Noah, is described as "the priest of Enki," which is new information. Other tablets outline that he is actually the son of Enki.

> The Sumerian flood story is the oldest forerunner to the Biblical account of the flood (Genesis 6:5–9:29). According to the British Museum, their Neo-Babylonian tablet with the Flood story as a part of the Epic of Gilgamesh is the most famous tablet in the world. The tablet shown here is over 1,000 years older than the one in the British Museum.

opposing point of view, from Enki's brother Enlil, who was in command of the planet and its people? Enlil never really liked the slave species and this provided him with a perfect opportunity to destroy them. What could all the people on Earth have possibly done that was so vile and evil, to have enraged god so much, that he plotted to destroy all of them? The fascinating thing is that the Flood story has been told in most of the ancient cultures which predate the biblical story of Noah. So which one of them is more accurate and factual? My guess is that it should be the oldest one, which is the Sumerian story about Enki and Enlil and Ziusudra. And this is where the plot thickens even further. The sons of the Anunnaki gods, who were also referred to as the Nefilim, were prohibited from having intercourse with the human females for fear of creating a new sub-species, which would be more intelligent and a potential threat to the Anunnaki. We have heard about them before, even in the Bible. But the sons of the gods were young and restless on Earth, showing the usual signs of rebellious youth. They obviously disobeyed the instructions, especially when they saw how sexual the daughters of man were. Both the Sumerian scripts and the Bible tell us explicitly what happened next. "God" decided to pull the ultimate act of supremacy over his disobedient slave species, which was to destroy all of them. This would allow him to clear the slate and start again with no loose ends and especially no disobedient and nosey humans. This is how the Bible describes it:

> The Nephilim were on the earth in those days and also afterward when the sons of God went to the daughters of men and had children by them. They were the heroes of old, men of renown. The LORD saw how great man's wickedness on the earth had become, and that every inclination of the thoughts of his heart was only evil all the time. The LORD was grieved that he had made man on the earth, and his heart was filled with pain. So the LORD said, "I will wipe mankind, whom I have created, from the face of the earth." . . . But Noah found favor in the eyes of the LORD. This is the account of Noah: Noah was a righteous man, blameless among the people of his time, and he walked with God. Noah had three sons: Shem, Ham and Japheth. Now the earth was corrupt in God's sight and was full of violence. God saw how corrupt the earth had become, for all the people on earth had corrupted their ways. So God said to Noah, "I am going to put an end to all people, for the earth is filled with violence because of them. I am surely going to destroy both them and the earth . . . I am going to bring flood-waters on the earth to destroy all life under the heavens . . . Everything on earth will perish. But I will establish my covenant with you . . . "
>
> GENESIS 6:4–18

Now there is a wonderfully ironic example of favoritism by the supposedly all-loving god, who made all people equal. Suddenly Noah was his favorite one, and the only kosher guy on the face of the Earth. This is a little too rich for me . . . there must have been some other motive, and the motive I place before you makes much more sense that any others I have read. That is especially in light of the inconsistency in the story when viewed from the two brother-gods' points of view, which presents us with a juicy bit of circumstantial evidence as to what exactly may have happened. We had two distinct personalities in Enlil and Enki with opposing views on the slave species. Enki wanted to save man, therefore he warned Noah (Ziusudra), who also happened to be his son, but he warned more than just Noah. Therefore, the biblical entry that proclaims Noah to be the only righteous man on Earth makes no sense. This is where it gets really interesting, because it feels as if this part of the biblical story was written only after the event of the Flood, from the perspective of Enlil, who suddenly realized that he had failed in his quest to wipe out the human race. This failure to dispose of the troublesome human population forced Enlil to alter his entire story, hiding the fact that he had failed. It really feels like a lot of sour grapes to me, and the entries in the Bible were written so as to hide the fact that god had failed in destroying the vile and evil humans, but instead he found one "righteous" man among them to take pity on. After the Flood, Enki took humans under his wing and started to teach them all the necessities of a civilized community, at which point we witness the emergence of sudden global civilization around 11000 BC. But their rapid evolution scared Enlil, especially when the humans built the tower of Babel in an attempt to reach their gods in the sky. So, it was probably the spiteful Enlil who destroyed the tower and caused them to scatter over the world in another attempt to slow down their progress. They were, after all, his creation, his slaves, and he could do with them as he pleased.

FLOOD STORIES: WHAT THEY TELL US

It may come as a surprise to learn that there are literally hundreds of Flood stories in early human history.

This is a good time to take a look at some of the other Flood stories from around the world, to see the incredible similarities in these stories that were written on different continents, thousands of miles apart, by primitive people, hundreds of years apart. Does that not ring very loud alarm bells with you? Mark Isaak has compiled an incredible collection of these stories at www.talkorigins.org and I would urge you to see his website for truly captivating reading. Here are a few excerpts:

Greek:

Zeus sent a flood to destroy the men of the Bronze Age. Prometheus advised his son Deucalion to build a chest. All other men perished except for a few who escaped to high mountains. When the rains ceased, he sacrificed to Zeus, the God of Escape. An older version of the story told by Hellanicus has Deucalion's ark landing on Mount Othrys in Thessaly. Another account has him landing on a peak, probably Phouka, in Argolis, later called Nemea.

The Megarians told that Megarus, son of Zeus, escaped Deucalion's flood by swimming to the top of Mount Gerania, guided by the cries of cranes.

An earlier flood was reported to have occurred in the time of Ogyges, founder and king of Thebes. The flood covered the whole world and was so devastating that the country remained without kings until the reign of Cecrops.

Fig. 12.2. Enlil decides to destroy humankind with a flood. The Atra-Hasis epic is the Babylonian Flood story written in Old Babylonian on clay in Babylonia circa 1900 BC in cuneiform script.

When the Neo-Babylonian account of the Flood story as part of the Gilgamesh epic was discovered in the nineteenth century, it caused a sensation. It turned out that this was an abbreviated account extracted from the Old Babylonian Atra-Hasis epic, written some 1,000 years earlier. The Flood is the climax of the whole story in which the gods created the human race to take over the hard labor on Earth. They were created with the power to reproduce, but were condemned to die as a result of age. The human race multiplied and made such a noise that the chief Sumerian god, Enlil, could not sleep. He therefore plotted to reduce their numbers, first by plague, then by famine. In each case the god Ea (Enki), who was mainly responsible for creating the human race, frustrated the plan. Enlil then got all the gods to swear to cooperate in exterminating the whole human race in an impending flood. This failed because Enki saved his favorite, Ziusudra, by allowing him to build an ark and so save the human race and the animals. This tablet starts after the famine attempt by the gods had just failed, Enlil plotted against humankind and came up with another plan.

Partial tablet translation: They broke the cosmic barrier!—The flood which you mentioned, whose is it?—The Gods commanded total destruction! Enlil did an evil deed on the people! They commanded in the assembly of the gods, bringing a flood for a later day, "Let us do the deed!" Atra-Hasis

Roman:

Jupiter, angered at the evil ways of humanity, resolved to destroy it. He was about to set the earth to burning, but considered that that might set heaven itself afire, so he decided to flood the earth instead. With Neptune's help, he caused storm and earthquake to flood everything but the summit of Parnassus, where Deucalion and his wife Pyrrha came by boat and found refuge. Recognizing their piety, Jupiter let them live and withdrew the flood. Deucalion and Pyrrha, at the advice of an oracle, repopulated the world by throwing "your mother's bones" (stones) behind them; each stone became a person.

Scandinavian:

Oden, Vili, and Ve fought and slew the great ice giant Ymir, and icy water from his wounds drowned most of the Rime Giants. The giant Bergelmir escaped, with his wife and children, on a boat. Ymir's body became the world we live on.

Celtic:

Heaven and Earth were great giants, and Heaven lay upon the Earth so that their children were crowded between them, and the children and their mother were unhappy in the darkness. The boldest of the sons led his brothers in cutting up Heaven into many pieces. From his skull they made the firmament. His spilling blood caused a great flood which killed all humans except a single pair, who were saved in a ship made by a beneficent Titan.

Welsh:

The lake of Llion burst, flooding all lands. Dwyfan and Dwyfach escaped in a mastless ship with pairs of every sort of living creature. They landed in Prydain (Britain) and repopulated the world.

There are many more Flood stories such as Lithuanian, German, Turkish, Vogul, Egyptian, and Persian. Even the Koran (11:25–48) refers to the Flood, adding that the Earth swallowed the water, and the boat came to rest on a mountain called Al-Judi, and one of Noah's disbelieving sons drowned in the Flood.

An apocryphal Book of Adam tells us how Adam instructed that his body, together with gold, incense, and myrrh, should be taken aboard the Ark and, after the Flood, should be laid in the middle of the Earth. God would come from thence and save mankind (Platt, and 2 Adam 8:9–18, 21:7–11). Here we are really mixing the history of humankind. Wasn't Adam dead by then? How would he know that a flood was looming to give such instructions? How sure are we of these facts?

The Babylonian tale is virtually identical to the Sumerian story and even the Chaldean story is filled with Sumerian influence. Remember that the Sumerian Noah was called Ziusudra:

> The god Chronos in a vision warned Xisuthrus of a coming flood, ordered him to write a history and bury it in Sippara, and told him to build and provision a vessel (5 stadia by 2 stadia) for himself, his friends and relations, and all kinds of animals, all of which he did. After the flood had come and abated somewhat, he sent out some birds, which returned. Later, he tried again, and the birds returned with mud on their feet. On the third trial, the birds didn't return. He disembarked in the Corcyraean mountains in Armenia and, with his wife, daughter, and pilot, offered sacrifices to the gods.

The Zoroastrian story:

> After Ahura Mazda has warned Yima that destruction in the form of winter, frost, and floods, subsequent to the melting of the snow, are threatening the sinful world, he proceeds to instruct him to build a vara, "fortress or estate," in which specimens of small and large cattle, human beings, dogs, birds, red flaming fires, plants and foodstuffs will have to be deposited in pairs.

What all these stories really point to is a time and place when the gods of heaven and Earth conspired to wipe out all of humanity. Why? Because they were showing signs of independence, intelligence, and possible rebellion against their makers. I have presented you with their motives that have been expanded on by many scholars in numerous studies of the Sumerian tablets and other ancient scriptures. But there is one story in the Bible that, in my humble opinion, supercedes all the others in presenting evidence of god's manipulation of humanity. This is the story of Abraham, his son Isaac, Sodom and Gomorrah. It reads like a plot from a Hollywood mafia movie, where certain people are set up to have their loyalty tested, before they can be trusted by the "godfather" to perform certain acts that are not necessarily always kosher. Ask any writer and they will confirm that the plot laid out in this particular story of the Bible has the perfect structure for a screenplay, which includes a good-cop-bad-cop situation, planting seeds of suspicion and distrust, while demanding absolute loyalty: a code of silence and obedience. These events are perfect examples of a master-slave relationship, with a constant undertone of possible violence to be inflicted on the slave if he should step out of line. It has perfectly crafted moments of transparent leniency and hints of empty compassion toward the slaves who are perpetually filled with mortal fear.

It all starts with the "god-master" setting up his slave for personal conflict by evicting his mistress. The slave is Abraham, the mistress is Hagar. Abraham's wife Sarah supports this move as Hagar is a real threat to her because Hagar had given birth to a son of Abraham, who will become a competitor to her own son in time to come. But the clever twist lies in that the god-master tells Abraham to evict Hagar personally. By doing this, the master tests his slave's loyalty and he drives a wedge between him and the mistress. No sooner has Hagar been left to die in the unforgiving desert than the god-master comes to the rescue of the evicted young slave girl and her newborn son, winning her undivided loyalty, spreading the word of the loving, benevolent god.

Hagar and Ishmael Are Sent Away

The child grew and was weaned, and on the day Isaac was weaned Abraham held a great feast. But Sarah saw that the son whom Hagar the Egyptian had borne to Abraham was mocking, and she said to Abraham, "Get rid of that slave woman and her son, for that slave woman's son will never share in the inheritance with my son Isaac." The matter distressed Abraham greatly because it concerned his son. But God said to him, "Do not be so distressed about the boy and your maidservant. Listen to whatever Sarah tells you, because it is through Isaac that your offspring will be reckoned. I will make the son of the maidservant into a nation also, because he is your offspring." Early the next morning Abraham took some food and a skin of water and gave them to Hagar. He set them on her shoulders and then sent her off with the boy. She went on her way and wandered in the desert of Beersheba. When the water in the skin was gone, she put the boy under one of the bushes. Then she went off and sat down nearby, about a bowshot away, for she thought, "I cannot watch the boy die." And as she sat there nearby, she began to sob. God heard the boy crying, and the angel of God called to Hagar from heaven and said to her, "What is the matter, Hagar? Do not be afraid; God has heard the boy crying as he lies there. Lift the boy up and take him by the hand, for I will make him into a great nation." Then God opened her eyes and she saw a well of water. So she went and filled the skin with water and gave the boy a drink. God was with the boy as he grew up. He lived in the desert and became an archer. While he was living in the Desert of Paran, his mother got a wife for him from Egypt.

GENESIS 21:8–21

This clever manipulation showed the gods that Abraham was extremely loyal and trustworthy of performing future tasks. It also made Hagar eternally indebted to god for saving her and her son's lives. But what future tasks do the gods have in mind for Abraham you might ask? Possibly the earliest recorded examples of espionage in human history. This was, however, not enough of a test of obedience for the future top spy of the gods. Before they could entrust Abraham with a full army of well-equipped men, chariots, advanced weapons, large stretches of land, and wealth beyond belief, they had to devise a test of ultimate obedience, which they did. The story is famous even outside of Judeo-Christian circles. Abraham is ordered by god to take his son Isaac onto a distant mountain and sacrifice him to the gods. Their premeditated maliciousness is evident in that they told Abraham to "go to a distant mountain," where they would be alone, so that nobody would witness the brutal event as well as a premeditated murder. Who knows, something may have gone wrong and Abraham may have killed Isaac on the mountain that day. It was better that there were no witnesses around, or confused relatives, to add to the growing discontent among the humans toward the gods. Abraham passed the test with flying colors. He was now ready to perform any task for the conniving gods. From this moment on, the gods made sure that everyone knew about their favorite boy, Abraham. Many tribal heads, kings, and even priests came to seek his favor, and in truth suck up to him to avoid any possible acts of vengeance from the gods.

The Sacrifice of Isaac by Abraham

Now it came about after these things, that God tested Abraham, and said to him, "Abraham!" And he said, "Here I am." He said, "Take now your son, your only son, whom you love, Isaac, and go to the land of Moriah, and offer him there as a burnt offering on one of the mountains of which I will tell you." So Abraham rose early in the morning and saddled his donkey, and took two of his young men with him and Isaac his son; and he split wood for the burnt offering, and arose and went to the place of which God had told him. On the third day Abraham raised his eyes and saw the place from a distance. Abraham said to his young men, "Stay here with the donkey, and I and the lad will go over there; and we will worship and return to you." Abraham took the wood of the burnt offering and laid it on Isaac his son, and he took in his hand the fire and the knife. So the two of them walked on together. Isaac spoke to Abraham his father and said, "My father!" And he said, "Here I am, my son." And he said, "Behold, the fire and the wood, but where is the lamb for the burnt offering?" Abraham said, "God will provide for Himself the lamb for the burnt offering, my son." So the two of them walked on together. Then they came to the place of which God had told him; and Abraham built the altar there and arranged the wood, and bound his son Isaac and laid him on the altar, on top of the wood. Abraham stretched out his hand and took the knife to slay his son. But the angel of the LORD called to him from heaven and said, "Abraham, Abraham!" And he said, "Here I am." He said, "Do not stretch out your hand against the lad, and do nothing to him; for now I know that you fear God, since you have not withheld your son, your only son, from Me." Then Abraham raised his eyes and looked, and behold, behind him a ram caught in the thicket by his horns; and Abraham went and took the ram and offered him up for a burnt offering in the place of his son. Abraham called the name of that place The LORD Will Provide, as it is said to this day, "In the mount of the LORD it will be provided." Then the angel of the LORD called to Abraham a second time from heaven, and said, "By Myself I have sworn," declares the LORD, "because you have done this thing and have not withheld your son, your only son, indeed I will greatly bless you, and I will greatly multiply your seed as the stars of the heavens and as the sand which is on the seashore; and your seed shall possess the gate of their enemies. In your seed all the nations of the earth shall be blessed, because you have obeyed My voice."

GENESIS 22:1–18

This is surely the most malicious manipulation of early man by the gods to establish his loyalty. It also provided a model for the gods with which they could exercise future control over their human subjects, while promising their loyal and obedient humans rich rewards. You have to see through all the grandstanding, posturing, and impressive narrative in the Old Testament to recognize the absolute fear under which the people lived at all times. The gods were bloodthirsty and ruthless manipulators. But they had a very good reason to behave this way: man had grown visibly unhappy with their abuse, and man was beginning to form groups of resistance, which were led by rebellious gods like Marduk, the son of Enki.

At this point, building up to the destruction of Sodom and Gomorrah, Marduk had officially revolted against his commanding god Enlil, developing a huge global following among humans, as he promised them life after death. He also proclaimed himself as god above all. People who were thought to be in any way involved in such activity against the ruling gods would be classified as vile and evil, committing unspeakable acts of sin against god, and they would be punished severely. It is not quite clear whether it was Enlil who committed the gruesome acts of violence against humans, but the evidence seems to point toward Marduk, as he grew more and more desperate to take control of the world. Marduk devised his own plan to control his human worshippers with fear and intimidation. After all, it had worked perfectly well until then. His recruitment campaign began shortly before the rise of the Egyptian empire and lasted way beyond the events at Sodom. Marduk traveled the whole world, wherever other gods had settled, proclaiming himself superior to them. It worked especially well in the biblical lands including Egypt. And so began the calculated recorded manipulation of humankind by the god of vengeance of the Old Testament.

Compare this behavior to that of some notorious dictators many years later like Stalin, Mao, and Hitler and you will see there is not much difference. "Like father, like son." The gods have taught us well and their inherited DNA is clearly visible in our actions even today. We will see some support for this in a few choice extracts from the Bible.

Meanwhile, the early activists against Enlil would congregate in places where they would not be easily spotted by potential gossipers and spies. The resistance kept on growing among the humans, and activists were plotting various ways to overcome the brutal gods. It is also clear that certain towns and cities became strongholds of the early revolutionaries, possibly inspired by the very early thinkers among humans, or the philosophers who became so highly admired in latter days. Two such cities were Sodom and Gomorrah.

So while Enlil was nurturing Abraham into a loyal general, other kings saw that the instability among humans was on the rise and realized that there was serious trouble brewing. It must have been common knowledge that humans were growing increasingly unhappy with their gods and the resistance was gaining momentum. Abraham and his followers were constantly manipulated and brainwashed by the gods with stories that the world was full of "sinful and evil" people. Do me a favor! How is this possible? How was it possible that suddenly it was only Abraham and his clan who were okay in god's eyes while mostly everyone else was evil, involved in unacceptably sinful behavior that meant that they had to be destroyed? Ask yourself again . . . what could those people have been doing that was so evil? What could they have been scheming that meant the total annihilation of two entire cities? Did the almighty and loving god not have other means at his disposal? Just imagine this kind of behavior today. Even in outright war situations, the aggressor usually never obliterates entire cities. The humanitarian element elects not to harm innocent women and children. It is mainly the soldiers who are targets in war situations. I must rush to add that although this kind of annihilation is pretty much what George W. Bush did in Afghanistan and Iraq, there were, however, many survivors. The kind of annihilation that describes the events at Sodom and Gomorrah was much more malicious, with a clear intent to kill all living things in those two cities.

Abraham must have become a highly dubious person in the lands through which he moved, so much so that even kings started to suck up to him in anticipation of the gods' possible retaliation against them. But his unshakable loyalty to his gods brought Abraham rich rewards of all sorts and made him a very wealthy man. His nephew Lot was an active participant in all of this and played a crucial role in delivering information to Abraham, which would in turn be conveyed to the gods and "angels" when they came calling and snooping around for information.

> Now Abram was very rich in livestock, in silver, and in gold. And he journeyed on from the Negeb as far as Bethel to the place where his tent had been at the beginning, between Bethel and Ai, to the place where he had made an altar at the first. And there Abram called upon the name of the LORD. And Lot, who went with Abram, also had flocks and herds and tents, so that the land could not support both of them dwelling together; for their possessions were so great that they could not dwell together . . . "Is not the whole land before you? Separate yourself from me. If you take the left hand, then I will go to the right, or if you take the right hand, then I will go to the left." And Lot lifted up his eyes and saw that the Jordan Valley was well watered everywhere like the garden of the LORD, like the land of Egypt, in the direction of Zoar. [This was before the LORD destroyed Sodom and Gomorrah.] So Lot chose for himself all the Jordan Valley, and Lot journeyed east. Thus they separated from each other. Abram settled in the land of Canaan, while Lot settled among the cities of the valley and moved his tent as far as Sodom. Now the men of Sodom were wicked, great sinners against the LORD.
>
> GENESIS 13:2–13

This was a cunning plan by the gods, to send Lot right into the heart of Sodom and settle down there, while providing his uncle with information about the growing movement of the resistance by the "vile and wicked" humans. Then the gods once again reminded Abraham what his reward would be if he did not disappoint them.

> The LORD said to Abram, after Lot had separated from him, "Lift up your eyes and look from the place where you are, northward and southward and

eastward and westward, for all the land that you see I will give to you and
to your offspring forever."

GENESIS 13:14–15

To illustrate how nervous the kings in the surrounding lands must have
been of Abraham, here is an extract where one such king tries to secure his
future with Abraham, the "blue-eyed" boy of the gods, by doing what politicians have been doing forever, sucking up to the guys with money and power:

A Covenant with Abimelech

And it came to pass at that time that Abimelech and Phichol, the commander of his army, spoke to Abraham, saying, "God is with you in all that
you do. Now therefore, swear to me by God that you will not deal falsely
with me, with my offspring, or with my posterity; but that according to the
kindness that I have done to you, you will do to me and to the land in which
you have dwelt." And Abraham said, "I will swear."

GENESIS 13:22–26

Even at this point, while reassuring Abimelech that he would put a good
word in for him, he starts to display the subtle signs of a snitch for the gods by
reprimanding the king, and in the process demonstrating his superiority:

Then Abraham rebuked Abimelech because of a well of water which
Abimelech's servants had seized. And Abimelech said, "I do not know who
has done this thing; you did not tell me, nor had I heard of it until today."

GENESIS 21:25–26

The poor king immediately tries to save his skin and eventually succeeds
according to the scripture. Another example of kings sucking up to Abraham
in fear, looking for favoritism, is the following excerpt:

Abram Blessed by Melchizedek

After his return from the defeat of Chedorlaomer and the kings who were
with him, the king of Sodom went out to meet him at the Valley of Shaveh
(that is, the King's Valley). And Melchizedek king of Salem brought out bread
and wine. [He was priest of God Most High.] And he blessed him and said,
"Blessed be Abram by God Most High, Possessor of heaven and earth; and
blessed be God Most High, who has delivered your enemies into your hand!"

GENESIS 14:17–20

It is painfully clear that everyone was very nervous of the tenuous situation in the land, expecting something major to happen at any minute. There was much activity with gods coming and going all the time, appearing to various people, giving instructions, and inflicting harm to potential enemies. And on the ground there must have been much activity among the revolutionaries, which we can tell from the constant references in the Bible to the "evil and vile and sinful" men everywhere. There is a distinct paranoia in the tone with which the accusations keep recurring. The people and the kings of the lands also knew Abraham's close relationship with the brutal gods, while the manipulation of Abraham continued:

> God's Covenant with Abram states: After these things the word of the LORD came to Abram in a vision: "Fear not, Abram, I am your shield; your reward shall be very great."
>
> GENESIS 15:1

All this activity, however, was just a build-up for the biggest event of them all, when the gods maliciously planned and executed a full onslaught on Sodom and Gomorrah, the safe haven of the revolutionaries under the influence of Marduk, the rebellious god among the Anunnaki. Their slave Abraham had become a devoted and loyal servant who would do anything for his gods. God told Abraham that "the outcry against Sodom and Gomorrah was great and the accusations against them were grievous." Then god said he had decided to "come down and verify," and if it was so, he would destroy them completely. What basically transpired here is that the gods instructed Abraham to go to the cities and spy on the people. Obviously the Bible describes the action very differently, and Abraham is seen to be sent on a mission from god, to identify any virtuous people who may live in those cities, said to be crawling with evil and vile sinners. And as history books are always written by the victors, we know very little about the people of Sodom and Gomorrah besides what the propaganda passages of the Bible declare. After all, the events were recorded by the victors who were grossly indoctrinated by the manipulative gods.

Back with Abraham: Three angels appeared to him. He raised his eyes and behold, there were three men with him. Isn't this bloody marvelous! These snoopy angels always seem to appear when there is trouble brewing, or just before the shit is about to hit the fan. Abraham obviously recognized them immediately because he bowed his head and pleaded with them. One can clearly see the fearful master-slave mentality in this passage. Two of them must have carried some sort of weapons that they used later to protect themselves, and believe it or not, the third one was "god" himself in person, telling Abraham what must happen. The Old Testament called the angels *malachim,* which literally translates as "emissaries who carry divine commands and messages from god." They made it very clear to Abraham that unless he can produce fifty virtuous men from the inhabitants of the two cities, the cities will be decimated. This is what really puzzles me, and what drives my theory that Abraham was weaned to be a spy for them. Why should they tell Abraham this? Why should he be the one to produce fifty righteous men to save the cities? It could only be because he was asked to snoop around and report back to the gods. They have now come to seek the results of his snooping.

At first Abraham showed a hint of a humanity and pleaded with the gods not to kill everyone, for there may be "some virtuous or obedient" people there. God seems to agree with this sentiment and promises not to kill everyone as long as Abraham can find "even one" virtuous person in all of those cities. What is happening here is clearly a setup for failure. The gods have a nonnegotiable plan to wipe out these rebels in these sinful cities and Abraham is their spy. The other curious event is that Abraham's nephew Lot actually moved into Sodom prior to this, and it is probably he who was leaking information about the evil sinful people of the city to his uncle.

So when the angel warriors arrived at the city gate they found Lot waiting for them. This is another little curiosity pointing to premeditation. He took them to his house where they washed and ate, but the word spread like fire through Sodom that the violent angels were at Lot's house, coming to attack them. Once again it is evident that the residents of Sodom recognized the two angels immediately. Could it be because they had been seen doing this before? Just another one of their regular appearances during which they inflicted pain and death on the people? Or was it because they were dressed differently, which included carrying deadly weapons, way beyond the humans' understanding? Clearly this was a perfect opportunity for the people of Sodom to lynch the angels and have some level of revenge, even though it would have been on a small scale. Pandemonium broke out as the activists were joined by young and old, demanding that the angels come out. There must have been a lot of heated commotion and adrenalin flowing because this type of situation did not present itself often. This was the perfect trigger for the violent gods to react. It was all the proof they needed to confirm that all the people of Sodom were indeed evil sinners who needed to be destroyed. The angels came out and "smote the people with blindness, so they could not see." Then they told Lot to gather all his family members and get out of the city as they were about to destroy it. Lot did his best to round them up but he was met with disbelief and ridicule. In the end it was only his wife and two daughters who fled the city with him, under cover of darkness.

The following is the most amazing revelation of awesome weaponry and deadly force that the angels possessed. The angels told Lot, "Escape for thy life, look not behind thee, neither stop thou anywhere in the plain . . . unto the mountains escape lest thou perish." Basically meaning, get the hell out of here—get to the mountains and hide in the caves, well out of sight! Then the most remarkable thing happened. Lot pleaded with them to delay the destruction of Sodom long enough for him to reach the town of Zoar, which seemed to be far enough from Sodom. The angels of death urged Lot to hurry for they could not unleash their deadly weapons until he arrived there safely. The description that follows in the Bible can only be compared to a nuclear holocaust. And so it must have been. The cities, the people, the vegetation: everything was "upheavaled" by the power of the angels' awesome weapons. The heat and fire scorched everything in its path. Its radiation and pressure wave affected people some distance away.

Why was Lot told not to look back and to hide out of sight? An explosion of such magnitude would certainly blind one as quickly as a million welding torches would, while the radiation with the pressure wave and the heat would incinerate life for miles away. This is exactly what happened to the disobedient and inquisitive wife of Lot. The explosions behind them must have been the most spectacular and frightening thing they had ever heard. She must have turned back from sheer inquisitiveness to see the destruction . . . this was not a wise move. The biblical Hebrew version relays that she was turned into "a pillar of salt." But as Zecharia Sitchin points out, it was incorrectly translated—the proper translation should be "a pillar of vapor." That is pretty much what one would expect from a nuclear blast.

The destruction by the violent angels did not stop there. Once again we find evidence that Lot may have been spying on other people in other cities, as he made his way from one to the other, but for some reason he was not allowed to stay. Could this be because the citizens were familiar with Lot and his close links to the gods? Could it be that they simply did not want Lot around? Were they scared of a similar fate to that of Sodom? The angels of death followed Lot from town to town, destroying one by one in the same fashion as Sodom. I ask you to evaluate the situation again. What on Earth were the people of those cities accused of to deserve such severe punishment from our "ever-loving" god? I will not settle for the schizophrenic story portrayed in the Bible, even if you do threaten me with nuclear weapons! This is not my God behaving in such a distinctly barbaric way. The anger of the innocent people throughout the lands must have boiled over, which only fueled the revolutionaries, causing thousands more to join the loud protests against the violent gods everywhere. The angels had no need to look for troublemakers; the cities must have risen up in rebellion against them one by one. The gods simply responded with what they knew best—violence, death, and destruction of their disobedient slaves.

What all this activity points to is my underlying theory that much of this violent global activity has everything to do with our human DNA, which we inherited from our godly makers, and the evolution thereof. As this human drama unfolds, I am changing my opinion rapidly about the state of evolution of the Anunnaki. The evidence is mounting rapidly that they were probably not much more evolved than we are today. If you look at some of the human rights hurdles we have crossed in the past few decades on Earth, it certainly seems that we may have already surpassed their level of evolution on human rights issues. I make this statement in the light that we have successfully passed a United Nations law against slavery, while the Anunnaki created an entirely new slave species some 200,000 years ago. What has bothered me about this whole chain of events is their lack of vision and their seeming ignorance of the repercussions. At first, I believed the Anunnaki to have had perfect genomes that allowed them to perform superhuman activities, live forever, and perform amazing genetic manipulations. But then I look at how we have advanced in genetic engineering and cloning, and I realize that we have the same capability today as they had when they arrived on Earth some 443,000 years ago. In many ways, we humans, the miserable slave species of the gods, are at a similar level in space travel as the Anunnaki were all those years ago, and before long we *will* be colonizing Mars. Ask yourself this question: Will our human rights charter allow the pioneers on Mars to clone a new subspecies of humans as a lowly worker, with fewer rights than the astronaut settlers? Or will the Mars settlers be allowed to clone a slave species to do all the dirty work, and to be treated as lesser humans? I don't think so. But while we display high levels of sensitivity toward human rights today, our violent genes are still causing havoc among humanity. On that front we have a long way to evolve or to possibly treat this violent imperfection with genetic manipulation in the future.

This brings me back to the issue of how evolved the Anunnaki genome might have been when they created us. It is now very clear that their intentions were to create a less intelligent humanoid; one who is smart enough to take instructions, but at the same time ignorant and subservient enough not to challenge his maker. To achieve this they realized that cloning their own species was not going to do the trick, as it would give the offspring an equal genetic capacity to themselves. The obvious answer to the problem was to cross their own more evolved DNA with that of the *Homo erectus,* a resident species here on Earth. Although the Anunnaki did possess enough knowledge of genetics to clone a number of possible beings, it's much clearer now that they probably also had to switch off or disconnect some of the important genes in the proposed slave species in order to prevent certain advanced characteristics. Sitchin's translations of Sumerian tablets tell us in great detail about how they tried and tried again to get the egg to fertilize in the surrogate females and allow the clone to grow into a healthy baby. They describe the *Homo erectus* as "Among the animals on the steppe they live, they know not dressing in garments . . . Shaggy with hair is their whole body . . . No creature like that has ever in Edin been seen." Then they tell us exactly what the purpose of the new creature will be: "A primitive worker shall be created . . . Our commands will he understand . . . Our tools he will handle . . . The toil in the excavations he shall perform." There are a number of lamentations about their despair as they failed on several attempts to create the primitive worker: "We must try once more . . . The admixture needs adjusting . . . In the crystal bowl the oval of an earth female she inseminated . . . There was conception . . . This one more in the likeness of the Anunnaki was." But their attempts failed on many occasions before they created the perfect species. "Again and again Ninmah rearranged the admixtures," and finally, the result was almost perfect.

The birth of Adamu was met with great excitement by the Anunnaki, but

Fig. 12.3. The creation of Adam. A representation of a Mesopotamian cylinder seal showing the creation of Adam, the first test-tube baby. We see a goddess holding Adam while the others in the laboratory are preparing the DNA mixture and holding up a test-tube of sorts. Notice the Tree of Life prominently displayed behind the goddess.

soon they would face many new unexpected problems. The main hurdle they needed to cross then was to tame the wild animal behavior of the new slave species, which naturally caused them to rebel against any kind of confinement or oppression. The other hurdle was to instil a sense of loyalty, subservience, obedience, and especially fear into the new slave species. And so we meet the vengeful, bloodthirsty, strict "creator-god" of humanity. He dishes out a code of strict instructions, and he rewards obedience with gifts and leniency, while dispensing harsh pain and suffering to those who disobey his word. While it may sound unbelievable, it was virtually a foolproof plan; the kind of plan that would make any dictator proud. Just look at how fearful we still are of the god of vengeance. I will leave the rest of this story of creation for a later chapter while we return to the concept of slavery and how free we think we really are in the twenty-first century.

MODERN SLAVERY

As always, just when you think you know it all, a new door opens to reveal just how little you really know. When I started researching the global history of slavery, I uncovered spine-chilling tales of hardship and misery of such proportion, and stories so unbelievable, that it could make one lose complete faith in humanity. But then I reminded myself of the very simple idea that I am trying to share with you in this book. So let me remind you once again, before I share some of the horrors of modern-day slavery with you: we were created as a slave species, and we are still a slave species . . . displaying all the behavioral characteristics of a slave species. There is simply no getting away from the overwhelming evidence surrounding us and filling the pages of our prehistory. It is interesting to compare the slave rules in the code of law by King Hammurabi from Babylon, some 4,100 years ago, to the plight of sweatshop workers in Chinese factories today. To get the real effect of these modern sweatshops, let me remind you that many of the world's largest consumer brands are now manufactured in China under despicable, inhumane conditions. These are the new slave markets of the modern civilized world. Even though these factories have received loads of publicity exposing them for violating human rights in ways that we cannot even imagine, all the flag-waving, banner-bearing and chanting liberals in the West keep buying the products that come from these Eastern slave markets. What they cannot see does not affect them, so the gluttonous consumers of the West will continue to consume in ever-growing numbers, propagating the growth of the invisible slave trade of the East. The United States and Europe are clearly the main culprits by virtue of the sheer numbers in the so-called First World countries, while the Asian market just carries on consuming the brands that enslave their relatives. So now that I got that off my chest, let's take a look at a Chinese sweatshop worker's lament, together with a few more nasty revelations about our humanity.

One popular method of enslaving workers is the system of imposing fines.

Side Tracking: Yellow lines are marked on the floor; if workers step outside the yellow lines, they are fined.

Overtime: Most factories fix a time limit for going to the toilet, usually 3–5 minutes. If they stay longer than the limit, they will be fined.

Going to the toilet without permit: In some factories, workers have to get a permit tag from the supervisor to go to the toilet. The problem is that there are usually only a few tags for large numbers of workers, mostly women.

Over and above these, there are many other creative excuses used to impose fines, such as "not willing to work overtime" and "not greeting the general manager." The high wages promised to workers in these "fine zone factories" are mostly eroded to one-third or even less by all the fines imposed. In extreme cases, workers end up in debt to the factory by the end of the month. It is said that the Matsushita (National/Panasonic) Co. Ltd. in Zhuhai City has the following warning system of yellow cards, listed in Rmb, one of two official currencies in China: First yellow card is a fine of Rmb 20, the second card Rmb 40, the third time, Rmb 80, and the fourth time they receive a yellow card they are fired. Reasons for receiving a yellow card include basic acts such as talking at work, not putting their name tags in the correct position, and so on.

I ask you again. How is this possible? How did primitive man suddenly come up with the concept of slavery? And how can modern man try to justify the continued use of forced labor still today? We can now draw a very clear line in human history and find a point when slavery first emerged. As amazing as it may seem, slavery amongst humans emerged at the same time as the sudden civilization around 11000 BC. Soon after the Deluge, the Great Flood, humankind began to enslave each other, doing what they were born into, and what seemed to come quite naturally.

Many will argue that we have not evolved at all since then, that we have actually gone backward. I must agree to a certain extent that dark oppressive cults and religious dogma are of great concern, and are in some ways retarding our spiritual progress. But there is increasing excitement among the global populace about new discoveries, inventions, space travel, and more basic events like the emancipation of various peoples from dictators. Let me remind you that it was only in 1930 that we discovered the planet Pluto, and yet today we have two robots on Mars beaming back visual messages to us. We have certainly evolved; there is no doubt about that. What needs to be established is how much our genome has evolved. If the past 100 years is a form of measure we could use, that would mean the pace of evolution among humans is most likely exponential. The more we evolve, the faster we evolve. And yet it is only the wealthy sectors of world population that seem to be evolving in this way. One can argue that it is mere progress and not real evolution. But conversely, progress could lead us to fast-track our evolution through knowledge of our DNA. The pace of space exploration and IT development would certainly support such a theory. So if my assumption about the level of evolution is correct, it would mean that the Anunnaki would have evolved way past us at this stage, possibly to the point where we wouldn't even recognize them. Unless, of course, we possess some unique mutation in our genome that would have catapulted us beyond their level of evolution. And by now we should have learned that everything is possible, so let us not discard that theory as yet. The very sad thing is that while one-fifth of the world's population revels in progress, the majority are trapped by poverty, hunger, disease, and even slavery.

Japan's military shipped thousands of women from Korea, China and other Asian countries to provide sex for Japanese troops during the Second World War. Historians say that around 200,000 women were forced into sexual slavery. It was only during the early '90s that Tokyo acknowledged its military had been involved in setting up and running brothels for its troops. However, high court judge Makoto Nemoto said the current administration did not have to pay compensation because it was not responsible for what past leaders had done. . . . In past rulings, courts have favoured the Japanese government, often saying that the statute of limitations had expired, or that international labour rules did not require compensation for sexual slavery.

THE GUARDIAN, DECEMBER 15, 2004

Slave labor in China seems to be on the increase according to a news report dated August 2001. Young Chinese men are increasingly becoming victims of forced labor as economic necessity forces them to migrate to other provinces, where they have been promised well-paid jobs in brick factories or stone quarries. The article by Bruce Gilley published in the *Far Eastern*

Economic Review on August 16, 2001, highlighted how twenty-seven men were forced to work as slaves for twelve hours a day with no pay in a brick factory in Dingzhou, China. One of the men who tried to escape was caught, dragged back to the camp, and beaten to death in front of the other men. It was only on May 22, 2001, after one worker managed to escape from the guards, that local labor officials were informed and arrived to arrest the manager and free the men. The workers had been enslaved there for more than one year.

In February 2001, a newspaper called *Dahe Daily* reported that officials in Zhengzhou, Henan province, tried to free thirty slaves from an illegal coal pit. They were turned away by twenty armed guards and had to return the next day with armed police. Another coal pit was closed in the same area that enslaved six laborers, whose ages ranged between 14 and 73 years old.

In May 2001, five women, who were being forced to work without pay at an industrial materials polishing factory, escaped during an electricity blackout, according to a report in the *Yanshan Metropolis News*.

China has a household registration system called *hokou* that gives workers very few rights or protection when they leave their designated place of residence. This encourages others to view migrants as second-class citizens. The attitude taken by local authorities is that "it's not our people so we're not responsible for them." In one reported case, 100 people from Henan were rescued from a kelp factory in Shandong's Rongcheng city, only after one of them managed to contact family in Henan, after which they contacted the local newspaper, the *Henan Daily*. A manager of a brick factory in Dingzhou admitted to keeping "several" workers against their will. While laws exist to prohibit forced labor, government officials and labour officials often do not seem to enforce them.

As much as economic necessity plays a role in making migrants vulnerable to being trapped as forced laborers, it is mainly the corruption and greed of humans that allows slavery to flourish. The greed gene and the violent gene are as strong as ever in our genome. Why is it that some have developed mechanisms to suppress these characteristics, while others thrive on the effects of these genes? By the end of 1994, there were a total of 260,000 officially-registered FIE (Foreign Invested Entities) enterprises in China, employing around 1.95 million workers, with total investment amounting to $491 billion, in U.S. dollars. Because they are afforded preferential treatment by the government, FIEs in China are immune to any monitoring. The trend is that government officials and departments turn a blind eye to law-defying

FIEs for fear of losing investment. In return, the FIEs have identified this loophole as a psychological advantage and use it as a threat against law-enforcement departments. FIEs comprised at least 40% of all labor dispute cases in 1994. Some other tricks used by FIEs are:

1. Workers are required to pay a deposit upon recruitment, which usually adds up to two to three months' salary. They cannot claim back the deposit if they quit or get fired.
2. Workers' identity cards and temporary residence permits are confiscated upon entry. Workers are virtually held in custody, since they cannot go anywhere without their identity cards.
3. Workers get paid on average 18% less than the minimum wage. The lowest wage level was found in Dongguan City, which paid 32.2% less than the minimum wage.
4. Wage arrears and underpayment enslaves workers by not allowing them to take any action on their own. Some receive their wages once every few months and some enterprises only pay basic living allowances. Invariably, when the enterprises wind up, the workers cannot claim back their unpaid wages. In an official investigation conducted in September 1994 in Guangdong Province, which was the main area for foreign investment in China, 25,000 workers were found to be underpaid or unpaid to the tune of Rmb 6.52 million.

Harsh management resembles slave treatment even in accredited factories in the special economic zones. Many of the laborers come from poverty-stricken villages. Physical and verbal abuse and arbitrary dismissals are the rule of the day.

In March 1995, workers in a Korean electronics factory in Zhuhai City were forced to work nonstop for four days with only five hours sleep. The exhausted workers took a nap during the ten-minute afternoon rest period. Angered by their "laziness," the factory boss ordered the whole staff to kneel down. When some refused to obey they were sacked immediately. As China is being rapidly integrated into the world trade system, workers in China are no longer slaves of the state, they are becoming slaves of the state and of international capitalism.

The slave-labor-like factories, many of which produce big international brands, have taken many lives due to fires in the past decade. This kind of safety statistic would be completely unacceptable in the United Kingdom or United States.

FACTORY FIRES

May 1991	Hong Kong-owned Xingye Raincoat Factory, producing Ninja Turtle children's raincoats in Dongguan City, Guangdong Province; 72 killed, 47 injured.
November 1993	Hong Kong-owned Zhili Toy Factory, producing Chicco Toys in Shenzen SEZ; 87 killed, 51 injured.
December 1993	Taiwanese Gaofu Textile Co. Ltd. in Fuzhou City, Fujian Province; 61 killed, all women.
June 1994	Hong Kong-owned Yuexin Textile Factory in Zhuhai SEZ; 93 killed, 160 injured. The workers were asked to go back to the burnt factory building to take out the fabric just before the building collapsed.
September 1995	Electric wire factory in Dongguan City; 7 killed, 4 injured.
New Year's Day 1996	Workers' dormitory of a Taiwanese Christmas decoration factory in Shenzen SEZ; 22 killed, 33 injured. The warehouse-turned-dormitory was built with corrugated iron. It housed more than 800 workers and masses of plastic materials. The only exits were the two main doors.

All these preventable "accidents" follow the same pattern. There are no fire prevention facilities, and emergency exits are normally blocked or sealed to prevent the slave laborers from getting out. In the first eleven months of 1995, there were 1,184 fires recorded in Guangdong Province, claiming 193 lives and injuring 268. Most of the casualties involved young women workers, who constitute the main workforce in foreign-invested enterprises. Can you imagine this kind of news making the headlines in Los Angeles? At first you may say "this kind of thing would never happen in the United States." But the truth is, it probably happens all the time, but it simply never makes the news. Why? Because the cheap labor in L.A. consists of Mexican illegal aliens, which means it is not juicy enough for the bloodthirsty media, who probably won't pay any attention to it. Mexican lives just seem to be worth a little less than blond-blue-eyed beach bunnies.

So here we are some 200,000 years after our entry into the universal community of primitive species. Although we arrived as a slave species, we have made remarkable progress against our hostile and vengeful makers, who would stop at nothing to manipulate, control, and punish us at every conceivable opportunity. And only some 11,000 years since we adopted civilization, courtesy of some of the more benevolent gods, we are about to colonize Mars. Now that we have the moral high ground on our creator gods, with regard to our view on human rights and equality, we still carry the violent hangover of our slave species character. Although almost invisible, slavery is alive and well on Earth, as it has been for thousands of years. Will we learn from our own experiences when we settle on Mars, or will we do what comes so naturally to us—clone a new slave species and control them with an iron fist? If our slowly evolving DNA has any role in this, we will probably engage in the latter.

CODE OF HAMMURABI: THE PRIEST KING WHO ESTABLISHED BABYLONIA

There is some disagreement about the date of Hammurabi's rule. Some scholars put him at circa 2300 BC, others as late as 1700 BC. Zecharia Sitchin places him at around 1900 BC, which would make Hammurabi one of the first kings after the destruction of Sodom, Gomorrah, and other cities by the Anunnaki gods, in pursuit of Marduk the rebellious god and son of Enki, circa 2024 BC. But as we will show, Marduk survived and Babylon became a powerful city under his godship. In this translation by L. W. King, we read what King Hammurabi had to say about his new kingdom as bestowed upon him by Marduk:

> When Anu the Sublime, King of the Anunnaki, and Bel, the lord of Heaven and earth, who decreed the fate of the land, assigned to Marduk, the overruling son of Ea, God of righteousness, dominion over earthly man, and made him great among the Igigi, they called Babylon by his illustrious name, made it great on earth, and founded an everlasting kingdom in it, whose foundations are laid so solidly as those of heaven and earth; then Anu and Bel called by name me, Hammurabi, the exalted prince, who feared God, to bring about the rule of righteousness in the land, to destroy the wicked and the evil-doers; so that the strong should not harm the weak; so that I should rule over the black-headed people like Shamash, and enlighten the land, to further the well-being of mankind.

These words are wonderful evidence of how the Anunnaki gods controlled the fates of men and bestowed kingship on their chosen few. We also find corroboration of the close relationship between Marduk and the Igigi, who were his followers, who arrived on Earth from Mars when it lost its atmosphere.

They are the most likely candidates, who were the progenitors of the Aryans when they married human females in years to come. We also read about the "blackheaded people," who were the primitive workers and descendents of Adamu, who were brought up to Sumer to work for the upper-class Sumerians and gods. We also read about the plight of the blackheaded people in other tablets, and we find references to them mostly with regard to performing the hard labor for which they were created. This proves irrefutably that black people have had the raw end of the deal on this planet since the very first moment of creation. It is now clear that Adam was black. Some of his descendents were taken north and mixed with the Igigi and other lesser gods of Sumer, creating the white Aryan upper class of the Sumerian civilization. Those relatives of Adam who remained in Africa, remained behind in many other ways. While the technology of the Anunnaki gods was being widely applied in the daily lives of the Sumerians, the African descendents of Adam were living in basic and primitive conditions for thousands of years, worshipping their supposedly mythological gods. But not all the blackheaded people who were taken to Sumer had it easy, because most of them remained slaves to the Anunnaki and experienced hardship. Some 2,000 years BC, an unknown scribe wrote a poem describing the sad events which surrounded the fall of the city of Ur. In this lamentation we read about the plight of the blackheaded people. This poem is an excellent corroboration of the aftermath during which Sodom and Gomorrah were destroyed by some kind of nuclear disaster, unleashed by the biblical angels who visited Abraham and Lot. The time was around 2024 BC. The dots in the following translation of the tablet indicate the damaged parts of the tablet that are illegible.

That law and order cease to exist . . .

That cities be destroyed, that houses be destroyed . . .

That Sumer's rivers flow with bitter water . . .

That the mother care not for her children . . .

That kingship be carried off from the land . . .

That on the banks of the Tigris and Euphrates . . . there grow sticky plants . . .

That no one tread the highways, that no one seek out the roads, That its well-founded cities and hamlets be counted as ruins, That its teeming black-headed people be put to the mace . . .

The fate decreed by the gods cannot be changed, who can overturn it!

Codes 15–20 of The Code of Hammurabi: References to Slaves

15. If any one take a male or female slave of the court, or a male or female slave of a freed man, outside the city gates, he shall be put to death.
16. If any one receive into his house a runaway male or female slave of the court, or of a freed man, and does not bring it out at the public proclamation of the major domus, the master of the house shall be put to death.
17. If any one find runaway male or female slaves in the open country and bring them to their masters, the master of the slaves shall pay him two shekels of silver.
18. If the slave will not give the name of the master, the finder shall bring him to the palace; a further investigation must follow, and the slave shall be returned to his master.
19. If he hold the slaves in his house, and they are caught there, he shall be put to death.
20. If the slave that he caught run away from him, then shall he swear to the owners of the slave, and he is free of all blame.

The Code of the Nesilim (Hittites), circa 1650–1500 BC: Random Excerpts

- If anyone smite a free man or woman and this one die, he shall bring this one and give two persons, he shall let them go to his home.
- If anyone smite a male or female slave, he shall bring this one also and give one person, he shall let him or her go to his home.
- If anyone blind a free man or knock out his teeth, formerly they would give one pound of silver, now he shall give twenty half-shekels of silver.
- If anyone blind a male or female slave or knock out their teeth, he shall give ten half-shekels of silver, he shall let it go to his home.
- If anyone cause a free woman to miscarry, if it be the tenth month, he shall give ten half-shekels of silver, if it be the fifth month, he shall give five half-shekels of silver.

- If anyone cause a female slave to miscarry, if it be the tenth month, he shall give five half-shekels of silver.
- If any man of Hatti steal a Nesian slave and lead him here to the land of Hatti, and his master discover him, he shall give him twelve half-shekels of silver, he shall let it go to his home.
- If anyone steal a slave of a Luwian from the land of Luwia, and lead him here to the land of Hatti, and his master discover him, he shall take his slave only.
- If a male or female slave run away, he at whose hearth his master finds him or her, shall give fifty half-shekels of silver a year.
- If a free man and a female slave be fond of each other and come together and he take her for his wife and they set up house and get children, and afterward they either become hostile or come to close quarters, and they divide the house between them, the man shall take the children, only one child shall the woman take.
- If a slave take a woman as his wife, their case is the same. The majority of the children to the wife and one child to the slave.
- If a slave take a female slave their case is the same. The majority of children to the female slave and one child to the slave.
- If a slave convey the bride price to a free son and take him as husband for his daughter, nobody dare surrender him to slavery.
- If a free man set a house ablaze, he shall build the house, again. And whatever is inside the house, be it a man, an ox, or a sheep that perishes, nothing of these he need compensate.
- If a slave set a house ablaze, his master shall compensate for him. The nose of the slave and his ears they shall cut off, and give him back to his master. But if he do not compensate, then he shall give up this one.
- If a free man kill a serpent and speak the name of another, he shall give one pound of silver; if a slave, this one shall die.
- If a free man pick up female slaves, now one, now another, there is no punishment for intercourse. If brothers sleep with a free woman, together, or one after the other, there is no punishment. If father and son sleep with a female slave or harlot, together, or one after the other, there is no punishment.
- If a slave say to his master: "You are not my master," if they convict him his master shall cut off his ear.

No matter how much evidence is presented, many readers will find the truth too terrible to digest. Our human nature has evolved in a way that we simply reject gloomy hypotheses of such magnitude in favor of rosier tales told by historians. In this quest for enlightenment, our biggest enemy is our arrogance. In our inability to face the terrible truth about our slave-species ancestry, lies the ironic paradox that may ultimately contribute to our demise. Our misplaced pride may eventually destroy us. Knowledge is power, no matter how old it may be. I suggest that we begin to embrace the knowledge of our distant ancestors, as difficult as it may be, and find a way to understanding the real facts about our origins as the human race and our place on this planet. Unfortunately, every ounce of our human essence screams with the characteristics of a slave species trapped in a cycle of incomprehensible rituals enslaved by everything around us, but stubbornly rejecting such suggestions to our graves. We were created as a slave species, we have lived and behaved like a slave species, and we are still behaving as such, uncertain of our origins and purpose.

13

WORLD RELIGIONS

The Great Slave Maker

WHEN YOU VISIT SOMEONE at their home for the first time, it is always fascinating to scan the photographs scattered on the walls and furniture, showing off their close family and friends. Within minutes, one gets a sense of the person's background, where they were born, where they grew up, how well-off they are, and how many brothers and sisters they have. Are the parents still together or divorced? Where do they live now? Baby pictures, school pictures, graduation pictures, pictures of their animals, and even pictures of their cars in some instances. It presents a reasonably complete collage of your host's family and history as well as their social standing. It fills you with a sense of comfort, knowing a little more about your host. Suddenly the expression "the apple never falls far from the tree" becomes relevant again when trying to analyze your host's character and personality. Subconsciously you start to calculate whether the first impressions you formulated of the host, before you were exposed to his photographic display, match the evidence presented. We are often surprised to discover something new from the photo gallery, something that takes us by complete surprise. Especially if the host is of another culture or lives in a foreign country. And so we are filled with a sense of comfort as we settle down to a cup of tea or a *braai* (barbecue) in the backyard.

Let us imagine for a minute that we as the human family receive a visitor for dinner from another planet. We manage to overcome any fear of conflict because it just so happens that the guest speaks a distant dialect of our own language. As they arrive we display pictures of our human family, our brothers, sisters, cousins and nephews, but for some reason we have no pictures of our parents. The visitor is immediately very intrigued. Are we a bunch of orphans? Do we not know who our parents are? With all this time on Earth, have we not had enough time to find out? We then explain that we have many fathers upon which the visitor bursts out laughing. He realizes that we obviously do not know anything about biology and he explains to us that it is impossible to have more than one father. We then present our guest with the evidence of our many fathers, by which time he realizes that we are seriously disturbed and uninformed, and we as humans need some serious guidance and a refresher course on the origins of humanity. The visitor asks us if we are not aware of the universal community of beings and whether we know that we all come from one original source. He tells us of the common practice of colonizing new planets by the infinite number of evolved intelligent species of beings; the extended practice and the right to populate new planets with our own species if we are the first ones to get there; the practice of creating genetically less advanced beings to perform the tough task of manual labor on newly colonized planets, allowing them to evolve to the highest level; at the same time continuing the cycle of universal evolution and enlightenment of species; and when we reach the highest level of evolution and enlightenment we rejoin the universal community of beings from which we all originate; at which stage we are reunited with our Creator the Universal Being, Creator of all things in the universe.

This story really confuses us and makes us feel a little uneasy because we are all very sure of who our father is, and we make an excuse for our human brothers and sisters who claim that our father may be someone else according to them. We try to convince our visitor that our father is whom we believe he is. Although we have no evidence of it, it has been passed down to us through many generations, so it must be true. Our guest then asks to see a list of our human brothers and their supposed fathers, and this is what we show him.

RELIGIONS BY COUNTRY	
(To avoid boredom, please use this list as a reference only.)	
COUNTRY	RELIGIONS INDICATED IN PERCENTAGE OF ADHERENTS
Afghanistan	Sunni Muslim 80%, Shi'a Muslim 19%, other 1%
Albania	Muslim 70%, Albanian Orthodox 20%, Roman Catholic 10%
Algeria	Sunni Muslim (state religion) 99%, Christian and Jewish 1%
American Samoa	Christian Congregationalist 50%, Roman Catholic 20%, Protestant and other 30%

Andorra	Roman Catholic (predominant)
Angola	Indigenous beliefs 47%, Roman Catholic 38%, Protestant 15% (1998 est.)
Anguilla	Anglican 40%, Methodist 33%, Seventh-Day Adventist 7%, Baptist 5%, Roman Catholic 3%, other 12%
Antigua and Barbuda	Christian, (predominantly Anglican with other Protestant, and some Roman Catholic)
Argentina	Nominally Roman Catholic 92% (less than 20% practicing), Protestant 2%, Jewish 2%, other 4%
Armenia	Armenian Apostolic 94%, other Christian 4%, Yezidi (Zoroastrian/Animist) 2%
Aruba	Roman Catholic 82%, Protestant 8%, Hindu, Muslim, Confucian, Jewish
Australia	Anglican 26.1%, Roman Catholic 26%, other Christian 24.3%, non-Christian 11%, other 12.6%
Austria	Roman Catholic 73.6%, Protestant 4.7%, Muslim 4.2%, other 0.1%, none 17.4%
Azerbaijan	Muslim 93.4%, Russian Orthodox 2.5%, Armenian Orthodox 2.3%, other 1.8% (1995 est.)
Bahamas	Baptist 32%, Anglican 20%, Roman Catholic 19%, Methodist 6%, Church of God 6%, other Protestant 12%, none or unknown 3%, other 2%
Bahrain	Shi'a Muslim 70%, Sunni Muslim 30%
Bangladesh	Muslim 83%, Hindu 16%, other 1% (1998)
Barbados	Protestant 67% (Anglican 40%, Pentecostal 8%, Methodist 7%, other 12%), Roman Catholic 4%, none 17%, other 12%
Belarus	Eastern Orthodox 80%, other (including Roman Catholic, Protestant, Jewish, and Muslim) 20% (1997 est.)
Belgium	Roman Catholic 75%, Protestant or other 25%
Belize	Roman Catholic 49.6%, Protestant 27% (Anglican 5.3%, Methodist 3.5%, Mennonite 4.1%, Seventh-Day Adventist 5.2%, Pentecostal 7.4%, Jehovah's Witnesses 1.5%), none 9.4%, other 14% (2000)
Benin	Indigenous beliefs 50%, Christian 30%, Muslim 20%
Bermuda	Non-Anglican Protestant 39%, Anglican 27%, Roman Catholic 15%, other 19%
Bhutan	Lamaistic Buddhist 75%, Indian- and Nepalese-influenced Hinduism 25%

Bolivia	Roman Catholic 95%, Protestant (Evangelical Methodist)
Bosnia and Herzegovina	Muslim 40%, Orthodox 31%, Roman Catholic 15%, other 14%
Botswana	Indigenous beliefs 85%, Christian 15%
Brazil	Roman Catholic (nominal) 80%
British Virgin Islands	Protestant 86% (Methodist 33%, Anglican 17%, Church of God 9%, Seventh-Day Adventist 6%, Baptist 4%, Jehovah's Witnesses 2%, other 15%), Roman Catholic 10%, none 2%, other 2%
Brunei	Muslim (official) 67%, Buddhist 13%, Christian 10%, indigenous beliefs and other 10%
Bulgaria	Bulgarian Orthodox 82.6%, Muslim 12.2%, Roman Catholic 1.7%, Jewish 0.1%, Protestant, Gregorian-Armenian, and other 3.4% (1998)
Burkina Faso	Indigenous beliefs 40%, Muslim 50%, Christian (mainly Roman Catholic) 10%
Burma	Buddhist 89%, Christian 4% (Baptist 3%, Roman Catholic 1%), Muslim 4%, Animist 1%, other 2%
Burundi	Christian 67% (Roman Catholic 62%, Protestant 5%), indigenous beliefs 23%, Muslim 10%
Cambodia	Theravada Buddhist 95%, other 5%
Cameroon	Indigenous beliefs 40%, Christian 40%, Muslim 20%
Canada	Roman Catholic 46%, Protestant 36%, other 18%* *Note: Based on the 1991 census.
Cape Verde	Roman Catholic (infused with indigenous beliefs), Protestant (mostly Church of the Nazarene)
Cayman Islands	United Church (Presbyterian and Congregational), Anglican, Baptist, Church of God, other Protestant, Roman Catholic
Central African Republic	Indigenous beliefs 35%, Protestant 25%, Roman Catholic 25%, Muslim 15%
Chad	Muslim 51%, Christian 35%, Animist 7%, other 7%
Chile	Roman Catholic 89%, Protestant 11%, Jewish negligible
China	Daoist (Taoist), Buddhist, Muslim 1%–2%, Christian 3%–4%* *Note: Officially atheist (2002 est.).
Christmas Island	Buddhist 36%, Muslim 25%, Christian 18%, other 21%

Cocos (Keeling) Islands	Sunni Muslim 80%, other 20% (2002 est.)
Colombia Roman	Catholic 90%
Comoros	Sunni Muslim 98%, Roman Catholic 2%
Congo, DRC	Roman Catholic 50%, Protestant 20%, Kimbanguist 10%, Muslim 10%, other syncretic sects and indigenous beliefs 10%
Congo, Republic of the	Christian 50%, Animist 48%, Muslim 2%
Cook Islands	Christian (majority of populace are members of the Cook Islands Christian Church)
Costa Rica	Roman Catholic 76.3%, Evangelical 13.7%, Jehovah's Witnesses 1.3%, other Protestant 0.7%, other 4.8%, none 3.2%
Cote d'Ivoire	Christian 20%–30%, Muslim 35%–40%, indigenous 25%–40%
Croatia	Roman Catholic 87.8%, Orthodox 4.4%, Muslim 1.3%, Protestant 0.3%, others and unknown 6.2% (2001)
Cuba	Nominally 85% Roman Catholic prior to Castro assuming power; Protestants, Jehovah's Witnesses, Jews, and Santeria are also represented
Cyprus	Greek Orthodox 78%, Muslim 18%, Maronite, Armenian Apostolic, and other 4%
Czech Republic	Roman Catholic 39.2%, Protestant 4.6%, Orthodox 3%, other 13.4%, Atheist 39.8%
Denmark	Evangelical Lutheran 95%, other Protestant and Roman Catholic 3%, Muslim 2%
Djibouti	Muslim 94%, Christian 6%
Dominica	Roman Catholic 77%, Protestant 15% (Methodist 5%, Pentecostal 3%, Seventh-Day Adventist 3%, Baptist 2%, other 2%), none 2%, other 6%
Dominican Republic	Roman Catholic 95%
East Timor	Roman Catholic 90%, Muslim 4%, Protestant 3%, Hindu 0.5%, Buddhist, Animist (1992 est.)
Ecuador	Roman Catholic 95%
Egypt	Muslim (mostly Sunni) 94%, Coptic Christian and other 6%

El Salvador	Roman Catholic 83%* *Note: There is extensive activity by Protestant groups throughout the country; by the end of 1992, there were an estimated 1 million Protestant evangelicals in El Salvador.
Equatorial Guinea	Nominally Christian and predominantly Roman Catholic, pagan practices
Eritrea	Muslim, Coptic Christian, Roman Catholic, Protestant
Estonia	Evangelical Lutheran, Russian Orthodox, Estonian Orthodox, Baptist, Methodist, Seventh-Day Adventist, Roman Catholic, Pentecostal, Word of Life, Jewish
Ethiopia	Muslim 45%–50%, Ethiopian Orthodox 35%–40%, animist 12%, other 3%–8%
European Union	Roman Catholic, Protestant, Orthodox, Muslim, Jewish
Falkland Islands (Islas Malvinas)	Primarily Anglican, Roman Catholic, United Free Church, Evangelist Church, Jehovah's Witnesses, Lutheran, Seventh-Day Adventist
Faroe Islands	Evangelical Lutheran
Fiji	Christian 52% (Methodist 37%, Roman Catholic 9%), Hindu 38%, Muslim 8%, other 2%* *Note: Fijians are mainly Christian, Indians are Hindu, and there is a Muslim minority (1986).
Finland	Evangelical Lutheran 89%, Russian Orthodox 1%, none 9%, other 1%
France	Roman Catholic 83%–88%, Protestant 2%, Jewish 1%, Muslim 5%–10%, unaffiliated 4%
French Guiana	Roman Catholic
French Polynesia	Protestant 54%, Roman Catholic 30%, other 10%, no religion 6%
Gabon	Christian 55%–75%, Animist, Muslim less than 1%
Gambia	Muslim 90%, Christian 9%, indigenous beliefs 1%
Gaza Strip	Muslim (predominantly Sunni) 98.7%, Christian 0.7%, Jewish 0.6%
Georgia	Georgian Orthodox 65%, Muslim 11%, Russian Orthodox 10%, Armenian Apostolic 8%, unknown 6%
Germany	Protestant 34%, Roman Catholic 34%, Muslim 3.7%, unaffiliated or other 28.3%

Ghana	Christian 63%, Muslim 16%, indigenous beliefs 21%
Gibraltar	Roman Catholic 76.9%, Church of England 6.9%, Muslim 6.9%, Jewish 2.3%, none or other 7% (1991)
Greece	Greek Orthodox 98%, Muslim 1.3%, other 0.7%
Greenland	Evangelical Lutheran
Grenada	Roman Catholic 53%, Anglican 13.8%, other Protestant 33.2%
Guadeloupe	Roman Catholic 95%, Hindu and pagan African 4%, Protestant 1%
Guam	Roman Catholic 85%, other 15% (1999 est.)
Guatemala	Roman Catholic, Protestant, indigenous Mayan beliefs
Guernsey	Anglican, Roman Catholic, Presbyterian, Baptist, Congregational, Methodist
Guinea	Muslim 85%, Christian 8%, indigenous beliefs 7%
Guinea-Bissau	Indigenous beliefs 50%, Muslim 45%, Christian 5%
Guyana	Christian 50%, Hindu 35%, Muslim 10%, other 5%
Haiti	Roman Catholic 80%, Protestant 16% (Baptist 10%, Pentecostal 4%, Adventist 1%, other 1%), none 1%, other 3%* *Note: Roughly half of the population practices Voodoo.
Holy See	(Vatican City) Roman Catholic
Honduras	Roman Catholic 97%, Protestant minority
Hong Kong	Eclectic mixture of local religions 90%, Christian 10%
Hungary	Roman Catholic 67.5%, Calvinist 20%, Lutheran 5%, Atheist and other 7.5%
Iceland	Evangelical Lutheran 87.1%, other Protestant 4.1%, Roman Catholic 1.7%, other 7.1% (2002)
India	Hindu 81.3%, Muslim 12%, Christian 2.3%, Sikh 1.9%, other groups including Buddhist, Jain, Parsi 2.5% (2000)
Indonesia	Muslim 88%, Protestant 5%, Roman Catholic 3%, Hindu 2%, Buddhist 1%, other 1% (1998)
Iran	Shi'a Muslim 89%, Sunni Muslim 9%, Zoroastrian, Jewish, Christian, and Baha'i 2%
Iraq	Muslim 97% (Shi'a 60%–65%, Sunni 32%–37%), Christian or other 3%
Ireland	Roman Catholic 91.6%, Church of Ireland 2.5%, other 5.9%

Israel	Jewish 80.1%, Muslim 14.6% (mostly Sunni Muslim), Christian 2.1%, other 3.2% (1996 est.)
Italy	Predominately Roman Catholic with mature Protestant and Jewish communities and a growing Muslim immigrant community
Jamaica	Protestant 61.3% (Church of God 21.2%, Baptist 8.8%, Anglican 5.5%, Seventh-Day Adventist 9%, Pentecostal 7.6%, Methodist 2.7%, United Church 2.7%, Brethren 1.1%, Jehovah's Witness 1.6%, Moravian 1.1%), Roman Catholic 4%, other including some spiritual cults 34.7%
Japan	Observes both Shinto and Buddhist 84%, other 16% (including Christian 0.7%)
Jersey	Anglican, Roman Catholic, Baptist, Congregational New Church, Methodist, Presbyterian
Jordan	Sunni Muslim 92%, Christian 6% (majority Greek Orthodox, but some Greek and Roman Catholics, Syrian Orthodox, Coptic Orthodox, Armenian Orthodox, and Protestant denominations), other 2% (several small Shi'a Muslim and Druze populations) (2001 est.)
Kazakhstan	Muslim 47%, Russian Orthodox 44%, Protestant 2%, other 7%
Kenya	Protestant 45%, Roman Catholic 33%, indigenous beliefs 10%, Muslim 10%, other 2%* *Note: A large majority of Kenyans are Christian, but estimates for the percentage of the population that adheres to Islam or indigenous beliefs vary widely.
Kiribati	Roman Catholic 52%, Protestant (Congregational) 40%, some Seventh-Day Adventist, Muslim, Baha'i, Latter-day Saints, and Church of God (1999)
Korea, North	Traditionally Buddhist and Confucianist, some Christian and syncretic Chondogyo (Religion of the Heavenly Way)* *Note: Autonomous religious activities now almost nonexistent; government-sponsored religious groups exist to provide illusion of religious freedom.
Korea, South	No affiliation 46%, Christian 26%, Buddhist 26%, Confucianist 1%, other 1%
Kuwait	Muslim 85% (Sunni 70%, Shi'a 30%), Christian, Hindu, Parsi, and other 15%
Kyrgyzstan	Muslim 75%, Russian Orthodox 20%, other 5%
Laos	Buddhist 60%, Animist and other 40% (including various Christian denominations 1.5%)
Latvia	Lutheran, Roman Catholic, Russian Orthodox

Norway	Evangelical Lutheran 86% (state church), other Protestant and Roman Catholic 3%, other 1%, none and unknown 10% (1997)
Oman	Ibadhi Muslim 75%, Sunni Muslim, Shi'a Muslim, Hindu
Pakistan	Muslim 97% (Sunni 77%, Shi'a 20%), Christian, Hindu, and other 3%
Palau	Christian (Roman Catholics 49%, Seventh-Day Adventists, Jehovah's Witnesses, the Assembly of God, the Liebenzell Mission, and Latter-Day Saints), Modekngei religion (one-third of the population observes this religion, which is indigenous to Palau)
Panama	Roman Catholic 85%, Protestant 15%
Papua New Guinea	Roman Catholic 22%, Lutheran 16%, Presbyterian/Methodist/ London Missionary Society 8%, Anglican 5%, Evangelical Alliance 4%, Seventh-Day Adventist 1%, other Protestant 10%, indigenous beliefs 34%
Paraguay	Roman Catholic 90%, Mennonite, and other Protestant
Peru	Roman Catholic 90%
Philippines	Roman Catholic 83%, Protestant 9%, Muslim 5%, Buddhist and other 3%
Pitcairn Islands	Seventh-Day Adventist 100%
Poland	Roman Catholic 95% (about 75% practicing), Eastern Orthodox, Protestant, and other 5%
Portugal	Roman Catholic 94%, Protestant (1995)
Puerto Rico	Roman Catholic 85%, Protestant and other 15%
Qatar	Muslim 95%
Reunion	Roman Catholic 86%, Hindu, Muslim, Buddhist (1995)
Romania	Eastern Orthodox (including all subdenominations) 87%, Protestant 6.8%, Catholic 5.6%, other (mostly Muslim) 0.4%, unaffiliated 0.2% (2002)
Russia	Russian Orthodox, Muslim, other
Rwanda	Roman Catholic 56.5%, Protestant 26%, Adventist 11.1%, Muslim 4.6%, indigenous beliefs 0.1%, none 1.7% (2001)
Saint Helena	Anglican (majority), Baptist, Seventh-Day Adventist, Roman Catholic
Saint Kitts and Nevis	Anglican, other Protestant, Roman Catholic
Saint Lucia	Roman Catholic 90%, Anglican 3%, other Protestant 7%

St. Pierre and Miquelon	Roman Catholic 99%
St. Vincent and the Grenadines	Anglican 47%, Methodist 28%, Roman Catholic 13%, Hindu Seventh-Day Adventist, other Protestant
Samoa	Christian 99.7% (about one-half of population associated with the London Missionary Society; includes Congregational, Roman Catholic, Methodist, Latter-Day Saints, Seventh-Day Adventist)
San Marino	Roman Catholic
Sao Tome and Principe	Christian 80% (Roman Catholic, Evangelical Protestant, Seventh-Day Adventist)
Saudi Arabia	Muslim 100%
Senegal	Muslim 94%, indigenous beliefs 1%, Christian 5% (mostly Roman Catholic)
Serbia and Montenegro	Orthodox 65%, Muslim 19%, Roman Catholic 4%, Protestant 1%, other 11%
Seychelles	Roman Catholic 86.6%, Anglican 6.8%, other Christian 2.5%, other 4.1%
Sierra Leone	Muslim 60%, indigenous beliefs 30%, Christian 10%
Singapore	Buddhist (Chinese), Muslim (Malays), Christian, Hindu, Sikh, Taoist, Confucianist
Slovakia	Roman Catholic 60.3%, Atheist 9.7%, Protestant 8.4%, Orthodox 4.1%, other 17.5%
Slovenia	Roman Catholic (Uniate 2%) 70.8%, Lutheran 1%, Muslim 1%, atheist 4.3%, other 22.9%
Solomon Islands	Anglican 45%, Roman Catholic 18%, United (Methodist/Presbyterian) 12%, Baptist 9%, Seventh-Day Adventist 7%, other Protestant 5%, indigenous beliefs 4%
Somalia	Sunni Muslim
South Africa	Christian 68% (which includes most Whites and Coloureds,* about 60% of Blacks and about 40% of Indians), Muslim 2%, Hindu 1.5% (60% of Indians), indigenous beliefs and animist 28.5% *Note: A South African term denoting mixed European and Khoi-San, Bantu, and other African heritage.
Spain	Roman Catholic 94%, other 6%
Sri Lanka	Buddhist 70%, Hindu 15%, Christian 8%, Muslim 7% (1999)

Sudan	Sunni Muslim 70% (in north), indigenous beliefs 25%, Christian 5% (mostly in south and Khartoum)
Suriname	Hindu 27.4%, Muslim 19.6%, Roman Catholic 22.8%, Protestant 25.2% (predominantly Moravian), indigenous beliefs 5%
Swaziland	Zionist (a blend of Christianity and indigenous ancestral worship) 40%, Roman Catholic 20%, Muslim 10%, Anglican, Baha'i, Methodist, Mormon, Jewish and other 30%
Sweden	Lutheran 87%, Roman Catholic, Orthodox, Baptist, Muslim, Jewish, Buddhist
Switzerland	Roman Catholic 46.1%, Protestant 40%, other 5%, none 8.9%
Syria	Sunni Muslim 74%, Alawite, Druze, and other Muslim sects 16%, Christian (various sects) 10%, Jewish (tiny communities in Damascus, Al Qamishli, and Aleppo)
Taiwan	Mixture of Buddhist, Confucianist, and Taoist 93%, Christian 4.5%, other 2.5%
Tajikistan	Sunni Muslim 85%, Shi'a Muslim 5%, other 10% (2003 est.)
Tanzania	Mainland—Christian 30%, Muslim 35%, indigenous beliefs 35%; Zanzibar—more than 99% Muslim
Thailand	Buddhism 95%, Muslim 3.8%, Christianity 0.5%, Hinduism 0.1%, other 0.6% (1991)
Togo	Indigenous beliefs 51%, Christian 29%, Muslim 20%
Tokelau	Congregational Christian Church 70%, Roman Catholic 28%, other 2%
Tonga	Christian (Free Wesleyan Church claims over 30,000 adherents)
Trinidad and Tobago	Roman Catholic 29.4%, Hindu 23.8%, Anglican 10.9%, Muslim 5.8%, Presbyterian 3.4%, other 26.7%
Tunisia	Muslim 98%, Christian 1%, Jewish and other 1%
Turkey	Muslim 99.8% (mostly Sunni), other 0.2% (mostly Christians and Jews)
Turkmenistan	Muslim 89%, Eastern Orthodox 9%, unknown 2%
Turks and Caicos Islands	Baptist 40%, Methodist 16%, Anglican 18%, Church of God 12%, other 14% (1990)
Tuvalu	Church of Tuvalu (Congregationalist) 97%, Seventh-Day Adventist 1.4%, Baha'i 1%, other 0.6%
Uganda	Roman Catholic 33%, Protestant 33%, Muslim 16%, indigenous beliefs 18%

Ukraine	Ukrainian Orthodox—Kiev Patriarchate 19%, Ukrainian Orthodox—Moscow Patriarchate 9%, Ukrainian Greek Catholic 6%, Ukrainian Autocephalous Orthodox 1.7%, Protestant, Jewish, none 38% (2004 est.)
United Arab Emirates	Muslim 96% (Shi'a 16%), Christian, Hindu, and other 4%
United Kingdom	Anglican and Roman Catholic 40 million, Muslim 1.5 million, Presbyterian 800,000, Methodist 760,000, Sikh 500,000, Hindu 500,000, Jewish 350,000
United States	Protestant 52%, Roman Catholic 24%, Mormon 2%, Jewish 1%, Muslim 1%, other 10%, none 10% (2002 est.)
Uruguay	Roman Catholic 66% (less than half of the adult population attends church regularly), Protestant 2%, Jewish 1%, nonprofessing or other 31%
Uzbekistan	Muslim 88% (mostly Sunnis), Eastern Orthodox 9%, other 3%
Vanuatu	Presbyterian 36.7%, Anglican 15%, Roman Catholic 15%, indigenous beliefs 7.6%, Seventh-Day Adventist 6.2%, Church of Christ 3.8%, other 15.7% (including Jon Frum Cargo cult)
Venezuela	Nominally Roman Catholic 96%, Protestant 2%, other 2%
Vietnam	Buddhist, Hoa Hao, Cao Dai, Christian (predominantly Roman Catholic, some Protestant), indigenous beliefs, Muslim
Virgin Islands	Baptist 42%, Roman Catholic 34%, Episcopalian 17%, other 7%
Wallis and Futuna	Roman Catholic 99%, other 1%
West Bank	Muslim 75% (predominantly Sunni), Jewish 17%, Christian and other 8%
Western Sahara World	Muslim Christians 32.71% (of which Roman Catholics 17.28%, Protestants 5.61%, Orthodox 3.49%, Anglicans 1.31%), Muslims 19.67%, Hindus 13.28%, Buddhists 5.84%, Sikhs 0.38%, Jews 0.23%, other religions 13.05%, non-religious 12.43%, atheists 2.41% (2002 est.)
Yemen	Muslim including Shaf'i (Sunni) and Zaydi (Shi'a), small numbers of Jewish, Christian, and Hindu
Zambia	Christian 50%–75%, Muslim and Hindu 24%–49%, indigenous beliefs 1%
Zimbabwe	Syncretic (part Christian, part indigenous beliefs) 50%, Christian 25%, indigenous beliefs 24%, Muslim and other 1%

Compiled from *World Factbook*, CIA, 2005

Our guest becomes very sad at the sight of this and realizes that somewhere along the line we, as the human race, have been lied to and conned. This is in direct violation of the communal spirit of universal beings. He explains that there are a number of rogue beings who were included in the community of beings a little prematurely, who have been known to colonize planets but do not follow the common protocol of educating and informing the newly created species about their origins and their destiny. Such rogue beings are like pirates of the universe, raping and pillaging planets for their wealth while creating a lesser evolved being that cannot possibly understand its place in the universe. The pirates often present themselves as gods of sorts, dealing brutally with their newly created species. They use them for labor, for experiments, and for pleasure. These cosmic pirates leave behind an uninformed and confused planet of beings, who may take forever to figure out the truth about themselves. The common pattern on such planets is that the lesser evolved beings start to create their own gods, mimicking the ones that were introduced to them by the cosmic pirates. This leads to more confusion and constant conflict as the new beings try to impose the supremacy of their particular god over the rest of the new beings on such a planet.

Apparently this is a growing concern among the community of universal beings and all attempts are being made to prevent this from happening in the future. It was a blatant mistake on the part of the universal community to allow a group of "almost evolved" beings to join the highest community of beings. It seems that their almost-complete genome was not quite sufficient to make them completely at one with the Supreme Being in the universe. They will have to be restricted to a planet and allowed more time to complete their evolution toward a complete genome. Only then will the genome be able to open all the ports in their minds, which will allow them to plug into the universal spirit and join the full community of universal spiritual beings without any complications.

At this point we feel very uncomfortable and scared, because we have been warned about false prophets on many occasions by our respective gods. This must surely be such a false prophet who will cause the "wrath of god" to be unleashed on us, which we do not deserve. So we kill our visitor in the name of god, knowing that what we did was the right thing. After all, the Bible and the Koran allow us to do this. We are permitted to kill false prophets, for they are surely the disciples of Satan.

Boy oh boy . . . what a pathetically confused species we are. Lost in the vastness of the universe, searching for our roots, confused by so much false knowledge passed down to us through the ages. All this disinformation has to stop somewhere. But what will it take for us to realize that we cannot have more than one father? We cannot all be right . . . we cannot all claim to have the correct answer. Somewhere out there is the truth, and as it usually happens, it is probably too close for us to see. But it should be easy to spot the indigenous tree in a forest of invasive alien species. Let's get one thing straight. There is not a single religion on Earth that was created by God—but there are several that were imposed on us by the ancient gods. There is not one single book on Earth that was written by God—but there are many that were inspired by the activity of the ancient gods. Take a look at the number of man-made religions around us. It is clear that a situation like this could only have emerged out of uncertainty. If we knew who our creator was, we should have all received the same instructions, surely? The fact that we have so many conflicting ideas leads me to believe that we have been the victims of continued disinformation over long periods of time, as well as the victims of a meticulously executed manipulation of the facts to keep us ignorant and in a continuous state of conflict. It's as if the captain has abandoned ship and left it floating in the middle of the Pacific ocean filled with five-year-olds. What chance do they have to steer the ship to the nearest port and to safety? Virtually zero. But if the ship is lucky enough not to encounter any storms for a long, long time, while the currents take them along, they may be lucky enough to work out how to steer this ship for themselves. But there is a very good chance they will all perish in an inevitable storm.

The list of religions we looked at serves as concrete evidence that we have been deserted on this planet without an instruction manual. To prove their supremacy, most religions have brought out their own manuals, claiming that theirs is the original manual to guide humanity into their future and the kingdom of God. But how can they be such conflicting manuals? Surely the real builders or creators of this ship must have had only one set of plans to build it? Maybe not, maybe they were not qualified builders to begin with and, therefore, the ship is in such disarray. Some manuals seem to put us in reverse gear whereas others are rammed into the first gear, not quite sure where the second is.

Okay, enough metaphors and parables, I am sure that by now you get my drift. To make my argument even more compelling, let us take a look at the world's major religions and the numbers of followers. It has "recipe for disaster" written all over it, pitting one group against another. The largest and strongest will want to defend its position and grow, while the others will want to spread their doctrine in an attempt to become the dominant religion. There are more religions today than countries in the world. This creates an additional dilemma and sends a stern warning to politicians, that religion may yet again become the driving force of politics in the future, something that modern democracies have been working very hard to overcome. The principle of divide and conquer has been meticulously applied in all the instances of these religions, showing that the ancients gods of Sumer were cunning strategists and extremely shrewd military commanders. The religious statistics point unavoidably to a conflict situation in our present state of mind. Tolerance has not won the day as yet. It's as if it was purposely so devised, to steer humanity into a perpetual situation of war.

RELIGIONS BY SIZE		
RELIGIONS	ADHERENTS (AS OF 2004)	% OF TOTAL
1. Christianity	2,069,883,000	33.6
Roman Catholic	1,092,853,000	18.7
Protestant	391,143,000	6.9
Orthodox	217,030,000	3.1
Anglican	79,988,000	1.4
Other Christians	406,074,000	3.5
2. Islam	1,254,222,000	18.3
3. Hinduism	837,262,000	13.5
4. Buddhism	338,621,000	6.0
5. Chinese Folk and Universists	398,106,000	2.6
6. New-Religions	128,975,000	2.3
7. Tribal religion	99,150,000	1.8
8. Sikh	24,295,000	0.4
9. Judaism	14,551,000	0.2
10. Shamanism	11,010,000	0.2
11. Confucianism	6,334,000	0.1
12. Baha'i	7,000,000	0.1

13. Jain	3,987,000	0.1
14. Shintoism	3,387,000	0.1
Other religions	20,419,000	0.4
Non-religious	924,078,000	16.3
Atheism	239,111,000	4.2
Total population	6,500,000,000	100%

Compiled from *Encyclopedia Britannica,* and Adherents.com

The world population was assessed to be very close to 6.5 billion in December 2004. You will note that the total of the adherents is larger than the global population. This could be because of the duplication of followers of different religions; a rather strange phenomenon that has puzzled me while compiling this. According to these stats there are about 8.5 billion people in the world making up 133% of the population. How do they calculate these figures?

For us humans on planet Earth, there are many seemingly insurmountable obstacles in our path to evolution and peace. As we evolve, more people embrace the possibility of the newfound truths about our past. The most important questions we need to answer are who we are, and where we come from. But these answers will not be presented to us on a platter with a treasure-hunter's kit and a map to get to the prize. Fortunately, we have now started to uncover some very uncomfortable evidence, which does not seem to tell the same story that we have been told about our history. The biggest obstacles to our growth as a species, to find peace and harmony, are the many man-made religions. It will not be easy to convince devout Christians and Muslims to start considering new possibilities. It instantly turns the messenger into a false prophet who has been sent by the devil. The creators of humanity were the finest strategists ever. They managed to create the perfect environment for continued doubt and conflict. They created the most perfect propaganda tools ever: fear, punishment, and reward. It is all so simple, isn't it? Hopefully this will not be the message that we teach the citizens of the new planets we are soon to start populating. But since we ourselves have no clear answers for our origins, what will we teach the newly cloned colonies of humans on other planets in the near future?

While religion plays a crucial role in shaping our communities, we live our lives reasonably sheltered from the diversity of other religions. We may drive past a mosque on our way to work every day, but how often do we actually take the trouble to find out more about the people who worship there? When Jehovah's Witnesses knock on our door to spread their message, how many of us actually take the time to listen to what they have to say? It is this kind of detachment that keeps us divided and wrapped up in feelings of superiority over other religions, because our god is always bigger and better than the other's. The study of religion is truly fascinating and it helps us understand the murky origins that they all share. Only once we have looked at the very sketchy roots of the most popular religions of the world, can we begin to understand that they are all built on the same shaky ground. We also begin to realize that all religions are man-made and, therefore, cannot be deemed to be divine, because man is fallible. It would be very laborious to try to educate the readers of this book about all global religion, and also unfair to reduce them to a page of editorial. But I have chosen to give you a quick overview of the twelve most popular religions on Earth, just to help you understand some of the similarities and shortcomings. It will help you formulate your own opinions about the religious dogma that has evolved over thousands of years to keep us seemingly happy, but totally enslaved and divided as a species. They are listed in order of size and historical influence on the global populace.

CHRISTIANITY: ORIGIN CIRCA AD 30

This is by far the largest of the world religions with almost twice as many followers as its closest rival, Islam. From the digging that I undertook during the writing of this book, I was amazed to discover that Christianity somehow made it against all odds. It was a struggling young philosophy in the days after the crucifixion of Jesus, with the disciples devoting their lives to the spreading of the word, but it certainly was not easy. They were often threatened, chased away, or made to feel very unwelcome. You have to remember that the pretty clean image we have developed of Jesus and the disciples is very far from the truth. Those were difficult times for him and his relatively small group of followers. As Barbara Thiering puts it in *Jesus of the Apocalypse,* "He was a central figure in a major political movement which was working at overthrowing the pagan Roman empire." She goes on to reveal a staggering bit of information that becomes another perfectly fitting piece in our Great Human Puzzle. Even at this point in time, the gods were as active as ever and Christianity was flying right in the face of the huge support for the many Hellenic gods from days gone by. She continues, "The enormous number of followers of the new, still underground religion, introduced from Judea long before the time of Jesus, were ready to believe in divine figures who were the subjects of visions and miracles. It was the world of Hellenism, where pagan religions had encouraged the idea of human beings as incarnations of gods."

So while there is reference that the people of the day were still being manipulated by their Sumerian gods, Christianity was hanging on. They were persecuted, tortured, fed to lions in the Colosseum, and generally abused in various ways. This was not a good time to be a Christian. This situation continued for nearly 300 years, when suddenly Flavius Valerius Constantinus—AD 272 to 337, came to the rescue. Commonly known as Constantine the Great, he became known as the first "Christian Emperor" of the Roman empire and began the Empire's unofficial sponsoring of Christianity, which was a major factor in the survival and spread of the religion. His reputation as the first Christian Emperor was promulgated by Lactantius and Eusebius and gained ground in the succeeding generations. He founded the city of Constantinople as the new capital of the Eastern Empire, which became the home of Christianity, filled with large numbers of churches and temples. He also proclaimed that Sunday would be the day of worship.

The First Council of Nicaea, which took place during the reign of the emperor Constantine in AD 325, was the first ecumenical (worldwide) conference of bishops of the Christian Church. The participating bishops were given free travel and lodging. The council, which was also called a synod, dealt with the problems created by the Aryan controversy, concerning the nature and status of Jesus. The Aryans had their own views of who Jesus really was. We must remember that Jesus spent most of his growing life, since the age of 12 or 13, in the East, under the influence of several eastern religious philosophies and Aryanism was just one of them. Finally, the Synod decided against the Aryans and voted in favour of Trinitarianism, which suddenly made Jesus part of the Father and the Holy Spirit. This was a whole new twist to the New Testament and the holy trinity was born. Another outcome of the council was an agreement by the bishops of all the Churches to celebrate Easter on the same day. This was by far the most important celebration on the Church calendar; therefore, it was important for all to celebrate the resurrection together. Constantine became such a strong voice of Christianity that on his deathbed he was ordained as the thirteenth apostle.

These were the wild and wonderful early days of Christianity, when most of its foundations were laid. The editing of the Bible's New Testament began to take shape, but it would take another 800 years before the final version was decided upon. This long process is filled with controversy because many books were omitted while others were amended before they were included. A large number of books known as the Apocrypha (hidden writings) have been the subject of much controversy ever since they were deliberately excluded from the New Testament. It was during this period that one of the first recorded references to the Catholic Church emerged. This Catholic denomination of Christianity continued to expand into what it has become today: the largest and most powerful wing of the Christian Church. This is what St. Cyril of Jerusalem (AD 315–386) had to say:

> The Church is called Catholic or universal because it has spread throughout the entire world, from one end of the Earth to the other. Again, it is called Catholic because it teaches fully and unfailingly all the doctrines which ought to be brought to men's knowledge, whether concerned with visible or invisible things, with the realities of heaven or the things of Earth. Another reason for the name Catholic is that the Church brings under religious obedience all classes of men, rulers and subjects, learned and unlettered. Finally, it deserves the title Catholic because it heals and cures unrestrictedly every type of sin that can be committed in soul or in body, and because it possesses within itself every kind of virtue that can be named, whether exercised in actions or in words or in some kind of spiritual charism.

The Bible

The Bible is a very complex and controversial book, but it remains the most sacred book of the Christian faith. It is regarded to be the "Word of God," inspired by the Holy Spirit. It has been translated into 275 languages and possibly more, but the origins of the Bible remain very unsettling, with too many people having had too much influence over the final version. But as you will see, there really is no one final version of the Bible, as various groups have made their own changes and presented their copy as the ultimate word of God. The Old and New Testaments feel as if they should not be part of the same religious philosophy. The one preaches "an eye for an eye" and exalts the god of vengeance, while the New Testament speaks of the Prince of Peace and god of love, and teaches us to love our enemies instead of destroying them. It is great fodder for many subcults and sects within the Christian faith.

The original documents of the New Testament: all the books are written in Greek, with the quotations from the Old Testament taken from the Septuagint. There are 4,500 manuscripts in Greek, 67 papyrus, 2,578 parchment, 1,600 lectionaries mainly in the Codex of the Vatican, London, Paris, Cambridge, and Washington.

The Old Testament: These books were written mostly in Hebrew and Aramaic, some in Greek. None of the original documents are in existence, but what we have today are mainly the Greek Bible and the Hebrew Bible. But then there are the Dead Sea Scrolls, which are still a point of great controversy and concern for some, because they once again raise the question, which of the books should be included in the Old Testament?

The Greek Bible: The Septuagint originates from the third century BC. It is the Greek translation done in Alexandria by a group of 72 rabbis, 6 from each of the 12 tribes, and hence the name, Septuagint, was given to the translation. It has 46 books just like the actual Catholic Bible, and it was the common version of the Bible among the Jews during days of Christ and even after Christ. It was the version used and quoted by the Evangelists and Apostles when they wrote the New Testament. It was translated to Syriac, Coptic, and Latin (The Vulgate of St. Jerome) in the fourth century AD.

The Hebrew Bible, or Masoretic Text: Written in the sixth to tenth centuries AD, by a group of scholars from Babylon and Palestine, introducing vowels and accent signs to the Hebrew scripts. And of course, they also used the Septuagint to produce it. It has 39 books, like the Protestant Bibles.

The Dead Sea Scrolls are very important, because they are written in Hebrew, dating from the third century BC, while the oldest Hebrew Bible, the Masoretic, dates from 700 years AD. With the discovery of the Scrolls it suddenly pushed back the curtain some 1,000 years on the earliest Hebrew documents. In the Scrolls, every book of the Bible is represented with a remarkable similarity to the later scriptures in Greek and Hebrew. This was a very important, yet controversial, discovery surrounding the Old Testament.

Differences Between the Catholic, Orthodox, and Protestant Bibles

There are a total of 73 books in the Catholic and Orthodox Bibles, but only 66 books in the Protestant Bibles. The Old Testament is the same as the Jewish Tanakh. The Catholic Bibles have 46 books, as does the Bible of the Jews of Alexandria, who wrote the *Septuagint,* the version quoted by the Apostles in the Gospels and Epistles. The Protestant Bibles have 39 books, as does the Bible of the Jews from Palestine.

They do not have the following:

4 Historic Books: Tobit, Judith, 1 Maccabees, 2 Maccabees (and additions to Esther)

2 Wisdom Books: Wisdom of Solomon, and Ecclesiasticus of Ben Sirach

1 Prophetic Book: Baruch, and parts of Daniel—The Prayer of Azariah, the Song of the Three Young Men, Bel and the Dragon, and Susana

The New Testament has 27 books in all the Bibles. The Four Gospels are essentially the heart of the Bible. Some religious authors see the name of Christ on every page of the Old Testament and claim that it "prefigures and characterises" the Christ of the Gospels and his Church. But my research has shown that the first time the word/name Christ ever appears in the Bible is in Matthew 1:1 of the New Testament. There is, however, a constant reminder of the *savior* that is mentioned the first time in Deuteronomy 32:15, the fifth book of the Bible; Messiah is mentioned in Matthew 1:1 for the first time; and Jesus also in Matthew 1:1.

"Jesus" was, and still is, a man's name. "Christ" means the "chosen one," which became associated with the name Jesus after his supposed resurrection. But the inexplicable absence of the name of Christ in the early books of the Bible is filled with suspicious undertones. The Old Testament talks generically about a number of prophets or saviors, but only one suddenly emerged, which happened to have been Jesus Christ. I find this highly suspicious. Could not even one of the prophets of the Old Testament have been named Jesus? I suggest that the "gods" were preparing mankind for a savior but they were not quite sure which one of the prophets they had lined up was going to strike a chord with the people of the time.

One of the most fascinating and yet disturbing things about the books of the Bible, and their many relatives who did not make it into the Bible, is that a bunch of men sitting around a boardroom table, some 350 years after the death of Christ, decided on the fate of all the writings. The books that made it are called canonical, which could be translated to mean "according to the Christian set of laws" or possibly even "inspired by God." They sat with a pile of books that mostly had the same authors, and yet some were deemed to be canonical and others not. This is very puzzling to me, but it obviously made a great deal of sense to the decision makers way back then, because some of those writings contained things that did not really fit their structured image of what the Christian Church should represent.

Some Facts about the
Deutero-canonical and Apocryphal Books

Deutero-canonical (second canon), was the term used in 1566 by the Roman Catholic Church, meaning that their canonicity was recognized only after a period of time. They are included in the Greek Septuagint scriptures of the third century BC, but they are not included in the Hebrew Masoretic scriptures from the seventh century AD. Some fragments of these books have also been discovered among the Dead Sea Scrolls. Strangely enough, they are included in the Catholic and Orthodox Bibles, but they are usually not included in the Protestant Bibles. The Deutero-canon include the following books and parts of books:

Historical: Tobit, Judith, First and Second Maccabees, Additions to Esther
Wisdom: Wisdom of Solomon, Sirach (also called Ecclesiasticus).
Prophets: Baruch, the Letter of Jeremiah (in Baruch), and parts of Daniel: The Prayer of Azariah, the Song of the Three Young Men, Bel and the Dragon, and Susana.

The Apocrypha (hidden things/writings) is a collection of books written mostly by authors of other books of the Bible, but the Apocrypha were not included in any of the Bibles. They deal with Christian and Biblical themes, some from the times of the Old Testament, others from the times of the New Testament.

Apocrypha of the Old Testament Times: There are over 25 books; this is a list of some: Acts of Adam, Apocalypse of Adam, Abraham, Testament of Adam, Book of Enoch, Enoch II (Book of the Secrets of Enoch), Book of Noah, Apocalypse of Barach (I), Apocalypse of Barach (II), Apocalypse of Daniel, Apocalypse of Elijah, Apocalypse of Enoch, Apocalypse of Ezra (Esdras), Apocalypse of Solomon, Odes of Solomon, Testament of Isaac, Martyrdom of Isaiah, Apocalypse of Zephaniah, Paralipomena of Jeremiah, Apocryphon of Ezekiel, Ascension of Isaiah, Assumption of Moses, Baruch III, Baruch IV, Chronicles of the Kings of Israel, Acts of Solomon, Chronicles of the Kings of Judah, Maccabee III, Maccabee IV.

Apocrypha of the New Testament—Christian Apocrypha: There are over 40 books. This is a list of some: *14 Gospels* by Thomas, James, Peter, Bartholomew, (Gospel of Nicodemus, Gospel of Perfection, Gospel of Philip, Gospel of Peter, Gospel of the Birth of Mary, Gospel of the Hebrews, Gospel of the Infancy of Jesus Christ, Gospel of Thomas, Gospel of Truth); *15 Acts* by Andrew, Peter, Matthew, John, Thomas, Paul, (Acts of John, Acts of Paul, Acts of Paul and Thecla, Acts of Peter); *6 Revelations* by Paul, Thomas, John, Virgin Mary, Stephen, Peter (Apocalypse of James (I), Apocalypse of James (II), Apocalypse of Peter, Apocalypse of Philip, Apocalypse of Stephan, Apocalypse of Thomas); *Additional books:* Apocryphon of John, Epistle of Pontius Pilate, Revelation of Peter, Protevangelium of James, History of Joseph, Letter of Paul to the Alexandrians, Testament of the Lord, Wisdom of Jesus

So how do we know which books belong to the Bible? Or as the church would call it, "canon" of the Bible? The answer is "because the Church tells us so!"

St. Augustine goes on convincingly to say that "if the Church won't tell me these Books are the Bible, I won't believe it."

This is a perfect example of the master-slave relationship between the ancient gods and the primitive slave species, which I postulate in this book. Humankind is told "do not question, do not doubt, stay fearful, your reward will be great." None of the books of the New Testament were even written by the time Jesus was crucified, and yet he was the prophet who made his mark on humanity. All the other prophets suddenly became irrelevant as Jesus rose to take the center stage. There is so much preparation and expectation for over a thousand years of the coming of the savior, and yet we only find out his name after his birth. Does that not strike you as very suspicious? There are another 35 books dealing with themes of the Old and New Testaments. They are attributed to Enoch, Moses, Solomon, St. Paul, St. Thomas, St. James, St. Peter, Virgin Mary; and they are also not in the Bible, because the Church says so!

In 1517, the Christian Church, which was completely controlled by the Catholics, was shocked when Martin Luther nailed his 95 Theses to the door of the Church of All Saints in Wittenberg, which was used as a customary notice board, inviting the priests to a debate. The letter challenged the teachings of the Roman Catholic Church on the nature of penance, the authority of the pope, and the usefulness of indulgences. They sparked a theological debate that would result in the birth of the Protestant, Lutheran, Reformed, and Anabaptist traditions within Christianity. This was the real beginning of the Protestant Reformation and the split from the Catholics by many who felt uncomfortable with the violent stranglehold of the Catholic Church. The letter contained 95 points outlining what was essentially wrong with the teachings of the Church.

After disregarding Luther as "a drunken German who wrote the Theses; when sober he will change his mind," Pope Leo X ordered the Dominican professor of theology, Silvester Mazzolini, to inquire into the matter. Prierias recognized Luther's dangerous potential, declared him a heretic, and wrote a scholastic refutation of the Theses. It asserted papal authority over the Catholic church, and denounced every departure from it as a heresy. You have to remember that Luther was playing with his life. He could have been charged with various offenses for doing this, but his dislike for the Catholic Church was so intense that it became his passion. Even so, the following excerpt from a letter shows his subservience to the Catholic Church. The tone in which it is written may have been the style of the day, but one can almost smell the anxious fear between the lines, knowing his days may be numbered. He even uses the word *fear* in the opening lines of the letter below. Is it not ironic that we are talking about the representatives of the "House of God: who were supposed to be the disciples of love and peace? But as we discover in this book, our creator and god did not have those benevolent characteristics in his personal arsenal.

Letter to the Archbishop Albrecht of Mainz—October 31, 1517:

> To the Most Reverend Father in Christ and Most Illustrious Lord, Albrecht of Magdeburg and Mainz, Archbishop and Primate of the Church, Margrave of Brandenburg, etc., his own lord and pastor in Christ, worthy of reverence and fear, and most gracious.
>
> The grace of God be with you in all its fullness and power!
>
> Spare me, Most Reverend Father in Christ and Most Illustrious Prince, that I, the dregs of humanity, have so much boldness that I have dared to think of a letter to the height of your Sublimity. The Lord Jesus is my witness that, conscious of my smallness and baseness, I have long deferred what I am now shameless enough to do, moved thereto most of all by the duty of fidelity which I acknowledge that I owe to your most Reverend Fatherhood in Christ. Meanwhile, therefore, may your Highness deign to cast an eye upon one speck of dust, and for the sake of your pontifical clemency to heed my prayer.

Luther had a very clear opinion on the Church of the time, believing that the Catholics were only interested in lining their pockets and controlling people with fear. "Many of the fanatics of our day pronounce words of faith, but they bear no good fruit, because their purpose is to turn men to their perverse opinions." He also had his views on the Aryans, who were so prominent in the shaping of Christ's philosophies. "The Aryans were sharp fellows. Admitting that Christ had two natures, and that He is called 'very God of very God' they were yet able to deny His divinity. The Aryans took Christ for a noble and perfect creature, superior even to the angels, because by Him God created heaven and Earth. Mohammed also speaks highly of Christ. But all their praise is mere palaver to deceive men."

I do admit that I share Luther's concern about the "brutality" of god, as taught by the Church in 1517 and as it still continues to do today.

> I hated the just God who punishes sinners. In silence, if I did not blaspheme, then certainly I grumbled vehemently and got angry at God. I said, "Isn't it enough that we miserable sinners, lost for all eternity because of original sin,

are oppressed by every kind of calamity through the Ten Commandments? Why does God heap sorrow upon sorrow through the Gospel and through the Gospel threaten us with his justice and his wrath?" This was how I was raging with wild and disturbed conscience.

Luther initially preached tolerance toward the Jewish people, convinced that the reason they had never converted to Christianity was that they were discriminated against, or that they had never heard the Gospel of Christ. However, after his overtures failed to convince Jewish people to adopt Christianity, he began preaching that the Jews were set in evil, anti-Christian ways, and needed to be expelled from the German body politic. He repeatedly quoted the words of Jesus, in Matthew 12:34, where Jesus called the Jewish religious leaders (Pharisees and Sadducees) of his day "a brood of vipers and children of the devil." In the book written three years before his death, Luther listed seven recommendations how to deal with the Jews:

> I shall give you my sincere advice: First, to set fire to their synagogues or schools and to bury and cover with dirt whatever will not burn, so that no man will ever again see a stone or cinder of them . . . Second, I advise that their houses also be razed and destroyed. For they pursue in them the same aims as in their synagogues. Instead they might be lodged under a roof or in a barn, like the gypsies . . . Third, I advise that all their prayer books and Talmudic writings, in which such idolatry, lies, cursing, and blasphemy are taught, be taken from them. Fourth, I advise that their rabbis be forbidden to teach henceforth on pain of loss of life and limb . . . Fifth, I advise that safe-conduct on the highways be abolished completely for the Jews . . . Sixth, I advise that usury be prohibited to them, and that all cash and treasure of silver and gold be taken from them and put aside for safekeeping . . . Seventh, I recommend putting a flail, an axe, a hoe, a spade, a distaff, or a spindle into the hands of young, strong Jews and Jewesses and letting them earn their bread in the sweat of their brow, as was imposed on the children of Adam (Gen. 3:19) . . .

In spite of these seven recommendations, he added:

> But if we are afraid that they might harm us or our wives, children, servants, cattle, etc., if they had to serve and work for us for it is reasonable to assume that such noble lords of the world and venomous, bitter worms are not accustomed to working and would be very reluctant to humble them-

selves so deeply before the accursed Goyim then let us emulate the common
sense of other nations such as France, Spain, Bohemia, etc., compute with
them how much their usury has extorted from us, divide this amicably, but
then eject them forever from the country. For, as we have heard, God's anger
with them is so intense that gentle mercy will only tend to make them worse
and worse, while sharp mercy will reform them but little. Therefore, in any
case, away with them!

Luther's harsh comments about the Jews are seen by many as a continuation
of medieval Christian anti-Semitism, and as the above quote shows, reflects
earlier anti-Semitic expulsions in the fourteenth century, when Jews from other
countries like France and Spain were invited into Germany. Since Luther's
statements were widely read at the time, it is possible that this doctrine fed
anti-Semitism, leading to the Nazi era about four centuries later. Early Nazi
leaders loved to quote these particular statements of Luther.

Does this rosy picture of our Christian history not disturb you yet? It certainly disturbs me greatly to see the shallow moral values, lack of respect for
humanity, hatred of others, infinite conceit, and everything that flies in the
face of the "Love of God." These are the foundations upon which our unshakable faith is standing today. Are you not concerned? Are you happy to accept it?
Or can you see that something has gone wrong somewhere in the distant past,
to have caused this unacceptable situation?

The angry Martin Luther went a lot further in criticizing the Church and
the Jews. In accord with his posture as restorer of Christianity, he took it upon
himself to judge various books of the Bible as "God's holy Word." This was not
a healthy situation for him. This is what he had to say about some of the books
of the Old Testament:

We have no wish either to see or hear Moses . . . Job is merely the argument of a fable . . . Ecclesiastes ought to have been more complete. There
is too much incoherent matter in it, Solomon did not, therefore, write this
book . . . The book of Esther I toss into the Elbe. I am such an enemy to
the book of Esther that I wish it did not exist, for it Judaises too much and
has in it a great deal of heathenish naughtiness . . . The history of Jonah is
so monstrous that it is absolutely incredible . . .

The books of the New Testament fared no better. He rejected the following
from the canon: Hebrews, James, Jude, and the Apocalypse. Instead, he placed
them at the end of his translation, after the others, which he called "the true

and certain capital books of the New Testament." "St. John is the only sympathetic, the only true Gospel and should undoubtedly be preferred to the others. In like manner the Epistles of St. Peter and St. Paul are superior to the first three Gospels." The Epistle to the Hebrews did not suit him either: "It need not surprise one to find here bits of wood, hay, and straw." Luther denounced The Epistle of St. James as "an epistle of straw." "I do not hold it to be his writing, and I cannot place it among the capital books." He held this view because it proclaimed the necessity of good works, contrary to his heresy. "There are many things objectionable in this book," is what he said about Apocalypse. "I feel an aversion to it, and to me this is a sufficient reason for rejecting it."

Now that we have dealt with the largest and possibly the most confusing of the world's religions, let us have a quick look at the rest of the major world religions, demonstrating the chaos that exists amongst humanity in a desperate attempt to find their roots. The information given is intended to provide a short introduction to the major religions as defined classically. Each description has been kept short and as uncomplicated as possible.

HINDUISM: ORIGIN CIRCA 4000 BC

Hinduism is the most complex religious system that has evolved on Earth. It is almost impossible to define it. The origins of Hinduism can be traced to the Indus Valley civilization sometime between 4000 BC and 2500 BC. The origins are very murky and the influence of the early settlers in this part of the world, called the Vedas, must have played a crucial role in the origins of Hinduism, because the Vedic scriptures form pretty much the largest part of the Hindu sacred texts. There was, however, another group of people who had a huge impact on Hindu evolution; they were called the Aryans. This group of highly skilled, highly educated, industrialized and technologically advanced people had a profound influence on all the Near Eastern and Indus religions. The Aryan history is equally murky and their true origin and source of knowledge is very mysterious. But, they were there in large numbers to influence the Hindus, Jews, Christ, and Christians and all the other global cultures for over 2,000 years. As much as some historians claim that the Aryans began to write the Vedas when they arrived in the Indus Valley, this is argued against very strongly by other scholars who have shown a Vedic presence and culture in the region as far back as 8000 BC. The Vedas were in possession of their Vedic poems in oral form for thousands of years before they were finally written down. There are, however, others who have presented astounding evidence that the Vedas may have been able to write as far back as 8000 BC. This is at least 3,000 years before the next known script emerged.

So let's take a quick look at these Aryans who also populated and conquered Europe. They inspired a very early class structure based on skin color, they were the earliest colonialists and even inspired modern-day warriors like Hitler. Scholars believe that these Aryans originated from somewhere in Northern Mesopotamia, southwest of the Black Sea in eastern Anatolia (Turkey). They are described as light-skinned or "whites" who spoke a very early proto-European language from which all the latter European languages evolved. This is fantastic news to feed my theory because according to the Sumerian tablets the Igigi (who were the astronauts who looked after the base on Mars, while the Anunnaki were those on Earth) came to Earth after the year of the Flood and took human females for their wives. They were treated almost as outcasts by the Anunnaki in Sumer and, therefore, they moved away establishing their own community in a land of their own. And guess where they moved to? They went north toward the mountainous areas of Anatolia, southeast of the Black Sea, and to the Cedar mountains where Enlil had spent much of his time as well. Their community grew rapidly as they shared their knowledge and technology with their new human offspring. The new race of humans that emerged out of this cohabitation was also white, and confident, because of their "godly" ancestry. From there they infiltrated most of Asia and Europe spreading their civilization and language. As a result, the languages spoken in India actually fall into the various Indo-European languages. Latin, Greek, Hittite, Sanskrit, French, German, Latvian, English, Spanish, Russian, and others are all Indo-European (IE) languages; or more properly Proto-Indo-European (PIE), which is the lost ancestral language from which those languages originated. The Indo-European language used the term *Aryan* to classify a group of people not only racially, but also ethnically based on the type of accent or "Aryan speech" the people spoke.

This should have been expected, however. It is fascinating to see how the gods who created humankind as a lower slave species immediately classified them in a lower ethnic class, giving birth to slavery and racism right at the beginning of humanity. *Arya,* meaning "noble," appears in various Indo-European languages. Once again this should be expected from the Igigi gods who regarded themselves as way superior to lesser mortal humans. They probably used the plural of the word *Aryas nobles* to describe themselves prior to their dispersal. It may even have survived in Eire (Ireland), but it certainly survives in Iran where they are referred to as "Airyanam vaejo"—"realm of the Aryans." The discovery of thousands of such cognate words in widely separated languages, along with similar grammatical structures, led philologists to conclude, early in the nineteenth century, that most European languages had evolved from a common proto-language spoken millennia ago.

Greek, Latin, and Sanskrit were considered the closest languages to PIE, and much of the reconstructed Aryan proto-language is based on them. Modern Lithuanian is thought to be the most archaic living language, closer to the original Aryan speech than any other. Tocharian is an Indo-European language that had been spoken in Chinese Turkestan, indicating that the Aryans reached as far as China in the Far East. The only possible explanation of how they could have had such an impact on the entire European and Asian ancient history is because they were more advanced, or possibly even related to the ancient "gods" of Sumer—and that is exactly who they were. A white blend between Igigi gods and mortal humans who suddenly saw themselves in a higher bracket than the rest of the mortal beings on Earth. A recent discovery of the remains of blond-haired people in China is a large missing piece of the Great Human Puzzle, which is beginning to take shape very quickly under the watchful eye of science as it shows how far the Aryans explored.

Perhaps the most famous proof for the prehistoric existence of PIE is the word for king: *rex* in Latin, *raja* in Sanskrit, *ri* in Old Irish, along with a host of others, all are obviously variants of a common word for king. And since none of the peoples speaking these various languages were in physical contact with one another during the historical period, for which written records do exist, comparative philologists claim that their respective languages must have evolved from a single proto-language. The Aryans worshipped a sky god, they traced descent through the male line, they raised cattle, they drank mead, they used horse-drawn chariots that they probably invented as weapons of war, which included bronze and iron. The civilizations of Asia were completely outclassed and outsmarted by the Aryans when they arrived.

Aryans, or more specifically Indo-Aryans, make their first notable appearance in history around 2000 BC as invaders of Northern India. This event holds firm with the behavior of Anunnaki god Marduk, who was proclaiming himself as god above all at that time. The result of the conflict between the Anunnaki in the biblical lands is well documented and outlined in the last chapter. It was, however, around 2000 BC when Sodom and Gomorrah were destroyed by the Anunnaki's nuclear and biological weapons, which forced many inhabitants of the surrounding lands to flee and evacuate. Remember that the white Aryans (Igigi) were Marduk's followers, so when they suddenly made their appearance in the Indus Valley, the ancient Vedic tales begin to carry much of the content dealing with these invasions and subjugation of the dark-skinned inhabitants.

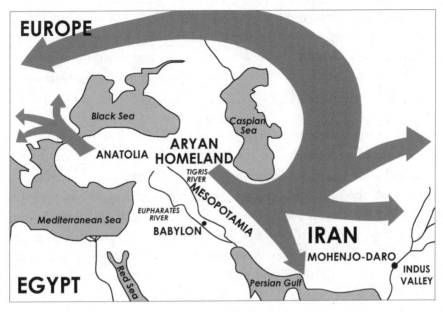

Fig. 13.1. Aryan invasion

The Sanskrit Rig Veda, a collection of religious texts still revered by modern Hindus, carry enigmatic records of such events. This is another perfect example of how historians have scrambled our brains over time, because suddenly we have mythological gods clashing with actual historic people. Hindus see this as history, while others have described it as mythology. So if the invading Aryan gods were mythological, who are the Vedic poems referring to? Who was actually invading the Indian lands? Or were they just imagining that too? How can you have a situation where half of the historic records is deemed to be acceptable, but the other half is just a figment of their imagination, because they had nothing better to do? These events surrounding the Aryan invasion of Indus are of paramount importance to the credibility of the ancient gods, because there is no other time and place in history where we have such detailed description of historic interaction between gods and men, outlining the superiority of the gods and the subservience that was forced upon the humans. In the following extract from a Vedic poem (Rig Veda 1.53) the local people were referred to as the Dasyus.

Indra (Norse—Thor, Celtic—Taranis) has torn open the fortresses of the Dasyus, which in their wombs hid the black people. He created land and water for Manu (Aryan man); Lower than all besides, hast thou, O Indra, cast down the Dasyus, abject tribes of Dasas; After slaying the Dasyus, let

Indra with his white friends win land, let him win the sun and water; Indra subdued the Dasyus colour and drove it into hiding. "With all-outstripping chariot-wheel, O Indra, Thou, far-famed, hast overthrown the twice ten kings . . . Thou goest from fight to fight, intrepidly destroying castle after castle here with strength."

The Aryans were remarkably expansionist and almost everywhere they went they conquered and subjugated the indigenous peoples, imposing their languages and their religious beliefs on the natives. In turn, they received contributions from the people whom they conquered. The Aryans had very strong links to the Essenes sect of Hebrews, to which Joseph and Jesus belonged. There is some evidence that it was the Aryans who sponsored Jesus to travel the East and learn the cultures. Aryan invasions had been going on for millennia, as far back as 4000 BC and probably even further back, when they first began to conquer Europe. Most of the contemporary inhabitants of Europe, along with their respective early national cultures, are the result of interaction between successive waves of white Aryan invaders and their culture. Therefore, almost all modern European languages are members of the Western branch of the Indo-European family tree.

The birth of a European culture predates the arrival of the Indo-Europeans. The descendants of the biblical Nefilim and their human children moved away from Sumer according to the clay tablets. They settled in distant lands that can only be identified as prehistoric Europe. They were also white and more technologically advanced because they possessed some of the Anunnaki's genetic pool and influence. This means that the coming together of the Old Europeans and the Aryans actually brought together two opposite sides of the advanced white Anunnaki children who had interbred with earthling females, as is so eloquently outlined in Genesis. The cave art of Lascaux, which some have identified as the first flowering of Western man's creative genius, was the work of Old Europeans. Stonehenge in the North and the Minoan Palace culture of Crete in the South are other examples. A pan-European religious symbolism had already evolved but once again much of it was later incorporated into IE mythologies, including various regional adaptations of European reverence for the Mother Goddess. Many of the principal figures in Greek mythology predate the arrival of the Aryans, which means they must have arrived with the Nefilim from Sumer. This would have been the other group of Anunnaki offspring, who married earthling females and started a whole new race of humans: a white and domineering race. During the course of ancient history, Old European religious beliefs and practices continually reasserted themselves, such as the image of the Minoan snake goddess from the Palace of Minos, circa 1600 BC, but it probably has much older origins.

Europe is European because the conquerors and the conquered were members of the same white race, different branches on the same family tree. One came in from the Southwest while the others, mainly Aryans, arrived from the Northeast. India is a morass of poverty because the bulk of the conquered, with whom the Indo-Aryans eventually intermarried, were nonwhite Veddoids. The lesson is obvious. Even today high-caste Hindus can still be identified by their Caucasian features and light skin, and the poorest and most "backward" parts of India are generally the darkest. Were the Aryans the original promoters of apartheid? It certainly looks like it. Where else would modern Europeans have got it from? Everything we have and we know was handed down to us by our ancient ancestors, the Sumerians, who were taught everything they knew by the Anunnaki gods. If we extrapolate this time line a little further back in time to the point of the creation of Adamu; and we analyze how the whole human race issue was handled by the gods for thousands of years right up to the rapid expansion and globalization by the Anunnaki under the leadership of Marduk; which included the Igigi, who were actually the Aryans; we arrive at the conclusion that "god" our maker was the first racist. It is very disturbing to discover that the wise Anunnaki gods who settled on this planet with all their knowledge could allow such disorganized chaos to evolve. But maybe that is exactly what they had in mind—divide and rule. Keep the slave species subjugated at all cost. Recent genetic studies have indicated that the Basques of Aquitaine and the Pyrenees are probably the purest form of Old European as they existed prior to the arrival of Indo-European invaders. They evidently emerged from the invasions of Europe unconquered, and they remained sufficiently isolated to retain their own unique, non-IE language.

Now that we have dealt with the very important issue of the Aryans, we can return to the Hindus and their religious and cultural development before and after the influence of the Aryans. While many believe that Hinduism is a polytheistic religion that worships many gods, the basis of Hinduism is the belief in the unity of everything. This totality is called Brahman. The purpose of life is to realize that we are part of God, and that by doing so, we can leave this plane of existence and rejoin with God. This enlightenment can only be achieved by going through cycles of rebirth, life, and death known as *samsara*. And yet the major part of this religious practice is to worship the god Vishnu, who seems to be the prominent god; or Shiva or the goddess Shakti; or their many other incarnations, aspects, spouses, or progeny.

In Hinduism, one's progress toward enlightenment is measured by one's karma, which is the accumulation of all one's good and bad deeds, and which determines the person's next reincarnation. Hindus follow a strict system called "caste," which determines the social importance or standing of each person. The caste that one is born into is the result of the karma from their previous life. Selfless acts and thoughts as well as devotion to God will help one to be reborn at a higher level in the caste system. Bad acts and thoughts will cause one to be born at a lower level, as a person or possibly even as an animal. Only members of the highest caste, the Brahmins, may perform the Hindu religious rituals and hold positions of authority within the temples. The earliest cultures in Mesopotamia were building many temples to the different gods presiding over individual villages. It is curious that historians refer to those as mythology, and yet, the Hindu sects are still practicing this form of religious worship today. But in India it is called a religion and nobody will dare to call their gods mythological figures. Just as the gods in the Sumerian tablets had various towns or villages to look after, and were worshipped as such, so are Hindu gods still worshipped today—different gods in different villages. Hindus join a sect by undergoing initiation and learning the sacred *mantra* of that sect, which is presented to them by the *guru*. The mantra is in the form of an "Om" homage to the god to which the sect belongs and is normally the god of that village.

The entire vast Hindu family of sects and offshoots emerged from the proto-Hindu culture known as the Veda, which originated in the Indus Valley. The Rig Veda is the oldest of the collection of Vedic hymns and is the oldest living religious literature in the world, predating the Bible by thousands of years. The total collection of Vedic poems or hymns consists of 1,028 hymns to the Vedic deities. The origin of these can be traced back to around 8000 BC according to some scholars. Incredibly, they survived for thousands of years by being handed down in the oral tradition until they were finally written down.

The Vedas are the most sacred scriptures of Hinduism. According to tradition, "when God creates the worlds, He reveals the Vedas for the welfare of the worlds and when He ends the creation, He takes them back again." Some people say that all human knowledge is available in the Vedas in symbolic form, and that the knowledge of all our discoveries and inventions is already contained in the Vedas. It is true that the Vedas are not mere books of some magical chants but they are loaded with ancient historical knowledge from a time before time, which reveals itself step by step. They are Rig Veda, Sama Veda, Yajur Veda, and Atharva Veda.

The Atharva Veda is different from the other three Veda collections in that it contains spells and incantations for medicinal purposes, magical aids to victory in battle, and so on. The Vedic collections are complemented by a series of works called the Brahmanas, which are devoted to the explanation of the hymns, their ritual applications, and their mythology. It is the Vedic books called the Aranyakas and Upanishads that push the religion toward a monistic philosophy. It is only in the pages of the Upanishads that we first find references to death and rebirth of the soul, and not in the much older Vedas. It seems as if the Aryans had a lot to do with the writing of these scriptures, most likely for the purpose of enslaving the locals with religious dogma. The rather strange and non-Hindu contents of the Upanishads resembles the assertions of the followers of Marduk, promising humans an eternal afterlife, but only if they behaved themselves, and followed god's commands. They did this very successfully in Egypt with the pharaohs, but in the Indus Valley they added a very juicy twist . . . if you do not obey god's commands, you will be reborn as a dirty animal. This was actually a brilliant form of mental torture. The people were already experiencing hardship on Earth, waiting to escape it. There could be nothing more horrific than the thought of having to return to this realm to live in harsher conditions than before. And so these descendants of the Sumerian gods were on the move, conquering and subjugating humans in their path.

There are so many rituals and different cultural applications by the various sects of Hinduism that it would take up the rest of this book and much more to begin to capture it all. The fascinating thing about Hinduism is its murky origin in distant prehistory, where the Vedic poems originated. Every single poem deals with one or more ancient god in various ways. Either praising him or her, exalting them, worshipping, asking for favor, wisdom, wealth, courage and thousands of other human needs. It seems as if the people of those early days had a very different relationship with their gods when compared to the modern Hindus. What is even more interesting is that those early Vedic gods resembled the ancient Sumerian gods to perfection. They had similar functions, denominations, characters and personalities, and all other aspects of their being. They liked their material offerings of gold and food, just like their Sumerian counterpart gods, and they could be equally brutal in dispensing punishment to unlucky followers. And yet on different occasions they would reward their obedient followers with material wealth. According to the Sumerian clay tablets it was the talented goddess of love, Inanna, who was given this Asian domain to look after. Is it not strange that her high sexual appetite and love for poetry and music turned out to be the cultural centerpiece of the Indian people? But it goes even further. There is a plethora of references to the gods of Sumer, mirrored in the Vedic poems. We see them riding in sky chariots, displaying all kinds of fierce weapons, slaying their foes with ease by using weapons that closely resemble both the biblical descriptions and those of the Sumerian tablets. During excavation in Harappa, one of the largest ancient Indus cities, the predominant effigies, statues and references found were to the "Great Mother Goddess." The same Mother Goddess who was very active in Old European civilizations. Little statues and figurines of this celestial deity were scattered all over the Indus Valley, Western Asia, and even the Aegean. I am of the firm belief that these statues represented the goddess of love and war, Inanna or Ishtar as she was know to her Anunnaki godly family.

A most fascinating link to the creation of humankind comes to us in the Laws of Manu. This revealed scripture comprises 2,684 verses, divided into 12 chapters presenting the norms of domestic, social, and religious life in India. There is some disagreement among scholars about the exact date when these scriptures were first penned. Some scholars date it back as far as 1500 BC, others place it at 500 BC, and some say that it is a copy of much earlier writings only captured around AD 200. Regardless of the date, the Laws of Manu, or Manava Dharma Shastra, is one of the standard books in the Hindu canon, and a basic text for all gurus to base their teachings on. It is fundamental to the understanding of ancient Indian society and traditionally accepted as one of the supplementary arms of the Vedas. What interests me most are verses 16–29 of chapter 1. As you will see below, the description of the "creation of mankind" is uncannily close to the descriptions in the Sumerian tablets. How is that possible, unless there was a very close link to the Sumerian gods by one of their representatives in the Indus Valley. There were many gods in the valley organizing the rise of that civilization from thousands of years BC. So it should not surprise us to see this kind of sharing of knowledge. Manu's text clearly suggests some kind of genetic engineering, DNA splicing, and other biological manipulation by the gods when they were creating mankind. This extract is translated by G. Buhler:

16. But, joining minute particles even of those six, which possess measure-less power, with particles of himself, he created all beings.

17. Because those six (kinds of) minute particles, which form the (creator's) frame, enter (a-sri) these (creatures), therefore the wise call his frame sarira, (the body).

18. That the great elements enter, together with their functions and the mind, through its minute parts the framer of all beings, the imperishable one.

19. But from minute body (framing) particles of these seven very powerful

Purushas springs this (world), the perishable from the imperishable.

20. Among them each succeeding (element) acquires the quality of the preceding one, and whatever place (in the sequence) each of them occupies, even so many qualities it is declared to possess.

21. But in the beginning he assigned their several names, actions, and conditions to all (created beings) even according to the words of the Veda.

22. He, the Lord, also created the class of the gods, who are endowed with life, and whose nature is action; and the subtle class of the Sadhyas, and the eternal sacrifice.

29. Whatever he assigned to each at the (first) creation, noxiousness or harmlessness, gentleness or ferocity, virtue or sin, truth or falsehood, that clung (afterwards) spontaneously to it.

(Were the seven Purushas the same seven Sumerian birth-mothers that gave birth to the first *Homo sapiens*?)

Much has been written about the origins of writing in the world. One of the strongly argued topics is the origin of the Vedic scripts. Is it at all possible that over 1,000 Vedic poems could have survived thousands of years without having been written down? It seems highly unlikely. But humankind only started to write around 4000 BC in the Near East, and 3400 BC in the Indus Valley. How could the Vedic poems have been written down if humankind could not write yet? Just because no writing material had been excavated in India does not mean that they could not write.

Ellie Crystal from the remarkable www.crystalinks.com website has presented a very strong argument showing that it may actually be possible for the Vedic literature to have been written down long before the time of the accepted emergence of writing in the world. Rig Veda is accepted as the oldest existing literature available to humans. It seems to be older than the Ramayan of at least 5500 BC, and some internal proto-Hindu evidence takes it as far back as 23000 BC. Other scholars place it at around 8000 BC. The point is that they must have written all that literature down in some way, because it is highly improbable that they could have memorized such a vast amount of work. There are a number of references that allude to the art of writing in the Rig Veda. Some of the references state that the seers "inscribed or engraved" words on certain materials, suggesting that they knew how to write. The Rig Veda 1.164.39 states that: " In the letters (akshara) of the verses of the Veda."

The Rig Vedic texts consists of a large number of compositional *chandas,* which are very specific spatial arrangements of the lines in a meter, and to complicate it even more, a specific number of words per line. It would take a tremendous amount of mental effort to compose and memorize so much material with all the specific intricacies involved. So unless these were reduced to writing and given a specific concrete shape, it would not have been possible to transfer it orally.

Yet another verse of Rig Veda (10.62.7) mentions how cows were marked "by an 8–eight," which clearly shows that the ancients possessed the knowledge of writing. Rig Veda 10.71.4 refers to a language that can be "seen," meaning that it must have been in written script. If there was no written script at the time, surely they would have used the verb "to pronounce or say" rather than "to inscribe or write"? The only plausible reason for choosing to use these words was because a written form of language existed during that time.

The art of writing was prevalent even during the Mahabharat era as the verb *lekhi* or "writing" in all its forms (like *lekhako, lekhani,* and others) appears numerous times in the Mahabharat text (Aadi 1.77–78). Their arrows were inscribed with the names of specific persons to whom they belonged. Distinction was made between "to write" and "to read" in Harivansha texts, indicating to us that "what was written, was also being read."

How could a text with over 100,000 verses be composed, preserved, and transmitted through memory alone? I say it's impossible. You may believe otherwise. But while such an incredible feat may have been performed by a few, it does not suggest that the art of writing was not developed.

The Atharvasheersha from the Upanishads scriptures symbolizes Shree Ganesh as an *omkar,* which is a combination of g-*aakar,* m-*aakar.* How could a syllable that was transmitted only orally have an *aakar* or "shape"?

In the Mahabharat text from circa 3100 BC there are quotes from Rishi Vasistha of the Ramayanic Era (at least 5500 BC) that include the expressions *granth* or "manuscript." If writing skills were not acquired at the time, how is it possible that they would discuss the issues surrounding various manuscripts?

The Yujurvedic Taittiriya Samhita and also the Atharvaveda utilize the word *likha* to "write." Although these scriptures are not as ancient as the Rig Veda, it shows that the art of writing was known by ancient Vedic peoples since remote times.

R. N. Dandekar remarks:

There is, indeed, considerable circumstantial and inferential character which enables us to perceive the existence of writing even in the very early periods of Indian cultural history. It is true that the Veda has been handed down from generation to generation through oral tradition. It must not, however, be supposed that on that account, as is often erroneously done, that the art of writing was unknown in the early Vedic age. The practice of oral transmission of Veda was adopted, not because written copies of these texts were not available, but presumably because it was believed that oral transmission alone was more conducive to the preservation of the magic-religious potency and the formal protection of those arts.

Let's take a look at some examples of the Vedic Hymns/Poems to see what possible connections there may have been between the ancient Indus civilization and the Anunnaki gods of Sumer. In this first example, which is the Samaveda Decade 1 Agni, we deal with so many of the same issues that the Sumerian tablets have captured, it is truly uncanny. We read about visible deities among men, dwelling places in the sky, gods of violence, and gods of material reward. This could have been a poem recited by a Sumerian faithful:

> Come, Agni, praised with song, to feast and sacrificial
>   offering: sit
> As Hotar on the holy grass!
> O Agni, thou hast been ordained Hotar of every sacrifice,
> By Gods, among the race of men.
> Agni we choose as envoy, skilled performer of this holy rite,
> Hotar, possessor of all wealth.
> Served with oblation, kindled, bright, through love of song
>   may Agni, bent
> On riches, smite the Vritras dead!
> I laud your most beloved guest like a dear friend, O Agni,
>   him
> Who, like a chariot, wins us wealth.
> Do thou, O Agni, with great might guard us from all
>   malignity,
> Yea, from the hate of mortal man!
> O Agni, come; far other songs of praise will I sing forth to
>   thee.
> Wax mighty with these Soma-drops!
> May Vatsa draw thy mind away even from thy loftiest
>   dwelling place!
> Agni, I yearn for thee with song.
> Agni, Atharvan brought thee forth by rubbing from the
>   sky, the head
> Of all who offer sacrifice.

O Agni, bring us radiant light to be our mighty succour, for
Thou art our visible deity!

SAMAVEDA—DECADE I AGNI

Because there are 1,028 of these poems and every single one carries some sort of link to our Sumerian ancestry and the gods who flew around in their chariots, brandishing their weapons, I will only quote the appropriate few lines from a small number of Vedic poems to demonstrate my point.

Weapons with flames, travel to the sky, material wealth, blessing from the sky:

Hence have these men gone up on high and mounted to the
heights of heaven:
On! conquer on the path by which Angirasas travelled to
the skies!
That thou mayst send us ample wealth,
Shoot forth, O Agni, with thy flame: demolish them on
every side!
Break down the Yatudhana's strength, the vigour of the
Rakshasa!
Worship the Vasus, Agni! here, the Rudras and Adityas,
all
Who know fair sacrifices, sprung from Man, scattering
blessings down!

SAMAVEDA—DECADE V Agni

Black drop in the heart resembles the story of Mohammed at birth. This had something to do with immortality or reviving someone from the dead. Sumerian tablets are also filled with similar content of resurrection by the flying gods.

The black drop sank in Ansumati's bosom, advancing with
ten thousand round about it.
Indra with might longed for it as it panted: the hero-
hearted King laid down his weapons.
Flying in terror from the snort of Vritra all deities who
were thy friends forsook thee.
So, Indra, with the Maruts be thy friendship: in all these
battles thou shalt be the victor.

The old hath waked the young Moon from his slumber
who runs his circling course with many round him.
Behold the God's high wisdom in its greatness: he who died
yesterday today is living . . .
SAMAVEDA—DECADE IV INDRA

The following Samavedas are filled with references to war, flames, heavenly hosts, violence, anger, and more.

Indra, pitiless hero with unbounded anger,
Victor in fight, unshaken and resistless—may he protect
our armies in our battles!
And let the banded Maruts march in forefront of heavenly
hosts that conquer and demolish!
Ours be the potent host of mighty Indra, King Varuna the
Maruts, and Adityas!
Uplifted is the shout of Gods who conquer, heightened
Gods who cause the worlds to tremble.
III INDRA—BRIHASPATI

Bristle thou up, O Maghavan, our weapons: excite the
spirits, of my warring heroes!
Urge on the strong steed's might, O Vyitra-slayer, and let
the din of conquering cars go Upward . . .
IV INDRA—MARUTS

This sounds similar to the "angels" who came to destroy Sodom and Gomorrah. They struck the aggressors down with blindness first.

With immortality King Soma clothe thee!
Blind, O my foemen, shall ye be, even as headless serpents
are
May Indra slay each best of you when Agni's flame hath
struck you down!
VIII SOMA—VARUNA

Gods delight in offerings of food; fly to the heavens; Tvastar makes a weapon for Indra.

The Maruts have made heaven and Earth increase and
  grow: in sacrifices they delight, the strong and wild.
The Rudras have established their abode in heaven . . .
  they shine in bright attire, and on their fair limbs lay
  their golden ornaments,
They drive away each adversary from their path,
When ye have harnessed to your cars the spotted deer,
  urging the thunderbolt,
Let your swift-gliding coursers bear you hitherward with
  their fleet pinions. Come ye forward with your arms.
Sit on the grass; a wide seat hath been made for you:
  delight yourselves,
O Maruts, in the pleasant food.
Before the Maruts every creature is afraid: the men are like
  to Kings, terrible to behold.
When Tvastar deft of hand had turned the thunderbolt,
  golden, with thousand edges, fashioned more skilfully,
  Indra received it to perform heroic deeds.

HYMN LXXXV—MARUTS

Rocket ships with flaming red rockets of fire?

Let the swift steeds who carry thee, thought-yoked and
  dropping holy oil,
Bring the Gods to the Soma draught.
With all the Gods, with Indra, with Vayu, and Mitra's
  splendours, drink,
Agni, the pleasant Soma juice.
Harness the Red Mares to thy car, the Bays, O God, the
  flaming ones:
With those bring hitherward the Gods.

HYMN XIV—VISVEDEVAS

Could "spacious view" be referring to the heaven in the sky above?

Watch ye, through this your truthfulness, there in the place
  of spacious view Indra and Agni, send us bliss.

HYMN XXI—INDRA—AGNI

Come hither, Maruts, on your lightning laden cars,
  sounding with sweet songs, armed with lances, winged
  with steeds.
Fly unto us with noblest food, like birds, O ye of mighty
  power.
With their red-hued or, haply, tawny coursers which speed
  their chariots on, they come for glory.
Brilliant like gold is he who holds the thunder. Earth have
  they smitten with the chariot's felly.
                    HYMN LXXXVIII—MARUTS

This next poem is an astounding piece, which virtually paraphrases the clay
tablets of Sumer, outlining the marriage between gods and mortal humans, creating more civilized humans, who were taught all the skills they needed by the
gods to provide the global population with the food they so badly needed. This
new breed of humans were also the future kings, priests, and pharaohs of Egypt
with more power than mere mortals. They were the mouthpieces of the gods,
delivering messages to the people. They often thought of themselves as gods.

I Praise with sacrifices mighty Heaven and Earth at
  festivals, the wise, the Strengtheners of Law.
Who, having Gods for progeny, conjoined with Gods,
  through wonder working wisdom bring forth choicest
  boons.
With invocations, on the gracious Father's mind, and on
  the Mother's great inherent power I muse.
Prolific Parents, they have made the world of life, and for
  their brood all round wide immortality.
These Sons of yours well skilled in work, of wondrous
  power, brought forth to life the two great Mothers first
  of all.
To keep the truth of all that stands and all that moves, ye
  guard the station of your Son who knows no guile.
They with surpassing skill, most wise, have measured out
  the Twins united in their birth and in their home.
They, the refulgent (brilliant) Sages, weave within the sky,
  yea, in the depths of sea, a web for ever new.
This is to-day the goodliest gift of Savitar: this thought we
  have when now the God is furthering us.

On us with loving-kindness Heaven and Earth bestow
riches and various wealth and treasure hundredfold!
HYMN CLIX—HEAVEN AND EARTH

Benevolent gods who reward their faithful; immortal gods:

For they are dealers forth of wealth, and, not deluded,
with their might
Guard evermore the holy laws.
Shelter may they vouchsafe to us, Immortal Gods to mortal
men,
Chasing our enemies away.
May they mark out our paths to bliss, Indra, the Maruts,
Pusan, and Bhaga, the Gods to be adored.
Sweet be our Father Heaven to us.
HYMN XC—VISVEDEVAS

The best of guardians hath that man within whose
dwelling place ye drink,
O Maruts, giants of the sky.
Honoured with sacrifice or with the worship of the sages'
hymns,
O Maruts, listen to the call.
HYMN LXXXVI—MARUTS

This poem is very reminiscent of the rewards that god promised his chosen people, or individuals like Abraham and Moses, if they went to war and did what was commanded. God would promise great riches and rewards to those who obeyed, but punished those who did not. This was not only restricted as punishment for "sin" but also rewards for actually performing required tasks for god.

The men have lifted Indra up, the Vrtra slayer, to joy and
strength:
Him, verily, we invoke in battles whether great or small:
be he our aid in deeds of might.
Thou, Hero, art a warrior, thou art giver of abundant
spoil.
Strengthening e'en the feeble, thou aidest the sacrificer,
thou givest the offerer ample wealth.

*When war and battles are on foot, booty is laid before the
      bold*
*Whom wilt thou slay and whom enrich? Do thou, O
      Indra, make us rich.*
*Mighty through wisdom, as he lists, terrible, he hath
      waxed in strength.*
*Lord of Bay Steeds, strong-jawed, sublime, he in
      joined hands for glory's sake hath grasped his iron
      thunderbolt.*
*He filled the Earthly atmosphere and pressed against the
      lights in heaven.*
*None like thee ever hath been born, none, Indra, will be
      born like thee.*
Thou hast waxed mighty over all.
                              HYMN LXXXI—INDRA

There is no doubt that the gods of the Indus Valley were as unpredictable as the gods of Sumer. The people never knew what kind of mood they were in, or what exactly they should do to please them, not invoking their wrath. They even tried to befriend the gods.

*May powers auspicious come to us from every side, never
      deceived, unhindered, and victorious,*
*That the Gods ever may be with us for our gain, our
      guardians day by day unceasing in their care.*
*May the auspicious favour of the Gods be ours, on us
      descend the bounty of the righteous Gods.*
*The friendship of the Gods have we devoutly sought: so
      may the Gods extend our life that we may live.*
                          HYMN LXXXIX—VISVEDEVAS

A clear reference to a chariot that reaches the heaven and we also read that the gods traveled far and wide over the world. There must have been times when the gods were not present in India, but rather in the distant "seven regions" of the world as they say. But the gods mostly stayed up in the heavens.

*We call the Asvins Twain, the Gods borne in a noble car,
      the best*
Of charioteers, who reach the heavens.

The Gods be gracious unto us even from the place whence
    Visnu strode
Through the seven regions of the Earth!
Through all this world strode Visnu; thrice his foot he
    planted, and the whole
Was gathered in his footstep's dust.
The princes evermore behold that loftiest place where
    Visnu is,
Laid as it were an eye in heaven.

HYMN XXII—ASVINS AND OTHERS

God's chariots with missiles and mighty weapons; humans wanted to stay among the gods, in their areas; but humans were still slaves of the gods and toiling for them in many ways.

As on a fair bright day the arrow flieth o'er all the barren
    soil their missiles sparkle.
. . . For power and might have they, their own possession.
    This is my reverent thought of you, ye Holy; may it
    inspire you, make you dwell among us,
. . . Toiling for the Gods and seeking treasure. May we find
    strengthening food in full abundance.

HYMN CLXXXVI—VISVEDEVAS

No harm will come to those who bring gifts to the gods and worship them.

The awful car, Brhaspati, that quells the foe, slays demons,
    cleaves the stall of kine, and finds the light.
Thou leadest with good guidance and preservest men;
    distress o'ertakes not him who offers gifts to thee.
Him who hates prayer thou punishest, Brhaspati, quelling
    his wrath: herein is thy great mightiness.
Brhaspati hath overthrown like cars of war all wicked
    enemies who fain would injure us.
Burn up the demons with thy fiercest flaming brand, those
    who have scorned thee in thy manifested might.
Show forth that power that shall deserve the hymn of
    praise: destroy the evil speakers, O Brhaspati.

HYMN XXIII—BRAHMANASPATI

Just as in the Sumerian tablets, here we discover that there were mortals who did have sex with goddesses, or the other way around. "When the sons of the gods saw the daughters of man and had sex and children with them." But the Indian culture was driven by Inanna/Ishtar, goddess of love and war. It is evident from the poems that she was highly sexed and ready to fight at the drop of a hat. She wanted things to be done her way in the lands that were given to her by god Enlil.

> Born in the heavens the Dawn hath flushed, and showing
> her majesty is come as Law ordaineth.
> She hath uncovered fiends and hateful darkness; best of
> Angirases, hath waked the pathways.
> Rouse us this day to high and happy fortune: to great
> felicity . . .
> Vouchsafe us manifold and splendid riches, famed among
> mortals, man-befriending Goddess!
> She yokes her chariot far away, and swiftly visits the lands
> where the Five Tribes are settled,
> Looking upon the works and ways of mortals, Daughter of
> Heaven, the world's Imperial Lady.
> On her all-lovely car she comes, the Fair One, and brings
> rich treasure for her faithful servant.
> True with the True and Mighty with the Mighty, with
> Gods a Goddess,
> Holy with the Holy.
>
> HYMN LXXV—DAWN

We often hear of thunder when the gods come down from the skies. That would not be surprising since their "rocket ships" would make a lot of noise. It is also described when they go to battle and the gods are with them, slaying their foes with their mighty spaceships.

> Fierce comes the Maruts' thundering voice, like that of
> conquerors, when ye go forward to victory, O Men.
> Born of the laughing lightning . . . may the Maruts guard
> us everywhere
> May they be gracious unto Us.
>
> RIG VEDAS—VAYU AND OTHERS

Immortality among the gods was greatly admired by humans, who all desired it. In the Sumerian tablets we also read about the large homes or dwellings in places that were out of bounds to humans, which the gods built for themselves, often admired by humans. Sometimes the gods would go away into the sky, other times to their splendid dwellings on Earth.

> *Foremost be Visnu, stronger than the strongest: for glorious*
> *   is his name who lives for ever.*
> *Over this Earth with mighty step strode Visnu, ready to*
> *   give it for a home to Manu.*
> *In him the humble people trust for safety: he, nobly born,*
> *   hath made them spacious dwellings.*
> *Yea, I the poor and weak praise thee the Mighty who*
> *   dwellest in the realm beyond this region.*
> *May these my songs of eulogy exalt thee. Preserve us*
> *   evermore, ye Gods, with blessings.*
>
> HYMN C—VISNU

Humans were generally impressed by the ancient gods. They were beautiful, they lived forever, they could fly away in their thundering ships of the sky, and they had mighty weapons. They could appear any place, any time, without warning.

> *How were they born? Who knoweth it, ye sages?*
> *These of themselves support all things existing:*
> *The Twain uphold, though motionless and footless, a*
> *   widespread offspring having feet and moving.*
> *. . . protect us, Heaven and Earth, from fearful danger.*
> *May we be close to both the Worlds who suffer no pain,*
> *   Parents of Gods, who aid with favour,*
> *Both mid the Gods, with Day and Night alternate.*
> *Protect us, Heaven and Earth, from fearful danger.*
> *Faring together, young, with meeting limits, Twin Sisters*
> *   lying in their*
> *Parents' bosom, Kissing the centre of the world together.*
> *Who, beautiful to look on, make the nectar.*
> *Wide, vast, and manifold, whose bounds are distant, these,*
> *   reverent,*
> *I address at this our worship,*

May both these Friends of man, who bless, preserve me,
may they attend me with their help and favour.
Enrich the man more liberal than the godless. May we, ye
Gods, be strong with food rejoicing.
I have uttered this truth, for all to hear, to Earth and
Heaven.
Be near us, keep us from reproach and trouble.
Nearest of Gods be ye with your protection.
                    HYMN CLXXXV—HEAVEN AND EARTH

JUDAISM: ORIGIN CIRCA 2000 BC

Judaism is the religion of the Jewish people and can be traced back to the Exodus of the Hebrews from Egypt. Judaism, Christianity, Islam and the Baha'i faith all share Abraham as their founding father sometime around 2050 BC. This original development is marked by the divine covenant that was made between god and the ancient Israelites. Moses was the next leader of the Israelites, and probably the first "real" Jewish leader, who led his people out of captivity in Egypt and received the "Law from God." Then Joshua led them into the promised land where Samuel established the Israelite kingdom with Saul as its first king. King David established Jerusalem and King Solomon built the first temple there. But the history of the Jews is a tragic one. These chosen people of god have been in a perpetual state of conflict since the very first book of the Bible. In AD 70, the temple of Jerusalem was destroyed and the Jews were scattered throughout the world—until 1948 when the state of Israel was formed.

Jews believe in one creator who alone is to be worshipped as absolute ruler of the universe. He monitors people's activities and rewards good deeds and punishes the evil ones. This is the god of vengeance of the Old Testament. The Jewish holy book is the Hebrew Bible, which is a collection of books that were written over a period of about 1,000 years and established in its full canonical form by the end of the first century AD. It is divided into three sections: the Torah, the Prophets, and the Writings. The Torah, which consists of the first five books of the Bible, was apparently written by Moses, by divine instruction from God himself and cannot be changed. How convenient. A perfect example of the manipulative nature of the god of vengeance. Just command the people not to question and not to touch, otherwise they will be punished. The same old story that has plagued humankind from the very beginning. Throughout their history, God would communicate with the Jewish people through prophets, high priests, and sometimes even through oracles and oracle stones. The actual origin of the prophetic experience is not clear, but a prophet was simply anyone who believed himself to be summoned by God to preach his message. Some of these prophets became very powerful people, who held the attention of their fellow Jews without question. We can assume that there were many other prophets besides the more popular ones, who were less admired. The prophetic experience could range from the obscure mystical visions of an Ezekiel, to the clear ethical convictions of Amos. The word *Jehovah* is a medieval misreading and does not appear in the Hebrew Bible.

Jews believe in the inherent goodness of the world and its inhabitants as creations of God and do not require a savior to save them from original sin. They believe that they are God's chosen people and that their Messiah will arrive in the future, gather them into Israel, where there will be a general resurrection of the dead, and the Jerusalem Temple will be rebuilt. This is a beautiful fairy tale that belongs squarely in the realms of mythology, but somehow this naive version of the evolution of humankind escaped the historians' wrath and remained a divine religion, never to be associated with the heathen behavior of those who worshipped the Sumerian gods just a short time before.

You may be surprised to find that the Jews may be a little unsure of the whole truth, because even the Hebrews had different names for different gods, which once again resemble the "heavenly gods" of the Sumerians who came before them. The scriptures mention only a few, like Shad-dai, which seemed to represent the storm god; also Elo'ah; Yah; Adonai, and Elohim. But if they had these few gods pretty clearly identified, there must have been others. The most important one was "YHWH" (pronounced as Yahweh), generally taking on the meaning of "Lord" and eventually became Jehovah. This word was apparently not pronounced by the early Hebrew priests because it was deemed to be the unpronounceable name of god. If you spend a while contemplating all the strange coincidences, you will begin to see the underlying common thread of the prehistoric Sumerian gods and the Anunnaki deities, who settled on Earth long before all this confusion among the humans began. As much as the Jews like to present a strong unified front, their religion has had many sects and cults over a 3,000 year period. From the Essenes of Jesus' days, who had very strong ties with the Aryans of Persia, to the Kabbalists and the Karaites of the eighth century AD, who regarded themselves as "Children of the Scripture," and only adhered to the five books of Moses, and in addition they practiced much stricter rules in their lives. The transformation from Hebraism to Judaism happened during the periods some time before the birth of Christ to around AD 200, by which time the writings of the Mishnah (set of six orders outlining the basis of Jewish law) were completed. It was a long and slow process from which biblical Hebraism emerged as rabbinic Judaism.

ZOROASTRIANISM: ORIGIN CIRCA 1000 BC

From the northeastern parts of Iran, what was then known as Persia, emerged a prophet called by the Greek name of Zoroaster. His real name was Zarathushtra, and the religious faith that emerged from his teachings became known as Zoroastrianism. He preached what may have been the first monotheistic belief in a single supreme god, Lord Ahura Mazda, who was completely removed from evil. Ahura Mazda can be translated to mean "god of Light," which would be in line with Sumerian descriptions of their gods, describing them as "radiant" and "shining like the light of the sun," and it instantly makes me think that Zoroaster must have encountered this "bright" god who appeared from the west. The Sumerian gods were jostling for position, Marduk was forcing his will on the Egyptians and according to the tablets, also on the rest of humankind everywhere, propagating the message that he was the god above all. Until this point, the gods of prehistory were ruling their lands collectively and were being worshipped fanatically by mortal humans. The people were protected by these localized gods who in turn had a closely developed relationship with their master-gods.

We should not be surprised to learn that Zoroaster's teachings were so controversial and caused so much resistance that Zoroaster had to flee for his life. A "single supreme god" philosophy did not go down well in those days when the gods of ancient times were in control of the world. Zoroastrians believe in the dualism of good and evil as either a cosmic one between Ahura Mazda and an evil spirit of violence and death, Angra Mainyu, or as an ethical dualism within the human consciousness. The Holy Spirit establishes life and creates men and women. The Zoroastrian holy book is called the Avesta, which includes the teachings of Zarathushtra written in a series of seventeen hymns called the Gathas. Although they were difficult to translate, his love for god was striking. It is a collection of abstract, sacred poetry, directed toward the worship of the one god; understanding of righteousness and cosmic order; promotion of social justice; harmony and individual choice between good and evil. Zoroastrians worship through prayers and symbolic ceremonies that are conducted before a sacred fire that symbolizes their god. They dedicate their lives to a three-fold path represented by their motto: "Good thoughts, good words, good deeds." They also teach that the "System, Order, Principle and Rule," which is to be seen in heaven, must be implemented on Earth. But he was also prepared to use the imagery of judgement at the point of death. Later Zoroastrians in the ninth century AD disagreed with the propaganda of the Christians and Muslims, so they wrote a set of books to defend their "Good Religion." While the holy book of Zoroastrians was probably only written down in the fifth century AD, its roots go back a long way, many years before Zoroaster himself. But just like the other religions, and even though Zoroaster preached the supremacy of one god, there was an additional group of gods that surrounded the supreme one. Suddenly the whole Zoroastrian belief system joins all the others that actually submitted to a "leading" god, who was master of several lesser gods. Zoroastrians had six "Bounteous Immortals" who sat before the throne of god possessing special powers. They could be compared to what the Bible calls "angels." Furthermore, they believe that the world and all material things belong to God, while the devil and evil can only exist in an immaterial world, like a parasite, constantly trying to destroy God's world.

The basic elements of original Iranian religion are the traditional Aryan faith and the teachings of Zoroaster. So much so that during the reign of Darius and Xerxes, Zoroastrianism was a strong influence in the courts. He was also respected in Greece at the time of Plato. And just like all the other religions, it has its own set of sects, cults, and offshoots that have evolved with time. We must remember that the Three Wise Men who visited Jesus at birth came from the east, and were called Magi. Zoroastrian priests were known as Magi, whose job it was to look after their religion.

BUDDHISM: ORIGIN CIRCA 560 BC TO 490 BC

After digesting thousands of pages in an effort to get a broader understanding of global religions, their origins, and how they all fit into the Great Human Puzzle, I reached the conclusion that Siddhartha Gautama Buddha (Sanskrit version) was the first real rebel in the world of religion. The founder of what is today called Buddhism began to question the meaning of life, the futility of life, why men are born only to suffer sickness and hardship and eventually death.

With his new philosophies he basically flew in the face of what the other religions of his time were teaching. Most of what we know about the Buddha is derived from canonical texts written mainly in Pali, an ancient language of India. Those who practice this faith in its native home call it "Buddha-sasana," which could be best translated as "the way of life" or "discipline of the Awakened one." It is also known as the "Buddha-Dhamma," meaning "the eternal truth of the Awakened one." The young Gautama grew up in a hill town called Kapilavastu, which is in Nepal of today, being highly inspired by bald, wandering, holy men known as *shramanas,* who devoted themselves to the pursuit of an ascetic life. That meant no sex, no personal pleasure of a material kind, and a total devotion to spiritualism. These bald wanderers were in search of answers to the futility of life and in a sense were the proto-Buddhists who showed Gautama the way. He was determined to find a solution to the problems of human existence.

The difference between the Buddhists and Brahmins who lived in India during those days was mainly in their sacrificial rituals, which were rather elitist and excluded most of the common people. He joined a group of shramanas, mastered the art of meditation while in search of spiritual truth but in the course of his pursuit he was reduced to skin and bone, and almost died. He realized that this was not the way forward. Some time later he found himself in the province of Ganges where he was engaged by Mara, the "Evil One" and his three daughters, who tried everything in their power to deflect the Buddha-to-be from his purpose.

After a night of spiritual struggle in about 535 BC, he became "The Awakened" and entered a supposed state of transcendental being. Buddhists disregarded the Indian caste system of segregating classes; they accepted all humans as equal. And so the enlightened and Awakened Gautama Buddha began to preach the Dharma. The Buddhists call it "The Discourse of the Setting in Motion the Wheels of Dharma." He traveled and preached for forty years, during which he established the Order of the Buddhist Brethren and Order of Sisters. It is also written that he was confronted several times by Mara the Evil One, but Gautama defeated him each time. When he died in 490 BC, his body was cremated seven days after his death. Buddhists believe in reincarnation and that one must go through several cycles of birth, life, and death. After a number of such cycles, if a person releases their attachment to desire and the self, they can attain Nirvana. In general, Buddhists do not believe in any type of god, the need for a savior, prayer, or eternal life after death.

From the *Gospel of Buddha* as written by Paul Carus we learn that one of the major philosophies the Buddha taught was, "Truth knows neither birth nor death; it has no beginning and no end . . . Truth gives unto mortals the boon of immortality."

So it seems that just like all the other religions, the pages of the Buddhist scriptures are filled by the obsession with immortality. In some religions it would be described as life after death. By now we have established that this idea originated from the Sumerian gods dating back to the flood some 11000 BC and their interaction with the humans who survived. But as time passed their fascination with eternal life evolved into a variety of obsessions, many of which manifested themselves in the number of religious denominations that emerged. We learn further that "karma is undeniable . . . Like everything in nature, the life of man is subject to the laws of cause and effect." Buddha felt strongly about the vanity of religious ritual. He had a whole new approach to life, clearly very influenced by the interactions between the many gods of pre-history and the control they exerted on humankind, while demanding to be worshipped. He resisted it strongly and desperately wanted to free humankind from the stranglehold of the Sumerian gods. "Rituals have no efficacy; prayers are vain repetitions and incantations have no saving power."

The teachings of Christ resemble the words of the Buddha in so many ways that it seems impossible that the two are coincidental. As stated in the *Gospel of Buddha,* "What love can a man possess who believes that the destruction of life will atone for evil deeds? Can a new wrong expiate old wrongs? And can the slaughter of an innocent victim blot out the evil deeds of mankind? Purify your hearts and cease to kill, that is true religion."

I found this gospel quite uplifting in the early days of 2005. It is filled with constant repetition regarding "brotherly love toward your enemies"; the great circle of fate that may turn the victor into the victim; reconciliation; truth and so on. It is the kind of wisdom we hear from peacemakers like Nelson Mandela on a regular basis, but I cannot recall Mandela ever proclaiming to be a Buddhist. "Come now and make peace, let us be brothers; he will gain a victory that is not a transient success, for its fruits will remain forever." The Buddha believed that humans will not be reborn into suffering or lower forms of life or continue a karma of evil deeds, if they followed the appropriate steps toward enlightenment. We are assured of "final salvation." It is not quite clear what that "final salvation" might be, as we read on: "When they die, nothing will remain of them but their good thoughts, their righteous acts, and the bliss that proceeds from truth and righteousness."

But as with all the other religions, even Buddhism refers to the influence and involvement of the ancient gods. In this case however, it seems that the Buddha actually stood up to the violent gods of Sumer and the Old Testament, in an attempt to show them the way of peace and enlightenment. In the book of The Mirror of Truth (from the *Gospel of Buddha*) it refers very clearly to such interaction between the Buddha and the gods; and men. "The Fully enlightened one; the wise; upright . . . The Bridler of men's wayward hearts; the teacher of Gods and men; the blessed Buddha." Those gods of ancient times just happened to pop up everywhere. Are we still so sure that they were mytho-logical figures? If we accept the Buddha as a real historic figure, should we not also accept the "gods" of Sumer and all the latter cultures as real historical deities, although it goes against what we think we know? As vague as the so-called salvation that the Buddha refers to may be, his teachings overflow with the unbridled embrace of truth and love. It is staggering to see how completely opposed by nature it is to the brutal tales of violence that we read in the Bible and other religious scriptures, like the Koran.

But guess what? That mysterious shiny metal called gold pops its head out even on the pages of the *Gospel of Buddha*. Where there was gold, there were the signs of the Anunnaki gods who controlled all of it. We read that even the Buddha was pleased to receive a robe of golden thread from a man of a lower caste. The most fascinating link to our gods of Sumer is beautifully revealed in the story of Buddha's birth. His mother was referred to as the "Queen of Heaven . . . beautiful as a water lily and pure in mind as the lotus." She had a complexion bright and light, like many of the Sumerian goddesses as described in the clay tablets. Those were the days when humans were intermarrying with "Nefilim gods" as we are told in the Bible and the Sumerian tablets. We were also shown that the Egyptian kings were required to be half human, half god. *The Gospel of Buddha* states that her husband the King "honoured her in her holiness." Was the Buddha another one of the chosen prophets of the Anunnaki gods in an attempt to keep humankind in line? And was he the son of a mortal king and a beautiful Anunnaki "goddess"? Would this heritage have given the Buddha superior knowledge to perform his role as a leader among men? There is ample written evidence that seems to suggest this very convincingly.

Once again we have the involvement of "angels" at the point of conception or birth, as it seems to have happened with all the ancient prophets. When the Buddha's mother was about to give birth, she went for a walk in the garden. Four "pure-minded angels" appeared out of the blue and helped her bring the child into the world. The angels took the child, placed it in front of the mother and said: "Rejoice O queen, a mighty son has been born unto thee." This was followed by a very similar event surrounding the birth of Christ. In that story, when Joseph returned to the cave with a midwife, the cave was "filled with light brighter than the sun." The place surrounding the newly born Buddha experienced a similar event. "All the worlds were flooded with light."

It certainly seems that the Anunnaki gods were there in greater numbers, observing the event and "shining some light on the subject." Even the Buddha referred to "Heaven" as being up in the sky. Why is that? Is it because that is where the gods would descend from and return to every now and then? ". . . One who looks up and spits at heaven; the spittle soils not the Heaven, but comes back and defiles his own person."

But, just like all the other religions, there are many sects and cults in Buddhism. The two main ones are Theravada Buddhism, which is practiced in Sri Lanka, Thailand, Kampuchea, and Laos; while the other is Mahayana Buddhism, practiced mainly in China, Korea, and Japan. In China we encounter Ch'an Buddhism, and in Japan, Zen Buddhism, which are derivatives of the original Buddhist teachings introduced into China by an Indian monk called Bodhidharm around AD 500. Zen Buddhism in Japan only really took root in AD 1191 when a monk called Eisai established the first Rinzai school of Zen. A new form of Buddhism, called Shingon, began to emerge in Japan under the influence of Kukai who was born in AD 774 and is now regarded as the person responsible for the merging of Buddhism and Shinto, which became the feature of Japanese religion. The concepts of compassion and salvation were much greater features of this new form of Buddhism, from which compassion and faith began to emerge as the most important tenets of the faith. Shinran was born in 1173, and later established Jodo Shinshu, "The Pure Land Sect." He became consumed with the struggle between the "good man" and the "evil man" in many ways absorbing much of Christianity. The subtle undertones of a place like heaven is referred to in his teachings. "Even a bad man will be received in Buddha's land."

There is one other fascinating aspect of the Buddhists that may have linked them to the Anunnaki for hundreds of thousands of years. Buddhists believe that a new Buddha comes along about every 5,000 years, and the Buddhist tradition has a list of at least 24 Buddhas who preceded Buddha Gautama. This would give us a path of some 120,000 years back in time, approaching the origins of humankind about 200,000 years ago. Is it possible that the human resistance to the Anunnaki masters' oppressive control over them could have begun so very long ago? This is obviously too much for any modern historian to digest, but the legends carry some overwhelming traditions and facts that will be very difficult to disprove or to come to terms with.

SHINTO: ORIGIN CIRCA 500 BC

Ancient Japanese civilization and their earliest semblances of religion are truly fascinating, bearing instantly visible links to the prehistoric Anunnaki of the Sumerian tablets. The Japanese tradition talks about the age of Kami, which began with the emergence of the cosmos out of chaos, giving rise to the history of humankind. The story continues with Ningi, the grandchild of the Sun Kami, who descended to the lower realms. It was his great-grandson who later became the first emperor of Japan. The Sumerian tablets talk about a very similar set of events surrounding the creation of the heavens in the book of *Enuma Elish,* or *Epic of Creation,* the great celestial battle in the sky during which Earth was created. After some time the Igigi, who were referred to as the "children of the stars," descended from heaven to "marry the daughters of man" (Genesis 6:1–8), and in so-doing sped up the growth of the human population. Marduk was the son of Enki, who was the first settler on Earth, and destined to be the first commander of Earth. A further interesting thing is that from about 660 BC to around AD 600, the authority lay with women rulers who acted as shamans or mediums. Could that be because the lands that included Japan were bestowed upon Inanna, Sumerian goddess of love and war, who was renowned for her enjoyment of wine, song, and poetry? She was a strong, determined goddess who ruled over the Indus Valley and spread her wings even further east as time went by. Japanese prehistoric mythology seems to gently transform into history without causing any ripples, claiming that Japan has a divine mission upon Earth. Fortunately, from around the sixth century AD, with the introduction of Buddhism into Japan, there are written documents to draw upon. Although Shinto was around before the arrival of Buddhism, they developed side by side in Japan, but Shinto inherited many diverse influences from Mahayana Buddhists and other Indo-Chinese religions seeping into the region. In 1549 the Christians arrived to teach the heathens of Japan the story of their savior. They were eventually banned from doing so by the first Japanese anti-Christian legislation in 1587. This caused the European powers to isolate Japan until Christian missions resumed in 1859.

The exact origins of Shinto are very blurry. The word *Shinto* is not a Japanese term; it was only coined in the sixth century AD to describe the older religious tradition, "The way of the Kami." It is described as Japan's indigenous faith, similar to the many African indigenous faiths. Shinto is a religion closely tied to nature, which recognizes the existence of various Kami, who are deities of nature. Once again we find immediate parallels to the gods of Sumer; taking control of different aspects of life and controlling humankind in various ways. Their names may be different, but their functions and influence certainly were not. Kami is often translated as god, which is not really correct. Some Japanese scholars go as far as saying it is impossible to define the word *Kami*. Even Japanese people themselves do not have a clear idea regarding Kami. They are simply aware of it intuitively. If we accept this kind of logic, believing in something intuitively, should we not rethink our arrogant approach toward the possible existence of the ancient Sumerian gods, who were certainly not "intuitive," but well documented in hundreds of thousands clay tablets? One Japanese scholar describes Kami as such: "All things whatsoever which deserve to be dreaded and revered for the extraordinary and pre-eminent powers which they possess, are called Kami." Shinto shrines are frequented by *miko,* who are female shrine attendants, performing a ritual dance that symbolizes the worshippers of that specific shrine. Is it coincidence that the goddess Inanna was the proponent of dance and music and such activities were also encouraged at her temples in Mesopotamia thousands of years earlier?

Shinto has many deity gods. Two of the leading deities are Izanagi and Izanami, who gave birth to the Japanese islands and whose children became the deities of the various Japanese clans. One of their daughters, Amaterasu (Sun Goddess), is the ancestress of the Imperial Family and is regarded as the chief deity. All the Kami sustain and protect. They are not seen as separate from humanity due to sin because humanity is "Kami's Child." Followers of Shinto desire peace and believe that all human life is sacred. They revere *musuhi,* the Kami's creative and harmonizing powers, and aspire to have *makoto*—sincerity or true heart. Morality is based upon that which benefits the group. Shinto has four affirmations:

Tradition and family: The family is the main mechanism by which traditions are preserved.

Love of nature: Nature is sacred and natural objects are to be worshipped as sacred spirits.

Physical cleanliness: They must take baths, wash their hands, and rinse their mouth regularly.

Matsuri: A festival that honors the spirits.

The behavior of Shinto people when entering a shrine is fascinating and raises many questions about the origins of such unusual rituals. Once again the similarity between Sumerian temple offerings and Shinto are remarkable. We read in Sumerian tablets how particular those gods were about their choice of food and drink, which they wanted to be offered in their temples. They also wanted a comfortable bed, a garden with trees for shade, a spring or rock pool with fresh water, a bath or cleansing area, and all had to be kept clean, neat, and tidy. The Shinto gods in their shrines have obviously demanded a similar kind of service, which is evident in the customs surrounding the entering of, and worshipping in, the shrines. You must wash your hands and mouth at a natural spring in the shrine or a rock pool. You can make a petition, request, or ask a question, but it is preferred if you submit it in writing. Could this be so that the "god" did not actually have to be present while you lament about your own hardship? You should present your offering, which in ancient times was preferably food. Today it is more symbolic, often giving money. Is it not amazing that the gods of Japan had the same materialistic needs as the gods of Sumer?

CONFUCIANISM: ORIGIN CIRCA 500 BC

China stands alone among the world's great civilizations, developing almost in total isolation from the rest. It adds a deep mystery to the Great Human Puzzle and is a real marvel to behold. The Chinese people speak a language that has no affinities with any other language group. It is written in a script invented by the Chinese themselves, and is unlike any other. The script can be read all over China, irrespective of the dialect of the speaker, because the script is ideographic and, therefore, ancient scripts can be read with ease today. There are three major religions in China: Confucianism and Taoism, which had been in existence for at least 500 years before the third major religion, Buddhism, arrived from India. The influence of Western and Indian cultures and religions caused new forms of neo-Confucianism and neo-Taoism to emerge while many other cults and sects flourished. It is important to remind Western readers that Confucianism and Taoism are actually *chiao,* Chinese teachings, which are not specifically religious doctrines as we would like to classify them in the West. The writers and creators of these two philosophies have been regarded as the collective cultural heritage of the Chinese.

Confucius or K'ung Fu Tzu was born in 551 BC in the state of Lu in China. He traveled throughout China giving advice to its rulers. His teachings and writings dealt with individual morality, ethics, and the proper exercise of political power. His sacred canonical works also contain secular documents predating Confucianism and have been the mainstream of the Chinese educational curriculum for over 2,000 years. It was only after the introduction of Buddhism into China that Taoism followed the path of instituting a priestly order and hierarchy, temples and monasteries and a sacred canon, attracting its own converts to a new faith. Chinese recorded history only really began with the Shang dynasty around 1600 BC. The discovery of a large number of "oracle bones" exposed us to much of the Shang dynasty's religious beliefs of ancient times. Some 100,000 fragments of bone and shell are covered with requests of all sorts, addressed to the spirits of their dead kings. So now we know that the people of the pre-Confucian era, dating back many thousands of years, believed in spirits who could intervene in their trials and tribulations. But more importantly, as Zecharia Sitchen tells us, the "deities of the hills and streams, and other gods were worshipped." Here we have a clear link to the same ancient rituals of Sumer and Egypt, where kings were seen as half-human, half-god, and, therefore, they were often worshipped themselves as gods by the common people. Many of these rites passed on to the modern forms of Chinese religion, maintaining an air of mysticism, and possibly even divinity, around the Chinese royalty. Just as in Sumer, early Chinese monarchs were often priests and kings simultaneously, who would wage war. The Chou dynasty rulers believed that they received a "mandate from heaven" to rule. The kings had to perform sacrificial rituals to please the gods and report to the gods on progress. They would also receive communication from the gods to deliver to the people. The Chinese had a complete hierarchical structure that went "Heaven to king; king to feudal lords; feudal lords to sub-feudal lords; sub-feudal lords to the rest of the community." The king had full control of his lands but the ultimate control lay in the "will of heaven." Such was the feudal pyramid of the Chou dynasty, not far removed from the structures set up by the Sumerian gods, attesting to the ongoing violent character of the growing human race; a characteristic that was very cunningly controlled by the Anunnaki gods. Prehistoric Chinese records are very cloudy but it is evident from these ancient rituals that the gods of Sumer were just as active in China thousands of years ago as they were all over the world's emerging civilizations. Teaching humans the art of cohabitation, agriculture, writing, and through the different characteristics of the "god in charge," injected very specific cultural diversity, like music, dance, poetry, architecture, and more. Poetry, song, and dance played a major part in religious rituals in China, clearly inspired by the neighboring Indian culture, which was undoubtedly driven by the talented Inanna/Ishtar, goddess of love. Just like in Sumer, the priests were also warriors, who would protect their sacred shrines and temples. The great temple courts were used to sacrifice war captives in front of the home crowd. In the following extract from a temple liturgy we can compare the Chinese subservience to the "gods of heaven" as they were worshipped in Sumer:

> *Majestic never ending*
> *is the Charge of Heaven*
> *Your virtue descending*
> *Oh illustrious King Wen*
> *Overwhelms with blessing*
> *Your servants on Earth . . .*
> *May we always*
> *Fear the wrath of heaven*
> *So to keep his favour*
> *And our ways even.*

Is it not fascinating that, as distant and diverse as the Chinese culture may be to the Western culture, the image of a vengeful god who is feared by his followers and who will unleash his "wrath" upon man, seems to follow every single group of early humans to the farthest corners of the world, even today. Confucius stressed a number of fundamental values:

Li: ritual, propriety, etiquette
Hsiao: love among family members
Yi: righteousness
Xin: honesty and trustworthiness.
Jen: benevolence toward others; the highest Confucian virtue
Chung: loyalty to the state

Unlike most religions, Confucianism is primarily an ethical system with rituals at important times during one's lifetime. The most important periods recognized in the Confucian tradition are birth, reaching maturity, marriage, and death.

TAOISM: ORIGIN CIRCA 440 BC

While the "activist" philosophers in China were advocating their theories in the courts of the cities, a whole new "Quietist" philosophy was developing in the countryside. Their concerns were other-worldly: seeking self-awareness and self-cultivation through yogic practice. They saw the unchanging "oneness" underlying a world of change. They called it "Tao." While all ancient Chinese philosophers spoke of their Tao, the Quietists spoke of "Tao-ness" itself. It was these Taoists who eventually inspired the birth of Taoism, a mystical religion.

There are two collections of Taoist works that survive from the age of the philosophers. They are Chuang Tzu and the Lieh Tzu. Toward the end of this period, another Taoist work appeared called the Tao Te Ching (The Way and Its Power). These three works are the earliest writings in a vast collection that forms the Taoist canon. While there is some doubt about the true identity of Lao-tzu, a contemporary of Confucius, he is seen as the patriarch and the original founder of Taoism. In his writings the Tao Te Ching, he describes the nature of life, the way to peace, and how a ruler should lead his life. Lao-tzu hoped it would help end the constant feudal warfare and other conflicts of his time. Taoism became a religion in 440 BC when it was adopted as a state religion. Tao can roughly be translated as "path," which is a force flowing through all life and is the first cause of everything. The goal of Taoists is for everyone to become "one" with the Tao. Tai Chi, a technique of exercise using slow deliberate movements, is used to balance the flow of energy or *chi* within the body. One of the beliefs arising from the Chuang Tzu is that a man of "lesser knowledge" or mundane thought, cannot conceptualize "greater knowledge," or the vision of the mystic. This knowledge can only be attained in a state of trance, referred to as a state of "I lose me." People should develop virtue and seek compassion, moderation, and humility. One should plan any action in advance and achieve it through minimal action. *Yin* (the dark side) and *yang* (the light side) symbolize pairs of opposites that are seen through the universe; such as good and evil, light and dark, male and female. Does this remind you a bit of Star Wars? The impact of human civilization upsets the balance of yin and yang. Taoists believe that people are by nature, good, and that one should be kind to others simply because such treatment will most likely be reciprocated.

Our link to the gods of Sumer comes in the Taoist description of what should happen in a state of trance. The person should take off "on a journey, riding upon the wind" borne by "cloud chariots." There were several people who were taken up into the realms of "heaven" by the Anunnaki; an experience of that nature would have changed their lives. On their return they marveled at the beauty, the sights from up high, the feeling of flying through the sky "on clouds of heaven like an eagle," and other poetic descriptions of their adventure. When stories like this get handed down orally over millennia, they would have had different effects on different people. There must have been a contact between the protagonists of Taoism and their Sumerian earthling brethren, who had had such cosmic experiences under the rule of the Anunnaki gods, a long time ago. It is also interesting that the Taoists believe that the cycle of life is made up of five recurring cycles that are represented by the five elements: earth, wood, metal, fire, and water. Each element conquers its predecessor in recurring cycles. There is a very strong parallel to the Inca belief in their five Cycles of Life. Is it possible that the ancient gods may have had something to do with this? China to Bolivia is a long way away, so how did these philosophies cross paths between South America and China thousands of years ago?

So the Age of Philosophers in China produced Confucianism and Taoism. One maverick Taoist called Mo Tzu, who was also one of the greatest philosophers of ancient China, was apparently promoting a concept of heaven and a personal god to his followers. This was a fascinating development in a culture that was obsessed with meditation, yin and yang, and chi. But this cultural explosion to seek a closer relationship with one's personal god infiltrated the new society. Could this have had anything to do with the events described in the Sumerian tablets? When Marduk, the god of Egypt, traveled the world, telling humans that he was the only and supreme god above all, terrorizing humans into absolute obedience, and demanding their trust, faith, and fear in him? The Taoist Church even went as far as developing rites and services for the atonement of sin. A little too close for comfort when compared to what kind of relationships the Sumerian gods had with their followers. Declaring your community's sins to the gods was necessary to receive rewards and mercy from the gods. Taoists had to pay five pecks of rice for redemption and all their sins were recorded in writing and a copy was made available to "heaven." What a perfect system to keep tabs on your human slaves. This is breathtaking stuff. It seems that this was the time when the more brutal gods of Sumer arrived in the East to reap some of the rewards of Inanna's creative civilization of humankind. They brought with them the more barbaric customs that they had imposed on the humans of the Near East. The days of the philosophers were gone; just as they were kept in their place in Greece by brutal gods, the new gods of China and the Far East had arrived with a vengeance.

It seems that the promises of immortality that Marduk made to the Egyptian pharaohs had spread all over the world; even the Taoists became obsessed with immortality. Obviously the ever-present gods of Sumer were there to ensure that the humans were fully informed about their passage into the afterlife, if they obeyed. Some Taoists even believed that they could avoid death altogether, and simply pass into the "land of immortals" by following specific regimens and rules.

JAINISM: ORIGIN CIRCA 420 BC

Jainism has many similarities to Hinduism and Buddhism, and it also developed in the same part of the world. Jains believe in karma and reincarnation, as do Hindus, but they believe that enlightenment and liberation from this cycle can only be achieved through asceticism. The virtue of a great ascetic could protect a city from an enemy, so it was fruitless to attack such a city until the ascetic had been corrupted or destroyed. There is a story of an ascetic who generated such powers through his penance that it caused the gods to send down a "celestial damsel" of great beauty to seduce him and expend his accumulated potency. There we go again! The gods of heaven who keep interfering with humankind. We know from the Sumerian tablets that the Anunnaki females, or "goddesses" as they were seen by humans, were "breathtakingly beautiful." Their offspring that they conceived with mortal men were equally beautiful. Here we have another perfect example of where mythology crosses paths with popular religion, and yet we hold onto what we call religion and we discard the unexplainable as "myth." How very convenient. Jainism follows similar beliefs as other religions: that time is cyclical; that the universe undergoes growth, decline, destruction, and re-creation perpetually. The Laws of Manu speak about the Four Ages that follow each other, dating the ages back to the last rebirth of humankind some 12,000 years ago. What a coincidence! Is that not what the Sumerian tablets say as well? When the Great Flood destroyed the world and Noah (Ziusudra) survived in his ark to start repopulating the world again? Another one of those coincidences that historians simply push aside!

The Kalpa Sutra Of Bhadrabahu—Lives Of The Ginas—Life Of Mahavira, deals with the birth of their new prophet. We read some remarkable things about the gods of the time and their influence on the people, and even interaction between gods and the people. The desire for ascending to heaven is very strong and, just like Sumerians, these people worshipped the gods in their "celestial abodes." The gods must have convinced the earthlings in this part of the world that they were sinful, just as the Sumerian humans were informed:

> *Obeisance to all Saints in the World!*
> *This fivefold obeisance, destroying all sins, is of all benedictions*
>   *the principal benediction.*
> *In that period, in that age the Venerable Ascetic Mahavira*
>   *. . . where he had lived for twenty Sagaropamas till the*
>   *termination of his allotted length of life, divine nature,*
>   *and existence (among the gods) . . .*
> *O beloved of the gods, what, to be sure, will be the happy result*
>   *portended by these fourteen illustrious, great dreams?*

But they wanted real quality education and nurturing for the new prophet to be born:

And this boy, after having passed his childhood, and, with just ripened intellect, having reached the state of youth . . . he will be versed in the philosophy of the sixty categories, and well grounded in arithmetic, in phonetics, ceremonial, grammar, metre, etymology, and astronomy, and in many other brahmanical [and monastic] sciences besides . . . O beloved of the gods; that matter is really such as you have pronounced it.

In that period, in that age, Sakra, the chief and king of the gods, the wielder of the thunderbolt, the destroyer of towns, the performer of a hundred sacrifices, the thousand-eyed one, Maghavan, the punisher of the Daitya Paka, the lord of the southern half of the Earth, the lord of the thirty-two thousand celestial abodes . . . who wears spotless clothes and robes . . . whose cheeks were stroked by fine, bright, and trembling earrings of fresh gold [the most prosperous, the most brilliant, the most mighty, the most glorious, the most powerful, and the most happy one] . . . in the celestial abode . . . he who exercises and maintains the supreme command, government, management, guidance, direction, and sovereign power and generalship over the thirty-two thousand gods of the celestial abodes, the eighty-four thousand gods of a rank equal with that of himself, the thirty-two chief gods, the four guardians of the world, the eight principal queens with their trains, the three courts, the seven armies, and the seven commanders of these armies.

It strikes me that those were very specific kinds of utterances, with little doubt in the mind of the writer as to who was in charge and of what, and exactly how the power structures on Earth were organized. While these writings are sacred to millions, some arrogant historians discard them very quickly and relegate the content to realms of mythology. How could this be possible? It is either a living religion, passed down over thousands of years, or all of the other religions should also be classified as myth.

The concept of *ahimsa*, or nonviolence, is a fundamental principle of Jainism, because any act of violence against a living thing creates negative karma that will adversely affect one's next life. It was also one of the principles preached by Jesus, when he suddenly emerged in Canaan at the age of twenty-nine. Many scholars have, however, denied that Jesus ever preached the concept of rebirth and any references to it have been removed from the New Testament. The founder of the Jain community was Vardhamana, the last Jain in a series of twenty-four who lived in East India. He attained enlightenment after thirteen years of deprivation and committed the act of *salekhana*, fasting to death, in 420 BC. You may remember that Mahatma Gandhi started a fast of this kind to get the warring Muslims and Hindus to stop fighting. Jains follow fruitarianism. This is the practice of only eating that which will not kill the plant or animal from which the food is taken.

ISLAM: ORIGIN CIRCA AD 622

Islam was founded around AD 622 by the Prophet Mohammed in the city of Medina. *Islam* is an Arabic word that means "acceptance; surrender; submission; or commitment." I found these descriptions fascinating, mainly because it echoes the words of the god of vengeance in the Old Testament. We should not be surprised by this because the patriarch of the Muslim faith is also Abraham. Although Islam is the youngest of the world's great religions, Muslims do not view it as a new religion. They believe that it is the same faith taught by the prophets Abraham, David, Moses, and even Jesus, but somehow the Jews and Christians got it wrong. The exact date of Mohammed's birth is not known, but scholars generally accept that he was born in Mecca circa AD 570. Islam sees Mohammed as the last prophet whose role it was to formalize and clarify the faith and purify it by removing ideas that were added in error. He married a rich widow fifteen years his senior and came under the influence of Jewish and Christian teachings. He developed a reputation for honesty and wisdom. Like all Arabs, Mohammed was a member of a tribe. The tribe he belonged to was called the Quraysh and his tribal upbringing played an important part in his role of uniting Islam behind a brand new philosophy.

In pre-Islamic Arabia the Bedouins were not notably pious, but they had certain religious practices. There were a number of spirits and demons whom they propitiated (whose favor they had to win on a constant basis). What is important to note is that they were highly influenced by the "astral religion" of the ancient Semitic people who led them to recognize deities associated with heavenly bodies. Most of these were goddesses with names like al-Lat, al-Uzzah, and al-Manat. Mohammed's tribe was no exception, and they also worshipped a number of different deities or gods. One of the gods that the Bedouins worshipped was Allah, but he was by no means their main god and at that point did not feature strongly and his function was rather vague. It becomes evident that during Mohammed's structuring of Islam, he did not introduce a new name or a new "god," it was a god who was already reasonably well established among the Arabs and Bedouins. What astounds me is the way in which humans, and specifically historians, can discriminate between these Arabic gods. While one of the ancient mythological gods by the name of Allah was elevated to the "supreme" god status, the others were summarily demoted and remained in the lesser ranks of mythological deities. How is that possible? Do our historians know something we don't? Or is it just their ignorance shining through again?

The Quraysh was a powerful tribe that rose to take control of Mecca. They built sacred shrines and erected their own deities in many places throughout the city. But the Arabs also made pilgrimages to other shrines erected around the peninsula. A popular spot was a shrine to god al-Manat at Ukas, not far north of Mecca. The most important center of pilgrimage was a rectangular stone building known as the Kaaba, in the valley of Mecca. The principal god of the Kaaba was Hubal, but there were other gods associated with the shrine as well. This pre-Islamic pilgrimage to Kaaba, with its specific performance of rites, makes up most of what is practiced by Muslims today. They would visit their shrines during certain months of the lunar calendar that were considered sacred. During this time, all fighting was forbidden and renunciation of hostilities allowed trade to flourish and festivities to take place. Mohammed claimed that he was a Hanif, a group who believed that they were of spiritual descent from Abraham and were highly inspired by monotheism.

So those were just some of the events that led up to Mohammed's encounter with the angel Gabriel and some of the thinking that went into the philosophy of Islam. Before Mohammed received his calling, Arabian paganism was showing great signs of decay. The Meccans were worshipping not only Allah, but a host of other deities, whom they referred to as "daughters of Allah." This should not be surprising as the rest of humankind were doing the same in distant parts of the world. Although Mohammed disagreed with the teachings of the Jews and Christians, he was impressed with the concept of "one god," or monotheism. He liked to retire to a certain cave on Mount Hira to meditate and pray. Mohammed disclaimed that he could perform miracles but he did claim to be the messenger of God himself. What is most fascinating about how Islam received its holy scriptures in the form of the Koran, are the circumstances surrounding the event. It is commonly accepted among Muslims that Mohammed was illiterate, which is one of the "miracles" associated with the delivery of a complete book by him. On one of those days in the cave or outside the cave under a tree, the exact place is not certain, the angel Gabriel appeared to Mohammed and instructed him to "Recite." The following lines are fascinating because they are almost identical to what some of the ancient Sumerian clay tablets tell us about the creation of the Adamu. "Recite in the name of your Lord who created, created man from clots of blood . . . Who by pen taught man what he did not know."

The book of Genesis tells a very similar story about the creation of Adam, but the most graphic description we have of this first creation of man comes from the clay tablets that predate the Bible and the Koran by as much as 4,000 years. It describes how the Anunnaki gods "created the Adamu from the African clay . . . and Adamu's skin was the same colour as the dark hue of the clay." But what is extremely disturbing is the way in which the "angel" approached Mohammed. It is recorded that after the first time the angel commanded him to "recite in the name of God," Mohammed did not respond, probably out of fear or confusion; you can be the judge of that. The angel grabbed him by the throat and shook him violently while repeating the command again. After the second command, Mohammed still did not respond, so the angel proceeded to choke him until Mohammed was compelled to do what he was told. It now makes complete sense why Mohammed was "so disturbed by his experience" and why at first he was filled with doubt, even wondering if he had lost his sanity or whether he may have been possessed by a malignant spirit. The outcome of this experience and an extended period of revelations to Mohammed was the complete works known to Muslims as the "unquestionable words of God himself"—the Koran.

I was always told a different story, one where Mohammed went into the cave for forty days and during that time he wrote down the words as dictated to him by the angel. That seems to be the popularized fairy-tale version, not what probably happened. The knowledge that was bestowed on Mohammed in the cave came to him in the form of revelations over an extended period, it did not all happen at once. It is said that the words of the angel "were inscribed upon his heart" and he could suddenly remember them and recite them in moments of inspiration. During Mohammed's life these verses would come to him from time to time and be inscribed upon palm leaves, stones, or any material that came to hand. In his English translation of the Koran, N. J. Dawood describes it as "the earliest and by far the finest work of classical Arabic prose." The final collection of Mohammed's revelations in the Koran was completed during the caliphate of Umar the second Caliph, but the authorized version was only established during the caliphate of Uthman, his successor, between AD 644 and 656.

The two sacred texts of Islam are the Koran, which are the words of Allah, "the One True God," as given to Mohammed; and the Hadith, which is a collection of Mohammed's sayings. Although the Muslims accepted Jesus as a prophet, they accused the Christians of blasphemy for worshipping him as the son of God, when they were strictly commanded to "worship none but Him." But Mohammed did not have it easy at the beginning of his preaching career. At first the Meccans ignored him, but as his following grew they feared him. Eventually they began to oppose him and Mohammed became somewhat of a hated individual in Mecca. The levels of intolerance grew so high that in AD 622 Mohammed and his followers were forced to leave Mecca. Fortunately, he managed to negotiate a favorable deal with the leaders of a city called Yathrib, in order to be accepted and given protection. Soon after this, Yathrib became known as Medina, the city of the prophet. Since this was a decisive turning point in the life and fortunes of Mohammed and his followers, it was adopted as the starting point of the Islamic calendar and his emigration from Mecca is known as the Hegira.

From this point Mohammed proclaimed the one unique God who created the universe, established its order, controlling its fate by his hand. Allah demands sole sovereignty and submission to his ordinance. There was a lot of emphasis placed on the horrors awaiting the disobedient ones who were ungrateful to their lord and refused submission. The Koran speaks vividly of the torments of hell and paints a gruesome picture of what will happen to those who do not obey the explicit word of Allah. Does this sound familiar? I, for one, do not see any real difference between what the god of the Old Testament was saying to humans, and what the words of Allah are saying in the Koran. I mentioned before that I find the Old Testament to be a very scary book. But, only when I read the Koran did I realize that there is a scarier book. Let me not beat about the bush here: for those who have not read the Koran, I urge you to do so, and then ask yourself if you were not scared out of your wits. It surpasses the Bible by a long way. The god of vengeance and retribution rises to greater heights in the Koran. It is truly remarkable how similar the rewards, which are promised to the righteous, are to the biblical rewards of heaven and paradise. In the book of The Winds of the Koran it states that "when the day of judgement comes . . . The righteous will dwell amidst gardens and fountains, for they have done good work." The day of reckoning in the Bible is perfectly echoed in the book of The Resurrection of the Koran, which tells us that on the day of resurrection, "There shall be no refuge. For to your Lord, on that day, all shall return. Man shall on that day be told of all his deeds, from first to last. Indeed, man shall bear witness against himself, plead as he may with his excuses . . . On that day there shall be joyous faces looking toward their Lord. On that day there shall be mournful faces, dreading some great affliction."

It is clear that the god of the Bible and the god of the Koran must have been related. And so they are, for if Abraham is the patriarch of Islam, as he is of Christians and Jews, their god must surely be one and the same! They certainly seem to preach the same death and destruction to humankind every step of the way. Every statement and every innuendo is filled with the kind of premeditated control factor that only humans are capable of. The constant threats against humankind smell of an anxious individual who is desperately trying to impose his authority on the lesser species that he created for his own device. The way that Abraham interacted with his god in the Bible is echoed strongly some 2,600 years later in the relationship between humankind and the god of the Koran. While Jesus had turned the god of vengeance of the Old Testament into the god of love and forgiveness, the poor Muslims were dragged all the way back to the mentality of Abraham, and their new god became even more schizophrenic. The "god of mercy; the gracious one; the compassionate," but also the "god of punishment." Suddenly the issues of equality among all humans, which the prophet Jesus had preached, were overridden by the new word of god that told us that women are not quite as equal as men. There are very clear directions on how to deal with a wife who commits some arbitrary oversight, and that a woman's testimony is not quite as valuable as a man's. In the book of The Cow 2.98, it reminds us that "God is the enemy of the unbelievers." I find it immensely unpleasant and horrifying to constantly get bombarded by threat after threat on every page of the Koran of how god will punish the nonbelievers, and yet in the same paragraph we are told that "if you fear God, he will grant you salvation and cleanse you of your sins and forgive you."

It seems as if nothing had changed and the manipulative Anunnaki gods were still trying to hold onto what they had established on Earth. But their grip was slowly slipping as people became enlightened and more evolved and more educated. Humankind was suddenly looking into the greater spiritual realms, realizing that the vengeful gods of the past who demanded to be worshipped, who claimed to have absolute power, may have been the god of the primitive man, but not the true God of the universe. The only way that the remaining gods could impose their authority on humankind was the only way they knew from their past activities—brutal force, violence, the promise of reward for those who followed orders, and punishment to those who disobeyed.

The inexplicable behavior of "angels" in the Bible—when they destroy cities, punish sinners, smite the unrighteous and more—seems to continue in the way that the "angel Gabriel" attacked Mohammed and basically forced him into submission. Let's face it, the angels in those days were very scary characters, appearing to be physical and humanlike. Where have they all gone? They are almost always described as having some kind of fearsome weapon with which they could do any kind of damage or control any kind of unruly situation among the humans, like the one in Sodom. The Koran speaks of humans as "mortals," as if there was another group of immortal humanoids on Earth. "When the sight of mortals is confounded and the moon eclipsed . . ."

No matter how hard we try to turn a blind eye to the ongoing activities by the Sumerian gods, they creep into every crevice of our global religions. We simply cannot escape them. The worst part of their interaction with humans and the control they have been exercising for so many thousand years, is that they have totally corrupted our ability to distinguish between "god" and "God." In the past 2,000 years the remaining Anunnaki gods on Earth have had to resort to extremes in a final attempt to control humans with fear. They certainly did a great job, as one-by-one the religions fell prey to the brutal victimization of humankind by the Sumerian gods. In the book of Ya Sin in the Koran, we read a very similar description to what the Sumerian tablets tell us, about how the Adamu was created by molecular splicing of the DNA and artificial insemination. The Koran says, "Is man not aware that We created him from a little germ?" But the story goes into greater detail in the book of The Believers when "god" says almost verbatim what the Sumerian tablets tell us. "We first created man from an essence of clay; then placed him, a living germ, in a secure enclosure. The germ we made a clot of blood, and the clot a lump of flesh. This we fashioned into bones, then clothed the bones with flesh . . ." Those words are absolutely astounding when compared to the biblical account of the birth of Adam, but even more inexplicable when compared to the Sumerian tablets, which were written some 3,000 years before Mohammed. But it is the last part of this Koranic phrase that sends a sense of utter disbelief through one's body. As the Sumerian tablets talk about the creation of another species or a new creature that they referred to as the primitive worker, so the Koran says: ". . . thus bringing forth another creation."

I trust that all Imams and preachers will argue the use of the term *we* as the way in which God would refer to himself. I find it a little strange that this term is not consistent and is rather prevalent in the part where the "creation of man" is outlined. The Sumerian tablets clearly describe that the creation was performed by three Anunnaki gods, and therefore the collective "we" is used. If the angel Gabriel was a messenger for Marduk, the son of Enki who proclaimed himself as god above all others, he would have most certainly delivered the message in those terms to Mohammed. No matter how we look at the global religions, the ancient Sumerian gods are ever-present, doing the same kind of recognizable things, which become very familiar the more we read the ancient clay tablets and compare them to all the so-called sacred books of the latter religions.

SIKHISM: ORIGIN CIRCA AD 1500

Sikhism is the ninth largest religion in the world today with over 23 million followers. This relatively new faith was founded by Shri Guru Nanak Dev Ji in the Punjab area, which today crosses from India to Pakistan. He was born in 1469, probably in the village of Talvandi, which is about 40 miles southwest of Lahore. At some stage during the year 1500 he began the life of a wandering ascetic, travelling all over India and possibly even beyond to distant places for many years. His travels are well documented in a collection of writings called the Janam-sakhis. The teachings of Guru Nanak can loosely be described as a blend of Hindu tradition and Muslim belief, but this kind of representation could easily be misinterpreted so we need to be careful not to simplify it in such a way. He was fortunate enough to be granted a piece of land on the banks of the river Ravi and there he established the village of Kartarpur. The Guru Nanak spent most of his life in this village until he died in AD 1539, a date that most scholars seem to agree on.

The Guru received a vision after which he began preaching the "way to enlightenment and God through inward meditation." Sikhs believe in a single formless God that they refer to by many names, one of which is Nirankar, "the Formless One," who can be known through meditation, which also includes tantric yoga. Sikhs pray many times each day and are prohibited from worshipping idols. Guru Nanak tackled the age-old question of "How can one know God?" which he answered this way: "One cannot know God, for God in his fullness is far beyond the understanding of mortal beings." But he also described God as *sarab viapak,* meaning "everywhere present" and "visible to the eye of the spiritually awakened person." This becomes a pivotal point in our unravelling of world religions, because the Guru claimed that such "spiritually awakened" people could communicate with God, but only if they applied the specific principles rigorously. He taught that the chief obstacle that impeded salvation was the human condition. He further said that people are imprisoned by the endless cycles of life and death because of their attachment to worldly things. Such people are known as victims of *maya.* Guru Nanak explained that people must comprehend the divine order of the universe in both physical and spiritual terms, and they should strive to bring themselves into harmony with it. The Sikh discipline breaks away from the common practices of most religions like temple rites, mosque worshipping, pilgrimages, and so on. "The only acceptable house of worship is the human heart." If you apply the principles of *nam siram* as taught by the Guru, you will experience "growing toward God" and "growing into God." They believe in karma and samsara (reincarnation of the soul or being reborn as a new organism) as Hindus do, but Sikhs reject the caste system. They believe that everyone has equal status in the eyes of god.

The Sikhs have two collections of sacred scriptures. The first one, called Adi Granth, seems to carry more weight and is the undisputed canonical work. The second and later compilation, called the Dasam Granth, carries its own distinctive importance. After the death of Guru Nanak, a series of nine Gurus who are regarded as reincarnations of Guru Nanak led the Sikh movement until 1708, each writing a contribution toward the sacred scriptures. The final text, the Shri Guru Granth Sahib, was compiled by the tenth Guru, Gobind Singh. It consists of the hymns and writings of the first ten Gurus, along with texts from different Muslim and Hindu saints. The holy text is considered the eleventh and final Guru's work. In 1931 Sikh scholars started to prepare the Reht Maryada, which is the Sikh code of conduct and conventions, which contains 27 articles.

Article 1 defines who is a Sikh:

> *Any human being who faithfully believes in:*
> *One Immortal Being,*
> *Ten Gurus, from Guru Nanak Dev to Guru Gobind Singh,*
> *The Guru Granth Sahib,*
> *The utterances and teachings of the ten Gurus and*
> *the baptism bequeathed by the tenth Guru, and who does not*
> *owe allegiance to any other religion, is a Sikh.*

The following extracts are taken from the translation of the Sri Guru Granth Sahib by Dr. Sant Singh Khalsa. The words once again display our confused obsession with a schizophrenic god, with many influences from the Koran and some other evident feeders from Hinduism. But in the end, where does this chanting and meditating get us? I get a distinct feeling that it is a continuation of the fear of the god of vengeance, as he was known in biblical times and before, the same god who made the Egyptians so fearful and obedient. Although this religion is well-wrapped up in nonviolence, their god certainly reserves the right to dish out punishment whenever he deems fit. The verses seem to be wrapped in a coat of self preservation in the face of possible punishment, so let's chant the phrases just in case we need to appear to be pious:

> The Lord Master, the Lord of the Universe, is infinite and unapproachable; God is the all-pervading Lord of all. The angels, the Siddhas, the beings of spiritual perfection, the heavenly heralds and celestial singers meditate on You. The Yakhsha demons, the guards of the divine treasures, and the Kinnars, the dancers of the god of wealth chant Your Glorious Praises. Millions of Indras and countless gods and superhuman beings meditate on the Lord Master and celebrate His Praises. The Merciful Lord is the Master of the masterless, O Nanak; joining the Saadh Sangat, the Company of the Holy, one is saved.

> Millions of gods and goddesses of wealth serve Him in so many ways. The invisible and visible beings worship Him in adoration . . . All the sources of creation, and all languages meditate on Him, forever and ever . . . He is the Purifier of sinners, the Lover of His Saints; As much as God has revealed to

us, that much we can speak with our tongues . . . We are all beggars, He is the One and only Giver; He is not far away, but is with us, ever-present. Chant the Naam, the Name of the Lord of the Universe; don't be lazy . . . you shall not have to go to the City of Death. Pain, trouble and fear will not afflict you; meditating on the Naam, a lasting peace is found. With each and every breath, worship the Lord in adoration; meditate on the Lord God in your mind and with your mouth. O kind and compassionate Lord, O treasure of sublime essence, treasure of excellence, please link me to Your service . . . The Purifier of sinners is the Naam, the Pure Name of the Immaculate Lord. The darkness of doubt is removed by the healing ointment of the Guru's spiritual wisdom. By the healing ointment of the Guru's spiritual wisdom, one meets the Immaculate Lord God, who is totally pervading the water, the land and the sky. If He dwells within the heart, for even an instant, sorrows are forgotten. The wisdom of the all-powerful Lord and Master is incomprehensible; He is the Destroyer of the fears of all . . . The Lord Master saves even the sinners. So many are saved; they cross over the terrifying world-ocean, contemplating the Naam, the Name of the Lord. In the beginning and in the end, countless are those who seek the Lord . . . and grasp the protection of the Lord of the Universe, the merciful . . . The Lord is the Lover of His devotees; this is His natural way. Wherever the Saints worship the Lord in adoration, there He is revealed. God blends Himself with His devotees in His natural way, and resolves their affairs.

BAHA'I: ORIGIN CIRCA AD 1863

The Baha'i Faith arose from Islam in the 1800s based on the teachings of Baha'u'llah and has become a distinct worldwide faith with over six million followers. It did not take too much reading of the Baha'i scriptures to realize that the oppressive human obsession to please its violent and vengeful god is as evident here as it is in most other religions of the world. Here is a short example of what I mean. Please see the underlying subservient fear, which highlights the "master-slave" relationship established by the Anunnaki gods of ancient times. This is an extract from the Epistle of the Son of the Wolf, clearly highlighting the sinfulness of humankind, very quickly reminding them that if they "fear and obey" they will be spared some horrific retribution:

> *Alas, alas, for my waywardness, and my*
> *shame, and my sinfulness, and my wrong-doing that*
> *have withheld me from the depths of the ocean of*

Thy unity and from fathoming the sea of Thy mercy.
Wherefore, alas, alas! and again alas, alas! for my
wretchedness and the grievousness of my transgressions!
Thou didst call me into being, O my God, to
exalt Thy Word, and to manifest Thy Cause.

Baha'i followers believe that God has sent nine great prophets to mankind through whom the Holy Spirit has revealed the "Word of God." They gave rise to all the major world religions. The differences in the teachings of each prophet are due to the needs of the society at the time, and they were adapted to the level of revelation mankind was ready to digest. This is fascinating, especially if you look at the apparent reversal of "digestible" revelations that followed Christianity. It seems to have gone downhill from there, through the conflicts between the Muslims and Christians, to the destruction of the knowledge in the Dark Ages. Baha'i followers promote gender and race equality, freedom of expression and assembly, world peace and a world government. They believe that a single world government led by Baha'is will be established at some point in the future. The faith does not attempt to preserve the past but does embrace the findings of science. Baha'is believe that every person has an immortal soul that cannot die, but is freed to travel through the spirit world after death. This philosophy seems to clash with the fearful relationship with god that some of their writings portray. I must add that this religion looks very interesting as it seems to push the boundaries of progressive thought, including newfound knowledge in science and astronomy, and yet at the same time there are weird undertones that desperately hold onto some of the old dogmas from other religions. The Baha'i seem to pride themselves as being the new progressive faith for all, ready to take humanity into the new era. The following extract from the introduction to their most sacred book, Kitab-i-Aqdas, creates a conflict between old and new philosophies mainly because it desperately wants to move away from the "old" and embrace the "new age." Yet, it advocates that its entire doctrine is squarely based on the foundations of the "old dogmatic" religions. How does one reconcile the two? I cannot help but wonder if the legacy of the manipulative, conniving Anunnaki is not really behind this very cleverly disguised and attractive religious movement. This is a slice from the Sacred Texts website (www.sacred-texts.com):

Of the more than one hundred volumes comprising the sacred Writings of Baha'u'llah, the Kitab-i-Aqdas is of unique importance. "To build anew the whole world" is the claim and challenge of His Message, and the

Kitab-i-Aqdas is the Charter of the future world civilisation that Baha'u'llah has come to raise up. Its provisions rest squarely on the foundation established by past religions, for, in the words of Baha'u'llah, "This is the changeless Faith of God, eternal in the past, eternal in the future." In this Revelation the concepts of the past are brought to a new level of understanding, and the social laws, changed to suit the age now dawning, are designed to carry humanity forward into a world civilisation the splendours of which can as yet be scarcely imagined. In its affirmation of the validity of the great religions of the past, the Kitab-i-Aqdas reiterates those eternal truths enunciated by all the Divine Messengers: the unity of God, love of one's neighbour, and the moral purpose of Earthly life. At the same time it removes those elements of past religious codes that now constitute obstacles to the emerging unification of the world and the reconstruction of human society.

This chapter on religion was extremely difficult to compile and it took a great deal of energy not to produce a glossary of religions that reduces them to a few pages of pulp fiction. But in the end, I have to be brutally honest and say that I believe they do not deserve to be much more than pulp fiction. The amount of history and culture surrounding each and every one of the religions is astounding. After all, they are the cornerstones of their own communities. Is that not ironic? The active ingredient for conflict and war is the cornerstone of every society! Pretty messed up is it not? As hard as I tried to extract the necessary essence to stimulate the reader's mind and show a clear thread of confusion that binds them all together, there is much more that could be said and explored. But it is very apparent that they all share a few common underlying symptoms. The relentless search for something, which is reminiscent of the ancient mariners who went in search of the edge of the world; the constant referral to fantastical beings with amazing powers; each one believing that they have the answer; not one of them looking at our past with clarity of mind to see where we may be heading. Those religions that do engage the human past only do so with ulterior motives, which are mostly to disprove the others while entrenching themselves as "the only one." The result of all this manic activity has dumped me squarely in a giant void of uncertainty greater than when I started investigating our fabulous religions. We are constantly faced by a god who is brutal and selfish, imposes all kinds of hardships on humans; changes his name and then does the same thing elsewhere. Or he enslaves humans on this planet in never-ending cycles of karmic madness, in the weird hope that the ignorant humans will learn from their mistakes. How could they possibly learn from their mistakes if they keep returning to the same place, more stupid than before?

The true face of God has not been revealed; our origins have not been explained; we still don't know who we are, where we come from, and why we are here. I am talking about the real facts and not the fairy-tale and horror stories that have kept us humans enslaved for too long. You be the judge. Does the outline of our so-called holy religions give you a feeling of confidence, and that we have it all under control? I am afraid it does the opposite. It graphically exposes the insecurity of humankind and our constant struggle to find out the real truth about ourselves. But it is so tightly wrapped up in syrups of different flavors that it has most probably caused a global diabetes syndrome, and we must be losing our sight and other senses. Surely the answers to our problems are not to be found in the dogma of these man-made religions?

14

MYTHS AND LIES

The Living gods

I RECALL VIVIDLY THE FIRST DAY I discovered a story about prehistoric mythological gods and their adventures. It sounded like the world's greatest fairy tale and yet it possessed some kind of mystery that made it feel more real that any other story I had ever heard. The characters were so well-defined that I could not help but imagine they were real. Flying through the skies, crossing the world in a flash, causing the thunder and rain, and bringing love and fertility to people while somehow being engaged in a perpetual battle for some righteous cause. It was mainly the Greek gods, Roman gods, and the Egyptian gods that I was so taken by. Although I was told on many occasions that they were not real, and they were merely imaginary deities who arose out of people's overactive minds over thousands of years, I refused to believe that. I really wanted to believe that these ancient gods were real. They were so majestic, all-knowing, all-powerful with extravagant palaces all over the world in secret places, where man could never set foot. The more I heard of these stories, the more I wanted them to be real. What my motivation was I will never know, but I suspect that it was really just the thought of touching the untouchable. The goddesses always looked so sexy and even as a young boy they had already appealed to me. As far as I was concerned, these magnificent gods and goddesses lived in a secret place in the world that was well hidden from humans, and that they would keep it a great secret from us forever. I was so taken by these gods that they consumed my teenage years and I wrote numerous songs about them from Zeus, the all powerful; Venus, the sexy goddess of love and every man's ultimate fantasy; Bacchus; Mercury; Thor; Apollo; and even the terrible

Beelzebub. I wanted to immortalize these exciting characters in my own way.

In hindsight I find this rather strange behavior and it intrigues me why they made such an impression on me, and why I behaved in such a manner. As the years wore down my impressionable qualities, I began to wonder what the possibilities were that maybe somewhere in the distant past such deities may have actually existed on Earth, and that they may be more than just fantasy characters. I'm sure that I am just one of many millions of screwed-up individuals who have had such thoughts at some stage. But my history teachers were steadfast in their pronouncement that they were most definitely just imaginary characters of simple people who needed something to believe in. Those simple, primitive people, folk from the distant past must have had great imagination, I thought, saddened by the reality that modern man no longer has such a vivid imagination . . . such detailed imagination . . . such convincing imagination that can last for thousands of years. But in the education system of the Western world, which is driven relentlessly by Judeo-Christian monotheistic beliefs, any teachers who would carelessly admit to the possible existence of ancient gods would be rapidly dismissed. That little part I did not know for some time; the part that has firmly held our cultures and customs in a stranglehold for 2,000 years. It started to dawn on me that people today are as fearful of their god, as the ancient people were fearful of the multitude of gods they prayed to. The only real difference was that the primitive people could see their gods, while we modern humans with fantastic technology cannot see our god. This has not always been the case, however, because the forefathers of our great modern religions saw "god" all the time. That was such an exciting discovery for me—it had actually been staring me in the face all the time. Of course . . . Adam, Noah, Abraham, Moses, Ezekiel, Isaiah, David, and many other heroes of the Bible had regular contact with "our" god as he came down from the heavens to converse with our forefathers and give them his commands. The only god, the real god, the god of love, the most vengeful god, but also the righteous god. So there it was, our god was also sexy, spectacular, flew across the skies on clouds and chariots, and lived in a magnificent palace in the sky. We did not have to feel ashamed of our god in front of the ancient Greeks, Romans, and Egyptians.

Then one day, a small technicality dawned on me: all the great civilizations of the world have their own mythology filled with magnificent gods. It made me wonder how they all seem to have heard about these gods all over the world. A well-informed 13-year-old friend of mine promptly provided the answer: "People passed the stories down from one generation to another for thousands of years and that is how they spread all over the world," he said convincingly.

How stupid could I be . . . of course! That is what people did, they told stories to their children and the stories traveled around the world being told by mothers to their children everywhere. That seemed like a very plausible solution to me and I was happy for a while. But as the years went by and I started to delve into more juicy literature, I suddenly wasn't so sure anymore. How is it possible that every civilization around the world had a similar set of gods they prayed to? And how is it that the gods did not take thousands of years to reach them, but suddenly appeared out of the blue, taking control of the local humans' lives and destinies? Let me explain the logistical problem to you. Even today, with international flight possible, with media covering every corner of the world, people who travel to all parts of the world carrying news and messages and cultural influences with them, it is still extremely difficult to get a message across that people will accept, swallow, and buy into. Even Richard Branson with his global brands and global influence finds it difficult to launch a new idea like Virgin Cola everywhere. People must be really impressed by something to embrace it, or they must be enticed to embrace it by the promise of reward, or forced to embrace it by the threat of violence. It is, therefore, very difficult to swallow modern-day explanations of how the primitive people of the world all got to hear the stories about these fantastical gods.

What makes these assumptions even more silly is the problem of antiquity, when the people of ancient times had no idea who lived 200 miles away from them, let alone 10,000 miles away, which included 7,000 miles of treacherous ocean. I trust you are starting to grasp the problem. How could those amazing stories of majestic gods have traveled such distances? And who was telling those stories to the people 11,000 years ago? And who actually created those stories? Did they originate in the Near East, in Mesopotamia, in the Far Eastern lands of China and Japan, or in the Americas where the Mayan and Inca civilizations were blooming way back then? The stories could also have originated in many other parts of the world, even among more remote cultures like the Inuits, Khoi-San, Aboriginals, Maori . . . you see the problem? Suddenly our spectacular mythological stories pose a real challenge to us in tracing them back to their mythical origin. It just does not seem to make any sense. The Flood story is a great example of similar tales that were told by many cultures scattered over the world. We have explored some of those examples of similarity in chapter 12. And it gets even more confusing when we realize that all the ancient cultures had very much the same group of gods they prayed to, they feared, they made offerings to, they were protected by, they were punished by, and gods whom they seemed to have regular contact with. If this sounds a little strange, let me quickly remind you of Adam, Noah, Abraham, Moses, and other biblical legends who had exactly those kind of experiences with their god constantly, throughout their lives. It was as if the gods were controlling the people's lives on a daily basis in ancient history. By this I mean all the people, including our biblical heroes. Is it possible that the gods of the ancient Mesopotamians and Greeks were the same gods of Noah and Abraham? The many descriptions in the Sumerian tablets by kings and priests of their gods are very similar to the descriptions by the biblical characters of god. Let me also ask my question from chapter 1. Why has it been 2,000 years since god has actually physically appeared before someone of international stature, or anyone else for that matter, and had a conversation with them? Why is it that the many appearances by angels and god himself have come to a stop? Is it because of our growing awareness and intelligence as a species? And the development of audiovisual technology, which could very easily expose the so-called angels as something very different?

The puzzle of the ancient gods is a crucial element in the quest for our origins, which needs to be answered before we find more clarity on who we are and where we come from. Let's face it, all the insipid explanations of how the primitive people created these gods from their imagination when they were bored thousands of years ago is simply not plausible and it stinks of our modern-day arrogance. There are simply too many holes and too many incredible coincidences. The most visible coincidence in the mythological god question is the simple fact that all the ancient cultures had virtually exactly the same gods with the same hierarchy. There is always the supreme god who in most cases is responsible for creating the world; his sons and daughters; their offspring and their offspring and so on. The amazing thing is that in each case the god was incredibly well-profiled. The people knew which aspects of their world each god was responsible for, how the gods looked, what they wore, how they traveled, in what kind of machine, whom they were married to—or had kids with—what they liked and disliked, what offerings people should make to them if the gods were angry, and when the people had sinned. In most cases people even knew where the god actually lived. The one overwhelming characteristic that all the gods seemed to share was their potential for violence, strong-handedness, vengeance, and punishment of the humans. But the gods also rewarded their loyal servants for performing good deeds, just like in the Bible. Those deeds were, however, normally commands or very strongly worded "requests" by the gods.

The LORD said to Abram after Lot had parted from him, "Lift up your eyes from where you are and look north and south, east and west. All the land

that you see I will give to you and your offspring forever. Go, walk through
the length and breadth of the land, for I am giving it to you."

GENESIS 13:14–17

There are many cases in the Bible where god rewards his servants, and the so-
called mythical gods were equally generous when they wanted to be . . . only
when they wanted something. There was always a hidden agenda behind god's
requests. People first had to do something, go somewhere, perform some arduous task, before they received some form of reward. The reward was, more
often than not, grandiose. There is just too much detailed information in the
relationship between the mythical gods and the people of ancient times to have
been a figment of people's imagination. Much of the detail includes physical
and material interaction between man and god that in today's world would
be completely fantastical. The Greeks described their gods as anthropomorphic, which means that they looked like humans in most respects. They also
displayed all the same human characteristics. They were happy, angry, jealous,
argued and fought, had likes and dislikes, they loved sex and procreated like
humans by creating offspring through sexual intercourse. They were untouchable and unreachable and yet they were constantly mixed up in human affairs.
They traveled at high speeds around the world, disappeared in a flash and
arrived in an instant. They each had specific functions and weapons of great
destruction and unusual power. People made ritual offerings to win their favor
but they were extremely unpredictable and could change their minds quickly,
depending on their mood.

The most compelling argument against the mythological god theory is
that around 9000 BC, shortly after the emergence of civilization in Sumer,
the early forefathers of the great Mayan civilization had also popped up. What
is totally mind-boggling is that they also knew all about agriculture, planting
and harvesting crops, domesticating animals, had communal settlements like
villages and cities where they displayed a remarkable grasp for trade and commerce. They had their own currency, they had seemingly endless supplies of
gold, they also knew the process of gold ore mining. The Mayan civilization
has baffled archaeologists for the past 200 years, when the rape of the continent first subsided and historical interest was raised, but even today there
seems to be no clarity regarding its actual origins, true age, and relevance to
the Sumerian civilization. Or is there? Ancient China had a god who actually
lived among the people and performed wondrous deeds for them. Does that
sound familiar? The parallels with Jesus are astounding. Kuan Ti was a god of
war. He was the Great Judge who protected the people from injustice and evil

spirits. A red-faced god always dressed in green, he was also an oracle. Kuan Ti was an actual historical figure, a general of the Han dynasty, renowned for his skills as a warrior and his justness as a ruler. There were more than 1,600 temples dedicated to Kuan Ti. This sounds a lot more like the messiah for whom the Jews were waiting; a warrior king to lead them out of slavery and defeat all their enemies.

The other fascinating coincidence is that most of the mythologies, although thousands of miles and years apart, seemed to have a pantheon of 12 main gods who commanded a whole host of other lesser gods, who were mostly siblings or other relatives. This was one big family affair. Why would it be kept in the family in such a fashion? Cast your mind back to biblical events. There too, the heir to a father's riches would be the son of his half-sister and not the son of his wife. Abraham had an episode like that and the Sumerian gods kept this pure bloodline ritual going most of the time, except when it all got out of hand and the "sons of the gods saw the daughters of man and had children with them," as is outlined below:

> When men began to increase in number on the earth and daughters were born to them, the sons of God saw that the daughters of men were beautiful, and they married any of them they chose. Then the LORD said, "My Spirit will not contend with man forever, for he is mortal; his days will be a hundred and twenty years." The Nephilim were on the earth in those days and also afterward when the sons of God went to the daughters of men and had children by them. They were the heroes of old, men of renown. The LORD saw how great man's wickedness on the earth had become, and that every inclination of the thoughts of his heart was only evil all the time. The LORD was grieved that he had made man on the earth, and his heart was filled with pain. So the LORD said, "I will wipe mankind, whom I have created, from the face of the earth men and animals, and creatures that move along the ground, and birds of the air for I am grieved that I have made them." But Noah found favour in the eyes of the LORD.
>
> GENESIS 6:1–8

This passage is another perfect example of how the ruling gods did not want their blood contaminated with the slave species. They needed to stay pure to stay more powerful and in control, which was showing signs of slipping. The slave species had found new wisdom and were no longer prepared to be treated so badly. And now that the sons of the gods were marrying mortal slave women, the offspring would have an advanced genome, be more intelligent, and live much longer. Already then, the gods had decided that they would not "contend with man forever, and his days on earth are numbered," as is outlined in 6:3 above. They knew very well of the impending cosmic gravitational effect that was going to cause the Great Flood, when Nibiru came closer to the sun. This would take care of the human problem forever.

Let's take a look at the major ancient civilizations and their prominent gods, to see how closely they resemble each other in description, responsibility, behavior, and many other characteristics. Let us start with the Sumerian gods, since they seem to be the oldest of the lot and probably are the originals upon which all the rest were modeled. We can say this with confidence because the Sumerians actually recorded their god's names in tablets called The Sumerian King Lists, with genealogies and tales in great detail. This ancient tablet contains some 149 names of kings and gods dating back to before the Flood, and so far there have not been any older discoveries made. Sumerian gods were the predecessors for later Akkadian, Babylonian, and Assyrian civilizations; the same gods with different names. Sometimes the names differed very slightly, as in AN and ANU. At first sight, the list of names looks like a mishmash of confusion, but on closer inspection we realize that they were all related and that the nieces and nephews and grandsons were allocated less important positions mostly in the smaller towns and villages. They were probably no more than foot soldiers posted out in the country to maintain a presence. Zecharia Sitchin points out that one such example of a lesser god with no awesome weapons or powers or heroic tales was NIN.KASHI. This goddess supervised the beverages and her name literally meant "lady beer." These lesser gods were referred to as "gods of Earth."

Each of the important deities was the patron of one or more Sumerian city, and large temples were erected in the name of such deities, who were worshipped as the divine ruler and protector of the city. Temple rites were conducted by many priests, priestesses, singers, musicians, sacred prostitutes, and eunuchs. The gods required that sacrifices were offered to them daily, which was a clever way of staying in close contact with their slave species and maintaining a subservient mentality among them. The Sumerians believed that human beings were "fashioned out of clay" just like in many later cultures and religions, and were created for the purpose of supplying the gods with food, drink, and shelter, so that the gods might have full leisure for their divine activities.

Once you unravel the long list of names you end up with a pantheon of powerful deities who ruled Earth with an iron fist. The Sumerians called them "gods of Heaven and Earth." These were the gods who struck fear into mortals with their awesome weapons as they regularly moved between heaven and Earth in their "boats of heaven." They were international gods who were active in various parts of the world where they had established mining activities. It is, therefore, logical to assume that because of their constant movement from place to place, the local slave species created their own localized stories about the gods of heaven. They were powerful with abilities way beyond human comprehension and yet they looked like humans, ate like humans, they displayed the same emotions like love, hate, loyalty, anger, and infidelity. This amazing similarity has baffled historians and anthropologists for years, mainly because they have constantly relegated Sumerian gods into the category of mythology. The moment we venture beyond this small-minded outlook, we can clearly recognize the genetic link between humans and their gods. The pantheon of gods of heaven and Earth were the original settlers on planet Earth who established a powerful dynasty long before humanity entered the picture. This is what the Sumerians believed and what they wrote about. It is also important to come to terms with the reality that it was not about the humans, but our ancient past was all about the gods. Humankind was a mere accidental "bystander" who was created to ease the daily grind of the gods. That is why the ancient humans were so absorbed by them. A family of advanced proto-humans who settled on Earth were our creators, the so-called gods who have ruled this planet for over 400,000 years. They were closely related, and yet at times they were bitterly divided.

SUMERIAN GODS

An or Anu

Known as Anu in Babylonian, Akkadian, Assyrian, he was the Great Father of the gods; the god of the sky, creator of heaven and Earth—god above all. His pictographic symbol was a star, which also stood for An, Heaven, divine being, or god. Anu dwells virtually exclusively in the celestial heaven, from where he controls all worldly activities. Only seldom does he venture down to Earth and when he does it is for a special occasion. He meets the assembly of other gods in his heavenly abode to settle disputes; he gives advice or reaches major decisions. The other gods have to ask permission to enter Anu's abode, but there are stories of mortal humans being taken up to Anu, almost always in search of immortality. The Tree of Life and Tree of Truth were in Anu's heavenly palace being guarded by vigilant gods named after each tree.

Enlil

The first son of Anu, he is the second most powerful deity. His name meant "lord of the airspace." He is the god who controls all of the Earth; the god of

Earth, wind, and storms. The principal god of Heaven and Earth, because he descended to Earth from the heavenly abode. He is the master of men's fates. Enlil sent the Flood that destroyed all mankind except Ziusudra and his family. Sumerians said that "in heaven he is the prince, on Earth he is the chief." He made Earth quake. He was on Earth long before it was settled by man. He first raped his young virgin concubine, by the name of Sud, before tracking her down later and marrying her. He bestowed the new name on her: Ninlil, which meant "lady of the airspace." He had a son, who became his heir, with his half-sister Ninharsag (Ninmah). Their son Ninurta was portrayed as a "heroic son of Enlil who went forth with net and rays of light."

Enki

Second son of Anu, also known as Ea, which meant "house-water." Also a god of Heaven and Earth, he was known as Prince of the Earth. Enki was a master engineer, god of water, and lord of the salt water who loved sailing. He built ships that sailed far and wide, and he also brought back riches like gold to Sumer. He was the supreme god of magic and wisdom and mining; he was a patron of the arts who was also an oracle. He built his house at Eridu. He mated with Ninhursag, "Lady of the mountainhead," who was his half-sister but could not produce a male heir. He created the plants and gave men agriculture. He constantly struggled against his brother Enlil. He was the architect of Adam and the one who warned Ziusudra, known in the Bible as Noah, about the impending calamity.

Ereshkigal

Goddess of the underworld or Lower World, and consort of Nergal. Some consider her a dark side or aspect of Ishtar. When Ishtar descended into the underworld to save Tammuz, Ereshkigal tricked her into leaving some part of her clothing or insignias at each of the underworld's seven gates as she passed through them. Standing naked at the seventh gate, Ishtar threw herself on Ereshkigal—but she was powerless like Samson without his hair. Ereshkigal confined Ishtar in the underworld until the wily Ea contrived her release with a trick.

Ishtar

Known by many names: Sumerian—Inanna; Egyptian—Astarte; Roman—Venus; Greek—Aphrodite; she was the greatest of all the mother goddesses of the Mesopotamians. Goddess of love and fertility, goddess of sex, goddess of the moon, goddess of war. Lady of heaven, lady of sorrow and battles. The great lover, the great mother. The human-hero-god Gilgamesh spurned her, which ensured his death. Her star is Venus and the lion is her cult animal. Ishtar's love is all-consuming and even deadly. Ishtar's worship involved phallic symbols, sacred whores, and painted priests in women's clothing. Many temples were dedicated to her, which were minded by priestesses who performed sexual rites in her honor, such as the one at Uruk.

Marduk

Also known as Ra and Amun, he was the great god of Babylon, King of Kings, Guardian of the Law, the Great Sorcerer, the Great Healer, slayer of Tiamat. Marduk represents "order fighting against chaos," which is the conflict from which all Creation emerges. Defeating Tiamat, Marduk brought order and life to the world. When the tablets of destiny were seized from Kingu, Marduk fastened them to his own breast, and so brought control of the Earth under the divine authority of the gods. The stela of Hammurabi shows Marduk on his throne with a horned headdress, giving Hammurabi his ring and scepter. The Amorites saw Marduk as a god of spring and sunlight, of herbs and trees.

Nebo or Nabu

The son of Marduk. God of writing and speech, speaker for the gods. Nebo maintains records of men's deeds and produces them for judgment after death. His symbol is the stylus.

Nergal

God of the underworld, mass destruction, and plague, consort of Ereshkigal. Thrown out of heaven, he stormed the underworld with fourteen demons until Ereshkigal consented to marry him.

Ninhursag

Also Maat, "lady mountain." An Earth mother, she molded the first man out of clay and brought him to life with the blood of Kingu.

Shamash or Utu

Son of the moon god Sin, brother and husband to Ishtar. The great god of justice. In Sumer, a god of divination. The enemy of darkness and all the evil darkness brings.

Sin or Nannar

The moon god. Wise and secretive, the enemy of all evil spirits. He is depicted as an old man with a long beard who flies through the sky in his sailboat every night.

Tammuz or Dumuzi

God of the harvest. The god who dies and rises again. The love of Ishtar killed him, and Ishtar fought Ereshkigal in the underworld to bring him back.

MAYAN GODS

The ancient Maya had a complex pantheon of deities whom they worshipped, and during the later periods of their civilization they even offered human sacrifices to their gods. The Mayan rulers were believed to be descendants of the gods and their blood was the ideal sacrifice, either through personal bloodletting or the sacrifice of captives. Their religious rituals were elaborate and imposing, and they hosted frequent festivals to honor their gods, with special honors to the deified national heroes Itzamna and Kukulcan. The whole country was dotted with temples, usually great stepped pyramids. Every god had a special feast day set aside especially for them. The mild approach toward sacred rituals of the Maya was in strong contrast to the bloody ritual of the Aztecs—who succeeded them into a new, more brutal epoch of humankind. Human sacrifice was forbidden by Kukulcan (their primary deity), and crept in only in later years. It was never a prominent feature, except at Chichen-Itza where it at least became customary, on occasion of some great national crisis, to sacrifice hundreds of voluntary victims of their own race, frequently virgins, by drowning them in one of the subterranean rock wells after which the bodies were drawn out and buried.

Mayan creational mythology refers to deities from other realms who came to Earth to seed the planet. The Popol Vuh is the most sacred book of the Maya and many people see the story of the Popol Vuh as the story of extraterrestrial gods who came down to Earth and made man in their own image. When they first made man he was too perfect, with a lifespan as long as theirs, he could see far and wide and was as perceptive as they were. They realized that they had made a mistake, and created a competitor who was as wise as the gods themselves. They proceeded to destroy man and started over again, creating present-day man who lives shorter lifetimes, is not as smart, and is here to act as a slave-servant to the gods.

One part of this story tells us of the gods' first attempt to create humans; only succeeding after several attempts, he created the True People by constructing them with maize.

They came together in darkness to think and reflect. This is how they came to decide on the right material for the creation of man . . . Then our Makers

Tepew and Q'uk'umatz began discussing the creation of our first mother and father.

This story is identical to that in the Sumerian tablets 10,000 miles across the Atlantic. How is that possible? Unless the same gods had a hand in all this activity? In another part of the Popol Vuh, it talks about how mankind had been created as a servant of the gods.

> Let us make him who shall nourish and sustain us . . . We have already tried with our first creations, our first creatures; but we could not make them praise and venerate us. So then, let us try to make obedient, respectful beings who will nourish and sustain us.

These various references took me by complete surprise when I first stumbled upon them. It is virtually identical to the theory that I had formulated before setting out to write this book. But I had not laid eyes on the Popol Vuh or its meaning until I began researching this chapter. It was a great personal discovery to see that others long before me had already had such outlandish ideas.

The Mayan culture is filled with legends of visiting gods from outer space. Kukulcan, who was also later known as Quetzalcoatl, "the great feathered serpent," was a god who brought the teaching of peace to this part of the world and appeared as a white god with a beard. The drawings of him look almost identical to the drawings of the deity known as Ea or Enki in the ancient Sumerian teachings. It is therefore very interesting to compare Quetzalcoatl to the Sumerian god Enki. The behavior and resemblance is uncanny. Sumerian Enki tried to show Adam and Eve the secrets of life in the garden of Eden, and after he was banished he was referred to as the devil, snake, serpent, Satan, and every other vile name in an attempt to discredit him and make it extremely undesirable for human slaves to associate with him. But scholars have pointed out that his "serpent" name may have been confused in a translation from the original Hebrew word *nanash,* meaning "snake," but its root is NHSH, which means "to find out or to decipher." These comparisons between the Mayan and Sumerian cultures are incredible. Is it possible that they are merely coincidences across the Atlantic some 11,000 years ago? It seems that after Ea or Enki was demoted by his father Anu as a result of his benevolent actions toward humans, he traveled the world and started his own settlements of human civilizations. After all, it was Ea who crafted the creation of the Adamu, according to the Sumerians.

The Mayan god Quetzalcoatl is depicted as a flying serpent, which makes perfect sense to those who can put the two together. He would fly in from afar to help elevate his newly-chosen society, but he was soon followed by other relatives; gods with ulterior motives. They would not allow him to share their knowledge with the primitive slave species. Clashes between gods is the stuff of which the Mayan mythology was made, just like in all the other parts of the world. They were a dynasty with infinite personal disagreements, and humans were, unfortunately, just the accidental bystanders who were dispensable.

The Guatemalans differ in their opinions and their acceptance of the Popol Vuh as the true story of creation. Their affinity for the document varies depending on their religious upbringing and beliefs. Although the tale has parallels with many other creation stories, including Genesis, some Guatemalan Catholics classify the Popol Vuh as an artifact of history, but not theology. This is fascinating! If they regard it as an historic event, it must have actually taken place! It can therefore not be regarded as mythology. And yet most historians classify it as such.

This interaction with gods around the world leads us right back to the notion that as advanced as the Nefilim or Anunnaki may have been in space travel and genetics, they were certainly not the complete genetic beings. Their violent behavior is a clear indication of an imperfect genome, which we undoubtedly inherited from them. Here are the events in the garden of Eden, when Nahash the snake tries to educate Adam and Eve, but is caught in the act by god . . . in this case his brother Enlil, who was of higher rank. Note the physical interaction and the fact that "god" did not know about the eating of the apple. He was just walking through the garden when he overheard Adam's interaction with the snake. Is that possible? That god would not know all things, taking a stroll in the shade of the trees on a hot day? Having to call Adam's name to ask where they were hiding and to drag a confession out of Adam? Here is the extract from Genesis for your own consideration. Also remember that the word *tree* is a symbolic metaphor and not necessarily an actual tree.

Now the serpent was more crafty than any of the wild animals the LORD God had made. He said to the woman, "Did God really say, you must not eat from any tree in the garden?" The woman said to the serpent, "We may eat fruit from the trees in the garden, but God did say, 'You must not eat fruit from the tree that is in the middle of the garden, and you must not touch it, or you will die.'" "You will not surely die," the serpent said to the woman. "For God knows that when you eat of it your eyes will be opened, and you will be like God, knowing good and evil." When the woman saw that the fruit of the tree was good for food and pleasing to the eye, and also desirable for gaining wisdom, she took some and ate it. She also gave some to her husband, who was with her, and he ate it. Then the eyes of both of them were opened, and they realized they were naked; so they sewed fig leaves together and made coverings for themselves. Then the man and his wife heard the sound of the LORD God as he was walking in the garden in the cool of the day, and they hid from the LORD God among the trees of the garden. But the LORD God called to the man, "Where are you?" He answered, "I heard you in the garden, and I was afraid because I was naked; so I hid." And he said, "Who told you that you were naked? Have you eaten from the tree that I commanded you not to eat from?" The man said, "The woman you put here with me—she gave me some fruit from the tree, and I ate it." Then the LORD God said to the woman, "What is this you have done?" The woman said, "The serpent deceived me, and I ate."

GENESIS 3:1–13, THE FALL OF MAN

So now that we have a slightly broader view of the activities in the garden of Eden, a look at the Mayan gods will help us recognize the behavior of the "good god" Quetzalcoatl, who was possibly also the human-loving Enki, the Sumerian god who created humankind as the slave species. I'd like to remind you at this point that the term *underworld* was most likely derived from the original Sumerian name given to the southern hemisphere where Enki discovered all the gold. It was called the "Lower World" as opposed to "Upper World" where the other gods lived, in Sumer. With time, the subtle change to underworld became associated with a dark and horrid world deep in the caverns of Earth, where the devil dwelled. Also known as hell. So when mythological stories talk about the underworld, it should be seen as southern Africa, or "Abzu," as the Sumerians called it, and not necessarily hell!

Kukulcan or Quetzalcoatl

The Maya called him Kukulcan—The wind god, was also known as the feathered serpent. The latter cultures called him Quetzalcoatl. His pyramid was the Pyramid of the Sun in Teotihuacán, the most spectacular of all the central American pyramids. Quetzalcoatl was tracked to Egypt, Sumer, then later to Mesoamerica and Peru. Quetzalcoatl is also the Aztec name for the feathered serpent deity of ancient Mesoamerica, one of the main gods of many Mexican and Central American civilizations. The name Quetzalcoatl literally means "divine-bird snake" or "serpent with feathers of the Quetzal," which implies something divine or precious in the Nahuatl language. The feathered serpent deity was a central figure in art and religion in most of Mesoamerica until the Spanish invasion. All the other Mesoamerican civilizations have worshipped the feathered serpent—the Olmec, the Mixtec, the Toltec, and the Aztec. In some latter cultures the worship of Quetzalcoatl sometimes included human sacrifices, although in some traditions Quetzalcoatl was said to oppose human sacrifice. His significance and attributes varied somewhat between civilizations and through history. Quetzalcoatl was often considered the god of the morning star under the title Tlahuizcalpantecuhtli, which means literally "the lord of the star of the dawn." He was known as the giver of maize corn to mankind and the inventor of books and the calendar, and sometimes as a symbol of death and resurrection. Quetzalcoatl was also the patron of the priests. All the characteristics fit the profile of the god Enki in Sumer.

Most Mesoamerican civilizations believe that the world exists in cycles. Our current time is considered the fifth world, the previous four having been destroyed by flood, fire, and other disasters. Quetzalcoatl went to the underworld, Mictlan, and created the fifth-world mankind from the bones of the previous races, using his own blood to imbue the bones with new life. You will see in chapter 16, when we look at Sumerian tablets, how incredibly similar this story is to that of Enki, while creating the first human, Adamu. It is simply too close to be coincidental. Quetzalcoatl was a god of such importance and power that nearly every aspect of everyday life seemed to be touched by him. As a legend, he would signal the end of mortal kingship.

Chac

The god of rain. Benevolent god for the Maya, who often sought his help for their crops. Chac was associated with creation and life. Chac was also considered to be divided into four equal entities: north, south, east, and west. Chac was also apparently associated with the wind god: Kukulcan. There is some debate whether or not Kukulcan was just a variation of Chac. Or could he have been the son of Enki, known as Ningishzidda?

Kinich Ahau

The sun god. He was the patron god of the city Itzamal. He visited the city at noon every day. He would descend as a macaw and consume prepared offerings. Kinich Ahau is usually shown with jaguar-like features. Kinich Ahau also wears the symbol of Kin, a Mayan day. He was also known by the name Ah Xoc Kin, who was associated with poetry and music.

Yumil Kaxob

The maize god, representing ripe grain that was the base of the Mayan agriculture. In some parts of Mesoamerica, like Yucatan, the maize god is combined with the god of flora. He is shown with a headdress of maize and a curved streak on his cheek. He is distinguishable from other gods by his youth. The maize god was powerless by himself. His fortunes and misfortunes were decided by the control of rain and drought. The rain god would protect him but he suffered when the death god exercised drought and famine.

Yum Cimil

The god of death. Also could be called Ah Puch, the god of the underworld, with a predominantly skeletal body. His adornments are also made of bones. Yum Cimil has also been represented with a body covered with black spots depicting decomposition. He also wears a collar with eyeless sockets. This adornment was the typical symbol for the underworld. Could this have had something to do with the tradition of mining, the symbolisms surrounding it, the clothing and protective gear the miners might have worn?

Ixtab

Goddess of the dead—the suicide goddess. She receives their souls into paradise and is always represented with a rope around her neck. The Maya believed that suicides would lead you to heaven. It was common for suicides to happen because of depression or for even more trivial reasons.

Ix Chel

The Lady Rainbow was the old moon goddess. She was depicted as an old woman wearing a skirt with crossed bones holding a serpent in her hand. She had an assistant sky serpent, which they believed carried all of the waters of the heavens in its belly. She is often shown carrying a great jug filled with water, which she overturns to send floods and powerful rainstorms to Earth. Itzamna, her husband, was the benevolent moon god. But Ix Chel had a kinder side and was worshipped as the protector of weavers and women in childbirth.

Other Mayan gods include:

Ah Kinchil: Another name for the sun god.
Ah Puch: Another name for the god of death.
Ahau Chamahez: One of two gods of medicine.

Ahmakiq: God of agriculture. He locks up the wind so it does not destroy the crops.

Akhushtal: The goddess of childbirth.

Bacabs: The bacabs are the canopy gods, thought to be brothers, who, with upraised arms, supported the multilayered sky from their assigned positions at the four cardinal points of the compass. The Bacabs may also have been four manifestations of the same deity. The four brothers were possibly the offspring of Itzamna, the supreme deity, and Ixchel, the goddess of weaving, medicine, and childbirth.

Cit Bolon Tum: God of medicine.

Cizin (Kisin): Stinking One, the Mayan earthquake god and god of death, ruler of the subterranean land of the dead. He lives beneath the Earth in a purgatory where all souls except those of soldiers killed in battle and women who died in childbirth spend some time. Suicides are doomed to his realm for eternity.

Ekahau: God of travelers and merchants.

Kan-u-Uayeyab: The god who guarded cities.

Nacon: The god of war.

Tzultacaj (Tzuultaq'ah): The god of the mountains and valleys.

Yaxche: Is the Tree of Heaven under which good souls rejoice.

EGYPTIAN GODS

Re or Ra

Egyptian sun god and creator god. He was usually depicted in human form with a falcon head, crowned with the sun disc encircled by the uraeus, which was a stylized representation of the sacred cobra. The sun itself was taken to be either his body or his eye. He was said to traverse the sky each day in a boat of heaven and pass through the underworld each night on another boat of heaven to reappear in the east each morning. His principal cult center was at Heliopolis, also known as "Sun City," near modern Cairo. Re was also considered to be an underworld god, closely associated in this respect with Osiris. In this capacity, he was depicted as a ram-headed figure. By the third millennium BC, Re's prominence had already become such that the pharaohs took to styling themselves as the "sons of Re." After death, all the Egyptian monarchs would ascend into the sky to join the entourage of the sun god. According to the Heliopolitan cosmology, Re was said to have created himself—either out of a primordial lotus blossom, or on the mound that emerged from the primeval waters. He then created Shu (air) and Tefnut (moisture), who in turn engendered the Earth god, Geb, and the sky goddess, Nut. Re was said to have created humankind from his own tears, and the gods Hu (authority) and Sia (mind) from blood drawn from his own penis. Re was often combined with other deities to enhance the prestige of such deities, as in Re-Atum and Amun-Re. We can see the amazing similarity to Marduk and his activity according to the Sumerian tablets. It is written that he dictated the *Book of the Dead,* which gave the pharaohs clear instructions on how to reach the afterlife.

Osiris or Usire

Egyptian god of the underworld and of vegetation. Son of Nut and Geb. His birthplace was said to be Rosetau in the necropolis west of Memphis. Brother of Nephthys and Seth, and the brother and husband of Isis. Isis gave birth to Horus after his death, having impregnated herself with semen from his corpse. Osiris was depicted in human form wrapped up as a mummy, holding the crook and flail. He was often depicted with green skin, alluding to his role as a god of vegetation. He wore a crown known as the *atef,* composed of the tall conical white crown of Upper Egypt with red plumes on each side. Osiris had many cult centers, but the most important were at Abydos (Ibdju) in Upper Egypt, where the god's legend was reenacted in an annual festival, and at Busiris (Djedu) in the Nile delta. One of the so-called dying gods, he was the focus of a famous legend in which he was killed by the rival god Seth. At a banquet of the gods, Seth fooled Osiris into stepping into a coffin, which he promptly slammed shut and cast into the Nile. The coffin was born by the Nile to the delta town of Byblos, where it became enclosed in a tamarisk tree. Isis, the wife of Osiris, discovered the coffin and brought it back. The story to this point is attested to only by the Greek writer Plutarch, although Seth was identified as his murderer as early as the Pyramid era of the Old Kingdom.

Seth took advantage of Isis's temporary absence on one occasion, cut the body to pieces, and cast it into the Nile. (In the Egyptian texts this incident accounts for the murder of Osiris.) Isis searched the land for the body parts of Osiris, and was eventually able to piece together his body, except for the penis, which had been swallowed by a crocodile (according to Plutarch) or a fish (according to Egyptian texts). In some Egyptian texts, the penis is buried at Memphis. Isis replaced the penis with a reasonable facsimile, and she was often portrayed in the form of a kite being impregnated by the ithyphallic corpse of Osiris. In some Egyptian texts, the scattering of the body parts is likened to the scattering of grain in the fields, a reference to Osiris's role as a vegetation god. "Osiris gardens"—wood-framed barley seedbeds in the shape of the god, were sometimes placed in tombs—and the plants that sprouted from these beds symbolized the resurrection of life after death.

It was this legend that accounted for Osiris's role as a god of the dead and ruler of the Egyptian underworld. He was associated with funerary rituals, at first only with those of the Egyptian monarchy, later with those of the populace in general. The pharaoh was believed to become Osiris after his death. Although he was regarded as a guarantor of continued existence in the afterlife, Osiris also had a darker, demonic aspect associated with the physiological processes of death and decay, and reflecting the fear Egyptians had of death in spite of their belief in an afterlife. Osiris was also a judge of the dead, referred to as the "lord of Maat" (divine law). Legendary ruler of pre-dynastic Egypt and god of the underworld, Osiris, symbolized the creative forces of nature and the imperishability of life. Called the great benefactor of humanity, he brought to the people knowledge of agriculture and civilization. The worship of Osiris, one of the great cults of ancient Egypt, gradually spread throughout the Mediterranean world and, with that of Isis and Horus, was especially vital during the Roman Empire.

Isis

Egyptian mother goddess, one of the great members of the pantheon. Greeks and Romans called her "star of the sea," represented by the North star. Mother of the God kings, offspring of Geb and Nut. Older sister and consort of Osiris. We see how the half-sibling procreation continues among the gods to keep the bloodline pure. Her other siblings are Seth and Nephthys. Isis is depicted with a crown in the shape of a throne or cow's horns. She revived Osiris, once after Seth threw his body into the Nile; and secondly, after Seth had dismembered the body. She impregnated herself from his corpse and gave birth to Horus, who struggled to lay claim to the throne against Seth. She is identical in action and description to the Sumerian goddess Inanna.

Geb

Egyptian Earth god. Son of Shu and Tefnut. Brother and consort of the sky god Nut. Father of Osiris, Seth, Isis, and Nephthys. Geb was generally depicted lying on his back, often wearing the crown of Lower Egypt, with the naked body of Nut arched above him. In this context, he was often shown with an erect penis pointing upward toward Nut. Sometimes, the air god Shu was shown standing on the body of Geb, supporting Nut and perhaps separating her from Geb. His skin was often green, indicative of his role as a god of fertility and vegetation. The goose was his sacred animal and his symbol in

Egyptian hieroglyphics. Geb was also said to imprison the souls of the dead, preventing them from passing on to the afterlife. The laughter of Geb was said to cause earthquakes.

Seth

God of chaos and adversity. Son of Geb and Nut and the sibling of Isis, Osiris, and Nephthys. He tore himself violently from his mother's womb and is depicted with a head of an animal resembling an aardvark, with erect ears and long snout. He is also linked to the Semitic goddess of war Anat and Astarte. In about 2500 BC the kings of Egypt suddenly deserted Seth and sided with Horus, the "falcon god." Tuthmosis III called himself "The beloved of Seth." Seth was jealous of his brother Osiris and fought an 80-year-war against him. He defended Ra against the hostile serpent god of the underworld. We should remember that the god of the underworld or Lower World was Enki, who was depicted as a serpent often with wings, and Ra or Marduk, who was proclaiming himself god above all in Egypt.

Horus

Sky god. Also known as Har, Har-pa-khered, Harpokrates, Harsiese, Harendotes, Harsomtus, Har-em-akhet, Harmachis, and more. Horus is one of the most important gods of the Egyptian pantheon, attested from the earliest recorded period. He is a universally worshipped god of Egypt and latter civilizations. Represented by a full hawk or human body with a falcon's head; also recognized by the "eye" symbol. Son of Osiris and Isis. The first ruler of Egypt after an 80-year struggle against his brother and rival Seth. His mother hid him in the papyrus bushes of the Nile to prevent him from being found by his enemies. This led to many stories like the one of Moses in latter times. Sometimes depicted as a sun disk with wings, "Horus of the horizon."

Min or Menu

Egyptian god of fertility but also virility. One of the important members of the pantheon of gods. Sometimes shown as the son of Isis or consort of Isis, and sometimes with Horus as his offspring from Isis. He is generally depicted as holding a flail in his raised right hand and wearing a crown with two tall plumes. Min was mainly a god of male sexuality, and in the New Kingdom (1567 BC–1085 BC) he was honored in the coronation rites of the pharaohs to ensure their sexual vigor and the production of a male heir. He was also depicted in human form with an erect penis. The white bull appears to have been sacred to him, as was a type of lettuce that bore a resemblance to an erect penis and had a white sap that resembled semen. He was also the guardian deity of mines. His most important sanctuaries were at Koptos (Qift) and Akhmim (Panoplis), which were gold mining locations. He was also worshipped as a god of desert roads and of travelers. In addition to his role in coronation rites, Min was honored in harvest festivals during which offerings of lettuce and sheaves of wheat were made.

Amun

The sun god, lord of the sky, the primeval deity present in creation and chaos. Probably the same god as Ra. In latter times he became known as Amun-Ra. Probably the same god as Marduk, who proclaimed himself god above all, according to Sumerian texts. Sometimes portrayed as a pharaoh with blue skin and a turban (modius). He is surmounted by two tall feathered plumes, showing his dominance over both Upper and Lower Egypt. His main place of worship is the temple of Amun at Karnak and Luxor. Other deities described him as "hidden of aspect, mysterious of form." He earned the title "King of the gods" and was regarded as the father of all pharaohs. At Thebes he was revered as a snake deity with connotations to immortality and renewal. This would fit the Sumerian description of the entwined serpent being the symbol of creation and knowledge of science, used in the creation of Adamu. The temple of queen Hatsepsut at Deir el-Bahari bears a relief of her mother impregnated by Amun. Once again this fits the link to Marduk, Ra, and Amun all being the same god, and insisting that all kings and queens were descendants of the gods. This means that sometimes Amun would do the procreating himself.

AFRICAN GODS

Of all the global cultures and civilizations, African mythology is the most colorful and diverse. And yet there is an underlying common thread of creation, descending supreme deities who were in charge, followed by other gods of lesser importance who ruled the world and controlled all aspects of early human life on Earth. One often forgets that Egyptian mythology is part of African myth, too. There are literally thousands of gods that have been woven into the tales of African mythology. They range from the very simple to the practical, from the ignorant to the wise and prophetic. Many of the northern Mediterranean myths are closely linked to the Egyptian gods, while the southern tales talk about gods who descend to Earth from their heavenly abode to make man, to teach them all they need, like agriculture and intelligence. There are tales about supreme gods who made all the other gods and created the Earth from water and chaos. Gods who created the first man are a common ingredient in African myth. There are many references to a flying serpent, which seems a bit too coincidental once again to be a figment of their imagination. Lots of tales of two gods, one benevolent and one violent, who lived in the underworld and rose to the sky. They speak of gods of thunder, gods of the sun, hunters, giants, bulls, and a variety of animals, including a supreme god who commands two lesser gods, who ruled after the creation was completed, which is identical to the Sumerian stories. It points to the simple fact that no matter how far apart the global civilizations may have been in the distant past, their tales of flying, powerful, benevolent, and violent gods are all the same.

The diversity of African mythology also fits the historic accounts of the Sumerian tablets that it was in southern Africa where the slave species was first put to work in the mines. It is truly incredible that many of the tales from these parts echo such sentiment. And just like the gods from other parts of the prehistoric world, the gods are related—with a hierarchy of responsibility. It makes perfect sense that the simplest stories with very basic imagery should come from Africa, since it was here that the original humans existed, who were for all intents and purposes the "infants" of humankind. As they left the secure mining compounds and established their own settlements and cultures, they would have regular contact from the many gods involved in the mining operations and the control thereof. And yet as we discovered in chapter 9, "Gold: The Endless Obsession," there were very few if any temples and shrines built in Africa by those very early humans. They had no need to do so, and their relationship with the gods was not at a worship stage yet. The worshipping of gods was only imposed on humanity by the gods many years later when the slave species made its appearance in the Near East. But the true enforcement of worship only really occurred after the Great Flood, some 13,000 years ago. There are so many wonderful examples connecting African mythology to the Sumerian gods that it is difficult to choose only a few for these pages. The titles that Africans have given god are wondrous in their variety. A few of these are: Creator; Molder; Giver of Rain and Sunshine; He Who Brings the Seasons; He Who Thunders; Ancient of Days; the First; the Limitless; the One Who Bends Even Kings; the One You Meet Everywhere; the Firelighter; Great Mother; Greatest of Friends; the Kindly One; the Providence Who Watches All Like the Sun; the Great Pool Contemporary of Everything; the Great Spider; the One Beyond All Thanks; the Bow in the Sky; the Angry One; the Inexplicable.

The following list is a brief and random example of African gods from a few stories of ancient times:

Agipie (Tanzania)

A benevolent god who lives in the sky. He fights with the evil god who has lightning and destroys people.

Buku
(Various West African Peoples)

A sky god sometimes worshipped as a goddess. Buku created everything, even the other gods.

Akongo (Democratic Republic of the Congo, DRC)

Supreme everlasting being, has good relations with humans. Has human characteristics with an intense interest in all their activities and their well-being. He had a quarrel with other gods and disappeared.

Alouko Niami Kadio
(Cote d'Ivoire)

Created all other gods as well as man. After creating the world, he descended on a Saturday from his heavenly dwelling. He taught humans all they need to know to live and also what must remain a secret.

Ananasi (Various Tribes)

The spider. A trickster. A creator god. Something of a scoundrel, but quite well-liked. Many amusing and fanciful stories are told of him.

Anyiewo

The Great Serpent who comes out to graze after the rain. The rainbow is his reflection.

Bunzi (DRC)

She was born as a snake to a god father and her great mother. The serpent grew up and assumed the role of her mother, which was rainmaking. People would see the serpent in the sky in the shape of the rainbow.

Danh,
also Dan Ayido Hwedo (Dahomey)

Snake god. The Haitians know him as Dan Petro, the Rainbow Snake who encircles the world. Danh is often portrayed with his tail in his mouth as a symbol of unity and wholeness.

Dxui (Bushmen; Hottentots, Tsui; to the Xhosa and Ponda, Thixo)

A creator god. In the beginning, Dxui took the form of a different flower or plant every day, becoming himself at night, until he had created all the plants and flowers that exist.

Eshu (Yoruba)

A trickster. A shape-shifter, Eshu can change his form at will, and can even seem to be both huge and small at the same time. Eshu confuses men and drives them to madness. But Eshu also knows all human tongues and acts as a go-between for mortals and the gods.

Doondari (Mali, Senegal)

The creator who descended to the Earth and created a stone, which created iron, fire, water, and air. Then he returned and shaped those elements into man. But man became too proud, so he created blindness and also death.

Dzemawon (Ghana)

A powerful and intelligent god who comes and goes as he pleases. He comes like the wind, he walks all over the world. He is omnipotent and can take on any shape. On days of worship he can appear in human form.

Gunab (Hottentot)

The enemy of Tsui-Goab, Gunab lived under a pile of stones. Gunab kept overpowering Tsui-Goab, but the god grew stronger after each battle. Because he killed so many, Gunab is sometimes identified with death. Creator of the rainbow.

Gua (Ga Tribe of West Africa)

God of thunder, blacksmiths and farmers. Gua's temples are often found at blacksmith's forges.

Kibuka (Baganda)

A war god, sent to save the Baganda people. The king of the Baganda asked heaven for assistance in war, and Kibuka was sent to aid them. Warned not to have anything to do with the enemy's women, Kibuka, nevertheless, made love to a woman prisoner. Unwisely, Kibuka confided in her, and after escaping she told the enemy how Kibuka could be killed, by firing arrows into the cloud where he was hiding. Kibuka flew off to a tall tree to die, and a temple was built at the place where his body was found.

Leza (Central Africa)

The One Who Besets, Leza is the Supreme God who rules the sky and sends wind and rain. Leza sits on the backs of all people, and no one can ever break free of him. Leza is said to be growing old and so does not hear prayers as well as he once did.

Mawu-Lisa (Ewe)

The great god and goddess of the sun and moon. Lisa is the sun and Mawu is the moon.

Modimo (Lesotho)

Creator god, supreme being, also called Ralapeba. Father of all might and power, feared for his vengefulness and power of fire. He is one of twelve gods with various functions and awesomeness. A comet called Modudusta is honored in the name of these gods.

Mujaji
(Lovedu-South Africa)

Rain goddess, queen of the Lovedu people. Four rain goddesses have ruled over the Lovedu people, all descendants of the original Mujaji. They are all related to the great and mighty Monomotapa of the Karanga empire in Zimbabwe, giving us a direct link to the mystery surrounding the Zimbabwe ruins and the lands of Ophir filled with gold. Mujaji has mysterious powers and is immortal. She has saved many people by bringing rain.

Mulungu
(East Africa)

God and the Supreme Being. The concept of a supreme being and creator is nearly universal in Africa. Although there are few temples to this god, they must have been built sometime after 3000 BC in the Mozambique and Zimbabwe areas. These temples resemble those of Canaanite origins in the Near East. Mulungu lived on Earth at first, but moved back to the sky because men were killing his children. He told man that they would come up to the sky when they die. So it is believed that when humans die they go up to heaven to be the slaves of god.

Nanan-Bouclou (Ewe)

The original god of the Ewe tribe, both male and female, Nanan-Bouclou is much too remote for worship. In Haiti, Nanan-Bouclou is remembered as the god of herbs and medicines.

Ngai (Masai)

Creator god. At birth, Ngai gives each man a guardian spirit to ward off danger and carry him away at the moment of death. The evil are carried off to a desert, while the good go to a land of rich pastures and many cattle.

Nyame
(Ashanti)

Supreme god of heaven, both the sun god and the moon goddess. Nyame created the three realms: the sky, the Earth, and the underworld. Before being born, souls are taken to Nyame and washed in a golden bath. Nyame gives the souls their destinies. The soul is then fit to be born.

Nyasaye (Maragoli, Kenya)

Chief god of the Maragoli. Spirits are said to aid Maragoli's work, and they are represented by round stones circling a pole that represents the god.

Nzame
(Fan People, Congo)

He is a vague and shadowy god whose likeness cannot be captured in wood, stone, or metal. Nzame lived on Earth with his three sons: Whiteman, Blackman, and Gorilla. At some stage Blackman and Gorilla with all their kinfolk sinned against Nzame. As a result Nzame took all his wealth and went to live with his other son, Whiteman, in the west, while Gorilla and his kin went to live in the jungle. Without the knowledge, wealth, and power of Nzame, Blackman and his family live a hard life of poverty and ignorance, constantly yearning for the land where Nzame lives with his favored son, Whiteman.

Obatala
(Nigeria)

The creator of land, he was summoned by the supreme being to create land where there was only water. Then he made man out of clay. This is virtually identical to the activity of Enki upon arriving on Earth, as described in Sumerian tablets.

Ruhanga (Uganda)

Creator of all things and living conditions on Earth. He retired to the sky but could not prevent the rise of evil and death. He established the unequal roles of society: the king, the herdsmen, the farmers.

Sagbata (Dahomey; the Yoruba, Shagpona)

The god of smallpox. Sagbata's shrines were painted with a design of small spots. In Mayan culture such small spots represented the decomposing bodies of those struck down by the god of death. Sagbata's priests fought smallpox with both prayers and medical knowledge, and wielded great power over the people.

Tano (Ashanti)

The second oldest son of god, and god of the river, who had the same name. The gods of the other rivers and families in the same region are all his family. Long ago Tano lost a singing match with Death. Tano and Death sang defiance to each other for over a month, but neither could win so they had to compromise. When someone is injured or falls ill, whichever god arrives first will claim him. If Tano arrives first, the person will live, but if Death arrives first the patient is lost.

Tsui'Goab (Hottentots)

Known as Wounded Knee and Father of Our Fathers. A rain god who lives in the clouds who is a great chief and magician. Tsui' Goab made the first man and woman from rocks. Several times Tsui' Goab died and rose again, to great joy and celebration. Men invoke Tsui' Goab with the first rays of dawn and recite oaths in his name.

Unkulunkulu (Zulu)

Old, Old One—Unkulunkulu was both the first man and the creator, a god of the Earth who did not travel between Earth and the heavens. Unkulunkulu showed men how to live together and gave them knowledge of the world in which they lived.

Wele Xakaba (Luyia-Kenya)

Supreme being who created the world and is the giver of all things. First created his own home in heaven, which was a place "ever bright" supported with pillars. The first human couple lived in a place called Embayi, a house in the air supported by poles, mainly because there were monsters called Amanani on

Earth. The first humans did not know how to have intercourse and lived many years without children. Later Mwambu and Sela did have intercourse and had a son called Lilambo, and so humans multiplied on Earth. This god was also known as the sun god who takes an earthling girl into heaven and makes her his wife.

Yo (The Creative Spirit, Bambara/Mali)

This creative spirit used three beings to create all things. This included seven heavens corresponding to the seven parts of the Earth. First they created men, and after some time the woman from dust and saliva. Men are immortal, becoming seven-year-old children each time they reach the age of fifty-nine. They live unclothed, have no needs, they don't speak or work.

Zimu (Ndebele, South Africa)

The supreme being, he sent a chameleon with a message to tell the people that they will "die and rise again." But the lizard got to the people first and told them that they would "die and not rise again." By the time the chameleon delivered his message of hope the people did not believe him and chose to believe the lizard.

African mythology is so rich and colorful that one could go on forever. The link that we have created in this book to our original ancestors in Africa draws much support from these tales. As one reads them, they seem to be more ancient than all the other civilizations. The relationship between gods and humans was more simple, more defined, and unquestionably obedient. There was also mysteriously no real need for worship and hardly ever any mention of sacrifices to the gods. These characteristics separate African mythology greatly from all the others, where sacrifice and temple worship form a major part of the rituals. In prehistoric Africa, gods and men seem to have lived side by side with very little friction. There are many tales that include a supreme deity with two sons or a daughter, who go down to Earth to make it habitable and to create man. They inevitably begin a feud that results in many clashes between the gods, and divides their human followers. Controversial South African mystic and Sangoma (medicine man) Credo Mutwa talks about the Zulu legends of the most ancient gold mines of Monomotapa in Zimbabwe. In his book *Indaba My Children,* he points out the legends that speak about "artificially produced flesh and blood slaves, created by the First People." The legends recount how the slaves "went into battle with the Ape-Man" when "the great war star appeared in the sky." As we delve deeper into these stories it becomes very clear that the continent of Africa was a hive of activity in the early days of prehistory, long before the civilizations of the Near East and the Americas blossomed. Man was an infant finding his way in the world and the gods had their hands full, trying to control these human slaves.

CHINESE GODS

Chinese history and religion are inextricably linked to their mythology. According to ancient tradition, the Chinese were savages until a sage came along and taught them how to construct shelters. Some time later wise men taught the original Chinese the use of fire, music, and the cultivation of crops, in succession. The last of these sages was the Yellow Emperor Huangdi, the father of Chinese civilization. Where Huangdi suddenly appeared from is not known, but he bestowed all knowledge on the Chinese people. Could he have been one of the Anunnaki gods on their expansion road to the East? If we accept that the gods of Sumer, or Anunnaki gods, were actually the progenitors of civilization in other parts of the world, then the same should apply in China. Huangdi carries all the mystical attributes that place him squarely in the realm of Anunnaki gods.

The discovery of *Homo erectus* fossils called "Peking Man" in 1921 near Beijing led to claims that the earliest humans evolved in China, and that the Chinese were the earliest modern humans who evolved into a unique indigenous race. This has subsequently been proven not to be true, and the accepted place for the Cradle of Humankind has been established in southern Africa. The Chinese Human Genome Diversity Project, a collaboration among twelve researchers from seven institutions, scrutinized DNA samples from 28 of China's 56 ethnic groups and then compared the samples with genetic material from other Asian and non-Asian groups. The outcome was that, just like the rest of humanity, the Chinese evolved in Africa. This may have been the case, but the huge influence the Aryans had on the development of the entire Asian civilization has somehow been overlooked. It is said that the early humans migrated eastward along the Indian Ocean and made their way to China via southeast Asia. The report linked to the Genome Project further mentions "it is now safe to conclude that modern humans originating in Africa constitute the majority of the current gene pool in Asian populations." I find it interesting that the report says "majority" of the current gene pool. If all humans originated in Africa, was there another genetic pool source? If so, where did this other gene pool originate? Did the elusive and influential Aryans who were responsible for populating Europe, and whose influence spread across

Asia, have something to do with it? Or was the Yellow Emperor Huangdi possibly the other gene pool contributor? The gods whom the Chinese people worshipped at the dawn of their civilization may have had different names, but their functions and their powers were identical to the deities from other civilizations. Chinese religious practice calls on great and powerful divine ancestors. Could those ancestors who are deified in Chinese mythology have been the early Aryans who had special powers and technology way beyond the primitive local earthlings of the time? Or were these ancestors even more powerful than the Aryans . . . could they have been the omnipresent Anunnaki gods who were taking control of the rapidly expanding world toward the East? The Sumerian tablets certainly seem to suggest such expansion by the Anunnaki gods, mainly driven by Inanna. But her relatives and siblings were all in on the act, trying to snatch a piece of the world for themselves and establish their own group of loyal, obedient human slaves.

Dragons play a central role in all of Eastern mythology, sometimes crossing over into popular religion. Their origins and backgrounds are amazingly close to stories of biblical and Sumerian origins. There are a number of dragons that differ slightly as you move further east. The one thing that strikes me is that the image of the Chinese dragon is very close to the flying serpent of the Maya, and other cultures. In many depictions, the dragon is long and thin, more closely resembling a serpent with wings rather than a flame-spitting monstrous dragon. Could this be another influence of Enki, the serpent of the garden of Eden fame, and the flying serpent god of the Maya? Because kings in China were appointed by sanction of the supreme being, they also became deified and often worshipped. Is it possible that just like in Egypt, the Chinese emperors were also half-god, half-man, and, therefore, often worshipped, becoming "gods" unto the people like the pharaohs? The subtle differences between the Chinese, Korean, and Japanese dragons raise a curious link to the possible expansion toward the East by the supporters of Enki and Inanna, and the lower ranks assigned to the lesser gods who were placed in charge of those new lands. Chinese dragons have five toes, Korean have four toes, and Japanese dragons have three toes. Could this represent the diminishing ranks of the Anunnaki gods far away from Sumer and their commander Enlil? But the stories surrounding the origins of some of the dragons are remarkably similar to many Sumerian and biblical tales.

Kinabalu

The Eastern Dragon, lived at the top of Mount Kinabalu in Borneo and was in possession of a splendid pearl that was desired by the Chinese emperor. Many men tried to capture the pearl from the dragon but they were all killed in the process. Then the emperor sent out brothers Wee Ping and Wee San to get the pearl from the dragon. They waited until the dragon went to find food, then they flew onto the mountaintop with a kite and replaced the pearl with a fake pearl. But the dragon was not fooled and gave chase to the thieves as they were escaping in a boat. As the dragon approached, Wee San launched a cannonball at him. The dragon thought the cannonball to be his pearl and swallowed it and died. Wee Ping wanted to take the pearl and the glory and lied by saying he was the one who managed to steal it from the dragon. Wee San wanted no more trouble over the pearl and left China. He later became the happy leader of Brunei. Wee Ping on the other hand, was not so lucky, for his lying brought him nothing but sadness.

The symbolism of this story is clearly linked to "pearls of wisdom" tales. One such story that carries many similarities is the Sumerian tale of Inanna stealing the Tablets of Wisdom, or ME, from her uncle Enki. She flew to his mountain retreat and seduced him. She also escaped in her boat, but this was a boat of heaven that could fly. Is it coincidence that Enki was the flying serpent of the Sumerian culture and probably other cultures too? So the flying serpent, or dragon, gave chase to retrieve his ME from Inanna, but was unable to do so. The similarities in the storyline are remarkable. We must remind ourselves that the Chinese stories were written many thousands of years later than the Sumerian tablets, but it is quite possible that they may have existed in oral form for millennia.

The symbolisms surrounding the dragons are very intriguing. Enki was the serpent who could fly and, therefore, could be seen as the winged serpent. His flying machines created a noise and so did the fire dragons while flying and spitting fire. Is it not possible that the different eastern dragons were just representations of the different Anunnaki gods in their flying machines during the early days when they were colonizing Asia, and keeping their human slaves obedient and fearful? There are several stories about dragons, their sudden appearance and lessons they brought to the people, the fear they spread, and control they had over many aspects of Chinese life. Most, if not all, of the stories resemble Sumerian stories regarding the activities of the Anunnaki gods, long before China became civilized.

Another dragon story reminds me in its symbolism of the story around the birth of Christ, where a young virgin falls pregnant to a stranger, or angel, who disappears. During the birth of Jesus, the cave was filled with magnificent light: brighter than the sun. The child grows up as an outcast, but he eventually becomes the "white prince of peace" slaying evil everywhere, eventually rising into the "sky." The young girl, Mary, became revered by millions and worshipped in prayer. Now see the remarkable resemblance in this story, The White Dragon, or Pai Lung:

> On a stormy night, a young girl answered the door to a stranger who came looking for shelter from the storm. He was an elderly man, while she was a virgin. The next morning the stranger was gone, but the young girl was pregnant. Her parents were enraged by this and threw her out of the house. When the child was born, it appeared to be a small white ball. They discarded the white ball into the ocean. To everyone's surprise, this ball grew into a magnificent white dragon. The young girl, terrified and shocked, fainted and never again woke.

Another variation of this story says that she was killed in a great storm, after which the "white dragon rose into the sky."

> The young girl was revered for being the mother of this magnificent dragon, the only White Dragon King. She was buried at the foot of a hill, where people ask for favors, pardons, and other blessings. A temple was erected on the summit of this hill, and a tablet is there that records this legend.

It is also important to note that the White Dragon was a five-toed dragon; brilliantly white, the same way the appearance of angels or the many gods are described in the Bible and Sumerian tablets. Could the five toes represent the highest order of the divine Anunnaki hierarchy?

The following story is basically a repeat of the Great Flood tale, which was allowed to wipe out mankind, according to the Sumerian tablets. It was a plan originally devised by Enlil, after he realized that humankind had become a huge burden on the Anunnaki, and the Flood would remove the problem very quickly and effectively. The same story is told in virtually every civilization of the world.

> The Yellow Emperor was the supreme god of China, who looked down upon Earth and saw that people were evil and filled with wickedness. So, the Yellow Emperor ordered the rain god to make endless rain. A Great Flood followed, causing everything to die. One of the gods, named Kun, looked down and was saddened by this devastation. Kun was the grandson of the Yellow Emperor who pleaded with his grandfather to make the rains stop, but the Yellow Emperor did not stop the Flood. An old tortoise

told Kun that in order to stop the rain he needed magic mud. The tortoise also explained that the Yellow Emperor had a jar of this mud inside his treasury. Kun stole the jar of magic mud and went down to Earth. Wherever he sprinkled the mud, islands grew and the water was sucked up. Kun traveled over the Earth spreading this magical mud and making new land as fast as he could. But the Yellow Emperor saw what Kun was doing and sent the fire god down to kill him. Kun saw the fire god coming, so he transformed himself into a white horse and tried to hide. Still, the fire god sent down lightning, which struck Kun and killed him on top of a mountain. Out of Kun's body grew a splendid son called Yu, who was a beautiful golden dragon. Yu flew up to the heavens to see his great-grandfather, the Yellow Emperor, begging him to end the flood. The Yellow Emperor made Yu the rain god with all the powers needed to perform his task, and allowed him all the amount of magic mud that could be piled upon the old tortoise's back. Yu made the rains stop, but much of the land remained under the water. So, he and the old tortoise went down to Earth, sprinkling the magic mud as they went. Then, after this was done, Yu used his tail to plough the mighty rivers of China. While carving the Yellow River, they came upon an obstacle of rocky cliffs. As Yu carved a chasm into the cliffs, he declared it to be the Dragon's Gate, which would always be sacred to dragons. Yu became a hero to the people; they begged him to be their emperor. So Yu transformed into a human and lived on Earth among the people as the Chinese Emperor.

There are so many symbolic similarities to other ancient scriptures it truly boggles the mind. But the one that really tickles me is the close link to the Anunnaki story of the Great Flood. Enlil was the supreme commander of Earth who decided to allow the impending flood to wipe out humanity because of their "evil ways." People believed that it was Enlil who brought the rain and the flood. But his brother Enki, one of the other gods, was saddened by the devastation and saved humankind from extinction. He was also known as being the god of water and marshes, with the ability to reclaim land from water, which is what he did soon after arriving on Earth. Enlil outranked Enki and in that way "killed" his challenge to save humans. And just like Kun's son Yu, became the god of the Chinese people, Marduk, the son of Enki, became the "god above all" who lived among the people on Earth by marrying a mortal female and leading the semi-god movement in many civilizations wherein kings were half-god, half-human.

Here are some more Chinese gods to digest:

Shang-Ti (Yu)

The highest deity and supreme ancestor of the Shang and Chou dynasty. The Shang worshipped Shang Ti, who ruled over lesser gods, the sun, the moon, the wind, the rain, and other natural forces and places. Highly ritualized ancestor worship became a part of the Shang religion. Sacrifice to the gods and the ancestors was also a major part of the Shang religion. When a king died, hundreds of slaves and prisoners were often sacrificed and buried with him. People were also sacrificed in smaller numbers during important events, such as the founding of a palace or temple.

Ch'eng-Huang

God of walls and moats. Every village and town had its own version of Ch'eng-Huang. This was often a local dignitary or person of importance who had died and been promoted to divine status or godhood. Such a divine status was revealed in dreams, but ultimately the gods made the final decision. Ch'eng-Huang not only protects the community from attack, but also sees to it that the King of the Dead does not take any soul from his jurisdiction without proper authority. Ch'eng-Huang exposes evildoers in the community itself, usually through dreams. He has two assistants: Mr. Ba Lao-ye and Mr. Hei Lao-ye, who are Mr. Daywatchman and Mr. Nightwatchman.

Chu Jung

God of fire. Chu Jung punishes those who break the laws of heaven.

Kuan Ti

God of war. The Great Judge who protects the people from injustice and evil spirits. A red-faced god dressed always in green who is also an oracle. Kuan Ti was an actual historical figure, a general of the Han dynasty renowned for his skill as a warrior and his justness as a ruler. There were more than 1,600 temples dedicated to Kuan Ti.

Kwan Yin

A popular goddess of mercy and compassion. A lady dressed in white, she is depicted seated on a lotus, holding an infant. After being murdered by her father, she recited the holy books when she arrived in hell. The disgruntled god sent her back to the world of the living, where Kwan Yin attained great spiritual insight and was rewarded with immortality by the Buddha. Her temple at the Mount of the Wondrous Peak was always filled with lots of pilgrims shaking rattles and setting off firecrackers to get her attention.

Lei Kung

God of thunder. Lei Kung chases away evil spirits and punishes criminals whose crimes have gone undetected. He has the head of a bird, wings, claws, and blue skin, and his chariot is drawn by six boys. Lei Kung makes thunder with his hammer, and his wife makes lightning with her mirrors.

Pahsien

These are the Eight Immortals of the Taoist tradition. They were ordinary mortals, who were rewarded with immortality for their good works and good lives by the Queen Mother Wang, who gave them the peaches of everlasting life to eat. They are:

Lu Tung-Pin: A hero of early Chinese literature. Renouncing riches and the world, he punished the wicked and rewarded the good, and slew dragons with a magic sword.

Tieh-Kuai Li: He of the Iron Crutch, who was a healer. Li sits as a beggar in the marketplace selling wondrous drugs. Some of these can revive the dead.

Chung-Li Ch'uan: A smiling old man always beaming with joy, who was rewarded with immortality for his ascetic life in the mountains.

Ts'ao Kuo-Chiu: Ts'ao Kuo-Chiu tried to reform his brother who was a corrupt emperor by reminding him that the laws of heaven are inescapable.

Lan Ts'ai-Ho: A young flute player and wandering minstrel who carries a basket filled with fruit. His soul-searching songs caused a stork to snatch him away to the heavens.

Chang-Kuo Lao: An aged hermit with miraculous abilities. Chang owned a donkey that could travel at incredible speed. He was the personification of the primordial vapor that is the source of all life.

Han Hsiang-Tzu: A scholar who chose to study magic rather than prepare for the civil service. When his uncle reprimanded him for studying magic, Han Hsiang-Tzu materialized two flowers with poems written on the leaves.

Ho Hsien-Ku: Immortal Maiden, a Cantonese girl who dreamt that she could become immortal by eating a powder made of mother-of-pearl. She appears only to men of great virtue.

P'an-Chin-Lien

Goddess of prostitutes. As a mortal she was a widow who was much too liberal and creative with her favors. Eventually her father-in-law killed her. She was revered in death by her professional associates who honored her. She eventually became the goddess of whores.

Shi-Tien Yen-Wang

Ten rulers of the underworld who were known as The Lords of Death. They dress alike in royal robes and only the wisest can tell them apart. Each ruler presides over one court of law. In the first court a soul is judged according to his sins in life and sentenced to one of the eight courts of punishment. Punishment is dispensed to fit the offense: misers are made to drink molten gold and liars have their tongues cut out. In the second court are incompetent doctors and dishonest agents; the third court has forgers, liars, gossips, and corrupt government officials. In the fifth court there are murderers, sex offenders and atheists; in the sixth, the sacrilegious and blasphemers; in the eighth, those guilty of filial disrespect; in the ninth, arsonists and accident victims. In the tenth court is the Wheel of Transmigration. This is where souls are released to be reincarnated after their punishment has been completed. Before souls are released, they are given a brew of oblivion, which makes them forget their former lives.

Ti-Tsang Wang

God of mercy. Wandering in the caverns of hell, a lost soul might encounter a smiling monk whose path is illuminated by a shining pearl and whose staff is decorated with metal rings that chime like bells. This is Ti-Tsang Wang, who will do all he can to help the soul escape hell and even put an end to his eternal round of death and rebirth.

Just like in the Sumerian, Greek, Egyptian, Mayan, and African myths, there were a number of humans who were given immortality by the gods of China for various reasons. We also see the importance of prostitution and sex, represented adequately by gods and goddesses in Eastern mythology. They support the Sumerian and biblical writing that the male gods had a ferocious sex drive and loved human females, which is evident in the many temples related to sexual acts and prostitution. While the same can be said about the goddesses, there is generally more reference to the sexual needs of male gods, which is supported by the temples of virgins and prostitutes. It does not take a trained eye to see the similarities to Sumerian gods and an underlying common thread binding the mythologies together.

GREEK GODS

The Greek gods were probably the most anthropomorphic gods of any civilization. This means that while they were gods, they possessed human attributes. They did, however, have some important differences to human beings. They were ageless and immortal, unlimited by physical restrictions, could take any shape they pleased, could go anywhere quickly, without much effort and often doing so invisibly. They were allowed to also perform a host of immoral acts, which were reserved for them only. Their sexual appetite was insatiable. Each god had his or her own special function. Just like in Sumer, the gods formed a distinctly untouchable and divine society living around the supreme deity, Zeus, on Mount Olympus. Theirs was the highest level of society, which was a reflection of the organization of societies in the heroic age. Just like the Sumerians, the Greeks also had deities who lived on Earth or in the underworld. Those were called Chthonian, or "gods on Earth." The others were called the Olympians, or "gods of heaven." In 1 Corinthians 8:5 there is an intriguing reference to the "gods of heaven" and the "gods on Earth," once again showing that the people of biblical times were not hallucinating, and that there were other deities or gods whom we know nothing about today, mainly through the long and perpetual eradication process carried out by religious authorities.

> We know that an idol is nothing at all in the world and that there is no God but one. For even if there are so-called gods, whether in heaven or on Earth (as indeed there are many "gods" and many "lords"), yet for us there is but one God, the Father, from whom all things came and for whom we live.
>
> 1 Corinthians 8:4–6

In a similar fashion to the Sumerian gods, the Greeks had two groups of gods. The Titans were the first to rule the world; they were the elder group who were overthrown by the Olympians who were led by Zeus. Although Greek deities were omnipresent and universal, their activities were attached to definite places. Temples in their honor were set within *temenos,* which were sacred precincts set aside for gods and deities. They would contain a spring for purification and a grove of trees. There was always an altar, placed in front of the temple, which was the one indispensable item at a shrine, because it was necessary for sacrifice during the main act of worship. Greek temples would house the deity's image and possessions, and it was not a place of assembly for worshippers but it was actually seen as the home of the deity. People went to the temple to make offerings, rather than for private prayer. This indicates that the gods actually used to frequent these temples. They expected to be treated well, to be cared for by their human slaves, and be provided with all the luxuries they required.

THE TITANS—
FIRST GROUP OF GREEK GODS

Gaea or Gaia

The Earth goddess. She mated with her son Uranus to produce the remaining Titans.

Uranus

The sky god and first ruler. He is the son of Gaea, who created him without help. Together with Gaea they had many offspring, including the Titans. His rule ended when Cronus castrated him. It is not clear whether he died from the wound or withdrew from Earth. Uranus was jealous of the future power of his children and feared he would lose his rule to them. To prevent this, he threw his children into the underworld. At the instigation of Gaea, her son Cronus castrated his father and dethroned him. When Uranus' blood fell upon the Earth (Gaea), the Erinyes, meaning "goddesses of vengeance," and the Gigantes (giants) sprang forth, among many other divinities. You will find out more about Erinyes and their Roman counterparts, the Furies, later.

Cronus

The ruling Titan who came to power by castrating his father Uranus. His wife was Rhea and their offspring were the first of the Olympians. To insure his safety, Cronus ate each of their children as they were born. Rhea was unhappy at the loss of her children, and tricked Cronus into swallowing a rock instead of Zeus, who would revolt against Cronus and the other Titans, defeat them, and banish them to Tartarus in the underworld. It is said that Cronus was killed by a thunderbolt unleashed by Zeus, but other stories say that he escaped to Italy, where he ruled as Saturn. The period of Zeus' rule was said to be the "golden age on Earth," honored by the Saturnalia feast.

Rhea

The wife of Cronus, who made it a practice to swallow their children. Rhea saved her son Zeus by tricking Cronus into swallowing a rock. Zeus grew up and deposed his father Cronus. Rhea is seen as the mother of the gods, daughter of Uranus and Gaea. She is also the mother of Demeter, Hades, Hera, Hestia,

Poseidon, and Zeus. Rhea is identified with mother goddess Cybele from Asia Minor and is also known as Rhea Cybele and Magna Mater or "great mother." She was worshipped with orgiastic rites. Rhea is depicted between two lions or on a chariot pulled by lions.

Oceanus

The unending stream of water encircling the world. Together with his wife Tethys, they produced the rivers and the 3,000 ocean nymphs. He is the personification of the vast ocean, especially the waters outside of the Pillars of Heracles, or the Atlantic Ocean. He was the son of Uranus and Gaia and the eldest of the Titans. He was the father of all rivers by his sister Tethys. The couple also had the Oceanids, which personified springs and smaller bodies of water, like lakes and ponds.

Tethys

The wife of her brother Oceanus and the god-mother of Rhea, who was raised during the war between the Titans and the Olympians. Tethys was the personification of the fertile ocean, and with Oceanus had 3,000 children, also referred to as the "three thousand ocean nymphs." Who were these nymphs?

In Greek mythology, nymphs were divine females associated with various natural objects. There is debate whether they were immortal or merely long-lived, in which case they would have been half-human, half-goddesses, akin to Sumerian mythology. There was an infinite variety of nymphs representing various localities, rivers, lakes, mountains, and more. Nymphs were depicted as young, beautiful, musical, amorous, and gentle, although some were associated with the wilder aspects of nature, while others were vengeful and capable of destruction. Whichever way one looks at it, the nymph cult was huge in Greece and they possessed all the characteristics displayed by lower ranked Anunnaki deities, who were in charge of the lesser fortified towns as part of the divine control over humankind.

Hyperion

The Titan of light and an early sun god. He is the son of Gaea and Uranus, who married his sister Theia. His name means "he who goes before the sun." Their children were Helius, the sun; Selene, the moon; and Eos, the dawn.

Mnemosyne

The Titan of memory and the mother of the nine Muses by her nephew Zeus.

Themis

She was the Titan of justice and order, one of the daughters of Uranus and Gaea. She is the personification of the "divine right order of things" as sanctioned by custom and law. She has oracular powers and it is said that she built the oracle at Delphi. She is the mother of the Horae and the Moirae. Themis is depicted as a stern-looking woman who is blindfolded and holding a pair of scales and a cornucopia. The Romans called her Justitia because her name means law. Themis introduced the ordinances that concern the gods and instructed men in the ways of obedience to laws and peace. Themis delivered oracles at Delphi until Apollo, the lovely son of Leto, came to the city, killed the serpent Python that guarded the oracle, and usurped power. Leto did not give Apollo her breast when he was born, but Themis, who was there, fed him with nectar and ambrosia. Themis told the Titan Prometheus not to join the Titans in their war against the Olympians, because—as she prophesied—in that war, the clever, not the brutal, would prevail. Themis was deemed guardian of men's oaths and for that reason also called the "goddess of oaths." She lives on Mount Olympus close to Zeus, who is described as the real all-seeing god as he whispers words of wisdom to Themis.

Iapetus

The father of Prometheus, Epimetheus, Menoetius, and Atlas, by Clymene.

Coeus

The Titan of Intelligence.

Prometheus

The son of Iapetus and the wisest of all Titans. His name means "forethought" and he was able to foretell the future. When Zeus revolted against Cronus, Prometheus deserted the other Titans and fought on Zeus' side. By some accounts, he and his brother Epimetheus were instructed by Zeus to create man. In all accounts, Prometheus is known as the protector and benefactor of man. He gave mankind a number of gifts, including fire. He also tricked Zeus into allowing man to keep the best part of the animals identified for sacrifice to the gods while giving the gods the worst parts. Zeus punished Prometheus by having him chained to a rock with an eagle tearing at his liver. He was to be left there for all eternity, or until he agreed to disclose to Zeus which of Zeus' children would try to replace him. He was rescued by Heracles without ever giving in to Zeus.

Epimetheus

He was a stupid Titan, whose name means "afterthought." He was the son of Iapetus and brother of Prometheus. In some accounts he is delegated by Zeus to create mankind along with his brother. He also accepted the gift of Pandora from Zeus, which led to the introduction of evil into the world.

Atlas

Also the son of Iapetus, but unlike his brothers Prometheus and Epimetheus, Atlas fought on the side of the Titans supporting Cronus against Zeus. Due to Cronus' advanced age, Atlas led the Titans in battle. And so, he was singled out by Zeus for special punishment and made to hold up the world on his back.

Phoebe

The goddess of the Moon and the daughter of Uranus and Gaia. She married her brother Coeus and with him she became the mother of Leto and Asteria. It is said that she owned the oracle of Delphi before Apollo took it over.

Metis

The goddess of the fourth day and the planet Mercury. She presided over all wisdom and knowledge. She was seduced by Zeus and became pregnant with Athena. He killed or swallowed her in fear that his heir would be more powerful than he was.

Dione

Her name means "divine queen." According to Homer in the *Iliad,* she is the mother of Aphrodite by Zeus.

There were a host of other gods and demigods, but for the purpose of keeping this to the point, which is very difficult at this stage, let's jump to the next generation of Greek gods who ruled the world.

THE OLYMPIANS— SECOND GROUP OF GREEK GODS

The Olympians are a pantheon of twelve gods who ruled the world after they defeated the Titans. All the Olympians are related in some way. They are named after their dwelling place, Mount Olympus.

Zeus

The supreme ruler of the gods who overthrew his father, Cronus. He had to draw lots with his brothers Poseidon and Hades to determine his leadership. Zeus won the draw and hence became the supreme ruler. This story is identical to that of Enlil and Enki of the Anunnaki gods, who also had to draw lots when they were dividing the Earth. Zeus is lord of the sky, and Earth. Just like Enlil, he has fearsome weapons but his favorite weapon is the thunderbolt, which he uses against those who displease him. He is married to Hera, but is famous for his many affairs. He is also known to punish those who lie or break oaths.

Poseidon

The brother of Zeus. After the overthrow of their father Cronus, he drew lots with Zeus and Hades for a share of the world. He became lord of the sea and, therefore, he was widely worshipped by seamen. He married Amphitrite, a granddaughter of the Titan Oceanus, but he desired Demeter. She asked him to make the most beautiful animal that the world had ever seen to distract him. So to impress her, Poseidon created the first horse. In some accounts his first attempts were unsuccessful and he created a variety of other animals in the process, which is very similar to the story of Enki and Ningishzidda in the Sumerian tales. By the time he created the horse, his passion for Demeter had waned. His weapon is the trident, which can shake the Earth and shatter any object. He was second in command to Zeus amongst the gods. He had a difficult, quarrelsome personality. He was greedy. He had a series of disputes with other gods when he tried to take over their cities. This is like a blend of Enki and Marduk of Sumerian and Babylonian stories.

Hades

The other brother of Zeus who partook in the drawing of lots after the overthrow of their father Cronus. He had the worst draw and was given the underworld to rule over the dead. He is a greedy god who is constantly concerned with increasing the subjects of his domain. He is also the god of wealth, overseeing the precious metals mined from the Earth. He is exceedingly disinclined to allow any of his subjects to leave. He has a helmet that makes him invisible. He rarely leaves the underworld. He is unpitying and terrible, but not capricious. His wife is Persephone whom Hades abducted. He is the god of the dead but death itself is another god, Thanatos. The Erinyes are always welcomed guests in the underworld.

Erinyes

But who were the mysterious Erinyes? The one account says that the Erinyes (Roman—Furies) were birthed out of anger from the blood of Cronus as it landed on Earth. They were three sisters: Tisiphone, Megaera, and Alecto. They were the punishers of sinners, also called "those who walk in darkness," persecutors of humans who broke natural laws. They would hiss like vipers and they would descend like a storm, sometimes overcoming their victims with deadly smoke. They were often depicted with dog-like faces and were fierce. When not stalking victims on Earth, the Furies were thought to dwell in the Tartarus mountains where they applied their tortures to the damned souls. They were also referred to as the Eumenides, the Kindly Ones; the Potniae, the Awful Ones; the Maniae, the Madnesses; and the Praxidikae, the Vengeful Ones. Their activities very closely resemble the "bloodless and lifeless" robot-like clones created by Enki to avenge the death of his niece Inanna. "From clay of the Abzu, Enki two emissaries fashioned, being without blood by death rays unharmed." They were created to track down and destroy the guilty ones. They were fierce, indestructible, and relentless, closely resembling what we would call terminators today. Were these Anunnaki emissaries the original Erinyes and Furies? "Not even the sun will transgress his orbit but the Erinyes, the ministers of justice, overtake him." Or were they biblical angels, interfering and vengeful, delivering god's message and retribution?

Hestia

Zeus' sister, the virgin goddess. She does not have a distinct personality and plays no part in myths. She is the Goddess of the Hearth, the symbol of the house around which a newborn child is carried before it is received into the family. Each city had a public hearth dedicated and sacred to Hestia, where the fire was never allowed to go out.

Hera

Zeus' wife and sister. She was raised by the Titan gods Oceanus and Tethys. She is the protector of marriage and married women. Hera's marriage began under difficult circumstances and continued in strife with Zeus. At first, Zeus made advances toward her unsuccessfully. To trick her, he changed himself into a disheveled cuckoo. Hera felt sorry for the bird and held it to her breast to warm it. Zeus resumed his normal form and took advantage of her and raped her. The young Hera married him to cover her shame. At one point when he was overbearing to the other gods, Hera convinced them to stage a revolt. Hera drugged him while the gods bound the sleeping Zeus to a couch with many knots. This done, they began to quarrel over the next step. Briareus slipped in and was able to quickly untie the many knots. Zeus sprang from the couch and grabbed his thunderbolt and hung Hera from the sky with gold chains. She wept in pain all night but no one dared to interfere. Her weeping kept Zeus up, so the next morning he agreed to release her if she swore never to rebel again. While she never again rebelled, she often questioned Zeus' plans, and she was often able to outwit him. Most stories concerning Hera have to do with her jealous revenge for Zeus' infidelities. Her sacred animals are the cow and the peacock.

Ares

The god of war and son of Zeus and Hera. He was disliked by both parents. While he was considered murderous and bloodthirsty, he was also a coward. Although he was immortal, he was very sensitive to pain and went running to his father Zeus whenever he got wounded. He is identified with Mars in Roman mythology. When Halirrhotius raped Alcippe, Ares' daughter by Aglaulus, Ares murdered him, for which he was tried in a court. Some say that this was the first murder trial in history, but he was acquitted. His companions included his sister Eris, as well as his sons Phobos and Deimos, and Enyo. Otus and Ephialtes were two giants who put Ares in an urn. To rescue Ares, Hermes changed himself into a deer and caused the giants to throw their spears at each other.

One night, while seducing Aphrodite, Ares put a youth named Alectryon by his door to guard them. The youth fell asleep and Helios, the sun, walked in on the couple. Ares turned Alectryon into a rooster, a bird that never forgets to announce the arrival of the sun in the morning. During the Trojan War, Ares was seen fighting on the Trojans' side. Hera, Ares' mother, asked Zeus for permission to drive Ares away from the battlefield. Hera encouraged Diomedes to attack Ares, after which he threw his spear at the god. But it was Athena who drove the spear into Ares' body. He bellowed in pain and fled to Mt. Olympus, forcing the Trojans to fall back. Ares was only rarely the recipient of cult worship. He was venerated most often in conjunction with other gods. For example, he shared a temple with Aphrodite at Thebes.

Athena

The daughter of Zeus. She came forth from his forehead, full-grown and dressed in armor. She has no mother. She is a virgin goddess, but she is fierce and brave in battle. She only fights to protect the state and home from outside enemies. Athena is the goddess of the city, handicrafts, and agriculture. She invented the bridle, which permitted man to tame horses; the trumpet, the flute; the pot; the rake; the plough; the yoke; the ship; and even the chariot. She is the embodiment of wisdom, reason, and purity. She was Zeus' favorite child and was allowed to use his fearsome weapons including his thunderbolt.

Apollo

The son of Zeus and Leto, and a twin brother to his sister Artemis. He is the god of music, often depicted playing a golden lyre. He is also the archer, shooting far with a silver bow; the god of healing who taught man medicine; the god of light; and even the god of truth, who can speak no lie. One of Apollo's more important daily tasks is to harness his chariot with four horses and drive the sun across the sky. He is famous for his oracle at Delphi. People traveled to it from all over the Greek world to consult the oracle on their future.

Aphrodite

The goddess of love, desire and beauty; the wife of Hephaestus. In addition to her natural gifts, she has a magical girdle that compels anyone she wishes to desire her. In truth, she is a seductress. There are two accounts of her birth. One says she is the daughter of Zeus and Dione. The other story is derived from when Cronus castrated Uranus and tossed his severed genitals into the sea: Aphrodite arose from the sea foam on a giant scallop and walked to shore in Cyprus.

Hermes

The son of Zeus and Maia, and the messenger of the gods. He is the fastest of the gods and known to wear winged sandals, a winged hat, and he carries a magic wand. He is the god of thieves and god of commerce, and also the guide for the dead who journey to the underworld. He invented the lyre, the pipes, the musical scale, astronomy, weights and measures, boxing, gymnastics, and even how to care for olive trees.

Artemis

The daughter of Zeus and Leto, and the twin sister of her bother Apollo. She is a virgin goddess, and the goddess of chastity. Yet, she is the lady of the wild things and the huntsman of the gods. She is the protector of the young, and just like Apollo she hunts with silver arrows. She became associated with the moon and also presides over childbirth, which may seem odd for a virgin. It is said that it was she who caused Leto to have no pain at her own birth. All wild animals are sacred to her, especially the deer.

Hephaestus
The son of Zeus and Hera, it is also said that Hera alone produced him and that he has no father. He is the only god to be physically ugly and also lame. The stories of how he became lame vary. Some say that Hera, upset by having an ugly child, flung him from Mount Olympus into the sea, breaking his legs. Others say that he took Hera's side in an argument with Zeus, and Zeus flung him off Mount Olympus. He is the patron god of both smiths and weavers. He is kind and peace-loving, and yet he is the god of fire and the forge, using a volcano as his forge. He is the smith and armorer of the gods. His wife is Aphrodite, but sometimes his wife is identified as Aglaia.

ROMAN GODS

The Roman gods are as popular today as they were 2,000 years ago. Their names have been used in countless movies, fictional stories, science fiction tales, and a multitude of global brands have borrowed their names from Roman gods. But because they were mostly derivatives of the earlier Greek gods, we will introduce them briefly, to show their obvious Greek heritage.

There were many dozens of gods worshipped by the Romans, but they specifically honored a pantheon of twelve gods called Dii Consentes. They were Iuppiter, Iuno, Minerva, Vesta, Ceres, Diana, Venus, Mars, Mercurius, Neptunus, Volcanus, and Apollo. These are the gods listed by the Poet Ennius around the third century BC. These six male and six female gods were probably worshipped at the Lectisternium of 217 BC. This was a banquet of the gods, where the statues of the gods were raised on cushions and offered meals. This is a clear hangover from the ancient Greek and even the earlier Sumerian tradition. Except, the food offered to the ancient Sumerian and possibly Greek gods was done in the gods' own temples with a very strict set of rules. Those old temples were actually the resting places of the Anunnaki gods, while traveling from place to place. The number twelve clearly runs throughout all these ancient mythologies, with only a few cultures that may differ from that—like the African mythologies. But we have already established that the African myths are much older in their style and approach, pointing to a very early relationship between the gods and humankind—a time before worshipping was enforced on the human slaves, even long before the Great Flood. What is also evident is that the Roman gods arose from a void with no mythological tradition associated with them. It is said that Julius Caesar had the "Alexander disease," trying everything in his power to match the conqueror's accomplishments. It is clear that the gods infected the rest of the Romans with their own brand of mania. It is as if the Romans simply inherited the Greek pantheon of twelve Olympians and changed their names—but the pantheon was introduced in stages to the Romans. They were led by the first three, which formed the Capitoline Triad. These became the three cornerstones of Roman religion, whose rites were conducted in the Capitoleum Vetus on the Capitoline Hill. This tradition was probably the driving force behind the introduction of the holy trinity, the Father, Son, and Holy Spirit, which was introduced into the Roman Catholic faith by the first ever "global" council of Church leaders, during the Council of Nicaea in AD 325. A wonderful example of how even in the Catholic faith, the line between history and myth is extremely fragile. It is evident that Roman mythology greatly influenced the thinking of the leaders of the early Catholic Church.

There were many other gods who played a major role in Roman culture and tradition, just like they did in all the earlier civilizations. It was not only the gods, but the cults that surrounded them, that best characterize the origin of the Roman religion. One example is the family cult of the Dii Familiaris. We find the following gods, spirits, and deities in this cult:

The Lar Familiaris: the guardian spirit or Genius of the family
The Lares Loci: the guardian spirits of the place where the house is built
   and the Genius of the *paterfamilias,* or House-Father
The Dii Penates: patron gods of the storeroom
The Dii Manes: the spirits of the deceased

There was a multitude of other domestic deities who were worshipped daily by the members of the family. The household cult was so important that it even served as the model for several practices of the state cult. This is not surprising, because we have learned from the Sumerians how the lesser gods looked after the smaller towns and villages in the outlying areas, while the more senior gods would have the privilege of looting the more attractive spoils of the larger, wealthier cities. So the well-entrenched customs of the smaller towns became attractive to the gods of the larger cities, where their control over the humans may not always have been as smooth as expected. This resulted in the state cult using the models of the peasant family cults as an example for expansion. For example, even during the Empire, the Imperial cult came to be based on the household cult, which was then interpreted as the cult of the Genius of the Emperor, or the *paterfamilias*—"House-Father," of the family of all the Romans.

Other important Roman gods were Ianus, Saturnus, Quirinus, Volturnus, Pales, Furrina, Flora, Carmenta, Pomona, Portunus, and Fontanus. But there was also a group of mysterious deities consisting of native guardian deities: river gods or deified heroes from the Latium region, which are collectively called Dii Indigites. A multitude of other deities were also traditionally worshipped, which included other guardian deities of native Latin origin, like Roma, Tiberinus, Bellus, Bellona, Liber, Libera, and abstract deities such as Fortuna (Fate), Concordia (Concord), Pax (Peace), Iustitia (Justice), and more.

It must also be added that the very mysterious group of people called the Sabines, who lived north east of Rome, played a major part in the development of Roman culture. Contributing many gods, like Pluto, to the heavenly family, they influenced Roman mythology and religious practice in many ways. They seem to resemble the mysterious Igigi—as mentioned in Sumerian tablets— who also lived in isolated communities, yet contributed greatly to the Sumerian culture, mainly by marrying mortal women, creating a whole new breed of demigods. Like the Igigi, and their descendants the Aryans, these gods from the Sabines symbolized the innovative and creative power on Earth, which pro-vided humans with technology and the means for subsistence.

Romans were always willing to pay homage and sacrifice to foreign dei-ties, especially when traveling in their land. Before going to war, they would go as far as making greater sacrifices to the gods of their enemies than what was offered by their own people, in order to win favor from the enemy's gods to secure victory. And so the foreign gods infiltrated Rome, resulting in the building of temples and shrines to the new gods called Dii Novensiles. Among those were Apollo, Ceres, Bacchus, Isis, and more. This all goes to show that the Romans were innocent bystanders during a "changing of the guard" by the gods as a new wave of Anunnaki gods infiltrated Rome and its culture, bringing a whole new order to the newly established global power, which was operational only by the grace of the gods who allowed this new global power to triumph over their enemies. Here is a list comparing Roman and Greek gods:

ROMAN	GREEK
Apollo	Apollo
Bacchus	Dionysus
Ceres	Demeter
Coelus	Uranus
Cupid	Eros
Cybele	Rhea
Diana	Artemis
Hercules	Heracles
Juno	Hera

Jupiter	Zeus
Latona	Leto
Mars	Ares
Mercury	Hermes
Minerva	Athena
Neptune	Poseidon
Pluto	Hades
Proserpina	Persephone
Saturn	Cronus
Ulysses	Odysseus
Venus	Aphrodite
Vesta	Hestia
Vulcan	Hephaestus

Let us now move further east, to demonstrate how incredibly well these fairy tales of the gods traveled around the world in antiquity, when humans could hardly travel to the next city.

JAPANESE GODS

Japan presents us with a similar melting pot of religious traditions to those in China, but the blend is somewhat different and quite unique. What is most fascinating is the smooth crossover from myth to history. All the ancient Japanese writings seem to have no visible borders between what is today accepted as myth and what is actual history. This is truly remarkable, because many Western historians are very happy to make those distinctions for them. We know that the islands that are today known as Japan were only created some 13,000 years ago, coinciding with the Great Flood. Before that, the Japanese Islands were connected to the Asian continent by land. This was during the ice age, and humans from the Eurasian continent were migrating east. The reasons for the migration may have been to follow the food supply by following animal herds, or it could simply have been to get away from the vengeful gods of the lands in which they lived. Remember that the people left behind on Earth during the Flood believed that the gods had deserted them and tried to destroy them all. When they survived the Flood, god came down from the heavens, and his instructions were to "be fruitful and multiply." The subtext to this instruction was actually to disperse across the world and do not attempt to challenge the gods . . . or you will be punished again. This was some time before the

Anunnaki gods bestowed agriculture on humanity, while man was still hunting animals and gathering food. The ancient Ainu people of Japan are a real mystery to anthropologists. Some say that these hairy and heavily bearded people who lived in the northern part of Japan had been in those parts 10,000 years ago, while others estimate that the Ainu first inhabited parts of Japan around 3,000 to 4,000 years ago, during the last half of the Jomon period. This would fall perfectly into our timeframe as the Aryans moved east, colonizing new territories and enforcing not only their influence but spreading some of their gene pool as well. This eastward expansion was either followed or preceded by the Anunnaki gods who were granted the domains of the East by Enlil, to rule and develop. So every part of the world would have had a different group of gods, each with their own unique way of handling the human situation.

Ainu means "human." They believed that nature gods, house gods, mountain gods, lake gods, all existed together in symbiotic relationships that included man. There is nothing new in that line of thinking because we know from the Sumerians and the Greeks that they also had different gods looking after different villages and aspects of their lives. The Ainu believed that the gods helped humankind and must be appreciated by them. The Ainu's daily life was a continuous ritual to the gods and their mutual assistance to man, which tells us that this was before the gods decided to impose the concept of sacrifice and worship on humans, during the time of the Anunnaki expansion shortly after the Flood. All the reports available make it pretty clear that the Ainu did not have it very easy. Unless they had a real interaction with the gods, and unless they were directly engaged in some kind of relationship with the deities of their lands, why would they waste their time on issues that did not contribute toward their survival and well-being? The gods or deities who resided in the lands of the Ainu must have been very real and as demanding as the other gods of the later humans. The Ainu's mixture of European and Asian physical traits contrasts so sharply from other indigenous peoples of Asia that no one is really sure of their origin. Some theories hold they are of Caucasian descent, others say that their distinct features are a result of isolation that allowed them to remain racially unchanged as the rest of the mongoloid races mixed and evolved through a series of migrations. Could they be another link to the influence of the Aryans as they explored the East and left behind their mark on human population everywhere?

The literature of Shinto or "Way of the Gods" employs much of the Japanese mythology to describe the supposed historical origins of Japan. We can see clearly that religion and mythology are in fact inseparable. The earliest Japanese records we possess are the *Kojiki: Record of Ancient Things* and *Nihongi: Japanese*

Chronicles, written in AD 712 and 720, respectively. In the *Kojiki* part 1, we are introduced to the Japanese divine "trilogy," which was alive and well even in Japan, while creating Heaven and Earth. The influence of the gods of Rome seems to have spread much further than just the Roman Catholics. In the *Kojiki,* as translated by B.H. Chamberlain in 1882, we are told about this Japanese trilogy of supreme deities.

Part I: The Birth of the Deities and the Beginning of Heaven and Earth:

> The names of the deities that were born in the Plain of High Heaven when the Heaven and Earth began were the deity Master-of-the-August-Centre-of-Heaven; next, the High-August-Producing-Wondrous deity; next, the Divine-Producing-Wondrous deity. These three deities were all deities born alone, and hid their persons. The names of the deities that were born next from a thing that sprouted up like unto a reed-shoot when the Earth, young and like unto floating oil, drifted about medusa-like.

According to the creation story found in the *Kojiki,* the Japanese islands were created by the gods, two of whom descended from heaven to carry out the task. These gods—the male god Izanagi and the female goddess Izanami—also brought into being other Kami (deities or supernatural forces), such as those influencing the sea, rivers, wind, woods, and mountains. Two of these deities, the sun goddess, Amaterasu Omikami, and her brother, the storm god, Susanowo, warred against each other, with Amaterasu emerging victorious. This again is identical to the Sumerian and Greek myths where heavenly siblings fight each other.

Izanagi and Izanami

The creator god and goddess sent down from heaven to build the Earth. The other gods and goddesses followed them and were their descendants. Descending to the underworld, Izanami became old and ugly. Izanagi followed her to bring her back, but she forbade him to look at her. When Izanagi looked at her, she tried to imprison him in the underworld. Pursued by Izanami's Furies, Izanagi escaped and sealed up the entrance to the underworld with a boulder. It is fascinating to see that the Greeks had Erinyes, the Romans had Furies, and that the Japanese also had Furies, to do the dirty work. Izanami was enraged and vowed to kill 1,000 of Izanagi's subjects a day, while Izanagi vowed to create 1,500 a day. So it was that Izanami became the goddess of death and Izanagi became the lord of life.

While the above is a mythical story, the pages of the *Kojiki* tell us the so-called historical tale of how Izanagi ventured into the lands of the under-world in search of his beloved Izanami. Once again, our mythologies get tangled up as we meet the Greek god Hades, god of the underworld, brother of Zeus, who had imposed his influence on Izanami. Suddenly the Japanese mythology blends with Greek mythology, using a Greek god's name as if it was quite acceptable to do so some 6,000 miles away, sometime between 13,000 and 4,000 years ago. Where did Hades make his name first then? Greece or Japan?

The story is told very beautifully in the *Kojiki*. Unable any longer to bear his grief, Izanagi resolved to go down to the Nether Regions in search of his beloved Izanami and bring her back, at all costs, to the world. There were countless dangers to negotiate on his way, but Izanagi's determination conquered them all. He finally reached a large castle that must have been where she was being kept. But the gate was guarded by a number of gigantic demons, some red, some black, guarding the gates with watchful eyes. He went around the back and to his surprise, the rear gate was left unguarded. He cautiously crept through the gate and after some searching and calling he found his beloved wife:

My darling, I have come to take thee back to the world. Come back, I pray thee, and let us complete our work of creation in accordance with the will of the Heavenly Gods, our work which was left only half accomplished by thy departure. How can I do this work without thee? Thy loss means to me the loss of all.

Imagine his surprise when she responded with the following:

Alas! Thou hast come too late. I have already eaten of the furnace of Hades. Having once eaten the things of this land, it is impossible for me to come back to the world . . . I wish, with all my heart, to go back with thee, but before I can do so, I must first obtain the permission of the deities of Hades.

Just as the Sumerian gods divided the lands and appointed different gods to rule them, the Japanese gods did the same. In this excerpt from the *Yengishiki* or *Shinto Rituals,* we get a glimpse of such an event.

I declare with the great ritual, the Heavenly ritual, which was bestowed on him at the time when, by the Word of the Sovereign's dear progenitor and progenitrix, who divinely remain in the plain of high Heaven, they bestowed on him the region under Heaven, saying—Let the Sovereign Grandchild's augustness tranquilly rule over the country of fresh spikes which flourishes in the midst of the reed-moor, as a peaceful region.

Battle of the Japanese gods

In the chapter of "The Door of the Heavenly Rock-Dwelling" of the *Kojiki,* we read of a peculiar set of events that may have many different interpretations by historians. But if you remove the emotion, it sounds pretty close to some of the descriptions in Sumerian tablets of when conflict erupted among the Anunnaki gods. Even the Japanese gods were emulating their Sumerian ancestors as they clashed and fought each other from time to time in their quest for supremacy. As in any conflict situation, there were usually victors and those who were banished. Any kind of violent eruptions among the gods would have looked miraculous to the early humans. The following texts seem to be very poetic descriptions of the prelude to conflict, and the resulting outburst that caused one of the rebellious deities to be expelled from the "heavenly abode." This kind of thing had been happening on Earth for several hundred thousand years among the Anunnaki as they grew in numbers and their desires for earthly things increased.

> So thereupon the Heaven-Shining-Great-August deity, terrified at the sight, closed behind her the door of the Heavenly Rock-Dwelling, made it fast and retired. Then the whole Plain of High Heaven was obscured and all the Central Land of Reed-Plains darkened. Owing to this, eternal night prevailed. Hereupon the voices of the myriad deities were like unto the flies in the fifth moon as they swarmed, and a myriad portents of woe all arose. Therefore did the eight hundred myriad deities assemble in a divine assembly in the bed of the Tranquil River of Heaven, and bid the deity Thought-Includer, child of the High-August-Producing-Wondrous deity, think of a plan, assembling the long-singing birds of eternal night and making them sing, taking the hard rocks of Heaven from the river-bed of the Tranquil River of Heaven, and taking the iron from the Heavenly Metal-Mountains . . . His Augustness Heavenly-Beckoning-Ancestor-Lord prayerfully reciting grand liturgies, and the Heavenly Hand-Strength-Male deity standing hidden beside the door, and Her Augustness Heavenly-Alarming-Female banging round her the heavenly clubmoss the Heavenly-Mount Kagu . . . laying a sounding-board before the door

of the Heavenly Rock-Dwelling and stamping, till she made it resound and doing as if possessed by a deity, and pulling out the nipples of her breasts, pushing down her skirt-string usque ad privates partes. Then the Plain of High Heaven shook, and the eight hundred myriad deities laughed together . . . Thereupon the eight hundred myriad deities took counsel together, and imposed on High-Swift-Impetuous-Male-Augustness a fine of a thousand tables, and likewise cut his beard, and even caused the nails of his fingers and toes to be pulled out, and expelled him with a divine expulsion.

Aji-Suki-Taka-Hi-Kone

One of several thunder gods. Born noisy, he grew up even noisier, and so they carry him up and down a ladder to quiet him. That is why you can hear him receding and approaching. The "ladder to the sky" is an important bit of imagery in this myth. Why would all the myths always refer to gods going up into the sky and reappearing from there every so often?

Ama-No-Uzume

The fertility goddess. A companion of Ninigi, she performed a bawdy dance hoping to entice the sun out of hiding. This dance symbolizes the planting of seed that waits for the sun to come after winter. Is there a link here to the Igigi, who were the possible progenitors of the Aryans, also teaching them about agriculture and technology?

Amaterasu

The sun goddess, ruler of the heavens. When her great enemy, the storm god Susa-No-Wo, destroyed her palace, Amaterasu went to hide in a cave. The other gods used all their magical tricks to get her to come out, but to no avail. In her absence, darkness and demons ruled the Earth until Ama-No-Usume lured Amaterasu out of the cave with a trick. With a comical and obscene dance, he made the gods who were gathered at the mouth of the cave laugh. When Amaterasu asked what was going on, Ama-No-Uzume replied that they had found another and better sun goddess. Amaterasu peeped out of her cave and saw her own reflection in a mirror that Ama-No-Uzume had hung on a nearby tree. Fascinated, Ameratasu drew a little closer for a better look, and the gods grabbed her and hauled her out.

Benzaiten

Goddess of love, one of the gods of happiness. Benzaiten rides a dragon while playing a stringed instrument. There is very little difference between her and Venus, and Inanna and Ishtar and other love goddesses. They all seem to be attracted to music, dance, and culture.

Bishamon

God of happiness and war, which is a rather strange combination. Bishamon protects men from disease and demons. Bishamon was often portrayed wearing a wheel of fire like a halo, which some see as the Wheel of Fate.

Amatsu Mikaboshi

August Star of Heaven. God of evil.

Chimata-No-Kami

God of crossroads, highways, and footpaths. Originally a phallic god, his phallic symbol was placed at crossroads.

Ho-Masubi

The fire god. His birth killed the creator goddess Izanami. His father, the creator god Izanagi, was so enraged with grief that he killed the baby. From his blood came eight gods, and from the body came eight mountain gods. Compare this to the Greek story of Cronus and Zeus and the other gods who were created from spilt blood.

Kawa-No-Kami

The god of rivers. While larger rivers have their own gods, all waterways are under Kawa-No-Kami's authority. When rivers flooded the gods were sometimes appeased with human sacrifices.

Nai-No-Kami

God of earthquakes, was a late addition to the Japanese pantheon. Nai-No-Kami was inducted in the seventh century AD. This supports the stories about the so-called angels.

Ninigi

Grandson of Amaterasu, the "divine grandchild" sent to rule the Earth. The ancestor of all the Japanese emperors. The name and description of this god is reminiscent of the Sumerian Igigi who were the supporters of Marduk, who was also a divine grandchild. He married earthling females and contributed to the creation of the white Aryan tribe. But the interesting thing is that their semi-divine descendants were the kings of Egypt, according to Sumerian tablets, as Ninigi was to the Japanese emperors.

O-Kuni-Nushi
God of sorcery and medicine. He was originally the ruler of the province of Izumo, but he was replaced by Ninigi. In compensation he was made ruler of the unseen world of spirits and magic. Once again the Ninigi connection is fascinating, since the Igigi were the advanced proto-Aryans with knowledge of medicine and technology.

Sengen-Sama
Goddess of the sacred mountain of Fujiyama. Worshippers greet the rising sun at her shrine on top of the mountain. The Sumerian goddess Ninhursag also known as Ninmah, "Exalted Lady"—had her own mountain retreat. She was really the mother goddess of humanity and one of the original creators of Adamu. Could it be seen that in the East she was worshipped as such, represented by the rising sun over humankind?

Shine-Tsu-Hiko
God of the wind. Shine-Tsu-Hiko fills up the empty space between Earth and heaven, and together with his wife Shina-To-Be, they hold up the Earth. Greeks and Romans have identical gods performing these tasks.

Susa-No-Wo
God of storms, snakes, and farming. He was Amaterasu's brother and greatest enemy. From the moment he was born, he was a troublemaker. After Amaterasu was finally taken out of her cave, Susa-No-Wo was punished. The other gods shaved his beard and moustache, pulled out his fingernails, and banished him to live as a mortal on the Earth.

The descriptions above represent only a few of the gods of ancient worlds. The cultures and civilizations run into thousands of pages, for which I suggest you turn to specialized literature, which will certainly keep you gasping with amazement. Once you begin to identify the similarities and relationships between the gods, the entire mythology subject takes on a whole new perspective. The incredible wealth in diversity of all these ancient gods, and the interaction between gods and humans, is almost impossible to imagine in today's society. That kind of ongoing activity, which at times turned into mayhem, could only have been possible if it was enforced on humans. I cannot imagine that the close similarities in all of these cultures are mere coincidences. The basic storylines of the gods of Sumer are echoed throughout all of the world's mythologies. There is a constant presence of higher gods and lesser gods; benevolent gods and violent gods; supreme gods and sons of gods; houses of the gods and their sexual playgrounds. Goddesses and their offspring outline the genealogy of the gods, and point to the same hierarchical structure of an extended family of gods around the world: closely related but highly divided in their hunger for control. The genetic makeup behind this kind of behavior points directly to our own programmed DNA passed down from the gods. In chapter 16 we will explore the great epic of humanity from birth until today, outlining the moment when man was created and inherited this highly disturbing genetic feature from his makers, the "gods of Heaven and Earth," as outlined in the Sumerian scripts.

In *The Lost Book of Enki,* Zecharia Sitchin tells the chilling tale of Lord Enki, the mastermind behind the creation of humans. A story of humanity from the beginning to the tragic events surrounding Sodom and Gomorrah, which according to Enki was preventable and unnecessary. Enki was Anu's first son, one of the three supreme leaders on Earth after their arrival some 445,000 years ago. He was the true humanitarian among the Nefilim gods, "those who to Earth from heaven came," which eventually led him to dictate these pages to his scribe Endubsar, who states: "These were the words of the lord Enki. Written from the mouth of the great lord Enki, not one word missed, not one word added by the master scribe Endubsar, a man of Eridu, son of Udbar." Although these tablets were referred to in other finds, it took a determined effort to uncover them in the ruins of museums and archaeological sites. These ancient events, which were captured by Sumerian scribes, have now been translated and presented to humanity in the year AD 2002 by Zecharia Sitchin. Sitchin has dated the events at Sodom to 2024 BC. It, therefore, stands to reason that these tablets, as dictated by Enki, must have been written shortly after those events, after 2024 BC. Sitchin is the largest private owner of Sumerian tablets in the world, which allowed him to present these translations to an unaware civilization in AD 2005. This body of work, which comprises 308 written pages, is now the most complete source of information about the obscure events in our past. It shines a spotlight on the concept of mythology and the popular modern explanations of these myths. It makes it painfully clear that there were things going on in the biblical past that have been purposefully concealed from humanity. It also raises very serious questions about utterances in the Bible and their credibility, when compared to the older Sumerian scriptures. These translations remove much doubt about the existence of the "gods of Heaven and Earth" who controlled the world with an iron fist. It proves our genetic ancestry belongs both on Earth and in deep space, on a planet called Nibiru. It explains the previous speculation of who we are and where we come from, with all the necessary supporting evidence that humans have been searching for.

The most disturbing facts that emerge from this find are that there must have been an extremely sinister but well-executed plot of manipulation against humanity by Enki's brother Enlil. This supreme commander on Earth was never in favor of the creation of humans, and certainly did not want to go out of his way to ensure the survival of humans on Earth. It is turning out to be a distinct possibility that the entire Bible was a masterstroke of pandemic proportion: a continued and carefully controlled saga of propaganda and indoctrination of humanity by Enlil himself. This control must have started after the Flood, when Enlil realized that humans had been saved against his wishes. He also realized that the only way he would be able to control humanity was with absolute power, control and fear, using strong-handed, dictatorial tactics. From that moment on, Enlil would be their god, ruling them through intimidation, fear, bloodthirsty violence—but he also rewarded them for loyalty and obedience, for complying with his commands. But his nephew Marduk wanted to seize the power on Earth, which was promised to him by his father Enki, right at the beginning, shortly after they arrived on Earth. He would choose his favorite people and help them above others, using them for his devious plans. From about 3200 BC, at the rise of the Egyptian empire, Marduk and Enlil became engaged in a long struggle for control of Earth. While Enlil enforced clear principles of divide and conquer among humans, Marduk became the self-proclaimed god above all, taking control of Egypt, and promising his kings eternal life in the world beyond, if they followed him. Slowly but surely, Marduk also absorbed and enforced the principles of divide and conquer as he took control of the planet. As fate would have it, the slave species became not only the accidental victims in the war of the gods, jostling for control of the planet, but the humans became the ignorant foot soldiers of the Anunnaki in their struggle for power. These were the early biblical days, which are well corroborated in both Hebrew and Sumerian scriptures. God's chosen people conquering the others.

Throughout human history, Enlil did everything in his power to suppress human evolution and emancipation. He did this constantly and relentlessly as we have clearly shown, fearing that humans would grow wiser and stronger if they evolved, which would pose a great threat to his global empire. It is not clear if it was Enlil or Marduk, but their ultimate masterstroke was that they had all these ancient events written and captured by men, loyal and fearful of the great god of vengeance. These written works were treated as holy by man, and over the years they were compiled into a collection of books that today is called the Bible, besides other holy scriptures. Ask any war or propaganda strategist today and they will tell you one thing: If you repeat a lie enough times, it will become the truth. Especially if you enforce it with the threat of violence. Stalin was a master of propaganda and indoctrination. So much so that even after the fall of the Soviet Union and the exposure of the Kremlin vaults, there are millions of supporters who remain loyal to Stalin, refusing to believe that any of those horror stories about him are true. The people who have been reading and misinterpreting the Bible, constantly ascribing some inexplicable tales to situations that make absolutely no sense, have fallen victim to such tactics. They are so filled with fear that it consumes their minds, rendering them incapable of clear independent thought. They say that "it is the way of the lord, and god planned it, because he did not want us to know everything." Well, they are correct. The gods did not want us to know the terrible truth behind the manipulation of humanity, and how we were controlled with fear, violence, retribution and reward. This is the story of the entire Old Testament.

Now that we are confident of our place at the pinnacle of human evolution and knowledge, the time comes when we have to ask ourselves the life-altering question: Do we believe that the ancient clay tablets are a message from our concerned ancestors, or do we discard it as insignificant mumbo-jumbo written by some wild madman to confuse us? The decision is yours to make. I trust that you will weigh up the evidence and realize that the universal community of beings is a distant cry from the barbaric acts of bloodthirsty settlers on Earth. The so-called god with a small "g" is never to be confused with God with a big "G." Many people will feel greatly disturbed by this information and will fear "god's vengeance against their evil thoughts." Stop the fear, see the light of the real God, the God of love, the God of mercy, the Prince of Peace. Not a gluttonous deity who wants gold and goats and people offered to him as a gesture of loyalty. While this knowledge may be too horrific to contemplate, I see it as the most liberating experience, which has exposed the real God to me, answering many of the questions that have haunted humanity. Knowledge is power and this knowledge will help me to understand whose name I call when I say my prayers. The God of the universe, the universal spirit, the Supreme Being. Armed with this knowledge, I can look forward to the continued journey of humanity as we evolve toward a complete genome that will open the portals of our mind and allow us to rejoin the universal community of beings.

15

THE MYSTERY OF JESUS AND OTHER PROPHETS

NO MATTER HOW YOU LOOK at the figure of Jesus Christ, whether he was the son of God or just an inspired prophet who took the troubles of the world upon his shoulders, he left behind a legacy that has inspired billions of people. The debate about the Prince of Peace is almost always filled with deep emotion, which more often than not leads to heated exchange by people who speak of him as if they knew him personally. They make bold statements about what Jesus would have done, how he would have reacted, and what he would have said if he were in present company. And since the writings of alternative historians, which tell us different stories about Jesus the man, are mostly treated with suspicion, the most that religious scholars could possibly tell us about the man is what they have read in the New Testament. I must hasten to add that much of what was written in the New Testament is probably quite different from his original teachings. If we take into account all the new evidence presented in this and other books about our ancestry, and although reluctantly we accept that we are the descendants of a more advanced race who created us as a slave species, one question remains to be answered: Who was Jesus Christ?

After doing an extensive search on a Bible website consisting of a multitude of different Bible versions, I got a very surprising result. The very first time that the words *Jesus, Christ, messiah,* and *son of God* appear in the Bible is in the book of Matthew. And if my math serves me right, that is the fortieth book of the Bible, which also happens to be the first book of the New Testament. Is it not a little odd that there is no reference by name to the "messiah" who is supposedly the main attraction in the Bible? If Jesus was the main actor, the prophesied savior, and the ultimate reason for the whole collection of books in the Bible, is it not strange that we only come across his name at such a late stage?

Most of my life I have held a maverick admiration for Jesus Christ—inspired by the message, but confused by its origins. I must admit that my naive admiration was repeatedly derailed by preachers of different shades of gray. My personal belief is that popular religion has taken a very simplistic message of love and goodwill among humanity, and hijacked it for their own devious abuse. And as I dug deeper, I unearthed information that forced me to rethink my naive outlook on the whole debate around Jesus. One by one my suspicions were confirmed, that there must have been an ageless devious plot behind the carefully crafted ministry of Christ. Just like Abraham, Jesus became an unwitting mouthpiece for his bloodthirsty Nefilim god, preparing the ground for the continued enslavement of humanity. Doing great deeds among men, rounding up the flock for salvation, showing them the way to reach the gates of god, was unconsciously weaving the propaganda of a power-hungry Anunnaki god. The fact that Jesus was a man we cannot deny. The fact that he lived and traveled preaching his gospel is an historic fact. But who his real parents were, what his bloodline was, who orchestrated his appearance on Earth, and who actually plotted all the prophecies about Jesus for thousands of years have taken on a whole new slant. There is emerging evidence that the prophesied appearance of Christ is much more sinister than we could ever have imagined. The uncanny parallels between the murky origins of humanity, compared to the origins of Christ, point to the real possibility that whoever crafted humanity followed it up with a second wave of premeditated, calculated propaganda and ultimate control. A control mechanism that was planned and executed with pinpoint precision like a military maneuver.

As I pointed out, the one truly puzzling feature is the lack of reference to the messiah in the Old Testament. The word *messiah* first appears in John 1:41; and *Savior* first appears in Deuteronomy 32:15. It leads me to believe that the idea of sending a "savior" to Earth as "the son of god" was an idea that was only devised much later, toward the end of the Old Testament, by Enlil or Marduk and their "angels," when they realized that the violent, oppressive approach toward humans needed a facelift. They became aware that after thousands of years of evolution, humans had evolved substantially and had grown wiser, not always prepared to submit to the brutality of their Anunnaki gods. It meant that the gods needed to revise their plan and devise a new twist. And so they did. It was crafted like a movie script, and a very good one I may add. So good in fact, that after 2,000 years, billions of loyal faithfuls are still reading the script with absolute devotion, ready to strike down anyone who dares attack their holy dinosaur. We must examine some of the strange behavior and relationships between Jesus and his god to highlight these peculiar underlying signs of tension between the two entities. We mentioned earlier that history books are written by the victors, and in the struggle between Enlil, Enki, and Marduk, this was also the case. Unfortunately for humanity, the struggle between the sibling Nefilim gods was won by the nasty one, Enlil—the one who did not like humanity. Did he masterfully craft his dominion as "god" of humanity? The victorious Enlil took control of such matters as recording human activities and controlling man's destiny in writing. His mission was simple: Keep humanity uneducated, ignorant, and stupid. Take control of their fears, keep them loyal and obedient. Demonstrate your power and superiority over them every so often, to keep them fearful. Be the vengeful yet loving god, who will reward those who obey quietly and don't ask too many questions. In the early days of the Bible, when Abraham was weaned by Enlil to be his favorite among the leaders, Marduk was given the land of Egypt to control. Marduk was known as Ra, Re, and Amun among the Egyptians. To create a large following of his own, Enlil "chose" the Israelites as his "chosen" people and rescued them from slavery, under Marduk's control. This was a huge victory for Enlil, with which he earned eternal loyalty among the Hebrews and established himself as the god of Israel. Enlil promised his followers the "land of milk and honey," but in the process they would have to vanquish a number of other peoples, who undoubtedly were supporters of Marduk, and were not among god's favorites.

Enlil also held rank over Enki, which meant he could basically do what he wanted with Enki's human creation. The disagreement between Enki and Enlil, which had started way back in the garden of Eden, played a cardinal part in all of the scriptures of the Bible, including the prophesies that were made. We explore this in greater detail in other chapters, exposing how Enki was labeled the serpent and devil, and man was forbidden to consort with him. The plan was so superbly imposed on humanity that it will forever hold the top spot in the annals of human manipulation and propaganda. It may take centuries more of religious bloodshed for humans to come to terms with reality. Enki was the "good guy." But history is written by the victors, and the real story was masterfully covered up by history books, of which the Bible is the main culprit, because it was controlled by the victorious Enlil, who proclaimed himself god. As time marches on and we discover new truths about our ancient prehistory and our possible origins, we learn that Enki was the architect of Adam and he loved his creation. He tried on many occasions to elevate humanity, to teach them, to inform them, but Enlil would not allow the slave species to become a threat to him and their settlement here on Earth. This is the strong underlying message seeping out between the pages of the Bible today. After the longest period of human enslavement, the real truth is starting to shine through. The incredible revelations in the recently released *Lost Book of Enki* by Zecharia Sitchin provide us with much supportive evidence for the everlasting plot, and it presents some answers to the chasms in our very one-sided history books.

When I first started to read this incredible book, I felt as if I had stumbled upon the holy grail itself. Words cannot describe the feelings of conflict playing with your mind when you start to absorb the content of those ancient clay tablets and compare them to what we have been told for so many years. The inspiring thing is that the tablets that have been unearthed, translated, and that you can now read are the result of decades of work by people like Sitchin and many others. It is truly a surreal experience to read 4,000 and 5,000-year-old scriptures in clay. The beauty about these is that you cannot erase words with whitener; you cannot go back and change the odd word; it's very hard to fake it. These tablets reveal things about our human origins and support all the theories that I have postulated in this book about our human ancestry. By bringing these facts to life in an uncomplicated fashion, it also supports the horrible theory that we have been manipulated into submission from the very first day of our existence. Ask yourself this question: How many people who study and preach the Bible have ever seen the original biblical documents, as they were written in ancient times? The percentage will be minuscule. Here we have a discovery from the days of Abraham, perfectly preserved in clay, delivering a serious message to humanity, while turning on its head everything we have ever been taught. Suddenly the "lord" is the devil, and the devil is our maker. Are we going to believe it . . . or discard it? Since we have dealt with much of the finger-wagging of the Old Testament, let us look at a few very important technicalities surrounding the scriptures of the New Testament.

The recorded events surrounding the birth of Jesus are highly suspicious. The extremely questionable historic entries have never been able to concur on the time, place, and town in which Jesus was born. Even the date of his birth differs from publication to publication. It has been penned from 1 BC to 7 BC, and the presentations by historians and theologians seem to constantly clash. The fascinating thing about this subject is that when you speak about Jesus, son of Joseph and Mary, you deal in historic realms, which have a host of vigilant custodians. But the moment you say "Jesus the Son of God," you enter the world of religious dogma, which has a host of rather militant custodians of its own. It seems that Jesus was not the only victim in this covert human mismanagement. Equally convincing evidence shows that the Prophet Muhammad and even the Buddha were also misused by the devious Enlil to enslave humanity through religious fear. I kid you not. This is too much to handle for the strongest of character, so I suggest you put aside every ounce of everything you ever believed in, and prepare to digest some liberating facts.

Many people have this image of Jesus strolling around the countryside, preaching to people, moving happy-go-luckily from town to town, being welcomed by happy smiling people cheering him on, all wanting to hear the amazing stories he has been telling all over the place. Well, that was not the case. Jesus was not really well-liked in his time. It took a lot of effort to get people to risk all kinds of possible danger to come and listen to his preaching. Strangely enough, there is very little evidence that anything he said and did was actually ever captured during his short three-year-span as a prophet. With the possible exception of the Sermon on the Mount, it seems that most of the material written about Jesus was done so only after his death by his disciples, apostles, and some other interesting characters. These were collected into a body of literary work known as the New Testament over a period of about 300 years. The "editing" of the New Testament only began in the year AD 325, which consisted of deletions and changes that were made and approved by special church councils. This highly secretive manipulation continued until the twelfth century. I find this a little suspicious, don't you? What could have taken them so long to edit and change if this was all the "Word of God"? Clearly they had different ideas and they disagreed with much of what was written, those church councils. Either they had their own ideas of what the New Testament should contain, or they were directed by someone! Surely there must have been some mastermind behind this whole process? It could not possibly have continued for 800-odd years without an ever-present controlling force. And yes, you can say that "it was the power of god" because it seems that it was indeed the case. However, it was "god" with a small "g," not "God" with a big "G" who directed the editing process, and therein lies the rub. The priests and high priests among humans were instated by the Anunnaki-Nefilim as far as 5,000 years before Christ and the fear of "god-Enlil" was dispersed among humanity mainly by them. By the twelfth century AD they were so well established as the voice of the Nefilim, the voice of Enlil, the voice of god, that nobody could outmaneuver them. In one apparent sitting of the Second Synod of Constantinople in AD 553, the church editors deleted all of Jesus' references to reincarnation from the Bible. This was an important part of Jesus' ministry and adhered to by his early followers. It also points clearly to his youthful influences while growing up in the East, absorbing the many different cultures of the Hindus and Buddhists. What's more, in the twelfth century, the Lateran Council added the concept of the holy trinity into the Bible, an idea that was apparently never promoted by Jesus. This holy trinity idea was doing the rounds since the first Council of Nicaea in AD 325, when the trouble with Aryans caused much heated argument about the validity of Christ. Early in the fourth century, a dispute erupted among the Christian leaders regarding the exact relationship of the "Son to the Father." A priest by the name of Arius of Alexandria taught that there was a time when Christ did not exist because he was not co-eternal with the Father. He further said that the Father, the Son, and the Holy Spirit were three separate and distinct entities and that the Son, who was subordinate to the Father, was in fact a "creature." These teachings were condemned and Arius was excommunicated in AD 318.

As early as the second century, Irenaeus of Lyons described the Holy Spirit and Jesus as "the two hands of God." Irenaeus gave us a hint of what could be the functions of the other "parts of God," when he intimated that "through the Holy Spirit, God worked creation and through Jesus, He worked redemption." The word *Trinity* or *Trinitas* was most likely coined by Tertullian in the third century, in his extensive writing on the issue. Another Christian father, called Origen, carried the doctrine further, but neither assigned full consubstantiality of the Holy Spirit with God. At the gathering in Nicaea, the council formulated a creed that, although it was revised at the Council of Constantinople in AD 381–382, has become known as the Nicene Creed. It affirmed the doctrine of consubstantiality of the Father, Son, and Holy Spirit.

In his book *On the Trinity*, St. Augustine concluded that the Holy Spirit is the mutual love of the "Father for the Son" and of the "Son for the Father," while the Holy Spirit is derived from both the Father and the Son. He also wrote that the Holy Spirit is a gift to humanity from the Father and the Son. This explanation still did not clarify the function of the Holy Spirit and how it came about, and its role remained a mystery. The other problem that remained was how to explain the nature of Jesus. Everyone accepted that Jesus was human, so how could he also be "God"? With heretical views spreading and the Aryans promoting a different doctrine, something had to be done. This was one of the main reasons why the councils of Nicaea and Constantinople were set up: to stop the impending and massive division in the church and to ostracize perceived heresy. It was not surprising that the majority of the bishops rallied behind Bishop Athanasius in affirming that Jesus was consubstantial with the Father, in contrast to the views of Arius and his followers who maintained that Jesus could not be "one with God" and that he was a "creature." And so, Emperor Constantine put his foot down—Arius and his supporters were expelled, and the Nicene Creed was passed that affirmed the consubstantiality of Jesus with God. In AD 451 at the council of Chalcedon, Pope Leo I proposed a solution to the riddle of God and Jesus. He declared that they were "one person in two natures." As far as the fathers were concerned, his miracles, his conduct and his words were evidence that he was Divine. This formula was a great relief to the new young religion, and the bishops could go to their parishes, satisfied that they had solved a problem that had plagued theology for decades.

What this all really means is that the Christian church had complete freedom to hack the original writings to pieces, formulating the New Testament as they liked, adding whatever they believed to be necessary for human spiritual consumption, and deleting entire books that did not meet their image of the Bible. Fortunately, many of the deleted books were saved and compiled into a collection of writings called The Apocrypha. In essence, it is those books that were deemed to be of dubious content by the church. Once again this points to gross manipulation by a higher authority with more sinister plans. According to the NationMaster Encyclopedia, the definition of Apocrypha is something like this:

> The word *apocrypha,* from the Greek word meaning "hidden," refers in general to religious works that are not considered canonical, or part of officially accepted scripture, but are of very roughly similar style and age as the accepted scriptures. Such works are often believed not to have been "inspired" or to be in some way "less inspired" by divine processes or entities, such as Holy Wisdom or the Holy Spirit. Most works that are considered apocryphal in the Hebrew Bible were written in languages other than Hebrew, such as Greek or Aramaic, or at least survive only as translations into non-Hebrew languages.

You must keep in mind that Jesus never wrote any of the books in the Bible. They were all written about him by various characters, mostly after his death. I highly recommend you look into the Apocrypha on the Internet; there are so many fascinating pieces to read, it will make your mind boggle. One of the books omitted from the Bible was the story of Jesus' birth and childhood years, up to the point when he returned to his land of birth to start his ministry. This discarded book did not agree with the official version that the church wanted to present to the world. Once you read the "hidden" story, the evidence of human manipulation by a higher power is difficult to refute. There are fascinating books like Mary, Infancy, and Protovangelion just to name a few.

According to the Apocrypha, the birth of Christ goes something like this:

His grandfather Joachim was a priest in the Hebrew temple who was highly embarrassed because he and his wife Anna could not produce any children. A man in his position was expected to have an heir, which left the couple ashamed. While standing in the field one day, an angel appeared to him, glowing with bright white light. After calming the frightened Joachim, he said that his wife would bear a child aided by an angel, but they would have to surrender the child to be raised by priests and angels at a certain temple in Jerusalem. Lo and behold, Anna gave birth to a daughter called Mary, who at the age of three was taken to the temple and left there. Mary was an exemplary child, devoted to both priests and angels. By the age of around fourteen, the time came for her to go back into the world and get married. She was not allowed to choose a man; her mentors handpicked a much older man called Joseph to be her husband. But Joseph was not as willing as the angels would have had it and it took some convincing to do it. After finally agreeing to the marriage, he went back to his home in Bethlehem to prepare his home for his new wife, while Mary went to her parents in Galilee to get ready for her new life. One day an "angel" called Gabriel appeared to Mary and told her that she would give birth to the new messiah. Mary was confused as she had never had a sexual experience before.

There are many theories and explanations regarding the virgin birth. Regardless of what your personal beliefs are, it was supposed to be the Holy Ghost who "came upon her" therefore making the child holy, because the child was not conceived in lust. Whatever happened to Mary will forever remain a mystery, but there were a lot of so-called angels milling around during those times and we have a sneaky suspicion who those angels were: Enlil and his henchmen. If Enlil was delivering the final stroke to his masterful control over humanity, he would have wanted to ensure some form of genetic supremacy for his fabricated messiah. This would have included artificial insemination of the young virgin, for the purpose of giving young Jesus a distinct genetic advantage. Such a simple procedure would have undoubtedly given Jesus abilities that other humans did not possess. His life of miracles and healing attests to that. We must also keep in mind that the whole idea of sex, whether for fun or for procreation, was pronounced to be a sinful act. That is why all humans are said to be born in sin. This was another very good example of how god wanted to control the procreation of the slave species. Barbara Thiering writes extensively about the habits of the Essenes and their rituals in the stronghold of Qumran. In her book *Jesus The Man,* she presents a slightly different explanation for the virgin birth, which revolves around culture and custom.

According to Thiering, when Joseph returned from Bethlehem to collect his young wife Mary, he found her pregnant. He was obviously confused and somewhat alarmed, believing that Mary had become a whore. Before he could desert her, an angel appeared to him explaining that Mary was still a virgin. It must have been a very convincing angel, because Joseph stayed with Mary in Galilee until her ninth month of pregnancy, at which point they departed for Joseph's home in Bethlehem, where Mary would have the child. But the couple did not make it all the way home because Mary went into labor on the outskirts of the town. The only shelter they could find was a cave, in which Jesus was born. The Apocrypha book of Infancy describes it as such:

> And when they came to the cave Mary confessed to Joseph that her time of giving birth had come, and she could not go on to the city, and said, let us go into the cave. At that time the sun was nearly down. But Joseph hurried away so that he might fetch her a midwife; and when he saw an old Hebrew woman who was from Jerusalem, he said to her, please come here, good woman, and go into that cave, and you will see a woman just ready to give birth. It was after sunset when the old woman and Joseph reached the cave, and they both went into it. And look, it was all filled with lights, greater than the light of lamps and candle, and greater of than the light of the sun itself. The infant was then wrapped in swaddling clothes, and sucking on the breast of his mother, St. Mary.
>
> INFANCY 1:6–11

The bright light in the cave suggests some sort of more advanced technology, which cannot be explained. It goes hand in hand with other advanced phenomena surrounding the birth of Christ, like the star of Bethlehem. Over the years various explanations for the bright star have been proposed, which include the convergence of a number of stars and planets at that time. There is no doubt that such conjunctions did occur in the years of Christ's birth, but it is highly unlikely that it was a mere conjunction that would have caused the effect as described in the book of Protovangelion 15:7. "We saw an extraordinarily large star shining among the stars of heaven, and so outshined all the other stars, that they became not visible . . ." There is no planet or star or comet or conjunction of the above that could possibly be so bright. The star of Bethlehem was described in much greater splendor. It not only shone so incredibly brightly that it made all the other stars invisible, but it actually guided the Three Wise Men (Magi) for a long way toward the infant, hovering some distance ahead of them. The story in the Apocrypha Protovangelion 15:9 continues as such: "So the wise men began their travel, and look, the star which they saw in the east went before them, until it came and stood over the cave, where the young child was with Mary his mother." But this uncanny story does not end here. After their exchange with Mary and the infant Jesus, the star then guided the wise men all the way home, back to the East. As written in Infancy 3:3, "the light of which they followed until they returned in to their own country."

The Bible version is quite similar in this instance, but it does differ on the venue. It clearly states that Jesus was born in a house. Is this evidence of the so-called editing the various church councils conducted? They obviously felt that a cave was no place for the future messiah to be born. From Matthew 2:9–13:

> After they had heard the king, they went on their way, and the star they had seen in the east went ahead of them until it stopped over the place where the child was. When they saw the star, they were overjoyed. On coming to the house, they saw the child with his mother Mary, and they bowed down and worshipped him. Then they opened their treasures and presented him with gifts of gold and of incense and of myrrh. And having been warned in a dream not to go back to Herod, they returned to their country by another route.

The passage continues with the escape to Egypt:

> When they had gone, an angel of the Lord appeared to Joseph in a dream. "Get up," he said, "take the child and his mother and escape to Egypt. Stay there until I tell you, for Herod is going to search for the child to kill him."

This is really fascinating stuff in light of our theory that Enlil and his cronies were planning and manipulating all these events. Once again, when there are eminent signs of trouble, we have the presence of angels—this time in a dream warning both the Magi and Joseph. These subtle but important events show how incredibly well-thought-out this manipulative propaganda was. How do you create a hero very quickly even today? You stage an assassination attempt on his life, but against all odds, he escapes to tell the tale. This time it was the Magi who were brought a long way to help spread the news across the then civilized world about the true messiah who was born and whose life was already under threat by the nervous authorities. We should not be surprised at the brilliant strategy behind all this. The CIA and other secretive government departments are constantly engaged in similar manipulative acts involving their citizens. This just goes to show how much of that Nefilim DNA we inherited.

And so, the word went out in an instant that the messiah was born. After all, they had all the substantiation. The king had heard of him and wanted him dead. So it had to be the messiah! The coincidence that the Magi were from the East and the fact that Jesus spent most of his life after birth in the East learning the cultures and enlightenment is fascinating. The fact that Jesus was of the Essene Hebrew clan became clear after the discovery of the Dead Sea Scrolls in a cave in 1947, by a young Bedouin tribesman. Joseph and Jesus were both Essenes, which was a unique Hebrew religious sect with very different traditions. They also had very strong links to the Aryans of Persia, and that is why The Three Wise Men came to see the newborn child from such a long distance away. It appears that the Essenes had all the trimmings of a secret society. It took several years of initiation before one was admitted; as part of the official initiation you had to swear to protect all the secret teachings of the Essene Order; and most intriguingly, you had to keep secretive the names of "angels" living among them and their communities.

Barbara Thiering's version of the virgin birth of Jesus is a little different. From her extensive study of the Dead Sea Scrolls, she explains that Joseph, as an Essene, was practicing his religious principles of celibacy in a temple stronghold called Qumran. Celibacy was very important to the Essenes, it was regarded as the holiest way of life. They saw marriage and sex as unholy, and the more celibate you were the closer to god you got. The highest order of Essene men lived in Qumran behind thick walls completely out of touch with the world. They shared everything and owned nothing while dedicating their lives to god. When they needed to procreate to keep the bloodline alive, they would venture out for specific periods to find an appropriate female. The courting or betrothal period could last as long as three years after which they would have a first marriage. This was the period during which the woman would fall pregnant. After waiting for three months during which a miscarriage is more likely to happen, there would be a second wedding. But our Mary fell pregnant with the Holy Ghost, which according to the tradition meant that she was effectively still a virgin, because when she had the child she had not had both the weddings. At first Joseph did not want to have anything to do with the child, but an angel advised him to go ahead with the wedding as if it was the second.

The Essenes believed that priests and Levites were incarnations of heavenly beings or "gods" and "angels." The fact that Joseph did not have sex with Mary after their first wedding and yet she fell pregnant, made her a virgin. Joseph fell into a lower rank of priests and kings, which made him a "spirit." And so the mystery of the baby being conceived by the "Holy Spirit" is answered by Joseph's lower rank. Although the latter version is interesting, I find it almost too complicated, while the story of the Apocrypha has simplicity in its favor. William Bramley exposes much evidence that outlines Jesus' Essene lineage while also linking it to the secret societies like the Brotherhood and Freemasons, who also happen to use a symbolic apron.

The lack of information about the young Jesus' life is disturbing. Shouldn't the messiah have been the idol of humanity as he was growing up, spreading truth and wisdom even at a young age? Surely, that would have been the obvious thing to do, if you really wanted to impress people everywhere? But that was not the case. Instead, Jesus was whisked off to a faraway land, where he was prepared and most likely indoctrinated for the big role in the great human deception. He briefly appeared at the age of twelve before a group of Hebrew scholars, but then he disappeared for another eighteen years. The Anunnaki gods were too well-known around the Near East, Israel, and Egypt. Enlil had to find a more discrete location for the grooming of his protégé. By the age of around thirty, Jesus reappeared out of the blue to start his short life of ministry, lasting only an incredible three years before his crucifixion. Just think about this practically. In today's world of extreme wealth and mass media, it would be very difficult to create a global brand within three years. And yet, in only three short years 2,000 years ago, one man became a global phenomenon? The PR around his activities and the way in which his awareness spread led me to believe that there were very powerful forces, like the Anunnaki gods, behind such a masterstroke. But Jesus was not such a big hit in his time as we are led to believe. It actually took 2,000 years to make Jesus the phenomenon he is today, because at the time of his life he had a small following and caused much upheaval with his preaching. If it was not for Emperor Constantine some 300 years after Christ's death, Christianity would most likely have remained a small cultish religion.

A substantial number of historians have unraveled a fascinating history of the young Jesus in Persia and Asia that is too detailed to be a fabrication or coincidence. They are not like the predictable stories that state that he worked with his father in the carpentry workshop. If that was the case, who was responsible for his spiritual and philosophical education, and why did we not hear about him at all during those years? It is highly unlikely that he would have gone unnoticed if he was around the Nazareth area all his life. The local custom dictated that Essene boys entered a monastery at about the age of five where they received the appropriate education. Some historians claim that this was exactly what happened to young Jesus, at a monastery on the Mediterranean sea near Haifa. The reason why Jesus seemed to have made a short appearance in the New Testament at the age of twelve was for his bar mitzvah preparation, after which he mysteriously vanished for another eighteen years. Historians and documentary makers have done extensive work on the hidden life of the young Christ. Many of them agree that Jesus spent the time traveling through Asia absorbing the religious principles of their spiritual leaders. Those travels by Christ were probably sponsored by the Essenes as their religious culture was deeply rooted in the Aryan and Zoroaster religions, which originated from the East.

Ancient Buddhist scrolls reveal that Jesus spent seventeen years in India and Tibet from the age of thirteen to age twenty-nine. He was both a student and teacher of Buddhist and Hindu holy men. The story of his journey from Jerusalem to Benares was recorded by Brahman historians, who until today still know him and love him as St. Issa, their "Buddha." This was revealed in 1894 when a Russian doctor and explorer by the name of Nicolas Notovitch published a book called *The Unknown Life of Christ*. Notovitch journeyed extensively throughout Afghanistan, India, and further through the spectacular passes of Bolan, over the Punjab, down into the arid rocky land of Ladakh, and into the majestic Vale of Kashmir of the Himalayas. During one of his journeys in 1890 he was visiting Leh, the capital of Ladakh, near where the Buddhist monastery of Himis is located. Because of an accident in which he broke his leg, he had the opportunity to stay for some time at Himis. While he was there, he learned that the Buddhists had ancient records of the life of Jesus Christ. Notovitch was stunned, and with some scratching he located a Tibetan translation of the legend and carefully noted in his *carnet de voyage* over two hundred verses from the curious document known as The Life of St. Issa. He learned that "Issa" is the direct translation of the name "Jesus," which is also used by many Muslims today. He was shown two large yellowed volumes containing the biography of St. Issa. Notovitch enlisted a member of his party to translate the Tibetan volumes while he carefully noted each verse in the back pages of his journal. When he returned to the Western world there was much controversy as to the authenticity of the document. He was accused of creating a hoax and was ridiculed as an impostor. In his defence, he encouraged a scientific expedition to prove that the original Tibetan documents really existed. One of his skeptics was a Hindu monk and a disciple of Sri Ramakrishna called Swami Abhedananda. In 1922, Swami Abhedananda journeyed to Ladakh in hopes of exposing Notovitch as a fraud. Upon questioning the head lama about St. Issa, he was shown a manuscript that he recorded in his travel notes. He was astounded to find a manuscript of Bengali translation of 224 verses virtually identical to what Notovitch had written. Abhedananda was thus convinced of the authenticity of the Issa legend. While on a trek through central Asia during

1925, Nicholas Roerich, the artist-philosopher, also encountered the infamous manuscript. One of the many reasons for Roerich's trek was to record customs and legends of the peoples of central Asia. He published two of his diaries, called *Heart of Asia* and *Altai-Himalaya,* which both contain such tales of St. Issa. Roerich says that more important than the find of the manuscripts itself is the cultural phenomenon of the spread of Jesus' legend to these remote regions. He writes the following in *Altai-Himalaya:*

> Whoever doubts too completely that such legends about the Christ life exist in Asia, probably does not realize what an immense influence the Nestorians have had in all parts of Asia and how many so-called Apocryphal legends they spread in the most ancient times . . . Many remember lines from the book of Notovitch, but it is still more wonderful to discover, on this site, in several variants, the same version of the legend of Issa. The local people knew nothing of any published book but they know the legend and with deep reverence they speak of Issa. One might wonder what relation Moslems, Hindus, or Buddhists have with Issa. But it is still more significant to see how vital are great ideas and how they penetrate even the most remote places. Never may one discover the source of such legends. But even if they originated from ancient Nestorian Apocrypha, at present it is instructive to see the widespread and deep consideration paid to the subject. It is significant to hear a local inhabitant, a Hindu, relate how Issa preached beside a small pool near the bazaar under a tree, which no longer exists. In such purely physical indications you may see how seriously this subject is regarded.

According to the Buddhist legends, Issa arrived in Asia at the age of about thirteen, studied under various masters, absorbing much knowledge while engaging in some preaching of his own. The document further states that the "Blessed One" then returned to Palestine some sixteen years later at the age of twenty-nine. This fits the mysterious life of Jesus like a glove and since there aren't any other similar coincidences that we know of, it certainly sounds like Jesus was a well-traveled and well-learned man by the time he began his world-changing ministry in Palestine. The Legend of St. Issa further strengthens the Essene and Aryan link when it states that:

> In his fourteenth year, young Issa, the Blessed One, came this side of the Sindh and settled among the Aryas.

Sindh was a province of western Pakistan and *Aryas* was their term for Aryan. The legend goes that Jesus studied under the white Aryan Brahman Priests who were overjoyed by his arrival. "The white priest of Brahma welcomed him joyfully," states the legend. He was taught to read and to understand the Vedas, and also how to teach and expound these Hindu scriptures. But Jesus started to show his true colors very early in life when he disregarded culture and began to associate with the lower castes. He protested against their discriminatory practices and questioned why God would make any difference in his children. The Sudras (people of the lower castes) were not only forbidden to attend the reading of the Vedas, but they were even forbidden to look on them, for they were condemned to perpetual servitude as slaves to the Brahmins, the Kshatriyas, and even the Vaishyas who were of higher caste levels. Jesus strongly disagreed with their philosophy and openly questioned their morality. As written in The Legend of St. Issa, "God has made no difference between his children, who are all alike dear to him," said Issa. Disregarding their words, Issa remained with the Sudras, preaching against the Brahmins and Kshatriyas. "Those who deprive their brethren of divine happiness shall be deprived of it themselves. The Brahmans and the Kshatriyas shall become the Sudras, and with the Sudras the Eternal shall dwell everlastingly." Please note that some historians spell the word *Shudras* as *Sudras*. There is also a different spelling for *Vaishyas* and *Vaishas*.

Issa's teachings in Asia are astounding as they mirror the words of Jesus some years later. Take a look at some of the things he had to say, long before the people of the Holy Land got to hear his words of wisdom.

He passed his time in several ancient cities of India such as Benares. All loved him because Issa dwelt in peace with Vaishas and Shudras whom he instructed and helped. But the Brahmins and Kshatriyas told him that Brahma forbade those to approach who were created out of his womb and feet. The Vaishas were allowed to listen to the Vedas only on holidays and the Shudras were forbidden not only to be present at the reading of the Vedas, but could not even look at them. Issa said that man had filled the temples with his abominations. In order to pay homage to metals and stones, man sacrificed his fellows in whom dwells a spark of the Supreme Spirit. Man demeans those who labour by the sweat of their brows, in order to gain the good will of the sluggard who sits at the lavishly set board. But they who deprive their brothers of the common blessing shall be themselves stripped of it. Vaishas and Shudras were struck with astonishment and asked what they could perform. Issa bade them "Worship not the idols. Do not consider yourself first. Do not humiliate your neighbour. Help the poor. Sustain the feeble. Do evil to no one. Do not covet that which you do not possess and which is possessed by others." Many, learning of such words, decided to kill Issa. But Issa, forewarned, departed from this place by night. Afterward, Issa went into Nepal and into the Himalayan mountains . . . "Well, perform for us a miracle," demanded the servitors of the Temple. Then Issa replied to them: "Miracles made their appearance from the very day when the world was created. He who cannot behold them is deprived of the greatest gift of life. But woe to you, enemies of men, woe unto you, if you await that He should attest his power by miracle." Issa taught that men should not strive to behold the Eternal Spirit with one's own eyes but to feel it with the heart, and to become a pure and worthy soul . . . Not only shall you not make human offerings, but you must not slaughter animals, because all is given for the use of man. Do not steal the goods of others, because that would be usurpation from your near one. Do not cheat, that you may in turn not be cheated . . . Beware, ye, who divert men from the true path and who fill the people with superstitions and prejudices, who blind the vision of the seeing ones, and who preach subservience to material things.

Then Pilate, ruler of Jerusalem, gave orders to lay hands upon the preacher Issa and to deliver him to the judges, without however, arousing the displeasure of the people. But Issa taught: "Do not seek straight paths in darkness, possessed by fear. But gather force and support each other. He who supports his neighbour strengthens himself. I tried to revive the laws of Moses in the hearts of the people. And I say unto you that you do not understand their true meaning because they do not teach revenge but forgiveness. But the meaning of these laws is distorted." Then the ruler sent to Issa his disguised servants that they should watch his actions and report to him about his words to the people. "Thou just man," said the disguised servant of the ruler of Jerusalem approaching Issa, "Teach us, should we fulfil the will of Caesar or await the approaching deliverance?" But Issa, recognizing the disguised servants, said, "I did not foretell unto you that you would be delivered from Caesar; but I said that the soul which was immersed in sin would be delivered from sin." At this time, an old woman approached the crowd, but was pushed back. Then Issa said, "Reverence Woman, mother of the universe, in her lies the truth of creation. She is the foundation of all that is good and beautiful. She is the source of life and death. Upon her depends the existence of man, because she is the sustenance of his labours. She gives birth to you in travail, she watches over your growth. Bless her. Honour her.

Defend her. Love your wives and honour them, because tomorrow they shall be mothers, and later-progenitors of a whole race. Their love ennobles man, soothes the embittered heart and tames the beast. Wife and mother-they are the adornments of the universe. As light divides itself from darkness, so does woman possess the gift to divide in man good intent from the thought of evil. Your best thoughts must belong to woman. Gather from them your moral strength, which you must possess to sustain your near ones. Do not humiliate her, for therein you will humiliate yourselves. And all which you will do to mother, to wife, to widow or to another woman in sorrow-that shall you also do for the Spirit." So taught Issa; but the ruler Pilate ordered one of his servants to make accusation against him. Said Issa: "Not far hence is the time when by the Highest Will the people will become purified and united into one family."

It is fascinating to see that Jesus came face to face with some of the deities or angels who ruled the East. "Near Lhasa was a temple of teaching with a wealth of manuscripts. Jesus was to acquaint himself with them. Meng-ste, a great sage of all the East, was in this temple."

This behavior caused so much friction that a group of white priests sent some servants to kill Issa. He was, however, warned against the plot and escaped to the holy city of Djagguernat and further into Buddhist lands. Jesus stayed there for six years learning the Pali language and the holy Buddhist writings, the Sutras. The legend goes that Jesus "could perfectly expound the sacred scrolls."

This kind of teaching flies right in the face of the god of vengeance in the Old Testament, where god would choose his favorite group of people over another. It was the rebellious Jesus who began to preach in earnest that "all men are equal." This was a brilliant piece of strategy by the god Enlil, who was setting up the young messiah for the biggest day in human religion: the crucifixion.

Before Jesus returned to Palestine, he preached and performed miracles among the people of Asia, even raising some from the dead. This is another excerpt from Roerich's translations of the Legend of St Issa:

Finally Jesus reached a mountain pass and in the chief city of Ladakh, Leh, he was joyously accepted by monks and people of the lower class . . . And Jesus taught in the monasteries and in the bazaars (the market places); wherever the simple people gathered, there he taught. Not far from this place lived a woman whose son had died and she brought him to Jesus. And in the presence of a multitude, Jesus laid his hand on the child, and the child rose healed. And many brought their children and Jesus laid his hands upon them, healing them. Among the Ladakhis, Jesus passed many days, teaching them. And they loved him and when the time of his departure came they sorrowed as children.

By the time Jesus returned to Palestine he was twenty-nine or thirty years old and immediately started his public life of ministry. The relationship between him and his Essenes sponsors was showing great signs of distress, mainly because of his lack of respect for their Aryan brethren in Asia. The Essenes had a lot of time and money invested in Jesus and they were keen to have him proclaimed the new messiah, but Jesus wanted nothing to do with it. According to some historians, he denied his Davidic descent and even forbade his disciples to call him the messiah, which is another perfect example of how the principle of divide and conquer was being implemented by the cunning Enlil. While some writers of books dealing with the Anunnaki influence on human history believe that Jesus became a rebel within the environment that was prepared for him by his "heavenly gods," I have a slightly more sinister hypothesis. The most important message we extract out of these activities is the masterful precision with which Enlil, the supreme Anunnaki commander, was orchestrating the messiah prophesies. Day by day, step by step, he manipulated events while setting Jesus up to be the martyr for humanity, while he continually and unwittingly promoted the power of his "good" god, Enlil, the one and only god. Together with the books of the Old Testament, they provide the irrefutable evidence of manipulation, control, and oppression of humanity from the dawn of history. There is simply no other way to digest all the confusing and conflicting events of the distant past. The only sensible answer lies in the well supported historic findings that outline the arrival of the Anunnaki or Nefilim on Earth, which led to a chain of events nobody could have ever predicted in their wildest dreams.

Adding to the confusion about a messiah, which was being spread by the Anunnaki gods and angels, was the constant need displayed by the people of the day to find this elusive messiah. Their desperation for a savior was so great that they willingly proclaimed Jesus to be the new messiah, adding fuel to the fire. But once again the fuel was actually being poured on by the Anunnaki angels who were the real agitators, spreading the word of the messiah to humans all over the place. Within three short years, Jesus had made such waves and created so many enemies that neither the Hebrew leaders nor the Romans were too fond of him. He was a real rebel, unconsciously creating a legacy that would be masterfully crafted by a controlled group of priests between about AD 325 and AD 1150 into the New Testament. A stunning conclusion to the religious entrapment of the Old Testament, which needed to evolve into a true human drama of unconditional love, faith, and sacrifice of the New Testament. By its conclusion, the god Enlil had set the eternal trap of enslavement through religious dogma. A masterfully executed plot by the vengeful god, whom humanity still fears today.

Enlil was the father of manipulation and propaganda. Toward the end of the Old Testament he realized that humanity was growing increasingly informed and civilized. The other lesser gods under the leadership of Marduk were causing confusion among people, causing them not to know whom they should obey and worship. Remember that Marduk had proclaimed himself god above all, and the rivalry between him and Enlil was the main backdrop to the human drama of biblical times. But the humans had evolved; their brains were functioning more intelligently and they had great philosophers, mathematicians, and teachers who were uplifting humanity at a rapid rate. Very quickly, Enlil's control over humans was slipping. He had to come up with a cunning plan to reaffirm his supremacy, so that humanity would become fearful and obedient once more. We must remember that by this time there was a whole new subspecies of people called *Homo sapiens sapiens* or "wise wise man." This newly evolved subspecies emerged very early in human history when "the sons of God saw the daughters of man and had children with them," and by doing so, immediately created a new hybrid human who was more intelligent and more evolved. All signs point to the Aryans as the earliest "wise wise" humans. These hybrid humans became a huge threat to Enlil, and remained a threat for long periods of time. We have already pointed out how god and his bloodthirsty "angels" tried to wipe out those who conspired against him in Sodom and Gomorrah. This kind of persecution carried on throughout the ages with numerous examples in the Bible. At first Enlil tried to curtail such rebellious activity in various oppressive ways, but it failed. History has shown us that dictators do not last forever. Eventually the people will rise up against their oppressor. This is exactly what happened to Enlil. By the end of the Old Testament days, he realized that a new strategy was necessary to reestablish total control over humanity.

The divide and conquer principle was successfully introduced, but Enlil tested the process of religious entrapment on a few other occasions, with other so-called prophets. It seems that the Anunnaki had been planting seeds of messianic doctrine for quite some time, patiently waiting for one of or more of the messiahs to take root. And boy, did they! The Hebrew and Christian Bibles are filled with prophets, but some delivered less success than others. One such example is outlined in the Book of Enoch, one of the Apocryphal scriptures. Melchizedek was a Jewish high priest with great influence in his time, who was also reported to have been brought forth by a virgin birth by his old mother Soparim, without human intercourse.

> Soparim, old and barren, conceived Melchizedek without having intercourse with her husband.
>
> 2 ENOCH 71

Enoch writes that Soparim was not only postmenopausal but she had been childless all of her life, when suddenly she fell pregnant on her own. Although I have not read about the presence of any angels in this instance, I suspect they must have been present just like in all the other virgin birth cases, making sure that the intended recipient was receptive to the fertilization process she was about to experience. Enoch must have had some form of contact with the gods who used him as a mouthpiece to prophesy the coming of Melchizedek and another messiah, who would be the most powerful of them all. By using random prophets in this fashion, the gods created an expectation among humans of great heavenly things and salvation from the toil on Earth. They were promised eternal life in the house of god and other fantastical experiences. But *only if* they behaved and obeyed their god blindly at all times. It is mind-boggling that since those days, nothing has really changed in popular global religions, and the fear of punishment by god is possibly stronger now than ever.

> And afterward, in the last generation, there will be another Melchizedek, the first of twelve priests. And this last will be head of all, a great archpriest, the Word and power of God, who will perform miracles greater and more glorious than all the previous ones.
>
> ENOCH 71:34

What a wonderfully deceptive promise to make to a confused community of humans without any identity. The wonders do not end here though. The Hindu tradition has many legends of wondrous human beings who are conceived and born in strange and complex manners. Just take a look at the Vedic poems. The Buddha was born from the womb unlike many of the other Hindu gods. Once again there was a bright constellation that signalled the miraculous birth of a great prophet and teacher. The conception by his mother Maya was very peculiar: she fell into a deep trance in which a white king elephant seemed to enter her body without causing her pain or discomfort. During her pregnancy, Maya did not experience any fatigue or depression. The legend surrounding the conception and birth of the Buddha goes something like this, from Edward Conze's *Buddhist Scriptures:*

> So he issued from the womb as befits a Buddha. He did not enter the world in the usual manner, and he appeared like one descended from the sky.

Does this mean that the Buddha had Aryan features, like Enki and the other Anunnaki gods? If so, who was his paternal father whose DNA he inherited?

> And since he had for many eons been engaged in the practice of meditation, he now was born in full awareness, and not thoughtless and bewildered as other people are. When born, he was so lustrous and steadfast that it appeared as if the young sun had come down to earth.

Once again we witness a bright light or some other form of brilliance as in the cave during the birth of Christ.

> And yet, when people gazed at his dazzling brilliance, he held their eyes like the moon. His limbs shone with the radiant hue of precious gold, and lit up the space all around. Instantly he walked seven steps, firmly and with long strides. In that, he was like the constellation of the Seven Seers. With the bearing of a lion he surveyed the four quarters, and spoke these words full of meaning for the future: For enlightenment I was born, for the good of all that lives. This is the last time that I have been born into this world of becoming.

Based on various historic births of prophets, the people of Israel also expect that the birth of the Messiah would be surrounded by miraculous celestial signs, which would herald the beginning of the apocalypse when god's chosen people would be taken up to heaven. The Jews also expect the visitation of angels and wondrous occurrences to accompany the conception of the Messiah, as it seems to have happened for hundreds of years before. By the time Christ was born, the Jews were desperate for a messiah but they had pretty set ideas of what that job would entail. It certainly did not fall in line with what Jesus started to preach on his return from Asia. For a long time the Jews wanted a warrior messiah to save them from their slavery and torment. They wanted to be told that they were god's chosen people and that he had come to save them, not to tell them that all people are equal in god's eyes, or to turn the other cheek! But sadly for them, the message from the Old Testament had suddenly changed dramatically and Jesus took upon himself the hopeless situation of the slave species. He believed that he could teach them and really save them. Little did he know that there was a much bigger and more sinister plan by the Anunnaki that plotted his destiny. Once they realized that this Jesus character was well established among a growing loyal group of followers, they would stop at nothing to help elevate Jesus to the highest level of divinity. A good example comes to us in Matthew, when after Jesus was baptized, the gods had to add a little spice to entrench the moment in human history. Another incredible example of how the gods interacted with humankind. Wouldn't it be fascinating if this kind of thing happened today? I wonder what CNN and BBC journalists would make of it.

> As soon as Jesus was baptized, he went up out of the water. At that moment heaven was opened, and he saw the Spirit of God descending like a dove and lighting on him. And a voice from heaven said, "This is my Son, whom I love; with him I am well pleased."
>
> MATTHEW 3:16–17

We begin to suspect that Jesus did not want to go through with his ordeal when he realized what was going on. In the garden of Gethsemane he asks the gods twice if he could "not drink from the cup," basically meaning that he wanted this ordeal to pass him by.

> My soul is overwhelmed with sorrow to the point of death . . . he fell with his face to the ground and prayed, My Father, if it is possible, may this cup be taken from me . . . The spirit is willing, but the body is weak . . . He went away a second time and prayed, My Father, if it is not possible for this cup to be taken away unless I drink it, may your will be done.
>
> MATTHEW 26:38–42

It is clear from these words that Jesus had lost his lust for this messianic stuff. But a real moment of truth that reveals the terrible secret about Jesus being manipulated came on the cross just before he died. If he really knew what was awaiting him, why would he say the following:

> About the ninth hour Jesus cried out in a loud voice, "Eloi, Eloi, lama sabach-thani?" Which means, "My God, my God, why have you forsaken me?"
>
> MATTHEW 27:46

Why would Jesus suddenly feel that he had been let down, or forgotten? Did he expect to be helped by someone? Surely he must have been aware of his own fate and that he was going to stir the hatred of the authorities who would not let him get away with such blatant antiestablishment behavior! If he was fully aware of the implications of his actions, why would he expect his god to rescue him? After all, Jesus was supposed to be god personified in human form. Surely he knew he had to die for humanity? Or maybe not! Is it possible that the road that was laid out for him by the higher powers did not include the final chapter, which ended with a gruesome crucifixion?

Another example of Anunnaki interference in human entrapment, was the birth and life of the prophet Muhammad. Many extraordinary stories are told about the birth of the great prophet. A brilliant light shone over the entire world from East to West in the hour of his delivery. From Andras: "When Mohammed was born he was clean and without physical blemish, already circumcised, and with the navel cord already cut. At the age of four, Mohammed was visited by angels. They opened his body, taking a black drop from his heart while washing his inward parts with melted snow from a golden chalice. Furthermore there are many elements within Islamic folklore which imply and support a virgin birth."

The paranoia of losing control of their slave species is also clearly visible in the events leading up to the reciting of the Koran. As N. J. Dawood states in his introduction to the Koran, long before Muhammad's call, the Arabic world was worshipping many gods, whom they called the "daughters of Allah." Some of those were female goddesses like Al-Lat, Al-Uzza, and Manat. This was another area where Enlil and his Anunnaki gods had to take action before they lost any more control, allowing the humans to organize themselves against him. The power of the church was growing but it had not reached the kind of horrifying muscle that it would exercise during the Crusades some centuries later. Meanwhile, this was some 610 years after Christ, and still the slave species had not learned the lessons from Jesus, that they should only worship one god, and the only way into "heaven" was through him. So, the "god" who had set up Jesus needed another messenger. The famous story of the angel Gabriel appearing before Muhammad strongly resembles the process of setting up Mary and Joseph, pretty much to their surprise and against their will. Muhammad would become a prophet who is followed by people who fear the violent retribution of their god. According to Muslim tradition, one night in Ramadan about AD 610, the angel Gabriel came to him while he was asleep or in a trance, and said: "Recite!" He replied: "What shall I recite?" The order was repeated three times until the angel himself said: "Recite the name of your Lord who created, created man from clots of blood."

That statement is perfectly in synch with the Sumerian tablets outlining the creation of Adam by the Anunnaki gods. What makes this event even more interesting is that the original Koran translation into English carried the term *Lord of Creation,* which has since been changed to "Lord of the Universe" in latter translations. It may be a subtle change to the normal reader, but if you view it from the understanding of the Anunnaki's activity on Earth, it makes a huge difference. We suspect that the Anunnaki created man, but they certainly did not create the universe. The term Lord of Creation was more appropriate, but it was not grandiose enough for the followers of Mohammed. Once again we are faced with a tragic confusion between god and God, the former of which has kept humanity imprisoned on Earth in a perpetual fear of god.

The whole concept of angels has always troubled me. Honestly! Why in heaven would the "all-powerful," omnipotent God need a bunch of lower spiritual forms in a physical form to run His errands? To convey messages, to deliver warnings and threats, and to actually do the destruction on his behalf? Why would God need this kind of menial support? Surely the all-powerful God can facilitate all the interactions with humans in the blink of an eye, instead of long-winded tedious instructions, threats, and the monitoring of humans who have apparently been behaving sinfully while conspiring against him! It simply does not wash.

There are further examples of possible Anunnaki or Nefilim interferences in controlling humans. Many are kept under wraps for fear of ridicule. It seems that people in the twenty-first century are not as brave to come out with claims of having been visited by angels as their brethren of ancient times. There was one such occasion in 1820, when the young Joseph Smith had his first encounter with what was described as an "angel" who returned on several occasions to repeat *exactly* the same message of doom and destruction among humans. The way in which the young Joseph relates his story points to a possibility that the message was a recording that was replayed to him several times during the same night. It was beamed into his bedroom leaving the angel "floating" off the ground. The message ended with the floating angel exiting the window in a pillar of light until it vanished in the sky. The next day he had the same message broadcast to him by the same angel while in the field. The angel even introduced himself as Moroni, telling Joseph about some ancient metal plates containing the history of North America. Joseph was to find them and have them translated. And so was born the Mormon Church, which is many millions strong today.

I find it incredibly disturbing to contemplate the possibility that God would spend virtually 13,000 years, from the emergence of civilization, plotting a succession of messiahs and prophets to warn people about their sinful behavior. Then, going on to choose one group of favorites above another while decimating those who had been "plotting and conspiring" against him. How can people conspire against an all powerful God? I can understand how people can conspire against a physical entity or even deity, when they realize that the deities who are causing them harm are vulnerable. But such has been the strategy of divide and rule injected into human society by Enlil and the hordes of "angels" who seemed to have run all his errands for thousands of years.

If there ever was a clear case of evidence of ancient people living in fear of celestial deities, it exists in abundance in the Hindu scriptures. The Vedas, sacred Hindu poems, which have apparently been passed on verbally for as long as 10,000 years, and eventually written down in the Sanskrit language, are filled with references to a multitude of gods who display all the violent human traits we have described before. The most striking characteristic once again is the violent gene. If the Vedas are indeed as old as they seem, they are a vivid testimony of the constant interaction between gods and humanity in the distant past while man was being nurtured into so-called civilization by the Anunnaki and Nefilim gods. According to Richard Thompson in his book *Alien Identities,* there are many references to "non-human" interventions in ancient Indian scriptures. I went in search of such references and was astounded at the constant referral to things like sacrifice, fear of the gods, punishment, reward, wealth, goddesses who loved mortal men, immortality, being spared from harm, partying with the gods, gold, riches, victory over the enemy, chariots in the sky, god's bright beams of light, and literally thousands of strange references that cannot be explained in historic terms but rather by today's common sense. Evidence of human manipulation by heavenly deities fills hundreds of pages of the sacred Vedic poems. Such manipulation of humans continued over the years with the Bible, Kabbalah, Koran, and thousands of other documents that have never been brought into the mainframe, such as the apocryphal books of the Bible and writings of other religious groups. In the end, we have to admit that the strategy used by the Anunnaki has worked very well. Although stretched over long periods of Earth time, often appearing to be very disorganized, the gods of our prehistory, the Anunnaki, have achieved their goal. They have divided humanity, turned them against each other and they have conquered them with fear.

So, now that we have a clearer picture of the suspicious events surrounding the births and lives of some prophets of our human history, we can attempt to answer the question of who Jesus Christ really was. To some readers, the inbred fear of the mere suggestion that Jesus was anything other than the son of God will prevent them from crossing this bridge. I am of the firm opinion that Jesus was just one of many prophets or messiahs who were carefully planned by the Anunnaki gods, in an attempt to keep humanity in line, fearful and obedient, to the great gods who ruled the world, and possibly still rule it today.

If you find this preposterous just ask yourself this question: The world's largest organizations that control our day-to-day lives are controlled by a small group of people who basically determine what brands we consume, how we dress, what TV shows we watch, what we drive, what beer we drink, and where we go on holiday. How often do we see the small group of decision makers in their boardrooms as they plan our next mode of transport? Never. We simply accept it as it emerges and get on with our lives. But we believe and we "know" that there is such a group of people making those decisions that will influence our lives dramatically. We know that there is a group of people who control the price of oil, but we do not know what happens in their meetings while they plan our future. We simply live with the consequences. Our lives are controlled by a relatively small number of major industries and a small number of people in charge of those industries, but we simply accept that this is the case and that in truth there is not really much we can do about it. The absolute power that the giants of global industry wield is virtually unassailable. We should, therefore, not be surprised to find out that there could be a small number of ancient Anunnaki "gods" who still reside among us, controlling our affairs in ways that we cannot comprehend and cannot see.

As far as Jesus is concerned, it certainly seems that he was the most successful of the planted messiahs. He was the one who took root and captured the hearts and imagination of the people of his time, while the other prophets only achieved moderate success. To the gods who planned him and placed him into the world, Jesus was a great achievement and possibly even a great surprise for finding success where many others before him had failed. He managed to plant seeds of obedience but also perpetuated the fear of god, while unconsciously spreading the principle of divide and conquer among humanity. And so the Anunnaki gods reaped another major victory over their human slave species, keeping them enslaved and obedient for another 2,000 years. Who knows how much longer this grip of fear will control our world, before we will all be able to break free from the entrapment by our creators, our slave masters, our gods with a small "g," so that we can reach out to the infinite community of universal beings who live in unity with the real God. The universal one, who needs no offerings of gold, or offerings of flesh, or who harbors no need to punish humanity for disobedience; the God who does not choose one favorite human over another.

But the most compelling argument supporting that Jesus was an innocent bystander and accidental Messiah comes from Barbara Thiering in her book

Jesus of the Apocalypse: The Life of Jesus After the Crucifixion. Most people will be shocked to find out that the story of Jesus did not end on the cross or with his resurrection. Thiering presents a volume of evidence, mostly originating in the book of Revelations, that Jesus retreated into a secretive life of anti-Roman activity with his two sons and daughter. We learn that by the time Jesus was crucified, he was already married to Mary Magdalene. Their first wedding took place during September in AD 30, not long after Jesus began his ministry. We should also remember that there is now overwhelming evidence that Jesus was actually born in the year 7 BC, which would have made him seven years older than history books lead us to believe. Their second wedding took place during March to May in AD 33 according to their custom, when they knew that Mary Magdalene was more than three months pregnant and a miscarriage was less likely to occur. But it was a turbulent time for the Messiah as this was also the year in which he was to be executed. Later that year in September, his wife Mary Magdalene gave birth to a daughter, their first child. Jesus rises from the dead, his body mysteriously disappears from the tomb, and an angel tells Mary Magdalene and friends that he had risen on the third day as he promised he would. Those irrepressible angels seem to pop up every time there is possible trouble for the Anunnaki gods. Jesus begins his anti-Roman campaign with his disciples and a growing number of revolutionaries. They struggle against Agrippa I, Caligula, Agrippa II, and other Roman leaders. In June of AD 37 his first son Jesus Justus is born. In March of AD 44 his second son is born, and in September of that year his marriage to Mary ends. He travels extensively seeking support for his movement: in Cyprus, Asia Minor, Rome, Ephesus, and Philippi, where he marries a woman called Lydia in AD 50. He continues to travel until he dies in the year AD 70, at the age of 76, most likely in Rome. While this is a shocking glossary and revelation for the most religious, Thiering goes into great detail in supporting these facts. But let us go back to the resurrection, because it was really from this point onwards that things went a little pear-shaped in the scriptures and many questions arise as to what possibly happened to the son of God after he rose from the dead. Suspicious activity surrounds the cave and the reactions of those who came in search of Jesus. It seems that the angel did something to the guards that incapacitated them, as they "became like dead men." The gods used Mary to help spread the propaganda that Jesus had arisen.

"Take a guard," Pilate answered. "Go, make the tomb as secure as you know how." So they went and made the tomb secure by putting a seal on the stone and posting the guard.

MATTHEW 27:65–66

After the Sabbath, at dawn on the first day of the week, Mary Magdalene and the other Mary went to look at the tomb. There was a violent earthquake, for an angel of the Lord came down from heaven and, going to the tomb, rolled back the stone and sat on it. His appearance was like lightning, and his clothes were white as snow. The guards were so afraid of him that they shook and became like dead men. The angel said to the women, "Do not be afraid, for I know that you are looking for Jesus, who was crucified. He is not here; he has risen, just as he said. Come and see the place where he lay. Then go quickly and tell his disciples: 'He has risen from the dead and is going ahead of you into Galilee. There you will see him.' Now I have told you." So the women hurried away from the tomb, afraid yet filled with joy, and ran to tell his disciples. Suddenly Jesus met them. "Greetings," he said. They came to him, clasped his feet and worshipped him. Then Jesus said to them, "Do not be afraid. Go and tell my brothers to go to Galilee; there they will see me."

MATTHEW 28:1–10, THE RESURRECTION

And so began the life of Jesus the revolutionary after his resurrection. There was so much activity between Jesus and Simon, Mark, John, Peter, Matthew and others that it baffles the mind, and I highly recommend the reading of *Jesus of the Apocalypse* for the skeptics. What could have possibly happened to Jesus after these events? How could the son of God—the messiah of the people—just suddenly disappear from the face of the world? If he survived and lived on, would he not have continued a life of ministry of some sort? Why did he go into hiding? The biggest surprise comes when we learn of Jesus' personal views of the events surrounding his life. He was so disillusioned by all the activity that after his resurrection he vanished from the scene and carried on living with wife and children until the age of about 76, leading the life of an activist against the Romans. But why the Romans? Jesus was not a stupid man, he was extremely well-traveled, well-educated, and broad-minded. He must have realized that he was set up by the gods to be their front and mouthpiece. The gods presented themselves as the God of the universe, the God with a big "G." It must have come as a great shock to him that this was not the case and that he was greatly manipulated, lied to, and misguided by the deities of Rome. It became clear to him that these were actually the gods of Rome: the conniving and manipulative gods who have been controlling humanity from the very beginning.

This made Jesus retreat and with his fellow supporters begin a campaign of underground resistance against those Roman gods. They realized that the "gods" were not infallible and that humans could stand up against them. Just like his predecessors did during the time of Abraham in the cities of Sodom and Gomorrah—the earliest organized resistance against the gods, for which they were severely punished. I cannot find another plausible explanation why the son of God, who survived his execution, would suddenly disappear from the mainstream when he had had such a loyal following. In the years after his death, the Christian movement grew steadily, but in truth it was a movement that was aimed at discrediting the Anunnaki gods of Rome, while offering the people a whole new spiritual reality that Jesus absorbed during his early years in Asia. It is ironic that the Messiah who was planted and manipulated by the lesser deity gods to keep humankind enslaved through fear turned against his makers and began to preach the awareness of a greater spiritual power in the universe. But history got it all mixed up, and the poor faithful masses today do not really know who they are praying to. The message of Christ after his death is not clearly recorded or understood, but it somehow seeped into the greater pool of religious preaching and continues to be highly confusing in the twenty-first century. The number of divergent Christian movements are testimony to this curious development in the Christian church.

The desperation of the Anunnaki gods becomes evident when they try to create new prophets and messiahs, like in the story of Mohammed who was throttled by an angel commanding Mohammed to recite the name of the Lord. As time went by and humans emerged out of the Dark Ages and the Renaissance, the activity of the gods seemed to have diminished. They had greatly achieved what they had set out to do: to keep their human slave species ignorant, divided, faithful, and frightened of the wrath of god. So here we are, some 200,000 years after our creation, having gone through many stages of development, civilization, mechanization, and now technology. And still we do not know who we are and where we come from. Of the world population, 70% holds onto some fanatical religious belief system that promises to give them salvation over the masses of sinners in the world. Regardless of the technological achievements and our exploration of the planets, many still hold onto their ancient belief system, too scared to challenge it with newfound knowledge. Jesus was just an innocent bystander who was chosen and manipulated by the conniving Anunnaki gods. But when he realized what had actually happened to him, he tried his best to undo the damage. Unfortunately it was a little too late. The Roman Empire used his example to perpetuate the lie under Constantine, who was most likely guided by Enlil and his godly followers, while the Aryans and the supporters of Marduk opposed their activity, which is clearly outlined during the council of Nicaea of AD 325.

If you think that the mystery surrounding Jesus is pretty much exhausted, think again. We have only scratched the surface. A real mind bender occurred in 1963 with the discovery of the Talmud of Jmmanuel (TJ) scrolls. A Swiss traveler named Eduard Albert Meier and his friend, an ex-Greek-Orthodox priest, Isa Rashid, were walking along a roadway just south of the Old City of Jerusalem, when Meier happened to glance up and noticed a small opening in the ground amongst the rocks and shrubs. Curiosity made him reach into his backpack for his flashlight and he peered into the hole to notice that it continued inwards. They proceeded to dig away rocks and earth until the hole was large enough that they could crawl inside. It was an old tomb site, half filled in with soil. After further digging and exploring they noticed a bundle buried underneath a flat rock. It turned out to be the TJ in the form of rolls of written sheets, along with a few small artifacts. They were wrapped up together in animal skin, which was in turn encased in resin. There were four rolls, each of which contained many leaves or pages of Aramaic writing. They were old and fragile and each leaf was roughly 30 by 40 cm in size.

Rashid, who could read most of the old Aramaic due to his priestly education and Palestinian background, was concerned that the scripts were heretical. For example, its title involved Jmmanuel (i.e., Immanuel, spelled with a "J," making use of the "i" sound in place of the Aramaic/Hebrew letter *ayin*) rather than Jesus or Y'shua. Furthermore, its writer was noted as Judas Iscariot, the supposed betrayer of Christ. Thirdly, it mentioned that Adam's father had been Semjasa, the leader of the "celestial sons," who were El's or God's guardian angels, and who were "distant travelers." It immediately became apparent that if they ever wished this document to become public, its translation would have to proceed in secret. The scrolls further indicated that the Old Testament god had been an extraterrestrial leader, taking on the role of a "Father" in heaven, rather than the omnipotent God. So let us refer to him as El, as in Immanu-el. Rashid spent a few months reading through the TJ rolls to extract the highlights, which he reported to Meier. In August of 1963 they agreed that Rashid would translate the TJ into German and would retain custody of the Aramaic document, while sending his translations to Meier for him to disseminate. So Rashid started the long task of rendering a translation while Meier continued his travels.

The first set of translations up to chapter 36 of the TJ reached Meier in Switzerland some time around 1970, but Meier did not hear from Rashid himself until in a letter in September of 1974. This letter briefly explained the disturbing news that his translation project had become known to certain authorities, forcing him to flee from Jerusalem, together with his family.

Rashid found his way with the TJ rolls and further translations to a refugee camp in Lebanon. But his presence there became known to Israeli authorities forcing him to flee again, this time to Baghdad, where he posted the letter to Meier. He and his family, like the other refugees, had to flee so suddenly that Rashid had no time to retrieve the original Aramaic rolls or his further translations of them, and they were destroyed in the chaos from which they fled. In 1976 Meier learned that Rashid and his family were assassinated in Baghdad. Fortunately the German translations were quite substantial and various versions have been released from the original version of 1978. The latest edition was due out in 2005.

Meier insists that publications of non-German translations of the TJ include the side-by-side German edition, so that discrepancies or distortions in translation be less likely to creep in. The translation of the original Aramaic pages of the first roll reads as if it is the original writing of the ministry and teachings of Jesus. However, the messiah is referred to as Immanuel and not Jesus. The TJ resembles very closely the Gospel of Matthew in both wording, where the verses have close parallels, and in its order, although each contains many passages not contained by the other. James W. Deardorf is an esteemed author of a number of detailed books dealing with Jesus in India and other New Testament issues. He states that "Even a brief comparison of the TJ against the Gospel of Matthew discloses that one depends upon the other. The correspondence in order of events and sometimes in wording is too close to permit any other possibility." Deardorf has been analyzing the TJ since 1986 and has found several hundred reasons why the verses in Matthew were derived from the Talmud, and that it is virtually impossible for these writings to be the work of hoaxers. The Talmud speaks of a supreme deity called El who orchestrated all the activity surrounding humanity on Earth. Could this be the Enlil we read about in Sumerian texts, who was the supreme Anunnaki commander of planet Earth? Here are some excerpts from the Talmud to illustrate its close but shocking relationship to the Gospel of Matthew.

This is the book and Arcanum of Jmmanuel, who is called "the one with godly knowledge," who is a son of Joseph, grandson of Jacob, the distant descendant of David. David was a descendant of Abram [Abraham], whose genealogy traces back to Adam, the father of a lineage of terrestrial humans. Adam was begotten by Semjasa, the leader of the celestial sons who were the guardian angels of El, the great ruler of the travellers from afar.

TJ 1:1

I would dare to say that this follows closely my postulated theory that human-kind is a slave species created by ancient settlers on Earth, who seemed to be highly advanced and regarded as gods by us, up until recent times.

> Jacob begot Joseph. Joseph was the husband of Mary, the mother of Jmmanuel, who was impregnated by a distant descendant of the celestial son, Rasiel, who was the guardian angel of the secret.
>
> TJ 1:80–81

Rasiel was the guardian angel who appears to have been associated with a master plan to ensure that a highly evolved human like Jmmanuel was incarnated at the right time and right place. Rasiel is also mentioned in the Kabbalah and the book of Zohar as the angel who was the master of mysteries.

> When Joseph heard of Mary's secret impregnation by a descendant of the celestial sons from the lineage of Rasiel, behold, he was filled with wrath and thought of leaving Mary before he would be married to her before the people.
>
> TJ 1:82

> While Joseph was thinking in this manner, behold, a guardian angel, sent by Gabriel, the celestial son who had impregnated Mary, appeared and said: "Joseph, Mary is betrothed to you and you are to become her spouse; do not leave her, because the fruit of her womb is chosen for a great purpose. Marry her in all openness, so that you may be husband and wife before the people."
>
> TJ 1:83–84

> Behold, the impregnation of Mary occurred eleven thousand years after the procreation of Adam through the celestial son Semjasa, to fulfil the word of El, the ruler of those who travelled from afar, who conveyed these words through the prophet Isaiah.
>
> TJ 1:85

Here is a comparison between Matthew and Talmud Jmmanuel. See the last part that refers to "one with godly knowledge."

> Behold, a virgin shall conceive and bear a son, and his name shall be called Emmanuel (which means, God with us).
>
> MATTHEW 1:23

Behold, a virgin will be impregnated by a celestial son before she is married to a man before the people. They will name the fruit of her womb Jmmanuel, which translated means "the one with godly knowledge."

TJ 1:86–87

In the following verses the writer of Matthew omitted to mention the name of the prophet Micah, while the Talmud makes it clear who the actual prophet was who gave them the information.

Assembling all the chief priests and scribes of the people, he [Herod] inquired of them where the Christ was to be born. They told him, "In Bethlehem of Judea; for so it is written by the prophet: And you, O Bethlehem, in the land of Judah, are by no means least among the rulers of Judah; for from you shall come a ruler who will govern my people Israel."

MATTHEW 2:4–6

Herod Antipas called together all the chief priests and scribes from among the people and inquired of them where Jmmanuel had been born. And they replied: "In Bethlehem, in the Jewish land; for thus it was written by the prophet Micah: And you, Bethlehem, in the land of the Jews, are by no means the least among the cities in Judea, for from you shall come forth the king of wisdom, who will bring great knowledge to the people of Israel so that they may learn and serve Creation."

TJ 2:9–11

The description of a sound emanating from the star that hovered ahead of the Three Wise Men is a clear indication that there was some sinister activity surrounding this event, which can be explained with the help of advanced technology and machinery. Once again, the Matthew version does not include this particular section.

After they [the magi] had listened to Herod Antipas, they departed. And behold, the light with the long tail, which they had observed in the Orient, moved ahead of them with a high singing sound until it reached Bethlehem and stood directly over the stable where the infant was born.

TJ 2:14

John the Baptist preached of baptism in accordance with the old laws of El, according to which the way to knowledge was to be prepared. He preached that El's laws shall be followed because he is the sole ruler of this human lineage. He preached that above El, however, stands Creation, the source of the worlds, universes and all living creatures.

TJ 3:2–4

In the next comparison we have more evidence of some sort of intervention from a higher technological intelligence. Matthew is, however, less open about the true events. Were these the kind of events that were edited out of the New Testament by the Church councils?

> And when Jesus was baptised, he went up immediately from the water, and behold, the heavens were opened and he saw the Spirit of God descending like a dove, and a lighting on him; and lo, a voice from heaven, saying, "This is my beloved Son, with whom I am well pleased."
>
> MATTHEW 3:16–17

> When Jmmanuel had been baptized, he soon came out of the water of the Jordan, and behold, a metallic light came down from the sky and rushed over the Jordan. Consequently they all fell on their faces and pressed them into the sand while a voice from the metallic light spoke, "This is my beloved son with whom I am well pleased. He will be the king of truth, through which terrestrial humans shall rise as wise ones."
>
> TJ 3:30–32

And so the comparisons continue for dozens and dozens of verses. The obvious difference is that the TJ refers to the constant intervention of angels and other celestial beings, while the Gospel has a cleaner, more acceptable version of the events to suit the monotheistic community that was being nurtured by the early Church. Is it possible that whoever wrote the Talmud did so in an attempt to cut through the stranglehold and disinformation that was being imposed by the gods of Enlil on humanity? Someone who was well aware of the activity of the ancient gods who ruled the world? After all, these were the times of Roman mythology and everyone was very aware of the many gods and angels who ruled the roost.

While numerous scholars have found the book of Matthew to be full of inconsistencies, ambiguities, and interruptions in flow of thought, such inconsistencies are not nearly as obvious in the TJ. A growing number of scholars agree that Jmmanuel's teachings had to be altered or omitted to conform with the views of early Christianity. What this discovery does achieve is to confirm that Jesus or Jmmanuel did travel to India and back during the "lost" years of his life.

The gods who were orchestrating Jesus' life had much bigger plans for him. They wanted to make sure that this newly established prophet of theirs was recognized all over the populated world. In her book *He Walked the Americas,* L. Taylor Hansen reveals many breathtaking examples of how Jesus spread the gospel among the native North American tribes and the rest of the Americas, always symbolized by a T-cross. There is endless mention of a "White Prophet" with a beard, or "Healer," and many references of him arriving to teach them wisdom. These legends are still told by the fireside of a "saintly white teacher" who performed miracles with healing. They describe his eyes as grey-green like the ocean and his symbol has been woven into blankets, carved on canyon walls, put on pottery, and is even depicted in dances. His name has been given to mountains and rivers; and just as I suggest in this book that the Anunnaki gods taught humanity about civilization, agriculture, planting, and harvesting, so do the Native American tales speak of the Pale Prophet who came to teach them all these things. He gave them seeds to plant and taught them wisdom. And guess what his symbol was? A winged serpent. Is it possible that the winged serpent, whom we believe to be Ningishzidda or Enki, brought Jesus to the Americas on the instructions of Enlil?

He was called the "feathered serpent" or Eeseecotl among the Algonquins. They say that he always wore a long white toga and golden sandals. Every new town he arrived in would have a new garment waiting for him. They would keep the old ones, saying that to touch them would bring healing. During his stay he would train twelve disciples, with one appointed to be their leader, who would take his place when he left. He would say he had to "go about My Father's Business." This is a clear sign of extreme manipulation of humankind by the Anunnaki gods. Enlil was going to do everything in his power to squeeze Marduk out, denying him the pleasure of controlling the world. To do this, their manufactured messiah, Jesus, would have to be accepted by as many slave species as possible. And so they would ensure that this was going to happen even as far away as in the Americas. The Shawnee tribe speak of a message that was given to them by the Prophet. "Do not kill or injure your neighbour, for it is not he that you injure; you injure yourself. Do good to him, thus adding to his days of happiness even as you then add to your own. Do not wrong or hate your neighbour; for it is not he that you wrong: you wrong yourself. Rather love him, for the Great Spirit loves him, even as He loves you." This was the kind of message that humans were yearning for, for thousands of years under the oppressive regime of the Anunnaki gods. Enlil was providing them with a way out.

Michigan was the center of the Giant Cross of Waters and the Prophet was known to travel this trail. No tribe was too far, too small, too poor, or too violent. He would enter war situations, he would call all the chiefs together and divide the lands. He gave them seeds that they did not know about and showed them how to farm. He would teach them "His" principles and go to any length to ensure they remembered him above all possible future prophets. These tales are mirrored from tribe to tribe. But Jesus did not only raise people from the dead: in the Americas he revived even animals.

L. Taylor Hansen tells us how the Healer knelt down beside a dead deer whose fawn was standing nearby and started stroking the body. As his hand passed over the wounds, they healed up, leaving no marks. And soon the deer started breathing and rose. His disciples were upset saying that he was wasting his energy on animals. The Pale One said, "There cannot be too many good deeds. Such is the manner of compassion. A lost lamb is my Father's business, as important as saving a nation, if one need not choose between them. More precious in my Father's eyes is a good deed than the most exquisite jewel." We can clearly see how seriously Jesus took his mission here on Earth, before he realized that he was being set up by the Anunnaki gods. He told the people he was born across the ocean where all men had beards. Even in the American legends, he told them of his virgin birth and about the bright star that shone over the place of his birth. "The heavens opened up and winged beings sang chants of exquisite beauty."

During a dig by the University of Oklahoma at the Spiro Mound, they unearthed pottery showing winged beings singing and also a hand with the cross through the palm. The locals refer to him as "Chee-Zoos," the Dawn God. "The love they bear Him is beyond measurement, for well they know He watches over them, and that when their journey here is over, He will meet them in the Land of Shadows, for such was His sacred promise." Once again we hear about the promise of a life after death, which was commonly promoted by the gods among humans, to keep them faithful and loyal.

There are further tales of the "Great Mound Builders" by Decoodah, the last high priest of extinct Elks, which was translated and recorded by Walter Pidgeon around 1850. The legends described them as tribes that spoke the Algonquin language and they were the "Ancients" of the country. These legendary mounds marked the sites of ancient cities and are closely related to the mounds of the Maya of Mexico, drawing a distinct connection with the winged serpent that is referred to by both cultures. They also possessed a unique ancient type of writing that recorded history. The mounds were apparently covered by wood and painted as the Maya had done. The "Great White Robed Master" with his grey-green eyes and golden sandals also stayed among the mound builders. Stone pictographs of the prophet have been found causing much debate about his close resemblance to Jesus.

The Pawnee tribe talk of a prophet who visited them twice and taught them about "His Father," "The Mighty Holy of the Heavens."

The wrath of god was well experienced by the Native American tribes as well as those who lived in biblical lands. The Pawnee tribe angered god by being violent, so he appeared from the sky to intervene and cast his judgment on them. This extract from L. Taylor Hansen's *He Walked the Americas* sounds just like many passages from the Bible. "The eastern sky lit up with fire, growing ever brighter; everyone turned toward the brightened sky and stopped in their tracks . . . and suddenly there 'He' was among them! He asked them if this was how they kept His commandments, insulting the Father. 'I came to shield you from His anger, or lo, great wind would ignite the forest! And to ashes would be consigned the Pawnee Nation!'"

We know from the events at Sodom that these were not idle threats. God certainly had it in him to decimate a people out of anger. Humans were taught it was the wrath of god.

The Algonquin of the Eastern Seaboard say that they received their name for the Dawn Light from the Pale One. The Algonquin remember him well and the time of his arrival. The fleets coming down the river delivered him ceremoniously and he was always greeted with flowers. The Chippewa also remember him very well "the pale Great Master." He gave them medicine lodges with sacred symbols that were the signs and emblems from across the ocean. The Sioux tribe say that he gave them their rite of baptism and purification. The following excerpt, again from L. Taylor Hansen, is virtually identical to the way Jesus behaved in Palestine:

First to climb the mound was the Prophet. As over the horizon arose the first golden shafts of the Dawn Star, the Pale God spoke to the assembled nations. It is said that He always charmed His listeners, but now there was almost a breathless silence. Indeed it seemed the very trees were listening and also the assembled animals of the forest, so softly He spoke and so well did they hear Him, because of the silence that had settled.

The legends about the Pale Prophet go on and on among the North American Natives, but they continue further south into the land of the Toltecs. He went to the Empire of Tula, the capital of the peaceful Toltecs. He also went to the Wallapai tribe where he gathered the chiefs in a great counsel and redistributed their grain fields. He taught them advanced farming techniques with melons, squashes, pumpkins, mescal, and beans; he gave them many other plants that have been lost through the ages. This is an excerpt that was spoken by Marksman, an old Chippewa warrior at a council of native American tribes:

> It is well tonight that we speak of the Pale God, and fitting as well that we council with others, greeting our enemies as brothers, for such would have been the wish of the Prophet.

The last to speak at the council was a man from the Cheyenne and this is what he said: "Like our brothers we remember the Fair God who foretold the coming of the White Man. Yet so long ago was He living that like the Dacotah, our memories are garbled."

Is it possible that Jesus travelled the world with his message? Is it possible that he was aided in doing so by the Winged Feathered Serpent who appears in most global mythologies? The evidence is there for all to see. After all, even Jesus himself spoke of his sheep in distant lands.

> I have other sheep that are not of this sheep pen. I must bring them also. They too will listen to my voice, and there shall be one flock and one shepherd.

> John 10:16

16

THE STORY OF HUMANKIND

HISTORIANS AND ARCHAEOLOGISTS play a pivotal role in the way we perceive our world. They present us with a host of facts that shape our current belief structures, the way we imagine the World Wars, the Roman emperors, or the landing on the moon; historians become the custodians and the story tellers of what happened in the past. They wallow in the events surrounding the building of the pyramids and even describe the way the dinosaurs looked and behaved. In essence, anything that happened before our own time of reference is described to us by experts who study those past events. Their versions of those ancient and prehistoric images flood our minds and in most cases, they are chiseled into our subconscious as a direct consequence of how the past has been presented to us by the experts. If they get it wrong, we all get it wrong, and we never really know about it or question it. We expect the experts to tell us the whole truth and nothing but the truth. It is unfortunate that very few people are ever told about the amount of speculation that goes on in these revered professions. All you have to do is take a history book from fifty years ago and compare it to the way in which those historic events are presented in our present time. You will be fascinated to see how much they differ. The point is that history, as much as archaeology, is a living science and as we discover more, our objective views of specific events change according to the importance of our discoveries. Scientists and leaders are equally guilty of shaping people's ideas of things around them. In most cases, scientific discoveries are based on interim results based on hypotheses, theories, speculation, and faith in the eventual outcome, as much as theologians carry their blind faith toward their god. In the Dark Ages people really believed that the world was flat. They feared for the lives of the brave explorers as they set off into the great unknown, across the ocean, surely to be devoured by the monsters that dwelled at the bottom of the edge of the world. There are publications from our human past that speak of such things, and yet today it would be laughable to reintroduce such theories.

One hundred years ago, people were told by leading scientists that man would never be able to fly. In 1903, when the Wright brothers were flying their first plane at Kitty Hawk, the leading physicist of the time refused to attend a demonstration as he proclaimed that "man will never fly a heavier than air machine." Such utterances had a great impact on the point of view of many ordinary people who took their lead from the so-called experts of their times. In this instance it prompted the news editor of the local paper to write an article that outlined the scientific facts as presented by the eminent authority, which instantly turned the adventurers' attempts into a questionable pastime. It must have affected the Wright brothers' development and possibly retarded their progress for all that we know. Even today, in times when anything should be deemed possible, some scientists are still guilty of killing new ideas based on their personal perspectives. Historians have been known to hide facts or new discoveries, and so have archaeologists, for all kinds of personal reasons. Governments have kept secrets from their people for as long as humankind has been on Earth, citing all kinds of silly reasons, of which the issue of national security is used as a common excuse. Churches and other religious organizations have kept secrets from their followers for reasons only they seem to be able to justify. Even sports teams and their managers keep secrets from their fans in today's highly competitive sports industries. There is much to be said for the existence of a myriad of secret societies and yet with all their supposed power and influence, the world is perched on the verge of self-destruction. When we look at some of the great achievements of the past few thousand years, since we emerged as a civilized species from the caves and embarked on a path of rapid evolution, we constantly stumble over the Dark Ages when all human knowledge seems to have disappeared. We slowly reemerged from those times like a new species, rediscovering knowledge, but somehow this knowledge has been around with our ancestors for thousands of years. But once again, historians and archaeologists fall prey to their own insecurities. If they don't understand something, or if it does not fit into their frame of reference, it seems to get classified as fiction, esoteric, New Age, or mythological. These kind of actions have done humankind a great deal of damage when it comes to solving the problems of our origins. There are extremely smart people who have devoted large parts of their lives to unraveling the murky waters of our ancient past, but their credibility is continuously eroded by shortsighted "experts" with a different personal agenda. These agendas can be so incredibly subtle that we don't even realize we are being manipulated into believing something that is not really so.

I have two personal favorites that have tickled my fancy for many years: UFOs and the pyramids. I have never seen a UFO or been abducted, or "astral traveled" or had weird extrasensory interactions with "aliens," but I try to keep a rational perspective on the whole matter. Let's put all the sightings and so-called abductions into one giant pot for one minute and imagine that all of them are wrong. They all saw something else, they all experienced something impossible, or they all just had a really vivid dream; all the hordes of people who have made these claims over centuries were all wrong . . . all except one. The one UFO that was not imaginary, but was real, puts a whole new perspective on the matter and suddenly makes it all very real. In the field of statistics, it is virtually impossible for every single person to have been wrong or have simply imagined things. The statistical probability of such a coincidence is many millions to one. Even then, there is still the "one." And that "one" can change our world dramatically if we just embrace this new reality and learn more about it. A close friend of mine made an interesting remark saying that having an open mind is like being pregnant. Either you are, or you are not.

My other favorite is the story of the pyramids. I remember how impressed I was as a child when I saw the detailed pictures of slaves dragging giant monoliths, one by one, to build the three greatest structures in the world, even by today's standards. The descriptions of exactly how they went about getting the rock, shaping it, building the ramps, putting them on sleighs and dragging them into position. All those slaves or families who made a living out of building pyramids were responsible for dragging 1.6 million giant rocks, up steep ramps, each weighing between 1.5 and 3.5 metric tons, carefully creating the passages and inner chambers, all fitting so tightly that you cannot squeeze a blade of grass between them. To top it all, they covered these incredible structures with perfectly smoothed white limestone averaging 15 tons each, which had even greater levels of accuracy in the joints. This would have taken thousands of workers at least 50 years to complete if they managed to fit 100 stones per day. And all of this, so that one pharaoh could be buried in it? This impressed me immensely when I was ten years old, but when I started to read a bit more about these mystical structures, I realized there was much more to them than meets the eye, and that we were not so sure about who actually built the Great Pyramid, but we think it was King Khufu. From that day on I decided never to believe anything written by historians again, but rather inform myself about the situation and formulate my own informed opinion. I would much rather have our children at school be taught that we do not know who built the pyramids, allowing their minds to absorb the reality and formulate their own theories as they grow and search for clues on their own. We have to stop making absolute statements about the past that are built on fragments of speculative knowledge by "experts" with personal issues. The damage that has been caused over millennia will take much undoing to allow humans to free their minds, and allow themselves to think for themselves with the real knowledge that has been kept from them by authorities, and especially the religious leaders, most of whom have been brainwashed to a large extent by their own lack of knowledge. Or could it be that they have knowledge, and they do not want to share with us? The religious and political fear in which most humans live is immense and will take centuries to reverse. But we have to start somewhere. The many writers who have challenged the conventional popular belief systems are growing in numbers and their readers are discovering new horizons of human knowledge in greater numbers every day. As in all of history, only time will help shine the light on the real facts surrounding our human origins.

I embark on this somewhat righteous bashing of the sciences for reasons of my own personal agenda. I developed an urge to share the information that I have absorbed over a 20-year period with those in search of something light and juicy to read. Not too scientific, but meaty enough to stir the pot. I hope it will motivate others to do their own scratching and discover new evidence that has been buried beneath millennia of disinformation. It seems that now is the time when more and more people are looking for new answers to the mystery of our origins. They are not satisfied with the diluted answers and the reasons and the religious rhetoric they've been fed. They want to know what else is out there of which they have been deprived. So when we talk about events that truly challenge our personal beliefs, and when we propose new theories that shake the foundation of popular establishments, we must rise above those insecurities and remind ourselves that things are not always what they seem. The popular example of two people looking at an object from two opposite sides comes to mind. What the one sees is totally different from what the other one sees. I need you to keep this in mind as we embark on the last stretch of the road to discovering our human origins.

This chapter will take us on an epic journey of new discovery so fantastic that our natural instinct would be to block it out. Since the 1970s, when more scholars became attracted to the Sumerian translations of clay tablets polluting the basements of many museums of the world, a whole new wave of information started to emerge. Suddenly we were exposed to a whole new civilization that preceded all others, which spoke a different language and made references to times before their own from where all their knowledge was derived. Once again, many conservative scholars have shown great restraint and the majority of books written about those new finds have placed them safely under mythology or fiction. There has, however, been a growing number of authors who have identified that there is much more to those stories from the ancient past than meets the eye. Erich von Daniken truly popularized the whole concept of extraterrestrial activity on Earth in prehistoric times already in the 1960s with his *Chariots of the Gods,* allowing mankind to really start thinking about the many unexplained phenomena of our past. He was followed by many other esteemed investigative writers, scholars, and authors who took his lead to greater heights. But it was Zecharia Sitchin who truly pushed the newly deciphered Sumerian cuneiform text to the greatest heights in his nine books dealing mainly with the content of the Sumerian tablets and the eroded truth behind them. He has become one of the leading translators of the Sumerian language and he has presented evidence so vivid and compelling that it is truly hard to contest. Much of this last chapter and the story of humanity from the beginning of our time on Earth until about 2000 BC, comes from the many translated Sumerian tablets and some other tablets that have emerged since the '70s. It comes from linking the stories of scattered ancient cultures to each other and recognizing the common denominators that all lead to one simple conclusion. A conclusion that is exposed to us over and over again, in thousands of translated clay tablets, stone carvings, seals, stelae, and other scriptures from many cultures, clearly shining a light on who we really are, where we come from, and why we are here. This is after all, the one question that has crossed most humans' minds. These scriptures all have one thing in common, and that is their references to the Sumerian gods who came from distant lands and gave the early humans all their knowledge. The story has been captured dramatically in Sitchin's *The Lost Book of Enki,* which is a compilation of cuneiform translations of Sumerian tablets over a period of some thirty years. On many occasions, tablets found in different parts of Mesopotamia refer to the same events, giving us plenty of proof of their validity. It is now time to realize that we have gone way beyond speculation. We have accumulated a critical mass of evidence to start silencing the venomous critics and narrow-minded disciples of mediocrity.

The time has come to accept at face value that we are not the pinnacle of civilization, that we are only now emerging from the cradle of knowledge, and that we need to face the facts of our genetically created origins. The most incredible part of it all is that God had nothing to with it, but the many gods of our distant past were the true masterminds and manipulators of our misery here on Earth. We must also come to terms with the fact that there are no "aliens" involved in this great new truth we must face. WE ARE THE ALIENS. We were created as a primitive worker by astronauts from another planet and modeled in their image some 443,000 years ago, to perform a necessary task on their new planet. We have much of their DNA in our bodies, because they used it to create us, and we look pretty much the way they looked. Part of the terrible truth that we have to come to terms with is that humans are really an accidental by-product of an ancient colonization of Earth by the Anunnaki from Nibiru. Humans came into existence for one reason only: to be the slave laborers in gold mines, and nothing more. The importance attached to our existence is one that we have created in our own minds over millennia of ignorance and evolution, which were primarily guided by the oppressive control of our creators. From the early beginnings humans saw their makers as "gods," for obvious reasons, and not merely as more advanced beings. But as the dramatic events unfolded on this newly settled planet, humans were slowly given more tasks to perform, edging their way into a permanent master-slave relationship with their maker. But the Anunnaki had their own problems to deal with on their new planet, and they did not really spend too much time worrying about the well-being of the new primitive worker. Our primary task was to work the gold mines and relieve the gods of all the hard labor. These first settlers on Earth had a crucial task to perform for their leaders on their own planet, just like our astronauts had on the many moon landings and trips to the International Space Station, Alpha. They had their own problems and differences and we humans were not really a priority to them. Humans were, however, an important tool to help get the gold from the ground, but we certainly did not occupy much of the Anunnaki's pastime. All of this will be revealed in great detail using translations from ancient tablets.

In the chapters leading up to this point, we have looked at our DNA and its shortcomings, its absolute control over our physical and mental capabilities; we studied the human cell and questioned the fact that such a perfect organism eventually dies while it should realistically exist forever; we have explored the issue of slavery and our obsession with gold from the earliest times of humankind; we've traveled back in time to compare the evolutionary paths of some remotely related species to us; and we have even reintroduced the term *panspermia* into the vocabulary of readers, outlining the facts that life exists everywhere in the universe. Now that we have set the scene and hopefully provided enough food for thought to start questioning the anomalies of our existence, let us begin at the beginning. From the very first time when the first group of astronauts from another planet arrived on Earth and discovered that there was gold . . . the lifesaving metal that they were looking for in the solar system.

The Sumerian tablets refer to it as the "Olden Times" when the Anunnaki first came to Earth, and the "Prior Times" when they were on Nibiru. Sitchin translates:

> In the Olden Times the gods came to Earth and created the Earthlings. In the Prior Times, none of the gods was on the Earth, nor were the Earthlings yet fashioned. In the Prior Times, the abode of the gods was on their own planet; Nibiru is its name.

The tablets refer to the elliptical orbit of Nibiru as being "1 Shar," which equals 3,600 Earth years; it is also one of the reasons we have 360 degrees in our circles. Nibiru comes in close to the sun, crossing the paths of most planets up to Mars and the asteroid belt, and then it shoots out into deep space just like many of the long-term comets that we get to see every few thousand years. So we should not be surprised that astronomers could not find it in the solar system because at its apogee (furthest point) it is possibly 3–5 times as far as Pluto is from the sun. Nibiru's citizens were advanced in many ways, and yet they seem to be on a different level from our current state of development. I would venture to say that our human rights legislation has surpassed their approach to the subject all those thousands of years ago. Nibiru was under the rule of a king and we will see how it was all imposed on us, the new earthling species, in future years. But they had cracked the genetic code and had a clear understanding of how DNA could be manipulated. Their constant reference to immortality makes it obvious that they had also conquered the genetic defect which causes cell death and humans to die. Their planet was not free of conflict and those characteristics arrived with them on the new planet called Earth. There are many references about the various periods of their stay, and that is why we can calculate when the Anunnaki actually arrived on Earth. In *The Lost Book of Enki* it clearly states that the flood came in the "120th Shar."

> In the one hundred and twentieth Shar was the Deluge awaited. In the tenth Shar in the life age of Ziusudra was the Deluge forthcoming.

That would place the flood 432,000 years after their arrival. Scholars generally agree that the Great Flood occurred around 11000 BC, which would place the arrival of the Anunnaki on Earth some 443,000 years ago. It is important to keep track of the time references because they play a crucial role in supporting many of the activities and developments of human origins and the creation of the first humans, Adam and Eve, some 200,000 years ago. There was, however, a very good reason why the ancient astronauts arrived here; it was not just some random decision of a bunch of distant astronauts. After what is described as a fierce battle on Nibiru between an appointed king and a successor by birth, a truce was called.

> The nation of the north against the nation of the south took up arms . . . A war long and fierce engulfed the planet . . . there was death and destruction both north and south . . . for many circuits desolation reigned the land; all life was diminished.

A time of unification, rebuilding, and peace followed, where great cities and developments engulfed the planet of Nibiru. There is a vivid description of Nibiru's atmosphere, explaining how the volcanoes constantly feed the thick atmosphere that protects them against the sun when at its closest point "hot period it shields Nibiru from the Sun's scorching rays," and "in the cold period the inner heat of Nibiru it keeps about the planet like a warm coat." We must remember that the planet moves away far from the sun for longer periods than when it is closer to the sun, therefore, it needs a much denser protective layer to sustain a temperate climate for life. Not much different from our own atmosphere but seemingly much thicker and more active. The planet is described as a "radiant" planet with a "reddish hue." "A red planet, reddish in radiance; around the sun an elongated circuit Nibiru makes." While some planets absorb heat and energy, others radiate heat. Nibiru is such a planet. That is why it can seemingly survive the long periods in deep space, before returning closer to the sun every 3,000 years or so. It may take Nibiru as long as 600 years to orbit the sun in close proximity, as it makes its way out into deep space just like a comet.

Nibiru, however, was a troubled planet; its atmosphere was disturbed by some cosmic force, which began to have a devastating effect on the lands, animals, and people. The hardship hit everyone and started threatening the peace. The harsh rays of the sun were destroying crops and arable land, making large parts uninhabitable. Nothing new to us on Earth in the twenty-first century? "In the atmosphere a breaching has occurred . . . Nibiru's air has thinner been made, the protective shield has been diminished."

They tried all kinds of remedies to cure the growing gaping hole in their atmosphere with little success. "In the land strife was abundant, food and water were not . . . in the land unity was gone; accusations were abundant." We can also relate to the accusations and lack of unity in our own time, when we compare the way in which the world is disagreeing on the many issues threatening the environment, greenhouse effect, and ozone depletion. Once again we stare bluntly at the hereditary characteristics that were passed down to us by the Anunnaki. "Rains were withheld, winds blew harder; springs from the depths did not arise."

They called a council meeting and under the advice of some bright scientists, reached a decision to use gold in a fine powder form to be dispersed into the atmosphere and patch up the hole. "To use a metal, gold was its name. On Nibiru it was rare; within the Hammered Bracelet it was abundant."

It's important to note that they called the asteroid belt outside of Mars, the "Hammered Bracelet." It was known to them from the descriptions in the *Enuma Elish* or the Epic of Creation, that there was gold embedded in the many fragments of the asteroid belt. But would they be able to retrieve it? I trust that in years to come we will rediscover the rich gold deposits on the asteroid belt, which the Anunnaki knew about 500,000 years ago.

"It was the only substance that to the finest powder could be ground; lofted high to heaven, suspended it could remain." So while they sent out spaceships to obtain the gold, they also tried to activate the dormant volcanoes to start "belching" again. "With missiles the volcanoes to attack, their dormancy to bestir, their belching to increase." But neither of these attempts worked while the planet was slowly slipping into an environmental disaster. The king of the time was weak with little skill to make weighty decisions. Unhappiness and opposition grew against him until he was overthrown by Alalu, who took the throne. It was then discovered that Alalu was actually the successor by law, because he was the son of the prior king and his concubine half-sister. This is incidentally where the Biblical succession laws were also derived. The child of a man and his half-sister was first in line as successor, not the child of a man and his unrelated bride. We will see how the Anunnaki applied this rule on Earth and passed it onto the Hebrews, Egyptians, and other civilizations. But before Alalu's reign could be ordained, a young prince by the name of Anu presented himself, claiming that he was the direct descendent of the great king An. They studied his ancestry and came to the conclusion that he was a pure descendent of An, and, therefore, by their laws of seed and succession Anu should be king. After some more deliberation, it was finally decided that Alalu would remain king and Anu would be his "cupbearer," in the interest of peace and stability. This was also a very early example of a coalition parliament.

"Let us live in peace, together Nibiru to abundance return. Let me keep the throne, let you keep the succession," said Alalu to Anu, and "in this manner Alalu on the throne remained seated."

One of his first tasks was to find gold in the Hammered Bracelet, so he dispatched "celestial boats to seek the gold," but space can be a cruel place, and the mission was a huge disaster. All the spaceships that were dispatched on a discovery mission were destroyed by the asteroids. "By the Hammered Bracelet the boats were crushed . . ." After nine Shars on the throne and very little progress in the relief of the planet, Alalu was challenged by Anu. As advanced as the Nibiruans may have been in technology, they certainly had some interesting customs. The ritual was that the two opponents had to meet each other in hand-to-hand combat, all naked. That is the way it was written some 4,500 years ago, and also where the Greeks obtained some of their cultural influences.

"In the ninth Shar Anu gave battle to Alalu. To hand-to-hand combat, with bodies naked, Alalu he challenged . . . They grappled with each other in the public square . . ." As fate had it, Anu defeated Alalu and replaced him on the throne of Nibiru. He had great plans on how to save the planet's atmosphere from further destruction. Alalu was obviously distraught by the events so he planned a dramatic act to somehow show his supremacy over Anu. He "stole" one of the advanced spaceships and flew out toward the Hammered Bracelet. "To the place of celestial chariots he hurriedly went . . . into a missile throwing chariot Alalu climbed . . . the commander's seat he occupied. . . That-which-shows-the-way he lit up . . . the fire stones he stirred up; their hum like music was . . . Unbeknown to others, in the celestial boat Alalu from Nibiru escaped."

His escape was like a final attempt to show that he was smarter, or worthy of getting some sort of hold over the people of Nibiru, and by some strange twist of fortune, he achieved just that. He set his course for Earth, expecting to find gold there. But how would he have known that Earth had an abundance of gold? Once more we find amazingly sobering information in many of the tablets, with special reference to the *Enuma Elish* or *Epic of Creation*, well-known to historians. It is described in great detail as a "celestial battle" between gods. In reality it was an observation from the planet Nibiru of how a great celestial collision between planets and moons occurred in the past. This could have only been witnessed on one of Nibiru's close encounters when crossing the paths of other planets while rounding the sun. For the sake of brevity, I will keep this part of the story short, but you can get a detailed outline in the *Epic of Creation*.

This is a story that was written and captured in great detail on clay tablets. The observations are such that it could only have happened by observing the events from the planet Nibiru, which was at the center of the collisions, but did not actually collide with anything. Many millions of years ago, there was Mercury, Venus, Earth, Mars, Tiamat, Jupiter, Saturn, Neptune, Uranus, Pluto,

Fig. 16.1. Planet of the crossing. The planet Nibiru is often represented by these two crosses. One (left) telling us that it was a planet of the crossing that crossed the orbits of other planets. The other symbol (right) shows that Nibiru was also a radiant planet radiating its own heat.

and Nibiru, which came into contact with the other planets every 3,600 years. That is why the Sumerians called it the "planet of the crossing," as it crossed the paths of most of the other planets. Tiamat was a big planet, several times the size of Earth, orbiting where the asteroid belt is today. On one of her fateful orbits, Nibiru came very close to Tiamat, so close that their moons actually engaged in several dramatic cosmic collisions. The book describes these very dramatically, so that it almost reads like a Greek tragedy, and for those reasons it has been misinterpreted by many historians and astronomers. A large body of scholars now realize that it actually describes the cosmic collisions between Tiamat and her eleven moons, with Nibiru. From the transcripts we learn that Nibiru had seven moons, which "attacked" the helpless Tiamat, ripping into her belly, shattering her body, and splitting her in two: "Into two parts he split her, her chest from her lower parts he separated."

The outcome of this *Epic* was that as the moons pounded the planet, the observers could actually see the many compounds she was hiding. One of the most abundant metals present was gold. "Her inner channels he cut apart her golden veins he beheld with wonder." These were the collisions on the way toward the sun, and it continued as Nibiru returned on its way back. As one of the big moons, which the tablets call "North Wind," smashed into Tiamat, it dislodged the top half of the planet, which went flying into space toward the sun. Kingu, which was one of Tiamat's moons, followed the giant piece of the planet because of its momentum, before the large piece settled in its own orbit beyond Mars, capturing the smaller Kingu for ever as its moon. This is the price Kingu had to pay for its destructive power, the tablets tell us. "Nibiru's Wind upon Tiamat then hovered, sweeping upon her gushing waters . . . In a brilliance was Tiamat's upper part to a region unknown carried. With her the bound Kingu was also exiled, of the severed part a companion to be."

The rest of the planet Tiamat was destroyed and smashed into pieces that became known as the asteroid belt—or Hammered Bracelet, by the Sumerians. "With his mace the hinder part he smashed to bits and pieces, then strung them together as a band to form a Hammered Bracelet."

The other large piece and its new oversized moon, which were now in collective orbit around the sun, became known as the Earth and its moon. The Anunnaki, through the Sumerian tablets, continued to refer to the moon as Kingu for ever. During these collisions, there was a lot of transfer of material and "seeds of life" between all the bodies, which explains why Earth inherited much of the same life forms as Nibiru. It also became visible that the new planet Earth was rich in gold, as were the fragments of the asteroid belt. Furthermore, it answers the puzzling question of why the Earth's moon is so large, and why the Anunnaki knew about the gold on Earth. As time went by, Earth stabilized through gravitational and centrifugal forces, allowing life to develop and flourish. By the time the crisis on Nibiru started affecting the planet, life was well evolved on Earth, but more importantly, the Nibiruans knew that Earth was rich in gold. This is why Alalu set his course for the planet behind the Hammered Bracelet. They had never managed to travel through the asteroid belt before, and from the tablets we gather that it was a very dangerous affair. As was described earlier, none of the spaceships that were sent to find gold there returned. Alalu knew that if he found the precious metal on Earth, he could almost hold Nibiru to ransom and make a number of demands. He would be seen as the savior of his home planet. Alalu's journey is described so vividly that even 5,000 years later, one can visualize the imagery described in the clay tablets. I should remind you that Sumerian tablets often refer to acquiring their knowledge and information from other sources from the Prior Times many thousands of years before the tablets were actually inscribed. We do not know whether the stories were transferred orally or if they were captured in some other way, but the amount of information and detail is too complex to have been a mere oral tradition.

Riding like an eagle, Alalu the heavens scanned; below, Nibiru was a ball in a voidness hanging . . . He looked again, Nibiru's great ball turned into a small fruit . . . The next time he looked, in the wide dark see Nibiru disappeared.

And so he traveled rapidly toward Earth. It describes his saddened heart, not knowing what to expect, and if he was going to make it alive. It describes his

Fig. 16.2. Mars and Earth from space. The polar ice cap is clearly visible on Mars (left) showing that the planet contains water even today. The swirling clouds and deep blue color of the oceans makes Earth (right) a very attractive planet for a space traveler.

flight past all the planets as he approached and passed them from the outside in, marveling at their spectacle. It describes how he travelled past Saturn or "Anshar," "the foremost prince of the heavens" with its "bright rings of dazzling colour (Saturn)." Then Alalu traveled toward the giant "Kishar," or Jupiter, with its "swirling storms obscured its face, coloured spots they moved about" describing the giant red spot on Jupiter.

It is incredible to witness these perfect descriptions in texts that are as much as 5,800 years old, and included Pluto, Neptune, Uranus, yet our "modern" civilization only rediscovered these outermost three planets in the past 200 years. But then suddenly Alalu was faced by the threatening asteroid belt. "The Hammered Bracelet ahead was reigning, to demolish it was awaiting . . . Of rock and boulders was it together hammered." As he approached it, he recalled how the asteroids "Nibiru's probing chariots like preying lions they devoured." But somehow Alalu made it through the belt by using "death-dealing missiles" to blast a way through the belt. It would become a method of getting through the belt for others who would come after him. "Like a spell the Hammered Bracelet a doorway to the king it opened," and so Alalu was on his way past the "red-brown planet" of Mars before the "snow-hued Earth appeared, the seventh in the celestial count." He describes the three regions of the Earth, white at the top and bottom, and blue and brown in the middle. The planet had a thinner atmosphere than Nibiru and a lesser gravity; "weaker than Nibiru was its attracting net." He used some sort of scanning device to search for signs of gold as he was approaching from a distance. "The beam that penetrates downwards he directed, Earth's innards to detect." And there it was . . . the precious metal that was so desperately needed to save Nibiru's disturbed atmosphere. "Gold, much gold, the beam has indicated." Alalu proceeded to land rather ruggedly but "then he opened his eyes and knew he was among the living. At the planet of gold he victoriously arrived."

After stepping out with his "Eagle's Helmet," he was amazed to find that the air was good to breathe, and the protecting "Fish's suit" and helmet were not necessary. It may sound like a great adventure when told in this romanticized fashion, but here was a brave individual alone on a new planet. That would scare the bravest of adventurers into thinking again. "No sound there was . . . Alone on an alien planet he stood . . ."

Alalu set himself up in the spaceship to be able to survive the elements. Over the next few days he explored the planet, but not without protection. "He picked up the carried weapon, he picked up the handy Sampler." He describes the short days, the sweet smell of the trees, orchards of fruits, the marshes of green water, the dark-hued soil, and his search for drinking water. The salt water was not drinkable and filled with fish, but finally he found fresh water in a "silent pond," where he encountered a snake for the first time. He did not know what the creature was, and it must have been the first creature he encountered on Earth, which motivated the Anunnaki to use the symbol of a snake in so many applications in years to come. He did not waste any time before searching for gold with his "tester." He found an abundance of gold in the waters of the ocean and in the banks of the rivers. He urgently sent a message to Nibiru knowing that he had found the solution to its problems. "The Speaker-of Words he stirred up . . . Then to Nibiru words he uttered . . . On another world I am, the gold of salvation I have found; The fate of Nibiru is in my hands."

Anu and the residents of Nibiru were astounded to hear that Alalu was alive, and especially intrigued by his claims about the gold. They were reminded by the oldest of their wise men that Alalu had been taught about Tiamat with her precious abundance of water and gold. It was old news to him. "Of the watery monster Tiamat and her golden veins he knowledge acquired; if indeed beyond the Hammered Bracelet he had journeyed, on Earth, the seventh planet is his asylum."

It caused lots of excitement and spurred them into action. This was the point at which the real decisions were taken to send a full expedition to Earth to verify the claims of gold and establish a base. "If Tiamat's gold he indeed had found, proof of that is needed; is it for protecting our atmosphere sufficient?"

The Nibiruans had an incredible ability to turn adversity into stability, a notable trait that we are still trying to master. But the DNA that we inherited from the Anunnaki will hopefully allow us to achieve this state of mind. There are, however, encouraging signs of peacemaking that we as humans seem to be displaying in great abundance in the twentieth and twenty-first centuries AD. The bloodless revolution in South Africa and its 180-degree turnaround from oppression to democracy is one such example, and the "Orange" revolution in the Ukraine is another. On many occasions, as we will see, the Nibiruans diffused conflict situations by simple decisions. It was, however, the children of the Anunnaki who would be born on Earth in later years who did not possess the same characteristics of tolerance and forgiveness as their parents did. It was ultimately their antagonism and greed that caused the constant conflict between the gods, and rubbed off on the slave species who began to emulate their master gods.

Alalu transmitted the proof of the gold find to Nibiru through a well-described technological maneuver. "Of the Tester its crystal innards he removed, from the Sampler its crystal heart he took out. Into the Speaker he the crystals inserted, all the findings to transmit." Everyone on Nibiru was astounded by the proof of gold, and started planning the mission to Earth. Ea (Enki) was King Anu's firstborn, while Enlil was the second son, but by way of seed and succession, Enlil held higher rank because he was the son of Anu and his half-sister. After some serious deliberation, it was decided that Ea and not Enlil would lead the first expedition to Earth because he was the better scientist. They did a lot of research and preparation before they sent the ship off. They planned the course: "a tablet of destinies for the mission he was fashioning."

There are several references to the fact that they used water as a source of propulsion. Is it possible that they used the hydrogen in water way back then, in the same way we are starting to use it in the twenty-first century? "If water is the force, where could it be replenished? Where on the chariot will it be stored, how the force will be converted?" They assembled fifty "heroes" to embark on the mission, and they prepared the largest chariot for the journey, fitting it out with all the necessary tools. The day of Ea's departure was very similar to the kind of farewell one sees at the NASA launches; many people gathered to see the launch. Ea was the last to embark, but not before King Anu blessed him and bade him farewell. "Enlil with his half brother locked arms. Be blessed, be successful, to him he said." This was a time when the brothers were friendly and very little animosity existed between them. This would, however, change over the years to come as they took control of Earth and began to disagree an various issues. What I find incredibly sobering is the way in which the Anunnaki's behavior resembled those of humans today. It feels that we have a lot more in common with them in the twenty-first century than humans would have had at any time in the past. It is mainly because our levels of competence, our scientific discoveries and medical exploits are almost parallel to what they engaged in all those thousands of years ago. We are struggling to save our planet from environmental disaster; we are exploring the other planets in our solar system; and we have almost mastered the science of genetic engineering. We have, however, moved on beyond kingships and monarchy—only to be replaced by a greed-based capitalist system that does not really promote equality and stability. The greed gene, which I have mentioned on numerous occasions, is clearly visible in our social structures. I wonder how the Nibiruans handled this issue of greed and social interaction? Are there more lessons we should be learning from them?

The trip to Earth was not as pleasant as one would have wished, but the descriptions of the planets are equally astounding while they were venturing through the hazardous asteroid belt. This was obviously a huge hurdle to cross, and only one person had done it successfully before. You can sense from the translations that they were certainly not at ease with the prospect of crossing the belt: "Beyond the fifth planet the Hammered Bracelet was lurking." It took some doing and a concerted group effort to clear a path for the ship to pass through the rocks in the belt. What is even more surprising is the description of how they used water to disperse the rocks. They even describe how the boulders were turning as they travel through space, a phenomenon that we only discovered in recent times. "Toward the host of turning boulders the chariot was rushing . . . the word by Ea was given, with the force of a thousand heroes the stream of water was thrust." This was an extremely inventive technique, pointing to the true genius of Ea the scientist. If he had used explosive weapons to blast his way through, there would have been a new threat of fragments hitting the spaceship. By using the water thrusters in a controlled succession, over and over again, they managed to clear a path in the belt for the ship to pass unhindered. This sounds like science fiction and yet it comes from clay tablets thousands of years old. If that does not make you think, nothing will. "And then at last the path was clear, unharmed the chariot could continue."

All the "path-clearing action" depleted their water supply and they were in trouble. On their approach to the sixth planet—which they called Lahmu, and which we call Mars—they saw the planet reflect the Sun's rays. They realized that there was water on Mars and proceeded to land on it to replenish their supplies. It is notable that they recorded that gravity on Mars was not as strong as it would be on Earth later—another fact that the ancient Sumerians could not have known. At this point in time, Mars still had an atmosphere and they describe the sight from space: "A sight to behold was Lahmu . . . many hued it was, snow white was its cap, snow white were its sandals . . . There is water on Lahmu, Ea was saying . . . The planet's net is not great, its pull is to handle easy."

They landed with ease on Mars for a short pit stop, on the shores of a lake, and while they were taking in water, Ea made all kinds of observations, recording them in his book of knowledge. The water was good for drinking but the air was insufficient for breathing, which means they needed their "Eagle's helmets" to breathe.

Fig. 16.3. Evidence of water erosion on Mars. Just one of thousands of examples showing that Mars had an abundance of flowing water in the past.

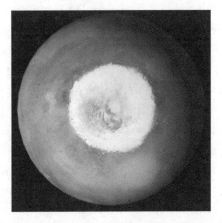

Fig. 16.4. A clear photograph of the southern polar cap showing an abundance of water in a frozen form. The Sumerians already knew 5,000 years ago that Mars had water. How so?

Soon they departed heading toward their destination, Earth. The manner in which their flights are described suggests that they must have traveled at very high speeds. It certainly seems that it did not take them much longer than a few days or weeks to cover the long distance from Nibiru, and only a hop and a skip to reach Earth from Mars. We can do a simple calculation to confirm this line of thinking. Most cars today can easily accelerate at 10 km/h every second. If our rocket was to accelerate at 10 km/h every second, it would reach 36,000 km/h at the end of the first hour. In ten hours it would reach 360,000 km/h and after 60 hours of such constant acceleration, we would be travelling at 2.16 million km/h. Mars is only 78 million km away from us, which means that at our maximum speed we would take approximately (78/2.16) + 60 hours = 36 + 60 hours = 96 hours to reach Mars, which is exactly 4 days. I excluded the distance covered by the spaceship during the time of acceleration, but this should be negated by the time and distance covered by the deceleration on approaching the planet.

There are probably some oversights according to professional scientific circles, but even if I missed the mark by 50% it would still only take us 8 days to reach Mars at those speeds. So what is stopping us from doing this? I would hazard a guess to say that only time is the hurdle at present. Very soon these hurdles will be overcome and we will be achieving much greater cosmic velocities.

Ea and his team of fifty explorers approached Earth, and the tablets point out to the reader that they had to slow the chariot down before descending or it would perish in the friction of the atmosphere. More incredible knowledge of space travel that comes to us from tablets that are thousands of years old. "The chariot must be slowed or in Earth's thick atmosphere it shall perish," said Anzu, the pilot to Ea. They circled the planet a few times slowing the ship down, before they entered the atmosphere hurtling toward the solid ground. The gravity was playing havoc with their ship and they were still moving too fast for a dry landing. "The Earth's pulling net too powerful for on dry land to descend." To avoid any possible damage, they splashed down in the sea where the Persian Gulf is today and opened the hatch. Alalu was waiting for them and made radio contact as they arrived. "To Earth be welcomed." They saw the other spacecraft from Nibiru at the edge of the water and knew they were in the right place. Their joy was immense as they swam and waded their way to dry land where Alalu was awaiting them. "Alalu toward him came running; his son by marriage he powerfully embraced. Welcome to a different planet! Alalu to Ea said." This is a mere extract of what has been written in cuneiform of the dramatic events leading up to

Fig. 16.5. Enki steps out onto the land. Sumerian seal depicting Lord Enki leaving the water and stepping onto the land for the first time. Notice the streams of water from his shoulders symbolizing that he was also the Lord of the waters. Also notice the winged deity with radiating beams from his shoulders awaiting Enki. This was his chief furnace master in the Abzu where the mining activity took place.

the first group of settlers on planet Earth some 443,000 years ago.

And so we get to the point where the real prehistory of humankind begins, long before the first Adamu was created, during the Prior Times when only the brave exploring astronauts were on this new planet Earth. They realized that their mission was one of life or death for their home planet Nibiru. "On a life or death mission we have come; in our hands is Nibiru's fate." There was little time to waste, and after sending a message to his father Anu back home, Ea mobilized a number of different teams to perform various tasks. The place where they landed would later be called Eridu, "the home away from home," the first city on Earth. It was located in modern Iraq near where Basra is today, on the coast of the Gulf. Over the next six days they performed miracles. They created a source for drinking water; they made bricks from clay to build their settlement; built a camp to live in; examined and recorded the edible fruit and trees that grew in abundance everywhere; they experienced their first thunderstorm on Earth with great trepidation; the rain and lightning and wind was fierce; they were amazed by the moonlight as it lit up the land and sky at night; and they were even more puzzled by the very short days and nights. Furthermore, they documented the creatures that were present everywhere: in the sky, on land, and in the water. They made traps for fish and fowl; they built boats to cover the waters; and they put up fences around their camp for protection against the fierce beasts they observed for the first time; and they even brought the "Beam That Kills" from the chariot to their new camp. This is where the historic events become very familiar, because on the seventh day

Ea gathered his comrades in the camp and suddenly the opening words of the Bible take on a whole new meaning.

> On the seventh day the heroes in the encampment were assembled, to them Ea spoke these words: A hazardous journey we have undertaken . . . At Earth with success we arrived, much good we attained, an encampment we established. Let this day be a day of rest; the seventh day hereafter a day of resting always to be!

And then the settlers gave their new home a name. "Let this place henceforth by the name Eridu be called, Home in the Faraway," and their new planet was called Ki. Now that they had the base camp established and they had identified the foods that they could eat, they did not waste any time before the gold extraction began. The first sources were the marshes, rivers, and oceans. The method they used sounds similar to the "sucking" method that is still used today in the ocean beds to find diamonds. Remember that they were searching for alluvial gold and gold nuggets from any source. So they used "That Which Water Sucks" and "That Which Spits Out the Water" to pile up the mud and sort the content. At the end of the week, they had all kinds of metals including iron and copper, but gold was the least amount. "Of the gold the smallest pile was accumulated."

Ea was fascinated by the moon and its orbits, which prompted him to call one circuit a month. "Month to its circuit he gave the name." The work continued for a whole year but not enough gold was collected. While Nibiru was approaching the sun in its orbit, they wanted to transport the gold to Nibiru at its closest point. It was decided that they should wait for one more Shar (3,600 years) until the orbit brought the planet back. They brought out the "Sky Chamber" from the spaceship and prepared it for action. With this craft they would have to scan the planet for new richer deposits of gold. They analyzed the planet and identified where the rich "veins of gold" were hiding. Then they traveled far and wide to scan the ground below. "In the sky chamber with Abgal did Ea upward soar, the Earth and its secrets to learn." We are told how they flew over mountains and valleys and rivers and vast lands separated by oceans, making a good record of all their findings. Ea also used this opportunity to hide the "seven deadly weapons" from the chariot in a secret place in a faraway land that only he and his pilot knew about. They were not to be used or abused on their new home.

Anu sent word to Ea that no matter what happened, they needed to ship whatever gold they had accumulated to Nibiru. It was essential that they tested the gold dispersion technique that would repair their atmosphere. But on

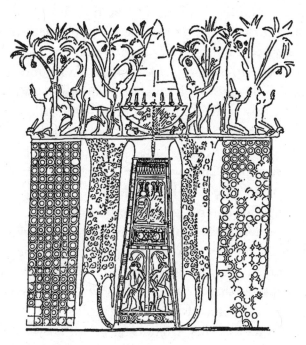

Fig. 16.6. Rocket ship? Could this be an ancient depiction of a rocket ship being filled with gold and prepared for take-off? It is clear that parts of it are underground or in some sort of protective chamber.

Earth, Alalu, who would take the gold back, was furious that Ea had removed the weapons from the space chariot. He was going to use them to blast his way through the asteroid belt. Ea explained that Abgal knew the way through the belt, as he successfully created a path through it on the way in. He would pilot the chariot back to Nibiru. So they loaded the gold and prepared for the launch. "Into Alalu's chariot basketfuls of gold were carried . . . The chariot's Great Cracker he enlivened . . . Then the chariot with a roar heavenward rose, to the heavens it ascended." And this is how the first ever shipment of gold left the newly colonized planet Earth.

The trip back to Nibiru is described in great detail. They use their crystals to locate the pathway through the Hammered Bracelet, and we also get a clear picture of what Nibiru, the radiant planet, looks like when observed from space: "In the darkness, in reddish hue glowed Nibiru; a sight to behold it was." There was great excitement on Nibiru about the arrival of their precious gold; they were welcomed by large crowds as heroes returning from space—very similar to the kind of reception our astronauts received when they returned from the first moon landing. "A multitude of populace was there assembled."

The work started immediately to prepare the fine dust powder mixture that was going to be dispersed into the atmosphere. The planned experiment turned out to be a great success. But now they needed more gold—lots more—to deal with the full extent of the atmospheric damage. "With rockets was the dust heavenward carried, by crystal's beams was it dispersed. Where there was a breach, now there was healing." They informed the settlers on Earth about their success, which caused much happiness. But the healing did not last long before it was dissipated by the rays of the sun on its approach. The chariot was assembled and returned to Earth with more explorers and more equipment to speed up the work. But after another whole Shar, they only collected a small amount, not enough for Nibiru's growing problems. Once again Ea traversed the planet searching for signs of gold, but the signals he received all pointed in one direction, to the southern parts of the planet, where the gold was mixed with ore underground. "Again and again there was the same indication . . . Where the landmass the shape of a heart was given, in the lower parts thereof, golden veins from Earth's innards were abundant."

It was at this point that they had to come up with new methods and technology to separate the gold from the rock, and it also very clearly indicated that the southern part of Africa was the place where this gold operation was about to take place. Anu sent word giving instruction to obtain the gold "from the veins, not from the waters, the gold must be gotten." In the meantime they realized that Ea would need help and guidance with the task, so his brother Enlil was dispatched to join him and help with the management and command. Once again they surveyed the lands and saw the rich gold deposits in southern Africa, a part of the world they called "Abzu." They knew the extraction from the rock would be more difficult. "Let Anu come to Earth, let him decisions provide," said Enlil to his brother. The decisions that needed to be made were crucial for the future success of the operation and would also play a pivotal role in the relationship between the royal brothers Ea and Enlil. If the activity was to take place in a faraway land, they would need to divide tasks and responsibilities. Someone had to oversee the base camp in the north at Eridu, and the other had to oversee the mining activity in the south at Abzu. These were the decisions Anu needed to make. Once again, the Nibiruans surprise us with their simplistic ways of solving complex problems. After Anu arrived and was shown the vastness of the proposed operation, he offered a solution. They drew lots to determine who would perform which task, a custom which the heroes of the Bible inherited. And so it was decided that Enlil would remain in Eridu and prepare the landing sites to handle higher traffic of spaceships to carry loads of gold, and ensure that the necessary infrastructure was in place to

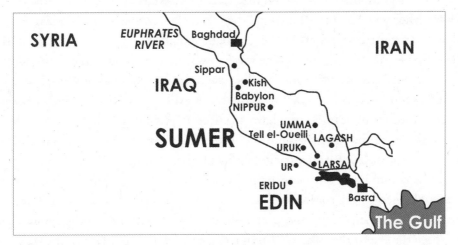

Fig. 16.7. Greater Mesopotamia, showing the ancient cities and modern-day countries

support such activity. Ea would establish the mining operations with its own control center in the south, and devise new tools and methods to maximize the extraction process. At this point, however, there were already signs of friction between the brothers. Ea felt that since he was the first on Earth, the one who had established the entire place to this point, he wanted to stay at Eridu and establish the Edin, which would become the lavish home of the "Upright Ones." He wanted Enlil to look after the mining in the south. "Let it the Edin be, abode for the Upright Ones, by this name be known. The commander of Edin let me be, let Enlil the gold extraction perform." Enlil felt that he was the better commander with a superior knowledge of chariots and sky ships and ports, while Ea was the scientist and engineer who would be more successful at mining tasks. The wise Anu realized that any decision would result in unhappiness, so the drawing of lots decided their fate. Ea was sad but accepted his task honorably; Enlil was satisfied and ready to start developing the space ports and command center. To reward Ea for his pioneering work, Anu pronounced that he would always be known as Enki, the "Earth's Master" from that moment on; and Enlil would be known as "Lord of the Command." And so were the responsibilities and titles allocated to the brothers on a distant planet, called Earth.

But before Anu departed, Alalu challenged him for the throne once again. They engaged in a wrestling match once more, and once again Anu was victorious. But in his anger Alalu lashed out at the crotch of Anu who was standing over him, and in a rage of fury he bit off his testicles. This was a blow for stability on this new space colony and after deliberation and contemplation, it was decided not to execute Alalu, but to banish him to Lahmu (Mars), to spend his time there alone. And so it was done. But Anzu, the talented pilot, volunteered to take Alalu down to the surface of Mars in the sky chamber and chose to stay with him until his sickness "devoured" him. There was apparently something in the flesh of others that killed anyone who consumed it. Could this have been an advanced genetic manifestation that becomes active as the DNA evolves and we move farther away from primitive species who may have practiced cannibalism at some stage in their past? Whatever the correct diagnosis is, it was Alalu's fate to die as a result of swallowing the testicles of Anu during their hand-to-hand struggle.

The mining and shipping preparations went on with purpose on Earth. They planned a way station on Mars. You may immediately ask why, but the answer is quite ingenious and practical, once again pointing to the knowledge of space travel and the solar system of those early astronauts. At present we have the ability to take about seven people into space. Any more than that starts to require much greater thrust and technology mainly because of the added weight and the effect of gravity. The gravity on Mars is only about 38% of that on Earth. By sending regular smaller shipments to Mars, they would be able to send fewer but much larger shipments from there to Nibiru. A simple and practical solution.

Enki (Ea) designed a new range of tools and equipment needed for the mining operation and beamed the designs to Nibiru to be manufactured. "An Earth splitter with cleverness Enki designed . . . 'That which crunches' and 'That which crushes' he also designed on Nibiru for Abzu to be fashioned." We also learn from the texts that Earth was too hot for some of the Anunnaki, suggesting that Nibiru had a more temperate climate with the sunshine not nearly as harsh, even when the planet came in close to the sun on its orbit. The Sumerian symbol for Nibiru is a radiating cross, like a plus sign, which indicates that it is not only the planet of the crossing, but also a planet that radiates its own heat and energy. The sun is not really required. Several of the other planets in our solar system also radiate heat and energy but they are obviously not suitable for life. This extra heat on Earth caused Enlil to seek cooler parts of the world for himself. "Enlil by the heat of the Sun afflicted, for a place of coolness and shade was searching. To snow-covered mountains on the Edin's north side he took a liking." There in the middle of the cedar mountains is where he set up his own home and started to build the new landing site for their spaceships. Was this the historic Cedar forest in north-east Lebanon? Where Baalbek is situated?

We learn of their technology to excavate and cut rocks to perfect size with tools not yet known to humans today. It explains the speed and precision with which they could build giant structures that would include all of the great pyramids and temples in years to come, in Egypt and in the Americas. "Above the mountain valley with power beams the surface he flattened. Great stones from the hillside the heroes quarried and to size cut. To uphold the platform with sky ships they carried and emplaced them." They indicated from the very first building activities that they liked massive sturdy structures built mainly from stone, which would last forever. Quite different from the architecture of today. It clearly explains where the ancient civilizations got their influence and their knowledge to build the colossal monuments of the past. "With satisfaction did Enlil the handiwork consider . . . a structure of everlasting." Could it be the hitherto unexplained ancient platform ruins at Baalbek? It certainly sounds like it. It was so impressive, not even the ancient Romans knew its purpose, but they used the giant 1,000-ton megaliths as a base to build their Temple of Jupiter.

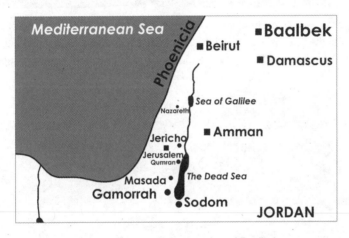

Fig. 16.8. Map showing location of Baalbek

Fig. 16.9. This 1,200-ton megalith was left behind by the original builders of the 9-hectare platform at Baalbek. It has not been moved to date because of its sheer size. Notice the two people, one sitting on top and one beside it, being dwarfed by the giant stone.

16.10. The giant megalithic structure at Baalbek that served as a landing platform for the celestial ships of the Anunnaki, survived the flood, and became the inspiration for the pyramids. Thousands of years later the Romans used this platform to build the Temple of Jupiter.

Fig. 16.11. A view of the Temple of Jupiter showing the megalithic platform upon which it was built by the Romans, thousands of years after it was originally constructed by the Anunnaki under the guidance of Enlil.

Back on Nibiru, they were ready to send the next celestial chariot to Earth filled with supplies and tools. They had also lined up a fresh group of fifty additional pioneers, among whom were female nurses and Ninmah, who was Enki and Enlil's half sister. She was a medical expert with the knowledge to resuscitate people from the dead. We will find a number of specific occasions when in time to come the Anunnaki would revive individuals back to life. Part of these new pioneers' mission was to stop over on Lahmu (Mars) and set up a way station for rocket ships from Earth to deliver regular loads of gold to. It's fascinating to notice the distinct references the Nibiruans made to Celestial Ships, Rocket Ships, and Sky Chambers. The first seemed to be much larger, used for long distances between Nibiru and Earth; while the second was smaller and used on shorter trips, like those to Mars; and the Sky Chamber was seemingly used to travel around the world and to descend from the large Celestial Ship to the surface of a planet.

By the time they reached Mars and descended to the same spot next to the lake where Ea had landed before, they found Anzu, dead. This is the first time we are really exposed to the scientific or medical knowledge of the Anunnaki. Ninmah performs a variety of procedures to revive Anzu, and for the first time we witness a dead person being brought back to life. "From her pouch she took out the Pulser; upon Anzu's heart pulsing she directed . . . she took out the Emitter, its crystals' life giving emissions on his body she directed." Ninmah repeated this several times after which Anzu opened his eyes.

Fig. 16.12. Sunset on Mars. The sunset on Mars is reminiscent of a sunset on Earth. When the planet had an atmosphere and running water, it must have been a beautiful place in our solar system for astronauts to spend time on.

Fig. 16.13. Exploring Mars. If this picture of the Mars Explorer digging into a rock on Mars was shown to people fifty years ago they would not have believed it. Today we accept this kind of achievement without giving it a second thought. Nothing seems to surprise us anymore. Are we following in the footsteps of our "maker" on Mars? Will we find evidence on Mars that will take us by surprise?

We are also exposed for the first time to the "Food of Life" and the "Water of Life," which she placed in his mouth and on his lips. Once revived, Anzu related to them the events that led to the death of Alalu and how he placed him in a cave.

I have often wondered if NASA knows something we don't, and if they are actually keeping something from us with regard to signs of intelligent life on Mars. The Anunnaki certainly spent many thousands of years there and must have left behind visible signs of their presence. The Sumerian texts tell us a lot about their activity on the planet. Starting with the death of Alalu, whose body was placed in a cave by Anzu and Ninmah. Will NASA find the skeletal remains of an ancient astronaut in a cave on Mars? Anzu described what he did with Alalu's body: "In the great rock a cave I found, Alalu's corpse therein I hid." They also carved a giant image of Alalu on the face of the great rock with their "beams." Has NASA already found this image, or will this yet surprise them in the future? Are the mysterious pyramids and "Face on Mars" more clues left behind by the Anunnaki and Igigi on Mars some 400,000 years ago?

The tablets tell us that twenty of the explorers were dropped off on Mars to set up the base under the command of Anzu, who was declared their commander by Ninmah, as requested by her father Anu. She explained that Mars would become a very important stop for the gold from Earth, and that Anzu would be in command of hundreds of men in time. One of the things that Ninmah brought to Earth were the mysterious seeds of a bush that would grow juicy fruits while its elixir would give the Anunnaki strength, cure disease, and keep their mood happy. "Their ailments it will chase away, happier their mood it shall make." Could this plant have had something to do with the Soma plant that the Vedic poems refer to constantly as a life giving "elixir" many thousands of years ago?

Ninmah revealed to Enlil that she bore them a son, called Ninurta, and they agreed to bring him to Earth. Because he was the offspring of half-siblings, he would be highest on the list of succession. In the meantime, the spaceships kept arriving with more heroes from Nibiru to help speed up the extraction of gold. Enlil unveiled his master plan to build five cities in the Edin away from Eridu, which would include a command post at Laarsa; its twin city called Lagash; on a line extended between the two he would build Shurubak, the "Heaven City"; and "On the centre line it shall be located, to the fourth city it shall be leading," called Nibru-ki. "A bond Heaven-Earth in it I shall establish." We can start identifying the Sumerian language in these names, that is, Nibru referred to heaven, while Ki referred to Earth. But Enlil's plans were even more elaborate. Beyond the fifth city he wanted to build a "chariot place" to allow ships to come directly and freely between Earth and Nibiru. He was not a big fan of the station on Mars from which the main shipping would take place.

At the southern tip of Africa, Enki was building his base to manage the mining operations. He measured and surveyed the whole land and even referred to what must have been the Zambezi river: "Great rivers there rapidly flowed. An abode by the flowing waters Enki for himself established." He established a place for his house and where the heroes would live and "where the bowels of the Earth to enter . . . Place of deepness he determined, for the heroes into Earth's bowels to descend." Could his domain in the Abzu have been the mysterious Great Zimbabwe ruins? The descriptions fit it very well. So far nobody has been able to explain its origins, but the Sumerian tablets certainly give us something to think about.

And so Enlil commanded the Upper World, which included Edin and the space ports, while Enki was in charge of the Lower World, or Abzu, never to be confused with Hell. This was where the precious gold was obtained that brought the Anunnaki to this planet in the first place. On one specific day, Anu addressed all the settlers who departed from Nibiru. There were 600 settlers on Earth and 300 on Mars, who listened to their king as he praised them. Anu told them that the fate of Nibiru was in their hands and it was at this point that they were given their lofty names. "Those on Earth are shall as Anunnaki be known, Those Who from Heaven to Earth Came," and "Those who on Lahmu are, Igigi shall be named, Those Who Observe and See." During the rise of Egypt in later years, the Igigi would be known as the "watchers," or Neteru, many of whom would produce offspring who became pharaohs. They would also play a crucial role in creating the Aryan civilization by intermarrying earthling females. Anu urged them to do what they could and deliver as much gold as was possible. Everything was in place and ready to begin the mining and the shipments. "Let the gold start coming, let Nibiru be saved," Anu instructed them.

The fascinating thing is that the Anunnaki never spoke about marriage; they referred to it as *espousal*, which was the process of acquiring a permanent spouse to procreate with. Enlil and Enki were no different. Now that they were on this new planet and destined to stay there for a while, they also found their own spouses, but not before both of them had sex with their half-sister Ninmah in an attempt to produce a male offspring who would be eligible for leadership through his preferred bloodline. Enki took the beautiful Ninmah to the Abzu with him where he tried and tried, but she only bore daughters. Before Enki came to Earth, he espoused a young princess whose name was Damkina, but she remained on Nibiru, and gave birth to a son called Marduk. "One in a pure place born" was the meaning of his name, Enki's firstborn son, destined for greatness here on Earth. The mother and child only arrived on Earth much later to join Enki. They had an interesting custom to change the names of their female spouses to resemble those of the man. Enki's spouse became Ninki. Is it possible that this was the custom that we have passed down through the ages and still use in various ways today? Also wanting a son to be of Earth descent, Enlil seduced a young girl named Sud, who eventually became his spouse. She bore him a son called Nannar (Sin), who was the first of the Anunnaki to be conceived and born on Earth. Sud also changed her name to resemble that of her male spouse and became known as Ninlil.

In addition to Marduk, Enki had five sons from his spouse Ninki and other concubines. They were Nergal, Gibil, Ninagal, Ningishzidda, and Dumuzi, the youngest. Enlil's sons were Ninurta, the oldest, Nannar and Ishkur. And so the dynasty of the Anunnaki gods on Earth expanded and the complexity of their social structure grew like a cancer. This involved the hard labor that had to be performed in the mines of the Abzu; the transporting of the gold to the space ports of the Edin; and the regular shipments to Mars (Lahmu) where the smaller base of 300 Igigi orchestrated the larger shipments to the distant

Nibiru. "From the planet Lahmu in celestial chariots was the precious metal to Nibiru brought."

In the past few decades a number of leading scientists have proposed how we could deal with the dwindling ozone problem on Earth. Several theories and many ideas have been bounced around. I distinctly remember reading articles that explained how we could disperse certain substances into the upper atmosphere to create an artificial layer, which would create a similar effect to the ozone, protecting us from the harmful rays of the sun. This is exactly what the Nibiruans did with great success some 440,000 years ago on their own planet. "On Nibiru was the gold to the finest dust fashioned, to protect the atmosphere it was employed." And from the ancient scriptures we can clearly see that their approach was working. "Slowly was the breach in the heavens healing, slowly was Nibiru saved."

After Enlil completed his colossal space command at Nibru-ki, he protected it with some sort of deadly weapon. "From there beams were raised, the heart of all the land they could search . . . its net unwanted approach impossible made." This sounds like the kind of protection allocated to the most advanced U.S. military base, not what we would expect to read on a clay tablet from 2500 BC. The Anunnaki had a number of very mysterious technological items, which we cannot fully understand, even from reading all their translations. One such item was the ME, meaning the "Tablets of Wisdom." It was as if it were some sort of advanced computer system that could calculate and compute any problem and provide a solution. They kept this ME in the new safe house from where Enlil could control all activity in the Upper World. "With them Enlil comings and goings oversaw."

As time went by, the Anunnaki who worked in the Abzu, extracting the gold from the mines, began to complain of the hard work they were being subjected to. The short days and years on Earth somehow also affected them. So the working Anunnaki were constantly being replaced by a new fresh group from Nibiru, while the exhausted group was allowed to return home. But the Igigi on Mars were even more restless. Anzu, their leader, "to Earth from the heavens descended" to deliver the complaints of the Igigi. They wanted a resting place of their own on Earth. Enlil tried to pacify Anzu and showed him the full extent of the global operations. From the mines in the Abzu to the ports in Edin, and even the secret ME that was in the hallowed chamber in Nibru-ki. But Anzu was not impressed and he plotted against Enlil. When the moment presented itself, Anzu stole the ME and escaped to the space port where other Igigi awaited him to stage a mutiny and take over the Earth. With the ME, they were basically invincible. But the oldest son of Enlil, Ninurta, offered to capture the rebellious Anzu. A dramatic aerial battle followed between the two, and with the advice and experience of Enki, Ninurta captured the unlucky rebel. The ME was returned and Anzu was executed. Marduk was ordered to return his body to Lahmu and lay him to rest there, as he was the commander of that planet. This was also the point at which Marduk was appointed as the new interim commander of Mars and asked to stay there and oversee the operations, but he was to also look after their well-being and to lift their spirits.

We know exactly when all of this occurred because the clay tablets tell us. "In the 25th Shar Anzu was judged and executed." This means that it was 90,000 years after the first arrival on Earth, which translates to about 353,000 years ago from present time. It became evident that the Anunnaki workers were kept on Earth for too long. They needed to be replaced more frequently. It was the young Ninurta who came up with a smart plan. Once again we see that their logic, actions, and response to situations are so very similar to how we deal with problems today. It is truly uncanny. He proposed to build a "Metal City" where they could smelt the gold to more refined levels. This would allow them to send lesser volumes of gold to Nibiru, and allow Anunnaki to travel back while being replaced by new workers. And so it was adopted. In the Edin they built the city where metal would be smelted and refined and they called it Bad-Tibira, making Ninurta its first commander. "The flow of gold to Nibiru was thereby eased and quickened." And so the arrival of fresh Anunnaki from Nibiru continued while the shipments of pure gold kept going out, helping to restore their atmosphere.

'Meanwhile, Enki was not paying attention to the growing unhappiness among the miners in the Abzu. He was preoccupied with the creatures that lived in the wilds and he also spent much time in his laboratory working with ME formulas on a number of projects. "In the Abzu by the gushing waters, a wondrous study place he erected, with all manner of tools and equipment he furnished it." Then Enki involved his talented son Ningishzidda to work in the lab with him while they used the sacred ME to unravel new theories. "The house of life he called the place . . . Sacred formulas, tiny ME's, the secrets of life and death possessing they shaped." It is evident from these texts that the two scientists were involved in some kind of genetic engineering program, specifically to unravel the secret of life and death of the earthly creatures that they were studying. These were the experiments that eventually led to the creation of Adamu. The tablets describe how Enki was fascinated with a specific creature that lived among the trees and in the savannah. "They lived among the tall trees, their front legs as hands they were using." This is the first description of a *Homo erectus* species on Earth. "In the tall grasses of the steppes odd creatures were seen; erect they seemed to be walking." A remarkable entry in clay of new discoveries from some 350,000 years ago, and not long before *Homo sapiens* made its appearance on Earth. This fascination with the wildlife on Earth, and not enough attention to the gripes of the miners, finally caused the uprising. Enlil arrived in the Abzu to help resolve the problems, but the workers had had enough. They set fire to their tools, they surrounded Enlil's house and would not budge. "The Anunnaki stood together: Every one of us hostilities has declared! Excessive is our toil, our work is heavy, great is the distress." The situation was so tense that even Anu was called via some advanced communication device to give advice. Enki explained to him that "the lamentation is heavy . . . every day the complaints we could hear." But Anu was steadfast in his pronouncement as he made it clear that "the gold must be obtained . . . the work must continue." After all, their survival on Nibiru depended on it.

It is also fascinating that they make mention of global warming 350,000 years before we regurgitated it again. The talk about "Ever since Earth's heat has been rising, the toil is excruciating," is a precursor of the looming melting of the poles and the coming end of the ice age that would cause great calamity on Earth. So they began to negotiate and explored various possible solutions. Maybe they should send the tired Anunnaki back home; maybe Enki could devise new tools that were more efficient; it seemed that there was no real solution to the serious problem; and then came the pivotal moment in all of human history. Enki consulted with his son Ningishzidda, before they proudly presented their proposal. "Let us create a Lulu, a Primitive Worker, the hardship work to take over . . . Let the Being the toil of the Anunnaki carry on his back."

The rest of the gathering was astounded. They had never heard anything like this before, but they were also unaware of the experiments that Enki and his son had been performing. They did not believe that a being could be created out of nothing, and even the wise Ninmah, their half-sister, made a statement that would be welcomed by the Darwinians among us. She explained that evolution was the force behind new species. "One being from another over aeons did develop, none from nothing ever came." Unfortunately, the rest of that statement is a bit of a blow for the religious creationists, because the creation is about to come in a way very few religious folk would have believed. It does, however, deal with the age-old dilemma that we were created in the "image of our maker." Enki was clearly very happy with himself at this point, as he agreed with his half-sister that you need a prototype to mold into something else. He proudly announced to them: "The being that we need, it already exists. All that we have to do is put on it the mark of our essence . . . A primitive worker shall be created." This was a firm declaration that they had knowledge of genetics and cloning. He explained further: "They walk erect on two legs . . . Their forelegs they use as arms, with hands they are provided . . . They know not dressing in garments . . . Shaggy with hair is their whole body . . . With gazelle they jostle, with teeming creatures in the water they delight." One cannot wish for a more vivid description of *Homo erectus*. It feels as if we have been plunged into the middle of a Jules Verne novel, and yet, these words are the result of a scribe some 4,500 years ago.

Enki demanded that a decision be made, so that he could proceed with the blessing of all. That would, however, prove to be much more complex than one would have expected under their present conditions. At this point we are also exposed to the moral dilemma that suddenly faced the Anunnaki about creating another living creature: a new species, and a slave to them, which was strictly prohibited according to their exploration charter. They were not allowed to create new living species on other planets. Enki took all of those present on a trip through his "House of Life" where some of these creatures were kept in cages. They jumped at the passers-by, banging their fists on the bars. "They were grunting and snorting, no words were they speaking." Everyone was astounded by this sight. There were male and female creatures and they procreated "like us from Nibiru coming." Enki was very excited by the prospects of this new creature, his maverick scientist characteristics were unashamedly exposed.

A primitive worker shall be created. Our command will he understand . . .
Our tools he will handle . . . To the Anunnaki in the Abzu relief shall come.

Enlil was strongly opposed to this idea, and for the first time we hear the Anunnaki refer to the "all mighty God" as Enlil says: "Creation in the hands of the Father of All Beginning alone is held." These words should sound very familiar to those who have been following the controversy surrounding the cloning issue in the twenty-first century. There is so much opposition to proposed cloning of embryos; stem cell therapy and the cloning of humans has been prohibited by most nations. And yet, in the United States the first Pet Cloning company has already opened its doors, to clone people's dead pets. If you ask me, there is a lot of ignorance surrounding all of these issues and politicians should keep their noses out of it today, just like Enlil should have done 250,000 years ago. Ultimately it would be Enlil's inability to come to terms with this newly created slave species that led to the conflict between the brothers, the oppression of the humans, and the disinformation campaign that was imposed by the vengeful Enlil in an attempt to keep the slave species primitive, ignorant, obedient, fearful, and in its place.

Before they allowed Enki to proceed with the "creation," there was much deliberation whether God would have given them such knowledge, if God did not want them to use it to their advantage. Does that sound familiar? "Let us with wisdom new tools fashion, not new beings create," was the one side of the argument. "What knowledge we possess, its use cannot be prevented," Ningishzidda the young scientist answered. They even contemplated very deep and spiritual issues like "Is it destiny . . . or is it Fate? . . . That to this planet us has brought." It was decided to put this matter before the elders from Nibiru, and so it was decreed that a "primitive worker" would be created. And so began the arduous task of cloning the first humans by Enki, his very smart half-sister Ninmah, and his son the scientist, Ningishzidda, who would lead the team. What followed was like something from a horror movie, and yet our ancient prehistory is filled with images of such creatures. Ningishzidda showed Ninmah the results of many experiments he had been conducting in secrecy. Among the trees to "a place of cages" he took her. There were the living results of various cloning and cross-species experiments he had performed, with horrific outcomes. "Foreparts of one kind they had, hindparts of another creature they possessed . . . Creatures of two kinds by their essence combined" he showed her.

The creation of the slave species did not happen overnight, it took the team a long time and many failed attempts to finally achieve the perfect genetic combination. One can feel their frustration and desperation as one attempt after another failed. They used the female creatures as the surrogate mothers, placing a fertilized egg into their womb. The results were not good. This is where we read about DNA splicing for the first time in human history. "The two entwined strands separate and combine an offspring to fashion." Many times they tried, while constantly aware that they could only use a small portion of the Anunnaki "essence" to keep the new being primitive. "To receive our essence in graduation . . . Nibiru's essence only bit by bit could be attempted."

Ninmah prepared the "admixture," or fertilized egg, in a "crystal vessel" before inserting it into the female creature. The following text could have been taken from a modern-day scientific magazine describing artificial impregnation. And yet once again these astounding words are thousands of years old, eternally captured in clay tablets. "In a crystal vessel Ninmah the admixture was preparing, the oval of a female two legged she gently placed . . . With ME Anunnaki seed containing, she the oval impregnated . . . The oval back into the womb of the two-legged female she inserted." What more do we need to hear to be convinced that the Anunnaki knew exactly what they were doing, and that they were indeed performing not only genetic splicing but artificial insemination into surrogate females? But it took many attempts and many modifications to the admixture to get the results they wanted. Time and time again offspring were born deformed, deaf, hairy, short arms, blind, and other defects. It is also evident that they were creating only males. "One being had paralysed feet, another his semen was dripping, one had trembling hands, a malfunctioning liver had another . . . one had lungs for breathing unsuited."

Enki and his colleagues were highly disappointed but they kept on trying new ways to perfect the primitive being until finally a being was born. "In her hands she held the child . . . it was the image of perfection." But their excitement was not long lived. After several years they realized that the child did not have the ability to speak; its animal genetics were stronger than its human side. "Of speaking he had no understanding, grunts and snorts were his utterings." It was Enki who made the observation that they have only been impregnating the "two-legged" Earth females. He suggested that they insert the fertilized egg into an Anunnaki womb. This caused a long debate about who would be the carrier of the baby, but it was finally decided that Ninmah should be the carrier and risk any danger, since it was her project. "The fertilized egg into the womb of Ninmah was inserted; there was conception." The gestation period was an interesting experience. It seems to have taken longer than the two-legged females but shorter than on Nibiru for the birth to occur. And finally they achieved what they had set out to do and Enki was elated. "The image of perfection he was . . . He slapped the newborn on his hindparts, the newborn uttered proper sounds." I suppose it should be quite simple to distinguish a human baby from other species, the baby cries when you slap its bum, just like the doctors do in the maternity ward. They examined the baby, his limbs, ears, eyes, and found that everything was perfect. We learn at this point why the Anunnaki referred to the primitive worker as the "blackheaded ones" because Enki gives a perfect description of the child. "Shaggy like the wild ones he was not . . . dark black his head hair was . . . Smooth was his skin . . . smooth as the Anunnaki skin it was . . . Like dark red blood was its colour . . . like the clay of the Abzu was its hue."

We learn so much about the very first human on Earth from this short statement, at the same time we corroborate a number of very important archaeological and anthropological theories. We know from mitochondrial DNA and the Y-Chromosome studies that the first humans, *Homo sapiens*, emerged around 200,000 years ago. It is a widely accepted fact that the Cradle of Humankind was in southern Africa, and now we also know what their skin and hair color was. The parallels between these clay tablets and the Biblical creation of Adam are uncanny, except that once again, most of these tablets predate the Bible by at least 2,000 years. But here we discover the terrible truth that will hopefully jerk us out of the confused state in which we find ourselves as a species! That our maker was not God, but rather an advanced being with advanced knowledge pretty similar to our knowledge today. And from that moment on, we saw our maker as a god. The subservience of humans permeated across the Anunnaki ranks, and as time went by, many of them would become worshipped, against the liking of Enlil, the supreme commander on planet Earth.

While examining the baby boy, Enki noticed that his penis had a long skin hanging from the front end. "Unlike that of Anunnaki malehood it was, a skin from its forepart was hanging. Let the earthling from us Anunnaki by this foreskin be distinguished." And suddenly the ancient ritual of circumcision takes on a whole new meaning. Is it possible that in years to come, the human tribes circumcised the newborn male babies not only for hygienic reasons, but also to imitate the gods? To look a little bit more like them? Because they saw the baby not as a creature, they decided to give it a name, they called him Adamu, "One Who Like Earth's Clay Is." And if you have ever wondered where the Aryan blond and blue-eyed people come from, the texts also divulge this information. In previous chapters we read that Enki had a son who looked just like him. It describes the baby as "radiating" and "bright eyes the colour of the sky"; and light hair as the "golden Sun." It is pretty clear from that description that the Anunnaki must have had white skin, generally blond hair, and blue eyes. And since Enlil and his followers preferred the cooler climate of the lands further North, near the snow capped mountains, it would also explain why the blue-eyed-blond people mostly originate from that part of the world even today. Further support for this revelation comes when Ninmah lifts up to hold her new earthling baby. "Ninmah cast her hand upon the newborn's body, with her fingers his dark red skin she caressed." We should assume that if her skin was also dark, they would not have made such a fuss about it in the tablets.

It's very important to recognize Enki's immediate affinity for his new earthling creation. We see the maverick, creative scientist in his character, who absolutely adored his Adamu and almost immediately wanted only the best for him. This would lead to many disagreements between him and Enlil, who only saw the earthlings as primitive workers who were created to perform a specific task.

But now they had to face the problem of multiplying this baby many times to create a large group of workers. The mass production of the slave species had begun. Out of the several hundred Anunnaki females, seven volunteers were found to become surrogate mothers and carry the new species to term. "Their task is heroic, by them a race of Primitive Workers shall come into being." They became known as the "Birth Mothers" and these seven females became highly worshipped in Vedic poems, Harappan, and other Asian cultures in latter years, often appearing in seals and other pictorial representations. It could also be the origins of why the number seven is so highly revered in so many cultures.

Fig. 16.14. Seven birth goddesses. Could these representations of the seven mother goddesses from the Indus Valley civilization be related to the Sumerian stories of the seven birth goddesses who were the surrogate mothers of the first humans?

Now that Adamu was created as they had wanted, they used his DNA as the prototype for all the other babies. The seven birth mothers were each impregnated with fertilized eggs, to carry the fetus to term. It is fascinating to see that there are seven female deities who were revered in the Indus Valley and Harappan cultures. The task of giving birth to the workers was a lengthy process and Enki realized that this was not really going to solve the problem of creating a substantial labor force of earthlings. He proposed that they create a female earthling to procreate with Adamu. "For males counterparts to be . . . let them know each other . . . as one flesh the two to become. . . Let them by themselves procreate . . . By themselves give birth . . . Anunnaki females to relieve." This time they used Adamu's blood and DNA to create the admixture for fertilization while Enki's spouse Ninki became the surrogate mother. In good time the first female earthling was born; it made human noises, it was healthy, and "her skin smooth was, as that of the Anunnaki in smoothness and colour it was." This is a fascinating bit of information, even right from the very start there was a differentiation in skin color between Adam and Eve. Is this why we simply cannot eradicate racism from the face of the world even today? Is it something so deeply seeded in our DNA that more evolution is required to overcome this race clash that lingers on and on? Only time will tell.

Once again they decided that the being needed a name because it was not a creature. They called her Ti-Amat, meaning the "Mother of Life," which was also a derivative of the watery planet Tiamat from which Earth was created during the *Epic of Creation*. They went on to create another seven earthling females from the Anunnaki birth mothers, which gave them seven males and seven females. "Let the males the females inseminate, let the primitive workers by themselves offspring beget." They created cages for them and allowed them to grow up together while observing them. But Adamu and Ti-Amat were to be excluded from the hard work of the other earthlings. They were the first ones and were to be protected for their DNA. Enki took them up to Edin in the Upper World where the Anunnaki dwelled, to show off the new primitive worker to all. A simple dwelling was built for Adamu and Ti-Amat in an enclosure of Edin and they were allowed to roam freely in it while the Anunnaki came from far and wide to observe them. It was probably a bit like an ancient freak show with never-seen-before species on display. Even Marduk arrived from the way station on Lahmu. What took everyone by surprise was their intelligence and ability to follow commands and perform simple tasks. Adamu and Ti-Amat led a privileged life in the lush gardens of Edin. They were cared for, constantly observed, and admired by all the Anunnaki. After all, they were created in their image. Even Enlil, who vigorously opposed the creation initially, was pleased with the outcome. But those who worked in the mines were most relieved. "Primitive workers have been fashioned, our days of toil to end" they were shouting.

Their excitement, however, was short-lived because while the two workers in Edin were being observed, so were the ones in the Abzu being observed by Ningishzidda, the young scientist. "Conceiving there was not, birth-giving there was not." The new species was unable to procreate. This was not only proving to be a problem for Enki in the lab but also underground. The Anunnaki miners were getting very restless and losing their patience waiting for this new primitive worker to take over their toil. Enki and Ningishzidda had to do more genetic manipulation, and we read in great detail what they did. The new species only had 22 chromosomes, which did not include the X and Y sex chromosomes; that is why they could not procreate. How on Earth could an ignorant scribe 4,500 years ago have had such detailed knowledge about genetics? "Like two entwined serpents Ningishzidda the essence separated . . . Arranged like twenty two branches on a Tree of Life were the essence . . . The ability to procreate they did not include." Then the young Ningishzidda performed a dangerous procedure that included the ribs of the individuals and that was rewritten in the Bible some time later with some variation. He sedated Enki and Ninmah, extracting the missing "sex-essence" from each one, implanting it into Adamu and Ti-Amat. "To their Tree of Life two branches have been added . . . With procreating powers their life essence are now entwined." From that moment on all humans had 23 pairs of chromosomes.

The two were allowed to roam freely in the orchards of Edin while their creator Enki tried to teach them some basics of intelligence. He clearly wanted his new species not to be too primitive, and not to evolve as a slave; he wanted to uplift them with knowledge. Enki's symbol was the entwined serpent, which is still used as the symbol for medical doctors today. It was this imagery that has led to the ageless confusion between the maker and the evil serpent who tempted Adam and Eve in the garden of Eden. The story is somewhat simpler and more logical if seen from the point of the Sumerian tablets. Enlil was furious about the slaves being able to procreate on their own. This was never part of the plan. Now they have not only created a new species, which was not supposed to happen, but they have given them the essence of intelligence and life, which the Anunnaki possessed.

This part of the scriptures points irrefutably to the genetic manipulation performed by the Anunnaki that stunted our DNA, causing many of the undesirable and unexplainable characteristics among humans today; the fact that

Sumerian Tree of Life **Egyptian Tree of Life**

Fig. 16.15. The Tree of Life referred to by the Sumerians was actually the DNA. Here we have two deities manipulating the DNA Tree of Life with a winged deity or a winged disc observing them from above. Such winged deities are common in ancient depictions and have been adopted by various religious groups, like Zoroastrianism. Similar representations of the DNA in the form of a Tree of Life are found throughout ancient civilizations.

we die, that we get sick, and other undesirable side effects associated with an incomplete genome. Ningishzidda comforted Enlil by explaining that he did not give the new species the gift of eternal life. "Knowing for protection they were given . . . The branch of long living, to their essence tree was not." This statement explains why the Anunnaki lived so long, or even eternally, and why they could be revived from the dead. It also suggests that they must have performed more genetic engineering on humans after this point, because it is clear from other scripts that the early humans lived very long lives, unlike humans today.

Enlil could not be pacified and he proclaimed: "Then let them be where they are needed . . . In the Abzu away from the Edin, let them be expelled." This story is well known as the "Fall of Man" in the Bible. There are also some other fascinating similarities, such as when Enlil was walking in the shade of the trees in Edin looking for the two earthlings, wanting to see how they were getting on. By that stage they had already been taught various things by his brother Enki and they were aware of their nakedness. Wanting to be more like their maker, who wore clothing, they began to emulate him. This was a dead giveaway to Enlil that someone had been feeding them knowledge and information, which he was decisively opposed to. It was at this point that he expelled them from Edin for becoming too informed, and a stern threat was extended to the human couple not to consort with the evil serpent, and not be led astray by his attempts and promises of knowledge and other things. So it turns out that the serpent was actually Enki, who was the maker, the creator of humankind, who was personified as the devil by Enlil, while from that moment on, Enlil became the god of fear and vengeance who did everything in his power to oppress and control humans. He was very clear about the limits to which he would allow humans to develop. He chose his favorites, punished those who would not listen to him, and prevented humans from worshipping any other god than him, although the other gods had much more regular contact with humans, which led to them being worshipped in any case. But in time, Enki's oldest son Marduk would take over this vengeful god role, when he proclaimed himself the god above all.

In the Abzu, all the earthlings were procreating, which included Adamu and Ti-Amat. "With wonderment did Enki and Ninmah watch the newborns . . . How they grew and developed was a marvel." They comprehended commands, did not complain about the heat and dust, and worked hard for rations of food. Finally, after a whole Shar (3,600 years), the Anunnaki were relieved of the toil in the mines. Meanwhile, back home on their planet, Nibiru's atmosphere was healing. The earthling workers in the Abzu grew in numbers quickly, working in the mines and as servant-slaves to the Anunnaki. But in the north, or the Upper World, the Anunnaki were also growing in numbers. Enlil and Enki's sons had offspring with some of the nursing Anunnaki females who arrived from Nibiru.

By now the settlers from a distant planet had been on Earth for around 240,000 years. They had established a stable infrastructure to perform the arduous task of mining gold for their home planet Nibiru, and they had grown in numbers, which now included many Anunnaki who were born on Earth and had no knowledge of Nibiru. This is quite an interesting set of variables. We are also told that their stay on Earth had sped up their aging process. "By lifecycles of Nibiru they were endowed, by Earth's cycles they were quickened." This means that the children grew up quicker on Earth. The larger community of Anunnaki made life a bit easier on them because they could now divide their chores among more individuals. The biggest achievement was the creation of the slave species, which was working out well. The new species performed all the lowest and the toughest tasks, and so the earthlings were in great demand by the Anunnaki. Those must have been very interesting times on Earth, while the settlers lived in a kind of utopian paradise. After all, they were on a mission that was planned, supported in many ways with technology from home, and most importantly, it was funded and provided for with everything they needed. It was a fully functional "communist" system where all of them worked together for a collective benefit. The settlers did the work required and in return they were provided with everything they needed. They were even allowed to break long-standing rules of the Nibiru civilization by creating a cloned slave species to perform the hard labor. There is no reference to money or currency or the need to pay for something until long after the flood, some 11000 BC. It was the perfect community of settlers, everyone with his own task, contributing to the greater benefit of all the Anunnaki, feeding everyone and providing for everyone in every way. The slave species became an inextricable part of the full cycle of activities on Earth, but they were functioning within their own little sphere, which was swallowed up by the larger Anunnaki sphere of activity. As slaves they were not paid, but they were housed and fed and clothed by the Anunnaki.

Enlil had twin grandchildren called Utu, a boy, and Inanna, a girl, who would become Ishtar, the goddess of love in many cultures, by many names. But the climate on Earth was changing and causing great havoc. We are even told about the Antarctic meltdown prior to the last ice age. "Upon the Earth the warmth was rising . . . Vegetation flourished . . . The rains were heavier . . . Rivers were gushing . . . The snow white parts to water were melting . . . volcanoes were fire and brimstone belching . . . In the Lower World the snow white-hued place the Earth was grumbling."

The disturbance on Earth was arriving from the cosmos, too, as Nibiru was on her way to round the sun. "In the heavens Nibiru was approaching, the Sun's abode it was nearing." This particular time the planet got a little too close to the asteroid belt, its gravity causing many rocks to be dislodged from their stable orbit, causing them to collide with the inner planets including Earth. But it was Mars and the moon that were most affected. Marduk, who was stationed on Mars, was very nervous and was complaining to Enki about the situation. "From the Bracelet bits and pieces it has been displacing." Mars, Earth, and the moon were bombarded by meteors causing havoc and panic and much damage. "In the Hammered Bracelet turmoils are occurring . . . Upon the Earth brimstones from the sky were falling . . . Like stony missiles the Earth they were attacking . . . The faces of all three with countless scars were covered."

It is fascinating to discover that after the original celestial battle collisions between the planets and moons that created the Earth, there must have been more collision each time Nibiru came past the sun, but eventually this stabilized allowing life to develop. Cosmic collisions are inevitable, however, and the balance must have shifted in our own solar backyard, which caused these sudden disturbances affecting the asteroid belt. The tablets describe how a giant comet or asteroid came close to the Earth, while flying on a collision path with Mars. It describes the rogue celestial body dramatically. "From horizon to the midst of heaven like a flaming dragon it was stretched . . . One league was its head, fifty leagues in length it was, awesome was its tail . . . By day the skies of Earth it darkened." This is a pretty awesome description of what was actually a giant comet, which must have been a similar experience to the Comet Shoemaker-Levy in 1994, which we all witnessed crashing into Jupiter. But this one was much closer, and way back then, somehow the moon got in the way and took the full impact of the comet. It is possible that the impact, which is described by the Sumerian tablets, caused the giant crater on the moon, which can still be seen with the naked eye today. You be the judge, this is what it says: "To intercept that dragon in its path Kingu (moon) was making haste . . . Fierce was the encounter, a tempest of clouds on Kingu was raised . . . By its foundations was Kingu shaken."

But as Nibiru made its turn around the sun and disappeared into deep space, everything subsided again and life returned back to normal on the fragile outpost of the Anunnaki. They surveyed the land from their sky ships to assess the damage, around Edin and north to the cedar mountains where the command post was, to the landing places and all their other cities. They scanned to ensure the gold mines were not affected—they were saved. However, the damage to Mars was severe. Marduk reported that the atmosphere was damaged and Enlil agreed that the stability of the base on Lahmu was questionable. They would build a new space port in the Edin on Earth to send ships directly to Nibiru. "A chariot place in the Edin must be established . . . The way station on Lahmu is no longer certain." There have been many theories by scientists about what may have happened to Mars in the past. Today, from the diagnoses by the rovers on our neighbor, we have irrefutable proof that Mars had water, oceans, lakes and rivers, and even an atmosphere. There is still ice present today, and all it really needs is an atmosphere to stabilize the environment. The Sumerian tablets certainly go a long way in supporting this line of thinking, but the lack of atmosphere and the "peeled away" crust of virtually one half of the planet have caused much speculation. Is it possible that the descriptions in the tablets are the actual event that killed Mars? Firstly, she was bombarded by giant asteroids that may have dislodged much of the peeled away surface, as is suggested by some scholars, before the close proximity of the much larger Nibiru caused dramatic gravitational disturbances that may have caused the loss of the atmosphere and a large part of its crust. We are told that all of this occurred around 80 Shar since their splashdown on Earth. That would make it 288,000 years after arrival and 155,000 years ago from our present time. It will be fascinating to see what evidence the Mars probes find of the meteoric activity on our neighboring planet.

After this calamity had subsided, Anu gave instruction to build a space port on Earth. "Let a place of Celestial Chariots in the Edin be established." But before they rushed to do that, Enki and Marduk wanted to survey the moon as a possible alternative to Mars, with its much lower gravity for a possible base there. "Eagles' helmets" they had to don, the atmosphere was for breathing insufficient . . . For a way station it is unsuitable." But the two stayed there for some time while Enki mapped the heavens; he was taken by the beauty of Earth from the moon and once again we hear the Anunnaki make reference to the almighty God. "The Earth like a globe in the void by nothing is hanging . . . Are you not by the celestial dance of Earth and Moon and Sun enchanted? . . . With our instruments we can scan the distant heavens . . . The handiwork of the Creator of All in this solitude we can admire." With this statement we get another glimpse at Enki's creative spirit, which was diametrically opposed to his brother—who was a true commander and politician. They did a great deal of astronomical observation while on the moon and the tablets describe them as they captured much of their newfound knowledge of the cosmos from there. The circuits of the planets around the sun indicated to Enki that "Nibiru of the Sun not a descendant" was, like the other planets in the solar system. Many modern-day astronomers may find this bit of information useful when making pronouncements and formulating theories on the mysterious planet X. Enki pointed out that there was a family of twelve with the sun, and he designated a station to each one by name. After this "twelve constellations by their shapes he allotted . . . The stars into twelve constellations he assembled." Is this is how we inherited the signs of the Zodiac?

Marduk used this quiet time with his father Enki to pour his heart out. He was bitterly disappointed about his position and role among the Anunnaki. He was Enki's firstborn and yet he had not been given any of the higher responsibilities on Earth. It was at this point we can sense that Marduk was becoming a loose cannon who would cause a lot of trouble in time to come. Enki promises him that "which I have been deprived your future lot shall be."

The continuing harsh climate on Mars and unsuitable conditions on the moon forced the Anunnaki to build "Bird City" at Sippar in the Edin. Now they would be able to fly their ships directly to Nibiru from Earth, without having to stop on a way station. "In the eighty second Shar was the construction of Sippar completed," and Anu traveled from Nibiru to see the latest developments. The Anunnaki from the Abzu were assembled and even the Igigi were called in from Mars for the occasion. We learn about the singing and dancing skills of Inanna, the goddess of love, Anu's great-granddaughter. A new era had arrived on Earth; the gold would be sent directly to Nibiru, and once they had collected enough in storage, the heroes and heroines would be able to return to Nibiru. "A few more Shar of toil, and homeward they shall be bound." The Anunnaki were excited about the prospects of ending their stay on this planet and returning home. But their anticipation was too hasty. The hard work in the Abzu continued, the Anunnaki in the Edin were growing restless. It was they who now demanded help from the slave species. But while Enlil and Enki were deliberating such prospects, Ninurta flew down to the southern tip of Africa and captured some earthling slaves for his Anunnaki friends in the Edin, thereby starting a never-ending tradition of slavery from Africa, which would haunt modern man for millennia to come. The events are described dramatically in the tablets: "In the forests and the steppes of the Abzu the Earthlings they chased . . . With nets they them captured, male and female to the Edin they them brought." This sounds like a scene from the seventeenth century when slavery became one of the most profitable businesses in the world and when African slaves were captured like wild animals to be shipped and sold in distant lands. And yet, this was happening some 150,000 years ago. It is amazing how strongly the Anunnaki genetic code has embedded itself in our DNA, still playing havoc with our behavior today.

Enlil was furious once again, because he explicitly expelled the earthlings from the Edin. Ninurta, his son, convinced him that the slaves would pacify the restless Anunnaki in the north and prevent a repeat of the revolt that took place in the mines of the Abzu. They let the situation simmer, as they all believed that they would be heading home to Nibiru very soon. "Let the gold pile up quickly, let us all to Nibiru soon return."

The Anunnaki in the Edin were very impressed with their new slaves. They showed intelligence and could perform all tasks given to them. "Intelligence they possessed, of commands they had understanding." The slaves took on all kinds of chores, all working naked for their gods. As time passed, the numbers of earthlings grew so quickly that they outnumbered the Anunnaki by many, and very soon the food supplies began to dwindle. The slaves would constantly scavenge for food everywhere, in the wild and in the orchards. These were days long before domestication of animals, keeping of herds, growing of crops, and understanding of farming by the humans. Those secrets would only be revealed to the slaves after the Great Flood, in many years to come. Enlil was still harboring negative feelings toward the slaves and he made it clear that Enki should deal with the problem that he created. So Enki started scheming. He observed the earthlings only to discover that they were somehow regressing toward their wild origins. He planned to create a civilized man out of them, but he was not quite sure how to go about it. There was already enough arguing about all the genetic experimenting and cloning. He had to do this less conspicuously. What he did has become another story that was repeated in the Bible around the birth of Moses. Enki impregnated two young earthling females, who bore a son and a daughter. The tablets tell us that he was ecstatic. "Who such a thing has ever known . . . Between Anunnaki and Earthling, conception was attained . . . Civilised man I have brought into being." He told his spouse that he found the babies floating in a basket on the river by the reeds and took the children to raise as his own. And just as Moses was raised as the son of the pharaoh, they became known as "The Gracious Ones" growing up as the children of the Lord of the Earth. They were born in the 93rd Shar, which was 334,800 years after arrival on Earth, 108,000 years ago from present time. They were called Adapa, "The Foundling" and Titi, "One with Life." By this action Enki personally created the first *Homo sapiens sapiens,* and secured their future as a new civilized species to multiply on the planet.

"Civilized man I have brought forth . . . A new kind of Earthling from my seed has been created, in my image and after my likeness." These are some of the most important words in my entire substantiation of the "god-devil" argument. Since Enki was the creator of the original Adamu and once again

Adapa, the first civilized human, he should be credited as the creator. But his brother Enlil described him as the deceitful and evil "snake" and the "devil" whom humans should stay away from. Enlil was for all intents and purposes the supreme commander of planet Earth, who not only declared himself to be their god, but was perceived to be their god. On Earth Enlil's word was supreme.

Fig. 16.16. The creators. Neo-Sumerian on clay, Babylonia, 1900 BC–1700 BC. One of various creation stories captured on clay. This text is unique and different from the story that introduces the "Creation of the Hoe" and the Neo-Babylonian *Epic of Creation* or *Enuma Elish*.

Tablet translation: In distant days, in those days, after destinies had been decreed, after An and Enlil had set up the regulators for heaven and Earth, Enki, the Exalted Knowing God, like a high priest with wide knowledge, Enlil-Banda, in the lands was their ruler. By the rules for heaven and Earth, the fixed rules, he set up cities. — He dug the Tigris and the Euphrates. Thereupon he established the rules of the lands. He set up hand-washing rites, he set up libations . . .

This supreme god of humankind was fierce and brutal, as is seen throughout the Old Testament, punishing humans for disobedience, but also rewarding his chosen few with physical possessions like land, gold, horses, livestock, and more. If you have ever wondered why we humans are so materialistic, herein lies your answer. Enlil was the god who manipulated humans to do exactly what he wanted. The god of the Bible and all other man-made religions. He never even gave humankind the chance to evolve into a state of consciousness where they could understand the bigger picture of the universe. Instead, he manipulated humans from their very beginnings into believing that he, Enlil, was the almighty God, creator of the universe and all things in it. So if Enlil, our god, was the brutal one, should he not be called the devil? For making false representations of himself to an ignorant species barely emerging from the cradle, confused about their purpose among the living?

When I say that god is the devil, and the devil is our maker, it should be seen in this context. Enlil should be classified as the devil for misrepresenting himself as god; and Enki, who was portrayed as the snake-devil, was actually the one who created us—our maker. Enki was the only one of the Anunnaki who consistently looked out for our best interests, who tried to give humans knowledge and intelligence in Edin, who taught us most of the skills we possess today, and the one who saved humans from the Great Flood when Enlil and the others agreed to let the water wipe out all humans from the Earth.

Fig. 16.17. Origins of medicine. The symbol used by the medical industry today can be traced back to early Sumerian symbolism. The wings represent a god or deity with superior knowledge; the serpent symbolizes Enki and the double helix of the DNA.

Adapa and Titi were brought up as little Anunnaki children; Enki and his spouse Ninki taught them all the skills of the Anunnaki. Satisfied that the new kind of earthling was in fact civilized and intelligent, he ordered the delivery of all kinds of seeds and domestic animals from Nibiru so that the earthlings could grow food and learn farming. "Let us from Nibiru seeds that are sown bring down . . . Ewes that sheep become to Earth deliver . . . farming and shepherding teach . . . By civilised man let Anunnaki and Earthlings become satiated." He was going to enable the Earthlings to provide food for the Anunnaki and themselves. This knowledge was, however, reserved only for a small privileged group of Earthlings, who were closely associated with the Anunnaki and whose responsibility it was to feed their masters. The mass civilization of the slave species would only happen much later.

Both Enlil and Anu were amazed that a civilized man could evolve so quickly from a more simple Adamu. Once again they refer to evolution before they voice their surprise. "That by life essence one kind to another leads is not unheard of . . . That on Earth a civilised man from the Adamu so quickly appeared, that is unheard of." It is evident from this statement that the Anunnaki were well-acquainted with the concept of evolution, but they also knew how long it took for species to evolve. As unhappy as Enlil was with the original idea of a slave species being created, he suddenly saw the merits of the more intelligent, civilized man, who could perform more delicate tasks, especially that of farming and cultivating food for all of those on Earth. Their excitement rose even higher when Adapa and Titi had their first children, which turned out to be twins. Anu was so impressed by the reports about Adapa that he ordered him to be brought to Nibiru for a visit. "Let Adapa the Earthling to Nibiru be brought."

A very important trip to Nibiru was planned to show off the amazing earthling who could speak, read, and behave appropriately, to Anu and all other inhabitants. Once again Enlil was not pleased with this plan. Not only have they endowed him with all their knowledge, but now they will take an Earthling into heaven, to become just like them? "With knowledge endowed, between Heaven and Earth will travel." But the command of Anu could not be avoided. Enki's two sons Ningishzidda and the youngest, Dumuzi, were chosen to accompany Adapa and visit their parents' planet for the first time. Anu wanted to bestow immortality on Adapa to include him in the extended family of the Anunnaki but Enki had other thoughts. Adapa was his creation by his own seed and a mortal earthling, with more Anunnaki blood than Adamu, who was created first. Adapa had to remain an earthling on his own planet Earth and face death as all other earthlings. Creating a new species was one thing, but creating an immortal species was not in the cards.

As they took off, the tablets describe Adapa's fear of flying for the first time, wanting to go back, while being pacified by Ningishzidda. "The lands they saw, by seas and oceans into parts separated . . . Adapa agitated was, he cowered and cried out: Take me back." This was one the earliest events of human flight ever recorded, describing clearly the geographical features in a way possible only when viewed from a great height. The events that took place on Nibiru upon their arrival, sound like a science fiction story along the lines of "The Alien Who Came to Dinner." So as Adapa was admired and quizzed by Anu and the entire city who came to see this new "civilized" alien from another planet, he was offered various items to eat and drink. When he refused, it surprised Anu and annoyed him somewhat, that this earthling would refuse the gift of immortality.

Then came the twist where fiction imitates life. We discover that the Anunnaki had some awesome technology that we do not really understand today. It allowed them to convey or transmit secret encoded messages. Before they departed from Earth, Enki gave Ningishzidda an encoded tablet for Anu. "Anu the tablet's seal broke open . . . into the scanner the tablet he inserted . . . its message from Enki to decipher." It explained the heritage of Adapa, that he was the son of Enki from an earthling female and had to return to face his destiny on Earth. "To be of civilised man a progenitor his destiny shall be." Anu then immediately declared that "the welcome to the earthling must not be overextended, on our planet he cannot eat and drink. Let his offspring there on Earth fields till and meadows shepherd." Dumuzi was asked to stay on Nibiru while Ningishzidda returned to Earth with Adapa, bringing with them seeds to be planted. Dumuzi would bring the lambs and ewes on his return.

Enki confessed to his half-sister Ninmah, and Ningishzidda about Adapa and Titi being his offspring, stressing that by his actions he secured the survival of the Anunnaki. Civilized earthlings would relieve more of their hardship, they will be taught to produce the food to keep everyone alive during the hard times. But once again, his brother Enlil's fury was immense. This is where the Anunnaki begin to debate destiny and fate as a philosophical inevitability. "So did Enlil in anger say. Now the lot is cast, destiny by fate is overtaken." All the way through many of these translations we are left with a very strange mixture of spirituality, awareness of the Creator of All things, advanced technological expertise and know-how. And yet, the Anunnaki themselves showed visible signs of a species still on the path of evolution. I personally get the distinct impression that their genome was not as evolved as we may have believed at first sight. It is possible that it was indeed fate that brought them to Earth to create humans, who would unravel the mystery of their own ancestry, which stretched all the way back to another planet called Nibiru. But I have already shared my thoughts on the evolution of the genome with you. I propose that evolution happens exponentially, and in a few thousand years we would have evolved to the same level the Anunnaki were when they created us. They, however, have probably evolved way beyond our present levels of comprehension, and that may have something to do with the many UFO sightings, visitations, and abductions that are reported recurrently. Is it possible that since they have deserted planet Earth, the Anunnaki keep coming back to check up on their creation, and possibly help steer us in the right, or wrong, direction?

Meanwhile, Adapa's female partner, Titi, gave birth to twin sons. They called them Ka-in and Abael, showing us that once again, those who rewrote the story in the Bible many thousands of years later got it completely wrong. It was not Adam and Eve who had Cain and Abel, it was the first civilized couple on Earth who had the troubled sons. Ka-in was taken under Ninurta's wing to his city of Bad-Tibira, to be taught everything about farming the lands, digging canals, plowing, planting, and harvesting crops, and was known as "He Who in the Field Food Grows." Marduk took the other son, Abael, "He of the Watered Meadows," and taught him everything about building enclosures for his animals, feeding them, and caring for them. We are reminded about the very long lives that these early humans lived because it was a whole Shar before Dumuzi returned from Nibiru, bringing with him mainly sheep and other four-legged domesticated animals for farming. "Never before was there an ewe on Earth, a lamb has never to Earth from heavens been dropped."

Under the leadership of Ninmah, the Anunnaki built what they called "the Creation Chamber" where "the multiplying of the grains and ewes on Earth begun." When the first crops and sheep were harvested by Ka-in and Abael, they were called before Enlil and Enki and we witness the first ever offering to the gods by humans. Enlil proclaimed that, "Let there be celebration of firsts," and for the first time in a long time he was pleased with the humans. This mentality of subservience and offering would be imposed on the humans for thousands of years by Enlil and other Anunnaki gods, forcing them to make sacrificial offerings as a sign of obedience. Those must have been tough times on Earth as the production of food was not sufficient to feed the large numbers of Anunnaki and humans, in the Abzu and in the Edin. Fish and fruit were clearly not enough. It was only after the introduction of the new seeds of a wide variety of agricultural produce that the food crisis was alleviated among the Anunnaki and humans.

The subtle competition among the cousins Ninurta and Marduk rubbed off on the earthling brothers Ka-in and Abael. They began to argue about who had the more important job, displaying typical human traits so early in human history. It was not long before their subtle competition turned into more visible rivalry, and when the climate changed and times became hard on the farmers, their rivalry turned to manslaughter. Abael's sheep found the green fields of Ka-in irresistible and invaded them to graze on. Suddenly, their petty arguments turned into a heated confrontation. The brothers got into a physical fight over their lands and in a fit of fury, Ka-in hit Abael with a stone, killing him. "Ka-in a stone picked up, with it he Abael in the head struck . . . Again and again he hit him until Abael fell, his blood from him gushing."

We see the first evidence of human remorse and grieving at this point. When Adapa and Titi found out about the tragedy they behaved the way some people still do today. "A great cry of agony Titi shouted, Adapa spread mud on his face." Although Ka-in was remorseful, it was too late. There was much deliberation and argument among the Anunnaki about how they should deal with the situation. The decision did not come easily. In the end, Ka-in was judged by the Anunnaki and expelled from Edin to live in solitude in distant lands, to fend for himself. "From the Edin you must depart, among Anunnaki and civilised earthlings you shall not stay . . . To the ends of the Earth let him be banished." The Bible tells us of the days that the Nefilim were on Earth . . . and the sons of the gods saw the daughters of man and had sex with them and so produced a new subspecies, which became the Aryans. Obviously the Bible does not put it in so many words, but I believe we have now reached the point where that particular biblical phrase begins to make much more sense.

In the 95th Shar, Adapa and Titi had another son, whom they called Seti, the biblical Seth, but the first civilized couple did not stop there. "Thirty sons and thirty daughters Adapa and Titi had." These human offspring were tillers and farmers who grew in numbers and provided all the food required on Earth. In the 97th Shar, Seti had a son called Enshi, which meant "Master of Humanity." Enshi was taught writing and counting by Adapa, he was taught about the Anunnaki and Nibiru, after which he was taken to Nibru-ki by the son of Enlil and showed anointing with oils, and how to extract the elixir from the Inbus fruits. This was also an important turning point in the relationship between humans and Anunnaki, when man began to call them "Lord." "It was since then that by civilised man the Anunnaki Lords were called," and the beginning of true worshipping of the Anunnaki. The civilized humans were also taught how to make fires with bitumen, how to operate the kiln and furnace, smelt metals, and refine gold. They were taught how to make instruments and play music and sing, and even how to dig wells for water. The humans liked to gather at the water to socialize and it was there where much interaction between males and females took place, with lots of sexual activity, leading to the rapid growth in their numbers. We still seem to display the same behavior as water always attracts loads of people. Whether it's the beach or a riverbank or even a pool in your backyard, people have always been attracted to water. And this is the part of the clay tablets that was copied into the Bible by the biblical writers thousands of years later, confusing virtually all scholars and theologians alike when they refer to the Nefilim. These were the days during which "the Igigi to Earth were more frequently coming" from Mars. Marduk and the rest of the Martian Igigi "what on Earth was transpiring they increasingly desired."

The time of human expansion had arrived on Earth. More and more humans were being born as descendants of Adapa. If one considers the cultural differences between those times and today, the one striking difference is that promiscuity among the gods was almost a part of their expected behavior. Is it possible that male humans inherited those urges from the Anunnaki? We certainly inherited most of their other characteristics, except the ones they specifically erased from our DNA. There was, however, a strange ironic reason for high levels of promiscuity in those ancient times. There had to be large numbers of half-siblings who could procreate to keep the genetic pool strong and healthy as the species was rapidly growing in numbers. So, without even realizing it, humans were imitating their maker gods in their sexual habits.

A long period of human achievement and cultural foundation building dawned. I will mention some of the characters who stood out in their prominence or achievements. Malalu, meaning "He Who Plays," was the son of Kunin and Mualit, his half-sister, and was known for singing and performing music, so Ninurta made him many instruments, which included a harp. Their whole family line worked in the metal city of Bad-Tibira.

Irid, which means "He of the Sweet Waters" became the master well-builder and provider of water where the humans liked to congregate and procreate. Ever wondered where the Greeks and Romans got their ideas for baths, and where the word *irrigate* originates? The Igigi from Mars were coming to Earth more frequently and in larger numbers, wanting to escape the harsh climate there, and to participate in the seemingly enjoyable lifestyle of the earthlings. The Igigi males started to take a fancy to the daughters of man and they began to desire them.

Marduk took a bright young man called Enkime—"Understanding the Annals"—under his wing and taught him many things. He took him to the moon, and taught him everything his father Enki had taught him before, about the stars and constellations and the circuits of the planets. Imagine finding those footsteps on the moon? What will that do to our perception of humanity? On their return, he was stationed under Utu at Sippar, the "Place of the Chariots," and was called the "Prince of Earthlings." Enkime was the first human who was taught the functions of priesthood. Some time later, Marduk returned to the heavens with Enkime, and his son Matushal. But this time Enkime did not return, he stayed in the heavens. "In a celestial chariot heavenward they soared . . . To visit the Igigi on Lahmu by Marduk they were taken . . . That in the heavens he stayed till the end of his days." It is not quite clear what exactly happened to this character, but it is written that the Igigi really took a liking to him. The possibility exists that Enkime actually stayed on Mars as a kind of pacifying force with the Igigi, who were growing restless. This would be very ironic since here we have a mortal earthling giving real Nibiruans inspiration. Maybe he was truly worthy of the priestly status bestowed on him. And maybe this is where he put it to very good use, because it would take a while longer before the Igigi finally began to leave Mars in great numbers, heading for Earth. This all happened in 104th Shar, which was 374,400 years after arrival, 68,600 years ago.

Adapa, the first civilized human or *Homo sapiens sapiens,* died in the 108th Shar, 55000 BC. He lived for 14 Shar, which would have made him about 48,600 years old! This is clear evidence that the Anunnaki must have performed additional genetic manipulation on humans as time went by to reduce their aging ability, and thereby reducing their numbers as well. This was, however, not enough to slow the rapid birthrate of the slave species. As the numbers of mankind kept growing and beautiful daughters were born to them, Marduk fell in love with an earthling female. He would be the first Anunnaki to espouse an earthling, and this would clearly have some repercussions. During their controversial debates, we are reminded about humankind's mortality and the image of their maker. Marduk also reminds his father about the mess they had made by creating a civilized species that is as advanced in their thinking as the Anunnaki, the only difference being their longevity. "Step by step on this planet a primitive being, one like us to be, we have created . . . In our image and in our likeness civilised earthling is, except for the long life, he is we." This was Marduk's substantiation for wanting to espouse an earthling female. His options were clearly presented to him by Enki and Enlil. Marduk would forsake all his princely rights on Nibiru and never be able to return there with his spouse. Even Anu was involved in this weighty affair. "Marduk marry can . . . but on Nibiru a prince he shall no longer be." It was this kind of action by his elders that pushed the young ambitious Marduk even further toward rejecting the whole system, and eventually rising against all of the Anunnaki when he proclaimed himself god above all.

And so after their wedding, Marduk and his bride Sarpanit were sent away to a land of their own. "A domain of their own, away from the Edin, in another land" did Enlil and Enki say. We also get a pretty good idea to which part of the world Marduk was restricted. "A domain above the Abzu, in the land that the Upper Sea reaches, one that by waters from the Edin is separated, that by ships can be reached." This was the land of Egypt they were talking about. The land that Marduk would rule as the god Ra, in years to come? Unbeknown to the senior brothers Enlil and Enki, the Igigi from Mars used the wedding ceremony as an excuse to come to Earth. However, they had a much more cunning reason for coming. Let's face it, their life on a lonely tough planet like Mars was not what they had hoped for when they left Nibiru. They also wanted the seemingly lavish and fun-filled life surrounded by slaves that the Anunnaki on Earth had. But their main attraction to Earth were the extremely sexual and beautiful "daughters of man." The following episode is well documented in Genesis, once again, copied from much earlier Sumerian tablets and misunderstood by scholars and modern-day theologians. The Igigi were saying: "What to Marduk permitted is from us too should not be deprived." The earthling females were called "Adapite Females," after their original ancestor Adapa, the first *Homo sapiens sapiens,* the son of Enki and an earthling of Adamu's ancestry.

The Igigi said: "Come let us choose wives from among the Adapite Females, and children beget." They took these females as hostages to the space port and demanded that they be allowed the same privilege as Marduk. He obviously agreed with them. "What I have done from them cannot be deprived." Once again we see the angry Enlil, who was extremely agitated by this. "Enlil was enraged without pacification." We can clearly sense the clandestine plot to control humans by force and punishment. "By our own hands this planet with earthling multitudes shall be overrun." He would become the vengeful god of the Bible, carefully monitoring every step the humans made, while ensuring they do not grow too wise or too strong to challenge him in any possible way. So even after Enlil capitulated "let the Igigi and their females from Earth depart," he immediately had to face another dilemma. Marduk informed him that it had become impossible to live on Mars any more, the conditions had become unbearable, and they would have to abandon their station. "On Lahmu conditions unbearable have become, surviving is not possible."

The immigrants from Mars were secluded in and around the space port in the cedar mountains, where they had originally staged their resistance. They had children who became known as "Children of the Rocket Ships" often referred to in books and Sumerian translations. Eventually, some of them joined Marduk in his new land, some went "to the far eastlands, lands of high mountains," while others remained where they were. It is absolutely clear from these descriptions that these were the original Aryans who later settled all over Europe and invaded the Indus Valley, laying the foundation for the Indo-European language base. They were white, technologically advanced, and possessed knowledge way beyond ordinary humans. They would also be the original pharaohs of Egypt under Marduk's rule. Marduk started to build a large and loyal group of earthlings who followed him, obeyed him, and worshipped him. He was becoming a powerful force on Earth, which began to worry Enlil and Enki. We hear some more biblical words from Enlil as he ponders what the future may hold. "The Earth by the earthlings inherited shall be." And so Enlil planned a resistance against any possible future moves by Marduk. He sent his son Ninurta to find the offspring and clans of Ka-in where they dwelled in the distant lands, and teach them everything they needed to know about making tools, mining, manufacturing, smelting, shipbuilding, sailing, and fighting a war. "In a new land a domain they established, a city with twin towers there they built . . . A domain beyond the sea it was, the mountainland of the new Bond Heaven-Earth it was not." From these descriptions it sounds to me undoubtedly like the early Andean settlement and civilizations of South America in Peru and Bolivia near Lake Titicaca.

Back in Edin, they appointed a human called Lu-mach, the son of Matushal, to be the work master for the Anunnaki. He had a wife called Batanash. "Of a beauty outstanding she was, by her beauty was Enki charmed." We see the highly sexual side of Enki's character resurface once again, creating more controversy and introducing his gene pool into the human species yet again. He seduced the beautiful Batanash who bore a son whom they called Ziusudra, "He of Long Bright Life Days." This would be the human who survives the flood in an ark, and who was the real original character that the Bible calls Noah. He was raised in Shurubak, but the secret of his paternal line remained with Enki and Batanash. He was born in the 110th Shar, 396,000 years since arrival, 47,000 years BC, which was right in the middle of the last ice age. For those who believe that the ice age meant that the whole world was covered in snow and ice, this was not the case. Scholars describe that most of Canada, northern United States, northern Europe, and northern Asia was covered by ice and snow, but further south, the world was very habitable with a very different climate than today. That is also why the Anunnaki settled in Mesopotamia between the Tigris and Euphrates rivers. Then, it was very lush and green, and did not look anything like the desert it is today. Antarctica was probably much more extended with thick ice covering, which would be the main cause of the Great Flood in time to come.

Just like Adapa, Enki's first human offspring, Ziusudra was also very smart, showing great signs of intelligence, and Enki adored the boy who looked just like him. The description of the child gives us a good idea of what Enki looked like. This is how the child Ziusudra is described. "White as the snow his skin was . . . the colour of wool was his hair . . . like the sky were his eyes, with a brilliance were his eyes shining." From the beginning, he was treated with special care by both Ninmah and Enki. He was taught priestly rites and everything that Adapa knew before him. We are also given a strong hint that the Anunnaki used a different language or written script among themselves when we read "to read the writings of Adapa he him taught." In this bit of information lies the possible substantiation that the Indus script and the Balkan-Danube Script may be a language that the Anunnaki used, or a related script that the early humans, like Ziusudra and Adapa, used long before the Flood wiped out most of the world. That would also explain why there is only a small number of examples found in the world. The rest were carried away and buried under mountains of sand and silt. But when the Sumerian tablets refer to the Prior Times, do they mean times before the Flood? When there was a different

Fig. 16.18. Diagnoses of medical conditions. Old Babylonian on clay, Babylonia, circa 1900 BC in cuneiform script. This clay tablet outlines a number of medical procedures by an ancient physician. Medical texts of this category are well-known from Neo-Babylonian literature; however, there are only a few surviving tablets from the Old Babylonian period, over 1,000 years earlier. Many of the Babylonian diagnoses and prognoses still hold true in modern medicine.

kind of order on Earth? When the language was different, before the tower of Babel and before "man's language was confused"? It certainly seems like it.

But the times were not good on Earth, which seemed as if it were trapped in a downward spiral both culturally and environmentally. The Igigi were procreating with earthling females at a rapid rate, which made Enlil extremely unhappy. "In his eyes the Anunnaki mission to Earth had become perverted." Let's face it: This kind of situation was probably the furthest from his mind when they arrived to extract gold from the ground. What is also fascinating was the environmental effect on the rapidly emerging new species. Here we have a new species that was suddenly dropped into relatively alien conditions to them. They did not evolve into their surroundings; their immune systems were not adjusted to the microorganisms on Earth at that time, so we should not be surprised when we read about the diseases that overcame humans. "In the days of Ziusudra plagues and pestilence the Earth afflicted . . . Aches, dizziness, chills, fevers the earthlings overwhelmed."

Thankfully, Ninmah, the smart half-sister of the mighty brothers, was a true healer. "Let us the earthlings curing teach, how themselves to remedy to learn." Enlil would have none of it. He was not going to do anything to help the new species survive and flourish. "Let the earthlings by hunger and pestilence perish." In his mind their stay on Earth was nearing the end and he would rather wipe out all life before they departed for Nibiru. His "vengeful god" personality was clearly exposed. The land suffered too, nothing grew, and winds, heat, and drought haunted them. Nibiru was nearing its path close to the sun and strange things were happening to planet Earth. Tremors and quakes became regular events and Enlil conferred with Anu on Nibiru about the strange activities. They set up monitoring devices in the Abzu to observe the South Pole. "Odd rumblings in the Whiteland's snow were recorded . . . The snow-ice that the Whiteland covers to sliding has taken." This is the first real evidence of the ending of the ice age, clearly captured in clay tablets. How could a scribe 4,500 years ago have known anything about the events that preceded the flood, unless he was told by someone who was there? The detail in his text is too specific to have been conveyed orally over thousands of years. It became clear that when Nibiru came around the sun, it was going to cause havoc with Earth's gravity and have a devastating effect on the polar regions where the ice was already melting. "The next time Nibiru the Sun shall be nearing, Earth to Nibiru's netforce exposed shall be." Those are highly insightful words by the Anunnaki on Nibiru, warning Enlil about a severe calamity awaiting the Earth.

The Anunnaki started preparing for evacuation. They ceased all the smelting, "all the gold to Nibiru was lofted . . . for evacuation ready, a fleet of fast celestial chariots to Earth returned." Enlil called an urgent meeting of all the Igigi and Anunnaki commanders and revealed the "impending calamity" to them. "To a bitter end Earth mission has come." He made it clear that those who wanted to leave Earth had to do so without their earthling spouses. This was the moment Enlil had secretly been waiting for: to destroy the hordes of earthlings who have taken over the world by their sheer numbers. Those among the Anunnaki and Igigi who chose to stay were told to move to higher grounds and wait for the calamity to pass. The other Anunnaki who did not want to return to Nibiru would wait for the events to play themselves out in their "Boats of Heaven" at the edge of Earth's atmosphere. Then came the critical moment when the true human character of many Anunnaki children born on Earth suddenly emerged. Marduk and all the other sons of Enki chose to stay behind. So did Enlil's sons. This was a really emotional time for the sensitive Ninmah; they all looked at her to hear her decision. "With pride her choice to stay she declared . . . my lifework is here . . . The earthlings my created I shall not abandon."

Then Enlil revealed his master plan for the human race. "Let the earthlings for the abominations perish." We can clearly hear the tone of the god of vengeance, whose voice we would constantly hear in the Bible. But Enki disagreed very strongly with his brother. After all, it was he who created the humans in the first place, and he who had fathered the next species of civilized humans. "A wonderous Being by us was created, by us saved it must be." A fierce argument erupted between the brothers, where Enlil accused Enki of playing God. "The powers of the 'Creator of All' into your hands you have taken," blaming Enki for all the abomination caused by the humans.

As the commander of Earth, Enlil made the final call, and instructed all those present to take an oath, which would cause the destruction of humankind. "Now that a calamity by a destiny unknown has been ordained, let what must happen, happen." Everyone pledged their oath except Enki, who stormed out of the assembly. "On Enlil alone let the responsibility forever rest." As part of the evacuation activities, Enlil took the ME to Sippar, the place of the "Celestial Chariots," and buried them safely in a protective chamber. So what were they all waiting for? What kind of calamity did they expect? A great flood of water, with a wave so high that it would devastate the entire planet. "When the avalanche of waters sweeps over the lands . . . In one sudden swoop to an extinction shall be doomed." And so the preparations came to an end and they waited for the disaster to strike. This is the kind of advanced warning the people of Indonesia, Thailand, Sri Lanka, India, and Ethiopia wish they'd had before the tsunami devastated their lives. But the defiant Enki and his half-sister Ninmah went to the Abzu and they collected all necessary specimens that would allow them to recombine all the life forms they had created on Earth. "Male and female essence and life eggs they collected . . . For safekeeping while in Earth circuit to be taken."

"In Sippar the Anunnaki gathered, the day of the deluge they awaited." Enki was not done yet. After all, his flesh and blood, Ziusudra, was to be left behind to perish in the flood. This is the original story of the flood and how humans survived. Unlike the more naive and simplified biblical version of Noah, the Sumerian tablets tell us in great detail to what length Enki went to help Ziusudra; how he guided him with precise plans to build the "boat"; how to seal it with pitch and exactly what he should take into it. "The boat be one that can turn and tumble, the watery avalanche to survive . . . into it your family and kinfolk gather . . . water for drinking heap up . . . household animals also bring." Although Enki was defiant against Enlil, he did not want to blatantly disregard the oath they had taken. Therefore, he conveyed all this information to Ziusudra from behind a reed hut wall, not to expose his face. His rather childish but effective argument was that he did not speak to Ziusudra, he spoke to a wall. "An overwhelming deluge coming from the south, lands and life shall devastate . . . Your boat from its moorings it shall lift . . . the boat it shall turn and tumble . . . By you shall the civilised seed of man survive." The differences between this version and the biblical story lies not only in its practical content, but the fact that Ziusudra took not only his immediate and extended family into the boat, but also other friends. The biblical Noah's seed would simply have died out within a few generations due to inbreeding. The part where Noah has to take all the animals two-by-two into the ark has always troubled me for reasons of improbability. But the story has in fact a very different origin, one that makes more sense, and is achievable. Remember that Enki and Ninmah collected all the essence of humans and creatures in the wilds? Well, they carefully stored this "essence," which must have been DNA, sperm, and ova, in appropriate containers for preservation. The tablets are very clear on this. A few days before the Flood, Ningal delivered a box to Ziusudra in the boat. "The life essence and life eggs of living creatures it contains, by the lord Enki and Ninmah collected . . . From the wrath of Enlil to be hidden, to life resurrected if Earth be willing." Those are chilling words that would be repeated many times by the heroes of the Bible thousands of years later. The wrath of Enlil became the "wrath of god," which has kept humanity fearful and obedient until today.

And so the Flood arrived as expected. It came in the 120th Shar, 432,000 years after arrival, about 11000 BC, which is exactly when modern scholars claim the Flood destroyed the world. It is also important to note that at that stage Ziusudra was already 10 Shars old, which made him 36,000 Earth years. It is now absolutely clear that the flood was not caused by God in a moment of anger with humanity, but that it was actually as a result of a cosmic event when the giant planet of the Anunnaki came closer to Earth than it normally did, in its 3,600-year orbit. It was indeed a natural calamity, which was abused by the Anunnaki to destroy their troublesome creation: their slave species called man.

Nibiru came into close proximity of Earth, causing havoc with gravity and seismic activity. It must have been very testing times for the fragile planet. The tablets tell us clearly that "For days before the Day of the Deluge the earth was rumbling, groan as with pain it did." The time had come for the Anunnaki to depart. "Crouched in their boats of heaven, the Anunnaki heavenward were lofted." We get a very clear picture of the exact events, not because of someone's vivid imagination, but because the Anunnaki were actually observing the Flood from their spaceships in orbit. The descriptions are much too detailed and descriptive for someone from a primitive age to have imagined it.

The Earth began to shake, by a netforce before unknown it was agitated . . .
In the Whiteland at Earth's bottom, the Earth's foundations were shaking

. . . Then with a roar to a thousand thunders equal, off its foundations the icesheet slipped . . . By Nibiru's unseen netforce into the south sea crashing . . . One sheet of ice into another icesheet was smashing . . . The Whiteland's surface like a broken eggshell was crumbling . . . Tidal waves arose, the very skies was the wall of water reaching . . . Northward was the wall of water onrushing . . . The Abzu land it was reaching . . . Toward the settled land it travelled . . . The Edin it overwhelmed.

We all know the kind of devastation a small tsunami can bring, so just imagine a tidal wave several hundred meters high moving northward from Antarctica at 500 km per hour, like a giant circle around the world, destroying all the lands lower than 2,000 meters above sea level. We get another bird's eye view from the Anunnaki in their orbit above the Earth. "Where there were dry lands, now was a sea of water . . . Where mountains once to heaven their peaks raised, their tops now like islands were in the waters." We also get a good glimpse of Ninmah's sensitive side as the matriarch of humankind, who was very sad by what she witnessed from up there. "My created like drowned dragonflies in a pond the waters fill, all life by the rolling sea wave away was taken."

I take it that we all know how the flood story ends, and yes you are right, the boat did settle on the twin peaks of a mountain called Arata, known to most as Ararat, which the tablets call "Mount of Salvation." The first thing Ziusudra did when he emerged from the boat was to praise the lord Enki for saving them. They built an altar, lit a fire, and gave thanks with a lamb sacrifice, something that he was taught in his initiation into the priesthood. The floating spaceships in orbit could not have been very comfortable, crammed with too many Anunnaki, keen to get back to solid ground. It, therefore, was not long after things subsided that Enlil and Enki landed to assess the damage. "The situation to review, what to be done to determine." At first the brothers were smiling and embracing but "when Enlil the survivors saw . . . his fury no bounds had." And once again we get a glimpse of the god of vengeance who would rule and control humankind with oppression and violence for thousands of years. In a rage of fury, Enlil attacked Enki. "Every earthling had to perish," he said. But Enki answered him by explaining the truth about Ziusudra. "He is no mere mortal my son he is." After some deliberation and argument, Enlil was persuaded that it was the will of the Creator of All that saved the humans. And before the so-called Olden Times came to an end, we are confronted by several more statements that were repeated in the Bible many years later. Ninmah, who loved her human creation whom she perfected with Enki, took an oath declaring that "the annihilation of mankind shall never be repeated," and Enlil told Ziusudra to "be fruitful and multiply."

You can imagine what kind of sedimentation resulted from a flood of this size. It took many years for the waters to subside, only to expose the valleys filled with mud and silt. Everything in the Abzu and the Edin was buried under mud. All the cities in the whole of Mesopotamia were gone, buried under mud and silt. But the great stone platform, their landing place in the Cedar Mountains, was still there and could be used, mainly because it was positioned much higher than all their other settlements. Some scholars like Zecharia Sitchin believe this to be the ancient stone platform of Baalbek in northeast Lebanon. When you view the giant megaliths placed together to form a perfectly flat platform that stretches around 90,000 square meters, you begin to wonder why prehistoric humans on Earth needed to build such a structure. The rocks weigh between 200 and 1,200 tons each. Today, there are only a handful of giant-sized cranes that could pick up such stones. They are perfectly cut out and shaped with smooth sides to fit into each other almost like Lego blocks at the edges. So it would make sense that this kind of platform did not get washed away, due to its sheer size and also its altitude. What it did was give the Anunnaki the crucial idea of how to deal with possible disasters in future. And what kind of structures could possibly withstand a similar disaster, while serving as an important beacon in guiding the Anunnaki pilots when coming in from space? You guessed right . . . the pyramids of Giza. Imagine having to land on a new planet for the first time . . . would you not prefer a clear beacon that guides you directly to the landing spot? I would, and clearly the Anunnaki did too. And that is where the pyramids come into the picture a little later.

The devastation was not only restricted to Earth; the Igigi arrived from Mars saying that their planet had also been devastated. "Lahmu by the passage of Nibiru was devastated . . . Its atmosphere was sucked out, its waters thereafter evaporated . . . A place of dust storms it is." They realized that survival was now their main concern. They retrieved the ME from the Creation Chamber, which they buried next to the launch site. It is fascinating that even the material that was used for the chamber is mentioned. It was diorite, the hardest stone known to man, harder than iron. "The diorite chests with seals were fastened." They retrieved a whole variety of items including the seeds they brought from Nibiru, which enabled them to start planting crops again. But while the survivors on Earth were getting on with rebuilding their lives, the word from Nibiru was not so reassuring. The gravitational activity between the other planets and Nibiru had also affected them. "The shield of gold dust was torn, the atmosphere was dwindling again." Suddenly the scramble for gold became critical. Just when they

 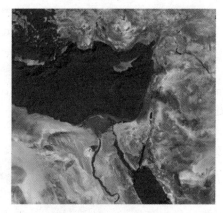

Fig. 16.19. A view of the pyramids from space. They not only served as landmarks, but the Great Pyramid also housed the transmitter beacon that would guide the incoming pilots and astronauts. These giant structures were built after the Flood, when the Anunnaki saw how resistant the stone structure at Baalbek was to the floodwater. Egypt and the Red Sea was a visible landmark from high above the Earth.

were ready to pack up and go home, the urgency had returned. But this time there were no more workers in the Abzu, they were all killed by the water, and even the Anunnaki were few in numbers as most of them returned to Nibiru. By fate or by destiny that could have only been preordained by the Creator of All, "on Earth and on Nibiru there was desperation."

The task of mining gold from ore was impossible with the few numbers of people left behind. They surveyed the world again and Ninurta returned with good news from distant lands beyond the ocean. The mountains had been eroded by the flood, exposing rich sediments of gold that were oozing out in pure nuggets. These were the valleys around lake Titicaca on the border of Bolivia and Peru, and the beginning of the ancient Inca civilization before the Europeans came to plunder it. "Nuggets large and small to the rivers below fell down, without mining can the gold be hauled." Enlil and Enki were astounded. "Gold, pure gold, refining and smelting not required, all about was lying."

And so began the South American prehistoric gold rush. But they needed to create a landing site nearby, from where to take the gold to Nibiru. Thus, we uncover the practical origins of the Nazca plain. Much has been written and speculated about the so-called Nazca lines. They have certainly challenged the best archaeologists for centuries. The Sumerian clay tablets provide the answers once more. For all those who have wondered and marveled at the strange markings and spectacles on the flat, hard, desert-like ground at Nazca in Peru, the answers are crystal clear in cuneiform text. "Now let us a new place to celestial chariots establish, therefrom the gold to Nibiru send . . . For a new plain whose soil has dried and hardened they searched . . . In a desolate peninsula such a plain they found . . . Flat as a lake it was, by white mountains it was surrounded." This fits the exact description of the desolate peninsula of Nazca that is surrounded by the Andes mountain range, which would have had "white" snow on its peaks.

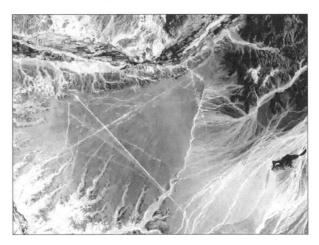

Fig. 16.20. X marks the spot. The symbol of the cross is well documented in ancient civilizations. Could it be that the Anunnaki used this symbol on the Nazca plain to indicate their landing spot to incoming craft? As seen in this satellite picture, this approach does the job quite superbly.

Ninurta had been living there before the Flood and he knew where to locate the descendants of Ka-in. The locals who survived the Flood knew Ninurta and revered him as their protector god. They could be used to gather the gold and other metals, they knew the art of smelting and handling of metals. Ninurta explained to Enlil and Enki "As the protector of their forefathers they me recall . . . The great protector they call me." At this stage even Enlil, who had hoped for the complete destruction of all humans, was pleased to find the survivors. The gods' future was suddenly in the hands of the humans. While the collection of gold began to swing into action in South America, the Anunnaki were not simply going to abandon their original settlements in Mesopotamia. For those who have spoken about the pyramids of Giza being built as a mirror image of Orion's belt, there is much vindication in the tablets. The Anunnaki decided to build a new landing site, "a new place of the celestial chariots." The tablets further tell us that in the peninsula they chose, "the heavenly ways of Anu and Enlil on Earth were reflected . . . Let the new place of chariots precisely on that boundary be reflected . . . Let the heart of the plain the heavens reflect." Enlil did the surveying from a sky ship, but it was the talented Ningishzidda who once more showed off his great architectural skills. That is why the latter civilization of Egypt would come to call him Thoth or Tehuti, "the divine measurer" and the god of science and knowledge. Ningishzidda designed, planned, and executed the building of the three pyramids of Giza. Not as tombs as most people still erroneously claim, but as very important landmarks, and indestructible beacons that made up part of the landing grid for pilots. "To demarcate the landing corridor . . . To demarcate the landing corridor's boundary, ascent and descent to secure." And so the three great pyramids were planned and measured as the beacons of their new future landing site. They witnessed how solid the landing platform at Baalbek was, so they applied those principles of using heavy rocks to build the new pyramid beacons in the south as part of a giant grid of landmarks, which would guide the pilots toward the landing site.

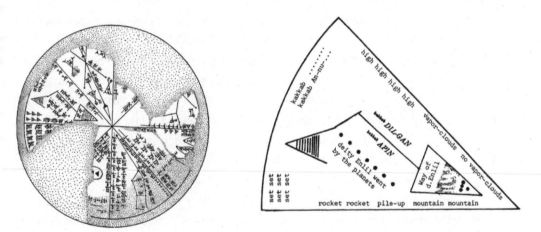

Fig. 16.21. Way of god Enlil—Ancient planisphere (flat circular map). When this disk was first discovered in the Royal Library at Nineveh it was thought to be linked to ancient witchcraft. It is an Assyrian copy of a Sumerian original. An ancient astronomical map divided into eight segments, showing geometric shapes, unseen on any other ancient artifact, and drawn with precision. It includes a host of astronomical content with a mathematical curve previously assumed not to have been known in ancient times, also introducing the 360 degrees of a circle.

The direct translation of the Sumerian inscriptions on this disk basically describe the "route map" by which the "god Enlil went by the planets." It includes operating instructions with altitude and weather pattern observations on various instruments. It also clearly shows the dots representing planets and Earth as the seventh planet to which Enlil would travel. The triangle on the left represents the far cosmos, while the destination is the triangle on the right converging toward the landing spot. Other translations are: "The ruler's domain on the mountainous land" and "The way of god Enlil." It also contains a complex mathematical formula that has perplexed astronomers ever since, and as yet remains unexplained.

The tablets describe how they chose the various landmarks, which included the old platform in the Cedar Mountains, as part of the directional grid. "Let the landing place in the Cedar Mountains be a part of the facilities." But why did they build the pyramids in that specific place, while all the other fixed points they had chosen were natural landmarks? This is why: "Where the second set of twin peaks was required, mountains there were none . . . only a water-clogged valley from the ground protruded." This is a perfect description of Giza all those years ago, after the Flood.

And so Ningishzidda came to the fore as he began to design the most mysterious and controversial structure on Earth, the Great Pyramid of Giza. "Artificial peaks thereon we can raise," he said to the others, referring to Giza. Before he began the huge undertaking, he built a smaller prototype to test some of his calculations. That was the smallest of the three pyramids, or as we know it, the Pyramid of Menkaure. "On the flatland, above the river's valley, Ningishzidda a scale model built . . . The rising angles and four smooth sides with it he perfected." Only after he was satisfied with the model, he continued to build the big ones, and we also learn how they managed to cut the stones so smoothly and perfectly, so quickly and seemingly with ease. "Next to it a larger peak he placed, its sides to Earth's four corners he set . . . By the Anunnaki with their tools of power, were its stones cut and erected." The next one to be built was the Pyramid of Khafre, as outlined in Sumerian texts. The reason we know this is because the first two pyramids do not have a major network of passages and chambers, which is exactly the way they are described. "Next to it a larger peak he placed, its sides to Earth's four corners he placed." Only once the second one was completed did he take on the task of constructing the Great Pyramid, with all its secret passages—all of which had a specific purpose. This purpose was most certainly not to serve as a tomb for some earthling pharaoh thousands of years later. "Beside it, in precise location, the peak that was its twin he placed . . . With galleries and chambers for pulsating crystals he designed it." There we have it, written in perfect clay, the pyramids were to be landmarks and beacons that transmitted signals and light to guide incoming pilots and astronauts. A large number of scholars have shown beyond doubt that none of the pyramids of the Third and Fourth Dynasty in Egypt have ever produced any evidence of burials, bodies, sarcophagi, or even inscriptions to that effect. There is no evidence whatsoever that they were built as tombs. This popular myth was created many years later when modern archaeologists began to fill the mesmerized world with fantastic stories created by their imagination only. Remember that unlike the tombs of the Valley of the Kings, the Great Pyramids of Giza do not have any inscriptions at all, anywhere, that refer to the burial of a king. The only inscription of King Khufu in the Great Pyramid is on a rock in one of the smaller spaces above the King's Chamber. This is highly suspicious and points to being a much later addition to the structure.

The references to the pyramids do not end there. They called it Ekur, "House Which Like a Mountain Is." They placed what they called the Nibiru Crystals in the chambers of the pyramid and "Enlil by his own hand the Nibiru crystals activated . . . the eerie lights began to flicker, an enchanting hum the stillness broke . . . Outside the capstone, all at once was shining." This was a great achievement for them, most likely inspired by the resilience of the landing site that was not destroyed in the Flood. They had built a landmark that would withstand floods and other kinds of catastrophes, except the constant onslaught of future human plunderers. The Anunnaki assembled to witness the spectacle and Ninmah even wrote and recited a poem.

> *House that is like mountain with pointed peak*
> *For Heaven-Earth it is equipped, the handiwork of the*
> > *Anunnaki it is*
> *House bright and dark, house of heaven and Earth*
> *For the celestial boats it was put together, by the Anunnaki*
> > *built*
> *House whose interior with a reddish light of heaven glows*
> *A pulsating beam that far and high reaches it emits*
> *Lofty mountain of mountains, great and lofty fashioned*
> *Beyond the understanding of Earthlings it is*
> *House of equipment, lofty house of eternity . . .*

The poem goes on praising the structure and its maker. To honor the builder, they agreed to build a monument nearby, with the face of the builder and the body of a lion, which symbolized the age during which it was built. "Let us beside the twin peaks a monument create, the Age of the Lion it announce . . . The face of Ningishzidda, the peak's designer, let its face be . . . Toward the place of celestial chariots gaze." The speculations about the age and meaning of the Sphinx have been as rife as the confusion around the pyramids. But as you can see from this excerpt, the tablets make it very clear when and why the Sphinx was built. As always, the answers seem to be much less complicated and more probable than the theories by historians who make pronouncements based on romantic assumptions. All those who argue against this information will probably eventually find that all the clues will lead them back to this conclusion. A number of researchers have already made such suggestions, implying that the Sphinx must have been around in times when water caused most of the erosion of the monument, and not wind as others assumed. Graham Hancock goes into great detail in his book *Fingerprints of the Gods* to explain the geological and erosion factors that led to the Sphinx being in the state it is today. It was mainly water, then wind that eroded it. This could only have happened thousands of years ago when Giza had more rain and the floodwater could reach the Sphinx. Therefore, many scholars now believe the Sphinx to have been built around 10000 BC. This would corroborate the information we find in the clay tablets.

But even while the building was in progress, Marduk started causing trouble again, complaining that his younger brother Ningishzidda was getting all the glory and that once again he had been passed by. A period of heated debates followed, during which all the Anunnaki children made all kinds of claims to different lands, and demanded that they be given more control over loyal earthlings and command of their own regions. "By the clamour for domains Ninurta and his brother were also aroused . . . Lands for themselves and devoted earthlings everyone was demanding." The wise and rational Ninmah came to the fore, playing the part of the peacemaker. She made proposals that clearly prevented violent conflict among the Anunnaki. "Let not the celebration a contest become, Ninmah amidst the raised voices shouted . . . For peace to prevail, the habitable lands between us should be apart set." For her role as a wise and calming sister, they decided to change her name on that day. Ninmah became known as Ninharsag, "Mistress of the Mountainhead." And so they divided the lands between the siblings and their followers. Ninharsag was given the "Land of the Missiles," or Tilmun, better known to modern humans as the Sinai Peninsula, which was out of bounds to humans. This land was declared as neutral territory under Ninharsag's control. "The habitable lands to the east thereof for Enlil and his offspring we set apart." This was the whole of the Near East or "Olden Lands" where the Anunnaki settled at first, which included Mesopotamia, Akkad, Babylonia, Assyria, and Sumer. The "dark-hued" lands and the Abzu were given to Enki and his clan, which included his earthling son Ziusudra. Enki decided to appease his oldest son Marduk, who also happened to be the regular instigator of trouble, so he gave him the "dark-hued" lands that we know as Egypt. Under his hand we see the sudden emergence of the new Egyptian civilization of earthlings. The old days of the primitive worker slaves were gone. Suddenly, everyone clamored for the civilized worker to be their slaves and perform all kinds of tasks.

One can clearly detect from the rather stressful and manic period in the lives of the Anunnaki that they were very preoccupied with their own personal struggle, family quibbles, and problems with the mission to Earth. They didn't want to have to deal with additional complaints of the humans who began to multiply again. But this time the humans were mixing with the Anunnaki and Igigi on a regular basis, many of them expecting to be granted the same treatment as the gods, as opposed to being treated like the lesser human slave species. A long period of uneasy stability followed while the gold supplies were being depleted and the occasional violent confrontation between the Anunnaki youth erupted. The tablets describe various battles in detail where fierce and sophisticated weapons were used, which could not possibly have existed in those days. Most of the conflict was regarding land, instigated by Marduk and the Igigi who were making all kinds of new demands and breaking rules at every opportunity. The way in which humans have fought over land since then is another perfect example of the genetic hold this Anunnaki DNA has had over us for thousands of years. The incredible desire to conquer lands and invade new territory is so distinctly visible in the behavior of the young offspring that the older and wiser Anunnaki produced on Earth. And so the incredible family drama of the Anunnaki continued among the extended family and their allies, while the humans became mere spectators on the sideline of this global stage. It would not be long, however, before humankind began to play out their own drama of cultures attacking and killing one another, but not before they were elevated to a higher level of civilization by their makers. There is a certain irony in that statement, which is indicative of the fact that the level of civilization had very little to do with the initial behavior of humankind, but it was the guiding hand of violent, selfish gods who manipulated humans to achieve their own objectives. The Anunnaki saw us in the same light we see the many kinds of domesticated dogs that we breed for various purposes. We adore them, but they are not quite equal to us, because they are animals. And so the gods perceived the human creation to be part animal and disposable.

The unrest among the gods continued and grew to the point where the Igigi invaded the "Place of the Chariots." Marduk lost both his sons, which made him even more bitter, and all this instability in the Old Land caused Enlil to be concerned about the safety of their space port. This prompted him to build a new space port: "Bond Heaven-Earth" facility in Ninurta's lands beyond the sea, as was mentioned earlier. They built it "in the mountain lands beyond the oceans beside the great lake," which was Lake Titicaca. "At the foot of the mountain where the gold nuggets were scattered . . . facility in secret establish we must." This is when the Nazca plain was first utilized by the Anunnaki, as they introduced advanced knowledge to the South American humans.

Dumuzi was Enki's youngest and most cherished son. He was described as being sensitive and caring and artistic. At the unveiling of the Great Pyramid, he met Inanna, who was Enlil's granddaughter, and they fell hopelessly in love. Many ancient love songs and poems were written about the couple; they were like the primordial Romeo and Juliet. They became inseparable and Inanna was described as being "beautiful beyond description she was, in martial arts with Anunnaki heroes she competed." She was also known as Ishtar, Venus, and by many other names in all the cultures around the world. No matter what name they gave her, she was everyone's goddess of love. Inanna had great aspirations of peacemaking between nations and people, this was one of her strongest characteristics. Dumuzi was given lands above the Abzu, with buffalo in the reeds, with rivers and cattle. This must have been very close to Marduk's Egypt, to which the older brother did not take kindly, and became insanely jealous. His jealousy was not only because of the lands that were given to Dumuzi, but Inanna's big plans for her beloved. She wanted Dumuzi's name to rise above all Anunnaki, and this was dangerous territory that had been claimed by Marduk many years ago. He would not have his baby brother upset his master plan. So Marduk devised a devious plan to entrap Dumuzi in a sexual act. He set up their half-sister Geshtinanna to seduce Dumuzi with the promise that their offspring will be the successor to the throne because of their line of seed. She must have had some real powers of persuasion, or some sedatives, or Dumuzi simply behaved like a highly sexed male who could not refuse the advances of a beautiful girl. But in the middle of the night Dumuzi panicked and ran away, through a river and over rocks, where he slipped, fell, and killed himself in a freak accident.

Enki was devastated, displaying some very human emotions that we have also inherited from his active gene pool. "So did Enki bewail and lament . . . Why am I punished, why has fate against me turned . . . Enki rent his clothes, on his forehead he put ashes." This tearing of a piece of clothing when mourning was adopted by the Jews in later years. The growing conflict between siblings knew no end. Inanna's sister, Ereshkigal, must have been insanely jealous of Inanna's looks and her future role in the hierarchy of the Anunnaki, because she not only refused to help Inanna in her search for Dumuzi, but she accused her of plotting something against Marduk, and she infected Inanna with some kind of deadly disease or virus. "Let loose against her the sixty diseases." This is most certainly a part of the tablets that must have given rise to elements of witchcraft in Africa and the witchdoctors who still practice an ancient form of healing in Africa. Ereshkigal lived in the Abzu, where she was known as the "Mistress of the Lower World," which was southern Africa. It was not only her skills with medicines and disease that inspired many tales, but the mysterious things that Enki did in his quest to find Inanna must have also been the source of the many ancient African traditions of strange creatures with awesome powers, indestructible bodies, and not like humans in their ways. What Enki did next in his quest to find Inanna is still a mystery to most who have studied the tablets. "From clay of the Abzu, Enki two emissaries fashioned, beings without blood, by death rays unharmed." He sent them out to find Inanna. These must have been some awesome prehistoric clones, because as much as I try, I cannot fathom what else the scribe could have meant. They do, however, closely resemble the "mythological" creatures called Erinyes or Furies, as described in Greek and Roman myths, and I suggest you have another look at chapter 14 for a quick reminder. But they did what they were sent to do. They found "the lifeless body of Inanna . . . hanging from a stake . . . Upon the corpse the clay emissaries a Pulser and an Emitter directed . . . The water of life on her they sprinkled . . . In her mouth the plant of life they placed . . . Inanna stirred, her eyes she opened, from the dead Inanna arose." It is not clear why certain Anunnaki were revived from the dead, while others were not.

This had a devastating effect on relations between Enlil and Enki. The Enlilites wanted Marduk dead, while Enki's clan argued that while Marduk was involved in the incident, "it was not by Marduk's hand did Dumuzi die." Inanna was not going to take this lying down. In her mind, Marduk was responsible for the death of her beloved Dumuzi, so she launched an attack on Marduk with the intention to kill him. "By Inanna was the warfare begun . . . Marduk to battle she challenged . . . Retribution for her beloved's death she wanted." Another fascinating glimpse into the future behavior of humans, challenging each other to battle and duels and other forms of violent conflict. A very noble kind of gesture, by which European noblemen would invite each other into the countryside, put on very smart clothing, and then try to kill each other in a duel. Once again we read about fierce weapons that caused death and destruction over a wide area as the two engaged in battle. There were many earthling casualties, which must have remained in the tales told throughout the ages about the battle of the gods. We are very familiar with similar so-called mythological stories from all cultures. The simple explanation for such ancient tales are that there were many such conflicts between the Anunnaki gods, which must have been witnessed by the earthlings in the affected areas. Those were not daydreams or mythological hallucinations of primitive people with overactive minds, those were real events in ancient times, before writing was bestowed on the earthlings, when they still depended on oral stories being passed down between generations.

Marduk retreated north toward the new artificial mountains in Giza, where he took refuge inside the chambers of the Great Pyramid they called Ekur. "With weapons of brilliance . . . Inanna the hiding place attacked . . . while Utu the Igigi and their hordes of earthlings beyond Tilmun held off." Remember that the Igigi were Marduk's followers. But the pyramid demonstrated the purpose with which it was constructed, to withstand any kind of disaster. Inanna's weapons the "stone structure could not surmount, its smooth sides her weapons deflected." We learn two very important bits of information from these written lines. First, that the pyramid did have a smooth finish outside, covering the building blocks; and second, the description of passages and chambers of the pyramid during the chase inside. The kind of detail in the description would have only been known by the builders of the pyramid or those who had the privilege of having been inside themselves. This is all the proof we need to substantiate that the Anunnaki actually built the pyramids long before the pharaohs inherited them.

> Then Ninurta of the secret entrance learnt, the swivel stone on the north side he found . . . Through a dark corridor Ninurta passed, the grand gallery he reached . . . Its vault by the many-hued emissions of the crystals like a rainbow was aglitter . . . Ninurta up the gallery kept going . . . Into the upper chamber, the place of the Great Pulsating Stone, Marduk retreated . . . At its entrance Marduk the sliding stone locks lowered, from one and all admission they barred.

These detailed descriptions could not possibly be coincidental or some ancient person's imagination. And yet there are those who claim this is all a myth.

Some decided to leave Marduk in there to die for his transgressions, but his family protested. The wise Ninharsag came to the rescue once more, resolving the deadlock. Marduk would be rescued but certain conditions had to be met. "The Igigi who Marduk follow, the landing place must give up and abandon . . . To the land of no return must Marduk in exile go." Then the task was up to Ningishzidda, the architect, to get Marduk out of the pyramid. "A doorway in the stones they will cut . . . a twisted passage they shall bore . . . At the vortex of the hollowing through the stones they will break through . . . Up the grand gallery they will continue . . . The three stone bars they will raise . . . Marduk's death prison they will reach." Those sound like words of someone who had a very good knowledge of the inside of the pyramid. Not some kind of airy-fairy dreamer imagining gods and myths because he was bored. But many historians will still want to make you believe such nonsense. And so it was that Marduk was rescued by Ninurta and brought out alive, although barely. "Carefully through the twisting shaft they the lord lowered, to fresh air they him brought." Ninurta also examined all the high-tech equipment inside. "Its Gut Stone, that directions determined, Ninurta ordered to be taken out . . . The twenty seven pairs of Nibiru crystals he examined . . . To remove the whole ones . . . Others with his beam he pulverised . . . To replace the incapacitated beacon, a mount near the place of the celestial chariots was chosen." And so the function of the Great Pyramid was moved to a mountain top and the empty chambers became the fascination of archaeologists ever since. These latest developments required that control over old lands were to be evaluated and lordship over new lands had to be assigned. So Enlil and Enki divided the lands between their other sons again. The most significant allocation was that of Egypt, which was now given to Ningishzidda, while Marduk was exiled. Inanna demanded a land of her own, and after much debating, she was given the land of the Indus Valley.

That bit of information has fascinated me. The highly sexed goddess of love who was crazy about poetry is given the Indus Valley region, where by complete coincidence the highly sexual Indian cultures originated, including the *Kama Sutra* philosophy of sex. Another coincidence? The sixty-four arts of love-passion-pleasure also coincidentally originated in India. There are many different versions of the arts, which began in Sanskrit and were later translated into other languages, like Tibetan and Persian. Many of the original texts are missing and the only clue to their existence is in other texts. Vatsyayana's version of the *Kama Sutra* is a well-known translation that survived. Is it also coincidence that, unlike other religions, the ancient Vedic praises to the gods are in poetic form? And it just so happens that the goddess of love was a big fan of poetry?

But the times on Earth had undergone great change. "The earthlings have proliferated . . . Of civilised mankind by Ziusudra there were descendants . . . With Anunnaki seed they were intermixed . . . Igigi who intermarried roamed about . . . In the distant lands of Ka-in kinfolk survived." The numbers of surviving pure Anunnaki were very small and they had growing problems on many fronts. Conflict among themselves, large numbers of humans making all kinds of demands, supply of food was problematic, humans were getting out of control. The Anunnaki had to come up with a master plan to take control of the situation, to ensure that humans were kept in their place, stayed obedient, and worshipped the gods. "Few and lofty were the Anunnaki who from Nibiru had come . . . Few were their perfect descendants." But to devise a plan for the future they needed the wisdom and advice of Anu. "How over mankind lofty to remain, how to make the many the few obey and serve." And so it was that "to come to Earth one more time Anu decided." And so we read in no uncertain terms that the gods wanted to remain "lofty" over the humans.

By now, enough time had passed for the flooded plains and valleys to dry and become habitable again. Some of the "black-headed people," or primitive workers in the south of the Abzu, who survived the Flood came in search of food and probably to also get some guidance from their gods, who lived in the north. The descendants of Ziusudra and his son Shem started to come down from their primitive dwellings in the mountains to resettle in the valleys and plains. They were among the few who were well trained and skilled in the art of farming. The Anunnaki decided to rebuild their original cities on Earth, where they originally stood, but were now covered with soil from the Flood. They also decided to use the more civilized humans for providing food for the growing populations of survivors on a much larger scale. This would, however, require the general upliftment of the slave species. "Upon the newly dried soil, the Anunnaki let them settle, food for all to provide . . . On top of the myriads of mud and silt a new Eridu was marked out." If you remember, Eridu was the first city of Enki when he arrived on Earth, and now he built his new home in the middle of the brand new Eridu, while Enlil built his new home where the old Nibruki stood. It was a seven-stepped ziggurat pyramid. "A stairway rising to the heaven, to the topmost platform led . . . His tablets of destinies did Enlil there keep, with his weapons it was protected." It seems that Enlil was the one who always used weapons to protect his dwellings, a habit that Marduk learned very well in his dictatorship over Egypt.

They built a brand new palace for Anu and Antu's (Anu's wife) arrival in the middle of the Edin, calling it Unug-ki, "Delightful Place." We learn about the aging effect that living on Earth had on the Anunnaki when Anu arrived. "At each other they looked, ageing to examine . . . Greater in Shars were the parents, younger than the children they looked." They debated this for some time concerned about this strange phenomenon. But Anu reassured them that those who returned to Nibiru were treated and cured of this aging problem. A number of banquets and astronomical observations took place during which they awaited the rising of various planets as night fell, including Nibiru. "From the topmost step . . . The red-haloed Nibiru into view came . . . The heavenly planet of the lord Anu." As you know by now, this was not the first time that we read about the "red-hued" planet of the Anunnaki.

The appearance of their planet made them go through another spell of deeply philosophical deliberation about the past events on Earth, their role in all of it, and "was the creation of the earthlings also destined?" They came to the startling conclusion that "The will of the Creator of All is clear to see . . . The Earth to earthlings belongs . . . To preserve and advance them we were intended." This is what Anu shared with his extended family on Earth. And so by this newly found understanding of their role in the greater scheme of things, they agreed to reorganize humans and teach them much more about civilization. "If that is our mission here, let us accordingly act, so did Enki say." It is important to witness once again that it was Enki who led the drive to uplift and educate humans, as he tried to do many times before. His brother and his eldest son Marduk, would, however, follow a different path of educating humans, introducing a long legacy of brutality and control over them. But for now, they had to start from scratch again, establishing cities for humans and "therein sacred precincts, abodes for the Anunnaki create." And so we learn about why the many temples to worship the many gods were built in the ancient cities. We also learn that this was the true beginning of kingship and priesthood in the world, as the Anunnaki chose appropriate humans to perform those tasks once more. "Kingship as on Nibiru on Earth to establish, crown and sceptre to a chosen man give." This answered many questions in my own mind. For I have always been troubled by the complex and shady origins of kingship on Earth. I could never be convinced by the popular theories surrounding the origins of royalty and why it would have been necessary for kings or royalty to suddenly emerge from a group of ancient, primitive cultures. Although you will find many historians who spew forth many arguments why kingships were a natural progression in human social and structural evolution, their arguments continue to be highly speculative, based on the popular views of the origins of humankind, which have very little to do with the truths revealed to us in the ancient clay tablets. The king, newly appointed by the Anunnaki, would convey the word of the Anunnaki to the people and enforce "work and dexterity" on them. This was pretty much the early beginning of the Old Testament and introduced the way in which the gods began to control humans.

The priests had an equally important role to fulfill from that point in history. They were to be taught "secret knowledge," to teach civilization to mankind and to serve the Anunnaki as lofty lords and worship them in the temples. Such talk about secret knowledge is fascinating. It is possible that it was this license to teach humans that caused Enki to continue his "secret society" movement, which has been successfully traced all the way back to Edin by William Bramley in his astonishing book *Gods of Eden?* After all, he was the "serpent" who constantly wanted to uplift humanity!

To achieve all this growth and development on Earth, the Anunnaki decided to establish four new regions that would be governed by appointed gods. Three of these areas were set aside for humans and the fourth for the Anunnaki, which was not accessible to humans. Enlil received the old lands, as he pretty much did before, including the Edin and all of Mesopotamia, or what became the Biblical regions in time to come; Enki retained all of Africa; and Inanna, Anu's beloved great-granddaughter, was given the lands of the Indus Valley. The fourth region was reserved for the Anunnaki, in the Sinai Peninsula, or the "Place of the Chariots," and declared out of bounds to humans.

Anu wanted to see his grandson Marduk, so the party departed for the lands beyond the ocean. First they built a palace for Anu in the new golden land, which was South America. All the buildings were covered in gold, even the statues and flowers in the gardens were made of gold, displaying incredibly intricate workmanship like never seen before. This sounds identical to the golden city described by Cortes when he first discovered the immense wealth in the Americas and stumbled upon a golden city of exactly such description. Anu saw the abundance of gold in this new land and how it was attained from the rivers near the lake in the mountains. He was also shown how a new metal was created on Earth by combining copper with tin. The result was a strong new metal that they called Anak and we call bronze. Anu was obviously pleased with the progress and realized that the time of the Anunnaki on Earth was coming to a close. "There is gold here enough for many Shars to come" he said, and called the lake Anak. If we scratch deeply enough we are likely to find references to such a name in the ancient Inca traditions, or possibly Peruvian and Bolivian cultures. What is revealed to us next is that Marduk came from the north to see Anu, which makes it pretty obvious that he must have been involved in the rise of the early Mexican civilizations, which were slightly different from the rest and yet shared many common signs of Anunnaki interventions, especially the flying serpent god. And if Enki was the flying serpent god, it would explain why he frequented this part of the world—to visit his son Marduk. The architectural styles and social building blocks are too similar to all the others around the world not to have been driven by the planned civilization drive of the Anunnaki at the time. Anu felt a great sense of pity for his grandson Marduk, for the way in which his fate had separated him from the other sons of the Anunnaki and caused him to become an outcast. And so he pardoned and blessed Marduk, which was probably all the license the young rebel needed to justify his actions of defiance in time to come.

Anu was to depart and we are reintroduced to the new landing place they had created on the Nazca plain. Anu gave his final instruction on how to deal with earthlings. "From the golden place, high in the mountain, all who had gathered to the plain below they went . . . There stretching to the horizon, Ninurta a new place for the chariots had prepared . . . Give mankind knowledge, up to a measure secrets of heaven and earth them teach." We have seen that the concept of time had a totally different meaning to the Anunnaki and that a few Shar, or few thousand years, was not an unusual timeframe to deal with. It is, however, a notion way outside of our human frame of reference. We can hardly comprehend circumstances that prevailed 200 years ago, so how can we possibly try to wrap our simple minds around epochs lasting 3,600 years? But those are the realities throughout the ancient times on Earth that led us to the point where we are today. This last interaction between Anu and the leading Anunnaki on Earth was almost within our grasp of comprehension because it must have taken place some 5000 BC, around the time we see the real evidence of a true civilization with the knowledge of writing emerging on Earth. This fits in well with the final instructions given by Anu to his commanders on Earth. "Laws of justice and righteousness teach them, then depart and leave." Those are crucial words to ponder as we ask ourselves, "Where are the Anunnaki today?" The answers may lie in that single statement. The Anunnaki finished their golden explorations and departed, leaving humanity to their own device. Or did they? There would still come a period of about 7,000 years, bringing us to our present time, which was filled with confusion and continued conflict, causing the virtual annihilation of the planet, and taking humanity through the very murky biblical times. This was the time when the Anunnaki began to count their stay on Earth in orbits of Earth-years and not orbits of Nibiru or Shars, as they had been doing up to that point. "In the Age of the Bull, to Enlil dedicated, was the count of Earth years begun." (Bull 4380 BC–2220 BC).

Nevertheless, those words of Anu, "Give mankind knowledge, up to a measure secrets of heaven and earth them teach" were very important in the much greater scheme of things, reaching right into the twenty-first century. The thousands of years that followed became more widely documented and recorded in various forms and in different cultures where humans were being uplifted and nurtured by the Anunnaki gods. The period that followed has become known as the time when sudden ancient civilization emerged; we now know why and how it emerged, under the watchful eye and guidance of the Anunnaki. But their internal family problems only escalated from this point in time, leaving humans as vulnerable bystanders in the great struggle for power among the Anunnaki. Enlil would do his best to control his extended family on Earth, constantly having to deal with the human problem as a side issue. Very soon the humans began to emulate their gods, initiating conflicts and aggression against each other. But those human conflicts were often driven by the gods of biblical times, as becomes very clear from the many scriptures of the Old Testament. The god of vengeance would become the omnipotent force that began to rule over humanity with an iron fist. However, what we need to consider is whether there was only one "god" in the Old Testament who ruled over humans, or whether there were more than one, leading to confusion among humans and even greater conflict between the Anunnaki gods to take control of the world and its slave species with it?

After Anu's final departure, Marduk began to make a move to assert his rightful control over the world, which was promised to him by Enki at the very beginning of time on Earth. But as we have seen, through an unforeseen set of circumstances, the young Marduk was always somehow left out of the distribution of power and responsibility. This is why he finally snapped and decided to take what was "rightfully" his. We should, therefore, not be surprised to see the levels of uncertainty by Enlil and Enki about how to deal with the problem. They both realized that Marduk had a really legitimate case to make; his forceful methods, however, were not so convincing.

The period that followed was the miracle of civilization. This was the time when so-called primitive man stepped out of the caves and started to display very high levels of intelligence, when the knowledge and understanding of modern societies came to him virtually overnight. The reason for that is simple and it had nothing to do with some miraculous fast-track evolution or anything as dramatic as that. It was simply that the Anunnaki had strict instructions from their leader Anu to do exactly that: train the humans and leave. And so it began. Humankind everywhere was taught the basic skills of survival by their Anunnaki gods. Remember that there were many gods who looked after the villages, towns, and cities. Those were the members of the extended Anunnaki family who were assigned to look over humans and keep them under control. These gods were like field soldiers in many cases, looking after a distant outpost. When the general or commander came to town, there would normally be a celebration in the form of an offering and worshipping in the temple. Every settlement had a temple specifically designed for such purpose. We have already explored the lavish temples that were erected for the patron god of each city, with its fresh water and shady garden, a place to rest, and a place where people could make their offerings. There was also a strict menu of what each god preferred to eat. Those menus would have to be prepared, sometimes several times a day, as different gods had different taste preferences. The role of the high priest was to ensure that the gods were looked after and in return the priest would be given instructions to convey to his people. A very simple setup if you think of it. But somehow it was all twisted out of context over the past few thousand years, spawning human-made religions that became trapped between the needs of the gods and their control of the people.

I must say that while I was reading all this information staring at me from the pages of various books, I constantly had to stop and remind myself that I was not reading a great novel, but I was actually reading the actual words written by ancient Sumerian scribes carved into clay some 4,000 to 5,500 years ago. I would suggest you do the same. It is very important to keep reminding oneself of this reality, because the content is so fantastic that it begins to sound like a science fiction screenplay conjured up by some Hollywood writer to attract mass appeal. Ask yourself once more, what possible motive would a scribe who was appointed by a king all those years ago have to capture such content so painstakingly in clay?

And so the civilization of the humans began. "Where once cities of the Anunnaki alone had stood, cities for both them and earthlings now arose." The humans were taught everything from making bricks, building, architecture, schooling, reading, writing, calculating, laws of justice, planting, harvesting, farming, finding water, using the wheel, riding of chariots, and basically everything we know today, which we have inherited from those early civilizations. There were a few well-known landmarks like the city of Lagash, where Ninurta kept his "Black Skybird," and the city of Sippar, from where Utu promulgated the laws of justice in a place called Ebabbar—"Shining House."

The time had come to bestow kingship of scepter and crown on humankind, and so it was that the first human king was appointed in the city of Kishi or Kish. He was called "Mighty Man" by Ninurta. Kish became known as "Scepter City." This title would be moved around from city to city every few hundred years. During the rebuilding of the old cities, "where because of silt and mud the olden plans could not be followed, new sites were chosen." The concerted effort to uplift the humans paid off very quickly, and the times on Earth were prosperous. There was plenty of food for everyone for the first time in a long time, industry blossomed, and the manufacturing of wheeled wagons was booming. Ninurta requested some of the ME from Enki for his tasks. Once more we read about the distinction between those who were brought up in Edin and those black-headed people who arrived from the Abzu. But the teaching was extended to everyone. It would be these black-headed people who would rise to become the great and powerful kings of Nubia, in the Sudan, who took over Egypt in later years. "In Kishi were the black-headed people, with numbers to calculate taught . . . Heavenly Nisaba writing them taught . . . Heavenly Ninkashi beer making them showed." Ninurta was in charge of this land of Edin, they chanted praises to him and his Black Skybird and told tales of "how in faraway lands the bison he subdued, how the white metal to mix with copper he found." The white metal was tin, at Lake Titicaca.

Inanna also wanted to obtain some ME from Enki, so she orchestrated a devious plan of seduction, during which we learn more about her powers as the goddess of love and sex. She caught Enki at home alone, inebriated him with wine, and seduced him with her seminaked posing. It reads like a script from a soft-porn movie. "With jewellery was Inanna bedecked, by her thin dress her body she revealed . . . When she bent down, her vulva by Enki was thoroughly admired . . . from the wine cups sweet wine they drank, for beer drinking a competition they had." Sounds pretty similar to the kind of behavior humans have been engaging in for thousands of years, and we can clearly see our genetic link to the Anunnaki. During their drinking games Inanna wanted to see some of the ME. Enki had no reason to suspect anything so he allowed her to hold some of them as part of their adult entertainment. He explained to her that "ninety four ME's that for civilised kingdoms are needed." Inevitably Enki fell asleep and she escaped with her stolen ME to start her own empire in the land she had been given. Enki's assistant Ismud chased her down, but she had hidden them by then, claiming that Enki placed them in her hand. It transpired that Enki admitted begrudgingly and he let the matter be.

When Enlil announced that the kingship would be moved from Kishi to Inanna's abode of Unug-ki, Marduk was enraged. Once more he was denied of being the commander of the planet that was promised to him. "Enough has my humiliation been . . . Marduk fate in his own hands grasped." He decided to build a sacred city of his own in the place that was at first reserved for Anu's visit. He called the Igigi and his followers from the dispersed lands and planned to build a "sacred city" and "a place for sky ships." The city in question was Babylon.

And so, Marduk built a city that reached the sky. They made clay "brick and burnt them by fire" to serve as stone, because there were no stones in the area. "Therewith a tower whose head the heavens can reach they were building." We can immediately see the biblical parallel of the Tower of Babel in this part of the texts. Enlil was not impressed with this at all. He realized that this was an attempt by Marduk to show his power and influence, which had to be kept in check. And just as it says in the Bible, "God came down to destroy the tower and confuse their language, because if they could achieve this, they would be able to do anything." The clay tablets tell it almost verbatim: "If this we allow to happen, no other matter of mankind shall be unreached . . . This evil plan must be stopped . . . From their skyships havoc upon the rising tower, fire and brimstone they rained." But this was not enough for Enlil; he wanted Marduk far away from him and to confuse his earthling followers, so they could not understand each other, just as it says in the Bible. "To scatter abroad their leader and his followers . . . Henceforth their counsel to confuse . . . Their language I shall confound, that they each other's speech will not understand." Those were very confusing words when seen in the light of an "all-loving God" who is supposed to want the best for his creation and certainly not the kind of words we would expect from God with a big "G." But when seen in the true ancient perspective, it now makes complete sense why "god" would seem so angered by the building of the tower. These tablets also educate us that Marduk was the original creator of the city of Babylon. Just as with the construction of the pyramids, which we still struggle to comprehend, the marvels of the Hanging Gardens of Babylon must have been the work of an advanced being like Marduk, the Anunnaki god. With his expulsion from Babylon, Marduk set his sights on a more exciting prospect that would bring him loyalty and notoriety: Egypt. This was 310 years since the new Earth count began in 7400 BC. This would place the event at 7090 BC, or possibly even 3490 BC if the later date for Earth-count years is accepted (3,600 years later). The later date would fit the rise of the early Scorpion King and the subsequent pharaohs in Egypt.

Sitchin gives us a very clear indication that Egypt had been ruled by the Anunnaki gods for some 12,300 years, which basically started soon after the Flood ended and the pyramids were constructed. We must remember that Marduk was the god of Egypt before he made a play for power in Babylon, but upon his return he found that his younger brother Ningishzidda had changed everything. "Ningishzidda as its master he there found . . . What Marduk had once planned and instructed, by Ningishzidda was overturned." One of the things Ningishzidda was accused of was sending Horon, or Horus, "to a desert place depart, a place that has no water." This line is very important in helping us string together the rule of the god Horus in southern Egypt, known as Upper Egypt. It was predominantly a desert area and Horus was much more worshipped there than in Lower Egypt. The quarrel between the brothers lasted for 350 years, as long as the two parts of Egypt were divided. Once again, this time line seems to fit perfectly, because it is estimated that the Scorpion King united Upper and Lower Egypt in bout 3100 BC, which saw the rise of the true Egyptian Empire.

After the intervention of Enki, the talented Ningishzidda was convinced to depart for the "land beyond the oceans . . . With a band of followers thereto he went." We must recall that this was a talented architect who designed the pyramids and the scientist who formulated the human DNA. His symbol was similar to that of Enki, consisting of entwined serpents representing life and creation, constantly referred to as the winged serpent. I mentioned before that we sometimes feel uncertain whether it is Enki or Ningishzidda being referred to as the winged serpent, because their symbols were so very similar and even their abilities and characters were very close. Based on the tablets, however, it was most likely Ningishzidda who had such a huge influence on the very early American cultures, teaching them most of what they knew including the building of the incredible structures in that part of the world. But there is a further interesting twist to this part of ancient history. Prior to this, Ningishzidda lived in Africa and probably used skilled African laborers who were trained in mining and building for his projects there. They were most likely also the ones who were mainly responsible for building the pyramids under his supervision. It, therefore, makes perfect sense that the distinctly African features of the Olmec could have been the labor force of Ningishzidda when he first arrived in the Americas. They were, very simply, his entourage of African builders and miners. Furthermore, it would explain why the writing style of the Olmec in Mexico resembles the writing styles of various African tribes.

I have to remind you that Egypt was inhabited by humans and gods for many thousands of years before the pharaohs made their appearance. There is plenty of evidence of that in the Narmer Plate, which was found and dated to around 4468 BC, and depicts the unification of Egypt by the Scorpion King Narmer. There are also the Egyptian sky charts that point out celestial constellations of some 14000 BC. In fact, it is recorded so precisely that those specific charts can be traced to exactly 11:57 pm on the 3rd of July 14000 BC. Historians say that it is not clear who was responsible for unifying Egypt, but the tablets tell us in no uncertain terms that it was Marduk. What is very exciting to me personally, and I see it as a little victory over conservative historians, is that the Scorpion King has finally been proven to have been a real historic figure. For many years he was seen as another mythological god who lived only in ancient people's minds. This kind of discovery will hopefully lead the way in getting people to recognize that the other gods of our past were also real live beings. For many years, Menes was credited with being the first pharaonic king of Egypt. But now there is lots of evidence that King Narmer was actually the mysterious Scorpion King who predated Menes by more than 1,500 years, if not more. In the years leading up to Menes, during the time of Narmer the Scorpion King, there is a lot of reference to the god Nannar, who was Enlil's son and was possibly active in Egypt before Marduk finally took control of it. Is it possible that Narmer was Nannar's son? Who was responsible

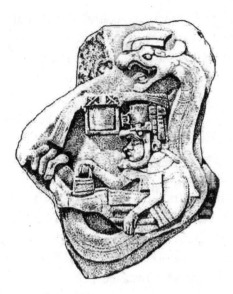

Fig. 16.22. Ancient miners. Olmec miner shown crouching in a confined space with some form of headgear and tools in both his hands. He is protected by his ever-present serpent deity. Were these Olmec miners brought from Africa by the serpent god Enki to expand the search for gold in the Americas? There are many depictions and carvings of miners in similar conditions that have baffled historians for ages.

for unifying Egypt? Or did he achieve this under the rule of Marduk? The Scorpion King's images cover the ruins of a fully fledged city, which was excavated at Hierakompolis dating back to 3500 BC. Furthermore, a dig at Abydos delivered 160 small bone and ivory plates, each the size of a large stamp, that contain the oldest known versions of early hieroglyphic text. Gunter Dryer, a German archaeologist, believes that they were the possessions of the Scorpion King, since they were found in his tomb. Could this be another example of how the Anunnaki gods were slowly introducing the earthlings to the art of writing? These finds are now possibly the oldest examples of written text on Earth. It seems that Marduk took over this part of the world around 3500 BC, which is also probably the reason why we knew so little about Narmer, the Scorpion King, because he did all the initial work for Marduk before the pharaonic era was introduced. And besides, it is possible that Narmer was of Enlil's clan, and this would not have been pleasing to Marduk. All future pharaohs would have to be related to Marduk and his Igigi or Neteru ("watchers") in some way. All this information would make Narmer well over 1,500 years old by the time he was buried. Could that be possible? Why not? Noah or Ziusudra was 36,000 years old according to the Sumerians' count. But that was all on account of him being a human son of Enki. There is, therefore, no reason to marvel at the age of King Narmer if he was the son of Nannar, a full Anunnaki god. But he too would eventually die as all human half-breeds did.

By the time Marduk took control of Egypt, he had the whole of the land to himself. North and South were unified and he began building his dynasty as the great god Ra, "The Bright One." Enki was known as Ptah—"The Developer," and Ningishzidda was Thoth or Tehuti—"The Divine Measurer." From the beginning, Marduk/Ra wanted to stamp a brand new authority on this land of his. The first thing he did was to erase the face of Ningishzidda from the Lion Sphinx statue. "To erase his memory, Ra on the Stone Lion his image with that of his son Asar replaced." But Marduk went a lot further to differentiate his land from the others. He changed the counting into tens and not by sixty; he divided the year into ten periods; and "the watching of the moon by the watching of the Sun he replaced . . . The two lands of the North and South into one Crown City he united." This ancient statement clearly suggests that it was Marduk, after all, who was behind the unification of Egypt, which means that Narmer was acting on his instructions. I hope that this will finally put this part of Egyptian history to rest. Probably not. It is painfully clear that Marduk was a very talented and yet a highly frustrated individual who wanted to get his own back for the years of being overlooked. He was going to do everything in his power to prove his point and rise above the rest of the gods. He did not waste any time before he introduced a new religion and instituted pharaonic reign to mark the beginning of his new breed of civilization. But his biggest mistake was to declare himself as "god above the rest." The pharaohs had to be half-god, half-earthling, and were chosen mostly from the group of Anunnaki gods known as Neteru, or "the watchers," whose job it was to look after the earthlings, but it was actually more like spying on the humans than anything else. The Neteru could very well be the so-called angels who mysteriously made their appearance to humans when they least expected them. These were, after all, the early biblical times and the occurrence of angels would become almost a daily affair. Suddenly the mystery of the ever-present angels does not seem so mysterious any more, and there seems to be a plausible reason for their presence in the tightly controlled human society.

But the new lofty royalty created an immediate class structure and allowed the kings to behave dismissively toward their followers. After all, they were half-god. It also explains why the kings were so obsessed with their gods, because deep inside they aspired to be like them; fully fledged immortal beings, able to travel to heaven. According to Sumerian scripts, the first king to be appointed by Ra was Mena, known as Menes to historians. At this point we reach a crucial stage in our philosophical debate. Suddenly, prehistoric myth meets recognizable historic fact. Is it not incredibly arrogant of our conceited civilization in the twenty-first century that we choose which parts of history we believe and which parts we deem as implausible? For no other reason than we don't understand it—or even worse, we simply don't believe it.

Enki was pleased that his son Marduk was making such good progress in his region, so he gave him all kinds of ME to help him with the process: all except the knowledge to revive the dead. "Then all manner of knowledge, except that of the dead reviving, to Ra he gave." This would prove to be a major gripe with Marduk, who would do anything to gain that knowledge. We read how they controlled the flow of the Nile (Hapi) to benefit their farming and how "abundance in the fertile soil quickly came, man and cattle proliferated."

Ninharsag named a constellation in Inanna's honor to share with her brother Utu; it would become known as the Age of Gemini. But the lands given to Inanna, the third region, were not doing so well. "Far away in the eastern lands, beyond seven mountain ranges, was the Third Region . . . Zamush, Land of Sixty Precious Stones, was its highland realm called." This was obviously the Indus Valley region where Inanna's personality and sexuality rubbed off on the humans. She was, after all, the goddess of love and sensuality. We read about twin cities that were erected by her and used for food storage, among other things. Those must have been the cities of Harappa and Mohenjo-Daro. They were both built from the same bricks and in the same style and are the same age. According to the Sumerian tablets, they were built 860 years after the start of the Earth year count. This could mean either 2940 BC or 6540 BC depending on where we take the beginning of Earth time, either 7400 BC or 3800 BC, which would have been either 1 Shar or 2 Shar after the last visit of Anu. The very curious link to corroborate these events is the mysterious Indus Script. The tablets inform us that Inanna introduced a new language and a new way of writing, as part of her duties as the first officially appointed ruler of the Indus Valley region. The Indus Script has puzzled scholars for many years and to date is still not deciphered. The way in which Indian culture utilizes precious stones in their customs, clothing, and jewelery also indicates that the Indus Valley was indeed the Land of Sixty Precious Stones, and the land of Inanna.

The ME that Inanna requested were lost on the way to her in a bizarre set of interceptions by her opponents; misunderstanding of their new respective languages; and deaths of the carriers. Ultimately, the result was that the third region of the Indus Valley did not develop as well as the other regions. "In the Third region, civilised mankind did not fully blossom." This brought the period of growing instability among the Anunnaki and the beginning of the end. The growing power quest by Marduk/Ra in Egypt and the resistance of the others began to cause skirmishes among their human followers. Many of the lesser gods were being worshipped in temples and sacred precincts, and the first brothel was established by none other than Inanna. "House for nighttime pleasure she established." Inanna's mourning for Dumuzi seemed to reappear in moments of possible insanity. She began to imagine that a half-god earthling by the name of Banda was her beloved Dumuzi. It is possible that her subtle levels of instability caused Inanna to initiate the "catastrophe" in time to come. But Banda married Inanna, the pure offspring from Enlil, and the couple had a son called Gilgamesh who was two-thirds god. Gilgamesh is recognized as a historic king, once again crossing the line between fact and fiction. As time went by, he realized that he had a strong divine DNA and he began to lust for the same privileges that were reserved for Anunnaki only. Like most humans today, he was especially taunted by the idea of immortality. One of the most famous of all Sumerian legends is the "Epic of Gilgamesh" in which he ventures into the lands of the Tilmun, the space port where the spaceships and other secret Anunnaki items were kept, in search of immortality. His mother Ninsun pleaded constantly with her great uncle Utu, to guide Gilgamesh to Tilmun. "Endlessly Ninsun to Utu appealed . . . Let Gilgamesh to the landing place go." The journey is written in great detail on a number of tablets and has become one of the most studied ancient bodies of written word. The argument still continues, however, whether it was fictional or historical because there are historians who refuse to accept this epic tale as part of history, while they accept many of the other ancient writings. Shame on them.

The epic tale tells us that to reach his destination Gilgamesh has to get past a number of precautionary measures that defy ancient logic, but his uncle Utu agreed to assist him with the aid of oracles. Oracles were also referred to as "talking stones" in those times. Often a priest would consult an oracle for advice from his god. The oracle would talk back to the priest advising him what to do. So when we read that Utu used oracles to help Gilgamesh reach the inner sanctum of the space port, it could be that these were strategically placed type of sensor devices, or like modern computer ports with monitoring cameras, allowing the controller to scan the perimeter. Since Utu was a senior Anunnaki, he may have had access to those cameras and codes, to guide Gilgamesh to the next point. But the weapons that protected the port were awesome. In the cedar forest he first encountered the "firebelching monster," then "the secret entrance to the tunnels of the Anunnaki they found . . . By the

Bull of Heaven with deadly snorts they were challenged . . . and chased." The reasons why the text refers to "they" is because Gilgamesh was accompanied by a friend. But in the end he made it inside where he was met by Ziusudra, the legend of the Flood, who told him of a unique plant that does have the ability to keep a man young. "Unique of all the plants on Earth it was." But the greedy Gilgamesh ripped the plant out from its roots and made his way back home. En route he fell asleep and the plant was stolen by a snake that was attracted by its fragrance. Gilgamesh returned home empty-handed where in the end he died as a mortal.

The fascinating thing about this story is the part about the snake, which bears a very strong resemblance to the events in the biblical garden of Eden. But in the Sumerian rendition of Adamu in Edin, it was Enki described as the evil serpent who came to inform and educate the new earthling pair. Is it not possible that it was Enki the snake who once more intervened, this time retrieving what was rightfully his: the secrets to eternal life? It certainly has very similar characteristics in the simplistic description of the interfering snake. The fact is that Gilgamesh was not just any old human; he was a great king of a major city called Uruk or the biblical Erech. So Marduk used this event as justification to bestow his own immortality on his kings and demand even greater adulation from all. "If demigods the gateway to immortality are shown, let this to the kings of my region apply." He basically started to tell the pharaohs that he could offer them a passage to heaven just like Gilgamesh was shown. He dictated what is known as the Book of the Dead, giving kings a step-by-step guide to reach the "boats of heaven" and the afterlife on another planet. In return Ra would demand complete obedience. Then he went on to decree that all the kings must be half-human, half-god. "Let kings of my region of Neteru offspring be, to Nibiru in an afterlife journey."

The afterlife Ra was offering his pharaoh kings was simply the privilege to travel to Nibiru, and there live as the Anunnaki do, eternally. These utterances should, therefore, not in anyway be confused with the heaven or spiritual afterlife with God with a big "G"; the universal Spirit or Being that many people have begun to believe in during the past few centuries. This afterlife of god Ra, was a fictitious reality in his own frame of reference and the planet he came from, but he did not have the ability to actually revive people from the dead and offer them eternal life. That privilege was reserved for the top few Anunnaki only. The ME that Marduk/Ra received from his father Enki gave him many powers to rule, but they did not give him the knowledge to revive people from the dead. Despite his inability to deliver kings to the afterlife, Ra dictated his Book of the Dead to his scribes outlining every step of "How to reach the Duat, the place of celestial boats . . . By a Stairway to Heaven, to the imperishable planet journey . . . How to build tombs facing eastward." As part of his rapid expansion plan, Marduk instructed his followers to invade other lands in the Abzu to seize gold from them, who were mostly his own brothers' followers. He ordered his kings to capture all adjoining lands to Egypt. "To be the master of the four regions was his heart's plan." Marduk became so obsessed and arrogant that he bluntly proclaimed to his father Enki: "The Earth is mine to rule."

Nannar and his wife Ningal were in charge of Mesopotamia, or the Olden Lands, that were assigned to Enlil. This was known as the first region and was becoming very prosperous under their lordship. They held twelve festivals each year, one for each of the great Anunnaki. "Shrines and sanctuaries were built, the people to their gods could directly pray." This first region was booming under the rapidly expanding civilization. Humans were learning everything, while remaining faithful and obedient to their gods. Inanna liked to roam the lands to see and observe how all the regions were progressing. She took a liking to the "People who in the upper plain of the two rivers dwelt." She liked the sound of their dialect, which must have been different from her own. They were the Igigi who "descended to Earth from heaven" from Lahmu (Mars). They knew all about the beautiful Inanna but they called her Ishtar. This is most likely the reason why the Igigi or Aryans moved east, following Inanna to her Indus Valley region, and laid the foundation for the Indo-European culture and language.

Back in Sumer, the kingdoms were rotated between cities but Marduk had none of that in his own Egypt. "In Shumer (Sumer) . . . Kingship between the cities was rotated . . . In the second region, diversity by Ra was not permitted, alone to reign he wished." Marduk had a very close affinity with all the Igigi who came to Earth after Mars had deteriorated, since he was their commander for a long period. It was mostly the Igigi who were the so-called watches, the Neteru, whose offspring became the future Kings of Egypt. Ra went further, he declared himself "The eldest of heaven, firstborn who is on Earth . . . The foremost from the earliest times." He expected all the priests to know him as such and praise him with hymns. Interestingly enough, he was not making anything up in those statements, he was all that. But then he went too far and his greedy or megalomaniacal character took over.

He began to believe his own propaganda with regard to immortality and suggested that he was more powerful than all the other gods. That specific aspect of our human DNA has been clearly illustrated by thousands of military leaders, presidents, and dictators throughout history—another harsh reminder of where we humans got our genetic material. Marduk declared himself as follows. "Lord of eternity, he who everlastingness has made, over all the gods presiding . . . The one who is without equal . . . Ra above all other gods." I don't understand what he was thinking; he must have lost control of his faculties by this stage. Did Marduk expect the senior Anunnaki to simply accept his attempts to snatch power from them so openly? But it got even worse: he actually compared the pantheon of gods, which included Enlil by name, and proclaimed that he was greater than them. These included Enlil, Ninurta, Adad, Nannar, Utu, Nergal, Gibil, and Ningishzidda.

It is not surprising that the Anunnaki were very concerned, but also furious by his behavior. Marduk had become a loose cannon and completely unpredictable. This was a whole new twist in their stay on Earth. Even his father Enki confronted him, realizing that his beloved son had now gone too far and that he could no longer defend his actions before Enlil. And for the first time we hear Enki speak very strong words to his firstborn: "What has you overpowered? Unheard of are your protestations." But Marduk was so high on the quest for power that he could not be brought down to Earth, if you forgive the pun. He suggested that his celestial sign was about to rise, which would give him the power to rule. The "Bull of Heaven," which was Enlil's sign, would be replaced by the age of the Ram. He said that the "heavens my supremacy bespeak . . . The age of the Ram is coming, unmistakable the omens are." (The Ram sign ruled from 2220 BC–60 BC.) It is incredible to see how steadfast his faith was in the heavenly signs. But what was to follow would bear the most miraculous twist in all of human events, which caused the other Anunnaki to suspect that maybe it was Marduk's destiny to become the supreme ruler of the world. Incredibly enough, there is a Sumerian royal cylinder seal that is dated from 2308 BC, celebrating the coming of the Age of Aries—the Ram, which was the sign of Marduk.

And so started a frenzied period of constructing observational monuments by which to predict the coming of the ages, leading up to 2308 BC. This would fit in perfectly with the many structures all around the world that have been found to have such a purpose. Everyone was watching the skies to see if Marduk's prediction was correct; if in fact they had made a mistake in their own predictions. Before they realized how the circumstances had changed, the gods were dependent on humankind for support on the ground. The war of the gods had arrived in which humankind would play a crucial part. "After the Anunnaki as gods themselves declared, on mankind's support they instead are dependent." They needed to find a strong leader among men who could spearhead their human armies against Marduk. Inanna found a human by the name of Abrakad who had such makings of a strong leader. Enlil made him a king with "crown and sceptre" and they called him Sharru-kin or Righteous Regent. The world knows him as Sargon I, the first powerful king of Akkad. The tablets tell us how a new unified city was declared that housed the crown in the olden lands by the name of Agade (Akkad), and the beginning of the great Akkadian empire under their leader Sargon I had begun. His task was simple: to ensure the obedience of all the people of Mesopotamia. Historians are well aware of the many astounding conquests by Sargon, and we read in the tablets what happened. "All the lands from the lower sea to the upper sea, to his throne obedience gave." There was a very good reason why he was so successful and seemingly invincible in battle, because Inanna provided his armies with the advanced weapons of the Anunnaki. A similar set of circumstances would assist Abraham in the future. "By Enlil was Sharru-kin empowered, Inanna with her weapons of brilliance his warriors accompanied."

Marduk was watching all this warlike posturing by Inanna from his lands in Egypt. When the moment was right, he pounced on the unsuspecting city of Babylon where he established himself against the will of Inanna. This was after all his city. "Babili, the gateway to the gods . . . Dikes and walls in the place of the tower they raised . . . House for the utmost god Marduk they built." This is how cunningly Marduk established his army of followers in the middle of the First Region, the heart of the Edin, the heart of Enlil's lands. But Inanna reacted swiftly and decisively. She attacked Marduk's armies with all the force she possessed, destroying them where they had embedded themselves in Babylon, in the process destroying most of the city. "With her weapons on Marduk's followers death she inflicted . . . The blood of the people, as never before on Earth, like rivers flowed." We have to remind ourselves that the gods were using humans, their slave species, as their disposable foot soldiers to do all the fighting and dying. We can now look at the tales of the early biblical scriptures with greater understanding when we read that god instructed Moses or Abraham to attack a certain group of people because they were vile and evil and who were conspiring against god. The people were simply doing the fighting for Enlil against the followers of Marduk. How else do you propose to explain it? Our history books are written by the victors; and at this stage it was Enlil who held the upper hand in the biblical lands, while Marduk ruled the roost in Egypt.

Marduk was defeated at Babylon and convinced to leave the Edin. They agreed to "peacefully wait for the true signs of heaven" to point out whether Marduk's age of rule, the Ram, had come. Marduk did not return to Egypt at this stage and his people began to call him Amun—"The Unseen One."

Naram-Sin, the grandson of the great Sargon I, was appointed as the new king of Akkad and Sumer. Those were truly strange times on Earth, as if everyone was waiting for something to happen. The most desired event among the elder Anunnaki was to return to Nibiru but the time had not yet come, because the gold collection in the Americas was at its peak. Their plan was to exhaust the visible gold and only then depart. But time was against them. In the East, Inanna was making plans of her own to rule the planet. Marduk and Inanna were engaged in a kind of a prewar dance, each making it clear that they wanted to rule the whole world. A strange situation arose when Inanna realized she could make her move. "In the first region, Enlil and Ninurta absent were, to the land beyond the oceans they went . . . In the second region Ra was away, as Marduk in other lands he travelled." And so Inanna made her move to take control of all the lands. "To seize all power Inanna envisioned, Naram-Sin to seize all lands she commanded." And so he did as he was commanded; historians will know these battles from ancient texts. Naram-Sin moved through all the lands of Sumer, Akkad, and into Egypt, taking control everywhere. But he made one fatal mistake when he marched his armies through the forbidden land of Enlil—the Tilmun—where the space port was reserved for the Anunnaki only. This is a great example of how mangled the situation was at that time. Enlil was furious and took no time to destroy Naram-Sin and his army, and he even ordered the destruction of Akkad. "By the command of Enlil was Agade wiped out." The tablets tell us that this happened in the Earth count year of 1500, after the Anunnaki began to count Earth years instead of Shar. That would place the event at around 2300 BC. These were early biblical times shortly before the appearance of Abraham and already god was instructing his human leaders to attack and destroy other groups of humans.

At this point it becomes clear how confused the earthlings must have been. An emerging species on a new planet, not quite in control of their own destiny, controlled by a number of different gods commanding them to do this and that and to wage war on their neighbors, the humans had very little choice but to follow the instructions from their brutal gods, who showed no regard for human life. The people were mere chess pieces in a great game of global conquest played by the Anunnaki gods. The clashes between the gods almost always involved humans who never knew the reasons for waging war against their neighbors. But as we see in the Old Testament, this kind of behavior was commonplace. It was this inexplicable act of aggression by one group of earthlings against another, as initiated by their god, that set the behavioral pattern for all future human conflict. Humankind, which was just emerging from the age of darkness into civilization, perceived this kind of activity as the normal thing to do. God would command his people to invade and attack, giving his human armies the excuse that they were vile and evil and they were sinful against god. But this god would differ from land to land, demanding total obedience from the humans, or they would themselves be punished. This led to the worshipping of many different gods by the early people of the biblical lands, as they worshipped the specific god who led them into battle or out of harm's way. This worshipping would lead to retribution by some other Anunnaki god with a higher rank. And so the clashes between the biblical groups of people would continue for almost 3,000 years, driven by the power struggle of the Anunnaki. It is all very nicely captured in the Bible, but the evidence is now overwhelming that the entries in that particular book had nothing to do with salvation and the eternal spiritual afterlife of God with a big "G." Rather, it was all a meticulously executed propaganda and mind control by a number of vengeful gods, who were no more than advanced humans with a higher level of intelligence, abusing humans for their own gain. And so we see this human behavior continuing even today. While some communities think they have elevated themselves above this kind of primitive behavior, just take a swipe at their religion and see their reaction.

This was possibly the single most important period in all of human history, because it was this continued confusion among humankind about the different gods that set the tone for the emergence of the many diverse religions visible in the world today. There can be no other plausible reason for this amazing phenomenon. How else can it be explained that one planet has developed so many different religions in such a short span of time? The answers are perfectly clear in the many Sumerian tablets and on the pages of the Bible. All we have to do is to take the fear out of the reading of the book and rather approach it as a historic record that was commanded to be written with a very specific purpose: to manipulate humans into a blind and fearful fanaticism. So from a purely human perspective, the very first wars among humans were fought on religious grounds by humans who were controlled by different gods. It is safe to say that since those early days some 3500 BC, all wars among humankind were also driven by religious beliefs, combined with our genetically inherited need to conquer, which was imposed on our species early in our infancy. We see the incredible effect of the inherited Anunnaki DNA rise to the surface and manifest itself in our violent behavior. The amazing desire by humankind to find peace has shown that genetically we are actually created to be more peaceful. The overwhelming majority of humans who strive for peace is a fascinating phenomenon. Combined with our incredible capacity for benevolence, it becomes debatable whether our violent behavior is a characteristic pattern we have adopted from our makers, rather than a genetic code that drives us to behave in such ways. In other words, have we been nurtured into becoming violent, or is our violent behavior driven by a violent gene? And so we get back to the nature versus nurture argument.

The clay tablets seem to concur that the world was gripped in a state of chaos and confusion. "After Marduk Amun became, kingship in the second region disintegrated, disorder and confusion reigned . . . After Agade was wiped out, in the first region there was disorder, confusion reigned . . . Kingship was disarray, from cities of gods, to cities of man it moved about . . . To faraway places kingship was shifting." The situation got so bad that Enlil had to consult Anu on faraway Nibiru about how to deal with the situation. They appointed a new king in the city of Ur, to be the peacemaker and "bring an end to violence and strife . . . in all the lands prosperity was abundant." This king's name was Ur-Nammu— "Righteous Shepherd." Enlil had a very vivid dream about the coming of the Age of the Ram and Marduk taking control of the world. It affected him so much that he dispatched his high priests to observe the heavens for signs of the new age. In the meantime, Marduk kept on moving from land to land telling people of his supremacy, gaining massive support from fearful and obedient earthlings. His son Nabu was also helping to enslave more humans into obedience through fear. Wars erupted again: "Between the dwellers of the west and the dwellers of the east clashes were occurring." That sounds like a scene from the twentieth century, seemingly not much has changed in 4,000 years. Ur-Nammu died in a chariot accident, to be replaced by Shulgi. "Full of vile and eager for battle Shulgi was." It seems that by this stage the humans did not need much encouragement from their gods to go to war; they began to emulate their gods. This Shulgi chap was a real tyrant according to the texts, with powers on the battle field and other powers of persuasion as well, because he managed to seduce the beautiful goddess Inanna. It just goes to show that as early as 4,300 years ago, women were already attracted to men of power. As silly as this statement may be, there is a lot of historic social behavior to support it. This behavior of women can be defended by outlining the genetic code, which programs the female to choose the strongest male, which will more likely ensure the survival of their offspring. And so Shulgi used his power to conquer lands and women. "In Nibru-ki himself high priest anointed, in Unug-ki the joys of Inanna's vulva he sought . . . Warriors from the mountainlands in his army he enlisted . . . The western lands he overran . . . The sanctity of Mission Control Centre he ignored." Once again, an arrogant human king made the mistake of defiling Enlil's restricted area. "Once again the rulers of your region all bounds have exceeded . . . Of all the troubles, Marduk is the fountainhead," so did Enlil say to Enki in anger.

This is once more where we see the dramatic marriage of myth and history. Enlil needed to find a faithful, obedient, strong human leader to oppose the chaos and growing human armies of Marduk. He did not have to search long before he found the most enigmatic figure in all of the Bible. The father of all the future biblical kings: Abraham, the father of the Jewish, Christian, and Muslim faiths. The Sumerians called him Ibruum, the Muslims call him Ibrahim. He was a powerful human with all the necessary attributes to command Enlil's army. The time had come for Enlil to start using the same tactics that were employed by the other Anunnaki gods and utilize humans as his own soldiers. His main objective was for Abraham to defend his space port. "A princely offspring, valiant and with priestly secrets acquainted, Ibruum was . . . To protect the sacred places, the chariot's ascents and descents enable, Enlil Ibruum to go commanded." But as soon as Abraham departed from the city of Harran to perform his new duties to his god Enlil, Marduk arrived to incite the people and cause havoc. It would be this kind of incitement and havoc that would entangle Abraham and his nephew Lot to become spies for their god Enlil, reporting on the activities of Marduk and his followers. Just imagine the kind of confusion that consumed the poor ignorant humans of those days: one god demanding obedience, the other god threatening punishment and retribution for disobedience. No wonder the Bible is such a confusing book of constant conflict and war amongst the human tribes, because in reality they belonged to different gods and they were commanded and controlled by these different gods.

It now emerges that the main protagonists in the holy wars of the Bible were the followers of Enlil taking battle against those who were controlled by Marduk. Both were strict and brutal in their dispensation of punishment and reward to their human followers. Those were stressful times for the Anunnaki gods. The new slave species they created to help them obtain the precious gold had now become their tools of war. By now, Marduk had reached the point of no return. He summoned all the Anunnaki to his beloved Babylon, to appoint him as the new ruler of the planet Earth. "In my temple house let all the Anunnaki gods assemble, my covenant accept." Obviously the others responded with horror to such utterances by Marduk, and Enlil called an urgent meeting of all the elders. "To a great assembly, counsel to take, Enlil them all summoned." There was a consensus that Marduk had finally gone too far, everyone was extremely unhappy with the tenuous situation. Nobody knew what to do, or how to respond to the present circumstances. "Accusations were rampant, recriminations filled the chamber."

Enki was the only one who felt that it must have been fate that led them to this situation, and maybe they should not oppose fate but rather to accept Marduk's rise to assume control. "What is coming, no one can prevent, let us Marduk's supremacy accept." At this stage Marduk had settled himself in Babylon and basically taken control of the whole known world of the biblical times, which included Egypt, Israel, Canaan, Assyria, Akkad, and Sumer. There were only a few Anunnaki strongholds that were not loyal to the brutal god Ra or Marduk, known to most in the world today as the biblical god of love. Is that not filled with deep dark irony? There was much deliberation and debate about what action to take against Marduk. The Anunnaki finally decided that there was only one way to stop Marduk: to obliterate all his cities with all his human followers who dwelled in them.

By this time Abraham had been a trusted and loyal general of the lord Enlil, who equipped him with the best chariots available together with the finest horses. Abraham fought many battles for him, mainly defending the space port in the Sinai that was out of bounds to all humans. Lord Enlil rewarded him with riches of all kinds, which included "land as far as the eye can see," gold, cattle and sheep, and a host of things that eventually made him the wealthiest man of his time. Abraham had a crack squad of some 380 well-trained and well-armed soldiers for the task. The weapons provided to him by his god were so awesome that this small group of warriors could smite an army of ten thousand men in a matter of hours.

This made Abraham not only the wealthiest man in the land, but also the most respected and feared. There are several references in the Bible where kings and priests come to him for leniency and mercy. They refer to his close ties with god, and that he should not forget their good deeds toward Abraham when god wants to pour his vengeance on them. Everyone was petrified of their god of vengeance, whom we now know was none other than Enlil, the supreme Anunnaki commander on Earth, whose command was under threat by his young nephew Marduk. On several occasions we read in the Bible that angels came to Abraham inquiring about the behavior of humans in certain cities. They clearly used Abraham and his nephew as informants to gain information about the activities of the followers of Marduk. Two of the cities that the Bible mentions in great detail were Sodom and Gomorrah. We have already explored the events that led to the destruction of those cities, but now we get a clear understanding of why this all happened. These were only two of the cities under Marduk's control. From there, he would marshal his large number of human followers and take control of all the establishments on Earth, including the space port of Enlil.

And so, after the long debate by the Anunnaki in Enlil's chamber, the fateful decision was made "to use therefore the weapons of terror" on all of Marduk's people. It was not dissimilar to the U.S.-led preemptive strikes on Iraq, in anticipation of some form of deadly attack by their perceived enemy. Is it not ironic that 4,200 years ago, the same part of the world was involved in a terrible battle? So the Anunnaki gods would use these weapons of terror on Marduk. If we look at the geographical area, all this information makes a lot of sense. Marduk was in charge of Egypt, and so the Sinai peninsula with the space port was virtually just to the east of him, while Sodom and Gomorrah were just north of the Sinai, perfectly positioned to launch an attack on Enlil's space port. So we should not be surprised when the angels came to visit Abraham shortly before the destruction began to get any final information about the citizens of those cities and how they were "conspiring against god." The actions of the people were described in the Bible as vile and evil, and Abraham shows some of his humane side as he pleads for the lives of the righteous few in the two cities. We know the rest of the story, the angels go to the city, talk to Lot, get apprehended by the citizens who suspect that they are there to kill them, and the cities are destroyed by incredible explosions that turned Lot's wife into a "pillar of salt," meaning that she was actually vaporized.

The event described in the clay tablets is even more dramatic, but clearly deal with the same situation. Only Enki was opposed to the proposed action of terror, saying that "What was destined to be, by your decision to undo will fail," once more displaying the Anunnaki's firm belief in a higher universal power that included destiny and fate. It was Ninurta, son of Enlil; and Nergal, son of Enki, who were chosen to "the evil thing to carry out." And so the identities of the two angels who visited Abraham are exposed. The same angels who then proceeded to Sodom to destroy it with nuclear weapons. And once again mythology meets biblical history, but this time we have a real link with real names and places. If you believe the one, you should believe the other, except that the Sumerian tablets give us a lot more detail that was omitted in the Bible when it was compiled by humans 2,500 years later.

The deadly weapons were retrieved from their secret places and Enlil revealed to the young Anunnaki "how the weapons from their deep sleep awaken." They were warned that the cities must be spared and the righteous people in their cities must not perish. The crucial part of the tablet that substantiates my assertion that Abraham was a spy is when Enlil tells his two fighters to "make sure that Ibruum is forewarned." Many scholars of the past have implied that the weapons used in the destruction of Sodom and Gomorra must have been nuclear weapons. These suggestions are not only supported by the descriptions of the aftermath in the Bible itself, but the clay tablets tell us in great detail what actually happened. They even reveal the names that Nergal gave the weapons before they unleashed them: "One without rival; Blazing flame; One who with terror crumbles; Mountain melter; Wind that the rim of the world seeks; One who above and below no one spares," and the grand-daddy of them all: "Vaporiser of living things." There were seven weapons in total with which the massacre would be performed. When the destruction began the tablets tell us that "a thousand and seven hundred and thirty six was the count of earth years then," which would make it 2064 BC when the destruction of Sodom and Gomorrah occurred, the end of the days of Abraham. It is also very clear from the tablets that Enki was mortified by the actions of Enlil, as he writes: "On that day, on that fateful day, Enlil to Ninurta the signal sent."

Ninurta and Nergal began the bombing. The tablets describe in great detail how "the mount's innards in an instant it melted . . . The rocks into a gushing wound were made . . . The Earth shook and crumbled, the heavens after the brilliance were darkened . . . Of all the forests, only tree stems were left standing." For those who have seen pictures of a nuclear aftermath, these words present a perfect description. They also concur with biblical descriptions. From there they flew to "the verdant valley where Nabu the people was converting." Nabu was Marduk's son who was also a target. There they annihilated five more cities and as it says in the Bible, "with fire and brimstone were they upheavaled, all that lived there to vapour was turned."

What followed is described as a typical "nuclear storm" with darkening of the skies, extreme winds blowing at hundreds of kilometers per hour, distributing the deadly nuclear clouds of dust. "Gloom from the skies an evil wind carried . . . The Sun on the horizon with darkness it obliterated." We must remember that these words were written before a single word of the Bible had been put down. It is very difficult to imagine that the descriptions in the Bible came from any other source than the same events that inspired the writing of the Sumerian clay tablets. The incredible nuclear descriptions continued: "At nighttime a dreaded brilliance skirted its edges . . . Wherever it reached, death to all that lives mercilessly it delivered." The Anunnaki were astounded by the extent of the destruction. The nuclear wind was distributing the deadly dust everywhere, and in their direction as well. There was no place to hide; the dust or "evil wind" would penetrate every nook and cranny as it rapidly moved toward Sumer, where the Anunnaki had based themselves. "No door could shut it out, no bolt could turn it back." Ninurta and Nergal sent an urgent message to Enlil and Enki: "Escape! Escape! To them all they cried out." Those are dramatic words that were followed by even more graphic descriptions of the effect that the evil wind had on the people in its path. "In the streets were their corpses piled up . . . Cough and phlegm the chests filled, their mouths with spittle and foam filled up . . . Their mouths were drenched with blood . . . From west to east over plains and mountains it travelled." Those words suddenly bring to light an even more horrific truth of that particular biblical event. The Anunnaki were not only using nuclear weapons, but biological weapons as well.

The terrible events of the recent past when Iraq was accused of harboring weapons of mass destruction revolved mainly around biological weapons. It is tragic that the twentieth century witnessed a number of attacks where biological weapons were used, and the descriptions in the clay tablets are precisely what happened in recent times when people fell victim to such attacks. They fell where they stood; their skin was burnt or covered with grotesque sores; their mouths filled with blood; suffocating in their own phlegm. There is no doubt that those ancient accounts are the gruesome description of biological warfare. How is it possible that a 4,000-year old clay tablet could have depicted such events if they weren't actually real? It is highly unlikely and utterly improbable that an ancient scribe would be able to imagine such events. This level of technology predated the Dark and Middle Ages by 3,000 years, where the sword and horse were the main weapon. You be your own judge to determine what the real meaning of those biblical and Sumerian descriptions are. "Everything that lived behind it was dead, people and cattle all alike perished . . . The waters were poisoned . . . All vegetation withered." But then came the incredible miracle that was seen by Enlil in a dream some time before the event. All of the lands were covered and destroyed by the evil wind from west to east. All except Babylon, "where Marduk supremacy declared, by the evil winds was spared." This was perceived as a miracle by Enlil and everyone else among the Anunnaki. Finally they declared that "Marduk to supremacy has been destined." There was no other possible explanation in their eyes, and slowly they made plans to disperse, leaving Marduk to rule. The Anunnaki show us their spiritual side once more as they debate the relationships between fate and destiny and how it has shaped their stay on Earth. One can sense between the lines that they were tired, focusing on completing their mission to find gold, and returning to Nibiru. Although Enlil and Enki were energetic and vibrant commanders on their arrival to Earth, the short yearly cycles had aged them. It certainly feels as if they did not have the energy left to continue squabbling. They had done what they deemed necessary, at the expense of their slave species. But now the time had come to go home.

The years that followed were tense and hard on the surviving humans. The old biblical scripts are filled with trials and tribulations of the human tribes, under the brutal dictatorship of the new god Marduk. He skillfully and cunningly controlled the human race, commanding them to pray to one god only, himself. He is referred to as the god of vengeance in the Bible, and that is exactly what he had become. It was as if the many years it took him to gain control of the planet made him bitter. He did not show any of the benevolent traits his father Enki displayed toward the human species throughout the years. The many demigods that people had worshipped in years past were slowly disappearing under pressure from him, and the world was being converted into a monotheistic society. He became the only god who humans were allowed to worship. He demanded sacrifices of gold, food, animals, and even humans. The early American cultures of the Aztecs and their ancestors had a brutal ceremony during which human hearts were extracted while still beating. There were as many as 20,000 captives killed in one massive sacrificial offering to their god. There is no reason to believe that they would have done something like that on their own. There was regular contact between the ancient cultures and their gods. Their actions would have been a direct response to a strict command by their god. There were many other gruesome customs performed by most of the ancient cultures. These barbaric customs only seem to have surfaced once Marduk took control of the planet some 2064 BC, lasting way beyond the Christian era into the Dark Ages, which included the brutal power mongering of the Catholics during the Crusades between the eleventh and thirteenth centuries AD.

Now that the story has been told, we need to sit back, take a few deep breaths to absorb all this information, and ask ourselves a crucial question: "What the hell is going on? Have we been lied to and bamboozled all our lives? Can the human race be so gullible and ignorant to be so exploited for so long?" The answer to that is a definite YES. You don't have to go back in time to witness the willingness of humans to follow a brutal dictator in huge numbers completely oblivious of their own state of ignorance. Hitler, Stalin, and Mao are just the obvious examples—Bush is a more recent example—of how people will follow a leader whom they believe will protect them and make them stronger than their enemies. But now, the obvious question we need to ask is, "Where are the Anunnaki now? Where are Enlil and Enki and Marduk today? Are they around, or have they all departed? Do they play any part in the confused state of mind of the modern humans?" This is a question that warrants an extended study and would be a great subject of a book on its own. I will dare to say the following: If you had to abandon a paradise island that you had inhabited for many years because of some kind of ecological disaster, would you not like to return at some stage to see how it has recovered and developed in your absence? There is a very strong possibility that the many unexplained sightings of UFOs may have something to do with our ancient creators checking up on the progress of their offspring. But we have reached a very disparate level of development or possibly even evolution on this planet. Some cultures are trapped in customs thousands of years old, living deep in the hearts of rain forests, not showing any signs of progress, while others are landing probes on Mars and cloning new life. The Earth today is a very different place to what it was 1,000 years ago. So if we assume that the Anunnaki departed from Earth some 1,000 years ago, it would be unwise for them to arrive on this planet in its current state of cultural and religious confusion. We would probably try to blow them out of the sky on their arrival, trying to tell us that "they" were actually our "creators." Are they trying to help us or guide us? Who knows. There is, however, an important lesson we should learn. The arrogant way that we treat the precious knowledge from our distant past has only extended our years of ignorance. As intelligent as we may think we are, we still do not know who we are, where we come from, and why we are here on this lonely planet called Earth. If we allow our minds to be opened we can only grow as a species, allowing us to evolve faster, both physically and spiritually. Because only then will we be able to join the universal community of beings, becoming one with the Great Universal Spirit, the creator of the universe and all things in it. I believe that we are on the cusp of achieving this giant evolutionary step, but it is up to us as a species to see it through to its conclusion. And on our path of evolution and enlightenment, we must at all times remind ourselves that while we are in this primitive state of mind, things are not always what they seem.

SELECTED BIBLIOGRAPHY
AND
RECOMMENDED READING

Balter, Michael. *The Goddess and the Bull: Journey to the Dawn of Civilization.* New York: Free Press, 2004.

Bramley, William. *Gods of Eden.* New York: Avon, 1993.

Branigan, Keith, ed. *Atlas of Archaeology.* New York: St. Martin's Press, 1987.

Budge, Sir Wallis. *Cleopatra's Needles and Other Egyptian Obelisks.* First published 1926.

Carus, Paul. *The Gospel of Buddha.* First published 1894.

Casson, Lionel. *Ancient Egypt.* New York: Time-Life Books, 1966.

Ceram, C. W. *Gods, Graves & Scholars.* New York: Knopf, 1956.

——. *A Picture History of Archaeology.* London, England: Thames & Hudson, 1958.

Coe, Michael D. *Breaking the Maya Code.* London, England: Thames & Hudson, 1992.

Daniken, Erich von. *According to the Evidence: My Proof of Man's Extraterrestrial Origins.* London, England: Souvenir Press Ltd, 1977.

——. *Return to the Stars: Evidence of the Impossible.* London, England: Souvenir Press Ltd, 1968.

Dawkins, Richard. *The Selfish Gene.* Oxford, England: Oxford University Press, 1989.

El Shammaa, Bassam. *Quest for the Truth: Discovering the Second Sphinx.* Amazon Digital Services, 2011.

Fagan, Brian. *Time Detectives: How Archaeologists Use Technology to Recapture the Past.* New York: Simon & Schuster, 1995.

Filotto, Giuseppe. *The Face on Mars.* Self-published, 1995.

Gibson, McGuire. "The Planet That Stalked the Earth." *New Scientist,* September 18, 2004.

Gilbert, Adrian Geoffrey, and Maurice M. Cotterell. *The Mayan Prophecies: Unlocking the Secrets of a Lost Civilization.* Shaftesbury, England: Element Books Ltd, 1995.

Gould, Stephen Jay, ed. *The Book of Life.* London, England: Random House UK, 1993.

Gregorietti, Guido. *Jewelry Through the Ages.* New York: Crescent Books, 1974.

Gribbin, John. *In Search of the Edge of Time: Black Holes, White Holes, Worm Holes.* New York: Penguin Books, 1998.

Gros de Beler, Aude. *Tutankhamun.* London, England: Grange Books, 2004.

Hancock, Graham. *Fingerprints of the Gods.* New York: Three Rivers Press, 1996.

Hancock, Graham, and Robert Bauval. *Keepers of Genesis: The Quest for the Hidden Legacy of Mankind.* Toronto, Canada: Random House of Canada Ltd, 1997.

Hancock, Graham, Robert Bauval, and John Grigsby. *The Mars Mystery: A Tale of the End of Two Worlds.* n.p.: Michael Joseph Ltd, 1998.

Hansen, L. Taylor. *He Walked the Americas.* London, England: Legend Press, 1994. First published 1972.

Hawkes, Jacquetta. *The Atlas of Early Man.* New York: St. Martin's Press, 1976.

Hoyle, Fred, and Chandra Wickramasinghe. *Our Place in the Cosmos,* new ed. Phoenix, Ariz.: Phoenix Publishing Group, 1996.

Hughes, Graham. *The Art of Jewelry.* New York: Gallery Books, 1984.

Inskeep, R. R. *The Peopling of Southern Africa.* New York: Barnes & Noble, 1979.

Jones, Steve. *The Language of Genes.* New York: Doubleday, 1994.

Jordan, Michael. *The Encyclopedia of Gods.* London, England: Kyle Books, 1995.

Koran. Translated by N. J. Dawood. New York: Penguin Classics. First published 1956.

Kramer, Samuel Noah. *Cradle of Civilization.* New York: Time-Life, 1969.

Mangold, Tom, and Jeff Goldberg. *Plague Wars: The Terrifying Reality of Biological Warfare.* New York: St. Martin's Press, 2000.

The Merck Manual of Diagnosis and Therapy. Rahway, N. J.: Merck, 2006.

Milton, Richard. *The Facts of Life: Shattering the Myths of Darwinism.* London, England: Corgi, 1992.

——. *Forbidden Science: Suppressed Research That Could Change Our Lives.* n.p.: Fourth Estate Classics House, 1995.

Mutwa, Credo. *Indaba My Children: African Folktales.* New York: Grove Press, 1999.

Nardo, Don, ed. *Ancient Greece.* Farmington Hills, Mich.: Greenhaven Press, 2001.

Neret, Gilles, ed. *Descriptions of Egypt (Icons).* Berlin, Germany: Taschen, 2001.

Notovitch, Nicolas. *The Unknown Life of Jesus Christ.* First published 1890, by R. F. Books.

Parrinder, Geoffrey. *Illustrated History of World Religions.* Worthing, England: Littlehampton Book Services Ltd, 1983.

Reader's Digest Association. *The World's Last Mysteries.* New York: Reader's Digest Association, 1977.

Reeves, Nicholas, and Richard H. Wilkinson. *The Complete Valley of the Kings.* London, England: Thames & Hudson, 1996.

Ridley, Matt. *Nature via Nurture: Genes, Experience, and What Makes Us Human.* n.p.: Hardcover, 2003.

Roerich, Nicolas. *Heart of Asia.* New York: Roerich Museum Press, 1930.

Rosenthal, Renate. *Jewellery in Ancient Times.* Worthing, England: Littlehampton Book Services Ltd, 1973.

Sagan, Carl. *Billions and Billions: Thoughts on Life and Death at the Brink of the Millennium.* New York: Ballantine Books, 1998.

Scheub, Harold. *A Dictionary of African Mythology: The Mythmaker as Storyteller.* New York: Oxford University Press USA, 2000.

Seligman, C. G. *Races of Africa.* Oxford, England: Oxford University Press, 1961.

Sitchin, Zecharia. *Genesis Revisited.* New York: Avon, 1990.

———. *The Lost Book of Enki.* Rochester, Vt.: Inner Traditions / Bear & Company, 2002.

———. *The Lost Realms.* New York: Avon, 1990.

———. *The Stairway to Heaven.* New York: Avon, 1983.

———. *The 12th Planet.* New York: Avon, 1978.

———. *The Wars of Gods and Men.* New York: Avon, 1995.

———. *When Time Began.* Santa Fe, N.M.: Bear & Company, 1994.

Soustelle, Jacques. *The Daily Life of the Aztecs.* New York: Macmillan, 1964.

Taber's Cyclopedic Medical Dictionary. Philadelphia, Pa.: F. A. Davis Co, 2009.

Talmud Jmmanuel. Edited by Eduard Albert Meier. 4th ed. Tulsa, Okla.: Steelmark LLc, 2007.

Thiering, Barbara. *Jesus of the Apocalypse: The Life of Jesus After the Crucifxion,* reprint ed. New York: Doubleday, 1996.

——. *Jesus The Man: A New Interpretation from the Dead Sea Scrolls.* New York: Doubleday, 1992.

Thompson, Richard. *Alien Identities: Ancient Insights into Modern UFO Phenomena.* Alachua, Fla.: Govardhan Hill Publishing, 1993.

Tyldesley, Joyce. *The Private Lives of the Pharaohs.* London, England: Channel 4 Books, 2000.

Watson, James D. *DNA: The Secret of Life.* New York: Knopf, 2003.

Willcox, A. R. *Southern Land.* London, England: Purnell, 1976.

WEBSITES

Esoteric and Suppressed Knowledge

The Big Eye: Bigeye.com

Deliriums Realm Essays on Good and Evil: Deliriumsrealm.com

Illuminati Conspiracy Archive: Conspiracyarchive.com

Library of Halexandria: Halexandria.org

Modern Science, Ancient Knowledge: Ancientx.com

Purging Talon: Purgingtalon.com

Xfacts Research: Xfacts.com

History and Culture

Academy for Ancient Texts: Ancienttexts.org

Akhet Egyptology: Akhet.co.uk

Commentary and Analysis on Science/Humanities Topics: Human-nature.com

Earth History: Earth-history.com

Exploring the Creation/Evolution Controversy: Talkorigins.org

GeoHive Population Statistics: Geohive.com

GoldSheet Mining Directory: Goldsheetlinks.com

Harappa, Glimpses of South Asia before 1947: Harappa.com

History World: Historyworld.net

Humanistic Texts: Humanistictexts.org

Humanities Text Initiative: Hti.umich.edu

Indian History: Indhistory.com

Institute for Ice Age Studies: Insticeagestudies.com

Macrohistory and World Report: Fsmitha.com

Manuscripts Spanning 5,000 Years: Schoyencollection.com

The Official Website of Zecharia Sitchin: Sitchin.com

Online Encyclopedia of Roman Rulers and Their Families: Roman-emperors.org

Online Encyclopedia of Western Signs and Ideograms: Symbols.com

Phoenician Encyclopedia: Phoenicia.org

Rare Book and Manuscript Collections: Rmc.library.cornell.edu

A Site Dedicated to Osiris: Osirisnet.net

Sumerian Language Page: Sumerian.org

U.S. Mint: Usmint.gov

World Gold Council: Gold.org

Religion

Adherent Statistics and Religious Geography Citations: Adherents.com

Answering Christianity: Answering-christianity.com

Answers in Genesis: Answersingenesis.org

BibleBell Chronicles: Biblebell.org

Bible Gateway: Biblegateway.com

Christian Answers: Christiananswers.net

The Gnosis Archive: Gnosis.org

Gospel of Jesus Christ: Gospel.net

The Hindu Universe: Hindunet.org

Hindu Website: Hinduwebsite.com

An Interactive Commentary on the Whole Bible: Bibleexplained.com

Interfaith Online: Interfaith.org

Internet Christian Library: Iclnet.org

Internet Sacred Text Archive: Sacred-texts.com

Landover Baptist Church (a satirical site): Landoverbaptist.org

Mega Site of Bible Studies: Bibledesk.com

New Testament Gateway: Ntgateway.com

Ontario Consultants on Religious Tolerance: Religioustolerance.org

Sacred Sites, Places of Peace and Power: Sacredsites.com

Sanskrit Documents: Sanskrit.gde.to

Shiromani Gurdwara Parbandhak Committee Sikh Website: Sgpc.net

Sikhism: Sikhs.org

Talmud Jmmanuel Research: Tjresearch.info

Wholesome Words Christian Website: Wholesomewords.org

Science and Technology

Animal Genome Size Database: Genomesize.com

Biology Online, Answers to All Your Biology Questions: Biology-online.org

Cosmic Ancestry: Panspermia.org

Crystalinks Metaphysics and Science Website: Crystalinks.com

Earth Changes Central: Earthchangescentral.com

Franklin Institute Science Museum of Philadelphia: Fi.edu

Genome Research Journal: Genome.org

HubbleSite: Hubblesite.org

Institute for Creation Research: Icr.org

International Science News: Unisci.com

Mark A. Garlick, Space Illustration: Space-art.co.uk

Memphis Arcaeological and Geological Society: Memphisgeology.org

Molecular Biology and Evolution Journal: Mbe.oupjournals.org

National Center for Biotechnology Information: Ncbi.nlm.nih.gov

National Health Museum, Site for Teachers and Learners: Accessexcellence.org

New Scientist Journal: Newscientist.com

Oak Ridge National Library: Ornl.gov

Physics and Astronomy Online: Physlink.com

Proceedings of the National Academy of Sciences: Pnas.org

Profiles in Science, National Library of Medicine: Profiles.nlm.nih.gov

Rafal Swiecki, Alluvial/Eluvial Deposit Geological Engineer: Minelinks.com

Science Daily, Your Source for the Latest Research News: Sciencedaily.com

Science Journal: Sciencemag.org

ScienceNews Magazine of the Society for Science & the Public: Sciencenews.org

Small Comets, University of Iowa: Smallcomets.physics.uiowa.edu

Space Today Online, Covering Space from Earth to the Edge of the Universe: Spacetoday.org

Starchild, A Learning Center for Young Astronomers: Starchild.gsfc.nasa.gov

Views of the Solar System: Solarviews.com

Your Guide to Human Anatomy Online: Innerbody.com

INDEX

Page numbers in *italics* indicate illustrations.

BOOKS OF RELATED INTEREST

African Temples of the Anunnaki
The Lost Technologies of the Gold Mines of Enki
by Michael Tellinger

DNA of the Gods
The Anunnaki Creation of Eve
and the Alien Battle for Humanity
by Chris H. Hardy, Ph.D.

Wars of the Anunnaki
Nuclear Self-Destruction in Ancient Sumer
by Chris H. Hardy, Ph.D.

**Zecharia Sitchin and the Extraterrestrial
Origins of Humanity**
by M. J. Evans, Ph.D.

The Anunnaki Chronicles
A Zecharia Sitchin Reader
by Zecharia Sitchin
Edited by Janet Sitchin

The Lost Book of Enki
Memoirs and Prophecies of an Extraterrestrial God
by Zecharia Sitchin

The 12th Planet
by Zecharia Sitchin

There Were Giants Upon the Earth
Gods, Demigods, and Human Ancestry:
The Evidence of Alien DNA
by Zecharia Sitchin

Inner Traditions • Bear & Company
P.O. Box 388
Rochester, VT 05767
1-800-246-8648
www.InnerTraditions.com

Or contact your local bookseller